Praise for the *Dictionary of Conflict Resolution*

"On behalf of the Society of Professionals in Dispute Resolution (SPIDR),
I am pleased to endorse the *Dictionary of Conflict Resolution*. I am certain
that the book will be an important contribution to the field of conflict resolution. It may very well become to the conflict resolution field what *Roberts'
Dictionary of Industrial Relations* has been to the labor-management literature. As such, it will become a standard reference for anyone who is a serious
scholar or practitioner in the field of conflict resolution and collaborative
decision making. One of the most important contributions that SPIDR has
made over the years is to contribute significantly to the intellectual capital
of the field. SPIDR's contribution to the development of the *Dictionary* is in
the best tradition of that intellectual enterprise."
—**Homer C. La Rue**, president, Society of Professionals in Dispute Resolution

"A crucial step in establishing conflict resolution as a distinct discipline,
this dictionary is a remarkable and ambitious work that makes sense out
of a 'tower of Babel' and successfully captures the diversity of meaning
in this rapidly expanding field. This will be an essential reference for the
profession."
—**William K. Slate, II**, president, American Arbitration Association

Dictionary of
Conflict Resolution

Compiled and Edited by Douglas H. Yarn

In cooperation with
The Society of Professionals in Dispute Resolution
and with the support of
The William and Flora Hewlett Foundation and
The Georgia Consortium on Negotiation and Conflict Resolution

Jossey-Bass Publishers
San Francisco

Jossey-Bass books and products are available through most
bookstores. To contact Jossey-Bass directly, call (888) 378-2537,
fax to (800) 605-2665, or visit our website at www.josseybass.com.

Substantial discounts on bulk quantities of Jossey-Bass books are
available to corporations, professional associations, and other
organizations. For details and discount information,
contact the special sales department at Jossey-Bass.

 Manufactured in the United States of America on Lyons Falls Turin
Book. This paper is acid-free and 100 percent totally chlorine-free.

Library of Congress Cataloging-in-Publication Data

Dictionary of conflict resolution/
compiled and edited by Douglas H. Yarn; in cooperation
with the Society of Professionals in Dispute Resolution and
with the support of the William and Flora Hewlett Foundation and the
Georgia Consortium on Negotiation and Conflict Resolution. — 1st ed.
p. cm.
Includes bibliographical references.

ISBN 0-7879-4679-6
1. Dispute resolution (Law)—United States—Dictionaries. 2.
Arbitration and award—United States—Dictionaries. 3. Arbitration,
International—Dictionaries. 4. Dispute resolution
(Law)—Dictionaries. I. Yarn, Douglas H. II. William & Flora
Hewlett Foundation. III. Georgia Consortium on Negotiation and
Conflict Resolution. IV. Society of Professionals in Dispute
Resolution (U.S.)
KF9085.A68 D53 1999   99-6149
347.73'9'03—dc21

FIRST EDITION
HC Printing   10 9 8 7 6 5 4 3 2

CONTENTS

To Lisa

PREFACE

I am a lawyer by training, a mediator by temperament, a teacher by choice, and a lexicographer by default. These sides of myself have often competed, occasionally warred, sometimes cooperated, and eventually collaborated to produce this dictionary. The internal conflict was inevitable. Law is a profession of words, and as a lawyer I believe that words and the meaning of words matter. This belief engenders profound prescriptivism—a tendency to ascertain and dogmatically assert an exact meaning and usage for acceptable writing and speech. As a mediator, however, I appreciate that usage determines meaning and that different people may claim validity for their use of the same term to describe different concepts; inversely, different terms may describe the same concept. This appreciation engenders uncontrolled relativism—a tendency to accept various meanings and usages. As a teacher, I sensed that this tension between my lawyer side and my mediator side presented an opportunity to learn and enhance my understanding of conflict resolution; however, I could not take advantage of this opportunity without compiling the terms and meanings at issue. Thus, by default I became a lexicographer of the vocabulary in the field of conflict resolution.

Lexicographers are "harmless drudges," according to Samuel Johnson, one of the earliest lexicographers of the English language. Drudgery inadequately describes the work that has gone into this dictionary. Fortunately I have been blessed with a number of fellow drudges who have graciously contributed their time, knowledge, and effort to the project. During the compilation phase I had a procession of talented graduate research assistants who painstakingly helped me extract terms and definitions from the vast body of literature that relates to conflict and conflict resolution. During the analysis and editing phases, several of my colleagues in the Consortium on Negotiation and Conflict Resolution (CNCR) slowly ploughed through early drafts to make suggestions and comments. Subsequent drafts were reviewed by chairs of specialized-practice sectors in the Society of Professionals in Dispute Resolution (SPIDR) and by its president at the time, Maria Volpe, to ensure that terms and meanings conformed to the range of specialized practice. After comments from SPIDR were incorporated, James Boskey reviewed and provided editorial comments for the final draft. I have long admired Professor Boskey for his breadth and depth of knowledge and for his contributions to the field. Although I am honored that he agreed to help, I had not expected the unflagging enthusiasm, good humor, and encouragement he brought to the project. His intellectual contributions to this book have been invaluable, but his faith in the value of the endeavor and his personal support have brought this book to fruition.

In the last two years of the project, my research assistant, Shinji Morokuma, patiently endured the worst drudgery—editing innumerable entries, tracking down dozens of incomplete citations, and achieving a consistent format. I am deeply indebted to Shinji. Gregory Bourne, former executive director of CNCR, played a crucial role in arranging the collaboration with SPIDR and in providing ongoing encouragement. I would be remiss if I did not thank my many friends at the American Arbitration Association (AAA) who supported this project. The AAA has a distinguished history of innovation and experimentation in the field, and despite growing economic and competitive pressures, it continues to value its educational role.

Finally, I am indebted to you—all of the many theorists and practitioners who contributed unknowingly to this work through your own efforts to make sense of the field or to create useful additions to the professional vocabulary.

By 1898, James Murray, compiler and editor of the first *Oxford English Dictionary,* had received more than five million slips of paper containing quotes from philological societies and volunteer readers from around the world. He sorted them into thousands of pigeonholes that lined an iron shed (the "Scriptorium") he had built in his backyard. Then, while he sat on a dais in the middle of the shed, his children read the quotations and he contrived and dictated the definitions. By 1996, I had entered thousands of quotes and citations into a database in my virtual backyard. Like Murray, but without his towering intellect, I sat in front of the screen contriving and pecking out definitions. One of the great ironies of conflict resolution is that practitioners who strive to improve understanding among disputants often fail to understand one another. If in the midst of this drudgery I have misunderstood, misquoted, or misinterpreted you, let me know so I may correct my mistake in future editions.

This dictionary is merely a snapshot of our vocabulary at one point in time. Like all photographs, someone had to hold and focus the camera and crop the picture. If something is not in the frame, is out of focus, or is obscured in the uneven light, blame the photographer. Bear in mind, however, that rather than the last word, this dictionary is merely part of the ongoing process of linguistic evolution in our field—a field intensely concerned with process. I enlist your help in this process because the way we talk about the practice and discipline of conflict resolution will determine the way it is. Please participate in the process by communicating with me and others through the electronic list server located on CNCR's Web site at law.gsu.edu/CNCR/ or by contacting me directly.

Douglas H. Yarn
Georgia State University
College of Law
Atlanta, Georgia 30303
(404) 651–2147
dyarn@gsu.edu

ABOUT THE *DICTIONARY*
OF CONFLICT RESOLUTION

The Consortium on Negotiation and Conflict Resolution (CNCR) started the Conflict Resolution Lexicon Project in 1989. CNCR is a program of the University System of Georgia and one of several conflict resolution theory-building centers initially funded by the William and Flora Hewlett Foundation. CNCR's mission is to bridge theory and practice in conflict resolution through multidisciplinary and interinstitutional activities and research projects. Its primary research focus is on the institutionalization of alternative dispute resolution processes.

A primary indicator of institutionalization is the establishment of a core language or vocabulary unique to the field and used by adherents to communicate shared values, concepts, and principles. CNCR members saw the need to create a specialized lexicon in response to the emergence of conflict resolution as a distinct profession and academic discipline. The ranks of arbitrators, mediators, and other professional conflict resolvers were starting to swell, and colleges and universities were beginning to establish conflict resolution curricula and degree programs. The emergence of the conflict resolution field has been accompanied by creative uses of new processes, a rapid development of theory, and an increasing institutionalization of conflict resolution mechanisms, particularly in relation to the courts. New terms are being created as familiar terms are being used in different ways.

Initially we at CNCR identified four primary objectives. First, we sought to increase knowledge and awareness of the wide range of conflict resolution terms and their meanings, nationally and internationally. If policymakers and others are going to use these terms, it is important that they appreciate the possible diversity of meaning among terms and not use them indiscriminately. Second, we wanted to improve dialogue and understanding among professionals and theorists in conflict resolution. People working in this field come from a broad range of backgrounds and disciplines and from different "speech communities," and they contribute language and meaning from their respective disciplines and practice contexts. We need to know what we mean when we talk to one another. In this same vein, our third objective was to preserve diversity in the range of meanings contributed by the many subcultures participating in the field and to avoid dominance by a single participating subculture. Our fourth objective was to promote uniformity and consistency in the professional language. Although this objective admittedly is in tension with the third, it is important to recognize that the field of conflict resolution constitutes its own speech community, and if it is to be a separate profession and discipline, it must have a distinct, broadly understood vocabulary for communicating the concepts of unique concern and usefulness to the field.

Subsequent to identifying these initial objectives we adopted additional objectives common to the science of lexicography and that overlap with our primary objectives. An overriding goal is to make a record of the rich language of conflict resolution, much of which has come into use within the last twenty-five years. In this sense, the dictionary is a sociological, cultural, and historical document that reflects an emerging vocabulary. It will be useful as a gauge for comparison as the language continues its evolution. Another objective in lexicography is to facilitate the general public's access to the language and to share rather than balkanize the language. Finally, we feel it is important to reflect, legitimate, and in some cases cause linguistic change. That purpose, too, is reflected in this work.

PROCESS

Although the project was conceptualized in 1989, we did not start compiling terms until 1992 when CNCR provided a small seed grant and the American Arbitration Association kindly lent us a rare copy of its *Dictionary of Arbitration* (Oceana, 1970) and encouraged us to bring that work up to date. Although we have strayed considerably from its format, that dictionary formed the base for this one. It also confirmed the need for a new dictionary. Reflecting the state of the field almost three decades ago, the *Dictionary of Arbitration* contains a fraction of the terms currently in use, most of which have emerged only in the last twenty years.

In an attempt to reflect the vocabulary of the field of conflict resolution as used by practitioners and theorists, we began compiling a citation database of terms, definitions, and usages from the conflict resolution literature, including all of the publications in the Jossey-Bass Conflict Resolution Series, the field's periodicals and journals (such as *Mediation Quarterly, Negotiation Journal, Journal of Dispute Resolution,* and *Dispute Resolution Journal*), and treatises and other texts. We also solicited contributions from practitioners and theorists. For the most part, all terms and definitions in the dictionary reflect how someone other than ourselves is using and defining them in the current literature and in practice. Some terms have only one definition and citation; others, such as *mediation,* for example, have one hundred or more definitions and citations. This edition of the dictionary includes materials compiled in our citation database through May 1996. At that time, with the continuing emergence of new materials in the field, we determined to declare a truce with the language; otherwise we would have gone on forever compiling the database.

The next task was to edit and write the first draft of the text. This involved distilling meaning from the citations and arranging the multiple meanings for some terms. At this point we were concerned about whether the distillation accurately reflected the range of meanings understood by practitioners working in different conflict resolution settings. It was time to "walk the talk" and make the lexicon project a collaborative, inclusive process.

REVIEWERS

In cooperation with the Society of Professionals in Dispute Resolution (SPIDR), we presented versions of the dictionary at two successive SPIDR conferences and solicited input from the membership. Subsequently we distributed a draft to the president of the organization, Maria Volpe, and to the chairs of several SPIDR specialized-practice sectors. These people agreed to read and review the draft. Although their agreement to participate did not constitute an endorsement of the final product, most of them provided comments and additions that we have incorporated. The original volunteer SPIDR readers were as follows:

Maria Volpe, professor, John Jay College of Criminal Justice–CUNY; SPIDR president

Michelle LeBaron, associate professor, Institute for Conflict Analysis and Research, George Mason University; SPIDR Commercial Sector cochair

Ben Carroll, executive director, Neighborhood Justice Center, Honolulu; SPIDR Community Sector cochair

Joe Paulk, mediator, Dispute Resolution Consultants; SPIDR Court Sector cochair

E. Wendy Trachte-Huber, regional vice president and national trainer, American Arbitration Association; formerly executive director, E. E. White Dispute Resolution Institute, University of Houston; SPIDR Education Sector Co-Chair

Robert Perkovich, mediator and arbitrator; SPIDR Employment Sector cochair

Phyllis Simon, family mediator, Family and Child Associates; SPIDR Family Sector cochair

Arthur Kaufman, Birch and Davis; SPIDR Health Care Sector cochair

Christina Merchant, conflict management systems design consultant

Several of my colleagues at CNCR also reviewed the work and provided their particular expertise:

Michael Elliott, professor, City Planning Department, Georgia Institute of Technology (Environmental and Public Policy)

Dorinda Dallmeyer, research director, Rusk Center for International and Comparative Law, University of Georgia (International Law and Relations)

Peter Shedd, professor, Terry College of Business, University of Georgia (Law and Business)

A number of graduate research assistants were engaged in compilation during the course of the project. The most important role of lead student editor was played by Shinji Morokuma, currently deputy director, Georgia Supreme Court's Office of Dispute Resolution.

Maria Volpe and Michelle LeBaron, previously mentioned, provided detailed readings of the complete draft of the manuscript, as did the following individuals:

Juliana E. Birkhoff, mediator

James B. Boskey, professor, Seton Hall Law School; editor, *The Alternative Newsletter*

Stephen K. Erickson, director, Erickson Mediation Institute

Michael Lang, editor, *Mediation Quarterly*

Christopher W. Moore, partner, CDR Associates

CRITICISMS AND CONTINUING THE DIALOGUE: AN ONGOING PROCESS

We anticipate and encourage criticisms of the dictionary. Valid questions can be asked about whether we have included all crucial terms and provided the full range of, or most authoritative, definitions used throughout the field. We did purposefully omit some terms, and some terms emerged after we closed the citation database, so I have no doubt we missed some. There may be a noticeable slant toward the international, legal, and arbitration terms that pervade the field, because these areas have been institutionalized for so long that they yield the most terms and the most consistent and concrete definitions. Other areas, particularly some subspecialties of mediation, have produced comparatively fewer terms or less definitive meanings. In some cases it was difficult to determine whether certain phrases constitute terms of the field or merely descriptions of a general problem or issue—for example, terms used to discuss aspects of the mediation process such as *time and timing, meeting needs and interests,* or *strategies to avoid impasse.* These phrases are excluded because we did not want the dictionary to evolve into a training manual. Our choices in this regard could, however, prompt valid criticisms.

Although we may have captured a term, we may not have used the definition that a particular sector of the field favors. In our decision making we have walked a fine line between favoring a definition as authoritative and including the full range of meanings currently understood for a single term. If we favor a particular definition as authoritative, someone will disagree, but if we allow for all definitions (no matter how inconsistent), we stand accused of promoting the fuzziness that currently pervades the use of so many terms in the field. Nevertheless, one of the objectives of the dictionary is to preserve meanings that represent the entire range of the field, and we are certainly open to criticism if we missed a meaning that is particular to a specific area of conflict resolution practice.

Additionally, there is a significant body of literature that is critical of many current trends in conflict resolution (Laura Nader's work for example) or that provides a different perspective influenced by other social theory developing mostly outside the field, such as feminist and diversity theories. Although these critical and social theory perspectives rarely create new terms in the field, they often shed a different light on the meanings of current terms and on the social and political significance of the semantics. Clearly, culture and diversity are central to the practice of many individuals in the field. To the extent that the definitions reflect a rational, analytical bias without incorporating terms and meanings emerging from these perspectives, the dictionary is subject to criticism.

Finally, participation in the creation of the dictionary was perhaps uneven. Although most of the readers and reviewers have significant experience in a wide range of conflict resolution theory and practice, there was probably less participation by those in the field who come from predominantly psychological or therapeutic backgrounds, who represent community and family mediation, or who work in the area of intractable or protracted deep-rooted conflict. Although a concerted effort was made to engage these groups and individuals to identify the terms and definitions relevant to them, there remains considerable room for improvement through more participation by individuals who work in these areas.

This is why we view the dictionary as an organic document subject to expansion and improvement. It must continually evolve and adapt as the field's vocabulary expands, changes, and coalesces. Even more important, we view the process of creating and updating the dictionary as part of an ongoing, participatory process—a continuing dialogue about language and meaning in our field. A core principle in the field is to engage in constructive dialogue. If you have criticisms, perceive gaps, or dispute meanings, you can help to improve achievement of the objectives of this dictionary by participating. We continue to seek input and have provided a site for contributions and comments on CNCR's Web site at law.gsu.edu/CNCR/.

GUIDE TO USING THE *DICTIONARY* *OF CONFLICT RESOLUTION*

This dictionary is distilled from a citation database—a compilation of terms and definitions used by practitioners and theorists, defined in the literature or in law or placed on the Internet. A draft containing the meanings distilled from the database was distributed to experienced practitioners and theorists for comments and additions, which were incorporated into the dictionary.

COVERAGE

There are approximately 1,400 headwords in this dictionary. Three criteria guided the inclusion or exclusion of a headword:

1. Is it unique to the vocabulary of conflict resolution professionals, either practitioners or theorists?

2. If it is not unique to the professional vocabulary, has it been adopted into the vocabulary?

3. If it is not yet a recognized part of the vocabulary, is it a potentially useful addition to the vocabulary?

Most of the headwords relate to particular processes, techniques, or concepts in conflict resolution. Specific conflict resolution organizations are included if their influence is so prevalent as to be commonly referred to in the field or if they are national or international in scope and recognized for some noncommercial reason—for instance, because they break new conceptual ground in dispute resolution administration or because they have particular influence in a specific area. Otherwise, because the dictionary is not an encyclopedia, it purposefully excludes historically significant events, people, organizations, and programs that may not yet have been coined as terms or that may not yet be part of the common vocabulary. Many of these organizations and programs are included in the list provided in the appendices. Statutes, treaties, and conventions are included if they are particularly influential, specifically focused on conflict resolution, or historically noteworthy. Generally, treaties, legal cases, and statutes are cited only as authority for a definition.

CULTURAL AND HISTORICAL FRAMES

Unless otherwise noted, the definitions reflect usage and meaning in the United States. Conflict resolution theory and practice in the United States have been influential outside the country in much activity in which these terms and meanings may be in use; it is important to note, however, that other cultural frames of reference may not be reflected in the entries. We have included terms and definitions from other countries and cultures if these terms were found in the conflict resolution literature published in the English language. As a result, some cultures are more represented than others; for example, there are many Navaho terms, but few terms from other Native American or First Nations groups despite the many relevant terms they may use. With respect to non-English terms, we have made no judgment as to whether they are correctly translated or understood by the authority cited. Historical and archaic terms and meanings are included if they are helpful to understanding the current meaning, if they reveal the evolution of meaning, or if they are otherwise interesting.

SCOPE

Conflict and its resolution encompass much of human history, behavior, and language. Virtually the entire language of the legal profession is related to disputes and dispute resolution; it would be useless, however, simply to absorb the vast *Black's Law Dictionary,* for example, into this dictionary. The terms found in a legal dictionary are included here if they have been adopted into the conflict resolution field and if the overlap of legal institutions with conflict resolution has necessitated their use. Numerous specialized terms are well handled in other reference material.

FORMAT AND TREATMENT

Headwords are printed in bold type. If the word is not naturalized in English, it is printed in bold italicized type. Words normally spelled with an initial capital letter are printed in this form when they appear as headwords. Variants and acronyms of the terms are generally in parentheses immediately after the headword. When the acronym or abbreviation is better known than the spelled-out term, the acronym or abbreviation is also used as a headword and the reader is referred to the spelled-out headword for definition.

The *Dictionary of Conflict Resolution* is not a dictionary in the strict sense and therefore not a guide to pronunciation or etymology. Designations as parts of speech such as noun or verb are included only when necessary to distinguish an important variation of usage. National, ethnic, and historical origins of some terms are noted in parentheses after the headword when the term is specific to a particular society or when such information is of particular relevance or interest. When the term has a specific meaning in a particular context or in a particular discipline, that context or discipline precedes the definition in italics (for example, *Labor*).

An entry may consist of several paragraphs. The first paragraph contains the broadest or most familiar or important definition. Subsequent paragraphs contain other usages, definitions in particular contexts (such as international relations), or discussions of the applicability of the underlying concepts. Paragraphs beginning with an italicized subject area indicate the cited authority's distinct and different uses of the term.

Throughout the terms and definitions section, we have used letter-for-letter alphabetization. To illustrate, what might seem to be an appropriate first entry under the letter *I* ("I-will-if-you-will proposition. . .," with its single letter *I* seeming to come before the entry "ICAR . . .") is alphabetized letter for letter and hence is in fact the last entry under the letter I (to follow "iterative dynamics," since the strict letter sequence *i-w* follows *i-t*).

Occasionally one or more authoritative definitions are inserted verbatim into the entry when they might help to illustrate the range of use. When these are part of a series each is preceded by a bullet (•).

SIGNALS

Signal words are used in the following manner:

Terms in all capital letters within an entry refer the reader to an additional headword for better understanding of the current headword.

At the end of an entry or at the end of subdefinitions within the entry occasionally appear terms in all capital letters preceded by a signal word, such as *compare* or *contrast*. These terms also appear as headwords in the dictionary and may help the reader to clarify distinctions and recognize similarities. In many cases these references substitute for antonyms and synonyms.

See precedes an authoritative reference or another term defined in the dictionary that was not used in the definition but that would help the reader better understand the headword.

Same as precedes terms that have the same meaning as the headword.

Compare precedes terms with meaning similar to that of the headword and that, while having some distinctions, aid in understanding the headword.

Contrast precedes terms whose distinctiveness from the headword aids in understanding the headword.

CITATIONS

Citations are used in a variety of ways. In some instances, they simply serve as sources for examples of usage, that is, they refer to a term used in a particular way in a particular work ("as used in"). In other instances, the definition may come directly from the work cited. When a term and its definition come primarily from a single source, we have opted not to change the author's original language very much for fear of distorting the intended meaning. If a definition was copied verbatim, it is in quotes or indented followed by a citation with a specific page reference. A paraphrase uses similar syntax and semantics to adhere to the meaning of the cited authority; in such instances, a specific page reference is given though without quotes or indent.

SOURCES

We used two citation forms. If the source is a statute or case law, we used the forms accepted in legal memoranda and scholarship. Otherwise we used the *Chicago Manual of Style* citation form recommended and used by Jossey-Bass Publishers.

With respect to terms of contemporary origin, we tried to cite authors and works of origin if the terms were coined specifically for conflict resolution. We traced origins for many terms coined in other disciplines and adopted for use in conflict resolution. In most cases, however, we tried to find out how the term is currently being used in practice and theory. The meaning intended by the originator may no longer match the current use of the term. Thus the reader may notice many citations of practice journals such as *Negotiation Journal* and *Mediation Quarterly* or of popular treatises such as Christopher Moore's *The Mediation Process* (1986). Sometimes these works are not the original source of the term; however, they reflect the way the term is currently used in practice or they are the publication that most popularized the term's use or best established its definition. Although the *Dictionary of Conflict Resolution* is intended to be a reference work, the extensive bibliography at the end can be used as a tool to research original sources. Bear in mind that citations often refer to a first edition or to the edition in print at the time of the database compilation. Subsequent and revised editions of the same works may now be in print. Notable examples include Fisher and Ury's *Getting to Yes* (1981) and Moore's *The Mediation Process.* We stopped adding to the citation database in June 1996; terms appearing in publications after that date are therefore not included, with a few exceptions.

SEMANTICS

One of the purposes of the dictionary is to provide a reference to the common and varied uses of terms relating to the resolution of conflict. Another purpose is to clarify differences between terms and to recommend accurate and precise usage. As noted in the introductory material presented earlier, these purposes are to some extent contradictory. As a result, when we define some terms, we may use other conflict resolution terms in the entry rather loosely, although at other times we might use the same terms with more precise meanings in other entries. The latter will be the case if we have recommended a particular use as more accurate or descriptive than other uses.

Many proponents of alternative dispute resolution practices eschew use of dyadic terms that emphasize difference or that reinforce contentious attitudes, such as *other, other side,* or *opponent.* Without commentary on this or other philosophies, this dictionary uses these terms for convenience in defining other terms and mostly when the common use of the term implies contention. For example, terms related to the adversary system, war, and positional bargaining carry this connotation.

Male and female pronouns are avoided where consistent with proper grammar. However, avoiding them is not always possible, so they are used alternatively throughout the dictionary.

ABBREVIATIONS

The following abbreviations are used frequently throughout the dictionary:

AAA	American Arbitration Association
ADR	Alternative dispute resolution
C.F.R.	Code of Federal Regulations
DOA	Dictionary of Arbitration
U.S.	United States
U.S.C.	United States Code
U.S.C.A.	United States Code Annotated
WAMR	World Arbitration and Mediation Report

Most other abbreviations are in the citations and refer to the codes of various states in the United States or to case law reporters.

Dictionary of Conflict Resolution

AAA   See AMERICAN ARBITRATION ASSOCIATION.

Academy of Family Mediators (AFM)   Nonprofit educational membership association established in 1981 for divorce and family mediators.

AFM holds conferences, certifies training for mediators, sponsors a periodical (*Mediation Quarterly*), and refers parties to mediators for a broad range of disputes. It has been very influential in the development of practice and training standards for divorce mediators. See FAMILY MEDIATION ASSOCIATION.

accommodating   Personality characteristic affecting conflict-handling preferences and identified by various psychological instruments, including the THOMAS/KILMANN CONFLICT MODE INSTRUMENT.

According to the Thomas/Kilmann instrument, the accommodating person is essentially the opposite of the COMPETING personality. Accommodating individuals are cooperative yet nonassertive and thus neglect their own concerns to satisfy those of another person. Accommodating individuals are characterized by self-sacrifice, selfless generosity, charity, yielding, or obeisance to the will of another, despite inner restraint [Thomas/Kilmann Conflict Mode Instrument, 1974]. Contrast AVOIDING, COLLABORATING, COMPETING, COMPROMISING. See ASSERTIVE, COOPERATIVE.

accommodation   Adaptation of one's goals or aspirations to meet the goals or aspirations of another person. It is not the same thing as making CONCESSIONS, because it is an internal psychological event, though it can lead to concession making. It is sometimes referred to as *yielding* [Thomas, 1976]; however, yielding may also connote both the internal psychological event of accommodation and the subsequent external strategic event of making a concession.

In the context of intranational ethnic strife, accommodation is a state strategy of responding to ethnic minority demands by making structural changes to formally recognize the minority. Contrast ACCULTURATION; compare CONSOCIATION.

accommodationist   One who favors the strategy of ACCOMMODATION.

International Relations: One who opposes militant internationalism yet supports cooperative internationalism [Holsti and Rosenau, 1984, p. 253].

accommodative strategy   *Negotiation:* Use of ACCOMMODATION to achieve goals.

According to Moore [1986, p. 69], parties pursue accommodative strategy when sacrifice of some interest is required to maintain a positive relationship, when it is desirable to demonstrate or foster cooperation, or when interests are extremely interdependent.

accord, accordance   To AGREE or CONCUR; to be in AGREEMENT or harmony with; to consent or grant. May also refer to the agreement itself or to the document containing the agreement.

accord and satisfaction   *Law:* Way of discharging or settling a legal claim. In this context, an accord is a contract made in settlement of a claim. The satisfaction is the performance of this contract. An accord and satisfaction may serve as a new contract to substitute for prior contract, thereby discharging it, or as a substitute for an obligation or cause of action, thereby settling the matter. Because the concept is rooted in contract law, a valid accord and satisfaction must have all of the elements of a valid contract.

accordion planning   *Public Policy:* Inclusive planning process for making decisions or policy.

All parties that would be affected by a given decision are engaged at the start of the planning process and work together throughout each of the phases, constantly returning to their own organizational bases to be assured of continual support. As a result, the process may expand and unfold like an accordion. This is in contrast to the conventional, or linear, way of approaching problems, in which a small group or single stakeholder plans an initiative or project and then attempts to sell it to others, doing its best to accelerate the process by ensuring that contending parties do not have an opportunity to exercise their power [Bradley, 1988, p. 54; Doyle and Straus, 1984]. See PUBLIC POLICY DIALOGUE, REGULATORY-NEGOTIATION.

accrued costs (AC) *Negotiation:* Costs of BARGAINING or other transaction costs already incurred at a particular point in time.

Because bargaining has its costs, the more one invests in carrying on a transaction, the greater will be the desire to resolve the conflict through that transaction rather than to incur a whole new set of transaction costs that may not produce a more favorable result [Goldman, 1991, p. 20]. See DATA ACCURACY (DA).

acculturation Adoption of elements of a dominant culture in order to function within it. This can trigger a process of steady disappearance of cultural distinctiveness as a consequence of what is essentially unforced ASSIMILATION. Acculturation can lead to as well as reduce the incidence of intercultural conflict. Contrast ACCOMMODATION and ASSIMILATION.

acquiescence Tacit agreement without objection.

Common and efficient form of DISPUTE RESOLUTION requiring no investment of effort, energy, or time in seeking adjustments of differences. Compare CONSENSUS.

action *Law:* Suit or formal complaint brought in a court of law and the resulting proceedings in that forum. Compare CAUSE OF ACTION.

action line Complaint-processing intake system, commonly through the use of telephones.

Action lines can be provided by individuals or organizations. However, most action line programs are provided by government agencies, private industries, or the media to handle citizen, customer, employee, and consumer complaints and to provide information. See MEDIA COMPLAINT CENTER, OMBUDSMAN.

active listening Generic term for a variety of similar but distinct communication techniques.

At one level, this term refers simply to good LISTENING skills, that is, being attentive, nonjudgmental, noninterrupting, and so on. At another level, it refers to a technique of listening for hidden messages and meanings contained in a communication and in the speaker's or sender's attitude and demeanor. Negotiators, for example, might use this technique to gain information that helps them determine credibility, the degree of interest in alternative solutions and proposals, or nearness to RESERVATION PRICE [Murray, Rau, and Sherman, 1989, pp. 116–117].

A more specific use of the term, however, denotes a technique whereby the listener seeks to decode the entire meaning and motive in verbal and nonverbal messages, beyond that which is obvious from the words used. The listener then conveys that meaning back to the sender, to confirm or correct the listener's understanding of the message and to make the sender more conscious of her own motives and emotions. In addition to helping the listener gain a better understanding of the sender, this form of active listening can be a therapeutic or psychological technique intended to benefit the sender. Counselors use the technique to build rapport and to encourage more open discussion. Mediators use the technique to help a disputant be aware of and thereby manage emotions that impair RECONCILIATION [Moore, 1986, p. 169].

Active and EMPATHIC LISTENING are often used interchangeably or together to refer to the same technique. However, empathic listening properly refers to a more passive listening technique. See LISTENING. Compare DIALOGIC LISTENING, EMPATHIC LISTENING, RESPONSIVE LISTENING.

ACUS   See ADMINISTRATIVE CONFERENCE OF THE UNITED STATES.

ADDR   See ALTERNATIVE DISCOVERY DISPUTE RESOLUTION.

ad hoc   "For a specific purpose only."
Used as a preface to many dispute resolution processes, for example, AD HOC ARBITRATION, and usually referring to the manner in which the process was invoked. Ad hoc dispute resolution processes are those created for a one-time use on a particular dispute, as opposed to processes that are institutionalized so as to be available for any referred dispute.

ad hoc arbitration   Arbitration in which the parties do not use an ADMINISTERING AGENCY or arbitral institution. The administrative functions and procedural aspects are managed and controlled by the parties and the arbitrators, and the entire arbitral framework is crafted for the particular dispute between the parties to the ARBITRATION AGREEMENT [DOA].
In disputes among states, ad hoc arbitration usually results from a special SUBMISSION AGREEMENT that defines the issues to be resolved, establishes procedure, and constitutes and empowers the arbitral TRIBUNAL.
Contrast PERMANENT ARBITRATION.

ad hoc arbitrator   ARBITRATOR jointly selected by the parties to serve in a single arbitration only.
Such an ad hoc arbitrator or arbitral TRIBUNAL is common in COMMERCIAL and INTERNATIONAL ARBITRATION.
In LABOR ARBITRATION, where PERMANENT ARBITRATORS are also frequently used, many employers and unions want each case decided strictly on its merits on an individual basis and feel that such decisions are more likely to be achieved if the arbitrator is chosen to serve in a single case only. Selection on an ad hoc basis also permits designation of specialists to arbitrate different types of cases. Even though an agreement establishes ad hoc arbitrators, the same individual

or board may be used again if both union and management are satisfied with the original selection. Such a continuation enables the parties to secure some of the advantages of PERMANENT ARBITRATION and at the same time retain their freedom to change or alternate arbitrators [DOA].

ad hoc conference of states   *International Relations:* Formal gathering of states called together for the sole purpose of negotiating a particular issue or group of issues.

adjudicate   To adjudge, decide, settle, or issue a decree in the exercise of judicial authority.

adjudication   Process of decision making by a third party with authority to determine a resolution through some form of JUDGMENT or AWARD. More properly, refers to the determination made through the use of an ADJUDICATIVE PROCESS. Some sample definitions:

- A process of decision in which the affected party is afforded an institutionally guaranteed participation, which consists of the opportunity to present proofs and arguments for a decision in that party's favor [Fuller, 1963, p. 19].
- The process of deciding by submitting a dispute to a third party neutral decision maker with the authority to issue a binding judgment [Lieberman and Lieberman, 1985, p. 69].
- Adjudication implies a high degree of rationality, some degree of institutionalization, formal procedure, norms of conduct, and means of enforcement. Adjudication by a judge in a court of law is the most familiar and formal form of adjudication. In this context, LITIGATION is often used interchangeably with adjudication (perhaps incorrectly, because litigation more properly refers to a process that may lead to adjudication). However, ARBITRATION, which is distinct from litigation, is also a form of adjudication. In addition, litigation may be used to invoke formal court mechanisms but may not necessarily lead to a final decision by a third party [Murray, Rau, and Sherman, 1989, p. 20].

International Law: Involves submission to determination by permanent courts or multinational bodies and may require the states involved to consent to adjudication by that body. In this context, arbitration is distinct from adjudication in that the former is usually an ad hoc procedure. See INTERNATIONAL COURT OF JUSTICE, PERMANENT COURT OF INTERNATIONAL JUSTICE. International adjudicative bodies may also have jurisdiction over defined categories of international disputes by way of treaty obligations. See ANDEAN

Court of Justice, Canada-U.S. International Joint Commission (IJC), European Court of Justice, International Tribunal for the Law of the Sea, World Trade Organization.

See ADJUDICATIVE PROCESSES. Compare ADMINISTRATIVE ADJUDICATION. Contrast CONCILIATION.

adjudicative Having the characteristics of ADJUDICATIVE PROCESSES.

adjudicative processes Class of dispute resolution processes characterized by the use of a third party with the power to impose a solution. A binding decision necessitates some form of social control, usually by the state, that enforces the determination. To be enforced by the state, the decision must be reached through a process that conforms to norms acceptable to the state. The characteristics that legitimate state enforcement include the rational application of a consistent set of known substantive and procedural rules to achieve a predictable result, an outcome insulated from bias and circumstances deemed irrelevant, and the opportunity for the disputants to present their cases and respond to each other's arguments [Stein, 1984, p. 14; Shapiro, 1981, pp. 1–37]. In the COMMON LAW tradition, the proceedings are formal and public, with an adversary presentation—often accomplished through the use of legal professionals—as the basis for decision making. Final decisions do not require party participation, nor do they have to be mutually acceptable, and they result in a clear winner and loser [Riskin and Westbrook, 1987, p. 2].

One of the most distinguishing factors of adjudicative processes is how the third party frames the conflict. The third party will look backward over time to reconstruct events and classify them in terms of applicable rules and standards (that is, norms). This requires the parties to formulate the dispute as a DISSENSUS, a diadic conflict of rights and principles framed within the applicable normative structure, before the adjudicator can make a determination [Eckhoff, 1966, p. 145; Aubert, 1963, p. 26]. In contrast to CONCILIATORY PROCESSES, which are *person oriented*, adjudicative processes have been described as *act oriented*.

adjudicator Third-party decision maker in an ADJUDICATIVE PROCESS, usually a stranger to the dispute and vested with some degree of official authority by the state or community. Common examples are JUDGES and ARBITRATORS.

adjudicatory Often used but grammatically incorrect version of ADJUDICATIVE.

adjuster One who investigates and negotiates the settlement of claims arising under insurance contracts, usually a salaried employee of the insurance company.

In some jurisdictions, adjusters may be legally defined as independent contractors who work on behalf of an insurer for a fee or commission and may not be salaried employees or attorneys engaged by the insurer. See, for example, Ala. Code § 27-9-1 (1993). Adjusters are frequent participants in negotiations and mediations involving disputed insurance claims and frequently the sole representative in such processes before suit is filed.

adjustment board   *Labor:* Decision-making board that consists of union and management and that frequently operates as the final stage of a GRIEVANCE PROCEDURE. An adjustment board may or may not be transformed into a BOARD OF ARBITRATION by the addition of a neutral member [DOA].

administered arbitration   Arbitration conducted by and under the rules of an ADMINISTERING AGENCY. Arbitration may be either *administered* or *non-administered.*

administering agency   Institution, trade association, government agency, or international body that, among other services, may administer ADR processes.

These services may be accessible to the general public (see PROVIDER) or they may be restricted to members of the institution. Such agencies generally operate under their own rules and maintain panels or rosters of NEUTRALS. Agencies may appoint a neutral or group of neutrals either as provided in their rules or by the agreement of the parties, or they may offer the parties lists from which to choose neutrals. A number of agencies maintain panels of arbitrators that are not selected by the parties but that are presented to them as a panel that acts as the arbitration board. The DOA used the term *administrative agency* in this manner. Today, however, administrative agency connotes a governmental unit responsible for administering regulations.

Prior to the 1970s, few such agencies provided processes other than arbitration, and thus were referred to as IMPARTIAL ARBITRAL INSTITUTIONS.

administrative adjudication   Adjudication performed as a function of an administrative agency of a government. In the United States, the ADMINISTRATIVE PROCEDURE ACT provides a format for adjudicative hearings that generally conforms to the court model but is less formal. Adjudicators in this context are known as ADMINISTRATIVE LAW JUDGES. In this context, federal law defines ADJUDICATION as "the agency process for the formulation of an order" [5 U.S.C.A. § 551(7)].

administrative agency   Governmental unit responsible for administering regulations. Increasingly such agencies are engaged in forms of ADR to resolve disputes over their regulatory authority (see, for example, REGULATORY NEGOTIATION) and personnel disputes. Not to be confused with an ADMINISTERING AGENCY that administers ADR processes.

administrative appointment   *Arbitration:* Appointment of an ARBITRATOR or ARBITRATORS by an ADMINISTERING AGENCY in a case under its administration when the parties cannot agree on the selection of an arbitrator or one of the parties fails to name its own arbitrator.

Most arbitration rules provide for the possibility of administrative appointments. The actual details of such a provision may vary from agency to agency. When parties have received lists of possible arbitrators and have failed to agree on an arbitrator, the agency may reserve the right to make the appointment itself. Under certain circumstances, the parties may invite the agency to make the appointment without such a preliminary submission of lists [DOA].

Administrative Conference of the United States (ACUS)   U.S. government agency that maintained a roster of neutrals for federal government dispute resolution. The ACUS was a key agency in the implementation of the ADMINISTRATIVE DISPUTE RESOLUTION ACT (1990). The ACUS was disbanded in 1995 under budget-cutting measures. However, its work provided much of the foundation for institutionalizing ADR in the federal government.

Administrative Dispute Resolution Act (1990 and 1996)   U.S. statute that explicitly authorizes and promotes the use of ALTERNATIVE DISPUTE RESOLUTION by federal governmental agencies and seeks to encourage a variety of alternative methods of dispute resolution in cases to which the federal government is a party. Pub. L. No. 101-552, 104 Stat. 2738, codified at 5 U.S.C. §§ 581-593 (1993) (not to be confused with the NEGOTIATED RULEMAKING ACT, also codified using the same starting code section number).

The act does not mandate the use of ADR; rather, the government and the private parties must consent to it. However, the law requires every federal agency to adopt an ADR policy. The law explicitly authorizes agencies to use ADR and greatly facilitates its use through amendments to the ADMINISTRATIVE PROCEDURE ACT and other statutes, including the FEDERAL ARBITRATION ACT. Specifically, the act encourages settlement negotiations, conciliations, facilitation, mediation, fact-finding, mini-trials, and arbitration or any combination thereof for nearly all types of federal disputes involving formal and informal adjudications, rulemaking, enforcement actions, licensing or permitting, contract administration, and litigation brought by or against the agency.

The original 1990 act had a sunset provision for October 1, 1995. However, the Administrative Dispute Resolution Act of 1996 permanently reauthorized and extended the 1990 act and eliminated further sunset dates and special oversight or reporting requirements. The 1996 act improves on the 1990 legislation by addressing problems that arose during implementation of ADR under the 1990 statute. The 1996 act (1) clarifies and enhances confidentiality protections by explicitly exempting most communications made in dispute resolution proceedings from disclosure under the Freedom of Information Act; (2) authorizes, for the first time, *true* binding arbitration for all federal agencies across the board by eliminating a one-sided provision in the 1990 act that had allowed agency heads (but not private parties) to overturn arbitral awards; (3) broadens the act's coverage by eliminating exceptions that had previously caused uncertainty as to the law's applicability to many workplace-related conflicts and to certain specific dispute resolution mechanisms, such as ombudsmen; (4) takes steps that should make it easier for agencies to acquire expeditiously the services of mediators and neutrals; (5) directs the president to find a new home in the federal government for some of the coordinating, consulting, and other functions that had been performed by the ADMINISTRATIVE CONFERENCE OF THE UNITED STATES before its elimination by Congress in October 1995; and (6) encourages greater use of NEGOTIATED RULEMAKING by promoting actions to simplify the procedures that agencies must follow in establishing the negotiating committees that craft the substance of proposed regulations.

administrative expenses   Costs for the administration of an ADR process charged by an ADMINISTERING AGENCY, usually as established in its rules.

Such costs may include an administrative fee, hearing room fee, and charges for clerical services but not usually for transcripts of hearings, and in some instances may also include the fees and expenses of the NEUTRALS [DOA]. Under the rules of most administrative agencies, arbitrators are empowered to allocate responsibility for administrative expenses in their awards.

administrative law judge (A.L.J.)   ADJUDICATOR in ADMINISTRATIVE ADJUDICATION appointed pursuant to specific statutory authority.

administrative law proceedings   See ADMINISTRATIVE PROCESS.

Administrative Procedure Act (APA)   Law providing rules of procedure to ensure due process in ADMINISTRATIVE ADJUDICATION and other government agency decision making. See ADMINISTRATIVE PROCESS.

administrative procedure alternative dispute settlement   Use of ADR, primarily MEDIATION and FACILITATION, to resolve disputes involving matters subject to regulation by government agencies. Term is most correctly used when referring to the use of ADR after parties have initiated an ADMINISTRATIVE PROCESS to resolve the issue [Price and Woods, 1990, p. 21].

administrative mediation   Process employed by government agencies and usually provided for by regulation to resolve disputes over an agency's exercise of power. See MEDIATION.

administrative process   Process by which government agencies exercise their rulemaking, investigative, prosecutorial, and adjudicative powers.

Typically, ADMINISTRATIVE LAW PROCEEDINGS refers to the adjudicative procedure presided over by judges selected and supervised by either the regulatory agency itself or a separate ADMINISTRATIVE AGENCY. See ADMINISTRATIVE LAW JUDGE, ADMINISTRATIVE PROCEDURE ACT.

administrator   Either an ADMINISTERING AGENCY or an official of that agency who is empowered to conduct and supervise an ADR process. When an ADR process is initiated by the parties under the rules of a particular agency, that agency is known as the administrator. Although expected to be impartial, under normal circumstances the administrator does not act as a NEUTRAL [DOA].

ADR   Most commonly recognized as an acronym for ALTERNATIVE DISPUTE RESOLUTION and often coupled with *processes* or *mechanisms* (see, for example, ADRMs) so as not to be confused with the resolution of *alternative disputes*. Also used as an acronym for the related but distinct concept of APPROPRIATE DISPUTE RESOLUTION. See ALTERNATIVE DISPUTE RESOLUTION.

ADRMs   Alternative dispute resolution mechanisms. See ALTERNATIVE DISPUTE RESOLUTION.

adversarial   Commonly used as an adjective in place of ADVERSARY to describe a system or process in which disputants are hostile or in opposition to each other as if opponents in a contest. Despite its common use, it is not found in dictionaries, and the correct term would be *adversary*. See ADVERSARY PROCEEDING, ADVERSARY SYSTEM.

adversarial methods of dispute resolution   Processes in which the disputants treat or are encouraged to treat each other as opponents or enemies contesting for mutually incompatible outcomes in which one wins and the other loses. Although often mistakenly used to refer to particular processes, such as ADJUDICATION, the term refers more to method than to mechanism. Therefore, parties can use adversarial methods in negotiation or mediation and conversely engage in nonadversary adjudication. See ADVERSARY, ADVERSARY SYSTEM. Contrast COOPERATIVE, COLLABORATIVE, PROBLEM SOLVING.

adversarial model, adversary model   See ADVERSARY SYSTEM.

adversarial society, adversarial culture   Society in which the culture favors or promotes adversarial methods of dispute resolution.

The United States is often cited as an example and described as a society of assertive, aggressive, rights-conscious, litigious people ready and eager to challenge one another and those in authority. Auerbach [1983, pp. 7–8] notes that in some societies (such as Scandinavian fishermen, Mexican Zapotec, Bavarian villages, certain African tribes, Sinai Bedouin, and Israeli kibbutzim) such attitudes might be considered psychologically deviant; in such nonadversarial societies or cultures, the importance of enduring relationships makes peace, harmony, and mediation preferable to conflict, victory, and litigation. Some research questions the extent to which the United States can be labeled an adversarial society [Galanter, 1983].

adversary   n. Opponent or enemy. A DISPUTANT is an adversary in an ADVERSARY SYSTEM. Condition resulting from the disputants' perceptions that they have mutually incompatible goals or that they stand as opponents in a contest. Approach to a dispute that values the vindication of rights or personal interests more than the discovery and accomplishment of shared interests or goals.

adj. System or process with the characteristics just described.

adversary proceeding   Proceeding under the ADVERSARIAL MODEL, in which the opposing parties are either contesting the issue or have been given notice and opportunity to contest the issue, as distinguished from an EX PARTE HEARING.

adversary system   Dispute resolution system within which each party presents its most favorable version of the dispute to an impartial, often passive ADJUDICATOR, who resolves the dispute by determining the "truth" after considering the competing versions. The system works on the premise that justice is most likely to result from the clash of proofs between contesting parties. The ultimate judgment involves the application of the determined facts and a weighing of the parties' competing rights. Often incorrectly referred to as *adversarial system.*

The formal judicial system in the United States and most other COMMON LAW countries subscribe to this model, which reflects certain assumptions of social contract theory: that individuals have certain rights, that the persons in possession of those rights are in the best position to guarantee their protection, and that individuals or their advocates are capable of vindicating individuals' rights. Not surprisingly, the adversary system has been called "the fight theory of justice" [Leeson and Johnston, 1988, p. 2].

In the United States, a unique balance of roles between the parties or their lawyers and the adjudicator (judge, jury, or arbitrator) is the essence of the adversary system of trial. The presentation of the case in a client's most favorable light is entirely the function of the lawyers, who decide which witnesses should be called, when they will be called, what questions they will be asked, and during cross-examination, what questions will be asked of witnesses called by the opponent. It is the adjudicator's function, often as representative of the sovereignty of the state, to maintain decorum and order in the forum; to rule on motions and objections raised during the proceedings; to instruct the jury, if there is one, concerning the principles of law applicable to its decision; and of course to deliver judgment. Except as required by these functions, the judge can and will do nothing that might indicate a lack of impartiality; the actuality and the appearance of impartiality are both preserved by the adjudicator's "passive" role [Cappelletti and Jolowicz, 1975, pp. 239–240].

There are many criticisms of the adversary system. The combative attitudes engendered by such a system increase tensions and hostility between the disputants. This is exacerbated by the ethical responsibilities of lawyers in such systems to "win" for the client using every tactic that is professionally allowable (or not explicitly prohibited). Rather than focusing on the disputants' present and future interests, the object of the process is victory in relation to a carefully defined question of rights or principle as applied to a definitive past incident or incidents. Thus the adjudicator issues narrow win-lose outcomes rather than problem-solving solutions that might take into account the context of the dispute, the merit on both sides, and the wider interests of the parties [Mackie, 1991a, p. 5].

Not all legal systems are based on the adversary model, and not all ADJUDICATIVE PROCESSES or ADJUDICATION is adversary to the extent implied by this definition. In some legal systems, formal adjudication is based primarily on an inquisitorial model in which the adjudicator directs the gathering of facts. Arbitration can be either adversary or inquisitorial or a little of both depending on the preferences of the participants. Compare INQUISITORIAL SYSTEMS.

advisory arbitration   Process in which the parties submit their dispute to a neutral person or persons who render an unenforceable decision that the parties may accept or reject. The decision provides the parties with information about the likely results if the dispute is resolved by binding adjudication. This "reality testing" gives the parties a neutral perspective on their case and a clearer notion of their risk exposure in a binding forum. In theory, this promotes settlement and overcomes previous negotiation impasses based on disparate predictions of outcomes in binding adjudication.

Advisory arbitration is the same as NONBINDING ARBITRATION except to the extent that it implies "advice." Traditional advisory arbitration, historically used to resolve public employee disputes, can result in one or more possible recommended solutions instead of a single award. In this sense, advisory arbitration is similar to some forms of proactive mediation.

advisory med-arb   Hybrid dispute resolution process starting with MEDIATION and shifting to ADVISORY ARBITRATION when the parties declare an impasse on an issue. See MED-ARB.

advisory opinion   Nonbinding determination rendered by an ADJUDICATOR.

Law: Most commonly associated with a legal opinion rendered by a court in response to a question of law submitted by some authorized body or party. The advisory opinion procedure differs from contested proceedings in that there are no parties formally before the court as plaintiff and defendant. In some legal systems, lower courts and arbitral tribunals are allowed, and in some cases are mandated, to submit questions of law to higher courts for more authoritative direction. In the United States, some state courts are empowered to render advisory opinions. However, federal courts may not.

Arbitration: Arbitrator's determination on the respective rights of the parties. Such advisory opinions are nonbinding and issued only in ADVISORY or NON-BINDING ARBITRATIONS. Contrast AWARD, which usually refers to a binding determination by an arbitrator.

International Law: International courts may be empowered to give an advisory opinion relating to an existing international dispute and referred by an international entity. For example, the United Nations (UN) Charter, Article 96, authorizes the General Assembly (and UN organs and agencies as authorized within the scope of their activities) or the Security Council to request an advisory opinion from the INTERNATIONAL COURT OF JUSTICE. In theory, advisory opinions can be issued on questions for which there is no related existing international dispute. Generally the procedure is the same as used in contentious cases and involves written and oral proceedings in accordance with the rules of the court in question. Advisory opinions are not binding on the requesting entity, or on any other body or state unless such entities formally approve the opinion. The formal, judicial character of the issued opinion, however, may persuade a state to regulate its conduct accordingly [*Handbook on the Peaceful Settlement of Disputes Between States,* 1992, p. 75].

advocacy   Supporting or speaking in favor of something or someone, usually associated with an attempt to persuade a third party through plea or argument. Disputants themselves are said to advocate their interests or position when arguing on their own behalf; however, the term is usually associated with a third party acting on behalf of the disputant.

advocate   Person supporting or speaking in favor of something or someone, usually not herself.

Law: Person with privilege to plead for another in court, (*archaic*) particularly before the admiralty and ecclesiastical courts in England or the appellate courts in Scotland.

AFCC See ASSOCIATION OF FAMILY AND CONCILIATION COURTS.

affidavit Sworn statement or written declaration made upon oath before an authorized magistrate or officer. Some state statutes explicitly permit the use of an affidavit as evidence in an arbitral proceeding [DOA].

afiesem **(Ghana)** Literally, "house court," form of dispute resolution in Ghana where an *odiasem* acts as a mediator between the parties. The process is relatively informal, but if a solution is reached both parties are asked to swear an oath that they no longer have a case. The process is reserved generally for civil suits and nonfelonious criminal cases [Lowy, 1978].

AFM See ACADEMY OF FAMILY MEDIATORS.

agenda, agenda development List of items or issues to be discussed at a meeting.

Negotiation: Parties develop agendas for positive reasons (to facilitate orderly discussion and problem solving by providing some structure and keeping participants focused and on track) and for negative reasons (to unduly restrict the issues or influence outcomes). One of the major tasks of facilitators and mediators is to help the parties develop agendas.

There are many different approaches to agenda development for negotiations. Drawing on Gulliver [1979] and Fisher and Ury [1981], Moore [1986, pp. 182–185] identifies and discusses the pros and cons of eight distinct approaches.

An alternative approach to determining meeting content is the AGENDALESS or OPEN SPACE MEETING.

agendaless meeting See OPEN SPACE MEETING.

agent-principal division Conflict of interest that can develop between an individual and his or her representative [Princen, 1992, p. 181].

aggression Unprovoked attack on another. Manifestation of the will to assert power over or hostile feelings toward others.

International Relation: Improper intervention or attack by one country against another.

aggressor-defender model   Model of CONFLICT ESCALATION in which the aggressor, whose goals directly conflict with the interests of the defender, proceeds to take the initiative with offensive, hostile tactics. The defender merely reacts, and the conflict escalates until the aggressor wins or gives up [Princen, 1992, p. 166].

agree   To concur or have a compatible opinion; to consent or mutually assent to, as to a proposal. To reach AGREEMENT or ACCORD, approve or adopt an agreement or settlement.

agreed award   *Arbitration:* AWARD that appears to have been made by the AR-BITRATOR but that has actually been arrived at by the parties concerned.
   Labor: Agreed award is considered a violation of the arbitration process. Such an award is also known as a *rigged award,* an *informed award,* or a *fixed award.* These are all alike in that someone who will be affected by the award is ignorant of the fact that the award was agreed to by the immediate parties to the contract and was not made by the arbitrator herself but with her knowledge and consent. The agreed award is perhaps most common in cases settling wage demands, a settlement that one or both parties feels unable to announce except through a third party, such as an arbitrator. Compare CONSENT AWARD.

agreement   Agreeing or the product of agreeing.
   AGREE and agreement can have a range of meaning, from merely sharing an opinion to reaching a mutual understanding to exchanging promises or entering into a contract (in the legal sense). The Latin root, *aggregatio mentium,* infers merely a meeting of the minds. Thus, agreement has a broader meaning than contract, although the terms are often used synonymously.
   Law: Typically refers to a concurrence over respective rights or obligations. Law recognizes various distinct classifications of agreements.
   International Relations: Usually refers to an undertaking that has binding force (without regard to its formal designation) among entities subject to international law that have entered into it. Iklé [1964, p. 7] defines the term as "an exchange of conditional promises between governments, by which each party declares that it will act in a certain way on condition that the other parties act in accordance with their promises." Compare CONTRACT.

aikido **(Japan)**   Japanese art of self-defense based on ethical considerations contained in Eastern religious and philosophical thought but differing from other martial art systems in its essential motivations and intents. The word *aikido* (composed of three characters) means the method or way (*do*) for the coordination or harmony (*ai*) of mental energy or spirit (*ki*). In contrast to other self-defense approaches, aikido, when used in its highest ethical forms, aims merely to neutralize and harmlessly redirect the aggression of the attacker; nobody is harmed in the encounter. Saposnek [1986–1987, pp. 119–120] has drawn parallels between aikido and MEDIATION, applying the techniques of the former to the practice of the latter.

aisatsu **(Japan)**   Formal greetings. In negotiations in Japan, an introductory meeting in which the highest-status representatives control the interaction and avoid task-related topics [Graham and Sano, 1989, p. 2].

A.L.J.   ADMINISTRATIVE LAW JUDGE.

alliance   Relationship or union between persons, groups, states, or other entities (such as an alliance of nations or an alliance by marriage), usually for the purpose of cooperating in a matter of common interest. Alliance connotes a more formal arrangement than COALITION, although the terms are often used synonymously.
   International Relations: The union between two or more states by treaty for purposes of offense or defense in war.
   Compare COALITION.

ally   Person or state that formally enters into an ALLIANCE with another. To enter into an alliance.
   Allies are those who can favorably influence the other party and its position in negotiation [Schoenfield and Schoenfield, 1988, p. 203].

alternate dispute resolution   Nonsense term often mistaken as the phrase from which the acronym ADR is derived. See ALTERNATIVE DISPUTE RESOLUTION.

alternation   *Negotiation:* Compromise technique whereby the parties decide to take turns in the possession of something that is difficult or impossible to divide [Moore, 1986, p. 210; Orme, 1989, p. 61]. Alternation can succeed only if the contestants have a minimal level of trust in each other, or failing that, if enforcement mechanisms can be put into place that will protect each side against betrayal and thus act as a substitute for trust [Orme, 1989, p. 64].

alternative conflict resolution methods   Negotiation, mediation, conciliation, and so forth [Goldman, 1991, pp. 15–17]. Same as ALTERNATIVE DISPUTE RESOLUTION.

alternative discovery dispute resolution (ADDR)   Use of neutral parties, other than the trial judge, to resolve disputed issues in the discovery phase of litigation.

Usually ADDR panels consist of senior judges and respected senior practicing attorneys who oversee the nagging problems that arise in complex DISCOVERY—when one party balks at turning material over, delays, or makes unconscionable demands. Unlike the trial judge, who is subject to many institutional restraints on time, resources, and scheduling, an ADDR neutral would have the time to learn the intricacies of the discovery issues and could meet more easily with the parties and under more circumstances—for example, during a deposition rather than days or weeks afterward. Moreover, because the litigants would be paying for the panelists' time, they would have marked incentives not to misuse or overuse the panelists' services [Lieberman and Lieberman, 1985, p. 121].

In addition to merely encouraging direct negotiation, an ADDR neutral may act as a mediator. The most common role, however, is that of the DISCOVERY REFEREE, who has limited decision-making or adjudicative powers on discovery matters and is empowered by court rule, statute, or party agreement. The best known model is used in California and has come under fire as subject to abuse [see, for example, Reuben, 1994].

See TRIAL ON ORDER OF REFERENCE.

alternative dispute resolution (ADR) Catchall generic term referring to ways in which a society with a formal, state-sponsored ADJUDICATIVE PROCESS attempts to resolve disputes without using that process. It is a class of DISPUTE RESOLUTION mechanisms and is commonly understood to include alternatives to the formal adversary method of trial or LITIGATION, as that process is understood in Western, particularly COMMON LAW, systems. Thus it includes NEGOTIATION, MEDIATION, ARBITRATION, and their variations. It is understood to exclude DICTATION, VOTING, FIGHTING, WAR, and WITHDRAWAL and is limited to procedural concepts. Therefore it does not include BLOCK SOLUTIONS (such as no-fault laws), which delete or control an entire class of disputes through adjustments to substantive law. Some representative legal definitions are as follows:

- "Methods, procedures, or techniques that are used to resolve differences voluntarily and that do not require a traditional or formal adjudicatory trial or a contested hearing. These methods include, but are not limited to, mediation, contractual arbitration, fact-finding, consensus-building, and neutral-expert evaluation" [Haw. Rev. Stat. § 613-1 (1992 Supp.)].

- "An informal forum in which mediation, conciliation, or arbitration is used to resolve disputes among individuals" [Tex. Civ. Prac. & Rem. Code Ann. § 152-001 (West 1993)].

- "Informal, consensual procedures which can be used by parties in a dispute to obtain a resolution in lieu of formal litigation. These procedures include settlement negotiations, conciliation, facilitation, mediation, fact-finding, mini-trials and arbitration or any combination" (Legislative history of the Minnesota ADR Act under "1. Purpose") [Minn. Stat. Ann. § 491.01].

- "The provision of an alternative system for settling conflicts between two or more parties, which operates both independent of or as an adjunct to the judicial-litigation system, through the intervention of a qualified neutral person or persons who are trained to intercede in and coordinate the interaction of the disputants in a settlement process" [Utah Code Ann. §§ 58-39A-1 (Supp. 1992)].

- "The term Alternative Dispute Resolution (ADR) refers to any method other than litigation for resolution of disputes" [Georgia Supreme Court Order on Alternative Dispute Resolution Rules, 1993].

- "Any procedure or combination of procedures voluntarily used to resolve issues in controversy without the need to resort to litigation" [48 C.F.R. § 33.201 (1992)].

The term is problematic. Clearly it refers to alternative mechanisms with which to resolve disputes (contrast DISPUTE and CONFLICT). There is a range of opinion, however, as to which processes are included. Although it is not clear who coined the term or when, ADR was first used when most of the processes encompassed by the term were private, voluntary, and provided independently of the judicial system as an alternative to litigation. Today, informal processes and procedures initiated and provided by the courts are also lumped under ADR. For a long time, arbitration was the most well-known ADR process leading to a distinction between *traditional ADR* (mainly arbitration) and *nontraditional ADR* (mediation, mini-trials, and so on). See, for example, WAMR 4(8). In contrast, Newton [1991] notes the increasing tendency when referring to ADR to mean processes other than arbitration and other adjudicative processes. Fiorino [1990] limits it to processes that direct parties toward a consensus. However, in contrast and consistent with the Texas provision quoted earlier, Applebey [1991] excludes unassisted, informal negotiation.

How does one determine whether or not a process is an alternative? If alternative implies choice, ADR processes would be characterized by complete party control and independence from the judicial system. Voluntariness and privacy would be primary determinants. Under this limited definition, ADR refers to any alternative to litigation that is provided privately, outside the existing judicial system, and subject to the complete control of the disputants. Some definitions emphasize proceeding privately without resort to litigation [for example, Practising Law Institute, 1987, p. 17]. This would exclude most of the COURT-CONNECTED or COURT-RELATED ADR programs, those informal DISPUTE RESOLUTION PROCESSES established, provided, and often mandated by law as institutional reforms designed to alleviate problems caused by the excessive burdens of litigation. Many of these processes are modeled after private, voluntary processes but actually constitute a form of judicial INFORMALISM. These processes are frequently involuntary and provided within or through the existing judicial system with limitations on the disputants' control over procedure. In most other respects, such processes can be identical to private, voluntary ADR but raise distinct issues because of their public administration and coercive nature.

Another approach is that *alternative* means choice between litigation and another process. This would limit ADR to those processes used only to resolve matters that are JUSTICIABLE, meaning capable of being contested in a court. This would exclude negotiation, mediation, and arbitration when used to resolve matters that are nonjusticiable. Some commentators would go further to imply that ADR refers only to processes used to resolve disputes that are already in litigation; for example, Applebey [1991] limits ADR to those processes that resemble a legal or paralegal process in connection with court activity and excludes informal settlement activities, particularly those that do not involve the use of an impartial third party. In its extreme this would include all court-related ADR and exclude not only negotiation (except in the context of a PRETRIAL SETTLEMENT CONFERENCE) but possibly all private, voluntary extrajudicial dispute processing.

Most definitions seem to focus on purpose and include any conflict-handling procedure that has as its goal any one or more of the following: improving relationships, avoiding the cost and delay of litigation, relieving court congestion, providing a more effective or constructive resolution between disputants, enhancing community involvement in the process of resolving disputes, and facilitating access to JUSTICE. Garth [1982, p. 185] distinguishes three sets of goals: (1) making rights effective, (2) conciliation, and (3) diversion. To advance these goals, the procedures that come under the heading of ADR usually are characterized as informal, fast, and inexpensive. Proceedings are usually held in private and the outcome is consensual, although participation in the process may be coerced. Many of these procedures tend to deemphasize ADVERSARIAL METHODS OF DISPUTE RESOLUTION by discouraging the use of lawyers, judicial involvement, and the application of substantive law, and by encouraging party participation. These goals and characteristics describe many court-connected processes as well as private, voluntary processes [Lieberman and Henry, 1986, pp. 425–426]. In determining whether court-connected processes qualify as ADR processes, Hensler [1995, pp. 1594–1595] includes only those that emphasize party control. Ultimately the definition is evolving to encompass a wide range of court-related initiatives designed to facilitate a more effective administration of justice and help overcome delays. It also includes many processes that may be used independently of court action even though litigation may or may not have commenced.

ADR processes are sometimes categorized as either ADJUDICATIVE, in which an independent party makes a decision as in arbitration, or nonadjudicative. The terms *nonbinding ADR* and *negotiation-based ADR* [Newton, 1991] are also used to distinguish some forms of ADR from adjudicative forms of ADR. Another class of ADR processes, including EARLY NEUTRAL EVALUATION and SUMMARY JURY TRIAL, has been identified as *evaluative,* although a more functional distinction may be between adjudicative and conciliatory ADR mechanisms. Contrast ADJUDICATIVE and CONCILIATORY.

Another distinction is made between *active ADR* and *passive ADR* [Practising Law Institute, 1987, p. 12]. Active ADR is affirmative risk-management activity that anticipates sources of conflict and puts in place systems to control costs and exposures to liability. Passive ADR is reactive risk management that seeks to settle or sidetrack expensive court litigation into other forums. The essential distinction between active and passive ADR is a party's ability to act unilaterally to make ADR happen. For example, placing ARBITRATION CLAUSES in all company contracts to require arbitration in any future disputes is active ADR, while proposing to settle or submit a pending lawsuit to arbitration or mediation is passive ADR because both require the other side's agreement to participate after the fact [Practising Law Institute, 1987, pp. 12–13].

ADR processes are alternatives to each other as well as to litigation. Litigation may be more suitable for some types of disputes. ADR and litigation are not mutually exclusive and often are complementary. See COMPLEMENTARY DISPUTE RESOLUTION.

alternative dispute resolution agreement   Agreement to resolve existing or future disputes through one or more methods of ADR.

An ADR agreement must be clear, explicit, and unequivocal and must not depend on implication or subtlety, particularly where the ADR process agreed on has terms that appear unfair on their face (such as terms binding on one party but not on the other). Some courts will hold the factual findings from an ADR process to be binding but not the legal findings unless the ADR agreement states that it should [*Thomas Crimmins Contracting Co.* v. *City of New York,* 1989].

alternative dispute resolution movement   Campaign undertaken by those with a common interest in the promotion and institutionalization of ADR processes. The idea that use of the official court system is only one among an abundant variety of ways of solving disputes.

The genesis of the current ADR movement in the United States was two-pronged: it emerged from the social reform movements of the 1960s and from ongoing efforts at civil justice reform. Often both complementary and contradictory, the social reform movements emphasized replacing ADVERSARY approaches with

RECONCILIATION, leading to "better" solutions and more satisfactory human relations. Ongoing efforts emphasize managing institutions more efficiently, clearing dockets, and reducing the delay and expense of and burden on judicial institutions. Informality is valued because it could result in speedier, cheaper, and less hostile DISPUTE RESOLUTION and a beneficial transformation of the disputants' interpersonal relationship [Murray, Rau, and Sherman, 1989, pp. 49–50].

alternative dispute resolution system   Institutionalization of one or more ADR processes, either singly or in combination, to resolve disputes that routinely arise in an organization or that are referred to a decision-making or judicial institution. *System* implies that the mechanisms are in place rather than AD HOC. According to the one legal definition, the ADR system is "an informal forum in which mediation, conciliation, or arbitration is used to resolve disputes among individuals, including those having an ongoing relationship such as relatives, neighbors, landlords and tenants, employees and employers, and merchants and consumers" [Tex. Civ. Prac. & Rem. Code Ann. § 152-001 (West 1993)].

Compare INTEGRATED CONFLICT MANAGEMENT SYSTEM.

alternative final award (England)   *Arbitration:* Practice of rendering two or more AWARDS, as alternatives, under a single arbitration proceeding. This practice is resorted to under English law when the arbitrator would rule differently based on the correct application of law and when she requests judicial advice on a point of law through the expedient of the special case-stated procedure [DOA]. The court's advisory opinion will determine which award becomes binding.

alternative means of dispute resolution   Less common alternative phrase meaning the same as ALTERNATIVE DISPUTE RESOLUTION. However, it could denote any and all alternatives, including political action, violence, AVOIDANCE, or BLOCK SOLUTIONS, such as no-fault laws. An illustrative definition is as follows: "Any procedure that is used, in lieu of an adjudication, to resolve issues in controversy, including but not limited to, settlement negotiations, conciliation, facilitation, mediation, fact-finding, mini-trials, and arbitration, or any combination thereof" [5 U.S.C.A. § 571(3) (West 1993)].

This term was more common in earlier days of the ADR movement and was adopted as the title for the American Bar Association's first committee to explore alternatives to litigation.

***althing* (Iceland)**   National assembly in medieval Iceland that met annually; as the forerunner of the current Icelandic assembly, it is perhaps the oldest continuous national legislative and judicial body.

The medieval *althing* exercised both judicial and quasi-legislative powers to resolve disputes. Within the *althing* were four courts, called Quarter Courts, which tried cases between litigants who did not belong to the same local *thing* and cases in which no judgment had been reached in the local *thing.* There also existed a Fifth Court, which acted as a court of appeals for cases ending in a divided judgment in the Quarter Courts. Each Quarter Court was presided over by a panel of thirty-six judges and required a concurrence of at least thirty-one judges for a determination. The Fifth Court judgment could be had by a simple majority. There was also a *logretta,* or court of legislation, composed of the chieftains, which was allowed to make or alter law and which decided what the law was if there was a disagreement about a rule [Miller, 1984, p. 97].

References to the *althing* in Icelandic sagas show its importance in resolving the violent, divisive blood feuds that pervaded early Icelandic society.

altruism   Concept of making a decision in which the decision maker voluntarily gives up something in order to increase the welfare of another person [Frohlich and Oppenheimer, 1984, p. 5].

The term *altruism* was coined by Auguste Comte, the founder of modern sociology, is derived from the Italian *altrui* ("the other"), and connotes an unselfish attention to the needs of others. It should be distinguished from empathy, which is an emotional feeling or state of concern for the other, because altruism implies an *altruistic act,* or behavior taken voluntarily and intentionally to benefit others, while empathy does not necessarily give rise to acts or behavior [Menkel-Meadow, 1992]. Many proponents of ADR claim that adversary litigation is contrary to, and ADR is suffused with, the concept of altruism.

ambiguous authority   *Negotiation:* Bargaining without clearly indicating that one has the authority to reach an agreement to bind one's client or constituents. This gives the negotiator the option of proposing risky concessions to test the extent of the other side's willingness to concede and then of walking away from a concession she appeared to have been authorized to make. See DISOWNABLE CONCESSION.

American Arbitration Association (AAA)   Oldest not-for-profit ADMINISTERING AGENCY in the United States primarily dedicated to dispute resolution. The AAA is a private organization that was founded in 1926 "to foster the study of arbitration, to perfect its techniques and procedures under arbitration law, and to advance generally the science of arbitration" (AAA, 1926, Preamble). It has pioneered the development and use of collective negotiations, arbitration, mediation, and other ADR processes, and works actively to publicize and promote these processes. Of far greater importance, however, has been its central role in the administration of much of the labor and commercial arbitration that takes place in the United States.

The AAA's dual mandate of education and administration distinguishes it from many of the more recently formed administering agencies and reflects its origins to some degree. The AAA resulted from a mediated settlement between two competing organizations, the Arbitration Society of America, founded in 1922, and the Arbitration Foundation, formed in 1924. Since then, the AAA has been an influential pioneer in the use of ADR.

amiable composition, amicable composition Form of equitable jurisdiction authority from French law in which ARBITRATORS are free, within limits traced by positive law, to decide in accordance with their basic sense of fairness. Associated primarily with international COMMERCIAL ARBITRATION, the term is rarely used in the United States, and English courts traditionally refuse to enforce awards arrived at by amiable composition.

Often used synonymously with *EX AEQUO ET BONO,* amiable composition is sometimes interpreted as requiring arbitrators to disregard the applicable law only when necessary to achieve a JUST result, while *ex aequo et bono* gives the arbitrator more latitude in ignoring the law. See *EX AEQUO ET BONO, AMIABLES COMPOSITEUR.*

amiables compositeur, amiable compounders French term for ARBITRATORS granted the POWER to decide using AMIABLE COMPOSITION.

The concept of *amiables compositeurs* is widely used in continental European legal systems. *Amiables compositeurs* are subject to the rules of *natural justice* and must observe the fundamental rules governing judicial procedure and material law. They are distinguished from other arbitrators in that they are permitted to decide on the basis of fairness and equity. The literal meaning of the term, "friendly" arbitrators, suggests that they are to CONCILIATE both parties rather than secure absolute fairness at the expense of one. Although this seemed to be the role of *amiables compositeur* under Roman law (see ARBITER), this is no longer current practice. In some countries, the parties waive the right of appeal if they authorize arbitrators to act as *amiables compositeurs* [DOA].

amicable settlement, amicable agreement Resolution of a dispute without recourse to the binding decision of a third party. Although parties may be able to reach an agreement amicably with or without third parties, the term is sometimes used in a more restrictive, technical sense to denote the resolution of a dispute prior to the involvement of third parties.

anchor, anchoring *Negotiation:* Used broadly to describe the phenomenon resulting from a party limiting its BARGAINING RANGE around a particular outcome, or to refer to that particular targeted outcome.

In some usage, anchor refers to the designated starting point for assessing whether an offer or settlement option is a gain or a loss, such as settlements in similar disputes or that can be achieved without the other side's cooperation [Putnam and Holmer, 1992, p. 132]. More specific usage refers to the phenomenon of a party, uncertain about the bargaining range, using the initial offer as the point from which to bargain. This may be used offensively by the more informed party to gain more from the BARGAINING process [Lax and Sebenius, 1986; Raiffa, 1982, pp. 127–128].

Related but distinguishable concepts include RESISTANCE POINT, RESERVATION PRICE, BOTTOM LINE, and BATNA.

Andean Court of Justice Dispute resolution institution established by the Agreement of Cartagena, a 1969 treaty entered into by Bolivia, Columbia, Chile, Ecuador, and Peru to initiate the process of subregional integration and formation of an Andean economic community. The court resolves disputes relating to the interpretation or implementation of the agreement or of decisions of the Commission, the administrative arm of the agreement. No issue over which the court has jurisdiction can be submitted to any other court or to arbitration. Decisions of the court are binding by treaty and prevail over domestic law [de Pierola, 1987, pp. 11–16].

anger Extreme displeasure. A standard negotiating tactic, a display of anger, real or feigned, may be used to convince others that the negotiator is serious about his position. Convincing displays of anger may evoke strong emotional responses from inexperienced negotiators, causing them to doubt the reasonableness of their position. Negotiators may be so intimidated by the display that they may make CONCESSIONS to avoid prolonged contact with the one using the tactic. Finally, an expression of anger may merely stimulate an angry response from an opponent, strengthening resistance and leading to a possible impasse [Edwards and White, 1977, p. 113].

annoy Anger slightly.

apex game In negotiation GAME THEORY, a game in which there is one player called the *apex* and a multitude of other players called the *bases,* and all legal winning coalitions must include either the apex or all other parties except the apex [Oliver, 1984, p. 128].

appeal Complaint made to a superior court to correct a perceived injustice by an inferior court or tribunal.

Arbitration: Often used in reference to a petition or motion to modify or to vacate an arbitration AWARD. When asking a trial court to make a ruling on an award, such use is technically correct but not as exact as a *petition to modify* or *petition to vacate.* See VACATING AN AWARD. One can appeal a trial court's ruling on an award to an appellate court, or a lower appellate court's ruling to a higher appellate court.

appeal boards of administrative agencies   Review procedure for challenging AWARDS in arbitrations that are administered by various commodity exchanges and trade associations. Typically provided as part of the standard rules rather than AD HOC, the APPEAL is administered by the agency in contrast to a review by a court.

A review procedure has long been established in Great Britain and in most of the commodity exchanges and trade associations in Europe, although there seems to be no uniformity among such practices [DOA].

appeasement   Act of making CONCESSIONS for the purpose of placating someone, usually a potential aggressor. Most commonly used in the context of international relations.

appellate alternative dispute resolution   Use of ADR, often INSTITUTIONALIZATION, at the appellate court level.

Many federal and state appellate courts now use ADR to encourage settlement negotiations pending appeal. Models vary by jurisdiction. Although appellate ADR goes by other names, such as *appellate settlement conference* or *appellate conference,* most models are based on the mediation process and incorporate coercion and neutral evaluation to varying degrees. Florida law, for example, provides for and defines *appellate court mediation* as follows: "Mediation that occurs during the pendency of an appeal of a civil case" [Fla. Stat. Ann. § 44.1011 (West Supp. 1992)].

appellate settlement conference   See APPELLATE ALTERNATIVE DISPUTE RESOLUTION.

applicable law   See GOVERNING LAW.

appointing agency   Another term for ADMINISTERING AGENCY, particularly as applied in the United States to such institutions as the AMERICAN ARBITRATION ASSOCIATION, the FEDERAL MEDIATION AND CONCILIATION SERVICE, and the various state mediation boards in their respective roles as ADMINISTRATORS of dispute resolution for labor disputes, for example, or for so-called LEMON LAW cases when statute or regulation grants them appointment authority [DOA].

appointment of arbitrators   Act of selecting ARBITRATORS.

Generally arbitrators are chosen by the disputing parties in the manner established in their agreement to arbitrate. Some agreements provide that each party appoints an arbitrator, with the third arbitrator to be chosen by these two arbitrators (see TRIPARTITE PANEL). If the two arbitrators cannot agree, the third arbitrator may be appointed by the agency administering the arbitration. A common practice at present is to select a single arbitrator whose appointment may be governed by the rules of an impartial agency or who can be designated in the agreement. Under MODERN ARBITRATION STATUTES, if the method specified in the agreement does not result in an appointment, a court may make the appointment on the motion of one of the parties. This is unnecessary when the parties proceed under self-executing arbitration rules, such as the AMERICAN ARBITRATION ASSOCIATION's Commercial Arbitration Rules, which allow the ADMINISTERING AGENCY to appoint the arbitrators when the parties fail to do so.

appraisal   Valuation of property by one or more especially qualified and impartial persons.

The appraiser makes her valuation according to her own skill, knowledge, and experience. Some courts have declared that an appraisal is not in itself an ARBITRATION proceeding, because no controversy exists. Unless such a specific provision is made in the agreement, an appraisal provision is not regarded as an intention to take evidence or to hear arguments in the presence of the parties. The distinction is prominent in English law [DOA].

appropriate dispute resolution (ADR)   Alternative meaning for ADR based on the proposition that the critical challenge in DISPUTE RESOLUTION is matching an appropriate process to a particular dispute. The term encompasses LITIGATION as well as those processes commonly referred to as ALTERNATIVE DISPUTE RESOLUTION processes, thereby putting all of them on an equal footing rather than designating some processes as second class or undesirable. Compare ALTERNATIVE DISPUTE RESOLUTION.

arbiter (archaic)   Term sometimes used in place of ARBITRATOR.

In the original use of the term, an arbiter was distinguishable from an arbitrator. Under old Roman law, arbiters were appointed by the *praetor* and invested with broad powers to decide causes of action, termed *bono fidei,* and to judge according to principles of equity. In contrast, the *iudex* was bound to decide according to strict law. Under later Roman law, the arbiter proceeded formally in imitation of the *iudicia* and served much like judges [Corpus Iuris Civilis, Dig. 4.8.1 and 4.8.13 §2]. This latter form of ARBITRATION, distinct from the older form of AMIABLE COMPOSITION (the informal practice of helping the parties to reach an accord), disappeared with the *iudicia* after which it was modeled.

The distinction between arbiters and arbitrators carried over into ecclesiastical law, which by the twelfth century stated that arbiters were expected to proceed formally in imitation of court and issue an ARBITRIUM or binding determination. An arbitrator, however, was expected to proceed informally and in a conciliatory capacity to reestablish harmony between the disputants. Relying solely on notions of equity, an arbitrator could give estimates on claims and suggest solutions but could not give sentence; the outcome was an ARBITRATUS or transaction composed by the parties. The distinction faded as arbitrators were invested with powers similar to those of arbiters, but it was retained in the notion that arbitrators can proceed wholly at their own discretion while arbiters are bound to decide according to rules of law and equity [David, 1985; Fowler, 1976].

Also, an arbiter may refer to an UMPIRE, who makes the decision when two party-appointed arbitrators cannot agree. The term arbiter is now rarely used.

arbitrability Legal standard determining that an issue in dispute between parties is subject to arbitration. Refers to circumstances and types of issues that may be within the authority of an arbitrator, and to whether the particular dispute falls within the ambit of the agreement—that is, whether the parties have agreed to submit the particular matter in controversy to decision by arbitration.

There are two kinds of arbitrability, substantive and procedural. SUBSTANTIVE ARBITRABILITY is whether the issue proposed for arbitration falls into a category of dispute covered by the ARBITRATION AGREEMENT. Determination of substantive arbitrability is based on the language of the arbitration agreement and applicable law. In some jurisdictions, the law may prohibit the arbitration of certain issues for reasons of public policy.

Procedural arbitrability is whether the issue proposed for arbitration is barred by a limitation of time or by failure to adhere to other procedural steps imposed on the particular claim by contract or statute. In labor disputes, the opportunity to arbitrate could be denied due to failure to file the grievance on time, to process it through the steps of the grievance procedure in timely fashion, to put the grievance in writing, or some other condition precedent. So, in addition to being time-barred, a matter could be procedurally infirm. Determination is usually based on compliance with the language of the agreement.

The question of arbitrability is distinct from the question of the validity of the arbitration agreement. Questions of arbitrability are usually raised before a court, arbitrator, ADMINISTERING AGENCY, or combination thereof. Precisely who determines arbitrability depends on statutes in force, rules of procedure, court decisions, or international convention, as ratified by the parties. Typically only the arbitrator or the courts, not both, may decide on arbitrability or on whether the decision may be referred to an international organization [DOA].

arbitral award See AWARD.

arbitral court (Africa) Ethnocentric term used by early ethnographers to describe the TRIBAL MOOT. Described as a type of court found in the ancient tribal law of sub-Saharan Africa and thought to be universal in all African societies, the arbitral court in Africa was recognized as an informal means of settling disputes through negotiation with or without the use of a third party—that is, ARBITRATOR. Usually such disputes were those within a family or an intrafamily group and were most appropriately settled by the head of the family or its elders. Issues apart from familial quarrels included the adjustment of property rights in land or cattle and the settlement of estates on the death of members of the family group [DOA].

arbitral immunity   Quasi-judicial, legal immunity for ARBITRATORS similar to that provided to judges in judicial proceedings. Arguably, the immunity extends to the ADMINISTERING AGENCY and to its directors, officers, and employees.

arbitral referee   Third party empowered by the disputants to dispose of issues that need immediate resolution prior to the empaneling and empowerment of arbitrators. Under the NEW YORK CONVENTION, the arbitral referee's decision may not constitute an enforceable award unless the parties agreed to be so bound.

arbitrament   Latinized form of ARBITREMENT.

arbitramentum aequum tribuit cuique suum   "A just arbitration renders to each his own." Before modern arbitration, courts required AWARDS in ARBITREMENT to provide something, no matter how nominal, for each disputant. See DOCTRINE OF MUTUALITY.

arbitrary decision-making procedure   *Negotiation:* Any procedural mechanism for automatically and arbitrarily deciding an issue in which the outcome is of little consequence to the disputants or in which they have an equal chance of winning or losing if a decision is made through some other means. The classic example is SPLIT THE DIFFERENCE, share equally in the benefits and losses of a particular resource [Moore, 1986, p. 237], or "flip a coin."

arbitrate   Act as an ARBITRATOR. See ARBITRATION.

arbitration   Generic term for a range of DISPUTE RESOLUTION PROCESSES involving the referral of a dispute to an impartial third party who, after giving the parties an opportunity to present their evidence and arguments, renders a determination in settlement of the dispute. Most commonly used in the United States to describe a private, voluntary, ADJUDICATIVE, and usually binding process established by mutual agreement of the disputants to resolve existing or future disputes. The term is difficult to define because it has been used loosely to denote many disparate processes whose only common element is third-party adjudication. Some authoritative definitions include the following:

- "The referral of a dispute to one or more neutral third parties for a decision based on evidence and testimony provided by the disputants" [Colo. Rev. Stat. Ann. § 13-22-302(1)(West 1996)].

- "Arbitration is closely akin to adjudication in that a neutral third party decides a submitted issue after reviewing evidence and hearing argument from the parties. It may be binding on the parties, either through agreement or operation of law, or it may be non-binding in that a decision is only advisory. Arbitration may be voluntary, where the parties agree to resolve the issues by means of arbitration, or it may be mandatory, where the process is the exclusive means provided" [1 C.F.R. § 305.86-3 App. (1993)].

- "A process whereby a neutral third party or panel, called an arbitrator or arbitration panel, considers the facts and arguments presented by the parties and renders a decision which may be binding or non-binding as provided" [Fla. Stat. Ann. § 44.1011 (West Supp. 1992)].

- "The process whereby a panel provides non-binding recommendation for the resolution of a dispute, unless the parties previously agree that the decision be binding" [40 C.F.R. § 131.7(f)(2)(ii) (1992)].

- "A consensual, voluntary contract entered into by parties to a dispute for the purpose of securing a final disposition in a speedy, inexpensive, expeditious, and perhaps less formal manner of one or more of the controversial differences between the parties" [*Barcon Assocs.* v. *Tri-County Asphalt Corp.*, 1981].

This entry outlines the evolution of the term and makes distinctions between the primary types of arbitration. For terms that are more precise, see the entries for terms in all capital letters.

Arbitration is a variant of the Old French *arbitracion,* whose root is in the Latin *arbitrari,* meaning "to examine or give judgment." It is difficult to determine how and when *arbitration* came into use as a legal term in England, was enshrined in the COMMON LAW, and was adopted by U.S. law. It may have been used in nonlegal contexts prior to its use in legal contexts; for example, "That a man . . . putte hym al outrely in the arbitracion and Iuggement . . . of hise enemys" [Chaucer, Melib: ¶ 787 (circa 1386)]. By the end of the thirteenth century, however, the phrase "put themselves upon" is found combined with ARBITRIUM, meaning "judgment." For example, *"Et partes petunt diem ad concordandum usque in crastinum et ponunt se in omnibus in arbitrio Bartholomei de Acre"* ("And the parties crave a day on which to make concord on the morrow, and

they submit themselves in all things to the judgment of Bartholomew of Acre")
[Records of the Fair Court of St. Ives, 1908, p. 18]. It is possible that the phrase
was adapted from the then-common formula *"ponunt se super patriam"* ("put
themselves upon the state") to signify joiner of issue and submittal of the dispute to determination by the state [Pollock and Maitland, 1895, vol. 2, p. 624].
Whatever the source of the term, it quickly evolved that parties would "submit
to an arbitrement."

Arbitrement, or the Latinized *arbitrament,* is defined in the earliest English
legal dictionaries as the AWARD or JUDGMENT itself. *Les Termes de la Ley* [1533,
p. 54] defines *arbitrement* as "an Award, Determination, or Judgement, which
one or more makes at the request of two parties at the least, for and upon some
Debt, Trespass, or other Controversie had between them. And it is called in
Latin *Arbitratus,* and *Arbitrium;* and they that make the Award or Arbitrement
are called *Arbitri,* in English *Arbitrators."*

By its tenth edition, *Jacob's Law Dictionary* [1797] did not even bother to define *arbitrement,* being content to lump the matter under *award.* Such old definitions provide little clue, however, as to the process that yielded the award
other than that it was a form of judgment. See ARBITREMENT.

Early legal commentators tended to define and distinguish the process by focusing either on the SUBMISSION (the agreement to submit to and abide by the
judgment of another) or on the award itself. One of the oldest treatises, West's
Symboleography [1601–1603], provides quite simply that "a Compromise or Submission, Arbitrium, Compromissum, Submissio, is the faciltie or power of pronouncing Sentence betweene persons at controversie, given to Arbitrators by
the parties mutuall private consent, without publike authoritie [Citing Y.B. 8
Eliz. 4, pl. 2.]." The first modern treatise on the subject also defines the process
by its elements: "That act, by which parties refer any matter in dispute between
them to the decision of a third person, is called a submission; the person to
whom the reference is made, an arbitrator; when the reference is made to more
than one, and provision made, that in case they shall disagree, another shall decide, that one is called an umpire; the judgment pronounced by an arbitrator,
or arbitrators, an award; that by an umpire, an umpirage, or, less properly, an
award" [Kyd, 1791, pp. 4–5].

To West, arbitration was clearly a private consensual process in which disputants gave another individual the power to determine a solution to their disputes. Modern treatises, however, cannot adhere to such a simple definition. In
1935, Lord Hailsham, formerly Q. M. Hogg, devoted nine pages to defining arbitration, which he summarized "with some hesitation" as follows: "Arbitration
is the reference for binding judicial determination of any matter in controversy
capable of being compromised by way of accord and satisfaction or rendered
arbitrable by statute between two or more parties to some person or persons
other than a Court of competent jurisdiction" [Hogg, 1935, p. 16, emphasis

added]. Hogg's definition was barely distinguishable from the definition of court judgment. In fact, he was forced to distinguish arbitration by noting that the decision maker is "other than a Court." In addition, he identified three kinds of arbitration classified according to the source from which the arbitration derives its binding character. Thus, "arbitration may originate" [Hogg, 1935, p. 16]:

(1) In an agreement between the parties, called a submission.
(2) In an order of the Court.
(3) In the provisions of an Act of Parliament.

"Unfortunately," observes one modern English treatise that devotes twenty-two pages to an attempt to define arbitration, "English law does not provide a comprehensive answer to the question, 'What is an arbitration?'" [Mustill and Boyd, 1987, p. 41]. American legal authority is not much better, and sometimes is contradictory. This is because there are many forms of arbitration in use today and a comprehensive definition of one will conflict with that of another.

Forms of arbitration can be divided roughly as either *voluntary* or COMPULSORY and either type can be *binding* or NONBINDING depending on the intended effect of the award. The most familiar form is voluntary arbitration, sometimes referred to as *private* arbitration because it is not conducted under the auspices of or by the state, or *contractual* arbitration because the process is created and defined by mutual agreement of the disputants. Some voluntary arbitration is not explicitly contractual, the agreement to arbitrate being implicit in the disputants' membership in a group or participation in an association, in which case the bylaws or other set of group norms require arbitration as a condition of membership. Because the agreement to arbitrate is not negotiable, this form is sometimes referred to as MANDATORY ARBITRATION, a good example of which occurs between employees and employers in the various stock exchanges and associations. Voluntary arbitration is characterized by party control over procedure, choice of adjudicator, effect of the award, and restrictions on arbitral powers.

Different types of voluntary arbitration are distinguishable by subject matter or type of disputant. For example, LABOR ARBITRATION involves disputes between organized labor and management over workplace and employment issues. The agreement to arbitrate is reached through COLLECTIVE BARGAINING and is contained in the COLLECTIVE BARGAINING AGREEMENT. In some labor-management contexts, arbitration may be imposed by statute (see COMPULSORY ARBITRATION). COMMERCIAL ARBITRATION involves disputes in business relationships. The agreement to arbitrate is usually contained in the contract that defines the business relationship or in the bylaws of a particular trade association or exchange. Arbitration involving business relationships that are transnational—that is, entities of different nationalities or contractual performance in another country—is often referred to as INTERNATIONAL COMMERCIAL ARBITRATION. Nation-states or other entities recognized by international law may agree to resolve their disputes through INTERNATIONAL ARBITRATION as established by preexisting obligations under international law, such as a treaty, or by agreement after the dispute arises. Some forms of voluntary arbitration are known as SPECIAL-FEATURE ARBITRATIONS, the best known of which is FINAL-OFFER ARBITRATION (also called LAST-BEST-OFFER ARBITRATION or BASEBALL ARBITRATION). When a voluntary written agreement to arbitrate must be enforced by statute, the terms *statutory arbitration* or *mandatory arbitration* may be used but should not be confused with the same terms as defined in the next paragraph. When an oral agreement to arbitrate is enforced under common law principles, the process may be referred to as a COMMON LAW ARBITRATION.

In contrast to voluntary arbitration is COMPULSORY ARBITRATION, sometimes referred to as MANDATORY ARBITRATION, in which the disputants have not agreed to arbitrate but are directed by court rule or by statute to submit their dispute to determination by a third party prior to or in lieu of formal adjudication by a judge. When arbitration is mandated by statute, it is referred to as STATUTORY ARBITRATION and is usually binding. Some dispute-specific forms of statutory arbitration include PUBLIC EMPLOYEE ARBITRATION (also called COMPULSORY ARBITRATION) and UNINSURED MOTORIST ARBITRATION. Arbitration directed by a court can be referred to as COURT-CONNECTED, COURT-REFERRED, or COURT-ANNEXED, and though usually nonbinding, is a precondition to formal trial before a judge. If the court actually administers the arbitration, it might be referred to as a *court-administered arbitration*. One form of compulsory arbitration common in U.S. courts is MANDATORY NONBINDING ARBITRATION, used to induce settlement of civil cases. Less common is JUVENILE ARBITRATION, used to determine appropriate action in minor criminal matters without the use of formal judicial proceedings.

Some types of arbitration may be subject specific. For example, MEDICAL MALPRACTICE ARBITRATION involves referral to an arbitrator of disputes over the negligence of health care providers. This type of arbitration may be compulsory and nonbinding and is sometimes referred to as a *case screening* procedure, or it may be voluntary and binding. Additional distinctions between forms of arbitration are illustrated by the contrasting terms AD HOC ARBITRATION and ADMINISTERED ARBITRATION, *binding* arbitration and *nonbinding* (or ADVISORY) ARBITRATION, RIGHTS (sometimes GRIEVANCE) ARBITRATION and INTEREST ARBITRATION, and TRIPARTITE ARBITRATION and PERMANENT CHAIRMAN or IMPARTIAL CHAIRMAN ARBITRATION. The term ARBITRATION SYSTEM is sometimes used to denote a particular type of arbitration conducted under a particular statute, regulation, or association rule and usually administered by an organization. Thus the commodities trade arbitration system is distinct from the labor arbitration system.

Arbitration is the most common adjudicative ADR process and is the process most similar to LITIGATION. Although arbitration can resemble a court proceeding with formal adversary presentations and the application of substantive rules of law to achieve a binding judgment, most arbitration is characterized as an informal, inexpensive, fast, and private adjudicative process that may consider custom as well as principles of fairness and equity to reach an outcome that is final and subject to very limited appeal. The neutral decision makers are not governmental officials appointed by the state or elected by the public to wield authority over disputes as do judges and officials of ADMINISTRATIVE AGENCIES. Formal rules of evidence and formal procedures such as discovery and motion practice rarely apply.

arbitration agreement   The part of a contract that pledges the parties concerned to use ARBITRATION as a means of settling any present or future dispute.

There are two types of arbitration agreement: the SUBMISSION AGREEMENT and the ARBITRATION CLAUSE. Parties enter into submission agreements after disputes arise in order to submit those existing disputes to arbitration. Parties place arbitration clauses in contracts to ensure the use of arbitration to resolve disputes that may arise in the future. The latter are also referred to as FUTURE DISPUTES CLAUSES. An arbitration agreement may take the form of an arbitration clause in a contract or it may be a separate agreement. Thus future disputes agreements (as opposed to clauses) can exist independent of a contract. However, such agreements must relate to a recognized legal relationship in order to be enforceable.

In the United States, under old COMMON LAW rules, oral or written arbitration agreements could be revoked by either party at any time prior to the issuance of an AWARD. Under older versions of arbitration statutes, some of which dated back to colonial times, submissions could not be revoked. Under MODERN ARBITRATION STATUTES, written arbitration agreements (submissions and clauses) are enforceable much like any other contractual agreement and cannot be unilaterally revoked. Additionally, legislatures have made arbitration agreements more readily enforceable by repealing older requirements that written agreements with arbitration clauses in them had to be very clearly marked as having such agreements.

Arbitration agreement is sometimes used interchangeably with *arbitration clause.* In practice, arbitration agreement is the more inclusive term, applying to both the submission agreement for existing disputes and the future disputes clause.

See ARBITRATION AND CONCILIATION TREATY, ARBITRATION CLAUSE, FUTURE DISPUTES CLAUSE, and SUBMISSION AGREEMENT.

arbitration and award   *Law:* Affirmative defense in a judicial proceeding that the subject matter of the proceeding has already been resolved in a previous arbitration. An ARBITRAL AWARD may have RES JUDICATA and COLLATERAL ESTOPPEL effects.

arbitration and conciliation treaty   International AGREEMENT establishing procedures for the use of either ARBITRATION (a binding decision made by judges chosen by the parties) or CONCILIATION (a nonbinding proposal of terms of settlement made by an impartial commission or single conciliator).

As in any arbitration agreement, the parties can specify scope and procedure. One area of interpretation concerns whether the parties have precluded referral to an international court by agreeing to arbitrate. Typically, international agreements to submit to the jurisdiction of an international court are labeled as such. The trend, however, is for arbitration and conciliation treaties to include voluntary, mutual submission to an international tribunal of choice, including international courts.

arbitration board   See BOARD OF ARBITRATION.

arbitration clause   Type of ARBITRATION AGREEMENT that exists as a provision in a contract (see CONTAINER CONTRACT) and by which the parties to the contract agree to resolve future disputes through ARBITRATION. Sometimes referred to as a FUTURE DISPUTES CLAUSE.

In U.S. practice, the arbitration clause is severable or separable from the container contract, allowing the arbitrators to rule on issues of contract validity. Other jurisdictions have found that the clause cannot be severed unless it is contained in a separate document constituting a separate and distinct agreement.

arbitration of consumer grievances   Use of ARBITRATION to resolve consumer complaints.

The Council of Better Business Bureaus pioneered CONSUMER ARBITRATION using a system in which the arbitrators served without compensation and the service was free. Much consumer arbitration today centers around the automotive industry and includes both voluntary and statutorily mandated arbitration, such as LEMON LAWS.

arbitration "on documents."   Form of arbitration in which an arbitrator hands down a binding decision decided solely on the basis of documents and submissions on paper made by the two parties. Also known as DOCUMENTS-ONLY ARBITRATION.

arbitration rules   Procedural rules adopted by the parties for the conduct of an arbitration. Typically such rules provide for how the ARBITRATOR will be appointed, how powers will be granted to the arbitrator and the ADMINISTERING AGENCY to conduct the arbitral proceedings from time of appointment to the rendering of the award, what the applicable limitations of time will be, and other matters of procedure. The term is most often used in reference to the standard set of rules developed by an administering agency and adopted by the parties when referring the matter to administration by that agency.

arbitration system   A particular type of arbitration conducted under a particular statute, regulation, or association rule and usually administered by an organization. Thus the commodities trade arbitration system is distinct from the LABOR ARBITRATION system.

arbitrator   Person who arbitrates; person selected to hear evidence and render a decision as a determination of a dispute. Depending on the form of ARBITRATION, the arbitrator may be chosen by the parties or by a court, may or may not be impartial, and may or may not have the power to issue a binding determination. In the most common forms of private, voluntary arbitration, however, parties choose an impartial arbitrator and define the arbitral powers by mutual consent.

Under Roman law and older ecclesiastical law, an arbitrator was not an ADJUDICATOR, and a distinction existed between forms of arbitration conducted by ARBITERS and arbitrators. An arbitrator was expected to proceed informally and in a conciliatory capacity to reestablish harmony between the disputants. Relying solely on notions of equity, an arbitrator could give estimates on claims and suggest solutions but could not give sentence; the outcome was an ARBITRATUS or transaction composed by the parties. The distinction faded as arbitrators were invested with powers similar to those of arbiters, but was retained in the notion that arbitrators can proceed wholly at their own discretion while arbiters are bound to decide according to rules of law and equity [David, 1985; Fowler, 1976]. Contrast ARBITER.

Another historic but important distinction is between an arbitrator and an UMPIRE. An umpire is a third party that usually intervenes and acts alone as a single arbitrator when two party-appointed arbitrators cannot agree on an award. In contrast, a third arbitrator appointed to a TRIPARTITE PANEL cannot act alone but must join one of the other two arbitrators in a majority decision. The intent of the parties will determine whether the third arbitrator is an additional arbitrator or an umpire, regardless of the nomenclature used in the agreement. This distinction harkens back to a form of early ARBITREMENT in which each disputant chose an arbitrator, both of whom attempted to construct a mutually acceptable award. See DOCTRINE OF MUTUALITY. If the parties appointing them failed to agree on the award they negotiated, the party-appointed arbitrators delegated their authority to a single umpire. See also REFEREE, PARTY-APPOINTED ARBITRATOR.

arbitrator-advocates   Party-appointed arbitrators who also serve as advocates for their respective appointing parties before a third, neutral arbitrator. Used in some LABOR ARBITRATION under TRIPARTITE PANELS and in maritime arbitrations, such as under the rules of the Baltic Exchange, to relieve parties who may live considerable distances apart from traveling to a hearing locale and from the cost of both an advocate and an arbitrator. See PARTISAN ARBITRATOR.

arbitrator's authority   Legal power or right of an arbitrator to hear and determine a dispute, an authority derived from law and from the will of the parties as expressed in their ARBITRATION AGREEMENT or COLLECTIVE BARGAINING AGREEMENT [DOA].

arbitratus   Resolution of a DISPUTE brought about by an ARBITRATOR, as opposed to an ARBITER, under twelfth-century canon law. An arbitratus was akin to a settlement agreement reached by the parties in an informal process in which the arbitrator suggested solutions, much like a CONCILIATOR in non–U.S. practice, but could not make a binding AWARD. See ARBITER and ARBITRIUM.

arbitrement (archaic)   "Law French" term referring to early forms of ARBITRATION recognized in English COMMON LAW. From the Latin root *arbitrari*, meaning "to examine or give judgment," it originally referred to the act of arbitrating, while ARBITRIUM referred to the determination or AWARD that resulted. English use changed the meaning. For example, arbitrement is defined in the earliest English legal dictionaries as the award or judgment itself. For example, *Les Termes de la Ley* [1533, p. 54] defines *arbitrement* as "an Award, Determination, or Judgement, which one or more makes at the request of two parties at the least, for and upon some Debt, Trespass, or other Controversie had between them. And it is called in Latin Arbitratus, and Arbitrium; and they that make the Award or Arbitrement are called Arbitri, in English, Arbitrators." By its tenth edition, *Jacob's Law Dictionary* [1797] did not even bother to define *arbitrement*, being content to lump the matter under *award*. Today, *Black's Law Dictionary* [1979] defines it as "the award or decision of arbitrators upon a matter of dispute, which has been submitted to them." Thus the term has been so closely associated with the award or the determination of the arbitrators that it is no longer used to refer to the act of arbitrating.

Older forms of arbitrement involved the selection of an arbitrator by each of the disputants. The arbitrators were often friends or influential acquaintances of the selecting disputant. After receiving a description of the dispute, the two arbitrators would retire to construct an award that would be mutually acceptable. In essence, this constituted negotiation by proxy. If the arbitrators failed to reach agreement among themselves, an UMPIRE might have been called in to make a determination. See DOCTRINE OF MUTUALITY, PARTY-APPOINTED ARBITRATOR.

arbitrium (archaic)   From the Latin, meaning "judgment." JUDGMENT or AWARD of ARBITERS, as opposed to ARBITRATORS, under Roman and canon law. See ARBITERS.

The term became connected with modern arbitration by the end of the thirteenth century, when combined with the phrase, "put themselves upon." For example, *Et partes petunt diem ad concordandum usque in crastinum et ponunt se in omnibus in arbitrio Bartholomei de Acre* ("And the parties crave a day on which to make concord on the morrow, and they submit themselves in all things to the judgment of Bartholomew of Acre")[Records of the Fair Court of St. Ives, 1908, p. 18]. It is possible that the phrase was adapted from the then-common formula *ponunt se super patriam* ("put themselves upon the state") to signify joiner of issue and submittal of the dispute to determination by the state [Pollock and Maitland, vol. 2, 1895, p. 624]. By the sixteenth century, the phrase evolved that parties would "submit to an arbitrement" and arbitrium was replaced in common use by *arbitrement* or *award*. See ARBITREMENT, ARBITRATION.

arb-med   Term used to refer to two very different hybrids of ARBITRATION and MEDIATION.

Most commonly it refers to a private, voluntary hybrid in which the parties agree in advance that the neutral is authorized to arbitrate, make an award, and then mediate. Typically the award is sealed in an envelope and concealed from the parties until such time as the neutral believes that further mediation would be fruitless. If and when the envelope is opened by the neutral, the revealed award becomes binding (or advisory as per the agreement). If mediation is successful, the award is destroyed without being revealed. This hybrid avoids the dangers associated with the confusion of roles in MED-ARB because the arbitration takes places before confidences are shared with the neutral in mediation. Because the neutral cannot go back and change the award, the parties can feel more comfortable in being candid with the neutral in the subsequent mediation. This hybrid has been used in labor negotiations, and several AAA offices have experimented with it in insurance claims disputes. The anecdotal evidence suggests that after venting and hearing each other's cases in arbitration, many parties are likely to negotiate a settlement with this "sword of Damocles" hanging over their heads [Yarn, 1992, p. 242].

Less commonly the term refers to a process that arises out of a single agreement to arbitrate one issue in a dispute and to mediate another issue in the dispute, with a fallback provision for referral of the second issue to a new arbitrator if the mediation of that issue does not succeed. Thus arbitration and mediation could proceed concurrently and independently on separate issues between the same parties.

argot   Special vocabulary and idiom used by a particular social, ethnic, or professional group.

Originally the term was associated with private communications among members of an underworld group. In a less nefarious context, argot can impair communication between persons who are unfamiliar with each other's specialized vocabulary and thereby exacerbate conflict or impede resolution. This lexicon is full of argot.

Argumentative Competence Instrument (ACI)   Test that assesses the competence of a person engaged in verbal persuasion.

Using traditional argumentation theory, the ACI analyzes both effectiveness and appropriateness of discourse. Effectiveness is a measure of "good" argumentation skills: logic, sufficient factual support, clear associations between facts and conclusions, persuasiveness, and clarity. Appropriateness is a measure of inappropriate behaviors: abusing and misquoting the opponent, interrupting, being arrogant and overbearing, and misuse of facts. By subtracting the appropriateness score from the effectiveness score, one calculates the overall argumentative competence [Keough, 1992].

arms race theory   Notion that mutual accumulation of nuclear armaments will eventually lead to war [Houweling and Siccana, 1988, p. 87–88].

Asbestos Claims Facility   Mechanism created to resolve asbestos-related personal injury claims in the United States.

Created in 1984 by an agreement (referred to as the *Wellington Agreement* because of Yale Law School Dean Harry Wellington's role in negotiating the agreement) among various insurers and manufacturers of asbestos, the facility attempted to lower the cost of resolving asbestos claims by providing a central place to file claims against all signatories to the agreement, by offering a neutral method of evaluating individuals' claims (nonbinding) and offering settlement without the discovery and legal costs associated with litigation, and by using mediation or expedited binding arbitration to resolve producers' claims against insurers [Marcus and Sherman, 1985, p. 834].

aspiration(s) level   Outcome that a party hopes to achieve through negotiation, which generally is an outcome better than that party's RESERVATION PRICE [Raiffa, 1982, p. 128].

assertive   Proactive in insisting on one's rights.

In the THOMAS/KILMANN CONFLICT MODE INSTRUMENT, assertive and COOPERATIVE are the two variables used to gauge conflict-handling modes. A COMPETITIVE mode is assertive but noncooperative. An ACCOMMODATING mode is cooperative but nonassertive. An AVOIDING mode is neither assertive nor cooperative. A COMPROMISING mode is partially assertive and cooperative. A COLLABORATING mode is both highly assertive and highly cooperative.

assessment   *Mediation:* Refers to two distinct processes used in the resolution of family, particularly divorce, disputes:

1. A screening process whereby client couples are initially judged on their readiness to enter mediation. Over time the term in this context has acquired two slightly different meanings. In general, assessment is treated as synonymous with *intake,* the INTAKE SESSION [Haynes, 1984], or the mediator's interpretation, after the initial telephone contact and one mediation session, of the clients' conflict and the way in which they currently deal with it. Occasionally *assessment* is used to refer to an evaluation of client behavior using a set of standard criteria with which the mediator plans subsequent intervention strategies [Walker, 1986; Irving and Benjamin, 1989, pp. 117–118].

2. A more INQUISITORIAL alternative to divorce mediation per se in which the neutral coerces family participation in analyzing their situation. In these forms of assessment, families are evaluated and recommendations are made to help a judge reach a decision regarding custody and access [Irving and Benjamin, 1992, p. 36].

The term carries some negative implications. Many practitioners are wary of engaging in any evaluation of a couple's readiness or the appropriateness of mediation. Instead they prefer to give parties an opportunity to make their own choices about participating.

assimilation   Strategy for resolving ethnic conflict by imprinting dominant language and culture on minorities.

Assimilation connotes proactive steps by the state, such as denying minorities opportunities for political and cultural self-expression or banning use of a minority's language in government activities. It can also refer to the voluntary adaptation of the national character or dominant culture by a minority. Compare ACCOMMODATION, ACCULTURATION.

Association of Family and Conciliation Courts (AFCC)   An international and interdisciplinary organization of judges, lawyers, counselors, mediators, custody evaluators, academics, parent educators, policymakers, and others interested in family law and domestic relations.

asymmetrically binding arbitration   Special form of arbitration in which one party to a dispute is bound by the arbitrator's decision while the other is free to reject the award and seek legal recourse through litigation. This form of arbitration may be used to counter any perceived imbalance of BARGAINING POWER or problems with adhesion contracts that may make enforcement of the arbitration agreement difficult. This type of arbitration is found in areas where consumers purchase goods or services without the meaningful ability to negotiate terms and conditions set out in the fine print of a form contract. Examples include insurance policy coverage disputes and automobile warrantee disputes (see, for example, AUTOLINE). A possible application is to employment disputes, where the employer surrenders its right of appeal while providing the employee with the option of being bound, thereby promoting fairness while possibly reducing litigation costs. Also referred to as CONDITIONALLY BINDING ARBITRATION.

attitudinal structuring   See subdefinitions under BARGAINING.

attorney   See LAWYER.

attribution bias   Tendency to attribute causality to personal rather than situational factors, even when there are clear situational causes for events [Ross, 1977].

As a consequence, conflicts that appear to outside observers to be caused by structural factors are often experienced by the actors involved as due to personality traits. Thus, apparent personality conflicts between individual organizational members may mask more central conflicts [Smith, Simmons, and Thames, 1989; Bartunek and Reid, 1992, p. 119].

attribution theory   Concept that the causes a person assigns for an injury will be important determinants of the action he or she takes in response to it. Attribution may affect an individual's tendency to transform an experience into a complaint. For example, people who blame themselves for an experience are less likely to see it as injurious or, having so perceived it, to voice a GRIEVANCE about it [Felstiner, Abel, and Sarat, 1980–81, p. 641].

auction bargaining   See BARGAINING.

auction procedure   Means of dividing a limited number of goods whereby each good is auctioned off to the recipient, who not only pays for the goods but receives an equal share of the money raised in the auction [Raiffa, 1982, pp. 289–290].

authority   Power or right to command, act, or commit oneself or someone else to a particular course of action or outcome. Authority may be inherent in a particular role or position or it may be granted by someone with authority.

Negotiation: Term most often refers to the power delegated by a principal to an agent, such as client to attorney. With respect to attorney-client relationships, the attorney needs the client's approval before finalizing an agreement or settlement. Within this guideline, Haydock and Mitchell [1984, pp. 46–47] identify various degrees of authority that clients may delegate to a negotiating attorney ranging from unlimited to none.

Authority can be *express,* that is, given explicitly either orally or in writing; *apparent;* or *implied.* For definitions of these and other legally recognized forms of authority, see *Black's Law Dictionary.*

Law: In the doctrine of STARE DECISIS, precedential weight or value of an opinion. Thus a particular ruling by the U.S. Supreme Court may be particularly authoritative on similar issues when handled by lower courts.

AUTOCAP (Automotive Consumer Action Program)   Informal third-party appeal program designed to improve dealer-customer relations by providing the mechanism for review and mediation of automotive complaints involving participating franchised new car and truck dealers or manufacturers. Voluntarily sponsored by state or local franchised automobile dealer associations according to the National Automobile Dealers Association's National AUTOCAP Standards.

AUTOCAP works to resolve automotive complaints in two ways. First, staff will attempt to settle the dispute through informal mediation between each party. Approximately 80 percent of all complaints handled by AUTOCAP are equitably settled in this way. Unresolved disputes are arbitrated by an impartial panel consisting of dealers and not less than 50 percent consumer professionals that recommends a solution based on the facts of the case. Participating dealers and manufacturers voluntarily agree to honor panel arbitration, which is nonbinding on consumers. See LEMON LAW. Compare AUTOLINE.

Autoline   Program established in 1982 by General Motors and other automobile manufacturers and administered by the BETTER BUSINESS BUREAU to resolve new-car warranty disputes.

Volunteer arbitrators from all walks of life who have gone through a short training program but who do not necessarily have a background in either the law or automobile mechanics, hear the consumer's claims under an automobile warranty issued by a manufacturer member of the Autoline program. These arbitrators cannot consider claims for consequential damages, such as for personal injury or lost wages. The consumer is not bound by the arbitrator's decision and is free to reject it and pursue any claim in court. The manufacturer, however, has usually agreed to be bound if the consumer so chooses. Funded by manufacturers, Autoline is designed to process complaints quickly and at no cost to the consumer.

Autosolve   Dispute resolution program run by the American Automobile Association in cooperation with various automobile manufacturers.

42

Similar to AUTOLINE, this program was discontinued in fall of 1993 when it came under investigation in Florida and California for alleged unfairness.

avoidance, avoiding   Dispute resolution technique associated with WITHDRAWAL. Authorities describing this technique can be divided into three groups. The first group focuses on relationships, for example:

- "A technique of acting on a dispute by withdrawing from contact with the other disputant. It is usually marked by a unilateral severance or shrinking of relations" [Miller, 1984, p. 100].
- "Avoidance has a particular meaning in studies of community disputing; it is usually defined as the withdrawal or curtailment of a relationship" [Nader and Todd, 1978, p. 9].
- "Avoidance involves the unilateral withdrawal of a social relationship" [Podolefsky, 1992, p. 53].

Using this focus, the coerciveness of the technique is gauged by the importance of the relationship. If the disputants highly value the relationship, avoidance is coercive, but not if the relationship is of little importance. Perceptions of the relationship's importance within the broader community may also be a factor. Thus, breaking off the relationship in a very public way may be an aspect of the technique [Podolefsky, 1992, p. 53]. In some cultures, avoidance is not perceived as coercive. Where the value of the relationship is great, avoidance provides a way to preserve harmony and save face by not dealing with the issues openly.

The second group of authorities focuses on the disputants' relationship to the conflict itself, for example:

- "When avoidance is set forth as a conflict management option, it is interpreted in the context of a particular conflict and not in terms of the overall relationship. Thus avoidance means simply the decision not to pursue a conflict, not to address an issue" [Thomas, 1976].
- "Avoidance represents a procedure of indirect confrontation in which one principal takes no action to obtain redress for a wrong or a curtailment of his interests, although his withdrawal tactics may induce his opponent to make amends" [Podolefsky, 1992, p. 52, citation omitted].
- "A means of resolving a dispute in which the incompatibility of goals, values, interests, or positions is perceived by both sides, and one or both then withdraw from a physical or bargaining position or cease the actions that originally caused the dispute" [Holsti, 1983, p. 406].

Compare WITHDRAWAL and LUMPING IT.

The third group of authorities focuses on the individual disputant's conflict-handling style and psychological preferences. The definition used in the THOMAS/KILMANN CONFLICT MODE INSTRUMENT [1974, p. x] is representative: "Avoiding is unassertive and uncooperative—the individual does not immediately pursue their own concerns or those of the other person. They do not address the conflict." Using this focus, outward manifestations of the technique, such as sidestepping an issue, postponing an issue, or simply withdrawing from a threatening situation, are seen as largely ineffective because they fail to satisfy any of the disputants' concerns and the conflict remains unresolved. Although most commentators are generally critical of this approach, one notes that it is useful when the issue is trivial or when the potential dysfunctional effect of confronting the other party outweighs the benefits of the resolution of conflict [Rahim, 1986, pp. 84–85]. Contrast COLLABORATIVE.

Finally, Pruitt and Lewis [1977] describe *conflict avoidance* as having many forms. In addition to withdrawal, in which one or both parties turn to some alternative activity or means of need satisfaction, these forms include SUBMISSION, in which one party makes a decision and the other follows it; *denial,* in which one or both parties come to believe that there are no differences between them; and *norm following,* in which parties resolve the problems that divide them by adopting ready-made and time-honored solutions instead of trying to develop new approaches.

award DECISION, JUDGMENT, or DETERMINATION, rendered by independent third parties and setting out the terms of settlement on a controversy submitted by the parties. Also refers to the written instrument containing the decision.

The term is most common in labor and commercial arbitration, where it refers to the final and binding decision by an arbitrator or arbitral tribunal in the full settlement of a dispute (compare ADVISORY OPINION). The decisions, however, of other private or extrajudicial decision makers such as REFEREES or of international dispute settlement bodies such as international arbitral tribunals, courts, and claims commissions may be referred to as *awards.*

In commercial arbitration, an award is usually given after taking testimony and hearing arguments from both parties (but see AGREED AWARD and ARBITRATION "ON THE DOCUMENTS") and must be in writing under modern arbitration statutes. In domestic matters, arbitrators in the United States and Great Britain generally need not state reasons for their award. In labor arbitration awards, reasons are generally given in the form of an opinion that accompanies the award but is not a component part of it, unless otherwise specified by the arbitrator. The practice varies by jurisdiction; for example, in France and the Netherlands an award given without reasons is invalid [DOA]. In international commercial arbitration and in the arbitration of disputes between states, reasons are essential for enforcement.

In both commercial and international arbitration, the arbitration agreement establishes the extent of the arbitrator's powers in making the award. Although most awards provide for monetary compensation, an award may require specific performance or grant a party injunctive relief unless the arbitration agreement expressly denies this authority. Awards may have COLLATERAL ESTOPPEL and *RES JUDICATA* effect and can be vacated only for limited reasons as provided by statute in each jurisdiction, such as the arbitrator exceeding the authority given under the arbitral agreement.

A definition of *award* in the context of international commercial arbitration was submitted for inclusion in the UNCITRAL model law but was not included. The definition is as follows: "Award means a final award which disposes of all the issues submitted to the arbitral tribunal which finally determines any question of substance or the question of its competence or any other question of procedure but, in the latter case, only if the arbitral tribunal terms its decision an award" [see Broches, 1984].

award by confession   AWARD by an ARBITRATOR, or by the agency or person appointing the arbitrator, that is made at the request of the parties for money due or for money that will become due before an award is otherwise made.

An award by confession may be useful when the parties wish to have the award legally confirmed, though no controversy over liability is involved. All that is required to initiate such a procedure is a verified statement by each party containing an authorization to make the award, the amount of the award, or the method of arriving at the amount, and any fact relevant to the liability. An award by confession is treated in the same manner as an award that has been arrived at through the full arbitration procedure. Such a method relieves the parties of submitting their dispute to the full arbitration process in order to arrive at the amount of money due [DOA].

award upon settlement   AWARD that an ARBITRATOR makes at the request of the parties on the terms of the settlement they arrived at themselves during the course of the arbitration [DOA]. Same as CONSENT AWARD. Contrast AGREED AWARD.

awase **(Japan)**   Japanese style of interaction that eschews dichotomous choices and focuses on interdependence and personal relationships. In negotiation, *awase* may place emphasis on the establishment of relations and on the existence of past favors and future obligations rather than treating the negotiation as an end in itself [Cohen, 1991, p. 31].

back channel communications *Negotiation:* Communications between a negotiator and the authority or constituency to whom he is responsible. Such communications can include progress reports, requests for and grants of negotiating authority, and strategy directions. Common usage often implies secret and informal communications that circumvent formal, recognized lines of communication for the purpose of reaching a higher authority directly.

In diplomacy, back channel communications is a process in which the members of a delegation report directly to their home office [Lall, 1985, p. 123].

Compare VERTICAL BARGAINING.

back pay awards *Labor:* Arbitration AWARD of lost pay benefits and compensation, given as a remedy for contractual violations. Unless deprived by the parties of the authority to do so, the arbitrator may award reinstatement, with the amount of pay lost as remedy and compensation, when finding discharge or wrongful layoff to be inappropriate or a violation of the contract. The idea is to place the aggrieved party in the circumstances that would have existed had no contract violation taken place. Arbitrators may qualify such a penalty by reinstating without awarding back pay, or with a specified portion or full back pay allowed. They may also frequently require deduction for any compensation the employee has been receiving in the interim, such as from a second job. Back pay may be awarded when a person is reinstated after having been laid off in violation of seniority rules. The awards of some arbitrators provide for back pay with deduction for any unemployment compensation received. Some arbitrators feel that because the employee has already lost his available eligibility for future benefits in the same year, to make him return the benefits without restoring his eligibility might be considered an injustice. Contracts sometimes state that any unemployment benefits received must be considered in computing the amount of pay lost [DOA].

background variables   *Negotiation:* Conditions that are external to the negotiation process and out of the negotiators' control but that have a significant effect on the process and outcomes. Some background variables are characteristics of the negotiators themselves, such as gender, age, nationality, race, personality traits related to "toughness" [Bartos, 1967], reputation, personal ambition, and experience as a negotiator [Iklé, 1964]. Other background variables are contextual, such as organizational context of the bargaining, position of the negotiator in the hierarchy, viability of the organization, and degree of interdependence [Douglas, 1962]. Because negotiators have little or no control over background variables introduced into the negotiation by another negotiator, they must anticipate and identify background variables and adjust their negotiating strategies or tactics accordingly [Edwards and White, 1977, p. 13].

backward induction argument   *Negotiation:* Tendency of parties to adopt a strategy of incremental concessions based on the anticipated or desired results. Most applicable in POSITIONAL BARGAINING when the number of rounds in a negotiation are known in advance. Such a strategy is likely to be competitive rather than cooperative [Schuessler, 1990, p. 478].

bad faith   Failure to act in good faith. See GOOD FAITH.

balance of power   Distribution of power among parties.
    Mediation: Sometimes discussed as a strategy used by mediators or as a goal of good mediation process. Depending on the mediation philosophy, the mediator either attempts to redistribute power to achieve a balance conducive to fair negotiation (see EMPOWERMENT) or seeks not to affect the existing balance through the intervention.
    International Relations: The conditions that either repress or promote aggressive action by a state [Pauling, Laszlo, and Jong, 1986, vol. 1, p. 85].

balanced partiality   Promotion of the disputants' shared goals, objectives, and interests by an INTERVENOR.
    Quakers who mediate often talk about balanced partiality rather than impartiality. By this they mean that they see themselves as advocates for both

sides or, more precisely, for overarching goals that both sides presumably prefer, such as the reduction of violence [Princen, 1992, p. 238]. Compare IMPARTIAL, BIAS, NEUTRALITY.

balanced and restorative justice (BARJ)   Juvenile justice concept giving equal weight to the basic RESTORATIVE JUSTICE principle of offender accountability, assurance of community safety, and providing the offender with skills to be able to engage in legitimate endeavors upon release. A balanced and restorative juvenile justice system gives victims and communities opportunities for involvement in the justice process. Many states are experimenting with the concept with the aid of the BARJ Project supported by the Office of Juvenile Justice and Delinquency Prevention of the U.S. Department of Justice.

BAPA   See BEST ALTERNATIVE TO THE PROPOSED AGREEMENT. Compare BATNA.

barangay **(Philippines)**   Traditional sociopolitical organization established in precolonial times that uses CONCILIATORY methods of dispute resolution.

Presidential Decree 1508, enacted in 1978, institutionalized the *barangay* justice system as a forum subordinate to the state judiciary. The *barangay captain,* the head or chairman of the *barangay* conciliation body, has fifteen days to help the parties arrive at an AMICABLE SETTLEMENT. Failing agreement, the matter is referred to a *Pangkat* (a panel chosen by the parties), which also has fifteen days to settle the dispute. A settlement has the force and effect of a final judgment of a court, unless a party timely repudiates. If the parties fail to settle before the *Pangkat* within the prescribed period, the case may be filed in court or proper office of the government for adjudication [Pe, Sosmena, and Tadiar, 1988, pp. 26–27, 43]. See also *JIRGA.*

baraza **(Congo/Kingwana)**   A calling together of people for the disposition or disputation and possible settlement of some knotty affair. A sort of colloquy of all those who matter, held whenever people could get ahold of a personage of authority to head the proceedings.

bargain   Mutual agreement reached through BARGAINING. To engage in bargaining. Compare AGREEMENT.

bargainer   Person engaged in BARGAINING.

bargaining   Exchange of tentative proposals or offers, usually in a pattern of CONCESSIONS, in an attempt to reach mutually acceptable terms on how to resolve a situation in which the parties' initial outcome preferences differ. Can be used as an adjective, as in *bargaining table,* or as a noun (although rarely).

A range of definitions includes Schelling's [1960, p. 21] broad definition of "any activity in which each party is guided mainly by his expectations of what the other will accept" and Nicholson's [1975, p. 233] more narrow description of "any process by which two (or more) parties come to some arrangement whereby their acts become consistent, where this arrangement is brought about by the parties involved in the conflict alone, and where the parties do not follow some procedure which by itself will determine the results of the bargain." There is Schoenfield and Schoenfield's [1988, p. 124] simple and direct definition of bargaining as merely consisting of an offer to exchange one specific item for another, that is, "I will give you X for Y." A sampling of other definitions includes the following:

- "An interdependent decision-making process characterized both by strategic interaction and imperfect information" [Princen, 1992, p. 32].

- "The manipulation of the information of others in the interests of improving the outcome for one's self under conditions of strategic interaction" [Young, 1975, p. 364].

- "A process of communication between two or more parties aimed at resolving initial differences in preference" [Pruitt and Lewis, 1977, p. 161].

- "Bargaining is a type of social conflict in which participants attempt to settle an issue of resource redistribution. The parties to bargaining will attempt—through their offers or through other, more esoteric machinations—to use various forms of social influence in order to gain a maximally favorable exchange rate vis-à-vis their opposite numbers" [Tedeschi and Bonoma, 1977, p. 213, citation omitted].

- "Bargaining entails two or more interdependent parties who perceive incompatible goals and engage in social interaction to reach a mutually satisfactory outcome" [Putnam and Roloff, 1992, pp. 2–3, citations omitted].

- "The process whereby two or more parties attempt to settle what each shall give and take, or perform and receive, in a transaction between them" [Druckman and Harris, 1989, p. 234, citation omitted].

- "Bargaining is a kind of game that can be defined as an interaction process that occurs when two or more persons attempt to agree on a mutually acceptable outcome in a situation where their orders of preferences for possible outcomes are negatively correlated" [Hamner and Yukl, 1977, p. 138].

The bargaining process consists of converging decisions that are construed as concession exchanges [Druckman, 1977, p. 26, discussing bargaining as "incremental convergence"] and of offers and communications that are intended to influence an opponent's perceptions of alternatives and utilities [Druckman, 1977, p. 26].

This range of definitions is problematic because the term is used indiscriminately, without regard to context, and is treated as synonymous with NEGOTIATION. The term is as likely to be used in the context of international disputes as in labor disputes, with no difference in meaning. However, the term, derived from the Old French or German for "haggling in the marketplace," is associated primarily with market transactions rather than with dispute resolution. As a result, Morley and Stephenson [1977, p. 23] note that most formal theories of bargaining behavior are confined to consideration of bargaining behavior in this narrow sense of arranging an exchange of goods in a given market. The solution to this tension is to focus on bargaining as an attempt to reach agreement and thereby to equate "reaching an agreement" with resolving a dispute as a transaction similar to that in a given marketplace. Thus Morley and Stephenson construct the following progression of definitions:

- To bargain is "to haggle over terms of give and take" [p. 18].

- "Bargaining denotes . . . the process of argument, persuasion, threat, proposal and counter-proposal by which the potential parties to a transaction discuss its terms and possibly reach agreement on them. In other words, bargaining may almost be said to denote the manner in which agreement is negotiated" [p. 19, citation omitted].

- "In the most general sense, bargaining refers to any activity whereby parties with conflicting and common interests determine the terms of their interdependence" [p. 21].

- "Bargaining involves a process of give and take, a willingness to make concessions in order to enhance agreement, or . . . a series of communication exchanges and compromises" [p. 25, citations omitted].

- "Bargaining is defined simply as the process of negotiating for agreement" [p. 26].

These definitions do not help to distinguish the process of negotiation from bargaining; in common usage these terms are treated as synonymous. Morley and Stephenson note unhelpfully that "negotiation may denote a special case of bargaining, or vice versa" [p. 23].

In dispute resolution, bargaining is best regarded as a more narrow concept than negotiation, referring only to the process of exchanging offers with the intent of finding an agreeable point of settlement. In contrast, negotiation is broader in scope and includes, in addition to bargaining, identification of issues, exchanges of information, and other activities that generally precede actual bargaining [Iklé, 1964, pp. 3–4], or according to Cross [1969, p. 7], *bargaining* is the process of demand formation and revision that provides the basic mechanism whereby the parties converge toward an agreement, while *negotiation* is the whole situation within which the bargaining occurs. Conversely, Stevens [1963, p. 1] argues that bargains may be stuck without negotiation, so negotiation is more restricted than bargaining.

Conditions for bargaining are similar to those required for negotiation. Outcomes must be indeterminant and parties must be interdependent to the degree that each requires the other's cooperation in order to achieve its goals and each can block the other from achieving its goals. This interdependence, combined with potentially antithetical goals and demands, sets up a mixed-motive relationship in which both parties cooperate by competing for divergent ends. Rules and normative practices of bargaining include specifying preferred outcomes prior to the negotiation, exchanging proposals and counterproposals, and engaging in dynamic movement through social interaction [Walton and McKersie, 1965].

Authorities have named and described several distinct forms of bargaining. Some of these classifications are similar to classifications of NEGOTIATION and some are based on the pattern of offers and demands or BARGAINING PATTERNS. For example:

- *Distributive or distributional bargaining.* Often called POSITIONAL BARGAINING to denote the pattern of positional demands, offers, and sequential concession making toward a mutually acceptable position (also called BIDDING). This pattern of bargaining emphasizes the series of positional commitments made by the parties and results in ZERO-SUM, a complete division of a fixed and limited resource or "pie" where one for me is minus one for you. The parties are competitors and alternate with demands and offers in an attempt to reach agreement on the division of the pie. The most common example is a straight division of money. Distributive and positional bargaining are not necessarily synonymous. Positional bargaining can be more a style of bargaining while DISTRIBUTIVE BARGAINING may be any attempt to allocate a fixed resource [Raiffa, 1982] regardless of the style used.

- *Integrative bargaining.* Sometimes called *interest-based bargaining*, this pattern of bargaining usually emphasizes a search for outcomes that satisfy the various interests of the parties and results in NON-ZERO-SUM or *positive-sum*, in which both sides may expand the pie and be made better off than before the resolution was achieved. Thus, if I get more, you do not necessarily get less; rather, both of us can get more. The parties are not strict competitors. They can cooperate to enlarge the pie that they eventually will have to divide [Raiffa, 1982, p. 131]. Typically, integrative bargaining occurs when there are multiple issues of varying values or when one party has something to which it attaches substantially less value than does the other side.

Some authorities note that both patterns may occur within a single negotiation. Describing a pattern similar to integrative, Karrass [1970, p. 66, pp. 128–129] calls the effort to seek joint improvement *problem-solving bargaining*. He observes, however, that every negotiation reaches a distributive point at which the gains of one party come at the expense of the other party and the parties must engage in SHARE BARGAINING [pp. 127–128]. Lax and Sebenius [1986] make a similar distinction between bargaining behavior that "creates value" and that which "claims value."

With respect to behavior in distributive bargaining, Craver [1988] uses *auction bargaining* to denote the use of extreme initial positions and the making of time-consuming concessions, while Midgaard and Underdal [1977, p. 332] use the term *pure bargaining* to mean trying to get the other party or parties to make the largest possible concessions while making the smallest possible concession oneself. See also HAGGLING. In contrast to these competitive behaviors in distributive bargaining, Pruitt [1981] describes a bargaining strategy of "heuristic trial and error" in which joint benefits can be realized when a bargainer frequently changes offers, concedes incrementally, and selects lowest priority issues first. Finally, Tutzauer [1992, p. 72] shows preference for the term *interactive bargaining* as accurately reflecting the fact that bargainers influence each other in concession making, that is, each bargainer's offers influence those of his opponent and vice versa.

Much of negotiation and bargaining theory is derived from the observation and experience of COLLECTIVE BARGAINING in labor negotiation and from international negotiations, both of which are usually conducted in teams. There are many terms that denote various negotiation team dynamics. The bargaining phase of a BILATERAL NEGOTIATION can be called *bilateral bargaining,* or in multilateral negotiation, *multilateral bargaining.* Moore [1986, pp. 287–288] uses *bilateral bargaining* to denote "official" communication between the two teams that occurs primarily between the spokespeople expressing either the consensus of the teams or the team position expressed by the hierarchical decision maker. Colosi and Berkeley [1986] describe the bargaining that takes place across the table as HORIZONTAL BARGAINING, which they contrast with the VERTICAL BARGAINING that takes place between the negotiators and their constituent groups or decision makers who are not at the negotiating table [called *intraorganizational bargaining* by Druckman, 1977, and Walton and McKersie, 1965, and *in-group bargaining* by Karrass, 1970, pp. 66, 132–134]. Colosi and Berkeley [1986] describe *internal* or *in-team bargaining* as that which takes place among members of the same team, and SHADOW BARGAINING as that which occurs when one or more members of a team informally, and possibly privately, explore alternatives for settlement with members of another team. Shadow bargaining can occur with the full knowledge of the team to promote more fruitful full-team bargaining [called *unilateral conciliatory bargaining* by Moore, 1986,

p. 288]. Shadow bargaining can also occur covertly, without the knowledge of other team members and for the sole benefit of one or more team members at the expense of the whole team, a wider constituency, or the organization at large [called *unilateral vested-interest bargaining* by Moore, 1986, p. 288]. Shadow bargainers can come from outside the team—for example, high-level executives from the disputing companies.

Finally, several other types of bargaining that are less easy to categorize should be noted. In the context of labor negotiations, *early-bird bargaining* occurs before the period for notice of reopening a contract to avoid undue time constraints [Maggiolo, 1971, pp. 103–104]. Karrass [1970, pp. 130–132] talks about *attitudinal bargaining* as a part of every negotiation; the attitudinal-bargaining process assumes that desired relationships, ranging from mutual degrees of aggression to accommodation to cooperation to collaboration, can be structured through negotiation with an opponent. He also discusses two types of *personal bargaining*—that which occurs when a negotiator bargains with his own team or decision-making group [Karrass, 1970, p. 66] and that which occurs within the negotiator as an internal psychological event—"It is evident that a negotiator must strike a bargain with himself" [Karrass, 1970, p. 132].

bargaining agent   Person authorized by a principal party to represent that party in negotiations.

The principal party establishes the extent of the bargaining agent's authority. An agent is often used to control the bargaining dialogue. For example, a lawyer may say to the other party, "I have given you every concession I am authorized to make. I can go no further." If such statement is taken at face value by the other party, that party may abandon his efforts to obtain further concessions, being convinced that he has to "take it or leave it" [Coulson, 1968, p. 57]. See AUTHORITY.

bargaining endowment   BARGAINING POWER acquired from the substantive and procedural legal rules that could be applied to resolve the dispute. The effects of the applicable rules are often used as bargaining chips by the parties. In a divorce negotiation, for example, the legal rules governing alimony, child support, marital property, and custody give each parent power to assert certain claims based on the outcome that the law would impose if no agreement were reached [Mnookin and Kornhauser, 1979, p. 968].

The bargaining endowment includes not only the substantive entitlement conferred by legal rules but also rules enabling those entitlements to be vindicated—for example, rules requiring production of documents or rules excluding evidence favorable to the other party or jeopardizing the claim of the other party, such as contributory negligence [Galanter, 1986, p. 213]. See IN THE SHADOW OF THE LAW, LITIGOTIATION, BATNA.

bargaining patterns   Discernable recurring sequences or archetypes of bargaining activity, such as POSITIONAL BARGAINING (see under BARGAINING), used by theorists to describe bargaining behavior and by practitioners to anticipate the behavior of other negotiators.

bargaining power   Ability of a negotiator to influence the behavior of an opponent [Karrass, 1970, p. 56]. See POWER.

Bargaining Process Analysis (BPA)   Interaction analysis system for the analysis of bargaining and competitive debate. All verbal behavior of negotiators is coded as falling into one of thirteen categories organized into five groups:

1. Substantive behavior (initiations, accommodations, retractions)
2. Strategic behavior (commitments, threats, promises)
3. Task behavior (agreements, disagreements, questions, answers)
4. Affective behavior (positive, negative)
5. Procedural behavior (subject changes and so forth)

The categories provide a set of conceptual building blocks that may have theoretical importance singly or when combined to form composite variables. The BPA instrument was designed to be applied and has been applied both to the behavior of subjects in a laboratory setting and to transcripts of real-world negotiations [Walcott, Hopmann, and King, 1977. p. 206].

bargaining range   Set of possible acceptable agreements in a given negotiation.

In some usage, an individual negotiator's bargaining range is independent of the other negotiators' bargaining ranges, that is, it is the set of possible negotiation outcomes that is acceptable to that negotiator without regard to the acceptability of particular outcomes in that set to other negotiators. Thus in pure POSITIONAL BARGAINING, the individual bargaining range consists of the continuum from the negotiator's opening offer to the position the negotiator has identified at which no settlement is preferred rather than moving closer to the opponent's goal [Harbaugh and Britzke, 1988, p. 36].

In other usage, the bargaining range is defined by that set of possible agreements that both sides prefer over their no-agreement alternatives. In this conceptualization, bargaining range is interdependent and limited to only mutually acceptable outcomes bound by both parties' no-agreement alternatives. Related terms would be CONTRACT ZONE and BARGAINING SET.

Under either usage, bargaining range is an important concept in understanding bargaining dynamics and behavior. Perceptions of bargaining range are determined by parties' perceptions of their own and each other's alternatives to a negotiated agreement. One implication is that the better one's alternative to agreement is, the better one's expected agreement will be. Therefore each party has an incentive not only to improve its own alternatives but also to take steps to lead its opponent to believe it has a high-value alternative and thereby influence the opponent's perception of the true bargaining range. For example, side A may claim that its alternative is very favorable and that unless side B can make an attractive offer, side A will take that alternative; or side A may try to show that side B's assessment of side A's alternative is unduly optimistic. In both cases, the bargainer tries to shrink the perceived bargaining range to favor itself.

With outcomes indeterminate and more than one possible solution in the bargaining range, the parties are inevitably faced with the dilemma of how to agree to a single point in the set when for each side some points are to better advantage than others [Princen, 1992, p. 32].

See also BARGAINING SET, SETTLEMENT RANGE, CONTRACT ZONE, ZONE OF AGREEMENT.

bargaining set   Range of possible outcomes that are defined by the RESERVATION PRICES of the involved parties. No bargaining set exists in which one party's maximum reservation point is lower than another party's minimum reservation point [Lax and Sebenius, 1986, pp. 247–248]. See also BARGAINING RANGE.

bargaining unit   *Labor:* Group of employees with common interests that bargains collectively with management or is represented by a single union.

barrister   See LAWYER.

baseball arbitration   Term sometimes used to describe FINAL-OFFER ARBITRATION. More specifically, a form of binding final-offer arbitration through which baseball players and team owners resolve players' salary disputes.

This form of arbitration is authorized under the COLLECTIVE BARGAINING AGREEMENT between the players and management. After reaching an impasse in salary negotiations, the player and management each submits a sealed settlement proposal, usually their last offer and demand, to the arbitrators for binding determination. After each party presents arguments and evidence in support of its proposal, the arbitrators open the envelopes and select the proposal that they think is most fair based on the arguments and evidence presented. The arbitrators may weigh only certain limited criteria in making their decision and must pick one of the offers submitted as their award. The award must be rendered within twenty-four hours of the end of arguments and is unaccompanied by written reasons [Arnold, 1994, pp. 47–48].

Baseball salary arbitration has been a controversial element of player-management relations. In theory, this form of arbitration eliminates extreme positions and promotes reasonable, good-faith bargaining because each side would want their offer to appear "reasonable" to an arbitrator, who would simply disregard extreme proposals. In practice, management believes the process forces them to inflate their proposals to avoid the risk of an arbitrator choosing a player's higher demand. Some see this practice as contributing, along with free agency, to the salary escalation that baseball has experienced since salary arbitration was first instituted [Fizel, 1994, pp. 42–43; Faurot and McAllister, 1992, p. 701]. It was primarily a dispute over the use of salary arbitration that led to the baseball strike of 1994 and to subsequent revisions of this arbitration system.

NIGHT BASEBALL ARBITRATION is when the arbitrator makes a decision without the benefit of the parties' proposals and then makes the award to the party whose proposal is closest to the arbitrator's.

Related terms: FINAL-OFFER ARBITRATION, LAST-BEST-OFFER ARBITRATION. Compare MED-ARB, MEDALOA.

baseball clause   Arbitration agreement contained in a contract and providing for BASEBALL ARBITRATION or FINAL-OFFER ARBITRATION to resolve disputes.

BATNA (Best Alternative to a Negotiated Agreement)   Best consequences of not reaching an agreement [Fisher and Ury, 1981, p. 99]. The most favorable remaining option once negotiation has failed to produce a settlement [Powell, 1991, p. 135].

Though often equated with BOTTOM LINE and RESISTANCE POINT, BATNA is a different concept. While these other terms refer to the lowest acceptable negotiated outcome, BATNA refers to the best outcome if there is no negotiated outcome. Thus BATNA may influence establishment of a bottom line or resistance point, but it is not necessarily equivalent. This is recognized by Raiffa [1982, p. 45] in his conceptualization of RESERVATION PRICE. In essence, estimating a BATNA forces a party to be more realistic about its bottom line. Having a BATNA prompts a party to ask itself what it will do without an agreement rather than what it ought to be able to get [Fisher and Ury, 1981, p. 99].

Although some authorities believe that the BATNA concept places undue emphasis on the utility of alternatives to negotiation while ignoring the value of relationships [Donohue and Ramesh, 1992, p. 209, citing Greenhalgh, 1987], the BATNA concept is expansive enough to include the utility of the relationship as part of its calculation.

bazaar bargaining   Same as HAGGLING.

BBB   See BETTER BUSINESS BUREAU.

BBB CARE   Consumer dispute resolution program of the BBB. See BETTER BUSINESS BUREAU.

behavioral decision analysis   Integration of analyses of what an opponent would do if completely rational (prescriptive analysis) and what he would be likely to do based on past behavior (descriptive analysis) in order to compose a model for the opponent's behavior for use in negotiation [Siebe, 1991, p. 202].

bench trial   Trial held before a judge and without a jury. Such trials are often less formal, and rules of evidence are relaxed. Judges in bench trials can be particularly effective at encouraging a negotiated settlement because a record of previous judgments makes it easier for the parties to predict the range of possible outcomes. A jury verdict, conversely, is harder to predict.

benchmark   Reference point used by negotiators to evaluate whether their sides would be better off or worse off by their accepting a certain term in an agreement [Iklé, 1964, p. 167]. See also BOTTOM LINE, BREAK-EVEN POINT, RESERVATION PRICE, RESISTANCE POINT, BATNA.

besara' **(Borneo)**   Informal method of dispute resolution used by the Pepen of Borneo. Meaning simply "to talk things out," it includes elements of negotiation, conciliation, and mediation. In the *besara'*, a person equally related to both parties—an uncle, for instance—acts as the head mediator. The parties meet with the head mediator and possibly other mediators to work out the problem. Fault and blame are very important to the Pepen, and great care is taken not to lay any blame on either party.

Best Alternative to a Negotiated Agreement (BATNA)   See BATNA.

Best Alternative to the Proposed Agreement (BAPA)   Broader concept than BATNA, inclusive of alternative agreements negotiated with other parties. Arguably, the term BATNA is limited to the extent that it implies that the negotiator's bargaining power depends on available forms of conflict resolution (that is, on something other than a negotiated settlement). The best alternative to a negotiated agreement with a party may be a negotiated agreement with a different party. As a result, Goldman [1991, p. 14] posits, the phrase *Best Alternative to the Proposed Agreement* more accurately describes what the negotiator must weigh in making bargaining decisions.

Bet Din (Judaism)   Generic term meaning "House of Judgment," an Orthodox rabbinical TRIBUNAL that decides disputes under Jewish rabbinical law. Historically, the origins of the *Bet Din* lie in the Torah (Deuteronomy 16:18), which commanded the Jews to create courts of law. During the early history of the Jewish people there were three categories of courts of law: civil courts, criminal courts, and the *Sanhedrin*, or Great *Bet Din*, which was the supreme ARBITER for the interpretation of Jewish law [Isaacson and Wigoder, 1973, pp. 49–50].

Following their Dispersion from Israel by the Romans in A.D. 70, Jews established a *Bet Din* wherever they settled, presided over by the chief rabbi of the region. These religious courts exercised authority over religious matters and the internal affairs of the Jewish community. The *Bet Din*, along with the synagogue, aided Jews in maintaining cultural and religious identity, as well as a sense of autonomy, while in exile. By the Middle Ages, the *Bet Din* in Eastern Europe and other areas of the Diaspora had established authority over all matters except serious crimes involving capital punishment. During the eighteenth and nineteenth centuries, the *Bet Din* lost its civil and criminal authority as Jews gained status in European communities and became subject to the secular courts. The jurisdiction of the *Bet Din* was relegated to religious matters only [Auerbach, 1983, pp. 77–78].

Bet Din dispute settlement maintained strict adhesion to formal Jewish law, including the precedents of other Jewish courts. However, *Bet Din* dispute settlement was also characterized by procedural informality. Disputes brought before the *Bet Din* were judged by rabbis, and parties presented their case without the assistance of counsel. The BINDING authority of *Bet Din* decisions was generated primarily by the effects of communal pressure, although the early *Bet Din* had the power of excommunication, or *herem*, at its disposal [Isaacson and Wigoder, 1973, pp. 49–50; Auerbach, 1983, pp. 77–78].

The *Bet Din* courts resurfaced in the Lower East Side of New York during the early twentieth century, reflecting a desire on the part of American Jewry to maintain its cultural and religious heritage and to keep its disputes within the community so as not to arouse any anti-Semitic sentiment in the United States. Within the New York Jewish community, the *Bet Din* could be found alongside other Jewish arbitral bodies, such as the Jewish Conciliation Board (see under JEWISH RABBINICAL TRIBUNAL), thereby offering a choice of forum. As Jews became more integrated into U.S. society, the authority of the *Bet Din* diminished within the community [Auerbach, 1983, pp. 79–88].

In the 1970s, the *Bet Din* was again revived in the United States as an authority over both matters of Jewish ritual law and matters submitted to voluntary arbitration. The *Bet Din* was perceived as a model for arbitration of disputes that aids maintenance of communal harmony and integrity [Fishkin, 1979, pp. 50–54]. In Israel, the *Bet Din* has been granted exclusive jurisdiction over marriage, divorce, and inheritance disputes [Isaacson and Wigoder, 1973, pp. 49–50].

Related term: JEWISH RABBINICAL TRIBUNAL.

Better Business Bureau (BBB)   Any of the many local and regional nonprofit, private organizations supported by businesses to combat unethical business activities, many of which administer ADR to resolve disputes between consumers and businesses.

BBBs offer private, voluntary CONCILIATION by a BBB staff member; MEDIATION; and both binding and CONDITIONALLY BINDING ARBITRATION. Many BBBs provide these dispute resolution services under the rubric of BBB CARE, to which member businesses can subscribe. Many problems, however, are simply handled on an AD HOC, case-by-case basis. BBBs also administer the AUTOLINE program to resolve automobile purchasing disputes.

Today's BBBs are descendants of the truth in advertising and business ethics vigilance committee movement of the early twentieth century and are coordinated by the national Council of Better Business Bureaus. See CONSUMER ARBITRATION, CONSUMER COMPLAINT MECHANISMS.

bias   Show of partiality or inclination to one side in a controversy. A predisposition to decide a certain way thereby precluding hearing a matter with an open mind, conducting a process evenhandedly, or exercising powers impartially.

Ethical standards for judges, arbitrators, and mediators provide that such third parties should be impartial and unbiased. In litigation, a judge's show of bias toward a party may lead to disqualification. In arbitration, any special show of bias by the arbitrator toward one party may result in his appointment or award being challenged by the other party. U.S. Arbitration Act § 10 provides that the court may vacate an award where "there was evident partiality or corruption in the arbitrators." In mediation, a mediator's show of bias can result in the offended party walking out or refusing to use or confide in the mediator.

One might question whether anyone is truly free from bias. See BALANCED PARTIALITY. Compare PREJUDICE; contrast EQUIDISTANCE, IMPARTIAL, NEUTRAL.

bicentric   Either a situation in which there are two possible "right" solutions or a situation in which there is an outcome that favors both parties in a bilateral dispute. Similar to WIN-WIN SOLUTION. Contrast POLYCENTRIC.

bid   To offer to buy at a specific price, especially at an auction. The offer to buy.

bidding   Series of competing offers that incrementally increases the price of an item until only a single potential purchaser remains.

Describes a pattern of positional bargaining involving a series of offers and counteroffers that move progressively closer until either settlement occurs upon reaching a mutually acceptable term, the parties agree to use a formula to determine the settlement figure, or they deadlock and resolve not to deal any further [Goldman, 1991, p. 201].

bilateral focus   Understanding the perspectives of both sides in a two-sided dispute or problem.

Conflict is often grounded in misunderstanding, not in or not limited to merely factual disagreement, nor simply a result of ambiguous communication, but rather stemming from different images of reality held by the parties. A strategy to improve bilateral focus is having each party state the position of the opponent to the opponent's satisfaction, state the conditions under which the opponent's position is meritorious, and identify a common ground where the opponents share common values [Walcott, Hopmann, and King, 1977, pp. 194–195, citation omitted].

Mediators employ similar techniques, including ROLE REVERSAL exercises, to improve mutual understanding and overcome impasses.

bilateral negotiation   Negotiation between two parties, as opposed to a multilateral negotiation.

bilateral treaty   Formal agreement made solely between two nations.

binding   Obligatory; creates a legal or social indebtedness of obligation, as in binding ARBITRATION.

bipartite board   Board consisting of equal number of representatives from labor and management that examines and acts on complaints as the last step in a GRIEVANCE PROCEDURE prior to arbitration.

The bipartite board in some industries may be the final step in the grievance machinery. Such a board is also sometimes referred to as a JOINT BOARD or an ADJUSTMENT BOARD [DOA].

blaming   Step in the dispute evolution process whereby a person attributes a perceived injury (GRIEVANCE) to the fault of another individual or organization [Felstiner, Abel, and Sarat, 1980–1981, p. 635]. See also NAMING, CLAIMING, DISPUTE.

blind bidding   Bidding without knowledge of the amount of competing bids. In public contracting, known as *sealed bidding*.

Also a technique employed by negotiators and mediators, usually as a final attempt to break an impasse in DISTRIBUTIVE, or POSITIONAL, BARGAINING. The buyer or respondent confidentially submits his highest offer to a third party. The seller or claimant also confidentially submits his lowest offer to the same third party. There are several possible ways to bring about closure at this point. For example, if the parties are within an earlier agreed-to amount of each other— say $20,000—then through prior agreement the third party is empowered to split the difference and settle the case. If the parties' bids overlap or create a previously unrealized CONTRACT ZONE, the third party can alert the parties to this fact and encourage continued negotiation without revealing the bids.

block solutions CONFLICT PREVENTION strategy of changing structures, laws, or policies so that the conflict cannot arise. A simple example would be so-called no-fault laws.

blocking techniques Techniques for controlling unintentional disclosure of information; more specifically, for avoiding answering an opponent's questions about highly sensitive areas. In negotiation, for example, a negotiator faced with an intrusive question could expressly refuse to answer by ruling it out-of-bounds. A negotiator could ignore the question and move toward another topic, answer only part of a complex question, or answer with a question. If a question is specific, a negotiator could respond generally. Conversely, if the question is general, a negotiator could respond specifically. Finally, a negotiator could purposely misconstrue the question so as to answer one that he would rather have been asked [Craver, 1993, pp. 92–98].

bluff Assertion or implication by negotiators that they will do what they do not actually intend to do at the time the assertion is made [Stevens, 1963, p. 89]; taking a position as if that position were absolutely fixed without the possibility of further modification when that is not really true. The negotiator is prepared to back down if strongly challenged [Schoenfield and Schoenfield, 1988, p. 136].

Bluffing positions may take two forms. The first form is a purportedly non-negotiable offer or counteroffer. The second is a threat, without intent or ability to carry it out, to cause an adverse consequence for the other party if it refuses to agree to certain terms [Schoenfield and Schoenfield, 1988, p. 136]. In this second form, bluffing is an example of a lie. Bluffing occurs when negotiator A wants negotiator B to believe that negotiator A has the capacity to implement a threat when in fact this capacity does not exist and negotiator A knows it [Gibbons, Bradac, and Busch, 1992, p. 161]. See LYING.

The obvious dilemma in bluffing is that once the negotiator has been caught bluffing, his credibility becomes either low or nonexistent. A common consequence is that the other negotiator is forced or encouraged to push hard on all of the remaining issues in order to determine whether other bluffs are being attempted as well [Schoenfield and Schoenfield, 1988, p. 136].

board of arbitration   Board (which may or may not be tripartite) established jointly by the parties and consisting of a chairman, sometimes referred to as a PERMANENT CHAIRMAN, and such other arbitrators as may be appointed with the approval of the parties to help the chairman hear and decide arbitration cases.

In labor disputes, a board of arbitration is one method of setting up a PERMANENT UMPIRE system, which may be particularly useful in large corporations that maintain many plants [DOA].

board of inquiry   See FACT-FINDING, INTERNATIONAL COMMISSION OF INQUIRY.

Board of Nine, Board of Nine Men   Court founded by ordinance in 1647 by the Dutch burghers of New Amsterdam, subsequently renamed New York, to arbitrate minor civil and mercantile disputes.

From this Board of Nine Men, three were chosen to serve together on each case. One man was to be a merchant, another a farmer, and the third a burgher. The three who were to serve and make their BINDING decisions as arbitrators were to meet on Thursday, which was the usual Burgher Court Day [DOA]. Primarily a mercantile court sanctioned and empowered by the state rather than a genuine arbitral TRIBUNAL empowered by the parties, the Board of Nine is often cited as an example of the historic tradition of COMMERCIAL ARBITRATION in the United States.

boilerplate   Standard or stereotypical clause that may appear in any contract and that negotiators often accept verbatim instead of creating a freshly worded clause to insert in their own particular contract [DOA].

The nondrafting party may not read the boilerplate and be surprised, even miffed, when the clause is invoked in a subsequent dispute. The use of ARBITRATION AGREEMENTS in boilerplate is controversial for two reasons. First, there is the notion that arbitration works best if the parties expressly consent to its use. Second, courts in the United States, influenced by the remnants of COMMON LAW hostility to arbitration, are loath to enforce what is perceived as an unknowing waiver of the constitutional right to a jury trial. Increasingly, arbitration agreements are found embedded in the boilerplates of consumer contracts or consumer agreements. Despite enforceability in stockbroker-customer agreements, the use of such clauses in other areas of the financial industry is being challenged.

bona fide dispute   See JUSTICIABLE.

bone throwing   Situation in which one gives an adversary something of relatively little worth to compensate for a major loss. Often this is done to assuage feelings when one has triumphed on a conflict in which one issue was dominant. In the manner of the master who throws a bone to a dog, the winner gives the loser an offering of some sort so that the loser does not go away empty-handed [Jandt and Gillette, 1985, p. 256].

bottom line   Minimum benefit a party must receive or the maximum cost a party will incur in order to agree voluntarily to a negotiated settlement [Murray, Rau, and Sherman, 1989, p. 103]. A party's worst acceptable outcome. If you are buying, a bottom line is the highest price you would pay. If you are selling, a bottom line is the lowest amount you would accept [Fisher and Ury, 1981, p. 98]. Sometimes referred to as the *walk-away point,* the point beyond which the negotiator is willing to cease negotiations, bottom line can be arbitrary, based on criteria, or informed by a party's alternatives to agreement. Bottom line should not be confused with BATNA. Compare RESERVATION PRICE, RESISTANCE POINT.

Some commentators have noted that a primary objective of many negotiators is to mask or distort their bottom line while attempting to discover the bottom line of their opponents. A danger exists, however, if each side is equally successful in persuading the other that his apparent bottom line is the real one. The result is no recognizable ZONE OF AGREEMENT and the parties will not settle, even though a zone of agreement exists between their actual bottom lines [Murray, Rau, and Sherman, 1989, p. 105].

Boulwareism   Negotiation tactic whereby a party makes its best offer first on a take-it-or-leave-it basis instead of starting with a figure from which it can make concessions. Named after Lemuel Boulware, vice president of public relations at General Electric Company in the 1950s, who had a policy of making first-and-final offers to the union, the tactic has since been associated with an unfair labor practice—refusal to bargain in good faith. See *N.L.R.B.* v. *General Elec. Co.* (1970).

Boulware believed that the traditional, time-consuming labor negotiation involving incremental positional bargaining from extreme initial positions merely achieved a bargaining agreement similar to that anticipated by the parties from the outset. Prior to negotiations, he formulated a "best offer first" package. The package was based on what the company was willing to commit to and on a survey showing employees' areas of compensation preference. After presenting the package to labor representatives, the company stated that it would modify its initial offer only if it was convinced of a miscalculation or change in circumstances [Craver, 1993, pp. 173–174]. The tactic was combined with a concentrated public relations campaign designed to compel the union to accept the offer.

Another form of Boulwareism is for one party to commit itself publicly to the opening offer so that it is unable realistically to accept anything less [Murray, Rau, and Sherman, 1989, p. 127].

Although the tactic may be effective against a weak opponent, it can evoke a strong negative reaction despite the reasonableness of the offer. The tactic may be perceived as paternalistic and as an affront to the other party's psychological need to engage in some bargaining to obtain the outcome, thereby obscuring the merits of the offer [Craver, 1993, pp. 173–174].

boundary dispute   Controversy between individual property owners, municipalities, or states over the specific demarcation line separating their adjacent properties, jurisdictions, or territories.

International Relations: A boundary dispute is closely related to a TERRITORIAL DISPUTE, which is concerned with conflicting claims of sovereignty over a territory rather than with the specific demarcation between two states. Boundary disputes constitute one of the three common types of disputes that are settled by means of INTERNATIONAL PUBLIC ARBITRATION. The other two are INTERNATIONAL CLAIMS and investment disputes between a state and a foreign nation. Under JAY'S TREATY of 1794 between the United States and Great Britain, the northeastern boundary of the United States was a subject of arbitration [DOA].

boundary role conflict   Conflict that occurs when a party has multiple roles and answers to different constituencies that are incompatible, when someone must respond to the demands of those both inside and outside an organization, that is, have a boundary role. When demands from both inside and outside make it difficult for the person to comply with both, there is a boundary role conflict [Turner, 1992, p. 235]. A negotiator is often caught between the expectations of his constituency and the needs of his opponent [Walton and McKersie, 1965, p. 284].

bounded rationality   Principle of decision theory meaning that human beings must make decisions without full information. Being limited in knowledge, tools, and intelligence, they cannot find the optimum solution to a problem no matter how hard they try [Karrass, 1970, p. 160].

Applied to dispute resolution, the concept implies that parties are constrained in their decision making by resources available (such as money, time, intelligence, and patience) to obtain information and must make decisions based on a certain number of assumptions.

brainstorm, brainstorming   Method of producing as many ideas as possible to solve a problem.

Method of separating invention of possibilities from the decisions over one outcome or another. Increases creativity in process of negotiations [Lax and Sebenius, 1986, pp. 133, 178]. Moore [1986, pp. 212–214] hints at two methods of initiating brainstorming. The mediator or negotiator can begin the process by framing an issue as a problem. The parties are then instructed to speak one at a time and suggest as rapidly as possible a list of alternative solutions that meet the needs of the parties. When the method is used in groups, the participants are encouraged to suggest the wildest solutions possible until they have exhausted the possibilities.

Although mediators often instruct parties to avoid stating purely self-serving options, the key ground rule is to postpone criticism and evaluation of ideas. The group or individual simply invents ideas without pausing to consider whether they are good or bad, realistic or unrealistic [Fisher and Ury, 1981, p. 60].

Brass Rule   In gaming theory, strategy of always defecting. Contrast GOLDEN RULE, SILVER RULE, TIT-FOR-TAT.

breach of contract   Breaking or violation of the terms of a contract [DOA].

break-even point   Reference point used by negotiators to determine whether their side will gain or lose by accepting a given proposal. Also referred to as BENCHMARK.

A frequently used break-even point is the status quo. That is, any arrangement that does not change the existing situation will be evaluated as resulting in neither a gain nor a loss. Because the world is always changing, however, maintaining the status quo on some isolated point may seem like a gain or loss from another vantage point [Iklé, 1964, p. 168].

Break-even point is distinguishable from BOTTOM LINE, RESERVATION PRICE, and RESISTANCE POINT, all of which imply some gain over the status quo. It may, however, inform or be the basis of these concepts, as with BATNA. Unlike BATNA, break-even point describes the most probable alternative to accepting the proposal. See PATNA.

breakthrough strategy   Various tactics recommended by Ury [1993] to overcome barriers to cooperation. Expands and adds to the concept of NEGOTIATION JUJITSU, going around your opponent's resistance instead of meeting it head on, introduced in Fisher and Ury [1981].

brief   Concise statement of fact and law in support of a party's case that is prepared by counsel or by the party itself and then submitted to a court or an arbitrator [DOA].

brinksmanship, brinkmanship   Negotiation tactic whereby a party threatens to abandon negotiations immediately and pursue more costly alternatives in order to force the other side to settle.

The word implies coming to the brink of using the alternative to settlement. The alternative could be war or trial or the severing of relations. Its effectiveness depends on the user's willingness to accept uncertainty of the alternative and the credibility of the threat.

The tactic is associated with international diplomacy because of its use in the 1950s by U.S. Secretary of State John Foster Dulles in threatening nuclear war.

broad arbitration clause, "broad form" arbitration clause   Agreement to arbitrate any and all future disputes that may arise between the parties. See AR-BITRABILITY. Such clauses are considered broad in scope. Contrast NARROW ARBITRATION CLAUSE, RESTRICTED ARBITRATION CLAUSE.

broker   Middleman; agent in buying and selling (such as agent in stock transactions).

In dispute resolution, brokers are middlemen who help define and manage problems, grievances, claims, and disputes. Informal brokers (family, friends, neighbors, and so on) and formal brokers (neighborhood and community service organizations) serve as a community's dispute gatekeepers [Ladinsky and Susmilch, 1983, p. 151–152]. Although the use of a broker can provide much needed insulation between disputants, brokers are not necessarily impartial or always interested in resolving the dispute.

bureaucratic constituency   Hierarchy of decision makers who may or may not be present at negotiations and who must sign or signify final approval of a settlement before it is considered valid. Bureaucratic constituencies are most common when one party is a governmental agency, a hierarchically organized company or industry, or a bureaucratically organized institution such as a hospital or social service agency [Moore, 1986, p. 289].

A bureaucratic constituency may complicate or confuse issues of authority and ratification of draft agreements. See VERTICAL BARGAINING, BARGAINING.

buy/sell provision   Agreement to avoid or resolve ownership disputes in commercial relationships involving co-ownership such as joint ventures or stock corporations. Typically it requires withdrawing or deceased owners to offer their interest at a particular price to the remaining owners, who may or may not be obligated to purchase [Hancock, 1987, pp. 705–708].

Calvo clause   Contractual provision that requires disputes to be referred first to a domestic court system. A clause used in CONCESSION contracts between South American governments and foreign nationals in which these nationals promise not to invoke the aid or diplomatic intervention of their own government but instead to abide by the local law of the country in settling claims arising out of disputes under their concession agreements. Failure to abide by the provision would result in forfeiture of the foreign national's interest to the state.

The Calvo clause was developed in the early 1900s by an Argentine jurist, Carlos Calvo, in the belief that a foreigner doing business in a country is entitled only to nondiscriminatory treatment. Therefore disputes between a foreign entity and a national were to be resolved in the same manner as disputes between nationals, without recourse to extraterritorial tribunals. Thus the effect of the provision was to avoid effective use of international commercial arbitration tribunals [DOA].

CAM   See COMPUTER-AIDED MEDIATION.

Canada–U.S. International Joint Commission (IJC)   Impartial, quasi-judicial body composed of three appointees from each nation. Established by treaty in 1909, the IJC meets at least semiannually, has mandatory jurisdiction over boundary waters projects, and reports on activities that might have transboundary effects.

capitulation   Surrender upon negotiated or stipulated conditions. Contrast COMPROMISE.

care perspective, ethic of care   Morality of care and responsibility as opposed to morality of rights. Within the care perspective, the central preoccupation is responsiveness to others that dictates providing care, preventing harm, and maintaining relationships. It contrasts with formal moral reasoning, the JUSTICE perspective, in which an autonomous moral agent discovers and applies a set of fundamental rules through the use of universal and abstract reasoning. Some feminist scholars suggest that the justice perspective typically dominates the moral development of men, whereas the care perspective is found predominantly among women [Kittay and Meyers, 1987, p. 3].

carry-over effect   *Negotiation:* Impact of one party's change in position on an issue in a previous session on that party's opening position on that issue in a subsequent session.

International Relations: Result of the fact that a government normally changes its position between the beginning and the end of a conference. If the conference ends without agreement and the same issue is taken up again in later negotiations (perhaps with some new participants), the government is likely to start out with a position that is closer to the one it held at the end of the previous conference than to the one it held at the beginning of that conference [Iklé, 1964, p. 22].

case evaluation   COURT-CONNECTED process in which a single lawyer or a panel of lawyers evaluates cases referred by a judge and provides an advisory opinion to the parties as to their respective case strengths, weaknesses, and value.

Often the term is used loosely and can denote any of several similar models of evaluative court-connected processes, including MICHIGAN MEDIATION and MANDATORY NONBINDING ARBITRATION (though rarely). In the Massachusetts federal district court, the term is used in reference to SUMMARY JURY TRIAL and other reality-testing devices [U.S. Dist. Ct. Rules, D. Mass., Expense and Delay Reduction Rule 4.03]. More often the term is used interchangeably with EARLY NEUTRAL EVALUATION, as in the following illustrative court rule:

> Case evaluation or early neutral evaluation is a process in which a lawyer with expertise in the subject matter of the litigation acts as a neutral evaluator of the case. Each side presents a summary of its legal theories and evidence. The evaluator assesses the strength of each side's case and assists the parties in narrowing the legal and factual issues in the case. This conference occurs early in the discovery process and is designed to "streamline" discovery and other pretrial aspects of the case. The early neutral evaluation of the case may also provide a basis for settlement [Georgia Supreme Court Order on Alternative Dispute Resolution Rules, 1993].

The California Family Court conflates the terms into *early neutral case evaluation* [Calif. Family Code § 2451].

Sometimes case evaluation is distinguished from early neutral evaluation. Although the original models of early neutral evaluation emphasized case management, thus streamlining the litigation for trial, case evaluation may be purely evaluative and have no case management characteristics in some jurisdictions [such as Tenn. Supreme Court Rule 31(f) (1996)]. In Maine, case evaluation refers to a distinct phase of early neutral evaluation in which the third party discusses the value of the case in CAUCUS [Maine Supreme Judicial Court Administrative Order to Establish Alternative Dispute Resolution Pilot Project, 1995].

The conflict resolution process of case evaluation should not be confused with the qualitative survey process known as *case evaluation* that is used in several federal district courts (the District of Columbia and the Southern and Eastern Districts of New York, for example). In the latter survey process, mediators are required to complete a case evaluation form after mediating a COURT-REFERRED case.

case status conference   Case-management function conducted by adjudicators or their surrogates, such as federal magistrates. The conference provides an opportunity for the parties to discuss settlement, often with the direct intervention and encouragement of the adjudicator.

cassation   Annulment or reversal in French law. Sometimes used to describe nullification of an international arbitral award by a court or sovereign authority [DOA].

See also COUR DE CASSATION.

caucus, private position   In MEDIATION, private, confidential meeting between the mediator and one or more participants that excludes other participants; sometimes called the PRIVATE POSITION. Also used to denote a brief meeting of a negotiating team conducted during bargaining, especially in labor negotiations, and impromptu discussions with a client during a hearing or court session, side-bar conference, and so forth. In the context of voting, a caucus occurs when members of a political party assemble to choose delegates or nominate candidates for office.

In a typical mediation, the mediator describes the caucus in opening remarks and tells the parties that she may initiate caucuses during the mediation. Some mediators encourage parties to initiate caucuses as well. Generally the purpose is to overcome barriers to settlement. Specifically, mediators will initiate caucuses to accomplish a variety of procedural and substantive objectives, including to build better rapport and trust in the process and mediator, to control negative negotiating behavior, to manage emotions, to improve attitudes and perceptions of the other, to search for hidden agendas, to promote candor, to uncover information that a party is unwilling to share with others in joint session, to clarify interests, to reality test, and to test the acceptability of various solutions [Moore, 1986, pp. 89, 263].

By caucusing, the mediator physically separates the participants and restricts their direct communication. Commentators have identified four basic advantages inherent in this separation: (1) Without the other party as a stimulus, the party in caucus should be less tense, angry, and defensive, and thus more flexible and creative. (2) Without the other party present to hear, the party in caucus feels freer to provide information about underlying interests and assumptions and to throw out tentative new ideas for possible solutions. (3) Because the other party cannot see or hear the mediator, the mediator may interact more intimately with the disputant without appearing partial, thus encouraging increased rapport and sharing of information. Caucusing also allows the mediator to make positive remarks about the other party without emboldening or seeming to curry favor with that party. (4) Without the other party available as a target for the diffusion of responsibility, the mediator can more effectively challenge the disputant to take personal responsibility for solving the problem [Pruitt, McGillicuddy, Welton, and Fry, 1989, p. 385, citations omitted; Welton, Pruitt, and McGillicuddy, 1988, pp. 184–186]. In POSITIONAL BARGAINING, caucusing is an effective method of helping the parties to save face and make faster concessional movements.

One crucial aspect of caucusing is confidentiality. The general rule, usually established at the beginning of each caucus, is that everything said in a caucus will be held in confidence. There are other schools of thought, however. Some mediators prefer that only information the party identifies as confidential remain so, while others prefer that nothing be kept confidential or that the mediator have discretion to use any information about the caucus that she deems useful. Another general rule is that each side receives an equal number of caucuses so that neither feels treated unfairly. Caucuses need not be equal in length. However, the parties not participating in the caucus can grow restless from inaction. Many mediators handle this problem by giving these nonparticipating parties a task to perform during the caucus.

Although most caucuses are between the mediator and one of the disputants, perhaps accompanied by counsel, mediators can meet with various combinations of participants, such as with the parties' counsel, with disputants exclusive of counsel, and with different combinations of disputants in a multiparty dispute. For example, the mediator can caucus with attorneys for one or both parties, individually or together, to consider matters that the attorneys are more comfortable discussing in their clients' absence.

Ethical concerns about caucusing center around the issue of trust. Any separate interaction with the participants can generate mistrust and concern about what is being discussed separately. Within the profession of mediators, especially family mediators, there is disagreement about the propriety of using this technique. Many divorce mediators have chosen to avoid caucuses and meet only with both husband and wife present because they believe that during a caucus with one spouse, the other spouse will become mistrustful. Many public policy facilitators also avoid caucusing. In labor mediation, however, holding caucuses is thought to be an essential component of a mediator's job [Engram and Markowitz, 1985, p. 25; Prather, 1990, pp. 57–58].

The word *caucus* has been traced to Native American origins, probably Algonquian, meaning "elder," "counselor," or "he gives advice to." An unsubstantiated story concerning its origins describes the caucus as a problem-solving meeting among tribal leaders. In such meetings, solutions were suggested first by lowest status leaders and last by highest status leaders so that the opinion of the highest status individual would not influence the opinion of the others.

cause of action   *Law:* Situation or facts giving a person the right to sue another.

CCRB   See CIVILIAN COMPLAINT REVIEW BOARD.

CDR   Acronym for COMPLEMENTARY DISPUTE RESOLUTION and center for dispute resolution.

Center for Dispute Settlement of the AAA   Now-defunct program of the AMERICAN ARBITRATION ASSOCIATION established to employ proven dispute-settlement techniques to solve community grievances such as landlord-tenant or parent-teacher disputes through the use of mutually acceptable neighborhood leaders [DOA]. The center was the successor to the National Center for Dispute Resolution (NCDR), formed with support from the Ford Foundation to promote the use of mediation and arbitration to resolve community disputes, particularly racial problems. NCDR helped create the first modern community mediation centers. It had nine offices across the United States and conducted dispute resolution work with Native Americans, in public housing, and in prisons. That program was a forerunner of the COMMUNITY DISPUTE RESOLUTION CENTER and NEIGHBORHOOD JUSTICE CENTER concepts funded and promoted by the U.S. Department of Justice in the late 1970s.

Center for Public Resources (CPR)   Founded in 1979, a nonprofit organization with members from major corporations, law firms, and law schools that seeks to develop private alternatives to litigation. Its mission is largely educational and it produces a number of publications, including an informative newsletter, *Alternatives to the High Cost of Litigation*. The large corporations that make up the bulk of its membership are asked to sign a pledge, known as the Corporate Policy Statement, that states, "In the event of a business dispute between our company and another company which has made or will then make a similar statement, we are prepared to explore with that other party resolution of the dispute through negotiation or ADR techniques before pursuing full-scale litigation." By the late 1980s and early 1990s, CPR began providing some administrative services and is now officially known as the CPR Institute for Dispute Resolution.

Centre for Dispute Resolution (CEDR)   Independent, not-for-profit organization for the promotion of ADR, located in London. Founded in 1990 and funded by industry and professional firm members, it provides mediation training and maintains panels of neutrals. CEDR aims to promote more effective resolution of commercial disputes in Europe by use of ADR techniques and provides advice and manages ADR dispute-resolution services.

cession   When part of a political entity is yielded to another entity through plebiscite, purchase, treaty, compensating agreement, or as a consequence of hostilities [Diehl and Goertz, 1988, pp. 105–106].

challenge of arbitrator   Right that a party may invoke to seek removal of an arbitrator either for cause or without cause. This right of challenge may be provided for in an arbitration agreement, in the rules of an administering agency administering the arbitration, or in a treaty [DOA].

challenge of award   Attempt by the dissatisfied party to set aside the decision of the arbitrator on specific statutory or other grounds [DOA]. See VACATING AN AWARD.

charette   Small-group, public discussion generally used to develop environmental policy [Montrose, 1984, p. 886].

charter party   Mercantile lease of a seagoing vessel. Contract by which owners lease a vessel, it often contains an arbitration clause. Subcharters are also common and frequently provide for arbitration.

Chartered Institute of Arbitrators (United Kingdom)   Professional membership organization of arbitrators, founded in 1915 and granted a Royal Charter in 1979 with the primary object "to promote and facilitate the determination of disputes by arbitration."

The Chartered Institute has become an international body with operating branches and members throughout the world. It is known for its education and training programs and it administers dispute resolution services, particularly several consumer arbitration programs in the United Kingdom. Along with the City of London and the London Chamber of Commerce, it controls the London Court of International Arbitration.

chicken   Someone who gives in to pressure; game in which pressure is created until one person backs down.

Negotiation: Strategy in which each party delays making CONCESSIONS until a deadline is imminent. The tension of intransigence may force a negotiator's will to fail so that she will make concessions rather than risk deadlock or negative costs should the deadline pass. Unfortunately, in some instances no party may be willing the break the cycle of resistance, in which case all parties are forced to carry out threats and endure unintended consequences [Moore, 1986, p. 245]. In his seminal research, Deutsch [1973] labeled one negotiation experiment the *chicken game* to induce in his subjects the impression that they were supposed to be competitive as opposed to being cooperative in the *problem-solving game.*

child-custody mediation   Mediation of disputes concerning the custody of and visitation with children. Such mediations can occur before, during, or after divorce proceedings or between unmarried parents, or they can be concerning other parental custody of a child. Although it can occur voluntarily, most child-custody mediation probably occurs through court order.

Arguably, the role of the mediator in child-custody disputes is different from that in other civil disputes. Bienenfeld [1983] describes three functional roles: (1) *counselor,* whose role is to "facilitate expression of feelings, concerns, and wishes"; (2) *educator,* whose role is to "focus on teaching parents about the process of divorce and about their children's needs"; and (3) *mediator,* whose role is to "help each parent, keeping the welfare and needs of their children in mind . . . [and to] facilitate communication, clarification, and discussion of issues that need to be resolved" [pp. 9–13]. Becker-Haven [1983, p. 3] describes four roles for a mediator: (1) *healer,* who promotes a therapeutic component of mediation; (2) *teacher,* who promotes an educational component of mediation; (3) *strategist* and *decision maker,* who promotes a rational or analytical component of mediation; and (4) *judge/inspector,* who promotes mediation as a normative and evaluative process. Although the first three roles correspond in both models, the judge/inspector role may be controversial [Balto, 1990, pp. 215, 218]. Although custody as determined by the court often focuses on who was the most fit or least fit parent in the past, many custody mediators prefer to move the couple toward determining what plan will allow them to be the parents they wish to be. In this vein, the term PARENTING PLAN MEDIATION has come into use in some jurisdictions and a number of states have passed parenting plan legislation reinforcing this emphasis.

Child Find of America Mediation Program   Program developed in Florida to facilitate return of children abducted by noncustodial parents or relatives. Begun as a pilot program in August 1986, it offers parents who are hiding with their children an opportunity to work out their differences with the child's other parent through the process of mediation. It can also prevent abduction by providing timely preventive counseling to a parent contemplating abduction.

Children's Creative Response to Conflict Program (CCRC)   Children's dispute-resolution training program of the New York Friends Meeting. CCRC developed a program that uses puppetry, games, music, discussion, and other activities to improve inner-city children's skills in cooperation and conflict resolution. Begun in 1972, CCRC has trained thousands of teachers.

Chinese mediation (Chinese People's Mediation, Neighborhood Mediation Committee [*Renmin Tiaojie Weiyuanhui*], Factory Workers' Mediation Committee, Chinese Mediation Committee, People's Conciliation Committee)   Institutionalized mechanism used in some Chinese communities to resolve private disputes among members.

The concept of Chinese mediation purportedly has roots in traditional Chinese Confucian principles that stress harmonious social relations through self-regulatory behavior and place a low value on law and litigation as means of dispute resolution. There is a high value on COMPROMISE, *JANG,* and the use of THIRD-PARTY INTERVENTION to promote compromise and restore social harmony. During the Ming dynasty, rulers encouraged village leaders and elders, *LI-LAO,* to solve petty disputes within and between families, but the solutions were nonbinding and parties were able to go to the local magistrate's office, *yamen,* as an alternative to mediation.

Today in the People's Republic of China, the process is no longer voluntary and the mediators take an active role in initiating their own investigations in search of disputes to settle. The focus is on settling the dispute, not on reaching a mutually satisfactory result as in Western processes. Nor is it a requirement that the mediator be neutral. Instead, disputants feel that a mediator's beliefs about who is correct actually expedite settlement [Wall and Blum, 1991, pp. 4–9]. The process differs in some respects from classic mediation in the United States, and practice may vary widely. In fact, earlier authorities referred to *Chinese conciliation,* which may be more like some forms of CONCILIATION in which outcomes are actively recommended by third parties. Rather than try to categorize the processes used under the label of Chinese mediation, this entry focuses on how conciliatory third-party intervention has been institutionalized in Chinese society.

The two primary manifestations can be found in expatriate or émigré Chinese communities and in the People's Republic of China respectively. In the

United States, for example, Chinese immigrants historically met with racial bias and language difficulties. To insulate themselves from an alien social and legal environment, they settled in close-knit communities (Chinatowns) in which they developed private means for dispute resolution. The historical use of these internal dispute resolution mechanisms is well documented by Auerbach [1983]. Silberman [1979, pp. 225–226] summarizes as follows:

> Chinese immigrant communities currently employ two primary dispute processing mechanisms: (1) Benevolent Associations, of both the business and family variety. Business associations typically encompass all of the businesses in a particular Chinatown community. Family associations may encompass all persons with the same last name (e.g., the family clan). Such associations represent the primary mode of dispute processing. (2) Go-Betweens. This mechanism involves a mutual friend of both disputants who informally attempts to bring about reconciliation or handles delicate business negotiations.
>
> The mediation that takes place in the benevolent association is handled by well-respected persons from the community, who usually have no legal training. Disputes ranging from business disagreements to personal arguments are processed without resort to rules of evidence, pleading, or precedent. After the Chinatown mediators have heard the case and applied their common-sense judgments to the facts and the parties' circumstances, they reach a decision. The only sanction applied to the parties is community pressure and moral persuasion. Appeals are rare, and the association's decision is almost always obeyed [pp. 225–226].

Mediation in the benevolent associations appears to be an ADJUDICATIVE PROCESS, although the lack of an enforcement mechanism other than moral and social suasion makes its taxonomy uncertain. The Chinese community can often exert considerable control over its members by threatening noncomplying members with ostracism [McGillis and Mullen, 1977, p. 14].

In China, the Communist Party institutionalized conciliatory processes through *People's Conciliation (or Mediation) Committees,* mass organizations for resolving civil disputes. Committees are also found within other institutions, such as rural villagers' committees and urban residents' committees. Depending on the size and needs of the institution, these committees are placed in industrial and mining enterprises or institutions at the factory, workshop, or group level. Thus People's Mediation Committees include Neighborhood Mediation Committees and Factory Workers' Mediation Committees. According to one commentary:

> [A People's Conciliation Committee] operates separately from the law except that a paralegal type records the ultimate resolutions and serves as a representative of the government. Basic concepts of fairness prevail, as opposed to application of any rigid legal principles. It uses no lawyers or judges, but it handles all

types of disputes, civil and criminal. (Very serious crimes, however, are handled by the court system.) This communal, grassroots method of dispute resolution differs from mediation in general in that there is more than one mediator. Each party is provided with a mediator who basically represents their interests. However, the method is not adversary per se since the judgment is determined through negotiated agreement between the mediators and acquiescence by the disputants. The mediators are typically supplied by the disputants' employers and/or are elected by the community. The mediators are trained laymen who work at the same place as their disputants and have been given time off during the mediation. The mediators often know the disputants. The mediations may occur where the dispute took place or they may occur at either parties' workplace. The process is quick and informal [BNA ADR Report, 1988, vol. 2, pp. 298–400].

Compare ARBITREMENT.

Other commentators contradict the notion that such mediation is free from the application of legal principles. The Bureaus of Justice at the local level are responsible for organizing mediation committees, formulating the rules, and training mediators. The nearly one million committees operate under the guidance of the local government and local court. Although the process is strictly voluntary, Li Mei Qin and He Wei [1988, pp. 324–328] note that the mediation must be conducted in accordance with the policies, laws, and regulations of the People's Government, and the contents of the compromise agreement should not run counter to the law and infringe upon third parties' rights or interests. Mediation committees are directed to support the parties' right to seek redress in the regular courts. In fact, the committees have some adjudicative-like functions because they can reject claims and issue DECISIONS that can be overruled by the courts.

Still other commentators describe a more politicized and coercive process only superficially related to traditional practices of community-level mediation. They describe a process designed as "the lowest level of the state control apparatus, whose members act as unofficial police spies against 'ideological enemies,' using as a powerful resource their own personal knowledge of the parties involved (or that of their neighbors)" [Marshall, 1985, p. 63]. Merry [1989] notes that mediators, elected by representatives of the residents, must be "politically upright." In addition to mediating, they conduct propaganda and educate the disputants about national policies and laws. Particularly during the Cultural Revolution, mediators operated "within a clear moral system and often deliver[ed] harangues on moral virtue and new ways of thought. The mediators can invoke sanctions either through the police and other cadres in the urban neighborhoods or through work supervision in factories and communes. Individuals from peasant or worker backgrounds fare[d] better than those whose families were bourgeois, reflecting communist values" [pp. 79–80, citations omitted].

Participants in recent junkets by Western mediators paint a picture of a more benign system. Indeed, Perkovich [1996] opines that during the post-Maoist period, mediation has returned to a more traditional base in which mediators no longer stress obedience to Communist Party principles. Such commentators do note, however, that mediators continue to exhibit a directive, authoritarian style unlike the primary model in Western societies. Mediation committees "investigate" disputes, make findings of culpability ("mediator's verdict"), and stress the importance of contrition for misconduct ("self-criticism"). There is considerable reliance on using authoritative elders as mediators who can interpose themselves and force mediation without the consent of the disputants. If the mediation is unsuccessful and the disputants pursue litigation, the mediator can provide information on the matter to the courts.

Undoubtedly there is much to learn about dispute resolution in Chinese society, but the range of authoritative descriptions indicates that changing political and social variables can and do affect the nature of conciliatory processes in a given society.

Chinese village anti-litigation societies   Societies that arose in China out of negative attitudes toward the law and law court. These societies sought to preserve the CHINESE MEDIATION as the predominant method of dispute resolution [Nader and Todd, 1978, p. 31].

choice-of-law clause   Contract provision specifying the GOVERNING LAW.

Christian Peacemaker Teams (CPT)   Collaborative program of MENNONITES and Church of the Brethren congregations and Quaker meetings (see SOCIETY OF FRIENDS) that focuses on international and civil war. Teams of trained peacemakers are sent into situations of violent conflict and areas of militarization to support local nonviolent efforts. CPT include full-time workers who make up the Christian Peacemaker Corps. Reserve Corps members are available for periods of two weeks to two months each year. Volunteers and Corps members also participate in special delegations to situations of conflict.

circuit court mediation   In Florida, mediation of civil cases, other than family matters, in a circuit court [Fla. Stat. Ann. § 44.1011 (West Supp. 1992)]. Florida was one of the first states to enact legislation authorizing judges to order participation in mediation as a condition precedent to further judicial process.

circularizing   When a mediator creates interdependence between the disputants to a conflict and their stories, as well as between the disputants themselves, by practicing circular questioning. Circular questions create descriptions of responsibility without blame via (1) a series of questions that collectively create descriptions of interdependence (such as "How did this problem begin?" and "When you noticed a problem, what did you do?"), and (2) one question that yields information about differences (such as "How were your attempts at resolution interpreted by the others?" and "What would they say is the most problematic emotion/thought for you?") [Cobb, 1993, pp. 255–256].

citizen complaint mechanism   System usually created by local governments to receive and process complaints about government services or actions. Examples include the classic government OMBUDSMAN and citizen complaint HOT LINE. A less accurate use of the term is for consumer complaints against businesses. See CONSUMER COMPLAINT MECHANISMS.

citizen diplomacy   *International Relations:* Contact between citizens of different nations through unofficial activity, such as religious, cultural, scientific, and educational activity, in which they are not representing their governments. It also includes unofficial negotiations and dialogue between citizens of nations in conflict. Also known as TRACK-TWO DIPLOMACY. Compare MULTITRACK DIPLOMACY.

citizen dispute settlement   Alternative dispute resolution process proposed by the American Friends Service Committee that drew upon a mixture of African tribal moots and mediation. Its underlying principle was the concept of disputes as a form of property that should belong to the community rather than to the formalized judicial system. The citizen dispute settlement was developed in the late 1960s and underlies some of the COMMUNITY DISPUTE RESOLUTION CENTER or NEIGHBORHOOD JUSTICE CENTER movement [Auerbach, 1983, p. 117].

citizens' conciliation council   *Labor:* Settlement procedure used in disputes of public COLLECTIVE BARGAINING AGREEMENTS. A board composed of residents from the jurisdiction of the public employer, after receiving written summaries from the disputants, makes a final decision on the settlement that is binding to the parties involved. The disputants must agree on both the issues to be submitted and whether to submit the issues to the citizens' council or other form of dispute resolution [Ohio Rev. Code Ann. § 4117.14 (c)(1) (Banks-Baldwin 1990)].

civil action   Court case other than criminal.
　　Such actions are brought to seek redress or protection for private rights. Currently used as synonymous with LAWSUIT.

Civil Appeals Management Plan (CAMP)   Prehearing intervention by an appeals court staff attorney to establish settlement conferences and scheduling orders and to facilitate settlement. See APPELLATE ALTERNATIVE DISPUTE RESOLUTION. The goal is to resolve pending appeals without the necessity of a full judicial hearing and to expedite the flow of those appeals that do go to hearing.

CAMPs have been found appropriate for all civil cases filed in federal appeals court other than original proceedings, prisoner petitions, summary enforcement actions of the National Labor Relations Board, and pro se appeals [Harter, 1987, p. 77]. In Local Rule 54, the Second Circuit has instituted a CAMP that empowers a court officer to direct the parties in a civil appeal to appear at a preargument conference "to consider the possibility of settlement" before their case is scheduled for argument. Conferences are held in approximately 90 percent of the cases assigned to CAMP. For a review of the debate over CAMP's success, see Hoffman [1982, pp. 60, 70, nn. 42–44]. For a discussion of the problems that arise when judges become deeply involved in pretrial attempts to facilitate settlement, see Resnik [1982].

civil diversion (macrojustice) Diversion of civil suits to alternative dispute resolution processes.

Also known as *civil case diversion*, it has become a major aspect of civil justice reform. The underlying premise is that attention should not focus exclusively on facilitating dispute resolution through the courts. Rather, dispute resolution should be viewed as a comprehensive system in which the courts are important but in which many other elements and techniques come into play [Johnson et al., 1977, p. ix]. See COMPLEMENTARY DISPUTE RESOLUTION.

As practiced, civil diversion is subject to criticism. In the United States, most civil diversion is accomplished by mass referral of whole categories of cases to COURT-ADMINISTERED ADR processes in which parties are mandated to participate despite having little control over the process and choice of NEUTRAL. Not only does this fail to shift the burden and focus of dispute resolution away from the courts, but it also coerces participation in processes that arguably work best with high degrees of party control and consent.

Civil Justice Reform Act of 1990 (CJRA) 1990 U.S. federal law that requires each federal district court to implement a "civil justice expense and delay reduction plan" to improve civil case processing and to appoint an advisory group of lawyers and clients to help develop the plan. District courts could frame their own plan or adopt a model plan developed by the Judicial Conference of the United States. A district court's plan might include provisions addressing the use of ADR processes, such as MEDIATION, EARLY NEUTRAL EVALUATION, MINITRIAL, and SUMMARY JURY TRIAL. Most COURT-ANNEXED ADR processes in the federal district courts are described in these plans [Pub. L. No. 101-650, 104 Stat. 5089 (codified at 28 U.S.C. § 471 et. seq. (1994)].

civil law Codified law of certain states that has roots in the Napoleonic Code or Roman law as provided in the *Corpus Juris Civilis*. Historically, Justinian's Institutes defined civil law as "that law which every people has established for itself." In this respect, it refers to the law of any given state, sometimes referred to as *municipal law*. It stands in contrast with the common law of England, with canon law, and with criminal law, because it is the law concerning private rights and remedies.

civilian complaint review board (CCRB)   Independent, nonpolice agency with the authority to investigate allegations of misconduct filed by members of the public against police officers.

CCRB's are common in major cities across the United States. In New York City's CCRB, a typical example, investigations are conducted by the board's investigative staff, which is made up solely of civilian employees. The CCRB is empowered to receive, investigate, hear, make findings, and recommend action on complaints concerning the use of excessive or unnecessary force, abuse of authority, discourtesy, or use of offensive language by city police officers. The board seeks to investigate cases expediently and fairly and to instill trust in the police department by the citizenry. Some CCRB's have been criticized as being too lenient on police officers.

claim   Assert a right or ownership over.

In litigation, a claim is a CAUSE OF ACTION. In arbitration, *claim* has similar meaning but is often understood as referring to each specific form of relief requested in the DEMAND FOR ARBITRATION. Compare COUNTERCLAIM.

claimant   Party who initiates an arbitration by giving notice to the RESPONDENT of his intention to arbitrate [DOA]. See also DEMAND FOR ARBITRATION.

claiming   Process by which an individual with a GRIEVANCE voices it to the person or entity believed to be responsible and asks for some remedy. A claim evolves into a dispute when it is rejected [Felstiner, Abel, and Sarat, 1980–1981, pp. 635–636]. Contrast BLAMING.

claiming value   Term used by Lax and Sebenius [1986] to describe competitive, distributive BARGAINING. Compare SHARE BARGAINING under BARGAINING. They note a fundamental tension between CREATING VALUE and claiming value in negotiations.

class action   Means provided by law for a large group of individuals with a shared interest or similar claim to sue or be sued.

clause compromissoire   Arbitration clause in French practice. See also ARBITRATION AGREEMENT, COMPROMIS, SUBMISSION.

Client Assistance Projects (CAPs)   Projects created voluntarily by state rehabilitation agencies, in part to help resolve disputes between state rehabilitation agency employees and service recipients. The idea for these projects originated in the U.S. Senate, and Senate members promoted them as representatives of client interests in their relationships with state agencies [Tripp, 1985, p. 86]. Compare OMBUDSMAN.

closed bargaining style Alternative term for COMPETITIVE bargaining style in POSITIONAL BARGAINING. Contrast OPEN BARGAINING STYLE.

closing argument Final oral statement made by each party in the HEARING phase of an arbitration or litigation.

coalition Temporary ALLIANCE to accomplish a common purpose or to engage in joint activity.

Viewed solely from the perspective of the coalition members, forming a coalition is a way to obtain payoffs that members cannot achieve acting individually. Viewed from the perspective of all stakeholders, the coalition is a subset of stakeholders that unites to determine an outcome for the entire group of stakeholders and that benefits coalition members more than other stakeholders [Brett, 1991, p. 303]. According to Gamson [1971, p. 5], a coalition is a social tool to win a competition. Members cooperate to gain advantage over other stakeholders. Although this view of coalition formation as a competitive strategy that comes at the expense of other stakeholders is accurate in purely DISTRIBUTIVE, ZERO-SUM situations, it does not necessarily apply to all coalitions. Coalition formation can be an effort by members to pool resources to achieve a better outcome than they could achieve alone. This leads to some distinctions between types of coalitions. A *positive coalition* may be formed to combine the necessary resources to implement a solution. A *negative coalition,* also known as a *blocking coalition,* may be formed to impede or frustrate action or agreement by other stakeholders. A *winning coalition* has the necessary resources to control and execute the decision and does so by achieving a competitive advantage [Gamson, 1971, p. 147; Axelrod, 1970].

Using a competitive, GAME THEORY approach, Gamson [1971, p. 148] determines that the following conditions must be present for coalition formation to occur:

1. More than two must make a decision while trying to maximize their payoff, but no single alternative will maximize everyone's payoff.
2. No participant can dictate the outcome.
3. No participant has veto power, that is, no member must be included in every winning coalition.

These conditions hint at some internal dynamics of coalitions. The inherent instability of coalitions derives from the fact that members do not have complete commonality of interests. Three or more stakeholders are required, and competition may occur among them. The members do not automatically give each other an equal share of the advantage of their joint efforts [Gamson, 1971, p. 5]. Disputes over conflicts of interest are likely. Stakeholders who are not coalition members can weaken a coalition by playing on the divergent interests of coalition members and encouraging their defection. This can destroy weak coalitions, such as a *minimum winning coalition* (a winning coalition such that the defection of any member will make the coalition no longer winning)[Gamson, 1971, p. 149]. The greater the commonality of interest, the more likely it is that a coalition will form, remain intact for a longer duration, and efficiently resolve its internal disputes. Size and distribution of resources among members also affect its stability [Axelrod, 1970]. [See also Midgaard and Underdal, 1977, pp. 340–344.]

code of arbitration procedure   Rules promulgated by a particular ADMINISTERING AGENCY, such as the American Arbitration Association, that govern the conduct of the arbitral proceedings.

coercion   Use of force or threat to control or compel obedience.
Some definitions by commentators in dispute resolution include the following:

- "An attempt by one party to influence the behavior of another party in desired directions by making him fear the consequences of not acting in the way demanded" [Greenstone and Leviton, 1987, p. 137].

- "The exercise of power through the use of particular tactics that aim to reward or punish the opponent" [Gibbons, Bradac, and Busch, 1992, p. 160].

- "A form of conflict resolution or, more accurately, conflict suppression. There is widespread agreement within the field of conflict resolution that genuine problem solving is incompatible with the utilization of coercive power" [Breggin, 1992, p. 73].

Between disputants, the use of coercion may aggravate the conflict and impede a settlement. As Rubin [1983, p. 140] notes, negotiators are reluctant to make CONCESSIONS unless they believe the choice is a result of their own competence. Coercion and intimidation, therefore, are likely to elicit defensive, noncooperative reactions rather than concessions. Contrast NEGOTIATION JUJITSU.

coexistence   Existing together at the same time and place without trying to destroy the other; an emerging subdiscipline or specialization in conflict resolution that focuses on bringing about changes in conditions and attitudes so that a party suspends or ceases attempts to destroy another or grants another party the right to exist.

Interest in concepts of coexistence increased with the end of the Cold War and the outbreak of old and new interethnic hostilities. Since many of these contemporary, seemingly intractable ethnic conflicts are exacerbated by ideologies that require the destruction of another group, mere acceptance of the notion of coexistence, allowing that the other has the right to exist, constitutes a significant decrease in hostilities. Simply allowing others to live and conceding that one must learn to live with them is a minimal condition precedent for seeking peace, cooperation, and reconciliation [Weiner, 1998]. Coexistence includes a wide range of relationships, other than those involving overt struggle, and varies by the extent of party interdependence, the degree of equality and inequality, and the subjective ways in which individual members of the groups regard members of the other party [Kriesberg, 1998a]. The related terms *competitive coexistence* and *peaceful coexistence* were used respectively to describe the overtly antagonistic and subsequently less antagonistic relationships between the Soviet Union and the West. Contrast RECONCILIATION.

collaborate, collaborating, collaboration, collaborative   Work together or jointly; in some contexts, working with the enemy. Merging resources to reach a common goal that will satisfy the parties' respective interests.

Parties are collaborating when their primary goal is to reach an accord that will provide both sides with mutual gains instead of mutual losses [Haydock and Mitchell, 1984, p. 128].

Term used to describe an individual's interpersonal conflict resolution mode or style. In the THOMAS/KILMANN CONFLICT MODE INSTRUMENT, collaborating is both ASSERTIVE and COOPERATIVE—the opposite of AVOIDING. Collaborating involves an attempt to work with the other person to find a solution that fully satisfies the concerns of both persons. It means digging into an issue to identify the underlying concerns of the two individuals and to find an alternative that meets both sets of concerns. Collaboration between two persons might take the form of exploring a disagreement in order to learn from each other's insights, concluding to resolve some condition that would otherwise have them competing for resources, or confronting and trying to find a creative solution to an interpersonal problem [Thomas/Kilmann Conflict Mode Instrument, 1974]. In this context, it is a unilateral activity or personal mode independent of whether the other side is collaborating.

collaborative negotiation   Approach to dispute resolution in which the parties to a conflict attempt to resolve their differences through a bargaining procedure that is not adversary. Rather than attempting to obtain their objectives by promoting their own positions, rebutting others' arguments, and threatening to bring their power to bear on each other, the parties engage in a mutual effort to discover solutions that will maximize the degree to which everyone's interests are met [Mayer, 1985, p. 70]. In this context, all parties must be engaged in collaborative behavior. Also known as COLLABORATIVE PROBLEM SOLVING (CPS).

collaborative problem solving (CPS)   Alternative term for COLLABORATIVE NEGOTIATION; sometimes used as a catch-all term for ALTERNATIVE DISPUTE RESOLUTION; more correctly used to describe dispute resolution processes or techniques that are neither adversary nor competitive, which some ADR processes can be. CPS requires parties to design a problem-solving strategy to reach decisions to which all parties can agree and, in the process, first come to agreement on the definition of problems at hand. See PROBLEM SOLVING.

collateral estoppel   *Law:* Doctrine stating that an issue that has already been legally determined cannot be reopened or adjudicated again in a subsequent proceeding.

Collateral estoppel applies in arbitration cases as well as in civil suits. Even when a point not central to the case has been determined, that point is considered to be decided for any further cases concerned with the same matter and involving the same parties [DOA]. The purpose of the doctrine is both to protect litigants from the burden of relitigating issues and to promote judicial economy by preventing needless litigation. *Offensive collateral estoppel* is used by a plaintiff to prevent a defendant from relitigating issues that the defendant previously lost against another plaintiff. *Defensive collateral estoppel* is used by a defendant to prevent a plaintiff from relitigating issues that the plaintiff previously lost against another defendant.

In determining the collateral estoppel and RES JUDICATA effect of arbitration, courts apply standards that include (1) whether the claim to be precluded is within the scope of the arbitration clause, (2) whether the previous award was final and binding upon the party to be precluded, and in some cases (3) whether the nonjudicial proceeding sufficiently resembled a judicial proceeding. The latter standard is meant to ensure that the party has a full and fair opportunity to contest the issue in the prior action [Wilkinson, 1990, pp. 419–420]. Because traditional COMMERCIAL ARBITRATION in the United States does not require the arbitrators to include their reasoning in the written award, there can be some debate as to the matters specifically determined. In labor and employment arbitration, some courts have ruled that the arbitrators' determination of certain federal statutory claims (Title VII, the Fair Labor Standards Act, Section 1983 of the Civil Rights Act) does not have collateral estoppel effect. The current trend, however, is toward finding collateral estoppel. If the arbitration award includes a statement that it is not intended to carry any preclusive weight, it normally will not [*United States* v. *Woodcrest Nursing Home*, 1983].

See also RES JUDICATA.

collective bargaining   *Labor:* Process of negotiation between representatives of labor and management to change contract terms and conditions of individual workers' employment [DOA].

In its broadest sense, it refers to any discussions relating to labor problems, and it either directly or indirectly affects a group of workers. Governments may or may not be involved, and FORUMS vary. Collective bargaining should be distinguished from joint committees, joint consultation, works councils, and other mechanisms in the workplace that promote cooperation on common interests. In collective bargaining, the object is for parties to compromise and agree on wages and other employment conditions [Sur, 1965, p. 9]. In a narrower sense, especially in the United States, the term denotes negotiations between trade union representatives and individual employers or representatives of employers' organizations. Collective bargaining involves representatives of groups. Interpersonal bargaining does not.

Much of the early theory building in negotiation was derived from studies of collective bargaining [such as Walton and McKersie, 1965]. Primarily a rule-making process involving a power relationship between organizations, collective bargaining should be distinguished from BARGAINING, particularly to the extent that bargaining connotes a market process that culminates in an act of exchange. In that sense, *collective bargain* is a misnomer. Morley and Stephenson [1977, pp. 22–23, 26], however, counter that there are collective bargaining processes that are in one sense nonnegotiated.

Simkin [1971, pp. 6–7] classifies two types of collective bargain: *crisis bargaining* and *noncrisis bargaining.* Crisis bargaining occurs near the time of contract expiration, after which there may be no limitation on strikes and lockouts. This creates a crisis atmosphere as expiration approaches and pressure mounts to avert a crisis by reaching agreement (see *early bird bargaining* under BARGAINING as a way to avoid the time constraints). Noncrisis bargaining occurs without the time pressures of contract expiration and over a specific issue of mutual importance that cannot be handled adequately in the grievance procedure. It may resemble BRAINSTORMING more than the POSITIONAL BARGAINING that typifies crisis bargaining, and it normally results in recommendations that require approval at other bargaining levels. This type of collective bargaining has been labeled *continuous bargaining.* Simkin uses the term *noncrisis dialogue* because it emphasizes that the bargaining is removed in time from contract negotiations and because such discourse is seldom continuous in a literal sense [pp. 313–314].

collective bargaining agreement   Contract between a union and a company that contains the terms and conditions of employment for a stated period. Might be called a *privately drawn code of laws* or the *common law of the plant.* An ARBITRATION CLAUSE is included in a great majority of such contracts [DOA]. See LABOR ARBITRATION.

collegiate tribunal   *International Relations:* Body established by TREATY and consisting of an uneven number of persons (three or five) with the power to decide a matter by majority. The treaty should provide for a manner of selection or appointment to the tribunal. Usually each party appoints one or more NATIONAL ARBITRATORS, then the parties agree on the remaining NEUTRAL members [Merrills, 1991, p. 83].

co-med-arb   Variation of MED-ARB in which the mediator and arbitrator proceed simultaneously and coordinate their roles.

Proposed in response to the role confusion criticisms of med-arb and the inefficiencies of MED-THEN-ARB, this variation might reduce the costs of using two separate NEUTRALS while maximizing the inherent advantages of the two separate processes. By having a mediator and an arbitrator cooperate as closely as possible without confusing their respective roles, one avoids the added expenses of having to bring the arbitrator up to speed if her adjudicative powers are required. Additionally, the parties can maximize the effectiveness of the two phases by selecting a mediator who is an expert in mediation and an arbitrator who is an expert in the technical aspects of the disputed subject matter.

To avoid jeopardizing the integrity of either phase, the arbitrator would participate only in the *open* segments of the mediation phase and not in those *confidential* segments in which the parties are engaged in confidential discussions with the mediator or in actual bargaining with each other. Thus the hypothetical co-med-arb would probably have three phases: (1) an information exchange similar to the hearing phase of a mini-trial at which both neutrals would preside, (2) a mediation phase during which the mediator may consult with the arbitrator on procedural matters but is otherwise prohibited from discussing the substance of the dispute, and (3) if necessary, an arbitration phase during which the mediator could remain available to facilitate settlement discussions before a final award or after interim awards [Buhring-Uhle, 1992].

See SHADOW MEDIATION.

co-mediation   Mediation conducted simultaneously or jointly by two or more mediators.

Co-mediation is sometimes used in cross-gender, cross-ethnic, and cross-cultural disputes when characteristics of a single mediator, such as gender, nationality, ethnicity, and culture, may match that of one of the parties and lead the other party to assume partiality or bias on the part of that mediator. Thus co-mediators are selected to represent the range of contrasting characteristics found among the disputants.

Also, co-mediation is used when a single mediator needs additional expertise to conduct the process effectively. Folberg [1982] describes *interdisciplinary co-mediation* as using a team composed of mediators with different professional backgrounds and experience that may be helpful in resolving the dispute—for example, a lawyer and psychotherapist in the context of some interpersonal disputes with mixed issues of emotional resolution and a comprehensive legal settlement. Although neither mediator should lapse into her respective professional role, the lawyer may be better at mediating the factual aspect of the settlement issues and the therapist may better mediate the interpersonal and emotional aspects. The therapist manages the therapeutic milieu and in that regard is attentive to issues of trust, fear, and safety. The lawyer provides information about the legal system and establishes legal parameters and guidelines for the mediation. Compare STRUCTURED MEDIATION.

Co-mediation might be used to describe a form of supervised mediation training in which an apprentice is officially assigned to the case and is responsible for conducting the session but mediates with the mentor mediator present. In discussing the use of co-mediation in divorce or family mediation, Haynes [1986a, pp. 13–14] describes something different: "a form of consultation in which the consultant and the mediator jointly mediate a couple from in-take through to the drafting of the memorandum of understanding." This appears to be a form of mentoring in which the consultant may merely observe the mediation while not actually participating, may participate with the mediator as a team, or may demonstrate while the mediator observes.

co-mediator   Mediator in CO-MEDIATION.

commercial arbitration   Voluntary, private arbitration used to settle disputes in the general commercial or business world [DOA].

There are two settings in which commercial arbitration occurs. Most commercial arbitration arises from a contract clause providing for the arbitration of future disputes arising out of the contract or from an agreement between parties in a commercial relationship to submit an existing dispute to arbitration. See ARBITRATION AGREEMENT. Another type of commercial arbitration arises within trade associations or exchanges that, usually through charter or bylaws, provide for the arbitration of member disputes as a condition of membership.

Commercial arbitration should be distinguished from LABOR ARBITRATION. The underlying rationales are the same—to save time and money, to minimize hostility in an effort to preserve relationships, and to achieve efficiency and rational results by referring the matter to adjudicators who have specialized knowledge of the norms and usages of the area. Additionally, the procedures are similar. Obviously labor arbitration occurs over conditions and terms of employment. This distinction is not always so clear. For example, in the United States labor arbitration arises only out of COLLECTIVE BARGAINING AGREEMENTS, while commercial arbitration arises out of individual employment contracts. Commercial arbitration is governed by a different set of laws in many countries.

For example, in the United States commercial arbitration is governed by the UNITED STATES ARBITRATION ACT or applicable state arbitration acts. In domestic practice, U.S. arbitrators issue reasoned awards in labor arbitration, but typically not in commercial arbitration. Historically, modern commercial arbitration grew out of mercantile traditions, while labor arbitration developed in the atmosphere of labor guilds. Although maintaining relationships was an important goal in both settings, arbitration of workplace disputes necessitated more sensitivity to the ongoing relationship of the parties. By contrast, in most commercial arbitration the relationship between the parties ended once one of them breached their contract. Consequently, arbitration awards in commercial arbitration rarely involve compromise, while those in labor arbitration are often seen as reflecting some "middle ground." See DOCTRINE OF MUTUALITY.

Although some commercial arbitration occurs AD HOC, most of it in the United States is administered by ADMINISTRATIVE AGENCIES such as the AMERICAN ARBITRATION ASSOCIATION or by administrative mechanisms provided by a particular trade group. Although the latter mechanism was established primarily to settle disputes among members, on either a voluntary or a compulsory basis, it is sometimes available to nonmembers doing business in the particular trade or to consumers of services in the trade, such as stockbroker-customer arbitration conducted by the New York Stock Exchange or the National Association of Security Dealers.

Although most commercial arbitration is between parties in a contractual relationship, there are exceptions. The American Arbitration Association, for example, classifies submissions of disputes between insurers and third-party claimants as commercial arbitration.

See ARBITRATION.

commission   Body composed of several persons acting under lawful authority to perform some public service. Although the term is used in many other ways, its public mission distinguishes it from a tribunal in conflict resolution. See TRIBUNAL.

commission of inquiry, commission of enquiry   *International Relations:* Independent FACT-FINDING body set up jointly by disputing states to conduct an impartial investigation of an international dispute, usually when the states concerned are unwilling to submit their dispute to arbitration.

The use of international commissions of inquiry was among the dispute settlement methods provided in the CONVENTION FOR THE PACIFIC SETTLEMENT OF INTERNATIONAL DISPUTES. Commissions of this kind are an alternate means of settling disputes afforded by the PERMANENT COURT OF ARBITRATION [DOA].

As with GOOD OFFICES and CONCILIATION procedure, a commission of inquiry formulates no recommendation but simply presents its findings on facts. These findings may then form the basis for subsequent direct negotiations or another procedure, or they may be ignored. As in other forms of fact-finding, the findings constitute not a resolution but rather a catalyst for subsequent processes [Umbricht, 1989, p. 26].

See INQUIRY, FACT-FINDING.

Commission of Investigation and Conciliation *International Relations:* Any COMMISSION authorized to resolve disputes through INQUIRY and CONCILIATION. More specifically, a dispute resolution body that helps settle disputes among states in the Americas.

The term encompasses standing commissions established by BILATERAL TREATIES and AD HOC commissions established by the Organization of American States (OAS) Council under the authority of the American Treaty of Pacific Settlement (PACT OF BOGOTA) of 1948. A commission may act only when requested by disputing states that are parties to one of these establishing treaties. Both standing and ad hoc commissions consist of five members—each party chooses two and the parties together choose a chairperson. Parties can select their own nationals for standing commissions but must select from a list of conciliators maintained by the OAS secretariat when forming an ad hoc commission.

Commission of Mediation, Conciliation, and Arbitration *International Relations:* Dispute resolution body that helps settle disputes among the members of the ORGANIZATION OF AFRICAN UNITY (OAU) and established under Article XIX of the OAU Charter. Applicable procedures depend on whether the commission is called on to serve as mediator, conciliator, or arbitrator.

commitment Choice to act in a particular fashion or to hold to a certain position. Associated with the BARGAINING phase of NEGOTIATION.

With respect to positioning, Lax and Sebenius [1986, p. 124] define commitment as a point within the BARGAINING SET beyond which settlements are deemed less attractive and that, if accepted, would result in self-imposed costs.

With respect to action, Fisher [1983a], who treats commitment as a form of power, notes that offers to settle contain both *affirmative commitments* to agree to and perform the conditions if accepted, and implicit *negative commitments* not to reach agreement if other conditions are proffered. THREATS are explicit negative commitments often used outside the context of a specific offer to stress the harmful consequences if the other side fails to agree. Willingness and ability to make a commitment and hold to it empowers a negotiator if they are exercised wisely in considering one's alternatives (see BATNA).

commitment-inducing procedures Voluntary and self-executing practices or measures that psychologically and structurally bind the parties to the negotiated settlement [Moore, 1986, p. 253]. These factors that induce commitment are distinguishable from merely a good, implementable solution that meets the parties' interests. A simple example would be the drafting and execution of an enforceable, written settlement agreement.

commitment points   *Negotiation:* Stages along the bargaining range at which a negotiator asserts a position, gives the opponent specific justification for the position, and resists further movement along the continuum toward the opponent's goal [Harbaugh and Britzke, 1988, p. 36].

common ground   Issues on which disputants agree.

Identifying the common ground helps resolve conflict in two ways. First, it reinforces the disputants' constructive interaction by showing that they either have common interests or have been capable of agreeing on some matters, usually more than they thought. Second, it helps highlight the points of disagreement on which they should focus their attention.

common law   Body of written or unwritten rules and principles that derive their authority solely from custom or secular court decisions, as distinguished from laws enacted by legislatures or from ecclesiastical law. Also, common law refers to the common law of England, including English statutes, that became part of the law of the thirteen original United States at the time of inception. All but one of the United States, as well as of certain nations associated with England, have adopted a considerable body of the common law [DOA].

In a broader sense, common law refers to the customary or positive law of general or universal application, as opposed to local rules or customs or rules of special application.

common law arbitration   Arbitration conducted under common law. Common law arbitration and all its procedures derive from court decisions rather than from statutes, although common law arbitration procedures may be codified in some states. Common law arbitration coexists, with little or no modification, with the various statutory arbitration systems.

Under common law arbitration, the parties voluntarily agree to submit their dispute to the decision of a mutually selected third person. Unlike in statutory arbitration, such a submission agreement may be oral and may be revoked at any time before the rendering of the award. Procedures include the agreement to arbitrate, the selection of arbitrators, the steps to be followed in the hearing and the form and making of the award, and enforcement or annulment of the award [DOA].

common law hostility   *Arbitration:* The common law doctrine in which courts refused to enforce agreements to arbitrate future disputes by declaring such agreements an "attempt to oust the courts" of their jurisdiction. The doctrine is attributed to Lord Coke's decision in VYNIOR'S CASE and is still applied in a few jurisdictions. Most jurisdictions, however, have adopted MODERN ARBITRATION STATUTES that nullify the doctrine.

commonality   Characteristic that parties have in common.

Identifying commonalities may help build trust and a cooperative attitude and erode the DEHUMANIZATION that often occurs in the escalation of disputes.

communicate, communication   Transmit information or express oneself so that one can be understood by another. In legal usage, a *communication* typically implies a deliberate attempt to communicate. In conflict resolution, persons might communicate information unknowingly or unintentionally.

community   In its broadest sense, a collection or congregation of individuals or entities with common interests either arising from their association or causing their association.

Another use refers to a locality or group of people living in a particular locality or in proximity to one another. The people in a community thus share some interests and often live under the same laws or customs.

The concept of community has important implications for conflict resolution. Members of the same community are more likely to resolve conflicts efficiently to the extent that they recognize shared norms, that they are subject to pressures from other parts of the community, that they are interdependent, and that they anticipate future interaction.

community boards   Dispute resolution programs focused on strengthening communities by using small, neighborhood-based boards of volunteers to hear disputes from community members and attempt to resolve them through the use of conciliatory processes, particularly mediation.

The predominant concept of community boards is typified by the *Community Boards Program* based in San Francisco. Using four-member, volunteer boards with at least one member of the same ethnicity or self-identified group as one disputant, the program tries to build communities in which diversity may create tensions. Disputes are referred to the boards by the police, by the courts, and through various community agencies. The Community Boards Program may be best known for its development of PEER MEDIATION programs in the schools. See CONFLICT MANAGER.

community dispute resolution, community justice system   Umbrella term for a wide variety of programs based on localism as an organizing principle, often originating and deriving their legitimacy from community consensus or religious norms rather than from the exercise of state power. These programs, subject to community control and direction, provide FORUMS where members of a community can get help in resolving their family, consumer, and neighborhood disputes without giving up decision-making power to the judicial system. Mediation and fact-finding are the methods most commonly used in community dispute resolution programs [Leeson and Johnston, 1988, p. 149].

Although most community justice systems start out as voluntary and free from state control, many come to rely on mandatory or coercive participation as directed by courts and become increasingly influenced by the state. See Merry and Milner [1993] and Tomasic and Feeley [1982].

community dispute resolution center, community justice center Facility in which COMMUNITY DISPUTE RESOLUTION programs are provided. The following legal definition of *community dispute resolution center* confuses program with place: "A program created to provide conciliation, mediation, or other forms and techniques of voluntary dispute resolution to persons as an alternative to the judicial process" [Mich. Comp. Laws Ann. § 691.1552 (West Supp. 1993)]. See also NEIGHBORHOOD JUSTICE CENTER.

community dispute resolution program Set or listing of DISPUTE RESOLUTION services provided to the public through a COMMUNITY DISPUTE RESOLUTION CENTER or otherwise, under principles consistent with COMMUNITY DISPUTE RESOLUTION. See DISPUTE RESOLUTION PROGRAM.

community mediation Mediation provided through a COMMUNITY DISPUTE RESOLUTION program. Also used to describe the process of mediation used in China and in similar cultures where mediation has become a social norm (see, for example, CHINESE MEDIATION).

community moot Term popularized by Danzig [1973] to denote what was thought to be the typical process of law in small tribal societies. This model emphasizes community involvement, party reconciliation, consensus, and the value of future social relations while it deemphasizes blame, judgment, and legal norms. See also TRIBAL MOOT.

Community Relations Service (CRS) U.S. federal dispute resolution program that uses mediation and conciliation to resolve community disputes involving discrimination based on race, color, or national origin. The CRS was established under the authority of the Civil Rights Act of 1964 and operates out of the U.S. Department of Justice. Under its congressional mandate, the CRS offers its services whenever, in its judgment, peaceful relations among the citizens of a community are endangered.

CRS mediators and conciliators lack enforcement authority, are precluded by law from investigating, and are governed by a confidentiality provision that makes it a federal offense to reveal information shared with them in confidence. Salem [1984, p. 65] notes that these factors make it easier for CRS personnel to gain the trust of parties to a dispute.

compact   Broadly, agreement or contract. Commonly used in international law to denote an agreement among states creating enforceable rights and obligations. Related terms: CONFEDERACY, TREATY.

comparative reciprocity   Process of increasing or decreasing CONCESSIONS in response to a higher or lower concession from the other party in the previous round of bargaining [Druckman and Harris, 1989, p. 236]. Compare TIT-FOR-TAT.

compel   Force or drive toward an involuntary response.

competence, competence-competence   *Arbitration:* The degree to which an arbitral TRIBUNAL may rule on its own jurisdiction as defined by the ARBITRATION AGREEMENT. Such a decision by the arbitral tribunal may be reviewed by the courts. If challenged, international commercial arbitrators are presumed to be empowered to rule on their own competence in most jurisdictions. Arbitrators of domestic commercial cases in the United States, however, must have express authority to so rule.

competing   Personal mode of conflict resolution that, according to the THOMAS/KILMANN CONFLICT MODE INSTRUMENT, is both assertive and uncooperative. Competing individuals pursue their own concerns without regard for others' interests and use whatever power seems appropriate to win [Thomas/Kilmann Conflict Mode Instrument, 1974]. Contrast AVOIDING, ACCOMMODATING, COLLABORATING.

competition, compete   Contesting, striving, or vying with others for scarce objects, status, a prize, or a resource. Contestants are normally referred to as RIVALS. Conflict is often concomitant with competition and may result in disputing. When the object is to be awarded by a third party, competition usually takes place according to established rules that strictly limit the competitors' behavior. For example, a football game played by the rules is competition until players begin to assault one another against the rules; then the game becomes a conflict [Mack and Snyder, 1971, p. 7]. Disputing may occur over the interpretation and proper application of the rules, in which case the third party may also become a disputant.

competitive   Theory, strategy, or personal style of negotiation usually associated with POSITIONAL BARGAINING.

The term is often used to describe a personality type in negotiation (see COM-PETING). In his study of lawyer-negotiators, Williams [1983, p. 24] defines a category of *competitives* who are perceived by opposing negotiators as "dominating, competitive, forceful, tough, arrogant, and uncooperative. They make high opening demands, they use threats, they are willing to stretch the facts in favor of their clients' positions, they stick to their positions, and they are parsimonious with information about the case. . . . [R]ather than seeking an outcome that is 'fair' to both sides, they want to outdo the other side; to score a clear victory."

Haydock and Mitchell [1984, p. 6] define the competitive negotiator as one who wants to win and who wants the opponent to lose and thereby attempts to maximize her position and minimize the opponent's position.

Other commentators make distinctions between *competitive theory, competitive strategy, competitive tactics,* and *competitive style.* Competitive theory, the underlying premise or assumptions through which the individual negotiator views the situation, holds that negotiations are over limited, fixed resources that must be divided through competition in an adversary world governed by egocentric self-interest. Each negotiator seeks to maximize his or her outcome in a situation that is purely DISTRIBUTIVE or ZERO-SUM—one side's gain is the other's loss [Murray, Rau, and Sherman, 1989, pp. 76–77; Riskin and Westbrook, 1987, p. 142]. Competitive strategy, the setting of goals and the general game plan for achieving those goals in negotiation, is largely dependent on the basic premise that gains come at the other's expense. Therefore most competitive strategies are to win as much as possible by lowering the other side's confidence and estimation of his settlement alternatives (see BATNA). Competitive tactics, the specific moves and actions used to carry out the strategy, are designed to force the other side as close as possible to one's aspiration level. Such tactics include high initial demands or low initial offers; concealment of information about preferences; arguing and various psychological attacks, such as threats; and firm positioning with slow and small CONCESSIONS. Competitive style corresponds more closely with the concept of a competitive personality type and refers to the personal behavior of the negotiator in carrying out the chosen strategy and tactics. In this sense, a negotiator who is confrontational, overtly hostile, and adversary is exhibiting a competitive style. As Murray, Rau, and Sherman [1989, p. 75] observe, the correlation between these distinct concepts is not direct. In carrying out a competitive strategy, a negotiator may exhibit characteristics that are far from hostile or adversary.
Contrast COOPERATIVE, COLLABORATIVE.

competitive strategy   See COMPETITIVE.

complain, complaint   Express dissatisfaction, expression of dissatisfaction.
In conflict resolution theory, a complaint is what a GRIEVANCE develops into when a sufferer asks others to forbear [Lieberman and Henry, 1986, p. 426]. In

this sense, it is very similar, if not identical, to the concept of CLAIMING as defined by Felstiner, Abel, and Sarat [1980–1981, pp. 635–636].

Law: Initial pleading that starts a civil lawsuit.

complainant   One who makes a COMPLAINT. A person who wishes to lodge a complaint, such as to an OMBUDSMAN, regarding, for example, the practices of superiors in an organization or of an administrative body. A complainant may later become a DISPUTANT, if and when a dispute between parties arises and some form of dispute resolution is begun. The term is a means of describing one who "perceives a problem, has a concern, complaint or grievance" [Rowe, 1995, n. 22]. Compare GRIEVANT.

complementarity   Concept that opposites are part of a whole that is bigger than the sum of its parts, and that these parts are engaged in a relationship of reciprocity with one another. Also, a structural family therapy technique used by divorce mediators to encourage both parties to see themselves as having an impact on each other's behavior instead of simply reacting in a linear, cause-and-effect manner [McIsaac, 1986–1987, p. 67].

complementary dispute resolution (CDR)   Concept that focuses on how methods of dispute resolution other than litigation can complement and be incorporated into the legal system. This is in contrast with the *extralegal, extrajudicial* thrust implied by the term ALTERNATIVE DISPUTE RESOLUTION (ADR).

Official use of the term CDR appears to have originated in New Jersey, where it is used to describe the state's COURT-CONNECTED ADR programs. The New Jersey programs range from UNINSURED MOTORIST and personal injury arbitration, pretrial intervention, JUVENILE CONFERENCE COMMITTEES, custody and visitation mediation programs, and matrimonial early-settlement panels [*WAMR* 5(3)].

compliance   Acquiescence, submission, yielding to demand.

In conflict resolution theory, the term refers to the act of obeying a court order (for example, to mediate or to pay child support) or conforming with a mediated or otherwise reached agreement. For example, it is important to understand the extent to which a mediated agreement is more "compliance prone" than a court order, particularly in divorce and child custody, in which there is often little compliance with court orders. Mayer [1989] and Menzel [1991, p. 8] discuss compliance in family mediation using Etzioni's [1980] organizational compliance theory, which points out three types of compliance, each motivated by different reasoning:

1. *Normative-moral:* based on a belief that the agreement is fair and in the best interests of the affected group

2. *Utilitarian-calculative:* finds the agreement more beneficial in terms of costs and rewards

3. *Coercive-alienative:* takes place to avoid potential legal problems

compliance officer   Individual within an organization, usually highly placed in the government or corporate structure, who has overall responsibility for seeing that the organization follows national compliance standards and procedures such as nondiscrimination laws, disabled access laws, environmental laws, and occupational-safety requirements. Sometimes called *ethics officers.* In organizations lacking an established OMBUDSMAN, complaints and grievances often gravitate toward compliance officers.

comprehensive mediation   Process for divorce mediation proposed as alternative to STRUCTURED MEDIATION. Unlike structured mediation, it does not involve a consulting attorney, nor does it require the participants to sign agreements to participate [Coombs, 1984]. Although it is more flexible than structured mediation, comprehensive mediation can resemble the traditional adversarial system because each party can have legal counsel in attendance and request individual, private sessions with the mediator [Carbonneau, 1989, pp. 194–195].

comprehensive rationality   Linear model of decision making using the following progression: identifying the problem, searching for alternative courses of action, examining the consequences or implications of each possible alternative to find the option that holds out the best prospect of maximizing values, and choosing the alternative that promises the best ratio of possible gains to losses. This model lies at the core of PRINCIPLED NEGOTIATION and other COLLABORATIVE PROBLEM SOLVING models.

compromis (archaic)   Agreement to submit to ARBITREMENT.
International Relations: Agreement between sovereign states to refer an existing dispute to arbitration or to a court, such as the INTERNATIONAL COURT OF JUSTICE. The compromis establishes the terms of arbitration and the jurisdictional limits of the arbitral TRIBUNAL by defining the subject of the dispute, setting forth the principles that are to guide the tribunal, and establishing the rules of procedure to be followed in deciding the case. The tribunal decides specific questions relating to its jurisdiction under the terms of the compromis. The compromis may also define the manner of appointing arbitrators and ascribe any special powers that may eventually belong to the tribunal, as well as the particular language to be used and all other determining conditions on which the parties are agreed. A clear definition of the question to be arbitrated should be given whenever possible. Although the compromis is a document used only in existing disputes, its subject matter is very similar to an arbitration agreement

for settling future disputes, an agreement that is an integral part of many BI-LATERAL TREATIES. Unless a compromis states otherwise, it is either an express or implied condition that the arbitrator shall apply international law as the basis of her decision [DOA; Convention on the Pacific Settlement of International Disputes, 1899].

Compromis exists in two forms: (1) the *ad hoc compromis,* by which parties submit a dispute between them to an ad hoc or institutionalized arbitral tribunal or to an international court; and (2) the *general, abstract,* or *anticipated* compromis, by which states submit all or definite classes of disputes between them to an arbitral institution, a court, or an ad hoc arbitral body. The general compromis is created by a general arbitration treaty or by an arbitration clause in a treaty. Many such general compromis simply obligate the parties to negotiate in good faith an additional compromis known as an *implementing compromis,* a *special agreement,* or a *protocol of submission.* By its nature, arbitration cannot take place unless a compromis is first established, regardless of whether the arbitration is agreed to ad hoc or is provided for in a treaty [*Encyclopedia of Public International Law,* 1992, pt. 1, p. 45]. Compare COMPROMISSORY CLAUSE.

compromise   Settlement of a dispute through mutual CONCESSIONS. Compromise requires mutual adjustment of initial positions and only partial satisfaction of parties' interests. Regardless of the gains one party may make over another, any settlement involving some sacrifice of each principal's initial position can be considered a compromise. Compromises may result from agreement to a simple decision scheme, such as SPLIT THE DIFFERENCE [Carnevale and Lawler, 1986, p. 638]. Contrast CAPITULATION, CONCEDE.

Arbitration: Settlement of a dispute when the parties reach their own agreement before the arbitrator's award [DOA]. This agreement may be converted into a CONSENT AWARD.

compromise and settlement   *Law:* Avoidance or cessation of a lawsuit by settlement reached through mutual CONCESSIONS (see COMPROMISE). In civil law, the term is sometimes but rarely used to refer to a COMPROMIS, an agreement to refer an existing dispute to arbitration.

compromising   Give-and-take style of handling interpersonal conflict whereby both parties give up something to make a mutually acceptable decision.

In the THOMAS/KILMANN CONFLICT MODE INSTRUMENT, compromising is intermediate in both assertiveness and cooperativeness. The objective is to find some expedient, mutually acceptable solution that partially satisfies both parties. It falls on a middle ground between COMPETING and ACCOMMODATING. Compromising gives up more than competing but less than accommodating. Likewise, it addresses an issue more directly than AVOIDING but does not explore it in as much depth as COLLABORATING. Compromising might mean SPLITTING THE DIFFERENCE, exchanging CONCESSIONS, or seeking a quick, middle-ground position [Thomas/Kilmann Conflict Mode Instrument, 1974].

Rahim [1986, p. 85] notes that the compromising style is useful when the goals of the conflicting parties are mutually exclusive or when both parties are equally powerful, thereby excluding INTEGRATIVE BARGAINING and making confrontation or power contests irrational.

compromiso arbitral (Spanish)   Term for COMPROMIS.

International Arbitration: Many Latin American countries have historically been hostile to foreign dispute resolution, especially INTERNATIONAL ARBITRATION (see CALVO CLAUSE), and have refused to enforce agreements to arbitrate future disputes. Consequently, parties have had to agree to submit a dispute to arbitration *after* the dispute has arisen, by means of a *compromiso arbitral* [*WAMR* 4(7)].

compromissory clause   *International Relations:* TREATY clause agreeing to submit all future disputes relating to that treaty to either arbitration, conciliation, GOOD OFFICES, negotiation, or adjudication, such as to the INTERNATIONAL COURT OF JUSTICE or other permanent TRIBUNAL. This approach contrasts with a general commitment between states to submit all disputes to arbitration or to a particular tribunal. States may also agree to submit existing disputes to arbitration or adjudication by means of a COMPROMIS. Compromissory clauses can range from short and simple to complex and containing detailed procedures for dispute resolution. The Statute of the International Court of Justice, art. 36(2)(a) of the UN Charter, specifically empowers the court to hear disputes referred to it regarding the interpretation of treaties. Compare COMPROMIS.

compulsion   Coercion, duress.

compulsory arbitration   Informal extrajudicial adjudication forced on at least one of the parties by statute without the party's consent. Except for the lack of consent, the process reflects most other characteristics of ARBITRATION.

Compulsory arbitration is most common in labor disputes, especially those involving public employees with critical safety roles, such as police or firefighters (see PUBLIC EMPLOYEE ARBITRATION). Compulsory arbitration preempts the right to strike. Typically, statutes mandating compulsory arbitration apply when the possibility of a strike seriously affects the public interest. Depending on the statute or other form of authority to compel, the parties may or may not have a voice in selecting the arbitrator, determining procedures, or defining the issues to be decided.

Compulsory arbitration has been accepted in Australia and New Zealand for many years [DOA]. In the United States during World War II, the National War Labor Board acted as a TRIBUNAL whose decisions were final and binding. The board was established, however, after a labor-management conference agreed that there should be no strikes or lockouts during the war, and that disputes affecting the war effort should be submitted to a national tribunal for settlement. So, to some degree there was consent from both labor and management to use this process. Some states, following the end of World War II, provided for compulsory arbitration of public-employee labor disputes. Subsequent U.S. Supreme Court decisions held that the federal government had preempted the field of labor-management relations insofar as these disputes affected interstate commerce [Britton, 1982, p. 11].

The term is sometimes used to refer to arbitration agreements in labor contracts that provide for arbitration should the two sides fail to reach agreement through the ordinary system of COLLECTIVE BARGAINING. Such use is incorrect (the correct term is INTEREST ARBITRATION) because the parties have consented to use arbitration and the applicable statutes merely enforce their previous agreement.

Historically, the term has also been used to refer to COURT-CONNECTED arbitration programs imposed to cope with congestion in small claims courts, especially in Pennsylvania [DOA], although the term MANDATORY ARBITRATION is more closely associated with such programs. Finally, the term is currently used to describe voluntary, private arbitration created by contract but enforced by a MODERN ARBITRATION STATUTE, particularly when one of the parties is resisting arbitration and claims to have had no opportunity to negotiate the arbitration agreement or to have been coerced into the arbitration agreement. Technically, such arbitration is not compulsory arbitration as provided by statute without a specific agreement; instead, it presents a problem of whether to enforce an arbitration agreement under statutes that enforce private agreements to arbitrate.

compulsory jurisdiction *International Law:* Power of an international TRIBUNAL or court to hear and decide certain classes of cases. The concept facilitates acceptance of legal means of dispute resolution among states.

Strictly speaking, international law does not recognize compulsory jurisdiction arising merely by operation of law or in the sense that a state is obligated to submit to adjudication without consent. Although in national legal systems, courts must have compulsory jurisdiction to operate effectively, competence to adjudicate with binding effect on nation-states is always dependent on some form of consent—either AD HOC after a particular dispute arises or by prior TREATY. With respect to the latter, the Statute of the INTERNATIONAL COURT OF JUSTICE provides for compulsory jurisdiction in its Optional Clause (Article 36), which specifies the following:

The states parties to the present Statute may at any time declare that they recognize as compulsory ipso facto and without special agreement, in relation to any other state accepting the same obligation, the jurisdiction of the Court in all legal disputes concerning: (1) the interpretation of a treaty; (2) any question of international law; (3) the existence of any fact which, if established, would constitute a breach of an international obligation; (4) the nature or extent of the reparation to be made for the breach of an international obligation.

Although compulsory jurisdiction is provided for in hundreds of international treaties, the concept conflicts with the doctrine of sovereignty. Thus many states have attached reservations to their acceptance of the Optional Clause. See, for example, CONNALLY RESERVATION.

computer-aided mediation (CAM)   Use of computers to facilitate mediation.
Computer models have been used to help define and resolve negotiation problems in a number of instances, such as in the Law of the Sea Treaty. Computer-aided mediation in litigation is alleged to have begun in November 1987, in a case involving a U.S. insurance company's product liability suit against a foreign electronics company in the federal court of the Northern District of Illinois. In the context of litigation, Nagel and Mills [1989, pp. 176–178] assert that a computer facilitates the dispute resolution process by working with many variables simultaneously. It can help with problems involving predicting, choosing, allocating, WHAT IF? analysis, PACKAGING criteria, multidimensionality, and missing information. Essentially, the computer program enables each side to clarify the benefits and costs of settling versus the benefits and costs of going to trial [Nagel, 1990, pp. 180, 181, 183]. See Nagel and Mills [1991].
 Beyond simple LITIGATION RISK ANALYSIS, mediators use computers to communicate between sessions and to draft single negotiating texts that can be projected on-screen and modified in real time by the disputants. Some larger organizations, particularly in higher education, have established computer-aided *decision rooms* with multiple terminals and a projection screen. The software allows multiple participants at the same time to contribute anonymously. Comments typed into the computers are merged on-screen for review and mediated discussion. In cooperation with the Carter Center of Emory University in Atlanta, Georgia, IBM supports such a decision-making room for the resolution of community disputes under the auspices of the Carter Center's Atlanta Project.

concede   Admit, acknowledge, grant, or give up. Though voluntary, it is often associated with defeat or an action taken in response to some pressure. See CONCESSION. Contrast COMPROMISE.

concert (in concert, concerted)   Agreement to act together; state of similarly directed purpose or feeling. In a legal sense, acting with others to achieve a preconceived goal. Often associated with crime involving an accomplice or conspiracy.

concession   That which is voluntarily relinquished. In negotiation, a yielding to a demand for purposes of reaching settlement, especially in POSITIONAL BARGAINING. According to Iklé [1964, p. 207], parties make concessions when they move their position closer to that of the opponent. The fact that parties have made concessions, however, means only that they have lowered the terms they first stated—not the ones they expected to get. Compare ACCOMMODATION.

concession-convergence   Alternative term to describe the movement toward agreement in POSITION BARGAINING in which the parties start out from different positions and approach each other in a series of concessions until they arrive at a compromise [Cohen, 1991, p. 86].

concession dilemma   A negotiator's difficult decision about whether to commit to a particular position. According to Walton and McKersie [1965], negotiators often find themselves in a mutual and potentially worsening concession dilemma. If the negotiator makes a concession, she loses both position and image. Position loss occurs because once a concession has been made, it is extremely difficult to go back on it. Image loss occurs because making a concession implies flexibility where previously there may have been attempts to convince the other side of one's inflexibility [Morley and Stephenson, 1977, p. 40, citations omitted].

concession magnitude   Difference between a bargainer's first offer and last offer [Tutzauer, 1992, p. 71].

concession pattern   Movement of the parties within a negotiation. The pattern involves the size, timing, and justification for each concession [Harbaugh and Britzke, 1988].

concession rate   Speed with which a bargainer concedes [Tutzauer, 1992, p. 71].

concession theory, convergence theory   Theories of negotiation that posit that the parties start at some point of stalemate and, in an action-reaction process of outcome, converge. The focus is on the rate of the parties' concessions, factors affecting that rate, and how the rate affects the process of converging toward an outcome [Habeeb, 1988, p. 12].

conciliate   Bring together; placate.

conciliation   Act of bringing together; attempt, usually by a third party who may or may not be neutral, to encourage the parties to settle their dispute.

Conciliation is an umbrella term used to describe many different and distinct processes. At one end of the spectrum, conciliation can be little different from some negotiations and an intervening third party is not required [see, for example, Lauer, 1930, p. 2: "Any process by which differences of the parties are eliminated by agreement of the parties themselves and the parties brought into harmony"; *Black's Law Dictionary*, 1979, p. 262: "The adjustment and settlement of a dispute in a friendly, unantagonistic manner"]. Most processes, however, to which this term attaches involve third-party intervention. No authoritative source equates conciliation with ADJUDICATION, because a conciliator is without the power to decide for the parties and is focused on encouraging their resolution rather than on interpreting the propriety of past practices. Conciliation is often difficult to distinguish from MEDIATION, which is also an umbrella term covering a range of third-party intervention processes. In common usage, there is little distinction between mediation and conciliation; the terms are used almost synonymously [see, for example, DOA]. The meaning of conciliation in international relations generally differs from its meaning in a particular country's domestic practice. In some countries' domestic practices, there is no distinction between mediation and conciliation, though the latter is usually the preferred term. In other countries, the terms imply different degrees of third-party intervention. This entry lists and summarizes the range of processes to which conciliation refers and its preferred meaning in different countries and contexts.

In U.S. domestic practice, conciliation is distinguished as a more passive, less structured form of intervention than mediation. Conciliators are focused on encouraging the parties to negotiate and reach agreement on their own. They act more as go-betweens to improve communication or reduce hostilities as a necessary prelude to negotiation [Sander, 1976, p. 115; Riskin and Westbrook, 1987, p. 5]. Their function may be limited to clarifying the issues for the parties. Unlike mediators, conciliators exercise little control over the dialogue process (contrast FACILITATION) and are not involved in the actual substantive bargaining, the adjustment of differences, or the assessment of settlement options. A mediator may offer settlement suggestions while a conciliator may not. A mediator may act as a conciliator at various points in the overall negotiation, but a conciliator is not as fully empowered to intervene as a mediator. Moore [1986, p. 124, citing Curle, 1971, p. 177] sees conciliation as the "psychological component of mediation in which the third party attempts to create an atmosphere of trust and cooperation that is conducive to negotiation." The following scholarly observations further elucidate the distinct role of the conciliator:

- "Conciliation is the more passive role. As is indicated by its Latin derivative, it is the act of 'gaining good will; to render concordant; to mollify'" [Maggiolo, 1971, p. 10].

- "Conciliation is conceived of as a mild form of intervention limited primarily to scheduling conferences, trying to keep the disputants talking, facilitating other procedural niceties, carrying messages back and forth between the parties, and generally being a 'good fellow' who tries to keep things calm and forward-looking in a tense situation. Mediation is frequently thought of as a slightly more affirmative function" [Simkin, 1971, pp. 25–26].

- "Conciliation involves a very limited role for the third party whereby the party simply attempts to encourage negotiation among the disputing parties. This encouragement can involve the conciliator serving as a 'go-between' in communications among the parties, providing a place for the negotiations to take place, etc. Conciliation in its pure form is likely to be relatively rare, because conciliators are often likely to be asked for advice on settlement of the dispute or to offer advice spontaneously. This form of active assistance in structuring the communication or offering recommended settlements results in the conciliator becoming a mediator. Because of the close gradation between conciliation and mediation, many scholars have chosen to treat conciliation and mediation as roughly interchangeable tactics" [McGillis and Mullen, 1977, pp. 10–11].

- "Not infrequently conciliation and mediation are regarded as different names to describe the same function. Technically speaking, however, there is a fundamental difference between these two methods of assisting disputing parties to resolve their own conflicts. Conciliators and mediators share the characteristic of being facilitators of communication between disputing parties, but the conciliator's function is usually thought of as being more or less limited to such services. In a strict sense, conciliators are not supposed to recommend solutions to the parties. By contrast, mediators not only facilitate communication between the parties, but they are expected to propose solutions" [Kanowitz, 1986, pp. 77–78].

- "Conciliation is an eclectic process, consisting of whatever steps seem to be appropriate to enable the parties to reach a mutually acceptable settlement of their dispute by themselves. The conciliator therefore always stops short of making substantive proposals, while at the same time assisting the negotiations between the parties in every possible way. . . . If conciliation is insufficient, then the third party's next step is mediation. . . . Whereas a conciliator's work is restricted to clarifying the views of the parties and providing technical advice on attitudes or on the implications of a particular option, the mediator takes the further step of suggesting various ways around the obstacles in the path toward a settlement" [Pauling, Laszlo, and Jong, 1986, vol. 1, p. 590].

The dominant theme is that U.S. conciliation involves concentrated effort on the interpersonal aspects of the conflict and less intervention on substantive matters than mediation. A primary distinction is that a conciliator has less authority, especially to make substantive proposals.

Such a distinction is generally ignored or unrecognized in other contexts. In U.S. labor-management relations, for example, the Taft-Hartley Act provides for the "conciliation" of labor disputes affecting commerce through the FEDERAL MEDIATION AND CONCILIATION SERVICE, an agency whose name either is redundant or implies that some distinction exists. In practice, however, little if any distinction is made, mediation being the preferred term at present. Other statutes in the United States, particularly state statutes, encourage government agencies to use conciliation typically if the dispute involves action by the government that meets with resistance from a community or another governmental agency. Examples include environmental matters and public resource conflicts. Such statutes provide little or no clarity, however, as to the particular process to be applied.

In many other countries and in certain international commercial arbitration FORUMS, *conciliation* is the traditional and dominant term (*mediation* being a U.S. import) for nonadjudicative third-party intervention. Typically it infers the more active role of making substantive suggestions associated with some mediation models in the United States, although the process may differ slightly from mediation as generally practiced in the United States (see, for example, CHINESE MEDIATION). In Chinese translation, there is no legal difference between the two words [Li Mei Qin and He Wei, 1988, p. 321]. In some societies, this nondifferentiated form of conciliation can be classified as either *people's conciliation* or *court conciliation.* People's conciliation is provided by conciliation boards, committees, or other voluntary associations if the parties consent to participate. Court conciliation is provided within the courts, usually by the judge in advance of proceeding to trial, and the parties' attendance is required [Pe, Sosmena, and Tadiar, 1988, pp. 40–41]. Similarly, Kanowitz [1986, pp. 77–78] notes that conciliation can be classified as either *voluntary* or *involuntary.* For example, a law or regulation may provide that conciliation be attempted as a condition precedent to a civil action. Kanowitz's example is the U.S. Equal Employment Opportunity Commission, which has the primary responsibility of administering Title VII of the 1964 Civil Rights Act. The commission stipulates that an employee may not sue an employer, labor union, or employment agency without first attempting conciliation.

In most other countries with COMMON LAW legal systems, conciliation has been the dominant term and indistinguishable from mediation. Singer [1990, p. 25] notes that in Canada, Great Britain, and Australia, *conciliation* is still used to mean "mediation." In some settings in Australia, mediation and conciliation are clearly distinguished [Pe, Sosmena, and Tadiar, 1988, p. 6–7]. In Great

Britain, *conciliation* has a broad legal meaning covering all peaceful methods of resolving disputes without adjudication. As such, it encompasses mediation. In labor relations, the British version of the Federal Mediation and Conciliation Service is the Advisory, Conciliation and Arbitration Service, established under the Employment Protection Act, 1975, Part I, to promote peaceful labor relations. In family relations and divorce, the term *conciliation,* long associated with divorce law in Scotland, first gained currency in Britain through its use in the government's Report of the Committee on One-Parent Families [1974]. This committee adopted the distinction between *reconciliation,* the reuniting of spouses, and *conciliation,* which they defined as "assisting the parties to deal with the consequences of the established breakdown of their marriage . . . by reaching agreements of giving consents or reducing the area of conflict upon custody, support, access to and education of the children, financial provision, the disposition of the matrimonial home, lawyers fees and every other matter arising from the breakdown which calls for a decision on future arrangements" [p. 176, as discussed in Dingwall, 1986, p. 6; see also Roberts, 1992]. Under the rules of the London Maritime Arbitrators Association, *conciliation* means any form of dispute resolution, including conciliation and mediation, other than litigation and arbitration. In other civil matters, a distinction between mediation and conciliation may be developing as a result of the recent interest in U.S. mediation practice.

In France and some other European countries with CIVIL LAW traditions, conciliation refers to a particular formal attempt by a justice of the peace (*judge de paix*) to reconcile the parties before proceeding in ADJUDICATION (see *court conciliation*). Sometimes known as a *cour de conciliation* (conciliation court), the process excludes criminal and commercial matters.

Conciliation has special meaning in the context of private international commercial disputes. The UN COMMISSION ON INTERNATIONAL TRADE LAW devised a model set of conciliation rules for commercial matters (recommended by Resolution 35/52 of the General Assembly, Dec. 4, 1980). The INTERNATIONAL CHAMBER OF COMMERCE (ICC) COURT OF ARBITRATION now provides for conciliation in its rules. In these rules, conciliators have broad powers of intervention, which include making recommendations for settlement, but they have no power to bind the parties. Most other international commercial arbitration centers have adopted similar conciliation rules, although it is noteworthy that the American Arbitration Association uses the term *mediation* in reference to its form of conciliation. In this context, the distinction between mediation and conciliation remains fuzzy. There is often, however, a high degree of formality attached to these conciliations, in which more weight is put on conciliators' ability to make substantive recommendations than on their interpersonal skills.

In international relations, conciliation refers to a distinct and well-defined process that contrasts significantly with its general meaning in U.S. practice as just discussed. In this context, conciliation combines elements of both INQUIRY and MEDIATION, as those terms are understood in dispute resolution among states. Created in the twentieth century under various bilateral and multilateral treaties and approved in the UN Charter (art. 33, para. 1), conciliation has two basic functions: to investigate and clarify the facts in dispute, and to attempt to bring the parties into agreement by suggesting mutually acceptable solutions to the problem. Some authoritative definitions provide the following:

- "The task of the Conciliation Commission shall be to elucidate the questions in dispute, to collect with that object all necessary information by means of enquiry or otherwise, and to endeavour to bring the parties to an agreement. It may, after the case has been examined, inform the parties of the terms of settlement which seem suitable to it, and lay down the period within which they are to make their decision" [Revised Geneva General Act for the Pacific Settlement of International Disputes, 1949, art. 15, para. 1].

- "A method for the settlement of international disputes of any nature according to which a Commission set up by the Parties, either on a permanent basis or an ad hoc basis to deal with a dispute, proceeds to the impartial examination of the dispute and attempts to define the terms of a settlement susceptible of being accepted by them or of affording the Parties, with a view to its settlement, such aid as they may have requested" [Regulations on the Procedure of International Conciliation, 1961, Art. 1].

Essentially, in international relations conciliation is a more formal legal process than mediation, institutionalized in a manner similar to inquiry and arbitration. As in mediation, the aim of conciliation is to convince the parties to accept a compromise solution often through suggesting possible compromises. Unlike mediation, however, which is usually conducted by a third state or other international legal entity not directly involved in the dispute but often in a position to exercise considerable political pressure, conciliation is conducted by an existing or ad hoc independent commission composed of individuals. (Theoretically, conciliation also could be conducted by a neutral government or by the Security Council as provided in the UN Charter.) In mediation, the scope of the process is usually broad and established by the parties; in conciliation, the parties more precisely define the commission's tasks, which are usually confined to the elaboration of the nonbinding conciliation proposal. Like inquiry, conciliation involves a formal fact-finding exercise from which the facts are elucidated. Unlike inquiry, the conciliator proceeds to make concrete proposals for settlement based on the facts found. Like arbitration, the third party makes a formal determination; unlike arbitration, the proposals are nonbinding, except to the extent that one or more of the disputing states agree to be bound. In sharp contrast to both inquiry and arbitration, the conciliator focuses on solutions that are "susceptible to being accepted" by the parties. Therefore, unlike inquiry, wherein a commission of inquiry will ascertain and report the facts despite objections from one of the parties, a conciliator may abstain from ascertaining facts in certain circumstances or be exceedingly diplomatic in articulating the facts. It also follows that unlike arbitration, in which the arbitrators' decision usually applies and conforms with legal norms, the conciliator attempts to articulate a mutually acceptable set of recommendations that emphasize equity and mutuality. Thus the conciliator's recommendations may not give full effect to the legal rights of the parties, but rather express an opinion as to what the parties deserve. The parties can reject or accept these recommendations. Although the outcome is not legally binding, the formal, quasi-judicial procedures help give the recommendations the persuasive weight of international opinion. Not surprisingly, conciliation has proved most useful for disputes in which the main issues are legal but the parties desire an equitable compromise [Merrills, 1991, pp. 59, 77].

It is possible for parties to give the conciliation commission power to lay down binding terms of settlement in the absence of an agreed solution. This procedure, however, is best classified as an arbitration, perhaps EX AEQUO ET BONO, and together with the conciliation procedures constitutes a hybrid such as MED-ARB or CONCILIO-ARBITRATION.

Conciliation may refer to a number of processes that are distinct from one another. For the disputants, these distinctions may be critical. Participants should be absolutely clear on the role and function of the conciliator.

Compare and contrast MEDIATION, INQUIRY, ARBITRATION, GOOD OFFICES, ADJUDICATION, RECONCILIATION.

conciliation commission, commission of conciliation   *International Relations:* Body formed to conduct CONCILIATION in an attempt to resolve disputes among states. The term is loosely but rarely used to denote a body engaged in the less formal process of MEDIATION.

conciliation courts   In certain jurisdictions in the United States, family courts that experimented with marriage counseling and now use mediation programs.

In the typical model, the action is stayed in response to either a petition for conciliation or a court-ordered referral and the parties meet with a court-employed counselor. Most conciliation courts offer some form of mediation as an option. Michigan and California are cited as pioneers in the conciliation court movement [Cramer and Schoeneman, 1985, pp. 33–35].

conciliation model for small claims   Term coined by Yngvesson and Hennessey [1975, p. 256] to describe early mediation experiments in small claims courts in the United States. According to their description:

The main feature distinguishing conciliation from adjudication is that the "judge" is not a judge, but an active agent in eliciting the true nature of the dispute and in bringing the parties toward a mutually acceptable resolution. The process is meant to be therapeutic rather than judgmental, and with this in mind the parties to the dispute are encouraged to express their feelings as well as telling the facts of the matter in dispute, with a view to increasing mutual understanding.

conciliator   Person or entity who conciliates. The nature and activity of a conciliator may vary by context. See CONCILIATION.

Standby conciliator: Second conciliator who may be included in the conciliation process by agreement of the parties. The standby conciliator is regularly informed about the progress (such as by performance reports) so that in case of need she is already familiar with the relationship and can act expeditiously. Compare SHADOW MEDIATION.

conciliatory   Behavior of someone attempting conciliation.

conciliatory processes   Umbrella term for processes characterized by voluntary, consensual participation; private, usually informal proceedings under party control; the application of norms selected by the parties or the creation of norms relevant to the situation; and a solution reached by consensus. A critical factor in classifying such processes is whether or not there is a third party with the power to impose a solution. If not, the process is conciliatory, as opposed to an ADJUDICATIVE PROCESS. Negotiation, conciliation, and mediation are examples of conciliatory processes.

Conciliatory processes settle disputes by adjustment or COMPROMISE between the parties. Compromise implies participation and choice in the resolution, which by implication will provide something for each disputant. The role of the third party is to help guide the parties, without exercising adjudicative powers, to an arrangement they will accept. As a result, the third party has no power over the proceedings or the outcome other than that granted by the parties themselves, either expressly or by implication. Such authority can effectively be revoked by the withdrawal of either party at any time. While an adjudicator frames the dispute as a diadic conflict of rights and principles in the context of an applicable normative structure, the third party in a conciliatory process, to facilitate agreement by consensus, seeks to frame the dispute as a conflict of the parties' respective interests [Fuller, 1978; Eckoff, 1966].

concilio-arbitration   Hybrid process in the MED-ARB family. The term derives from a contraction of *conciliation* and *arbitration* and reflects the European use of *conciliation* to describe a process substantially identical to mediation. See CONCILIATION for range of definitions.

Concilio-arbitration is being promoted in Great Britain and is a variation on ADVISORY MED-ARB. After attempting resolution through conciliation, the NEUTRAL produces a draft award, setting out his or her opinion of the outcome if the dispute were fully litigated. The parties have an opportunity to respond to the award, pointing out errors and presenting further arguments and evidence if they wish before the neutral makes a final award. If both parties accept the award, it becomes binding. If both reject, the award has no effect and is merely advisory. But if only one party accepts, which is likely, the rejecting party must pay all the costs of both sides in litigating the dispute unless it does better in the ensuing litigation by at least one third, or some other percentage set by contract [Williams, 1986].

concord   Harmony, agreement, accord, concurrence.
Law: Agreement in settlement of a right of action or legally recognizable claim, identical to COMPROMISE AND SETTLEMENT.
International Law: TREATY that ceases hostilities and establishes peaceful relations between states.

concordat   Agreement between two or more independent states. In ecclesiastical law, an agreement between the pope and a temporal state.

Concorde fallacy   Irrational rationalization that prior investment in itself should commit an individual to future investment. Derived from the development of the Concorde airplane in which the British and French governments continued to invest after it become clear that production and operation could not be profitable.
The concept has numerous possible applications to conflict resolution. For example, prior investment in a position or in a process, such as litigation, may impede resolution or prolong litigation because one is unwilling to abandon the investment and accept a compromise position or pursue negotiation. To avoid falling victim to such a fallacy, one should always consider whether to abandon a course of action now to avoid continued irretrievable losses in the future [Dawkins, 1989, p. 150]. Compare ENTRAPMENT, ESCALATION OF COMMITMENT.

concordia (archaic)   COMMON LAW term for CONCORD.

concur, concurrence   Agree, reach ACCORD or the same conclusion, or be of the same opinion; meeting of the minds.

conditional meetings   *Negotiation:* Initial or future meetings that are dependent on some event or action by the other party.
Conditional meetings are a common BRINKMANSHIP tactic, particularly in international negotiation, to force the other side to change its position in exchange

for the opportunity to continue negotiations. Maggiolo [1985, pp. 179–180] notes that when the condition imposed on initial or further meetings is that the other party be prepared to meet the last stated position, it not only invites the interjection of new issues but is also destructive of the future bargaining relationships. A surrender to such an ultimatum in current negotiations will encourage similar threats in the future.

conditional openness   *Negotiation:* Strategy in which a party is initially open to create value and seeks mutual cooperation, but is ready to claim value when one's counterpart claims value, yet is also ready to return to CREATING VALUE upon the counterpart's decision to be cooperative [Lax and Sebenius, 1986, pp. 157–164]. TIT-FOR-TAT is a simple form of conditional openness strategy [Axelrod, 1984].

conditional proposal   Offer that is contingent on either a particular event or action or on resolution of specific issues or all of the remaining issues in the negotiation. Differs from simple BARGAINING in that the tactic involves an offer of X for Y, but the offer is conditioned on subsequently reaching agreement on one or more other issues [Schoenfield and Schoenfield, 1988, p. 131].

conditional summary jury trial (CSJT)   COURT-CONNECTED ADR process that combines characteristics of MINI-TRIALS and SUMMARY JURY TRIALS. An abbreviated nonbinding trial is conducted by a trial judge and presented to a panel composed of that judge and representatives of the parties, usually chief executive officers, who have authority to settle. If the parties are unable to negotiate a settlement, the judge selects from the prepared dispositions submitted by the parties. A party who declines to accept the outcome of the abbreviated proceeding and who does not obtain a more favorable outcome in full trial must pay the adversary's litigation costs [Harter, 1987].

Like a mini-trial, the CSJT process is designed for large disputes between corporations and has high-level corporate representatives serve on the panel for purposes of reality testing prior to negotiations. Unlike mini-trials, which are voluntary and outside the judicial system, CSJTs are like summary jury trials— the matter must be in litigation and the process is conducted under the auspices of the court, which may have the power to mandate participation. One distinctive characteristic of a CSJT is that the parties must stipulate to file bond to secure payment of each other's litigation costs in the event that one party does not accept the CSJT outcome and the full trial outcome is not more favorable. The requirement to post bond depends on either a stipulation by the parties or a statute or court rule. This economic incentive to arrive at a settlement is a common characteristic of most MANDATORY NONBINDING ARBITRATION, as well as some models of summary jury trials and other court-connected, reality-testing processes.

The CSJT limits the hearing time and delineates a set of procedures under which the hearing takes place. To avoid prejudicing the trial judge in a subsequent trial if the CSJT fails, a different judge or a master paid by equal contributions from the parties conducts the CSJT and sits as the neutral on the panel. According to the CENTER FOR PUBLIC RESOURCES, cases that would take three weeks or longer to litigate are appropriate for a conditional summary trial. Large, two-party cases involving more than $1 million are the usual type [Harter, 1987, p. 1].

conditionally binding arbitration   Process in which two or more persons agree to arbitration but who are not all to be bound by the award. In much CONSUMER ARBITRATION, particularly under the auspices of the BETTER BUSINESS BUREAU, the consumer has the option of rejecting the decision, but the company has agreed to be bound by the decision if the consumer accepts it. Once the decision is accepted by the consumer, either party may compel compliance with the decision under any applicable state or federal law. See ASYMMETRICALLY BINDING ARBITRATION.

conduct   Lead, guide, manage, or direct. In dispute resolution, usually used in the context of a third party managing a process, as in "the arbitrator conducted the arbitration."

confederacy   Alliance or coalition of persons or states to accomplish a particular purpose. Outside of international relations, it often infers a nefarious or illegal purpose.

confederate   Member of a CONFEDERACY.

confer   Consult together, usually by comparing views.

conference   Meeting, usually involving more than two people, held to resolve disputes by conferring, discussing, consulting, expressing differences of opinion, and deliberating. Conference infers a formal and quasi-legislative process involving the selection of a chairperson, the adoption of standard procedural rules and a committee structure to expedite the work, and the use of some system for reaching decisions.

conference diplomacy   *International Relations:* Large, multilateral diplomatic negotiations in international meetings. Conference diplomacy is usually associated with peace negotiations subsequent to major wars. The process was institutionalized with the creation of the League of Nations and subsequently the United Nations, which essentially is a permanent session of conference diplomacy.

conference process analysis (CPA)   In the study of negotiation, method of dividing and classifying transcripts of the verbal communication in negotiations to determine how and what information is exchanged [Morley and Stephenson, 1977, p. 185].

confidential   Communicated under conditions or an understanding that further dissemination will be restricted; entrusted to another to be kept secret.

confidential communication   *Mediation:* Statement made privately to a mediator with the expectation that the mediator will not divulge the contents to the other side. Such statements are typically made in a CAUCUS with the mediator. As a general rule, mediators consider that all communications made in mediation will be kept confidential from those outside the process.
   Law: Statement made to a lawyer, doctor, spouse, or other party the contents of which the recipient cannot be forced to divulge in court. Although professional ethics may require that the recipient not divulge the information, certain evidentiary rules protect statements made in some professional relationships and statements made and materials prepared for settlement discussions and offers of settlement, including those made in mediation, from revelation at trial. See, for example, RULE 408. Increasingly, through statute, case law, court rule, or enforceable contract, statements made to mediators are considered confidential communications in this sense and may be excluded from evidence at trial or have even broader protections.

confidential listener mediation   Mediation technique that facilitates the search for and narrowing of the CONTRACT ZONE. The parties separately reveal to the mediator their maximum and minimum settlement figures. The parties agree that if their numbers overlap, they will settle the case by SPLITTING THE DIFFERENCE. If the numbers do not overlap, the mediator informs the parties of a lack of a settlement, and they can try the process again (*Corporate Counsel's Guide . . .*, 1989].

confirm   Make certain; make an agreement legally valid, binding, or enforceable, or ratify what has been done without prior adequate authority.

confirmation   Act of confirming, or a contract or written memorandum that confirms an indefinite agreement or clarifies an agreement in principle.

confirming letter   *Negotiation:* Letter directed to the other party that details the terms of the agreement. In the absence of a formal agreement or a response letter contradicting the terms stated in the confirming letter, it may be used as proof of an agreement if there is a subsequent disagreement over performance of the terms.

confirming the award Process of having an arbitration award confirmed by a court so that it can be enforced as a court judgment. The authority and procedure for confirming the award is typically provided in the applicable state or federal arbitration statute. See MODERN ARBITRATION STATUTE.

conflict Disagreement or incompatibility. Derived from the Latin *conflictus*, meaning "to strike together," it is used to denote both a process and a state of being. Here are some sample definitions of this sometimes subtle, complex concept:

- "A situation in which a choice must be made in the absence of dominance (i.e., a decision must be made that requires a tradeoff)" [Swingle, 1970, p. 222].

- "An inseparable part of social interaction. Conflict cannot take place without involvement of two or more parties. Mutually incompatible goals among parties amidst a lack of coordinating or mediating mechanisms give birth to conflict. In this broad sense, conflict is a generic social phenomenon involving individuals, societies, states and their collectives" [Azar, 1990, p. 5].

- "An expressed struggle between at least two interdependent parties, who perceive incompatible goals, scarce rewards, and interference from the other party in achieving their goals. They are in a position of opposition in conjunction with cooperation" [Kiely and Crary, 1986, p. 39].

- "When two or more individuals have preferences or goals which cannot be attained by all and a decision must be made as to whose preferences or goals will prevail. In conflict, each party desires to attain dominance, the state or position of being in control and, thereby, achieve the desired goal or preference" [Edwards, 1981, p. 82].

- "Conflicts involve struggles between two or more people over values, or competition for status power and scarce resources" [Moore, 1986, p. 16].

- "A situation in which authority or power is being exercised without the sanction or approval of those over whom it is being exercised" [Burton, 1969, p. 126].

- "A conflict arises when two or more people or groups endeavor to pursue goals which are mutually inconsistent" [Nicholson, 1975].

- "'Conflict' is a term with different meanings, depending on the user. For present purposes, conflict is defined as mutual hostility between or among individuals or groups. Hostility might be expressed in words (insults, name-calling, sarcasm, defamation, etc.) or in actions (killing, fighting, destroying another's property, withholding needed assistance, etc.). Obviously, this definition lacks great precision and does not outline the many possible subtle forms of conflict" [Nye, 1973, p. xi].

Conflict can also be defined as escalated natural competition of two or more parties who believe they have incompatible goals and whose aim is to neutralize, injure, or gain advantage over the other party or parties [Holsti, 1983].

In its more common use, *conflict* refers narrowly to a disagreement, the expression or manifestation of a state of incompatibility. In this sense, *conflict* connotes an interactive process involving some active or physical contest between parties, the act of disagreeing, disputing, or engaging in hostilities. When used in this manner, *conflict* is synonymous with DISPUTE. Distinctions between these two terms may be useful, and commentators have struggled with a variety of sometimes incompatible distinctions. Burton [1969, p. 2] describes conflict as a more extreme form of dispute, involving hostile action and the potential destruction of people and institutions. Disputes occur in situations where the issues are negotiable, while conflict is behavior that goes beyond "normal disagreements." Noting that some social scientists would differ, Starke [1968, pp. 74–75] believes that conflict requires an element of competition or rivalry over inconsistent values, claims, goals, or interests; thus conflict is a broad range of rivalries inclusive of a dispute, which in international relations normally means a disagreement on points of law, principle, or fact [p. 89]. Compare Costantino and Merchant [1996, pp. 4–5], who, from an organizational design perspective, attempt to distinguish conflict as a process of disagreement or dissatisfaction of which a dispute is one of several possible by-products.

In a less common use, conflict refers broadly to a state of incompatibility or disharmony. Generally this state requires conditions and behavior that give rise to a GRIEVANCE, as defined by Miller and Sarat [1980–1981, pp. 526–527] and Felstiner, Abel, and Sarat [1980–1981]. Examples of such conditions would be interdependence combined with scarce resources or divergent interests, and examples of such behavior would be competitive, uncooperative, or incompatible behavior. If one combines the notions of conditions and behavior, conflict is incompatible behavior between parties whose interests differ. In this context, *interests* refers to the recognized and unrecognized stakes, abstract as well as concrete, affected by the parties' interaction; incompatible behavior is action, real or perceived, that frustrates or opposes the other, purposefully or not. Take away either the difference in interests or the incompatible behavior and there is no conflict. This comports with Donohue and Kolt's [1992, p. 4] definition of conflict as "a situation in which interdependent people express differences in satisfying their individual needs and interests, and they experience interference from each other in accomplishing these goals." See also Levinger and Rubin, 1994.

When speaking of *conflict resolution,* it may be preferable to conceptualize conflict as a state rather than a process, thereby making it easier to distinguish between conflict resolution processes and the conflict that such processes are supposed to affect. For example, this use of the term simplifies the distinction between *conflict,* a state, and *dispute,* a process. A dispute is an articulation of the conflict, a symptom, so to speak, rather than the conflict itself. A conflict can exist without a dispute, but a dispute cannot exist without a conflict. For example, two sisters want the only orange in the house and begin arguing over who should get it. The conflict is that each wants the orange (interests differ), but neither is willing to yield it to the other (incompatible behavior). The dispute is their argument over it, and disputing is a method of resolving the conflict. In this sense, conflict that gives rise to a dispute is MANIFEST, while conflict that has not given rise to a dispute is LATENT.

Some other dichotomous classifications are being used. For example, Kolb and Bartunek [1992, p. 3] refer to *public* and *private* conflicts in a manner somewhat similar to the definitions of manifest and latent. Public conflicts are "in the open" enough to be handled by the applicable norms and conflict management machinery within the community or organization in which they arise. Although typically latent, private conflicts may be manifest to the disputants but not apparent to or perhaps not recognized as a dispute by the larger community or organization. Coser [1956] distinguishes between *realistic* and *nonrealistic conflict*. Whereas realistic conflicts arise from the frustration of specific demands, nonrealistic conflicts arise from the need to release tension. Other authorities note that incompatible behavior can exist merely when parties perceive their goals to be incompatible, when in fact no actual incompatibility of interests exists. Moore [1986, p. 174, citing Aubert, 1963] distinguishes between *consensual* or *interest-based conflict,* in which parties are in a sense collaborating to compete for the same limited resources, and *dissensual* or *value-based conflict,* in which parties are promoting incompatible norms or principles for application to a situation.

Without distinguishing dispute from conflict as described earlier, some social conflict theorists use the dichotomous classification of *constructive* and *destructive* conflict. Noting that these are easier to define at their extremes, Deutsch [1973, p. 17] focuses on outcome satisfaction, noting that a conflict is destructive if participants are dissatisfied with the outcomes and feel they have lost as a result of the conflict. Conversely, a conflict is constructive if outcomes are satisfying to all participants who feel they have gained as a result of the conflict. Noting that no conflict is wholly constructive or destructive, Kriesberg [1998b] explores the degree of constructiveness and destructiveness through assessing the way the conflict is waged as well as its outcomes. A conflict is increasingly destructive as the means used are more severe, as greater harm is caused to more people, as the scope of participation is larger, as the other side is viewed as increasingly illegitimate, and as characteristics tend to perpetuate the conflict. A conflict is more constructive when the means used tend more toward persuasion through promises of benefits rather than toward coercive threats or actions, the other side is increasingly viewed as a legitimate entity, and mutually acceptable outcomes are sought [pp. 21–22]. Although much conflict is so complex as to defy easy categorization, these constructs can help focus interventions on particular aspects of the conflict.

There are a number of subterms that distinguish different types of conflict by the setting in which it occurs. In psychology, conflict is generally used to describe an individual's internal state in which desires or impulses are in opposition. The term *intrapersonal conflict* may be used to distinguish this internal, psychological conflict from *interpersonal conflict* between two or more individuals. Conflict between two individuals or entities may be referred to as *dyadic conflict* or, when involving several actors, *multiparty conflict*. The term *interpersonal conflict* is commonly used to distinguish conflict among individual humans from conflict within and among nonhuman entities or states. Thus the terms *intraorganizational* or *intragroup conflict* are used to denote conflict between individuals within a group over issues relating to that group's purpose, organization, or action. *Interorganizational* or *intergroup conflict* denotes incompatibility or disagreement between groups, while *international conflict* is conflict between entities recognized under international law. An emerging term is *intercultural conflict,* which may occur between individuals or groups and involves incompatible perceptions, values, or behaviors resulting from differences in respective cultural preferences. Although *cross-cultural conflict* is sometimes used with the same meaning as intercultural conflict, it implies a comparative approach to understanding universals and differences in conflict-handling across different cultures (see CULTURE). *Multicultural conflict* refers to conflict usually found in multiethnic settings with many overlapping and interacting cultures.

Additional subterms include the following:

- *Diplomatic conflict:* Involves the use of formal methods by which states have traditionally dramatized differences of opinion nonviolently, such as by lodging protests, declaring diplomatic officials to be personae non gratae, and withdrawing ambassadors or officials of lower rank [Haas, 1974, p. 9].

- *Noninstitutionalized conflict:* Nonviolent, yet takes place outside polite channels for articulating demands and displeasure. Examples include severance of diplomatic relations and imposition of sanctions [Haas, 1974, p. 9].

In international relations, commentators often conflate the concepts of condition and process when referring to *international conflict.* For the most part, however, this term is used to refer to the consequences of the underlying incompatibilities rather than the incompatibilities themselves. In this sense, Wright [1971, pp. 349–350] notes that the term *international conflict* is used broadly to include all stages of a complete process, that is, (1) awareness of inconsistencies, (2) rising tensions, (3) pressures short of military force to resolve the inconsistencies, and (4) military intervention or war to dictate a solution. In a narrow sense, international conflict is a situation in which the parties are taking action against each other—that is, to the last two stages of conflict in its broad sense.

See also SOCIAL CONFLICT.

conflict analysis *Mediation:* Stage during which the mediator synthesizes and interprets data collected from interacting with the parties and other sources in an attempt to understand the elements of the dispute: people, dynamics, issues, and interests [Moore, 1986, p. 96]. The exercise is useful to negotiators and other third parties as well as to mediators. Compare CONFLICT MAP.

conflict audit *Conflict Management Systems:* Process by which the system designer identifies past, present, and anticipated types and sources of conflict in an organization along with the actual and potential costs of such conflicts. The purpose is to identify frequent and costly sources of conflict in order to prioritize design efforts.

conflict avoidance See AVOIDANCE.

conflict de-escalation See DE-ESCALATION.

conflict escalation See ESCALATION.

conflict-habituated couple Divorcing couple so invested in the conflict as its primary means of communication that it is very difficult for a mediator to promote problem solving. In such a situation, the goal of the problem-solving process—an agreement that terminates the formal spousal relationship—robs the couple of its vehicle to maintain the conflict addiction [Haynes, 1986b, p. 32].

conflict intensity Degree of goal discrepancies among disputing parties, including the degree of hostility parties bear toward one another [Donohue, Weider-Hatfield, Hamilton, and Diez, 1985, p. 389].

conflict intervention Strategy and behaviors of third parties attempting to resolve or manage conflict.

conflict management Study and practice of means by which to manage conflict and prevent or resolve disputes. In this context, *conflict* refers to the broader state of incompatibility that may or may not give rise to a dispute (see CONFLICT for the distinction). *Management* implies the ability to control a particular conflict or class of conflicts and the effects through either individual skill or institutional mechanisms. The underlying premise is that conflict is inevitable within organizations, so recognition and handling of the conflict is of great importance in making the conflict constructive rather than destructive.

Conflict management involves the application of theories from many disciplines, usually within the limited context of the workplace, as opposed to conflict at large within the broader community. It combines conflict analysis with attempts to control the dynamics of the conflict to yield the most positive organizational and personal growth and change. This may involve the use of a variety of dispute processing and conflict resolution mechanisms. Rahim [1986, p. 82] describes it as a process of maintaining an optimum amount of conflict. Thus conflict management may be used to promote constructive conflict as well as to intervene to reduce destructive conflict.

Walton's [1969, p. 105] early model of conflict management recognizes two phases inherent in most effective processes. In the first phase, differentiation, the parties acknowledge and clarify their differences and become motivated to engage in negotiation. In the second phase, integration, the parties recognize their commonalities and attempt to generate a mutually acceptable solution and means of implementation. The cycle of differentiation and integration may be repeated several times before parties reach an effective solution [Poole, Shannon, and DeSanctis, 1992, p. 50]. Compare and contrast CONFLICT PREVENTION, CONFLICT REDUCTION, CONFLICT RESOLUTION, CONFLICT TRANSFORMATION.

conflict manager Term associated with a PEER MEDIATION program developed by Community Boards of San Francisco (see COMMUNITY BOARDS PROGRAM) in 1982 and involving the training of fourth and fifth grade students to manage conflicts among their peers. After fifteen hours of training, students put on their conflict manager T-shirts and go into the playground in pairs during lunch and recess to assist fellow students in resolving disputes. Evaluation of the program's effectiveness indicated a decrease in conflict in the San Francisco schools [Kestner, Devonshire, and Kim, 1988, p. 86]. The concept and the term have been widely adopted by schools throughout the United States. Should not be confused with the concept of CONFLICT MANAGEMENT. See COMMUNITY BOARDS.

conflict map Conceptual road map of the dispute that details why a conflict is occurring, identifies barriers to settlement, and indicates procedures to manage or resolve the dispute. Tool recommended by Moore [1986, p. 26, citing Wehr, 1979]. Compare CONFLICT ANALYSIS.

ConflictNet Computer network (www.igc.org/igs/conflictnet) that serves as a general clearinghouse for information on practice and research in the dispute resolution field.

conflict of interest   *Law:* Situation in which duties are irreconcilable or in which private interest or self-interest conflicts with official or fiduciary duties.

conflict prevention   Study and practice of means by which to prevent the incompatibilities of interests and behavior that constitute conflict. In this sense, *conflict* refers to the broader state of incompatibility that may or may not give rise to a dispute (see CONFLICT for this distinction). Conflict prevention is more narrowly focused than CONFLICT MANAGEMENT and often involves structural adjustments such as legislation (for example, no-fault laws) or generic solutions (such as clarification of company policy or gender-sensitivity training). To be distinguished from CONFLICT AVOIDANCE wherein conflict exists.

conflict reduction   Term sometimes favored in lieu of CONFLICT RESOLUTION. According to Deng and Zartman [1991, pp. 299–300], conflict reduction means both reducing incompatibilities, where possible, and focusing the parties in conflict toward pursuing nonviolent or political means. One objection to the notion of *resolution* they raise is that some aspects of the incompatibility—underlying sentiments, memories, and interests—are rarely, if ever, fully resolved except by the passage of time. Conflict can be resolved only if *resolved* refers to the satisfaction of apparent interests. Compare DISPUTE PROCESSING.

conflict resolution   Study and practice of means by which to end the incompatibilities of interests and behavior that constitute conflict. In this sense, it refers to a professional field and academic discipline concerned with the nature of generic conflict (as opposed to a specific conflict) and with productive techniques to address conflict. Also, the term may be used to refer to an activity ("the parties are engaged in conflict resolution"), as in these illustrative definitions:

- "In psychology, process of reducing or removing antagonism among individuals, groups, organizations, or political entities" [Walker, 1991, p. 49].
- "The process where one attempts to reduce or eliminate conflict" [Rahim, 1986, p. 82].
- "The process by which two parties reconcile their goals to the extent that they are mutually consistent. The conflict is resolved when the two parties are willing to accept some position as a status quo, either because the costs of inducing further conflict would outweigh the benefits of any improved settlement which may result, or because, on some criterion or other, they are willing to accept the settlement as 'fair'" [Nicholson, 1975].

As a process, conflict resolution is inclusive of ALTERNATIVE DISPUTE RESO-LUTION, but may include other methods and techniques. It is rarely used to include hostile methods such as warfare. At a minimum, it involves a recognition of the conflict and a search for a mutually acceptable outcome or process to reach an outcome with or without the help of third parties.

Although the term is often viewed as synonymous with DISPUTE RESOLUTION, it is useful to distinguish conflict resolution as a broader concept. In this sense, *conflict* refers to the broader state of incompatibility that may or may not give rise to a dispute (see CONFLICT for this distinction). This definition thereby makes dispute resolution a subset of the more inclusive term *conflict resolution.*

Some authorities distinguish conflict resolution, which involves solving the underlying conflict between parties and establishing relatively harmonious relations, and CONFLICT SETTLEMENT, which entails ending a dispute by agreeing to terms that do not fundamentally alter the underlying conflict [Azar and Burton, 1986, pp. 153, 154]. In contrast, Fogg [1985, p. 331] adopts the reverse definition: *resolution* merely implies causing the fighting or contentiousness in a dispute to subside, and *settlement* entails solving the underlying conditions that gave rise to the quarrel. To be consistent with the prevailing use of other terms, the former distinction is preferred over the latter, bearing in mind other objections raised to the notion of *resolution* (see CONFLICT REDUCTION).

Contrast CONFLICT MANAGEMENT, CONFLICT TRANSFORMATION, DISPUTE RESO-LUTION, DISPUTE PROCESSING.

Conflict Resolution Board   Norwegian FORUM established by the state that may handle disputes if three conditions are met: (1) all parties to the dispute are known, (2) all parties agree to have their case handled by the board, and (3) the incident in question is not so serious that it could involve an active prison sentence. The focus of the subject matter that the boards handle is child welfare and teenage criminology, though the boards delve into other matters, too [Nergård, 1993, pp. 82, 83, 87].

Conflict Resolution in Education Network (CREnet)   A nonprofit, membership organization dedicated to the advancement of nonviolent conflict resolution skill building and curriculum in schools. Formerly known as the National Association for Mediation in Education (NAME) and currently associated with the NATIONAL INSTITUTE FOR DISPUTE RESOLUTION (NIDR).

conflict settlement   Sometimes used as a substitute term for CONFLICT RESO-LUTION.

Some authorities make distinctions between conflict resolution, which involves solving the underlying conflict between parties and establishing relatively harmonious relations, and CONFLICT SETTLEMENT, which entails ending a dispute by agreeing to terms that do not fundamentally alter the underlying conflict [Azar and Burton, 1986, pp. 153, 154]. In contrast, Fogg [1985, p. 331] adopts the reverse definition: *resolution* merely implies causing the fighting or contentiousness in a dispute to subside, and *settlement* entails solving the underlying conditions that gave rise to the quarrel. To be consistent with the prevailing use of other terms, the former distinction is preferred over the latter.

conflict spiral   Model of conflict ESCALATION in which disputants of roughly equal power engage in an ongoing cycle of contentious action and reaction. Each action is interpreted as a threat requiring protective reaction and retaliation, which in turn stimulate an increasingly hostile reaction. The conflict spirals in that the levels of antagonism and the propensity for violence escalate with the actions. The term is more commonly used in reference to the processes that lead nations to warfare [Princen, 1992, p. 167].

conflict transformation   Change in the characteristics of a conflict.

Lederach [1995] promotes the concept of transformation over CONFLICT RESOLUTION and CONFLICT MANAGEMENT as the former implies that all conflicts can and should be resolved while the latter implies that even if incapable of being resolved, the conflict involves parties who can be controlled or manipulated with the goal of reducing the conflict's volatility. In contrast, conflict transformation, as an intervening method of handling conflict, focuses on inducing constructive change in the parties' relationship through improving mutual understanding. The transformative approach is oriented toward understanding the dynamic interaction of the disputants' relationship and the conflict, and it better reflects the problems of protracted or intractable conflict.

confligology   Science that deals with the elements, origins, and causes of armed conflicts [Frangi, 1993, p. 1039].

conform   Adapt to the prevailing standard or be compliant. Just as the act of conforming may help resolve certain conflicts, the failure to conform may create conflict.

confront   Oppose or challenge directly or face-to-face.

congress   Formal meeting of representatives for discussion and action on some question.

congruence   See HALO EFFECT.

congruent   Conforming appropriately to the situation so as to be in harmony with it.

Connally Reservation, Connally Amendment   Reservation made by the United States in its 1946 acceptance of the Optional Clause of Article 36 of the Statute of the INTERNATIONAL COURT OF JUSTICE. It provides for an exception to the court's compulsory jurisdiction in "disputes with regard to matters which are essentially within the domestic jurisdiction of the United States of America as determined by the United States of America." Since the United States is free to determine what is or is not a domestic matter, the reservation renders the intended compulsory jurisdiction ineffective. Through either adoption of similar reservations or the application of reciprocity, other states have opted out of the court's compulsory jurisdiction.

conquest   Domination through the use of power rather than COMPROMISE. More properly associated with the use of armed force to achieve change without formal ratification by TREATY [Diehl and Goertz, 1988, p. 105].

Conseil de prud'hommes **(France)**   System of handling labor disputes established by law during the era of Napoleon I and considered one of the world's oldest continuously operating labor courts and conciliation boards. Members are selected in equal numbers by employees and employers. There is no neutral board member, and deadlocks are referred to judges of the local regular courts for final resolution [DOA].

consensus   General agreement or collective opinion by those most interested in the matter. In common use, the term can range in meaning from unanimity to a simply majority vote. In public policy facilitation and multilateral international negotiations, however, the term refers to a general agreement reached after discussions and consultations, usually without voting. Unanimity is required only to the extent that it means an absence of major objections. Compare ACQUIESCENCE.

consensus building, consensus decision making   Process or activity with the goal of reaching CONSENSUS. Usually parties seek consensus on shared norms and attitudes for application to specific issues rather than on specific solutions to specific issues, although they are not precluded from pursuing consensus on the latter.

consent   Voluntary approval of a proposal by another.

consent award   Award that disputing parties arrive at by themselves and that the arbitrator consents to make [DOA]. This should be distinguished from an AGREED AWARD, which is surreptitious and purports to have been reached by the arbitrator. Consent awards are made to ensure easy enforcement of a settlement reached by parties in arbitration.

consent decree   Decree entered with the consent of the disputing parties and adopted as such by the court. In criminal matters, an agreement by the defendant to cease allegedly illegal activities in return for the government's dropping the charges. Often associated with court recognition of an agreement reached by parties in divorce.

consociation   Coming together in a friendly association.

Describes any association of otherwise extremely diverse units in which there is a certain degree of unity but not necessarily uniformity or total ACCULTURATION or ASSIMILATION. For example, diverse units may seek a consociation in which representatives of each retain a veto to avoid a majority unit's domination and to promote joint, consensual decision making. A recent example of an attempt at consociation is the peace plan for Bosnia. An older example of a successful consociation is the canton system of Switzerland, which maintains federal unity in the face of linguistic and religious differences. Compare ACCOMMODATION.

consolidation   Result of making solid or whole for a single purpose, usually by gathering resources that have been devoted to other activity.

consolidation of cases   *Arbitration:* When two or more cases are heard as one.

Consolidation may occur when one party has initiated separate arbitral proceedings against one or more other parties and a party petitions the court or the arbitrators to combine the cases into one in order to promote efficiency. The power to consolidate may be given to the arbitrators by the parties or codified in the applicable arbitration law [see, for example, O.C.G.A. § 9-9-6(e) (1996)], as a power of the arbitrators or of the court. Consolidation may be granted for substantially the same reasons as for the consolidation of any legal action; that is, when the issues are the same and there is at least one party common to all of the arbitrations [DOA].

consortium   Association of entities; in law, the right of a spouse to the benefits of a conjugal relationship.

constituencies bargaining   See VERTICAL BARGAINING.

constituency   *Law/Politics:* Body of voters that elects a representative. A group of stakeholders with shared interests in a conflict or a problem that appoints a representative to negotiate. Commonly used in public policy dispute resolution and in labor relations.

constituent   Part of a whole. Person who gives another authority to act. Member of a CONSTITUENCY.

construction   *Law:* Process of determining intent, meaning, and effect of an agreement, will, statute, or other written instrument. Distinguished from IN-TERPRETATION, which is concerned with only the meaning and not the effect of the ascertained meaning.

constructive engagement   *International Relations:* Policy that foreign policy decisions with regard to a certain state should be weighted in favor of actions that would promote positive or helpful relationships rather than antagonistic ones. Coined to describe U.S. policy toward the Soviet Union in the 1970s.

consultation   Act of sharing information, seeking advice, or conferring.

International Relations: A technique in which a state anticipates that a proposed course of action will adversely affect another state and therefore initiates discussions to reach an amicable understanding. By exchanging views on the nature and effect of the proposed action, the initiating state may find a way to accommodate the other state's concerns or make adjustments so as to avoid conflict. Although generally viewed as a proactive method of preventing disputes, it is also used after a dispute arises, but typically in the early stages and before resorting to other forms of dispute resolution. In either case, it may be considered a form or preliminary stage of diplomatic negotiations.

Unlike MEDIATION or CONCILIATION, the parties meet directly and without the assistance of a third party. Unlike NOTICE or obtaining prior consent, two related ways of taking other states' interests into account, consultation implies more than mere notice, but less than giving the affected party veto power over the proposed action.

Article 33 of the UN Charter does not mention consultation, which has typically been AD HOC and not INSTITUTIONALIZED. A growing number of treaties, however, either mention or incorporate the process as an initial phase of dispute settlement. See, for example, article 41 of the Convention on the Succession of States in Respect of Treaties [1978] and article XI of the Antarctic Treaty [1959]. Even without treaty obligation, consultation has been important in matters affecting global commons, such as rivers, oceans, and outer space, and where other institutionalized forms of dispute resolution are not available

[*Handbook on the Peaceful Settlement of Disputes Between States,* 1992, p. 10; Merrills, 1991, pp. 2–3].

In mediation, consultation is a process whereby beginning mediators learn from those more experienced in the field, or when one mediator asks another to consult about a case or about another aspect of the mediation practice. Consultation thus involves (1) measuring the effectiveness of the mediator in general and specific strategies, (2) monitoring performance, (3) identifying dynamic issues that interfere with the mediator's effectiveness, (4) solving problems surrounding specific issues, and (5) creating a role model for good practice. Consultants may observe the mediation or take a more active role [Haynes, 1986a, p. 4].

consumer arbitration　Arbitration between individual consumers and manufacturers or other providers of goods and services (*sellers*). There are two types of consumer arbitration. One type is created by contract, the other is established by statute or regulation. In the contractual form, the consumer and the seller agree to arbitrate future disputes related to the goods or services. In contrast to other forms of voluntary, commercial arbitration, consumer arbitration involves a *consumer* (often defined by law), not a member of the particular industry or trade. In addition, much of the contractual form of consumer arbitration is established by an arbitration clause contained within a bill of sale or contract, often as part of the BOILERPLATE or preprinted provisions drafted by the seller. Court enforcement of these arbitration agreements is controversial in some jurisdictions where the contract may be considered adhesive or nonvoluntary, where there is a tradition of hostility toward arbitration, and particularly where the seller either has control over or actually administers the arbitration process. As a consequence, most consumer arbitration provided by a particular industry or seller, or through a more neutral administering agency such as the BETTER BUSINESS BUREAU, gives the consumer an option of rejecting the final award. Although not enforceable against the consumer in some jurisdictions, contractual consumer arbitration provided by the seller may be a condition precedent to the consumer pursuing remedies in the courts.

The second type of consumer arbitration is provided by law to handle a particular class of common disputes, for example, LEMON LAW arbitration for the resolution of disputes between consumers and the manufacturers of automobiles.

Consumer Arbitration Agreements Act 1988 (Great Britain)　Law in which when one party to a dispute is a consumer, and that party is given additional protection against the enforcement of arbitration provisions. Under the law, an arbitration cannot be enforced against consumers unless they have given their written consent to arbitration after the differences in question have arisen, or they have submitted to arbitration in pursuance of the agreement, or the court makes an order under Section 4 of the 1988 act referring the matter to arbitration. Such an order will not be made unless the court is satisfied that it is not detrimental to the interests of the consumer for the differences in question to be referred to arbitration [Burr and Lofthouse, 1992, p. 7].

consumer complaint mechanisms, consumer complaint office, consumer conciliation Terms inclusive of several different types of institutionalized mechanisms for handling consumer complaints. These agencies are usually independent of the provider of the goods and services at issue and include consumer complaint offices, media action lines, state and local government OMBUDSMEN and offices of consumer affairs, and private trade associations such as the BETTER BUSINESS BUREAU or the MAJOR APPLIANCE CONSUMER ACTION PANEL. In addition simply to educating either the provider or the consumer, all such mechanisms use informal means, such as facilitating communication when the consumer cannot get a response and persuading an uncooperative provider to rectify a situation. The private mechanisms persuade through either negative publicity or industry pressure in egregious cases, while the government mechanisms may be empowered by law to investigate, litigate, and take punitive action when appropriate.

Although many of these organizations use mediation, face-to-face meetings are the exception rather than the norm, and hearings are rare. Singer [1983] notes that although these agencies are attractive to many consumers because they are simple to use and often willing to represent the interests of complainants to large organizations, they have been criticized as ineffectual in representing the individual consumer's interests against large corporations.

Such mechanisms should be distinguished from CITIZEN COMPLAINT MECHANISMS designed to handle complaints about government services. Technically, citizens are users and beneficiaries, but not consumers, of government services. The terms, however, are often conflated and both types of mechanisms may be provided through the same agency or organization.

consumer protection restitution program Alternative method of dispute resolution in which a state negotiates with a business for a program providing restitution to consumers. In the state of Washington, for example, attorney general files suit against a business that has had a certain number of complaints filed against it. After filing, the parties—the attorney general's office and the business—may negotiate a restitution program for consumers. Basically they agree that if consumers can prove they were subjected to certain unfair treatment, consumers are entitled to money damages and possibly cancellation or modification of their contracts. For contested cases, the business agrees to be bound by an arbitrator's decision.

contact intensity   Extent to which disputants spend time on discussions aimed at settlement [Kritzer, 1991, p. 31].

container contract   Contract that contains an arbitration clause.

The importance of the container contract for arbitration is that under certain conditions the arbitration provision is regarded as separable from the contract in which it appears [DOA].

contentious jurisdiction   Power of the INTERNATIONAL COURT OF JUSTICE to hear only those matters that are in contention between states and, as in arbitration, only when the states in a given dispute have consented to its jurisdiction.

contest   Make something the subject of a dispute.

contingent agreement, contingent settlement   Settlement agreement that depends on the outcome of some event. In some cases, the agreement is void upon the contingency. In other cases, the agreement will vary in substance based on the contingent event. This allows for settlement when there may be different possible outcomes of an event; parties protect their respective interests by not being bound to certain terms if the outcome of the event would make adherence unfavorable.

contingent med-arb   Variation of the MED-ARB hybrid in which the arbitration phase is contingent upon the agreement of the parties after mediation begins. This process attempts to address the inherent problem of the mediators or arbitrators using their power to give binding judgments that force the parties to make a settlement during the mediation stage. If the parties are not bound to arbitrate, contingent med-arb is merely mediation in which the parties recognize the potential to arbitrate using the same NEUTRAL if the mediation fails. Compare and contrast MED-ARB2.

contingent moves   Responses to special or idiosyncratic problems that occur in negotiations or mediations [Moore, 1986, pp. 25–26]. Examples include specific interventions to manage emotions, dirty tricks, or poor communication, and common procedures such as the CAUCUS.

contract   Agreement, usually BINDING, between two or more persons that creates an obligation or duty to act or refrain from some action.

contract curve   Line that connects all points of intersection between the ISO-CURVES of two individuals. It represents the various values at which agreement between the two parties can be made [Raiffa, 1982, p. 158]. Compare CONTRACT ZONE.

contract zone   Region of the continuum of possible offers and demands where the parties' ranges of acceptable agreements overlap. Also the range of outcomes preferred by both parties to having no contract. Parties cannot reach an agreement unless there is a contract zone or they create one during negotiations [White and Neale, 1991, p. 380]. Compare CONTRACT CURVE.

contracting officer   Under federal U.S. law, a person who

- "By appointment in accordance with applicable regulations, has the authority to enter into and administer contracts and make determinations and findings with respect thereto" [41 U.S.C.A. § 601 (West 1987)].

- "Resolves disputes between the government and the contractor for federal public contracts. The contracting officer's decision on the claim shall be final and conclusive and not subject to review by any forum, tribunal, or government agency, unless an appeal or suit is timely commenced as authorized by statute" [41 U.S.C.A. §§ 605(a)–605(b) (West 1987)].

contractual arbitration   *Voluntary* or *private* arbitration. See ARBITRATION.

contractual mediation   Situation in which the mediator is an outsider with whom the parties contract for the specific purpose of helping them resolve their dispute. Used to distinguished from COURT-CONNECTED mediation that may be mandated by a court order rather than agreed to by the parties. Contrast EMERGENT MEDIATION.

controlled communication   As used by Burton [1969] in the international relations context, use of a third party to serve as a conduit for communication that makes communication more effective and constructive. It proceeds under the assumption that ineffective communication causes and exacerbates conflict. The role of the third party is to ensure that information is conveyed, received, and interpreted accurately and that the disputants understand the nature of the conflict. The third party makes no recommendations or decisions on substantive issues, but merely prepares the ground for more constructive direct negotiations along the lines of COLLABORATIVE PROBLEM SOLVING. The third party's role is similar to that in GOOD OFFICES. As a technique, controlled communication is fundamental to most mediation.

controversy   Discussion in which opposing views are expressed. Compare DISPUTE.
   Law: A dispute that is JUSTICIABLE.

convening   Calling or bringing people together for a meeting.

Public Policy: Technique used by a CONVENOR to identify and bring together stakeholders for negotiations over a disputed matter of policy or proposed regulation. The convenor will contact the stakeholders to understand their concerns and to assess the feasibility of undertaking formal discussions. Officially recognized in REGULATORY NEGOTIATION and in PUBLIC POLICY DIALOGUE and defined under U.S. federal regulations as "a technique that helps identify issues in controversy and affected interests. The convener is generally called upon to determine whether direct negotiations among the parties would be a suitable means of resolving the issues, and if so, to bring the parties together for that purpose" [1 C.F.R. § 305.86-3 App. (1993)].

convenor   Someone who convenes a meeting or conference. See CONVENING.

Public Policy: Defined under U.S. regulations as "an individual, government agency, or private organization, neutral with respect to the regulatory policies under consideration, designated by a government agency who advises the agency whether regulatory negotiation is feasible and determines, in consultation with the agency, who should participate in the regulatory negotiation" [1 C.F.R. § 305.82-4(3) (1993), 5 U.S.C. § 562 (1993)].

convention   Pact or written agreement that establishes a legal relation between the cosigning sovereign states.

A convention may be simply defined as a written instrument. States may, however, incur legal obligations other than through written agreements. Conventions are usually international agreements between more than two signatory nations (MULTILATERAL), while treaties are agreements between two nations (BILATERAL). Custom permits use of the term MULTILATERAL TREATY rather than convention. International organizations, such as the United Nations or the World Bank, may themselves have the authority to conclude international agreements with states.

Convention on the Execution of Foreign Arbitral Awards (1927)   Convention that provided for the enforcement of awards rendered according to an arbitration agreement covered by the Protocol on Arbitration Clauses of 1923 and adopted by the Assembly of the League of Nations on September 26, 1927. In arbitration circles, sometimes referred to as the *Geneva Convention*, but not to be confused with other, more famous conventions of that name.

Convention on the Pacific Settlement of International Disputes of 1899 and 1907, The Hague   July 28, 1899, 32 Stat. 1779, 187 Consol. T.S. 410, as amended, Oct. 18, 1907, 36 Stat. 2199, 205 Consol. T.S. 233.

International Relations: Multilateral, international agreement that provided for the peaceful settlement of international disputes. The convention resulted from the Hague Peace Conference of 1899 and was amended at the second Hague Peace Conference of 1907, called at the initiative of Czar Nicholas of Russia to elicit agreement on arms control and other measures for maintaining peace and making war more humane. In addition to codifying laws of war and neutrality (arms control measures were not adopted), the conventions established a framework for the Permanent Court of Arbitration and for international Commissions of Inquiry.

Although they have some significant shortcomings, not least of which is the failure to provide for any compulsory arbitration, the conventions have served as a model for binding arbitration procedures among states and are often incorporated in agreements among European states and occasionally referenced in ad hoc arbitration agreements. Commonly referred to as the *Hague Convention(s)*.

Convention on the Recognition and Enforcement of Foreign Arbitral Awards

Multilateral treaty drafted at a UN conference on international commercial arbitration. Commonly called the New York Convention and sometimes referred to in arbitration circles as simply the UN Convention.

The United Nations Conference on the Recognition and Enforcement of Foreign Arbitral Awards convened in New York City on May 20 and ended on June 10, 1958. The subject of international commercial arbitration had been under study by an ad hoc committee since 1954. The Convention on the Recognition and Enforcement of Foreign Arbitral Awards entered into force on June 7, 1959. Under the terms of the convention, each contracting state undertook to recognize as binding arbitral awards issued in other states, and to enforce them in accordance with the rules of procedure of the territory where the award was to be recognized. Arbitrations could be conducted according to existing rules, or special rules drafted for a specific arbitration, or under the law of the country in which the arbitration was to take place. A party seeking enforcement of the award needed only to produce the award, or a certified copy of it, including the agreement to arbitrate, in the country where such enforcement was being sought. The convention provided the primary legal framework for modern international commercial arbitration. Most states engaged in international trade are signatories.

Convention on the Settlement of Investment Disputes Between States and Nationals of Other States

Convention drafted by the International Bank for Reconstruction and Development that provides facilities for the voluntary conciliation and arbitration of investment disputes between member states and nationals of other member states.

A *national* is defined as either a private person or a corporation. The convention was one of several proposals designed to stimulate and protect the flow of private international capital into developing countries. It differs from three previous draft conventions in that it offers to member states and foreign investors a permanent FORUM for settling their disputes according to specific rules of procedure. The INTERNATIONAL CENTRE FOR THE SETTLEMENT OF INVESTMENT DISPUTES (ICSID) has been established with offices at the World Bank's principal office in Washington, D.C., but with its own autonomous secretariat for administering dispute-settlement procedures. The convention entered into force on October 14, 1966.

conversations   Oral, informal communications for the purpose of exchanging ideas.

International Relations: Communications between governments to explore a particular topic or issue. Conversations are a normal, usually ongoing activity undertaken to exchange information and views. Continuous conversations, which take place, for example, at the United Nations, allow diplomats to gauge the probable reaction of a state to a future action or initiative. Sometimes called *quiet diplomacy.* Contrast and compare CONSULTATION.

converting last offer to union offer technique   *Labor:* Negotiating technique of management in COLLECTIVE BARGAINING. The employer attempts to create a deterrent to the union's rejecting its offer by converting its last offer into a union offer. By framing its last offer as a union offer and accepting it, management puts the union negotiating committee in the position of having made the final offer. Therefore the onus is on the union committee to persuade membership to accept the package because it was the union's package to which the company acceded [Maggiolo, 1971, p. 89].

cooling-off clause   *Labor:* Contractual provision that provides for a COOLING-OFF PERIOD.

cooling-off period   *Labor:* Specified time provided by law or by contractual agreement during which the disputants can negotiate but must refrain from other particular actions, such as striking or filing a lawsuit. Typically included in collective bargaining agreements, cooling-off periods are triggered when one party provides the other with notice of a grievance or dispute.

cooperate   Work together.

Cooperation occurs when all participants work together toward a single goal, which all perceive as equally desirable, in a manner or by a process that all participants recognize as worthy and acceptable [Edwards, 1981, p. 82].

Contrast DEFECT, ADVERSARY.

cooperative   Willing to COOPERATE. Primarily used as an adjective but also used as a noun to mean someone who pursues a COOPERATIVE STRATEGY.

Has both a positive implication, as in working together instead of apart or at odds with one another, and a negative implication, as in being too compliant. Often used interchangeably with COLLABORATIVE and PROBLEM SOLVING; it should be distinguished from these, however. In the context of DISTRIBUTIVE or POSITIONAL BARGAINING, a cooperative negotiation style is often contrasted with a competitive negotiation style ["soft" and "hard" negotiators, according to Fisher and Ury, 1981], while the collaborative negotiation style is associated more with integrative, interest-based bargaining or PRINCIPLED NEGOTIATION. Under the THOMAS/KILMANN CONFLICT MODE INSTRUMENT, cooperative and AS-SERTIVE are the two variables that help define personal conflict resolution style preferences. Contrast ACCOMMODATING, AVOIDING, COLLABORATING, COMPETING, COMPROMISING.

cooperative antagonist   Label coined by Raiffa [1982, p. 18] to describe dis-putants who recognize that they have differences of interest but who under-stand that they would like to find a compromise. Such disputants fully expect that all parties will be primarily worried about their own interests, but they are not altruistically inclined and are slightly distrustful of one another.

cooperative reciprocity   Broad negotiating strategy whereby a party is coop-erative and continues to be cooperative as long as the other party is coopera-tive [Stoll and McAndrew, 1986, p. 316]. See, generally, RECIPROCITY. Compare TIT-FOR-TAT.

cooperative strategy   Affirmative negotiation technique in which a negotia-tor grants unilateral CONCESSIONS so as to establish a relationship built on trust and to create a moral obligation for the other side to reciprocate with similar concessions.

Williams [1983, p. 53] describes cooperative strategy as moving psychologi-cally toward the other side with a show of trust and good faith. A negotiator using this strategy believes that the other side is as motivated to establish a good negotiating relationship and to reach a JUST agreement as to maximize its own utilities. Therefore, the object of the strategy is to encourage cooperation, seek common ground, and achieve an objectively fair agreement through reciprocal concessions. Although making unilateral concessions involves some risk, ne-gotiators who adopt this strategy may believe that aggression and a competitive strategy undermine the negotiating relationship and result in even more costly impasses [Riskin and Westbrook, 1987, p. 144; Haydock and Mitchell, 1984, p. 6]. Compare COOPERATIVE STYLE. Contrast COMPETITIVE STRATEGY. Note that this strategy and its emphasis on concession making is conceptually tied to pat-terns of POSITIONAL BARGAINING.

cooperative style   Negotiation tactics and personal traits usually associated with the pursuit of a COOPERATIVE STRATEGY.

Because negotiators using a cooperative strategy are more likely to pursue that strategy using a cooperative style, it is common to conflate the concepts of negotiation strategy and style. Murray, Rau, and Sherman [1989, p. 75] make a useful distinction between theory, strategy, and style. Theory is the set of principles and assumptions used to understand the nature of a situation, strategy is the goals and pattern of conduct used to achieve those goals, and style is the personal behavior patterns of the negotiator used to carry out the chosen strategy. Cooperative strategy, therefore, is the general approach dictated by the individual's negotiation theory, while cooperative style is the way the strategy is manifested and the personality traits that dominate the negotiator's action. Thus style includes tactics and reflects personality. A negotiator, however, can exhibit aspects of a cooperative style while pursuing a competitive strategy.

corporate complaint system   Dispute resolution system used inside an organization and designed to resolve internal disputes typically involving nonunion employee complaints. Organizations use a variety of methods, such as chain-of-command systems, whereby employees are told to see their supervisors and then progress up the management ladder; and formalized systems, which involve step-by-step procedures modeled after the union grievance procedures [Westin and Feliu, 1988, pp. 4–5]. Some of these complaint systems incorporate a CORPORATE OMBUDSMAN.

corporate ombudsman   Neutral member of a corporation who provides confidential and informal assistance to employees in resolving work-related concerns and is outside the normal management structure. The corporate ombudsman may serve as a counselor, go-between, mediator, fact-finder, or upward feedback mechanism [Rowe, 1987]. See OMBUDSMAN.

costs of impending negotiations (COIN)   Term coined by Goldman [1991, p. 21] to describe a negotiator's perceived costs of continuing a transaction. The greater the cost that a negotiator expects will be required to continue to carry on a transaction, the greater will be the bargainer's motivation to abandon that transaction and seek the BEST ALTERNATIVE TO THE PROPOSED AGREEMENT (BAPA). Thus the perceived COIN adds to the attractiveness of the BAPA and detracts from the other side's perceived bargaining power.

council of conciliation (England)   Panels of elected employers (*masters*) and employees (*workmen*) empowered to resolve employment disputes submitted to them by the parties. A council's decision is much like an ARBITRAL AWARD. Unlike most forms of arbitration, however, the council has the power to apply to the court for enforcement of its own award [Acts 30 and 31 Vict., c. 105].

Council of Elders (Native American)   Traditional mechanism for resolving disputes.

counterclaim   *Law:* Claim or cause of action made by the defendant in response or in opposition to the claims made by the plaintiff [Fed. R. Civ. P. 13].

   Commercial Arbitration: Opposing claim made by the respondent in answer to the claim raised by the initiating party in his demand for arbitration.

county court mediation   Form of COURT-CONNECTED alternative dispute resolution in which certain courts in Florida are empowered by statute to order litigants to participate in mediation. The statutory definition is as follows: "Mediation of civil cases within the jurisdiction of county courts, including small claims" [Fla. Stat. Ann. § 44.1011 (West Supp. 1992)]. See COURT-ANNEXED MEDIATION.

Cour de Cassation   Supreme court of appeals in any country, such as the highest court of France, the judiciary committee of the House of Lords, or the U.S. Supreme Court.

court   Organ of government consisting of a person or persons empowered to hear and determine controversies through application of law—in short, to AD-JUDICATE matters properly brought before it. The term is often used synonymously with JUDGE.

   The adjudicative organ within certain self-governing organizations may also be referred to as a court, such as *honor court.*

court-administered arbitration   See COURT-ANNEXED ARBITRATION.

court-annexed   Type of COURT-CONNECTED alternative dispute resolution process or program controlled and administered directly by the court or courts from which the disputes are referred, in contrast to a COURT-REFERRED program managed by an entity mostly independent of the courts but to which the court may send cases.

   Also commonly used to describe any ADR process or program used by the courts to resolve disputes brought before it without recourse to further litigation. In this broad sense, the term has the same meaning as COURT-CONNECTED, COURT-REFERRED, and COURT-RELATED. The narrower meaning is recommended.

court-annexed arbitration (COA)   Informal pretrial adjudication required of certain civil litigants and resulting in a nonbinding determination that serves to encourage settlement without further litigation. See also MANDATORY NONBIND-ING ARBITRATION, COURT-ADMINISTERED ARBITRATION, JUDICIAL ARBITRATION, COURT-ORDERED ARBITRATION, MICHIGAN MEDIATION.

This SMALL-CAPS-COURT-CONNECTED ADR hybrid is a reality-testing device usually adopted under the aegis of civil justice reform for the purpose of diverting cases from a court's overcrowded docket. Although the practice can be traced back to Anglo-Saxon and early English equity courts as a method of fact determination in cases involving matters beyond the technical expertise of the court, the magistrates court in Buck's County, Pennsylvania, is credited with establishing the first modern program in the United States. Now found in jurisdictions throughout the United States, the typical model involves a panel of volunteer lawyers, usually three, who hear an informal presentation of the evidence and testimony of witnesses and then issue an award based on its findings of fact and application of law. The award is non-binding for a period, usually thirty days, after which it becomes binding and will be enforced by the court unless a party rejects the award and requests a trial de novo within the period. Technically this is not an appeal but rather a procedure of right in which the judge is not privy to the contents of the award.

The purpose of the award is to deflate unrealistic expectations of outcomes in litigation and to encourage a negotiated settlement without further litigation. As such, the success of these programs rests mainly on the extent to which the parties and their attorneys respect the opinion of the arbitrators. Most programs use only experienced litigators as arbitrators. Some systems discourage further litigation by requiring parties who reject arbitration awards to better their position at trial by some fixed percentage. If they do not, court costs or even attorney's fees are assessed against them. Most programs have case-selection criteria, often with a certain jurisdictional amount at issue. Cases with amounts in dispute below that limit are automatically diverted into the COURT-ANNEXED arbitration program, and cases with amounts in dispute above that limit may enter the program at the judge's discretion. Some programs exclude certain categories of cases, such as prisoners' civil rights or social security.

If true arbitration is voluntary and contractual, court-annexed arbitration is not arbitration at all but rather an administrative adjunct to the court or some form of judicial INFORMALISM. Unlike most contractual forms of arbitration, this process is neither voluntary nor binding, because the court's authority to compel participation is provided by statute or court rule. The parties must be litigants within the jurisdiction of the court, they can be ordered to participate without an agreement to do so, they have little or no choice of adjudicator, and they often must adhere to the formal procedural and evidentiary rules of the court.

court-annexed mediation Mediation program or process administered by a court and endorsed by it to resolve disputes brought before it in lieu of further litigation. The following statute provides a typical definition:

> The process by which a neutral mediator appointed by the court assists the parties in reaching a mutually acceptable agreement as to the issues outlined by the

court. The agreement reached is to be based on the decisions of the parties and not the decisions of the mediator. Any understanding reached by the parties shall not be binding upon the parties nor admissible in court until it is reduced to writing, signed by the parties and their attorneys, if any, and approved by the court [Kan. Stat. Ann. § 23-601 and 23-603(c) (1991)].

Although the term is used generically in reference to any COURT-CONNECTED MEDIATION program, technically courts exercise more administrative control over court-annexed mediation programs than over COURT-REFERRED mediation programs. The court uses public employees to administer these programs directly and parties may have little control over the choice of mediator (as in the statute just quoted), time and place of the conference, or procedures. Compare COURT-REFERRED mediation. Unlike pure mediation, the parties must be in litigation to access the process and in most cases are ordered to participate involuntarily. Although the court can require good-faith participation, it cannot order a party to settle.

court-annexed private judging   Form of TRIAL ON ORDER OF REFERENCE; when a judge, empowered by statute, rather than the parties, decides to present questions of law or fact to a private judge whose decision becomes that of the court. The private judge's decisions are open to appeal but are not subject to a trial de novo [Patterson, 1988].

court-appointed master   Same as SPECIAL MASTER.

court-connected   Any ADR program or process used in conjunction with a court and endorsed by it to resolve disputes brought before it in lieu of further litigation.

The term is broader than but inclusive of COURT-REFERRED and COURT-ANNEXED, and it is rarely used in connection with a specific program. An alternative term with identical meaning is COURT-RELATED. A distinguishing characteristic of most court-connected ADR programs is that the parties must first initiate litigation by filing suit before gaining access to the program. The primary goal of such programs is to alleviate pressure on judicial resources and court dockets.

court-connected arbitration   Nonbinding adjudicative process used in conjunction with a court and endorsed by it to resolve disputes brought before it in lieu of further litigation. See COURT-ANNEXED ARBITRATION.

court-connected mediation   Mediation program or process used in conjunction with a court and endorsed by it to resolve disputes brought before it in lieu of further litigation. See COURT-ANNEXED MEDIATION.

court of conciliation   Usually a SMALL CLAIMS COURT or other court of limited jurisdiction with informal procedure wherein the judge actively proposes terms of adjustment so as to avoid litigation, such as conciliation between debtor and creditor over disputed debt. In some jurisdictions, courts of conciliation focus on marital disputes. In the early nineteenth century, there was a movement in England to create a system of courts of conciliation that used conciliatory processes rather than adjudicative processes to resolve minor civil disputes. See Brougham [1831].

court of piedpoudre, court of pie-powder (archaic, England)   Slang for a now-obsolete lower court of record incident to fairs and markets that heard mercantile disputes.

Though it was an actual court with appeal to the courts at Westminister, it serves as a historical forerunner for modern COMMERCIAL ARBITRATION. With the mayor presiding, panels of merchants attending the fair served as judges, applying the applicable trade customs [Blackstone, 1765–1769, vol. 3, p. 32]. Although there are several possible origins for the name, Holdsworth [vol. 1, p. 538, n. 1] reports that procedure was so expeditious and justice was so swift that the flour dust on the feet of a baker would not have settled by the time a verdict was rendered. The French version, however, referring only to *pied*, or feet, predates the bastardization into the English *pie*.

court-ordered   Usually used in connection with an action or process mandated by a court, such as court-ordered mediation, court-ordered settlement conference, or COURT-ORDERED ARBITRATION. Although court-ordered ADR processes are often used in COURT-CONNECTED ADR programs, judicial coercion is not used in all court-connected ADR programs.

court-ordered arbitration   See COURT-ANNEXED ARBITRATION, JUDICIAL ARBITRATION.

court-referred   ADR programs that receive cases from a court but are administered by public or private agencies independent of court administration. A subset of COURT-CONNECTED. Contrast COURT-ANNEXED, which implies control and administration of the program or process by the court itself. Although court-referred programs require fewer judicial resources to operate, they usually are subject to similar standards and oversight as court-annexed programs.

court-related   Any ADR program or process used in conjunction with a court and endorsed by it to resolve disputes brought before it in lieu of further litigation, such as court-related mediation. The term is broader than COURT-REFERRED and COURT-ANNEXED. An alternative term with identical meaning is COURT-CONNECTED.

court-sponsored Same as COURT-CONNECTED and COURT-REFERRED when used in reference to an ADR program or process. Its use is much less common, however.

court-sponsored settlement conference Conference usually ordered by a judge for purposes of encouraging settlement without further litigation. Participation by the litigants, their attorneys, or both is required. The authority to order settlement conferences is increasingly found in rules of civil procedure. The judge's attendance and degree of participation seem to vary by jurisdiction and by judge. In some jurisdictions, the parties are ordered to MEDIATION (now more commonly referred to as a MEDIATED SETTLEMENT CONFERENCE) or to MANDATORY NONBINDING ARBITRATION. See SETTLEMENT CONFERENCE.

covenant Contract, agreement, or promise.
    Law: Used in reference to promises contained in written instruments relating to real estate. In legal use, there are several distinct classifications of covenants.

covenant not to sue *Law:* With respect to negotiated settlements, agreement by one who has an existing right of action not to sue to enforce that right against the other party to the agreement. Although it may be included as part of a release, a covenant not to sue differs from a release in that it is not necessarily a discharge or abandonment of the claim but rather an agreement not to prosecute the suit against the other signatories. Although the action is relinquished between the parties to the covenant, it is still viable as to third parties. Covenants not to sue avoid the COMMON LAW rule that the release of one joint tortfeasor releases all tortfeasors. Therefore, a claimant can settle with one or more parties without giving up rights to claim against others who do not participate in the settlement. Some jurisdictions have enacted statutes abrogating the common law rule. See also MARY CARTER AGREEMENT.

CPR See CENTER FOR PUBLIC RESOURCES.

CPS See COLLABORATIVE PROBLEM SOLVING.

creating value Term used by Lax and Sebenius [1986] to describe activities that "expand the pie," such as collaborative, integrative BARGAINING. Compare *problem-solving bargaining* under BARGAINING. Lax and Sebenius note a fundamental tension between creating value and CLAIMING VALUE in negotiations.

criminal mediation Mediation of criminal cases between victim and offender and referred by the court [Price and Woods, 1990, p. 16.]. See VICTIM-OFFENDER MEDIATION. See also RESTORATIVE JUSTICE.

crisis   State of most tense opposition; critical moment or turning point in a conflict or chain of events and therefore inherently unstable.

Psychology: Condition in which stress renders a person unable to cope or otherwise function and which may require intervention [Greenstone and Leviton, 1987, p. 40]. See CRISIS INTERVENTION.

International Relations: Turning point in relations between states that has the possibility of evolving into armed conflict. Typically a series of escalating events leads each side to become concerned that the other may commit an act of aggression. A sample definition: "a situation with three necessary conditions deriving from a change in its external or internal environment: (a) a threat to basic values, with a simultaneous or subsequent awareness of (b) a finite time for response, and (c) a high probability of involvement in military hostilities" [Wilkenfeld, 1991, p. 149].

crisis in the courts   See LITIGATION EXPLOSION.

crisis intervention   *Psychology:* Skilled and well-timed intrusion to defuse the CRISIS and return the person to normal precrisis functioning [Greenstone and Leviton, 1987, p. 41].

cross-cultural conflict resolution   See CULTURE.

Cuban Popular Tribunal   Postrevolution experiment in informal, popularly accepted courts that became the basis of Cuba's present national judicial system. The tribunals handle a wide range of "antisocial conduct" and make no distinction between civil and criminal cases. The lowest tier of tribunals is responsible for four to five thousand citizens, and in addition to giving frequent moral lectures and public admonitions, it issues sanctions that are restitutive and rehabilitative rather than punitive. The police enforce the tribunal's sanctions. Proceedings have a moderate degree of judicial formality. Lay people from the local community, however, serve on the tribunal and solicit participation from the audience. Legal representation is rare and all questioning is conducted by members of the tribunal in an inquisitorial process [Marshall, 1985, pp. 63–64]. Compare CHINESE MEDIATION, WORKER'S COURTS OF THE SOVIET UNION.

culture   Range of human activities that are learned and transmitted from generation to generation through various learning processes; custom and civilization of a particular, distinct group of people or society at a particular point in time.

Culture is a broad concept enveloping knowledge, language, beliefs, art, morals, custom, and other capacities and behaviors that one acquires as a member of a society. Culture is action, such as the behavior and products of a society; culture is the knowledge underlying action, such as ontology, innovation, and dissemination; culture is language, such as verbal instruction; and culture is the meaning attributed to knowledge and action, such as taboos. Generally the elements of culture are learned (not inherited), social (not individual), repetitive (not unique), and collective (not solitary). In addition to race and ethnicity, cultural difference may stem from gender, nationality, social and economic status, and sexual orientation [Duryea, 1992, p. 4].

A valid criticism of much of the modern conflict resolution movement is its dependence on American cultural paradigms. See, generally, Avruch, Black, and Scimecca [1991] and Lederach [1995]. Increasing numbers of theorists and practitioners are either working from their own cultural perspectives or finding themselves in other cultural settings where this paradigm is less useful. Thus it is not surprising that culture and the related concept of DIVERSITY is central to the work of many in the field. For an extensive bibliography, see Duryea [1992]. Various aspects of culture provide insight into the emergence and handling of conflict. *Cross-cultural conflict resolution* is a comparative approach to understanding universals and differences in conflict handling across different cultures. Differences among cultures of interacting peoples are often viewed as sources of conflict and barriers to peaceful resolution. *Intracultural conflict* is a dispute between at least two parties from the same or closely related cultural groups. *Intercultural conflict* is a dispute or series of disputes between at least two parties, and some element relates to the ethnicity of the parties or the parties belong to different cultural groups [Duryea, 1992, p. 6]. *Multicultural conflict resolution* is the resolution of conflict in multiethnic settings with many overlapping and interacting cultures. At some level, most disputes involve a cultural element that may not be readily apparent.

See also MULTICULTURALISM.

custody mediation   See CHILD-CUSTODY MEDIATION.

customary law   Traditional source of law that remains unwritten and that has been established by long usage through the collaboration and consent of ancestors.

In arbitration, the three traditional sources of law are customary law, statutory law, and judge-made law. Customary law in commercial arbitration is particularly significant in that it is frequently the reason for using arbitration instead of litigation, and because arbitrators, unlike judges, are familiar with the various trades and customs involved. Practice as it has developed in labor-management relations might be considered a customary law of a particular plant or factory. Customary law was often administered by English merchant courts in medieval times. See COURT OF PIEDPOUDRE. In folk societies, customary law usually denotes the unwritten law governing the various public aspects of that culture. In contemporary society, customary law is simply law that does not derive from official sources of decision making [DOA].

Czech Chamber of Commerce and Industry Arbitration Court Permanent, independent administering agency established to settle commercial disputes through independent arbitrators.

The arbitration court decides matters if it has been given jurisdiction on the basis of (1) an international bilateral or multilateral treaty, (2) a valid arbitration agreement entered into by the parties prior to the dispute, or (3) written declarations of the parties after the dispute has arisen that evidence their clear intention to submit the dispute to the arbitration court. The arbitration court makes a single decision, that is, one that is not appealable, and its awards are enforceable as judgments in the ordinary courts. This court is the descendant of the Czechoslovak arbitration court, one of many arbitration courts established throughout the former Soviet Union. The dissolution of Czechoslovakia and the formation of the separate Slovac Chamber of Commerce Arbitration Court has raised jurisdictional concerns.

dakhala (**Arabic**) Bedouin custom of providing and honoring sanctuary in conflicts that could escalate into blood feuds. Literally "entering protection," the custom of *dakhala* is to contain conflict and suppress violence.

In Bedouin society, vengeance is a customary duty when a kinsman has been injured or killed. Knowing this, the offender and his close kin flee the scene and take refuge in the nearest tent or house. Every home is like a sanctuary guarded by the honor of the owner, who is duty-bound to receive any fugitive who asks for protection. One can even safely demand sanctuary of his own enemy, because the obligation to respect the sanctity of one's own home takes precedence over the right to and temptation for vengeance. In such a situation, the *dakhal* (protector) must immediately assume the responsibility to ensure at all costs the safety of his *dakheel* (refuge seeker or supplicant).

Once a culprit has sought *dakhala* in a house in the community where the killing occurred, he and his kinsmen are given full protection for three days (*al-mahrbat,* or "escape days"), to allow the group to flee their *dira* ("tribal homeland"). On the first day, the *dakhal* is compelled to ride to the victim's group to inform it that the culprit is his *dakheel,* or in the local symbolized idiom, has "sought protection in their face." Thus all the adult male relatives of the victim are aware of the situation, so they no longer have an acceptable excuse if they violate the *dakhala* law. The success of *dakhala* lies in the fact that it is universally practiced, and thus everyone can offer it to others or seek it out when in need [Khalaf, 1990, pp. 227–228]. See also *JALI*; SULHA.

143

Danish Consumer Tribunals CONSUMER COMPLAINT MECHANISM in Denmark. A form of state-sponsored court often employing conciliatory, nonadjudicative processes [Marshall, 1985, p. 236].

DART See DISPUTE AVOIDANCE AND RESOLUTION TASK FORCE.

data accuracy (DA) Degree of certainty a party has of its ACCRUED COSTS (AC).
    In bargaining, uncertainty regarding accrued costs diminishes the role of AC in measuring bargaining strength [Goldman, 1991, p. 25].

Day of Concord See LOVEDAY.
    Contrast LAWDAY.

deadline See FINAL BARGAINING.

deadlocked Unable to agree. Similar to IMPASSE. Though impasses in bargaining might be overcome through various techniques or a change in circumstances, *deadlocked* denotes an irreconcilable impasse fatal to further negotiation. It also connotes more affirmative and purposeful action on the part of the parties than impasse.

deal-point price See DOORKNOB PRICE.

debate Open and usually formal discussion in which the different sides of a particular matter are voiced. Suggests ADVERSARY arguments made to influence a larger group, such as a legislature or public meeting. Compare DIALOGUE.

decide Bring to resolution; reach a determination or give judgment in favor of one or another party after deliberation.
    The term has different connotations depending on the DISPUTE RESOLUTION PROCESS used and the decision maker. For example, in a traditional, adversary, adjudicative process, the adjudicator has the power to decide, while in a conciliatory process, the parties themselves decide. See DECISION, DETERMINATION OF A DISPUTE.

decision Final determination or judgment in a matter that has been under deliberation or discussion.
    Decision connotes an intent to affect the matter under consideration. Therefore, decisions are made by those who have a direct interest in the matter or those who are otherwise empowered to affect the outcome, such as a judge or an arbitrator. Though they may form an opinion, those without power to affect the outcome cannot make a decision regarding the matter.

Law: Although popularly used ("The decision of the judge is final"), it is not a legal term with a technical meaning and thus may refer to the actions of any decision maker.

International Relations: According to Haas [1974, p. 492], a decision involves the formal selection of one of several possible policies with the intent to execute it. The same authority provides these subterms:

- *Preventive decision:* "The decision maker maintains a status quo and waits either for the decisional problem to become obsolete or for the decision making stimulus to disappear" [p. 122].
- *Promotive decision:* "A decision maker takes definite steps to bring about a new state of affairs" [p. 122].

decision aid   Formalized approach to information handling.

Two decision aids found to be effective in generating high-quality negotiated agreements are simultaneous consideration of issues, or packaging, and SEARCH MODELS [Brett, 1991, p. 305].

decision maker   Individual who has the power to decide.

Decision connotes an intent to affect the matter under consideration. Therefore, decision makers are those who are empowered to affect the outcome either through committing resources under the decision maker's control or through operation of law or other social institution. See DECISION.

decision-making process   Any process used to make a decision.

Processes can be purely private and individual, adjudicative, or political, varying by method and content. Thus, though an individual may decide a matter without regard to public decision-making conventions and public norms, a judge or jury must adhere to an established method of determining the facts and applying the law. Experts are expected to decide based on their own extensive knowledge and understanding of the problem, while politicians must consider the wishes of their constituencies.

decision-tree analysis   Graphic tool for outlining the range of possible choices and their consequences, including possible successive decisions, available to a decision maker.

In legal disputes, decision-tree analysis is a quantitative analysis of a case, often used as a form of LITIGATION RISK ANALYSIS, that helps counsel identify the uncertainty of outcomes for disputed legal and factual issues in a case. Once a range of outcomes for each issue is established, the ranges are matched with probabilities. The weight of probabilities helps determine the *expected value* of a case. Negotiators and mediators are increasingly using this tool for settlement purposes.

decree   Authoritative order issued with the force of law.

Decree and JUDGMENT are often used interchangeably. There is a difference, however. A sentence or order of a court of equity is a decree, a decision of a law court is a judgment. As distinctions between the two types of courts have eroded, the term *decree* has fallen out of use in favor of judgment. Scottish courts still use the term for a court's final sentence.

de-escalation   Gradual decrease of the intensity and scope of hostilities. Used mostly in the context of armed combat but applied to social conflict, generally to refer to decreases in the severity of coercion used and scope of participation [Kriesberg, 1998b]. Contrast ESCALATION.

deep-rooted conflict   See INTRACTABLE CONFLICT.

default   Failure; failure to fulfill an obligation.

Law: Party's state when she fails to defend a legal action; a *default judgment* may be entered against her without a hearing or trial. In arbitration, arbitrators cannot issue default awards. They can, however, issue an award when a party fails to appear and participate, providing they hear and consider the evidence and arguments of the parties that do appear and participate. See EX PARTE HEARING.

defect   Abandon one cause in favor of another.

Often used in GAME THEORY to denote the opposite of COOPERATE. Also used to describe leaving an ALLIANCE or COALITION and joining the opposition.

defendant   Person accused in a civil or criminal complaint before a court. Contrast PLAINTIFF.

dehumanization   Creation of negative stereotype depicting the other side as less human than one's self or group.

Though the process of dehumanization can be external, with the conscious intent of mobilizing the group against others, as in public propaganda depicting the enemy during wartime, it can also be an internal psychological process of denying recognition of human characteristics in an opponent that would otherwise invoke feelings of commonality and empathy. This allows one to engage more easily in hostilities. In either context, it tends to escalate conflict and inhibit resolution. Related term: ENEMY IMAGES.

delegation of authority   Assignment or transfer of decision-making POWER from one to another.

When parties are represented by others, negotiators and mediators should confirm that there has been sufficient delegation of authority to the representatives.

deliberate   Think carefully about, ponder, or carefully consider.

In ADJUDICATION, weighing the evidence and arguments presented in order to make a judgment or award.

delinking   Technique whereby the values held by a party are separated from the issues in an attempt to make the conflict easier to resolve.

In multi-issue disputes, delinking may help resolve some of the separate issues when resolution of the combined issues causes IMPASSE.

delivery of award   Transmission of an award to the parties in an arbitration.

The timing and manner of transmitting the award may be established by agreement, by the applicable procedural rules of the administrating agency, or by the applicable law. In U.S. domestic practice, the typical time between the hearing ending and the award delivery is thirty days. Delivery may also serve to start the limitations period for petitioning a court to modify or vacate an award.

demand for arbitration   Initial notice by one party to another of an intention to arbitrate his dispute under the arbitration clause in his contract [DOA].

Although in domestic U.S. practice the demand for arbitration often resembles a COMPLAINT in a civil suit, there are far fewer formal requirements for form and content.

deposition   Taking of sworn testimony in the form of answers to questions. The testimony is then transcribed for use in a trial or arbitration.

In a civil trial, depositions are used primarily in the discovery stage to gather evidence. In arbitration, depositions are often taken when it is inefficient or impossible for the witness to attend the arbitration hearing.

***dequitub* (Native North American)**   "Telling them gently what to do."

Salish Native American term describing the operating principle behind elders' advice, which was supposed to be guiding but not authoritative [Mansfield, 1993, p. 344].

desensus   See DISSENSUS.

destabilizer   Negotiating team member who resists movement toward settlement. One of three generic roles, identified by Colosi and Berkeley [1986], assumed by members of a negotiating team that also includes STABILIZERS and QUASI-MEDIATORS. Various team members may have different degrees of knowledge, authority, skill, or resources. They will always have different personality traits and negotiation styles. Because different team members have different interests, their roles could change as the issues under negotiation change; however, they could maintain the same roles throughout.

détente Relaxation of strained relations between nation-states. See RAPPROCHEMENT.

determination of a dispute Settling and ending of a dispute by a judicial or arbitral decision [DOA]. See AWARD, DECISION.

deterrence Strategy of raising the costs of hostile action or defection to discourage the same. More common in international relations. See RECIPROCITY. Contrast REASSURANCE.

deterrence theory Concept that nuclear weapons will maintain peace by deterring armed aggression.

Associated with MUTUALLY ASSURED DESTRUCTION (MAD), wherein neither the United States nor the former U.S.S.R. could escape annihilation by making a preemptive first strike.

detouring Shifting the conflict by picking a different or related issue and contesting it in a different manner or forum to gain advantage in the existing conflict [Lockhart, 1979, p. 102].

dialectical scanning Process whereby a mediator identifies the characteristics of the conflict at hand before selecting the appropriate technique for its resolution [Curtis and Bailey, 1990, p. 141].

dialogic listening Listening technique "to develop ideas and suggestions, tease out nuances, and help define incomplete ideas" [Stewart and Thomas, 1990, p. 202], which involves both focusing on the process of communication that is occurring between the communicators at the time they are communicating and focusing on the meanings that are being created, rather than only trying to understand the other person or get one's ideas across. This requires focusing on what is being said and how it is being said, not thinking about what to say next, and listening without presupposing any particular outcome [Howell, 1982]. The technique includes asking others to "say more" when they are unsure of what they mean, and summarizing what another person said in one's own words [Gudykunst, 1991, p. 39].

See LISTEN. Compare ACTIVE LISTENING, EMPATHIC LISTENING, RESPONSIVE LISTENING.

dialogue Conversation, usually between two parties, for a variety of purposes—building a relationship, defining a problem, developing approaches to the problem, or exchanging information.

Unlike processes with the goal of resolving a dispute, a dialogue may simply be used to improve trust and understanding and reduce stereotypes among opposing groups. Nor does it imply an attempt to influence others or have the adversary or formal connotation of DEBATE. Although duration and number of participants can vary considerably, participant continuity is stressed.

Use of dialogue as a structured, facilitated process is growing in a number of areas, particularly in international, intercultural and inter-ethnic, and public policy conflicts. Rothman [1996] describes dialogue as being either positional (focused on blaming and the maintenance of incompatible positions), human relations (focused on getting to know others better), activist (focused on bringing disputants together in a common cause requiring their mutual cooperation and assistance), and problem solving (reframing the conflict as a problem involving the parties' human needs and engaging in joint problem solving for ways to meet those needs).

International Relations: Connotes informal and ongoing discussions between representatives of two groups. Compare CONFERENCE.

dictation, dictatorial process   Form of dispute resolution in which an authoritative person or body simply instructs or imposes a solution. Connotes a lack of both due process and adjudicative deliberation. It contrasts with democratic forms of decision making in which people affected by the problem and the solution have some form of meaningful input.

differ   Disagree.

difference   Extent of disagreement.

difference maximizing   Concept of decision making whereby a person prefers the outcome that maximizes the difference between what he gets and what another person gets, with the latter getting the lesser amount [Frohlich and Oppenheimer, 1984, p. 6]. Compare DIMINISHMENT APPROACH.

diminishment approach   Technique whereby a negotiator may attempt to minimize the other side's position while remaining relatively neutral about a client's position. These negotiators want the other side to lose while preserving the status quo for their client. An example might be a labor negotiator who represents management in a union contract dispute [Haydock and Mitchell, 1984, p. 6]. Compare DIFFERENCE MAXIMIZING.

diplomacy   Art and practice of conducting relations with foreign governments through representatives in pursuit of the INTERESTS of a particular country. Sample definitions include the following:

- "'A process of representation and negotiation' based on information, communication, and interpersonal relationships" [Stern, Bagozzi, and Dholakia, 1977, p. 377, citation omitted].
- "The management of international relations by negotiation" [Powell, 1991, p. 137].

In its broadest sense, diplomacy encompasses the entire foreign relations process, including foreign policy formulation (ends as well as means). In a more traditional sense, however, diplomacy refers only to techniques whereby a state pursues its interests outside its boundaries (means, not ends). This definition includes all processes and techniques (see DIPLOMATIC MEANS OF DISPUTE RESOLUTION), either mutually constructive and overt or destructive and covert.

Some commentators view diplomacy as synonymous with NEGOTIATION, either by limiting the scope of diplomatic activities to negotiation or by expanding the concept of negotiation. Neal [1964, p. 201] proposes this syllogism: "Since negotiation aims at agreement, and agreement invariably means compromise, diplomacy may be defined as the art of making compromises in international political matters which promote rather than jeopardize the basic interests and security of a nation."

Diplomacy takes place at multilateral conferences but is mostly bilateral through foreign ministries and resident diplomatic missions. SUMMIT DIPLOMACY involves heads of government in the negotiation of critical issues. See also SHUTTLE DIPLOMACY.

Although traditional concepts of diplomacy exclude contributions to international peacemaking by nongovernmental actors, recent commentators have recognized these contributions in a larger conceptualization of diplomacy. See MULTITRACK DIPLOMACY.

diplomatic means of dispute resolution   *International Law:* Includes all processes, short of armed conflict, in which the parties retain control and may accept or reject any proposed settlements as they see fit. Some dispute resolution mechanisms included under this heading are NEGOTIATION, MEDIATION, GOOD OFFICES, INQUIRY, and CONCILIATION.

direct negotiation   Negotiation in which all parties involved are the principals [Rubin and Sander, 1988, p. 395].

The term denotes any negotiations in which the disputants are communicating with each other without the use of intervening third parties such as mediators, although direct negotiation can occur in mediation. In practice, negotiations between representatives who are not principals and who do not have a direct interest in the dispute, such as lawyer-to-lawyer negotiation, are loosely and incorrectly referred to as direct negotiations. If, however, the represented principals are present, direct negotiations may occur.

direct requests *International Relations:* In the enforcement of MULTILATERAL TREATIES, a confidential, private request made by the enforcing body to a signatory state for information about or for the abatement of minor or first-time deviations.

Although direct requests are confidential, nonconforming states that fail to respond to the satisfaction of the enforcing body risk public disapproval through comments published in the body's annual reports. On many occasions the body makes similar comments year after year as a means of continuing pressure on a state.

directional reciprocity Act of making a concession or a retraction in immediate response to and in the same direction as the other party's concession or retraction [Druckman and Harris, 1989, p. 236]. Similar to TIT-FOR-TAT. See also RECIPROCITY.

dirty tricks *Negotiation:* Tactics used by negotiators to achieve their objectives through unprincipled means, associated especially with competitive, aggressive, hard bargainers in positional bargaining.

Fisher and Ury [1981, pp. 132–141] divide dirty tricks into three categories: deliberate deception, psychological warfare, and positional pressure tactics. Most books on negotiation include a list of dirty tricks and a variety of responses. In addition to some of the most creative epithets, Craver [1988] has produced one of the more extensive lists of dirty tricks.

disagree, disagreement Having differences of opinion or inconsistent views; often used synonymously with DISPUTE.

In conflict resolution theory, the term has a narrower, technical meaning: "Conflicts concerning relationships or what to do in particular matters of interest which are dealt with by dyadic and private problem solving between the parties themselves" [Gulliver, 1979]. See DYADIC DISPUTE PROCESSING.

Anthropologists hold that a disagreement is distinguished from a dispute in that the former follows the definition just provided and the latter involves a disagreement in which the government or some other authority is brought in as a third party to help settle the matter [Miller and Sarat, 1980–1981, p. 528]. The anthropological definition for disagreement is nearly parallel to Miller and Sarat's definitions of GRIEVANCE and CLAIM. Compare DISPUTE, CONFLICT.

disagreement point Point at which the alternative to a negotiated agreement is preferable to what is being offered [Sebenius, 1992, p. 50]. See BATNA. Compare and contrast BOTTOM LINE, RESERVATION PRICE, RESISTANCE POINT.

discord Lack of harmony, strife.

discourse   Usually a formalized pattern of communication through which parties exchange information and points of view by engaging in alternating speeches or lectures. Compare DIALOGUE, DISCUSSIONS.

discovery   In U.S. litigation, legal procedure invoked before trial to inform the parties of the facts in a dispute. The goal is to narrow the issues and save time and expense.

Discovery as used in the United States is not traditional in most non–U.S. adjudicative processes. Nor is discovery traditional in COMMERCIAL ARBITRATION in the United States. Most arbitration statutes permit discovery to the extent that it is allowed by the arbitration agreement, or if the parties so stipulate during the arbitration. Compare INFORMATION EXCHANGE.

discovery referee   Neutral party, other than the trial judge, with limited decision-making or adjudicative powers on discovery matters and empowered by court rule, statute, or party agreement to resolve disputed issues in the discovery phase of litigation. The best known model is used in California and has come under fire as subject to abuse [see Reuben, 1994]. See, generally, ALTERNATIVE DISCOVERY DISPUTE RESOLUTION (ADDR). See also TRIAL ON ORDER OF REFERENCE.

discussions   Informal pattern of communication for the purpose of exchanging information and perceptions. Implies a more interactive process than DISCOURSE.

disownable concession   Negotiation technique of proposing concessions through an intermediary whose statements can be disavowed if the adversary is not interested in the proposal [Fogg, 1985, p. 353]. Compare AMBIGUOUS AUTHORITY.

disputant   Party to a dispute. Compare COMPLAINANT, PARTY, STAKEHOLDER.

dispute   Argue about, debate; subject matter of debate, CONTROVERSY.

In CONFLICT RESOLUTION, the term has a more specific, technical meaning, as illustrated by this representative list of definitions:

- "When one against whom a complaint is lodged fails to respond satisfactorily to the aggrieved party" [Lieberman and Henry, 1986, p. 426].

- "A specific disagreement concerning a matter of fact, law or policy in which a claim or assertion of one party is met with refusal, counter-claim, or denial by another" [Merrills, 1991, p. 1].

- "A specific disagreement which takes the form of claims between parties, which are met with refusals, counter-claims, denials, counter-charges, accusations, etc. A dispute relates to a question of material or moral interest, or concerns the interpretation of a point of law, usage, prevention of usage, abuse, violation of a right, etc." [Bailey, 1971, p. 7].

- "A dispute exists when a claim based on a grievance is rejected either in whole or in part. It becomes a civil legal dispute when it involves rights or resources which could be granted or denied by a court [Miller and Sarat, 1980–1981, p. 526].

These definitions suggest an important technical distinction between *dispute* and conflict, even though the terms are often used interchangeably. A dispute exists only after a CLAIM is made and rejected. A conflict is necessary for the articulation of a claim. A conflict, however, can exist without a claim being made. Thus, although a dispute cannot exist without a conflict, a conflict can exist without a dispute. Compare CONFLICT.

Law: Term used narrowly to refer only to those disputes involving legally recognized claims or rights. For U.S. federal government agencies, a dispute is "any question material to a decision concerning an administrative program, or, within the Conference's discretion, any other decision, about which persons who would be substantially affected by the decision or the agency disagree [1 C.F.R. § 316.101(c) (1993)].

International Relations: Situation that exists whenever states advance opposing viewpoints about a subject matter of common interest. The elements of an international dispute are that (1) it is between states, (2) it leads to some action by the aggrieved state ranging from diplomatic protests to overt hostilities, and (3) it relates to a reasonably well-defined, specific subject matter. Although the mere manifestation of a religious, political, or historical view by a state may conflict with that of another, it is not a dispute. Actions based on that view, however, such as claims over a specific territory or to specific rights, would constitute a dispute.

Compare CONFLICT, DISAGREEMENT.

Dispute Avoidance and Resolution Task Force (DART)   Multidisciplinary entity with the objective of changing the culture of dispute resolution in the construction industry through education.

Formed in 1991 under the auspices of the AMERICAN ARBITRATION ASSOCIATION and through the active support of liability insurers for design professionals and construction sureties, DART promotes the awareness, understanding, and use of private dispute prevention and resolution techniques, such as PARTNERING, DISPUTE REVIEW BOARDS, MEDIATION, and ARBITRATION, as standard practice for the construction industry. An industrywide coalition, DART represents public and private owners, architects, engineers, contractors, subcontractors, sureties, insurers, and lenders.

dispute management system (DMS)   Institutionalized framework of handling disputes within an organization. The design of a DMS involves examining the causes of disputing within an organization and then creating a process for constructively managing disputes as they arise. Also called DISPUTE RESOLUTION SYSTEM. See INTEGRATED CONFLICT MANAGEMENT SYSTEM.

dispute processing   Suggested by Felstiner [1974] as more accurate than DISPUTE RESOLUTION to describe the same category of processes because the objective of the process may not necessarily be to "resolve" the dispute or the underlying conflicts. Compare CONFLICT RESOLUTION, CONFLICT REDUCTION.

dispute resolution   Study and practice of resolving DISPUTES.

Although the range of possible dispute-handling processes is quite broad, including war and avoidance, the field of dispute resolution is primarily focused on ALTERNATIVE DISPUTE RESOLUTION processes, especially mediation and arbitration. For discussion on distinctions, see CONFLICT, DISPUTE, CONFLICT MANAGEMENT, CONFLICT RESOLUTION. See DISPUTE RESOLUTION PROCESS. Compare DISPUTE PROCESSING.

dispute resolution center   Location at which DISPUTE RESOLUTION PROCESSES using neutral third parties are made available, usually by government or not-for-profit entities.

Legal definitions such as the following define such centers as organizations and programs rather than as locations or physical facilities:

- "A not-for-profit organization which is exempt from the payment of federal income tax pursuant to §501(C)(3) of the Internal Revenue Code and which is organized to provide mediation services at no charge to disputants who agree to utilize its services" [710 Ill. Comp. Stat. Ann. 20/2 (West 1992)].
- "A program which is organized by one or more governmental subdivisions or non-profit organizations and which makes informal dispute resolution procedures available" [Iowa Code § 679.1 (1996)].

Although the term has evolved narrowly to refer only to those centers that provide ALTERNATIVE DISPUTE RESOLUTION processes, a dispute resolution center, as envisioned by Sander [1976, p. 131], would be a building wherein a complainant would be directed to one of many dispute resolution processes, including LITIGATION, depending on the complainant's needs and requirements. See also MULTIDOOR COURTHOUSE.

Dispute Resolution Journal   Periodical of the American Arbitration Association, formerly published as *The Arbitration Journal.*

Dispute Resolution Magazine   Periodical of the American Bar Association's Dispute Resolution Section.

dispute resolution organization   Any corporation or aggregation of individuals providing DISPUTE RESOLUTION services.
    Legal definitions include the following: "A private profit or non-profit corporation, political subdivision, or public corporation, or a combination of these, that offers alternative dispute resolution services to the public" [Tex. Rev. Civ. Stat. Ann. § 154.001 (West Supp. 1993)]. See also the definition from 710 Ill. Comp. Stat. Ann. 20/2 (West 1992) under DISPUTE RESOLUTION CENTER.

dispute resolution process, dispute resolution mechanism   Any process that may be used to resolve a DISPUTE.
    As illustrated by the following definitions (organized by decreasing inclusiveness), the term has acquired a fairly narrow legal definition in the context of COURT-CONNECTED alternatives to litigation:

- "Any process that assists persons with a dispute or a conflict to resolve their differences without further litigation, prosecution, civil unrest, economic disruption, or violence" [Ohio Rev. Code Ann. § 179.01 (Banks-Baldwin, 1990)].

- "A process voluntarily entered by parties in disagreement using mediation or arbitration to reconcile the parties' differences" [Minn. Stat. Ann. § 494.01 (West Supp. 1993)].

- "A process by which the parties involved in a minor dispute voluntarily agree to enter into formal discussion and negotiation with the assistance of a mediator or member of the Center's staff in order to resolve their dispute" [Iowa Code § 679.1 (1996)].

Use of the term in this narrow sense has led to its being used to denote only ALTERNATIVE DISPUTE RESOLUTION PROCESSES. Technically, litigation, voting, dictation, and warfare are also dispute resolution processes.

dispute resolution program   Set or list of DISPUTE RESOLUTION services provided to the public by a DISPUTE RESOLUTION CENTER or organization.
    The following legal definition is fairly inclusive, bearing in mind that such programs exclude noncollaborative dispute resolution processes such as litigation, voting, dictation, and violence:

Any process which may include one of the following:

(1) A program that provides or encourages dispute resolution and conflict management, including but not limited to a program that provides or encourages mediation or conciliation, a mini-trial program, a summary jury trial, or non-binding arbitration. The program may serve the legal community, business community, public sector, private sector, or private individuals, or any combination of them, and its scope may include disputes and conflicts in the domestic context, international context, or both;

(2) A program that provides education or training, in the primary and secondary schools, in colleges and universities of the state, as well as in other appropriate educational forums, about the elimination, prevention, resolution, and management of disputes and conflicts in the domestic and international context;

(3) A program that provides or encourages dispute resolution and conflict management and provides education or training [Ohio Rev. Code Ann. 179.01(B) (Banks-Baldwin, 1990)].

See also definition from Iowa Code § 679.1 (1996) under DISPUTE RESOLUTION CENTER.

dispute resolution provider   Person or organization, usually private, that offers ALTERNATIVE DISPUTE RESOLUTION services, typically for a fee.

A sample legal definition is as follows: "A person, other than a judge acting in his official capacity, who holds himself out to the public as a qualified neutral person trained to function in the conflict-solving process using the techniques and procedures of negotiation, conciliation, mediation, arbitration, mini-trial, moderated settlement conference, neutral expert fact-finding, summary jury trial, special masters, and related processes" [Utah Code Ann. § 58-39A-1 (Supp. 1992)].

The term appears to have been coined during the mid-1980s by insurance companies when referring to the various individuals and organizations marketing their dispute resolution services to the industry.

dispute resolution systems   Entire range and interrelationship of DISPUTE RESOLUTION PROCESSES available within a particular organization or for a particular class of DISPUTE or a particular group of people. See, generally, Ury, Brett, and Goldberg [1988]. See also INTEGRATED CONFLICT MANAGEMENT SYSTEM.

dispute resolution week   Same concept as SETTLEMENT WEEK. The first dispute resolution week was a statewide event in Texas under proclamation by the governor in 1985 [Singer, 1989, p. 111]. See SETTLEMENT WEEK.

dispute review board (DRB)   Standing group of experts who, during the course of a particular relationship, meet regularly or on demand to resolve disputes. Sometimes called *conflict review committees.*

Used on large projects in the construction industry, such as dams, stadiums, tunnels, runways, and highways, DRBs are often composed of individuals with different expertise if the project involves different aspects of engineering and construction. The authority and procedures of DRBs vary with the contract. Most DRBs, however, do not mediate and do not issue binding awards. Thus DRBs function more like ADVISORY ARBITRATION panels or neutral FACT-FINDERS. The great advantage of DRBs is the resolution of problems promptly on site, thereby saving time and money and preventing the escalation of adversarial hostilities that could delay or endanger project completion. The largest construction project to date, the English Channel tunnel (the "Chunnel"), involved DRBs.

dispute system design (DSD)   Ongoing, interest-based process of creating DISPUTE RESOLUTION SYSTEMS to handle clusters or *streams* of disputes to meet the needs of disputants and organizations. DSD, sometimes described as "the how of ADR," is a procedural framework that cuts across all substantive areas and all methods of ADR [WAMR 4(7)]. See, generally, Ury, Brett, and Goldberg [1988], and Costantino and Merchant [1996].

dissensus   Term coined by Aubert [1963] as the opposite of CONSENSUS and denoting methods of dispute resolution that rely on clearly defined differences between the parties, such as adjudication. Occasionally the term is misspelled DESENSUS.

dissonance theory   Theory that holds that it is not possible to hold one position and argue another conflicting or inconsistent position. Because the two are in dissonance, people will modify one or the other position in order to lessen the dissonance. Dissonance theory underlies the approach whereby mediators encourage disputing parties to try to understand each other's point of view in the hopes that doing so will cause the parties to alter their positions [Haynes, 1988, pp. 26–27].

distressed grievance procedures   *Labor Relations:* Accumulation of minor grievance cases that have reached the final step of ARBITRATION because they have not been resolved at any of the steps in the GRIEVANCE PROCEDURE.

Arbitration thus becomes a substitute for the grievance procedure rather than a means of strengthening it. Arbitrators themselves sometimes find ways of helping with short-cut procedures. Especially when the arbitrator is permanent, he or she may play a useful role in helping a union and company restore the effectiveness of the grievance procedure and reduce the case load [DOA].

distributive   Situation or condition in which there are few or no possibilities for joint gain in the resolution of a dispute, or in which the satisfaction of one party's interests is at the direct expense of another party's interest, thereby requiring a division or distribution of a contested resource. Roughly analogous to ZERO-SUM.

The term is also used to describe a style of negotiation associated with distributive situations. See DISTRIBUTIVE BARGAINING. Positional patterns of bargaining (and accompanying tactics) are also associated with distributive situations. In his critique of Fisher and Ury's [1981] PRINCIPLED NEGOTIATION, White [1984] notes that some situations are inherently distributive and therefore not suitable for principled negotiation, a technique he equated with concepts of INTEGRATIVE BARGAINING and INTEREST-BASED NEGOTIATION. For Fisher's response, see Murray, Rau, and Sherman [1989, p. 99]. A situation may be purely distributive, but rarely do parties have the same interests and utilities concerning the resolution of a particular issue. Whether or not a situation is distributive may be a function of the parties' perceptions and choices.

Contrast INTEGRATIVE AGREEMENT, INTEGRATIVE BARGAINING, and INTEGRATIVE ISSUES.

distributive agreement   Agreement to divide a fixed or limited resource, usually achieved through DISTRIBUTIVE BARGAINING.

distributive bargaining   Style of bargaining often called POSITIONAL BARGAINING to denote the pattern of positional demands, offers, and sequential concession making toward a mutually acceptable position (also called BIDDING). This pattern of bargaining emphasizes the series of positional commitments made by the parties in which a complete division is made of a fixed and limited resource, or "pie," whereby one for me is minus one for you. The parties are competitors and alternate demands and offers in an attempt to reach agreement on the division of the pie. The model example is a straight division of money. As a strategy, the goal is to elicit CONCESSIONS from the other side by lowering the opponent's expectations or the perceived utility of the opponent's options, by changing the opponent's attitudes [Pruitt and Lewis, 1977], and by using "adamant, directive, and controlled information processes" [Walton and McKersie, 1965, p. 381] in which the negotiators attempt to obtain information from the other side while attempting to withhold as much of their own information as possible. The resulting information is used to try to more realistically define the expectations of the other side and to modify the demands they are making [Edwards, 1981, p. 89]. Distributive bargaining tends toward ADVERSARIAL, competitive negotiations focusing on rights and power. Most DIRTY TRICKS are associated with this style.

This term and its opposite, INTEGRATIVE BARGAINING, are credited to Walton and McKersie [1965]. It is sometimes called *adversarial negotiation*. See BARGAINING for a more detailed discussion.

distributive issue   Issue that the parties to a dispute need never dispute again after settlement. Decisions regarding distributive issues are made only once and require no further interaction between the parties [McIsaac, 1985, p. 60]. Contrast INTEGRATIVE ISSUE.

diversity   Variability within a set or plurality; has a more positive connotation than *difference.*

In political parlance the term has come to denote a system or theory that values difference between and among individuals and groups in society under the belief that differences create a more dynamic and adaptive society. In conflict resolution, diversity often causes conflict. Competing interests of diverse groups can strain the plurality. Maintenance of the plurality requires that the interests of diverse individuals and groups be satisfied while all consent to and cooperate in the common objectives of the plurality. Similarly, awareness and respect for those who are different from oneself is considered to be a way to reduce conflict within the plurality.

Related terms: CULTURE, MULTICULTURALISM.

divide-and-choose procedure   Means of distributing a limited number of goods whereby one individual splits the goods into two groups and the second individual gets to choose first which group belongs to him [Raiffa, 1982, pp. 23–24].

divide and conquer   Negotiation strategy used to weaken opposing or blocking COALITIONS. The strategy is based on the idea that differences of interest among the members of an opposing coalition weaken their resolve and lessen their coordination [Pendergast, 1990, p. 138].

divorce mediation   Process whereby a third party helps divorcing couples to negotiate their own voluntary settlement.

Although typically the court retains jurisdiction over the divorce, the settlement terms are worked out in a mediation between the divorcing spouses rather than through negotiation between their lawyers. Divorce mediators help their client couples to identify the issues in dispute (child custody, support, property divisions, and so on), to identify and express their needs, to communicate their concerns, to generate alternative solutions, and to negotiate a resolution [Chandler, 1990, p. 331].

Technically, divorce mediation is a subset of FAMILY MEDIATION, the latter being inclusive of all family-related disputes and not just those accompanying divorce. Family mediation, however, is often loosely used synonymously with divorce mediation.

doctrine of mutuality (archaic)   *Law:* Now-defunct principle in arbitration law that required an award to provide something for both parties in order to be valid. There are current legal principles using the same term that are not as relevant to conflict resolution. See *ARBITRAMENTUM AEQUUM TRIBUIT CUIQUE SUUM*, ARBITREMENT.

documents-only arbitration   Arbitration held without an oral hearing and in which an award will be determined only on the basis of documents submitted by the parties. Although not common in commercial arbitration practice in the United States, it is common in other jurisdictions and in international commercial arbitration, particularly in matters where the costs of an oral hearing are not justified. Also known as *arbitration on documents.*

dominating   Using power to overwhelm the will of another; style of handling interpersonal conflict in which there is high concern for the self and low concern for others.

This style has been identified with a win-lose orientation or with forcing behavior to win one's position. A dominating or competing person goes all out to win his objective and, as a result, often ignores the needs and expectations of the other party. When the issues involved in a conflict are trivial, or when speedy decision is required, this style may be appropriate. It is also appropriate when unpopular courses of action must be implemented [Rahim, 1986, p. 84]. Compare COMPETITIVE.

doorknob price   *Negotiation:* Also called *deal point price.* Form of BRINKSMANSHIP. The doorknob or deal point price tells the opponent that he or she has only two choices: accept the last offer or allow negotiations to break down. In either case, the intent is to make the final decision entirely the responsibility of the opponent [Karrass, 1970, pp. 188–189; Edwards and White, 1977, p. 126].

dramaturgical analysis   Method of describing the development phases of any social process, including mediation, in theatrical terms.

In the dramaturgical view, the four phases of action are as follows: (1) providing a definition of the situation in the form of an idea to be acted out, (2) arranging for the staging by providing an area in which the action takes place and the resources, (3) recruiting the actors (if they are not already in place) and training them for their roles, and (4) enacting (in this case carrying out the mediation). There may be one or more instances of enactment, followed by a final phase in which the new meanings are assessed for the actors and the audience [Hare, 1992, p. 53].

dual mediation *Labor:* When the dispute is of such a nature that joint efforts by both federal and state mediators could be justified [Maggiolo, 1985, p. 53.]

dual-track strategy Dispute resolution strategy of pursuing two DISPUTE RESOLUTION PROCESSES at the same time, usually a binding adjudicative process, litigation, or arbitration, concurrently with a nonbinding conciliatory process. Though a dual-track strategy can create negotiating leverage (changing the other side's BATNA or using civil procedure to gain information through discovery), it can also raise the costs and increase hostilities.

***du-wrai* (Afghanistan)** Third party that performs mediator functions in *Waigali* society.

dyadic dispute processing DISPUTE RESOLUTION PROCESSES involving direct contacts between two parties, in contrast to unilateral actions by a disputant and third-party resolution techniques. Two major classes of options are available: COERCION and NEGOTIATION. Unilateral actions include inaction and active avoidance [McGillis and Mullen, 1977, pp. 6–24], while third-party resolution includes mediation and adjudication.

early neutral evaluation (ENE)   COURT-ANNEXED alternative dispute resolution process legally defined as "an early intervention in a lawsuit by a court-appointed evaluator, to narrow, eliminate and simplify issues and assist in case planning and management. Settlement of the case may occur at this stage" [Colo. Rev. Stat. Ann. § 13-22-302(2) (West 1996)].

Originally developed in the federal district court in the Northern District of California, the purpose of ENE is to help parties and their counsel determine the strengths and weaknesses of their case through a well-grounded neutral analysis. Although this process may promote settlement, the original and primary objective of the program is more to help the parties structure the litigation process by eliminating irrelevant issues and structuring more efficient motions and discovery activities to expedite an efficient resolution.

ENE is designed to target a case early in the formative stage of litigation before significant discovery has taken place. Usually, volunteer attorneys who have expertise in litigating the subject matter in dispute are appointed by the court to serve as evaluators. In a typical model, an evaluation session is scheduled approximately four months after case filing. At least seven days before the session, parties must submit written summaries of the case that identify the disputed issues and the preferred framework for discovery. The clients are ordered by the court to attend an evaluation session. The evaluation session begins with presentations by each attorney lasting fifteen to thirty minutes. Most conferences last approximately two hours. The case narratives and information exchange are extremely informal, the rules of evidence are not applicable, and the parties are not provided an opportunity for formal examination or cross-examination. The neutral identifies issues that are not in dispute and helps the parties enter into stipulations when appropriate. The neutral assesses the strengths and weaknesses of the parties' respective cases and evidence, then estimates, when possible, the probable outcomes with respect to liability and amount of damages. The neutral helps the parties plan future motions and discovery activities that will be more efficient and cost-effective.

Although the neutral's role in ENE is similar to that of a magistrate or SPECIAL MASTER in the organization of complex litigation, the neutral has no dispositive powers and is not involved with the case after the evaluation session. ENE appears to be most effective in tort and commercial contract cases, particularly where liability is clear and the only dispute is over damages. All communications in evaluation sessions are confidential.

ENE was specifically authorized under the CIVIL JUSTICE REFORM ACT OF 1990 and has now been adopted by many state and federal courts as a form of court-annexed ADR. Procedures vary considerably by jurisdiction. Although most jurisdictions use the evaluative function as a reality-testing device to encourage settlement, some jurisdictions stress the trial preparation functions of the neutral and allow evaluation only if expressly requested by the parties. ENE should not be confused with mediation, because the purpose in ENE is to get a third-party evaluation of the case to promote negotiation rather than to actively encourage the parties to fashion their own resolution. In practice, however, many neutrals engaged in ENE are trained to mediate and consequently lapse readily into mediation [Brazil, Kahn, Newman, and Gold, 1986]. ENE is sometimes referred to as *neutral case evaluation* or *case evaluation,* which might be distinguished either by not occurring early in the litigation or by its emphasis on evaluation rather than on pretrial case management. See CASE EVALUATION.

egalitarianism   Advocacy of equal rights for all.

Decision makers who adhere to this concept assess outcomes on their relative degree of equality [Frohlich and Oppenheimer, 1984, pp. 5–6].

elicit   Lure or draw out a response.

Term common in negotiation and mediation parlance and literature—for example, "elicit an offer." Also describes communication techniques of questioning and RESPONSIVE LISTENING designed to induce the subject to share information.

embargo   Governmental prohibition on trading with one or several countries; by analogy, used in negotiation to describe the refusal to deal with a particular issue.

Embargoes may range from total prohibitions to limitations applicable only to certain products. Embargoes are used to resolve conflict through economic coercion. By themselves, embargoes are rarely successful, requiring a strong COALITION of the target country's trading partners. Embargoes are usually accompanied by other techniques.

embeddedness Characteristics of relationships that reduce opportunities for misrepresentation and defection in negotiation.

In contrast to the GAME-THEORY view, negotiations are not carried out by anonymous parties making one-shot deals; they are *embedded* in a common social network. These people (1) have dealt with each other in the past, (2) know from personal experience how the other tends to act, (3) expect to have to deal with each other in the future, and (4) have a relationship overlaid with social content. To the degree that embeddedness is sustained, there is less opportunity for misrepresentation [Friedman, 1992, p. 151].

emergent mediation Informal mediation in which the parties and the intervener have ongoing relationships within the context of families, friendship groups, organizations of all kinds, and international relations. Most emergent mediation is done by people who do not formally consider themselves to be mediators but who voluntarily step in to resolve a conflict between their relatives, friends, and coworkers [Kolb, 1989].

emerging conflict Dispute in which no workable negotiation or problem-solving process has developed.

Moore [1986, p. 16] describes an emerging conflict as one in which the parties are known, the dispute is acknowledged, and most issues are clarified, but no dispute resolution process has been adopted. Such a conflict tends to escalate until a dispute resolution process is adopted, perhaps through the aid of third-party intervention.

empathic listening Technique of focusing on the other person and her perceptions and felt needs rather than on the overt communication or other communication going on between the communicating parties.

Sometimes used interchangeably with ACTIVE LISTENING but may more accurately connote a more passive technique. See LISTEN. Compare DIALOGIC LISTENING, RESPONSIVE LISTENING.

empathy Nonjudgmental understanding of another person's perceptions and viewpoint. It should be distinguished from ALTRUISM, which implies a voluntary act for the benefit of another, and from *sympathy*, which implies emotional identification with another person's plight. According to Mnookin, Peppet, and Tulumello [1996, pp. 218–219], empathy in negotiation involves the "capacity to demonstrate an accurate, non-judgmental understanding of another person's concerns and perspective." Thus empathy in this context involves more than merely an understanding of another's perspective; it involves the "non-judgmental expression of the other person's viewpoint in a way that is open to correction." In contrast, assertiveness is the ability to express and advocate for one's own interests.

empower   Enable.

empowerment   Result of enabling.

In conflict resolution, this term refers to the possibility and desirability of redressing POWER differences among the parties to the conflict [Avruch and Black, 1990, p. 221].

Cobb [1993, p. 250] defines empowerment as "a set of discursive practices that enhance the participation of disputants." From a narrative theory perspective, *participation* is the joint telling of the story by the disputants. Empowerment is a function of the narrative structures and narrative dynamics that shape the stories and their meanings. Empowering practices enhance the participation of the disputants in the co-creation of the story and its meaning, specifically by reducing the dominant effect of the first speaker's narrative and by avoiding the destructive narrative sequences that occur if the second speaker follows the natural tendency merely to attempt to rebut or otherwise respond to the first narrative with negative positions [Cobb, 1993, pp. 245–254].

Most commentators discuss empowerment in less complex terms and in the context of mediator practices. Empowerment activities by mediators include POWER-BALANCING TECHNIQUES (to encourage a situation in which each party has an equal ability to impose her will on the other), controlling the process (setting and keeping ground rules and moving through set stages toward agreement), and being NEUTRAL (that is, impartial or equidistant, so that the parties themselves feel in control of the dispute). In general, these activities allow the parties to deal with each other more effectively. Sometimes, however, they require the mediator to directly help the "weaker" party [Engram and Markowitz, 1985, pp. 23–24]. The extent to which empowerment, in this sense, by a mediator is acceptable practice may vary from one substantive area to another and is a source of considerable debate.

Along with RECOGNITION, empowerment is a crucial element in TRANSFORMATIVE MEDIATION and is defined by Bush and Folger [1994, p. 2] as "the restoration to individuals of a sense of their own value and strength and their own capacity to handle life's problems."

Law: Giving someone, such as an agent, the discretionary authority to act.

enemy images   Concept whereby internal factors (either within an individual or within a group) and external factors together create a mind-set in the parties that the opposing party is an enemy and should be treated as such, even though in reality the other party is not [Zisk, 1990, p. 687].

enforcement of award   *Arbitration:* Court enforcement of an arbitral decision.

The phrase, though common, is technically incorrect. In most jurisdictions, arbitrators cannot enforce their own awards because they are FUNCTUS OFFICIO after making the award and because they are not empowered to direct the police powers of the state to enforce the award. Instead, the party seeking to enforce the award may petition the appropriate court for confirmation of the award. By CONFIRMING THE AWARD, the court converts it into a court judgment, which it then enforces.

engagement agreement   Employment agreement, especially for independent contractors on a project of limited duration or scope.

Common term for the contract between mediators and disputants that usually details the role of the mediator, relationship to the parties, terms and responsibility for payment, and confidentiality. Also used by AD HOC ARBITRATORS in nonadministered arbitrations.

enlarged inquiry   See INQUIRY.

enmeshed couple   *Mediation:* Divorcing couple in which each partner has a heavy investment in the other's life, as expressed either through a desire to control or punish or through the inability to think in terms of an independent self [Haynes, 1986b, p. 32]. Used widely in behavior sciences and therapy and similar to codependence, enmeshment relates to a continuum, the opposite end of which is disengagement. It refers to a state in which family members lack firm boundaries, making it unclear, for example, whether they are speaking for themselves or for the other. Coined by family systems therapist Salvador Minuchin in 1974, the term is used by some divorce mediators to describe a particular type of couple susceptible to high conflict in divorce and difficult to mediate.

enquiry   See INQUIRY.

entrapment   Psychological process that occurs when an individual decides to continue with a course of action because she has already invested time, money, or other resources toward that course of action [Rubin, Brockner, Small-Weil, and Nathanson, 1980, p. 406]. Generally has negative connotations. Compare CONCORDE FALLACY, ESCALATION OF COMMITMENT.

This process makes it difficult for people to sever a relationship or to negotiate settlement of a lawsuit in which they are heavily invested, especially late in the litigation process after incurring much of the cost.

Law: Inducing people to commit a crime that they were otherwise not contemplating.

environmental dispute   Primarily disputes regarding specific projects or plans in a wide range of contexts: land use, natural resource management, air quality, and use of public lands, water resources, energy, and toxins [Sigurdson, 1986].

Often such disputes are prospective, concerning future policy or regulation of an environmental issue. They can also be retrospective, concerning something that has happened and how to repair the problem, such as who will pay for the cleanup of a toxic waste dump. Environmental disputes usually involve multiple stakeholders and complex technical issues.

environmental dispute resolution (EDR)   Alternative dispute resolution processes used to settle environmental disputes.

Most EDR involves some form of negotiation, facilitation, or mediation. EDR has proven increasingly popular in resolving disputes over the siting of hazardous waste facilities [Rabe, 1990, p. 3]. Through statutes or regulation, many U.S. jurisdictions either condone or mandate EDR for particular issues.

enunciation   *International Relations:* Procedure in which a third party clarifies the issues surrounding a dispute [Holsti, 1983, p. 421].

In clarifying, an outside party clearly enunciates its understanding of the issues involved and suggests basic principles, procedures, or mechanisms to achieve a solution or termination of the crisis. In essence, enunciation is third-party FRAMING that may help the disputants find common ground for DE-ESCALATION. It is useful only in a somewhat restricted range of situations and requires a quick and precise sense of timing and appositeness. Nevertheless, the resource requirements for this form of intervention are not great except in the area of knowledge and information, and the impact in successful cases might be substantial [Young, 1967, pp. 53–55].

equidistance   Extent to which a neutral third party can assist all parties equally.

Equidistance and IMPARTIALITY are generally considered the primary components of NEUTRALITY [Rifkin, Millen, and Cobb, 1991, pp. 152–153]. Equidistance relates to the evenhandedness of conducting the process and maintaining similar distance from the parties, while impartiality relates to the neutral's own ability to maintain an unbiased perspective. Compare IMPARTIALITY. Contrast BIAS.

equity   Principles of FAIRNESS, JUSTICE, and IMPARTIALITY.

Law: Application of principles of fairness to avoid unjust outcomes under strict application of law. In this sense, equity is distinguishable from the rules and procedures that developed as the COMMON LAW and were administered in separate *common law courts* as opposed to *courts of equity,* such as the Court of Chancery (now the Chancery Division of the High Court) in England.

erabi (Japan)   Negotiating attitudes associated with Americans that are incompatible with those of the Japanese.

Roughly, manipulation, a can-do attitude, or choosing. Used by Mushakoji Kinhide, a noted Japanese political scientist, who believes that the basic incompatibility between American and Japanese negotiators (which he, like many other Japanese observers, takes to be virtually axiomatic) derives from a fundamental philosophical difference in views about the relationship between humans and their environment. The American *erabi* style, he argues, is grounded in the belief that "man can freely manipulate his environment for his own purposes" [Cohen, 1991, quoting Kinhide]. This view implies a behavioral sequence whereby a person sets his objective, develops a plan designed to reach that objective, and then acts to change the environment in accordance with that plan. Little attention is paid by the *erabi* negotiator, according to Kinhide, to the need to cultivate personal relationships or to special circumstances. Choices are either-or and are made on the basis of instrumental or ends-means criteria alone [Cohen, 1991, pp. 30–31].

escalation   Sequential expansion of the scope or intensity of conflict [Geller 1990, p. 292; Pruitt and Zubin, 1986]; applied to social conflict generally to refer to increases in the severity of coercion used and the scope of participation [Kriesberg, 1998b]. Contrast DE-ESCALATION.

escalation of commitment   *Negotiation:* Tendency of negotiating parties to increase their commitment to the negotiation process, having invested substantially in preparation and actual sessions and often feeling pressure to reach an agreement.

Escalation of commitment sometimes involves rationalizing previous actions or psychologically defending oneself against perceived errors in judgment. In some cases, individuals may even go beyond mere distortion and actually enlarge their commitment or resources to a particular course of action as a means of justifying the ultimate rationality of an original course of action [Kesner and Shapiro, 1991, p. 373]. Compare ENTRAPMENT.

escrow   *Law:* Placing a document or other thing of value with a third party to be delivered to another upon the fulfillment of specified conditions.

escrow system   *Negotiation:* Technique of assuring the other parties that they will receive what is being offered by placing whatever it is in a position where those parties can reach it after fulfillment of certain conditions [Fogg, 1985, p. 347].

essence test   *Labor/Law:* Standard of judicial review for LABOR ARBITRATION awards.

The U.S. Supreme Court has stressed repeatedly that when courts are asked to enforce or vacate a labor arbitration award, they should not overturn the award merely because they believe the arbitrator was mistaken in his interpretation of the contract. But this deference has limits. According to the essence test, the arbitrator may look for guidance from many sources, yet his award is legitimate only as it draws its essence from the COLLECTIVE BARGAINING AGREEMENT. When the arbitrator's words manifest an infidelity to this obligation, courts have no choice but to refuse enforcement of the award [*United Steelworkers v. Enterprise Wheel and Car Corp.*, 363 U.S. 593, 597, 80 S. Ct. 1358, 4 L. Ed. 2d 1424 (1960)].

ethics   Relating to morals and moral choices; moral principles; a code of morality.

In the fields of mediation and arbitration, refers to professional conduct—the rightness or wrongness of the practitioner's actions. There are codes of ethics that have been developed by numerous dispute resolution organizations for many types of practitioners. None of these codes directly creates civil liability. Violation of court-connected codes, however, may result in the disciplining of the violating neutral, usually suspension or removal from the list of qualified mediators or arbitrators in the COURT-CONNECTED program.

ethics officer   See COMPLIANCE OFFICER.

Ethnic Conciliation Commission   Forum to address border and ethnic conflict in Central and Eastern Europe. Originally proposed by Raymond Shonholtz [1993] in 1991, these local commissions serve as forums for disputing parties to engage in productive dialogue based on needs, interests, and possible options, and to explore points of common or potential agreement. Each commission focuses on the creation of a physical place and visible process wherein disputing groups can express their needs. The first commission was created by the city of Plovdiv, Bulgaria.

ethnocentrism   View of things in which one's own group is the center of everything and all others are scaled and rated with reference to distance from one's own group. There are two facets to ethnocentrism. One involves orientation toward one's own group, or *in-group.* If one is highly ethnocentric, one sees one's in-group as virtuous and superior, and one sees one's in-group values as applying to everyone. The second facet of ethnocentrism involves one's orientation toward *out-groups*. If one is highly ethnocentric, one sees out-groups as contemptible and inferior, rejects the out-groups' values, blames out-groups for in-group troubles, and tries to maintain social distance from out-groups [Gudykunst, 1991, p. 66, citations omitted].

Ethnocentrism is a major contributor to conflict escalation. If acceptance of an out-group's legitimacy to deal, to be heard, or to have a point of view is crucial to the dispute resolution process, then ethnocentrism is a significant barrier to that process. As a result, identifying and managing ethnocentrism has become a major aspect of cross-cultural negotiation and mediation.

European Convention on International Commercial Arbitration   Treaty signed April 21, 1961, by many Western European countries in an attempt to harmonize domestic arbitration regimes and designed to supplement the enforcement and recognition of foreign arbitral agreements and awards under the NEW YORK CONVENTION. As a practical matter, this convention has had a limited impact, and many European countries have established unilaterally domestic legal regimes very favorable to INTERNATIONAL COMMERCIAL ARBITRATION.

European Court of Justice   Regional TRIBUNAL located in Luxembourg and empowered to decide cases arising under the treaties establishing the European Community, now the European Union.

evaluative mediation   See MEDIATION.

evasion   Act of AVOIDING, especially by artifice.
Negotiation: Utterance that maintains or increases the hearer's uncertainty about the speaker's intentions and, specifically, about the speaker's willingness to follow through on a threat or a promise. The speaker produces an utterance that influences the hearer not to form a belief about whether the speaker intends "W" or "not W" [Gibbons, Bradac, and Busch, 1992, p. 162].

evolutionary game theory   Repeat-play games used by game theorists in modeling social conflict. In the game, players are allowed to change strategy over time by trying different strategies and learning which ones work better than others [Schuessler, 1990, pp. 484–485]. Opposed to one-shot games. See GAME THEORY.

ex aequo et bono   "According to what is just and good."
Arbitration: Power explicitly conferred on arbitrators by the parties in their arbitration agreement or COMPROMIS, permitting the arbitrators to go outside the bounds of the law to reach a decision based primarily on concepts of fair dealing and good faith.

Parties in international disputes, public or private, must expressly state in the arbitration agreement that the arbitrator is authorized to decide *ex aequo et bono* to create this power. International legal authorities differ as to the definition of the term. Though generally used to describe a decision based on equity rather than on literal law, it is still guided by general principles and standards accepted by a majority of nations [DOA]. In this sense, the concept is somewhat analogous to EQUITY.

International Law: The International Court of Justice (ICJ) can make a decision *ex aequo et bono* if the parties agree [Article 38 of the Statute of the International Court of Justice]. Normally the ICJ applies rules of positive and customary international law. See AMIABLE COMPOSITION.

ex parte hearing, ex parte arbitration   Arbitration or hearing conducted without the participation of one or more of the parties. Most MODERN ARBITRATION STATUTES allow such arbitrations if the nonparticipating party has been given adequate notice. There is, however, no DEFAULT award in arbitration and the participating parties must present their respective cases.

ex parte proceeding   Proceeding that occurs without the participation of one or more of the disputants. Contrast with ADVERSARY PROCEEDING, in which decision makers have the benefit of hearing competing views.

exces de pouvoir **(French)**   *Arbitration:* "Excess of power." Basis on which the validity of an award may be challenged because the arbitrators exceeded the jurisdiction conferred on them by the arbitration agreement or compromis.

International Law/Arbitration: The question of excess of power or jurisdiction is a question of treaty interpretation. The award must be carefully compared with the relevant provisions of the compromis, which is the submission the powers have made of their dispute, and which is therefore the governing document in the arbitration [DOA].

exchange intensity   *Negotiation:* Numbers of demands and offers [Kritzer, 1991, p. 37].

exclusionary clause   *Labor/Arbitration:* Clause in a COLLECTIVE BARGAINING AGREEMENT that specifies that certain subjects, such as subcontracting, be excluded from the arbitration process [DOA].

Commercial Arbitration: Arbitration agreement that limits SUBSTANTIVE ARBITRABILITY might be referred to as a *restrictive* clause.

executive tribunal   Procedure whereby senior representatives of each party, generally with an independent chairman, form a tribunal. They listen to a presentation from counsel for each party and then try to reach a negotiated settlement. Also known as the MINI-TRIAL.

executory clause   *Arbitration:* Provision in a contract that provides for the arbitration of disputes that may arise in the future. Not enforceable under U.S. COMMON LAW, such clauses are now enforceable under federal and state MODERN ARBITRATION STATUTES. Same as FUTURE DISPUTES CLAUSE.

exhaustion of remedies doctrine   *Law:* Requirement that a disputant must exhaust other dispute resolution processes, usually administrative, before becoming eligible for judicial review, especially in administrative law.

existence conflict   Conflict in which the adversaries demand to be recognized as a distinct national entity [Agid-Ben Yehuda and Auerbach, 1991, p. 519].

expansion   Technique of improving communication and the flow of information often used by mediators who, upon receiving a message, expand and elaborate on it, feed it back to the listeners, and then check to verify their accurate perception [Moore, 1986, p. 169].

expected-satisfaction theory   Theory developed by Karrass [1970] to explain negotiating behavior. Willingness to negotiate depends on both sides' perception that there are potential gains in negotiation. Achieving satisfaction from an agreement must be more attractive than what might be achieved from not reaching agreement. The ability to achieve satisfaction is mutually dependent, that is, achieving a level of satisfaction through agreement that is greater than that of not reaching agreement depends entirely on allowing the other side to achieve an equivalent level of satisfaction. Negotiation can be described as a process of testing assumptions about the other side's satisfaction range [Karrass, 1970, pp. 144–145]. Compare BATNA, BOTTOM LINE, CONTRACT ZONE, PARETO-OPTIMAL, RESERVATION PRICE, RESISTANCE POINT, ZONE OF AGREEMENT.

expedited arbitration   Form of arbitration in which appointment of arbitrators, prehearing preparation, hearing, and award take place within a shorter period than is provided by statute or under the standard rules of the administering agency. Most arbitration laws give parties autonomy in setting times. Many administrative agencies have developed special procedures for expedited arbitration.

expert assessment   Process in which an independent third party with specific expertise is called on to give an opinion concerning a dispute.

This procedure is appropriate where the factual background to the dispute is relatively straightforward and the parties are relying on the particular expertise of the expert to settle their dispute. At times this decision is treated as final [Huleatt-James, 1992, p. 214]. Similar or equivalent to an ARBITRATION if the expert relies on the parties to present evidence and arguments. Compare FACT-FINDING.

expert fact-finding See FACT-FINDING.

FAA   See Federal Arbitration Act, United States Arbitration Act.

face   Positive social value, identity, image, or standing that one claims or perceives one has in the eyes of others, especially one's group.

Goffman [1955, p. 213–214] defined *face* as the positive social value that a person effectively claims by the role or characterization that he assumes during an encounter with others, who in turn acquiesce or accept the characterization. Thus the social value claimed is based on standing or identity that is tacitly negotiated and that is to the advantage of all the parties to maintain in social encounters. Face is a relational or situational concept that has the character of a social commodity.

In conflict, face issues are raised when people feel that their face is threatened, that is, when events, actions, or statements cast doubt on or have the potential to discredit a desired identity, such as capacity, strength, reputation, status, and so on, in the eyes of significant others. As conflict escalates, individuals are less likely to accept or maintain the other side's claims of face but are increasingly invested in their own. Threats to face may result from perceptions of public humiliation, personal disregard, unjustified intimidation, insults, patronizing airs, and contemptuous offers. Negotiators may have a significant investment in face, and third parties may be necessary to manage the resulting issues.

The term has roots in some Asian cultures where the development and maintenance of positive standing and image in the group has high value. Societies that stress face are characterized by an emphasis on relationships, family honor, and the personalization of transactions. Face plays a strong role in social stability, and loss of face can cause severe social disruption. Even today it is a prominent feature of both Chinese and Japanese cultures, in which elaborate mechanisms have evolved to protect not only one's own face but also that of others [Cohen, 1991, p. 24].

face maintenance   See FACE WORK.

face-restoration tactic   See FACE WORK.

face-saving tactic   See FACE WORK.

face-threatening tactic   Acts or statements that by their very nature run contrary to the face wants of the addressee, speaker, or both [Wilson, 1992].

One can distinguish acts that threaten negative face from those that threaten positive face [Wilson, 1992, citations omitted]. As a "tactic," the act or statement is consciously or subconsciously intended. Although face-threatening tactics might be including in FACE WORK, the latter seems to be used more in the context of face-maintenance activity and may imply "work" as a constructive activity, while the former has destructive connotations.

face work (face maintenance, face-saving tactics, face-restoration tactics)
Tactics employed to save, maintain, or restore FACE.

Goffman [1969, p. 12] defines face work as "the actions taken by a person to make whatever he is doing consistent with face" and distinguishes between behaviors that protect one's own face (*defensive*) and those that affect the opponent's face (*protective*). The following definition of face-saving tactics is defensive: "Anticipatory action taken by a party at risk to prevent, forestall, or block others from making him or her appear foolish, weak, or incapable" [Volkema, 1988, p. 6]. The following definition of face-saving tactics is protective: "The taking of an action or the making of a statement that permits the other party or its negotiator to back down from a position or to make additional concessions without being embarrassed. It is not at all unusual for a party or a negotiator to stubbornly refuse to act, even when that may be costly, rather than suffer personal embarrassment or a potential loss of respect from the other party, its negotiator, or others who might learn of the incident" [Schoenfield and Schoenfield, 1988, pp. 154–155].

It may be difficult to determine whether an action or statement is defensive or protective; in fact, some behaviors may be intended to serve both purposes. Also, it should be noted that actions can be oriented toward the destruction of an opponent's face. See FACE-THREATENING TACTIC.

In contrast to face-saving, which anticipates and prevents damage, *face restoration* is used to try to repair damage [Volkema, 1988, p. 6]. Another related term is *face maintenance,* defined idiosyncratically as follows: "In negotiation, the desire to project an image of capability and strength or conversely to avoid projecting an image of incapability, weakness or foolishness" [Brown, 1977, p. 276]. Examples of face-maintenance tactics include the following: "The development of rationalizations which the parties could use to justify withdrawing from commitments; demonstrations (sincere or contrived) of the present irrelevance of the commitment; the elaboration of mutual benefits to be had from moving beyond the fixated point of commitment; and the injection of a willingness to assume part of the responsibility for the ultimate termination arrangement" [Young, 1967, p. 43]. These and other tactics can be used by third parties as well as by the parties themselves to manage face issues that arise in a negotiation. As a term, *face maintenance* could be used as inclusive of both face-saving and face-restoration actions. This makes the term useful when, as so often is the case, it is difficult to determine whether the behavior is preventive or restorative.

facilitate   Make a process or action easier or less difficult. See FACILITATION.

facilitation, facilitator   Collaborative process used to help a group of individuals or parties with divergent views reach a goal or complete a task to the mutual satisfaction of the participants. "Facilitation helps parties reach a decision or a satisfactory resolution of the matter to be addressed" [1 C.F.R. § 305.86-3 App. (1993)].

In professional conflict resolution practice, facilitation is often closely associated with disputes over public resources or with the formation of public policy, in which there are many stakeholders formed into constituencies, each of which has representatives in the process.

Something or someone that facilitates is a facilitator. Definitions of facilitator are helpful in describing the process of facilitation:

- "A facilitator is someone at a meeting or the like who keeps the meeting on track, makes sure people get a chance to speak, enforces any ground rules, and stimulates discussion by asking questions" [Fisher and Ury, 1981, p. 61].

- "The facilitator functions as a neutral process expert and avoids making substantive contributions. The facilitator's task is to help bring the parties to consensus on a number of complex issues" [Kanowitz, 1986, p. 28].

Kanowitz's definition implies neutrality. It is important to note, however, that in common use facilitators include individuals who may have a stake in the substance. For example, many organizations have employees who serve as facilitators. The use of neutral facilitators is increasingly common, particularly by governmental agencies faced with public policy issues.

The distinction between a facilitator and MEDIATOR is often made. For example:

- "While often used interchangeably with 'mediator,' a facilitator generally conducts meetings and coordinates discussions, but does not become as involved in the substantive issues as does a mediator" [1 C.F.R. § 305.86-3 App. (1993)].
- "Facilitators are not expected to volunteer their own ideas or participate actively in moving parties towards agreement" [Singer, 1990, p. 24].

In practice it is hard to say when facilitation ends and mediation begins. During a mediation, a mediator may perform facilitator tasks, but this would be consistent with the definition and distinctions noted. In turn, however, many third parties engaged to facilitate use techniques associated with mediation when necessary. Compare GOOD OFFICES, CONCILIATION, MEDIATION.

facilitative mediation   See MEDIATION.

fact-finding, factfinding; fact-finder, factfinder   In the broadest sense, process of determining the facts relevant to the controversy and, as such, a crucial aspect of most dispute resolution processes.

In a narrower sense, fact-finding is an independent process in which a neutral third party, or fact-finder, investigates a dispute and issues a report establishing the relevant facts. Disputants may agree before or after the report to be bound by the conclusions, they may use it as a basis for settlement, or they may move to other processes.

Fact-finding operates on the principle that disputants tend to favor their own versions of the facts when the facts are contested. Fact-finding separates the function of defining the problem from developing a solution. It seeks to avoid the hardening of positions over contested facts so that parties can either move on to problem solving or seek agreement on a resolution based on principles. The fact-finder's neutrality lends persuasive power to the findings.

The fact-finder is a person or group usually with technical expertise who may be appointed by the disputants, as in joint fact-finding, or by a business, government, or court. The appointing body may limit the scope of the fact-finder's investigation and determination to particular areas in which the facts are controverted, especially highly technical areas. Legal definitions include the following:

- "A 'fact-finding' processing entails the appointment of a person or a group with technical expertise in the subject matter to evaluate the matter, present it and file a report establishing the 'facts.' The fact-finder is not authorized to resolve policy issues. Following the findings, parties may then negotiate a settlement, hold further proceedings, or conduct more research" [1 C.F.R. § 305.86-3 App. (1993)].

- "A process where a commission holds hearings to determine the facts revolving around an issue" [Wis. Stat. Ann. § 111.70(4) (West 1996)].

Fact-finding is becoming increasingly common in complex civil litigation, particularly in matters involving complex technical evidence or difficult computations. It has been used in class actions and mass tort claims.

Labor: Fact-finding is best known in the context of labor. In this context, there are variations of fact-finding in which the fact-finder also makes recommendations concerning settlement. Thus, the following legal definition holds: "An investigation of a dispute by a public or private body that examines the issues and facts in a case and may or may not recommend settlement procedures" [Colo. Rev. Stat. Ann. § 13-22-302(2.1) (West 1996)].

This kind of fact-finding is common in labor disputes, primarily those in public sector employment, in which the fact-finder recommends a resolution for each outstanding issue. An additional benefit of fact-finding in this context is that it prohibits changes in the status quo until the fact-finder has had an opportunity to investigate and report. Some statutes require INTEREST disputes to be submitted to a fact-finder, who issues recommendations either as a final stage in a series of processes or in advance of COMPULSORY ARBITRATION. See also INTEREST ARBITRATION. In addition to using an independent investigation and materials submitted by the parties, the fact-finder may hold hearings. In this context, fact-finding is similar to aspects of both MEDIATION and NONBINDING ARBITRATION. Mediators frequently make recommendations in the course of encouraging settlement. Advisory arbitrators use a quasi-judicial process to recommend a fair, just, and reasonable resolution to the dispute. Mediators usually couch their recommendations in the form of questions or suggestions, while neither mediators nor advisory arbitrators make their recommendations public. The unique feature of the fact-finding process in labor disputes, however, is that the recommendations of the fact-finder are usually made public under the rationale that public opinion will make the recommendations difficult to reject. [See, for ex-ample, 43 Pa. Cons. Stat. §§ 1101.801, 1101.802 (1993); Ore. Rev. Stat. § 243.722(3) (1993); N.J. Stat. Ann. § 34:13A-16 (West 1992)]. See FACT-FINDING BOARD.

International Law: Fact-finding is also well known in international disputes, where it is usually merged with the process of INQUIRY. Fact-finding is not specifically listed with the different steps of peaceful settlement in art. 33 of the UN Charter. In fact, only the word *inquiry* appears as a step between negotiation and mediation. In this context, and unlike fact-finding in labor disputes, fact-finding in international law is concerned only with ascertaining the facts and does not include the making of recommendations. This would be consistent with the limits on inquiry defined in the HAGUE CONVENTION FOR THE PACIFIC SETTLEMENT OF INTERNATIONAL DISPUTES of 1907 (Arts. 9, 35). Contrast CONCILIATION. Note, however, that many recent references to and uses of inquiry in international law refer to *enlarged inquiry* (see under INQUIRY), in which a finding of facts is accompanied by recommendations or conclusions of law.

Joint fact-finding refers to two different kinds of fact-finding processes. In PUBLIC POLICY DISPUTE resolution, facilitators often encourage the stakeholders to start by jointly gathering and determining the salient facts. In some cases, the parties will designate representatives to work together to develop responses to factual questions relevant to a controversy. In civil disputes, the parties may engage a neutral, mutually selected expert to make determinations on contested facts. This may avoid the impasses that arise in negotiation when the parties are using "dueling experts" in preparation for adjudication. In either usage, joint consideration of the results usually helps negotiators understand which alternatives are supportable.

fact-finding board, fact-finding panel   Group, panel, or committee appointed to engage in FACT-FINDING. Most commonly used in the context of fact-finding in labor disputes in public sector employment. The following is a legal definition:

> A process used in resolution of public collective bargaining agreements whereby the disputants select the members of the panel according to rules set by the labor relations board. The panel gathers facts concerning the dispute and makes recommendations for the resolution of the matter. The guidelines and rules of conduct are specified by the labor relations board, and the panel has the power to administer oaths. The recommendations of the panel may be rejected by either party, but failure to accept causes the dispute to be submitted to a conciliator for a final, binding decision [Ohio Rev. Code Ann. § 4117.14 (C)(3) (Banks-Baldwin, 1990)].

fairness   Being just to all parties; evenhandedness.

The concept of fairness permeates the dispute resolution literature and is fundamental to neutral THIRD-PARTY INTERVENTION. Fairness is explicitly articulated in the various ethical standards for mediation and arbitration practice (see citations under ETHICS). Commentators distinguish between PROCEDURAL and SUB-

STANTIVE FAIRNESS. While procedural fairness involves the relative fairness of the process used, substantive fairness involves the fairness of the content of the agreement or the outcome. In negotiations, Albin [1993, pp. 225–237] makes further distinctions between *structural fairness, process fairness, procedural fairness,* and *outcome fairness.*

There is tension between the need for and problems of trade-offs between fairness and efficiency, particularly in public policy disputes, leading some observers to include efficiency in determining the fairness of outcomes and others to equalize fairness with efficiency [Albin, 1993].

Although JUSTICE is often used synonymously with fairness, some commentators distinguish between the two concepts. Fairness is a more idiosyncratic concept, based in individual perceptions in the context of a particular conflict, process, and outcome. Perceptions of fairness may include partisan application of broader justice norms [Dworkin and London, 1989, pp. 3–6]. See also INTERNAL CRITERIA, IMPARTIALITY, PROCEDURAL FAIRNESS, SUBSTANTIVE FAIRNESS.

faksoro **(Rotuma)**   Literally, "to entreat, beseech; to apologize; to beg to be excused." A ritual of apology within Rotuman culture that, under most circumstances, must be accepted by the aggrieved party.

The island of Rotuma is located approximately three hundred miles north of Fiji in the South Pacific. The Rotuman people form a cultural enclave in the Republic of Fiji. Although Rotuman disputes are not infrequent and, in rhetoric at least, can be quite bitter, physical violence is a rarity on the island. *Faksoro* is a major factor keeping Rotuman disputes from escalating into violent confrontations. At least five gradations of *faksoro* can be distinguished:

1. A verbal apology in private (that is, on the spot) following an accidental occurrence in which one individual was in the wrong.

2. A verbal apology made in public. This lends greater weight to an apology because it constitutes a public admission of culpability. Typically such an apology would be made at a village or district meeting.

3. A formal presentation of a *koua,* "pig cooked whole in an earthen oven." Prepared this way, a pig is a sacrifice to the gods. Furthermore, according to Rotuman myth, a pig is a substitute for a human being.

4. A formal presentation of a *koua* plus a presentation of *kava,* the giving of a fine white mat (*apei*), or both. Both *kava* and *apei* are of central significance for Rotuman ceremonies.

5. The strongest *faksoro* an individual can make is called *hen rau'ifi,* "to hang leaves," referring to a garland of leaves that the person who

comes to *faksoro* wears around his neck. The person coming to *hen rau'ifi* is essentially offering his life in a plea for forgiveness.

When done properly, acceptance is virtually mandatory; aggrieved parties refusing a proper apology may be subjected to severe criticism. Those admitting culpability and accepting blame can gain compensatory status for doing *faksoro*, which is an honorable act. As far as disputes go, *faksoro* thus provides a means by which someone who finds himself in a weak or untenable position can escape the social effects of losing a confrontation and perhaps even gain a degree of status in the bargain [Howard, 1990, pp. 263–292].

false demand   *Negotiation:* Tactic in which a negotiator demands something of little or secondary utility in order to keep the other side from knowing what they want most.

family   Traditionally denotes a biological kinship unit, especially parents and children.

The term has been acquiring a broader, more inclusive definition in the dispute resolution literature, for example: "People who provide each other with emotional and economic support, protect one another, and intend to continue to do so permanently" [Lemmon, 1985, p. 6].

As the most fundamental unit in human society, the family provides a distinct arena for conflict and for conflict resolution skills acquisition. Many conflict resolution theorists and practitioners, especially mediators, focus on the family.

See, generally, Kantor and Lehr [1976].

Family Conciliation Service (Canada)   Social services program in the Province of Manitoba that helps resolve family disputes.

The service is a branch of the Department of Community Services and Corrections, the social services arm of the court. The court has the power to refer parties to a family conciliation officer, who helps them reach an agreement on disputed issues, such as the custody of children. The service operates independently of the court and includes both conciliation officers and family investigators [Helper, 1986].

family court   Court of law with limited jurisdiction to hear cases involving family-related matters. Some states have specialized family courts with jurisdiction over areas of *domestic relations law* such as divorce, child support, custody disputes, and other family-related matters (paternity, child abuse, and so on).

Some courts of general jurisdiction are referred to as family courts only when sitting in session as a special division specializing in family disputes.

family group conference (FGC)   Participatory process created as an alternative to formal legal proceedings before a court or government administrative agency for resolving family disputes and juvenile offender problems.

As a form of FAMILY GROUP DECISION MAKING, family group conferences were instituted in the late 1980s and early 1990s within the New Zealand legal system in order to match the expectations of the Maori culture and to build community responsibility for the resolution of youth and family problems. Youth crime concerns are now addressed primarily by the young person's family, the victims, their supporters, and the community, while child abuse and neglect cases are worked out by the family in collaboration with the social service agency. The family group consists of extended family members and close family friends, who meet privately to decide whether a child has been abused or neglected and to develop a plan for protecting the child.

Under the New Zealand child welfare law, the state is represented by a *care and protection coordinator,* who facilitates the meeting, represents the interests of the state, and monitors the conference in the best interests of the child. The coordinator sets the time and place of the meeting and has discretion over who should be in attendance. If the family members in the conference determine that the child needs protection, they can make recommendations and plans in accordance with the principles of New Zealand's child welfare law and are responsible for periodic review of the implementation. The coordinator seeks approval from the appropriate authorities to implement the conference recommendations. If consensus is not reached on implementation, the coordinator may reconvene the conference to enable its members to reconsider their plans. Out of 10,720 conferences in 1991, only 652 did not result in some agreement over what should happen with the child in question. If there is no agreement, or the coordinator is unable to obtain the agreement of implementing authorities, the coordinator reports to the referring authority, which in turn pursues appropriate recourse. Thus, while FGCs are the primary mechanism employed in child protection cases, they are not the final forum.

The process is drawing increased attention from RESTORATIVE JUSTICE advocates in the United States and other countries, and many jurisdictions are experimenting with various adaptations of it, particularly in juvenile offenses. Family group conferencing in New Zealand, however, has been criticized as ignoring the conflict of interests that may exist between family interests and the child's interests. The Mason Report expressed concern that "bringing the wider whanau [that is, the extended Maori family] and other players under the umbrella of the Act has increased the number of competing interests and in our view has rendered the child or young person increasingly vulnerable" and recommended administrators and coordinators of these processes stress the child's interests as paramount [Durie-Hall and Metge, 1992, p. 75].

Compare JUVENILE ARBITRATION, JUVENILE CONFERENCE COMMITTEES, SENTENCING CIRCLES, VICTIM-OFFENDER RECONCILIATION PROGRAMS. See also RESTORATIVE JUSTICE.

family group decision making   Concept that the entire family, including extended family and close friends, should participate in resolving disputes involving a family member, usually a child, and in which the state has intervened. The primary vehicle for this concept is the FAMILY GROUP CONFERENCE, in which the problems addressed may range from child abuse to juvenile delinquency. The concept is supported by FAMILY SYSTEMS THEORY and the belief that it is more efficient and in the better interests of the child and family for relatives to reach a consensus on the way to handle the problem rather than for the state to act unilaterally [Pennell and Burford, 1994].

family mediation   General category for all mediation between family members over a familial matter or domestic dispute as opposed to a business matter. Usually used interchangeably with its subset, DIVORCE MEDIATION, as in the following legal definition: "Mediation of family matters, including married and unmarried persons, before and after judgments involving dissolution of marriage; property division; shared or sole parental responsibility; or child support, custody, and visitation involving emotional or financial considerations not usually present in other circuit civil cases" [Fla. Stat. Ann. § 44.1011 (West Supp. 1992)]. Although most family mediation involves divorce, it can include disputes between parents and children or other family members and other types of domestic conflict such as disputes over inheritance. Although the term excludes commercial disputes between family members, it is often difficult to divide the familial relationship issues from the business dispute.

Family Mediation Association (FMA)   Predecessor organization to the ACADEMY OF FAMILY MEDIATORS, FMA focused on STRUCTURED MEDIATION, a form of divorce mediation.

Family Mediation Canada   Membership organization for family mediators based in Ontario, Canada.

family systems theory   Theory that postulates that family members are interconnected in such a system that when one member changes, it has an impact on the others. This is an important concept in family mediation. Virginia Satir [1964] is credited with coining and popularizing the term.

Some theorists use family systems theory to postulate that in spousal abuse cases the roles of abuser and victim are interrelated and have complementary needs that must be fulfilled to maintain the set patterns of a relationship [Corcoran and Melamed, 1990, p. 306].

farmer-lender mediation   During a farm finance crisis in the mid-1980s and early 1990s, the federal government supported, and many states facilitated and in some cases mandated through legislation, mediation between farmers and creditors to help resolve issues surrounding foreclosure on farms, such as debt restructuring, forbearance, and planned liquidation in some cases.

fast-track arbitration   Same as EXPEDITED ARBITRATION.

fatwa **(Islam)**   Formal statement of proper conduct based on the interpretation of religious laws [Ihromi, 1988, p. 155].

feasible outcome set   Method of displaying the collection of all possible settlements as a set of points in a plane.

The set is like a two-dimensional CONTRACT ZONE. The points in the feasible outcome set are not the settlements themselves but rather the utilities associated with the settlements [Tutzauer, 1992]. Compare PARETO-OPTIMAL.

Federal Arbitration Act   Term commonly used to denote what is officially referred to as the UNITED STATES ARBITRATION ACT.

Federal Mediation and Conciliation Service (FMCS)   Service established as an independent agency of the U.S. federal government under Title II of the Labor Management Relations Act of 1947 to mediate and conciliate labor disputes in any industry affecting commerce other than those occurring in the railroad and air transportation industries.

The United States Conciliation Service had operated since 1913 as a function of the office of the secretary of labor. One of the major responsibilities imposed on the service by the Labor Management Relations Act of 1947 was the prevention of labor-management disputes. In an effort to follow this concept of prevention, the service has sought to provide labor and management assistance in the form of PREVENTIVE MEDIATION on a year-round, voluntary basis. The service also makes available full and adequate governmental facilities for conciliation, mediation, fact-finding, and voluntary arbitration. These functions are in accordance with the service's own published regulations, or with those procedures specified in the labor agreements of the parties [DOA].

The service's mediators, located across the country, also mediate complaints brought under the Age Discrimination Act and has become increasingly active in DISPUTE SYSTEM DESIGN. The service can intervene on its own motion or by invitation of either side in a dispute.

fighting   Method of dispute resolution connoting a physical struggle as parties contend to assert their superiority so as to impose their solution. The term is commonly used to describe nonphysical clashes of power as well.

final bargaining   Flurry of bargaining activity and movement initiated by negotiators late in negotiations in an attempt to reach agreement before a deadline. The deadline may be dictated by external forces or arbitrarily imposed by the parties. Mediators might set deadlines in order to encourage final bargaining behavior [Moore, 1986, p. 227].

finalization   *Mediation:* Concluding stage of the mediation process in which the mediator prepares either a written memorandum of understanding or an outline of the agreement reached. Participants and the mediator discuss the agreement and make necessary changes. When the parties appear to be satisfied with the understanding, significant others (such as children, in the case of divorce mediation, but rarely) may be invited to participate [Cramer and Schoeneman, 1985, p. 45].

final offer   See TRANSMISSION OF FINAL OFFER.

final-offer arbitration   Form of SPECIAL-FEATURE ARBITRATION in which the arbitrator must choose between one of the final offers submitted by the two parties. This differs from conventional arbitration, in which the arbitrator is free to fashion any award she deems appropriate. Also referred to as BASEBALL ARBITRATION, LAST-BEST-OFFER ARBITRATION. See variations: MODIFIED FINAL-OFFER ARBITRATION, MULTIPLE-OFFER SELECTION, REPEATED-OFFER SELECTION.

The primary objective of final-offer arbitration is to encourage a negotiated settlement. By eliminating the arbitrator's ability to compromise, it increases the risk that one side will be completely successful at the expense of the other. The increased risk should cause the parties to be more reasonable in their settlement proposals because they are also trying to make them appeal to an objective, rational arbitrator if the negotiations fail.

fixed award   See AGREED AWARD.

fixed pie   Limited resource over which parties are contending and must find a way to divide among them. The notion of a fixed pie graphically describes a win-lose or ZERO-SUM situation in which every piece one side gets is one less piece the other will get.

fixed threat *Negotiation:* Communicated proposition to do something negative in the eyes of the other party from which, when made, it is difficult to back down. An example of this would be if a buyer is unhappy about the sale price for a house, the buyer can threaten to walk away from the sale entirely [Raiffa, 1982, pp. 15–16]. See BRINKMANSHIP.

FMCS See FEDERAL MEDIATION AND CONCILIATION SERVICE.

focal neutrality *Mediation:* Unlike absolute NEUTRALITY, involves mediator conduct that is case-specific and context-specific, with different interests deserving priority at different points in the same case. May entail intervening in the relations between disputing parties, or responding to the two parties differently. A response to feminist critique of divorce mediation, which maintains that absolute neutrality is unfair in situations characterized by power imbalance before mediation [Benjamin and Irving, 1992, p. 137].

focal point Those issues in a dispute that are particularly important to the parties jointly.

For Iklé [1964] and Lax and Sebenius [1986], focal points are particularly prominent alternatives for settlement rather than prominent issues:

- "These focal points are like a notch where a compromise might converge, a resting place where rising demands might come to a halt, or a barrier over which an initial proposal cannot be budged. In tacit bargaining, focal points help the parties to coordinate their expectations and positions. In negotiation, since coordination can be achieved through the exchange of proposals, focal points serve to reduce the alternatives that the parties might consider" [Iklé, 1964, p. 213].

- "A psychologically prominent position which negotiators naturally gravitate towards due to their ease to work with or compliance with social norms or principles of fairness (e.g., equal division, round numbers, compensation based on hours worked)" [Lax and Sebenius, 1986, p. 126].

The term comes from optical physics and describes a point at which rays can either converge or diverge.

focus/downplay *Negotiation:* Tactic of giving false clues to focus attention on items of less interest and to downplay items of real interest. In doing so, the negotiator makes it appear that the item of real interest has less value to the client than it really does. If successful, the negotiator will obtain the desired item at a lesser cost because the other party underestimates its value to the negotiator's client [Schoenfield and Schoenfield, 1988, pp. 149–150]. Compare FALSE DEMAND.

Ford Motor Company Consumer Appeals Board   Consumer dispute resolution program that provides an opportunity for Ford automobile owners to have service complaints judged by an independent authority without having to resort to court action.

The Board concept is relatively simple. Any owner of a Ford product whose dealer is in a state represented by a board and who has a service complaint about her Ford vehicle can request a board review of the problem regardless of the vehicle's age and mileage. Each FCAB consists of five members: three consumer representatives, a Ford dealer, and a Lincoln-Mercury dealer. Presentations to the board are in writing; oral arguments by customers, dealers, or company representatives may be made only at the invitation of the board. Importantly, Ford and its dealers are bound by the board's decisions, but customers are not and thus remain free to go to court if they remain dissatisfied [Henry, 1983] (see ASYMMETRICALLY BINDING ARBITRATION).

Many state LEMON LAWS, designed to give consumers direct recourse against car manufacturers, require consumers to go through these manufacturer's dispute resolution mechanisms before submitting to a state-sponsored panel or to a court. See also LEMON LAWS, AUTOCAP.

foreign arbitral award   Arbitration award made in one country and enforced in another.

There is no universally accepted definition of a foreign arbitral award. For various purposes, different legal systems depend on such differing criteria as the territorial principle, the nationality of the parties involved, or the nationality of the procedural law used in the arbitration [DOA].

Foreign Trade Arbitration Commission   Official dispute resolution body in the former Soviet Union established in 1932. It handled transactions in all types of commercial disputes in which one of the parties was a foreign national. Decisions were generally based on documents only, although witnesses were admitted at the arbitrator's discretion.

Most former Soviet states and satellite states had similar arbitration administration agencies with exclusive jurisdiction over transnational commercial disputes involving state agencies or between these states. Since the breakup of the Soviet Union and the democratization of Central and Eastern Europe, these agencies have lost jurisdiction and have been trying to redefine their roles.

forgive   Absolve or pardon.

forgiveness Willingness to abandon one's feelings of resentment, revenge, negative judgment, indifferent behavior, and condemnation toward one who unjustly injured oneself while fostering the undeserved qualities of compassion, generosity, and even love toward that person [Enright, Freedman, and Rique, 1998, p. 47.

Forgiveness involves a perceived injustice or offense about which the offended person willingly chooses to let go of negative affect. It is a unilateral act in which the offended person substitutes compassion for resentment, respect for condemnation, and goodwill for revenge. Some practitioners and theorists are examining forgiveness as a crucial phase in dispute resolution or an independent dispute resolution process. See RESTORATIVE JUSTICE, VICTIM-OFFENDER MEDIATION.

formula-detail approach *Negotiation:* Analysis developed by Zartman and Berman [1982] that presents negotiation as a three-stage process: the diagnostic phase, the formula phase, and the detail phase. The diagnostic phase includes prenegotiation activity, such as cost-benefit analysis, leading to the realization that a negotiated solution is possible. The formula phase is characterized by a search for general principles, or formulae, defined as "a shared perception or definition of the conflict that establishes terms of trade, the cognitive structure of referents for a solution, or an applicable criterion of justice" [p. 95]. In the detail phase, parties bargain over how they will implement the formula agreed to in the previous phase [p. 199]. This phase involves offers and demands, concession making, convergence, and formal conclusion. Because the detail phase consists of what most people associate with negotiation, it is often assumed to represent the entire negotiation process [Habeeb, 1988, pp. 28–31].

formulation Communication technique, sometimes exercised by mediators, of commenting on and offering interpretations of a conversation in progress, using such techniques as REFRAMING, PARAPHRASING, and summarizing. Formulations preserve relevant features of prior utterances while also recasting them. Formulations have five primary characteristics: they (1) preserve meaning, delete extraneous details, and transform information; (2) function to manage topical talk; (3) function to manage roles; (4) imply a decision from the recipient in the form of confirmation or disconfirmation; and (5) reduce emotional levels.

Mediators may use formulations to further mutual understanding and to define the conflict. In this context, formulations can be used to clarify meanings, soften or minimize the use of harsh language, change the topic, switch the conversation from one speaker to the next, reframe an utterance into a proposed solution, force a party to look carefully at statements she has made, emphasize points of agreement or disagreement, and maintain control of the mediation process [Wall and Dewhurst, 1991, pp. 65–67, citations omitted].

forum   Place for meeting or discussion; the meeting or discussion itself.

Though the term has long been used to refer to a court or tribunal, it is becoming increasingly used interchangeably with *process* to refer to any dispute resolution process involving a discussion.

fractioning, fractionating, fractionation   Problem-solving technique of breaking up a single issue into several smaller, more manageable issues. May be used several ways to facilitate resolution. By disengaging issues from one another, the parties may be better able to deal with matters on their merits. By reducing a dispute into elements, the parties can build trust for settling the more agreeable parts first or merely reach an agreement on issues while referring the more difficult issues to another process [Fogg, 1985, p. 339; Bailey, 1971, p. 18].

frame, framing   Conceptualization or behavioral principles or standards, as in "frame of reference." It can be the meaning or definition an individual assigns to an issue, or the decision maker's understanding of the consequences of actions and choices. Framing reflects individual biases and interpretative paradigms.

Each bargainer enters the negotiation with fields of vision or frames of reference that help her construct meaning or make sense of the situation. Although scholars differ in their exact definitions of *frame* and REFRAMING, both concepts refer to the way negotiators come to understand their situation. Framing is a key to deciphering how bargainers conceive of an ongoing set of events in light of past experiences, and it affects their substantive and procedural expectations and biases.

Framing can be discussed in the context of THIRD-PARTY INTERVENTION. In this context, third parties develop frames to guide them in choosing an intervention procedure. Four kinds of frames are associated with third parties:

1. *Right-wrong frame:* The problem requires identifying one party as right and one party as wrong, based on the rules or norms that apply to this particular dispute. In other words, a discrete choice is required.

2. *Negotiation frame:* Trade-offs and compromises can be made so that a negotiated solution is possible.

3. *Underlying conflict frame:* This particular conflict is only symptomatic of a more important, ongoing problem between the two parties.

4. *Stop frame:* This dispute must be stopped. Resolving the issues is of secondary importance to making the conflict go away.

These frames can be culturally based views of the world. Frequently such frames are fictions created by a third party either for some ulterior motive or out of habit [Sheppard, Blumenfeld-Jones, and Roth, 1989, citations omitted; see, generally, Putnam and Roloff, 1992].

Framing is also a communication technique. Framing includes attempting to influence another's conceptualization of an issue by conveying a message in a certain way. Thus Coulson's [1968, p. 40] definition: "The vivid use of language to describe an issue, such as the use of a metaphor, used in order to make the issue and solution stand out in an arbitrator's mind."

Reframe: In its broadest sense, a realignment of a frame of reference. In this sense, reframing is a mental or emotional activity in which a person changes his interpretation of the conflict. Qualitatively different frames may help reduce perceptions of conflict and promote resolution.

In a more specific use, reframing refers to a communication technique, sometimes used by mediators, to help disputants reframe (in the broader sense) the conflict to facilitate resolution. See FORMULATION.

frustration   Emotional response to perceived interference in achieving goals; dissatisfaction with the prevailing status quo. As such, frustration is either the same as or gives rise to a GRIEVANCE, may lead to a DISPUTE, and is indicative of CONFLICT.

functus officio   Task performed.
Arbitration: Any officer who has fulfilled the duties and functions of her office or whose term of office has expired becomes *functus officio,* that is, she no longer has official status or authority. The doctrine of *functus officio* as applied to arbitration has meant the termination of an ad hoc arbitrator's authority after rendering and delivering her award [DOA].

funnel approach   Graduated technique of questioning to elicit a broad range of information from uncooperative or reluctant sources. It begins with asking general, usually open-ended questions that evoke narrative responses. After these questions, accompanied by encouragement, exhaust the speaker's willingness or ability to disclose information, continually narrower, more direct questions are posed, seeking more specific or detailed information [Schoenfield and Schoenfield, 1988, p. 97]. As a last resort, the questioner may use leading questions.

future disputes clause   *Arbitration:* Clause in a contract that provides for arbitration to resolve disputes that may arise during the life of the contract. Also called an *executory clause.*

Historically, the courts deemed such clauses unenforceable under U.S. COMMON LAW as an "attempt to oust the courts of their rightful jurisdiction" and therefore contrary to public policy. This COMMON LAW HOSTILITY to arbitration in the United States was reversed with the passage of MODERN ARBITRATION STATUTES in most states and at the federal level during the twentieth century. Like all arbitration agreements, the future disputes clause should state what disputes or subject matter the parties will refer to arbitration. Clauses range from broad to narrow. A broad agreement makes any and all disputes subject to arbitration. There may be some issues that are neither subject to compromise nor arbitrable as a matter of corporate policy, such as ownership rights to intellectual property or quasi-criminal activities such as fraud. There may be types of remedies that one would want to be able to pursue immediately without consultation with the other party, such as a temporary restraining order for misuse of a confidential customer list. A clause that limits the scope of disputes referable to arbitration is NARROW OR RESTRICTED (also known as or accompanied by an EXCLUSIONARY CLAUSE in COLLECTIVE BARGAINING AGREEMENTS).

Future disputes clauses can range from being either *bare* or *detailed*. A bare clause simply states that arbitration is the process of choice, but it contains no details on applicable ground rules or procedures. A detailed clause contains specific ground rules and procedures to be followed in the process. Detailed clauses typically incorporate the rules of an ADMINISTERING AGENCY. For example, a typical, broad future disputes clause providing for binding arbitration under American Arbitration Association rules would read like this: *Any controversy or claim arising out of or relating to this contract, or breach thereof, shall be settled by arbitration in accordance with the Commercial Arbitration Rules of the American Arbitration Association, and judgment upon the award rendered by the Arbitrator(s) may be entered in any court having jurisdiction thereof.* An arbitration clause covering claims "relating to" the contract is broader than a clause covering claims "arising out of" the contract.

***gaiatsu* (Japan)**   Foreign negotiating pressure. Often arises in trade negotiations, especially with the United States.

The Japanese government has historically awaited the influence of *gaiatsu* before taking action on international trade matters. Foreign pressure gives Japanese politicians a means to justify, in the eyes of the Japanese public, action to open its markets to foreign products. In U.S.–Japan trade negotiations, the scenario often is the United States presses Japan for change of some sort and the Japanese government responds with some concession, portraying it as a victory over opposing domestic pressures.

game theory (theory of games, game-theoretic models, gaming, matrix games, distribution games, games of economic exchange, role-playing debates, substitute debates, game experimentation, utility-bargaining theory models)   Method of mathematical analysis applied to games of strategy to determine which of several choices of strategy is likely to maximize gain or minimize loss. Games of strategy, such as chess or bridge, are distinguished from games of pure chance, such as dice, by requiring players to anticipate outcomes of decisions made by both themselves and other players.

As an approach to understanding conflict, the goal of game theory is to model a conflict situation in a way that both captures and simplifies the fundamental elements of that situation [Kritzer, 1991, p. 80]. Game theory is not a theory of negotiation. Rather, game theorists approach negotiation as if it were a game of strategy, and they use game theory to analyze the efficacy of particular negotiation strategies in particular bargaining situations. Because of the complexity of most multiparty games, most game theoreticians focus on two-person games, typically expressed in the form of a matrix that sets different pay-offs for different choices of strategy by the players. The choice of strategy by each player will affect the payoff for the other. If the players play only one move, choice of strategy is based on anticipating the strategy of the other player. If, however, players know or believe there will be opportunities for repeat play, strategy can change in reaction to how the other side has played in previous moves. This consequence of *repeat play* underlies Axelrod's [1984] theory that cooperation results from the anticipation of reciprocal actions (see later discussion of Repeated Prisoner's Dilemma).

Game models provide some predictive insight into player behavior and strategy choices in negotiations, but the models otherwise have limited use. The fixed-payoff hierarchies are not necessarily consistent with real-world choices, and often there is no relationship between the predictions made in the mathematical models and the actual behavior of individuals in interpersonal situations. It boils down to differences between payoff and utility. Payoff is a concept expressed in quantitative terms, such as money, years in prison, or points. Utility, however, is a far more subjective concept because it refers to satisfaction or value. For one person, prestige may have far greater utility than money. The payoffs in the matrix may not reflect the utilities to the player. Additionally, game models assume player rationality and restrict the effect of communication between players. These characteristics ignore often important problems in real-world decision making.

Most games can be classified as follows:

Zero-sum or nonzero-sum. Game theory focuses on a payoff to the participants, and in a two-person game the payoffs fall into two categories. If a person's winnings equal the other's losses, this is a ZERO-SUM game. If the payoffs (both positive and negative) do not add up to zero, this is a NON-ZERO-SUM game.

Cooperative or *noncooperative*. Game-theoretic models of bargaining have generally been classified as either cooperative (*axiomatic*) or noncooperative (*strategic*). In cooperative games, parties have a shared interest, but in noncooperative games they have distinctly opposing interests [Kritzer, 1991, p. 87]. For purposes of understanding bargaining in the litigation context, noncooperative games are clearly the most appropriate, particularly noncooperative games under conditions of uncertainty. Stevens [1963, p. 154] defines cooperative games as those in which the players have complete freedom of preplay communication, whereas in noncooperative games the players are not permitted to communicate. The aspect of game theory to which the theory of negotiation is most closely related is preplay communication in cooperative games.

Static or *dynamic.* A static game is one in which the players choose strategies at a given point in time. Dynamic games, conversely, involve adopting strategies sequentially over time so as to obtain temporal optimality. Similarly, a one-shot or single-play game would be static, while a repeat-play or iterated game would be dynamic [Chatterji, 1992, p. 123].

Determined or *probabilistic.* Facts, constraints, and utilities are fixed in the determined game. In contrast, a game is probabilistic when random error in the utility function or constraint may exist due to lack of information [Chatterji, 1992, p. 123].

Strategic or *passive.* Strategic games are those in which the opponent is a rational, active player. Passive games are those in which the opponent is naive and does not retaliate [Chatterji, 1992, p. 123].

There are many different game models, each with its own name. However, the game that has had the greatest influence on negotiation theory is the Prisoner's Dilemma (or Negotiator's Dilemma)—a large class of games in which, if every player acts *rationally* in his individual interest, everyone is worse off than if each acts in the collective interest. The most common scenario involves two persons, A and B, taken into custody for collaborating in a crime. While in their separate cells and unable to communicate with each other, each can turn state's evidence and betray the other (*defect*) or remain silent (*cooperate*). Each prison sentence depends on what both prisoners do, and neither knows what the other has done. If neither defects, they will both be convicted of a minor offense with a minimal penalty (such as a brief jail term). If one defects and the other does not (that is, one turns state's evidence and the other pleads not guilty), the former will be released and the latter will go to jail for a long time. If both defect (that is, plead guilty so that there is no need for one to turn state's evidence), both will go to jail but will receive reduced sentences in return for pleading guilty. Without the ability to communicate, neither prisoner wants to "take the entire rap" and each is under considerable pressure to defect even though both will be better off if neither confesses than if both confess. Thus, according to Axelrod [1984, p. 7], "the pursuit of self-interest leads to a poor outcome for all."

Of particular interest is the Repeated (or iterated) Prisoner's Dilemma—a version of Prisoner's Dilemma in which the game is repeated an indefinite number of times with the same players. The game and strategy can change considerably if the players play (or anticipate playing) more than once. Each choice will influence the future choices of the other player, that is, strategies are interdependent and based on RECIPROCITY. To avoid endless punishment in the iterated version of the game, the players seek to establish some level of cooperation based on reciprocity. A reciprocal strategy would be to make choices that influence cooperation by the other side. One example of such a strategy is

TIT-FOR-TAT, in which a player cooperates on the first move. In each successive move, he mimics the previous move of the other player. If the other player cooperates, he cooperates, and if the other player defects, he defects. The player thereby sends a signal to the other player that he expects reciprocal cooperation. See Axelrod [1984].

Tit-for-tat is one of a great number of strategies identified through game theory. One influential strategy is known as GRIT or GRADUAL RECIPROCATION IN TENSION REDUCTION. In his work in evolutionary biology, Dawkins [1989] has coined a number of terms describing different player strategies. He divides players into *hawks* (aggressive, competitive, predatory) and *doves* (nonaggressive, cooperative).

See SIMULATION.

***Gamsabhawas* (Sri Lanka)**   Village councils exercising both conciliatory and informal adjudicative powers in Sri Lanka (formerly Ceylon).

With origins dating back to 425 B.C., these councils encouraged AMICABLE SETTLEMENT and had the coercive force of traditional village society. After the British took control in the late 1700s, *Gamsabhawas* were viewed as alternatives to official courts. Their judgments, however, could be appealed to official courts. The Charter of Justice of 1833 recognizes the *Gamsabhawas* as providing a legitimate alternative to regular judicial proceedings. Unfortunately, British and subsequent administrative and economic policies ultimately undermined traditional village structures and eroded the influence of the *Gamsabhawas*. More recently, the government of Sri Lanka has shown an interest in revitalizing the concept through village tribunals or conciliation boards and has passed several laws creating village councils or tribunals whose main function is to effect amicable settlement of disputes [Pe, Sosmena, and Tadiar, 1988, pp. 21–30].

GATT   See GENERAL AGREEMENT ON TARIFFS AND TRADE.

General Agreement on Tariffs and Trade   Commonly known as the GATT, this agreement regulated international trade among its member states. The GATT had as its principal purpose the reduction of tariffs and other barriers to trade among nation-states and provided for the resolution of trade disputes among signatory states. The GATT itself was never entered into force. Rather, the GATT formed the framework for a web of agreements to which GATT member states agreed. The last version of the GATT resulted from the so-called Uruguay Round, begun in 1986 and not completed until 1994. The Uruguay Round agreements made sweeping and controversial changes in the way international trade disputes are settled among nation-states and resulted in the WORLD TRADE ORGANIZATION. See also NORTH AMERICAN FREE TRADE AGREEMENT.

general dispute resolution   Rarely used term inclusive of a number of dispute resolution processes both within and outside the court system. Includes informal procedures common in state-sponsored adjudication, such as small claims court and minor offense procedures, judicial settlement conferences, and offers to settle, as well as court-annexed and court-referred ADR processes and private ADR processes [Gold, 1991]. Thus the term is broader than ALTERNATIVE DISPUTE RESOLUTION but not as broad as DISPUTE RESOLUTION.

general war   Military conflict that satisfies three criteria: (1) the participation of a leading power, (2) the participation of at least half of the other major powers, and (3) the attainment of a conflict intensity level exceeding one thousand battle deaths per one million population [Levy, 1985, pp. 344–374]. Compare WORLD WAR.

generic theory of conflict   Theory that conflict comes from unmet universal, human needs. Hence, studies of generic theory of conflict address human needs such as identity, security, recognition, and distributive justice [Kestner, Devonshire, and Kim, 1988, p. 60].

Geneva Convention   Generic term attached to any multilateral international agreement drafted or executed in Geneva, Switzerland.
   International Relations: Most commonly used to refer to an international agreement initially drafted in 1864 and subsequently revised that set forth standards of conduct for nations at war.
   International Commercial Arbitration: Refers to both the Geneva Protocol on Arbitration Clauses, September 24, 1923, 27 LNTS 157, and the Geneva Convention for the Execution of Foreign Arbitral Awards, September 26, 1927, 92 LNTS 301. These international agreements on international commercial arbitration were the forerunners of subsequent more effective conventions such as the United Nations CONVENTION ON THE RECOGNITION AND ENFORCEMENT OF FOREIGN ARBITRAL AWARDS.

German Social Courts   Courts of the former German Democratic Republic (East Germany) set up in 1953 as *conflict commissions* (KONFLIKTKOMMISSION) to settle industrial disputes. In 1968 they were renamed *social courts* with additional jurisdiction over criminal offenses and civil disputes. They were distinct from the SOVIET COMRADES' COURTS (see also WORKERS' COURTS OF THE SOVIET UNION) in being fully integrated into the formal legal system. The social courts were responsible to the formal courts, to which appeal was available; their procedure was highly regulated; and only the formal courts could enforce their decisions. Criminal offenses could be referred only from the law enforcement authorities. Compared to the Soviet courts, the social courts were also much less inquisitorial, depending instead on mediation and the voluntary cooperation of litigants [Marshall, 1985, p. 59].

global familism   Concept that all human beings on earth are members of a global family and jointly responsible for the maintenance of peace [Pauling, Laszlo, and Jong, 1986, vol. 1, pp. 370–371]. The term is not widely used.

global integration   Process whereby the world's diverse economic, communication, social, cultural, and political systems are purportedly gradually developing into a single unit [Pauling, Laszlo, and Jong, 1986, vol. 1, p. 373]. With respect to conflict, this *globalization* causes significant tensions and increased tribalism as entities attempt to resist integration and the threat of cultural and sovereign erosion. Conversely, the process increases interdependence, which deters violent and destructive means of conflict resolution.

global war   Military conflict that is the result of a system's periodic structural crisis. A long period of capability deconcentration leads to a lack of leadership and greatly increased competition among rising powers. The outcome is a sequence of interrelated wars of generational length in which all global powers become involved [Modelski, 1984]. Compare GENERAL WAR, WORLD WAR.

goal   Purpose or object of a given effort or endeavor, conscious or unconscious.
    In much of the literature, the term is often used synonymously with OBJECTIVE and INTEREST, but there are useful distinctions. For example, a goal has the connotation of an ultimate end sought, such as winning the war, while objectives are accomplishments necessary for the attainment of the goals, such as destroying the enemy's industrial capacity or defending this territory. Usually expressed as personal or group needs, interests justify the goal and are satisfied by the attainment of the goal (such as need for personal freedom or need for essential resources such as food or water).

goal congruence   Extent to which the private goals of the negotiator and the goals of the party that is represented by the negotiator correspond. Applicable whether a negotiator represents an individual or a particular group or class of stakeholders as in labor negotiations. The more congruence there is, the higher will be the probability that an agreement reached by the representative or negotiator will be accepted by the constituents and complied with. Contrast AGENT-PRINCIPAL DIVISION.

goal orientation   Factor that dictates a negotiator's strategy, thereby affecting the content and pattern of his tactics. As used by Brett [1991, p. 305], for example, a negotiator's goal orientation may be cooperative (focusing on maximizing mutual gain), competitive (seeking to maximize the difference between his own and the other party's gains), or individualistic (holding only his own gains as important). A particular goal orientation motivates the approach toward gain.

In common usage, goal orientation is a competitive style of negotiation, as in "he's so goal oriented."

Golden Rule   Guiding principle or basic principle of action; usually associated with a maxim in Christian doctrine to "do to others as you would have others do to you" (Matt. 7:12; Luke 6:31).

In GAME THEORY, it is the strategy of always cooperating. Considered a risky guiding principle because one cannot always depend on others to respond to one's lead, particularly in single, nonrecurring encounters.

Compare BRASS RULE, SILVER RULE, TIT-FOR-TAT.

good faith   Honest or sincere intentions; lack of intent to defraud; honesty in conduct or adherence to the norms of fair dealing.

In conflict resolution, good faith is an imprecise, abstract term, largely subjective in its interpretation and application. Disputants' perceptions of each others' good faith are usually crucial for agreement. According to Iklé [1964, pp. 111–113], negotiating in good faith means not taking a position certain to obstruct agreement and not being predisposed always to obstruct an agreement, but to propose terms that one would want accepted and to conform to customs of accommodation.

Law: There is no legal requirement per se to negotiate the settlement of a dispute in good faith except in labor negotiations. In *N.L.R.B.* v. *General Electric Co.*, 418 F.2d 736 (2d Cir., 1969), cert. den. 397 U.S. 965 (1970), a "take our initial proposal or leave it" tactic was found not to satisfy the requirement to negotiate in good faith under the Labor Relations Act (see BOULWAREISM).

In COURT-ANNEXED or COURT-REFERRED ADR processes, local rules and individual court orders directing the parties to participate may also impose a requirement of good faith participation and efforts to settle. Failure to comply may be sanctionable conduct. See BAD FAITH.

good guy/bad guy (good cop/bad cop routine, Mutt and Jeff play, Pat-and-Mike ploy, sugar-and-spice role play)   *Negotiation:* Tactic in which one negotiator plays the "bad guy" (unreasonable and aggressive) while his partner plays the "good guy" (reasonable and sympathetic). The bad guy takes a hard line and rejects the other side's concessions while the good guy apologizes and suggests additional concessions in order to placate the bad guy. A single negotiator can even use an "unreasonable" absent client as the bad guy. Fisher and

Ury [1981] describe this as a form of psychological pressure, which Craver [1993] classifies as a DIRTY TRICK.

good offices   *International Relations:* Dispute settlement procedure in which a respected third party (individual, state, or international organization) acting on request or on its own initiative seeks through diplomatic means to persuade the disputing parties to meet and engage in direct negotiation or establish bilateral relations [DOA]. Although used loosely in other contexts, the term is mostly limited to international relations and the resolution of disputes between states.

Good offices can be offered on the third party's initiative, at the request of one or both of the disputing states or other states, or in response to an obligation or an authority imposed or granted by international agreement. In the absence of treaty obligations to the contrary, the offer of good offices can be rejected by one or more of the disputants. Rejection does not create a right to intervene forcibly. Traditionally, internal or civil conflict is generally not a subject for good offices.

The term has been in diplomatic and judicial use for some time; Chief Justice John Marshall of the U.S. Supreme Court used the term as far back as 1812 [*The Schooner Exchange* v. *M'Faddon,* 11 U.S. 116, 3 L. Ed. 287, 7 Cranch 116 (1812)]. According to the definition of *good offices* in the PACT OF BOGOTA, the task of the third party is to bring the parties together so that they may arrive at a solution themselves [DOA]. The good offices of a third power were frequently used in the nineteenth century to start the process of reconciliation between two powers, and so the resolution of particular disputes. For example, the good offices of the British government were used to resolve the dispute between Portugal and Brazil over Brazilian independence in 1825, and between the United States and France over the interpretation of the Treaty of France. In recent times, this function has been more frequently filled by an international personage, such as a representative of the UN Secretary General.

The HAGUE CONVENTIONS FOR THE PACIFIC SETTLEMENT OF INTERNATIONAL DISPUTES of 1899 and 1907 contain specific provisions establishing good offices as a means of dispute resolution (Arts. 2–8). The UN Charter does not refer to good offices specifically. It has, however, become increasingly common for the UN Secretary General to perform good offices either in response to a request from a competent organ of the United Nations or on his own initiative within the competence of his office. The Secretary General's practice is limited to attempts to bring the conflicting parties to the negotiating table without interfering in the negotiations themselves [Raman, 1977, p. 591].

In its original legal sense, good offices denotes a particular step in a series of procedures that were established to settle international disputes peacefully and that flow from traditional public international law as ascertained by conventions, treaties, practice, and doctrine. In the most limited sense, a third, usually neutral state merely urges parties to begin direct discussions. In a broader sense, the state acts as a go-between and conduit of communications between states that had no direct diplomatic relations. Nowadays, the term covers a range of both legal and political activities taken to bring about or initiate negotiations, promote understanding between nations, or merely reduce the effects of conflict. Good offices, however, is not synonymous with mediation because it does not include active participation in the discussion of the substance of the dispute; but the terminology is not strictly applied, and good offices and mediation are sometimes used indifferently. Indeed, the Hague Conventions treat good offices as if it is interchangeable with mediation. The Pact of Bogota (Arts. IX–XIV), however, treats the two methods as distinct.

The *Encyclopedia of Public International Law* [1992, pt. 1, p. 67] makes a distinction between *technical* and *political* good offices, noting that the distinction is not clear-cut and that the two types may be combined. *Technical good offices* include activities that facilitate communication between the parties, acting as a go-between, inviting the parties to conferences, and facilitating the convening of such conferences. These activities are intended to restore bilateral direct contact between conflicting parties when diplomatic relations have broken off, and to represent the interests of one of the parties in the country of another. *Political good offices* is a much broader term that includes all intervention activities by states to facilitate a solution. This category would include appeals for peace or an armistice, calls for negotiations or the holding of a conference, and intervention into the substance of the conflict. Thus inquiry, conciliation, mediation, and arbitration would be other forms of political good offices. It seems useful, however, to maintain some distinction between good offices and these other third-party processes. Otherwise the term would include all third-party activities intended to bring about peaceful resolution of a dispute between states. So, to the extent that a mediating state is helping the parties reach agreement on the structure of the negotiation process, these activities would be included in the definition of good offices. Similarly, a third party helping the conflicting parties implement mutually accepted procedures for peaceful settlement is engaged in good offices. However, a third party engaged in functions unique to these other processes, such as determining the facts, making recommendations, or issuing awards, is no longer acting within the strict definition of good offices [Probost, 1989, pp. 1–6]. Sample definitions of good offices in this narrower sense include the following:

- "The procedures whereby third parties act as channels of communication between the opponents, passing messages between them. In addition, the third parties may propose sites for formal diplomatic sessions and urge the antagonists to begin formal discussions" [Holsti, 1983, p. 417].

- "Action to bring about or facilitate negotiations but without participation in the discussion in the substance of the dispute. Mediation is basically the same thing, only it includes getting involved in the substance of the dispute" [*Report of a Study Group. . .*, 1966, p. 31].

- "The action taken to bring about or initiate negotiations, but without active participation in the discussion of the substance of the dispute. In this restricted sense, good offices are a mediation of more limited scope. But the terminology is not exactly applied, and good offices and mediation are sometimes used indifferently" [*Report of a Study Group. . .*, 1966, p. 72].

- "A procedure for international dispute resolution whereby a third party is given the limited role of bringing the parties into communication and facilitating their negotiation" [Bilder, 1989, p. 481].

- "The role of the friendly third party is less active, being to tender its services in order to bring the parties in conflict together, and to suggest in general terms that the conflict be resolved, without itself actually participating in the negotiations or conducting an exhaustive inquiry into the various aspects of the dispute. Hence, once the parties have been brought together for the purpose of working out a solution of the conflict, strictly speaking, the party tendering good offices has no further active duties to perform" [Starke, 1968, pp. 95–96].

- "The good offices role is even more passive than mediation. It could be limited to providing a place for meeting, or a chairman of a meeting. Where the parties will not meet, it could be merely conveying of messages between them. It is the closest approximation to negotiation, and the farthest from judicial processes. Of all techniques it implies the least intervention in the dispute" [Burton, 1990a, pp. 155–156].

- "The efforts of one or more States (or organizations or individuals) directed, in the presence of a tense situation between other States, towards maintaining peaceful relations or, if necessary, inducing these other States to resume negotiations without, however, taking part in such negotiations themselves" [Probost, 1989, p. 2].

- "Good offices are preliminary procedures in which a third party attempts first, to bring together the disputants and then attempts to clarify the essential elements of a dispute. These techniques have been employed often in international diplomacy" [Zeif, 1983, p. 622].

The narrower definition of good offices provides a nice theoretical distinction and might be preferred so that the parties know the boundaries of the process they have chosen. There are practical reasons, however, for allowing the term its broader meaning, which includes mediator functions. The broader definition allows for the role of the third party to adapt to the changing circumstances surrounding the dispute [*Handbook on the Peaceful Settlement. . .*, 1992, pp. 33–40].

governing law   Substantive and procedural law applicable to a particular legal dispute. Determined by the application of conflicts of laws principles or specified by the parties to a contract in their CHOICE-OF-LAW CLAUSE.

In arbitration, the applicable procedural law governs the arbitral proceedings or procedure. Examples are laws of states or countries that establish procedures for conducting the arbitration, enforcing the AWARD, and guarantee due process rights for the parties (see LEX ARBITRI). If the arbitration agreement or the CONTAINER CONTRACT specifies the applicable procedural law or the governing law of the contract, through a choice-of-law clause, that law will usually prevail. See *Volt Information Sciences, Inc.* v. *Board of Trustees of Leland Stanford Junior University* [1988] (to the extent that it does not conflict with federal law, state procedural law in a choice-of-law clause prevails over the federal arbitration law). If the parties have not designated applicable procedural law but have designated a location for the arbitral proceedings, the procedural law of the country or state in which the arbitration takes place will usually prevail. If the parties have not determined in their agreement where the arbitration is to take place, the question is commonly decided by the arbitrator using conflicts-of-laws principles [DOA].

In contrast, the *applicable substantive law* is applied by an adjudicator in defining and determining the merits or issues in a dispute. In the United States, arbitrators are usually free to determine domestic commercial disputes without the strict application of substantive law unless the parties specify its application. In international commercial arbitration, application of substantive law may be required for subsequent enforcement. If the parties in their contract have not decided on the APPLICABLE LAW, the place of arbitration may become an important factor among others in determining what law the arbitrators should apply in resolving the dispute [DOA]. The term may also refer to the substantive law of arbitration that may limit enforcement of arbitration agreements and awards over certain issues that are deemed not to be arbitrable in the jurisdiction.

government mediation   Mediation between local or municipal governments.

In the United States, this form of mediation is usually over comprehensive planning conflicts. Some states, such as Florida and Georgia, provide for such mediation by statute [Price and Woods, 1990, p. 18].

gradual reciprocation in tension reduction (GRIT)   Strategy involving a unilateral commitment to incremental conciliatory actions or concessions over a period of time to reduce hostilities, initiate cooperation, and facilitate negotiation between bitter, long-term adversaries [Osgood, 1962, 1971].

Typically, the GRIT user announces an intent to cooperate, invites the other side to participate, and makes a series of announced, progressive, unilateral, and conciliatory actions to reduce perceived threats to the other side. The user is committed to continual incremental concessions over time, and reciprocal action by the other side is not a precondition to an announced conciliatory action. The objective is to foster enough trust to persuade the adversary to reciprocate and thus set in motion a spiral of tension reduction.

GRIT differs from TIT-FOR-TAT in that the latter strategy dictates cooperative moves, other than the initial move, only if the other side reciprocates with a cooperative move. The other side's failure to respond with a cooperative move will induce a punishing move. Compared to GRIT, tit-for-tat could more easily result in a continuous spiral of negative moves. In addition, it is harder to maintain a cooperative initiative with tit-for-tat [Betz, 1991, p. 678].

See GAME THEORY.

grievance   Real or supposed injury or circumstance that provides grounds for a complaint.

In common usage, the term can also refer to the actual complaint made by the aggrieved party. In conflict resolution theory, authorities maintain a distinction between grievances and complaints wherein the former gives rise to the latter. Some sample definitions of the former include the following:

- "An individual's belief that he or she is entitled to a resource which someone else may grant or deny" [Miller and Sarat, 1980–1981, p. 527].

- "A problem that affects a particular person but which may or may not have a particular person or group as the cause of the problem" [Lieberman and Henry, 1986, p. 426].

- "A grievance is a belief that one has a right, an entitlement, to corrective action with regard to a problem. A grievance is a state of mind, an opinion arrived at, presumably after reflection and discussion of the problem with others. The term 'complaint' often is used interchangeably with grievance" [Ladinsky and Susmilch, 1983].

Labor: Formal complaint made by an employee or his union representative against the employee's employer in the belief that the employee has been wronged in some area or aspect of his employment. The grievance may result from some harmful or disciplinary action against the employee by his employer. Any complaint of an employee relating to his job, pay, working conditions, or the way he is treated is generally considered to be a grievance. A grievance may also be a complaint that an employer has against a union or union officials [DOA]. Although in its broadest conception in the labor setting a grievance is any complaint about the employment relationship, the word may be more specifically defined by a labor agreement or statute. For example, a grievance is "any complaint by any employee or labor organization concerning any matter relating to the employment of any employee, or by any employee, labor organization or agency concerning the affect or interpretation, or claim of breach, of a collective bargaining agreement, or any claimed violation, misinterpretation, or misapplication of any law, or rule, or regulation affecting conditions of employment" [5 U.S.C.A. § 7103(9) (West, 1993)].

Thus, disputes involving the proper interpretation or application of the provisions of the collective bargaining agreement are grievances, and while an employee may have a complaint about an employment condition, it is not a grievance if it complies with the provisions of the agreement. So, all grievances are complaints, but not all complaints are grievances. Such definitions narrow the occurrence of grievances to unionized settings, although some labor agreements do not contain grievance procedures and some nonunion work settings have grievance-like procedures [Lewin and Peterson, 1988, p. 2].

grievance arbitration, rights arbitration   Use of arbitration to resolve grievances in employment relationships, especially where there is a COLLECTIVE BARGAINING AGREEMENT containing a GRIEVANCE ARBITRATION CLAUSE (see also GRIEVANCE). Grievances may range from discipline and discharge to minor violations of the contract, such as coffee breaks or wash-up time. The arbitrator acts as a quasi-judge to determine the meaning of the contract that the parties have established as the law of their relationship and to clarify and interpret its terms. He may also decide if the grievance in question is covered by the contract and if the penalties are just. The arbitrator's jurisdiction is frequently limited to those disputes involving the interpretation or application of the contract. However, the grievance procedure prior to arbitration may allow consideration of a wider range of disputes. Arbitration in almost all contracts is the last step in the grievance procedure [DOA].

INTEREST ARBITRATION is distinguished from grievance arbitration in that the former covers arbitration over new contract terms while the latter covers disputes regarding compliance with an existing contract [*International Bhd. of Elec. Workers* v. *Graham County Elec. Coop.*, 783 F.2d 897 (9th Cir. 1986)]. Contrast INTEREST ARBITRATION.

grievance arbitration clause   Provision in a contract between a union and a company that makes arbitration the last step in a grievance procedure [DOA]. A sample statutory definition is as follows: "A voluntary agreement by the two parties to engage in the process of arbitration over only the meaning or application of the terms of the actual written collective bargaining agreement" [Wis. Stat. Ann. § 111.70(4) (West 1996)].

grievance mediation Use of mediation to resolve grievances in employment relationships, especially where there is a collective bargaining agreement. Usually provided as a step in the grievance procedure in an effort to settle the dispute before it reaches arbitration [DOA].

grievance procedure Steps, usually established in a contract, for the effective handling of complaints made by employees or employers against each other [DOA]. An internal, multistep mechanism for an employee to complain about his work or working conditions and obtain a fair hearing without jeopardizing his job. Without a grievance procedure and the right to strike, the only forum left for resolving alleged contract violations is the court system.

Grievance procedures usually consist of a series of procedural steps to be taken within specified time limits. These procedural steps may vary from contract to contract. Most procedures found in labor agreements, however, are very similar. A grievance may be taken by the aggrieved employee to the foreman, and if no settlement is reached, the employee may appeal it through successive steps in the management hierarchy. The grievant may be represented by various union officials. Smaller companies tend to have shorter grievance procedures, consisting of two or three steps, usually concluding with arbitration. In larger companies, or in the case of multiplant contracts, the process may include grievance committees with union-management representatives, followed by joint boards, which are in turn followed by PERMANENT UMPIRE systems [DOA]. Grievances involving established policy and precedent are expected to be settled at lower steps, while grievances calling for new policy or precedent and grievances that are too "hot" for lower-step settlement end up in the higher steps.

The procedure should be orderly from the initial presentation of the grievance through varying levels of appeal, with the primary intent to settle the dispute before it reaches the final step of arbitration. In this sense, the grievance procedure recognizes that labor agreements are not easily applied and interpreted in the context of day-to-day operating problems. Thus it provides a forum for continuing collective bargaining to resolve questions and differences of opinion on how a provision should be applied to a specific situation [Simkin, 1971, pp. 7–8]. There is still debate as to whether the grievance procedure, up to and including arbitration, is actually part of the collective bargaining process, or whether it is essentially the administration or adjudication of particular established rights [DOA].

Because virtually all labor agreements contain a grievance procedure, it is not surprising that the term is used most in relation to unionized work settings and collective bargaining. In this narrow sense, the procedures may be available only to complaints that qualify as *grievances* under the labor agreement. See GRIEVANCE. The term is increasingly being used in a more general sense to denote any set of multistep, complaint-handling procedures based on similar principles. Thus the term might include mechanisms established by large governmental and private organizations for their nonunionized employees and even for their clients. With respect to the latter, a number of prisons, high schools, universities, and hospitals have adopted procedures for responding to clients' complaints.

Finally, Moore [1986, p. 253] has formulated an expansive definition that includes those mechanisms created by mutual agreement, such as but not limited to labor agreements. But the definition may exclude unilaterally created mechanisms for nonunion employees and clients:

> A grievance procedure is a process disputants identify to manage disagreements that arise during or as a result of the settlement's implementation phase. The establishment of a grievance procedure is often a functional prerequisite for initial settlement. Parties often believe that a grievance procedure gives them a way to redress new problems, to modify agreement if necessary, and to avoid abandoning the entire settlement because of difficulty implementing a small component of the settlement.

grievant   Individual with a GRIEVANCE.

Labor: Employee who registers a complaint against his employer. *Grievant* is a term used for the most part only in an employment setting where specific machinery has been established for the hearing of such complaints—usually a unionized setting [DOA].

grieve   Have or bear a GRIEVANCE.

Labor: To invoke the grievance machinery to correct a wrong that an employee believes he has suffered, especially in a unionized setting [DOA].

GRIT   See GRADUAL RECIPROCATION IN TENSION REDUCTION.

Grotius, Hugo (1583–1645)   Dutch scholar known as the "father of international law."

In Books 2 and 3 of *De Jure Belli ac Pacis,* his famous work, Grotius proved the antiquity of, and demonstrated the reasonableness of, international arbitration as a dispute settlement method. "For if," he wrote,

> in order to avoid trials by judges who were not of the true religion, both Jews and Christians appointed arbitrators of their own, and it was recommended by St. Paul, how much more ought to be employed to avoid war, which is far more injurious? . . . And for this reason as well as for others, it would be profitable,

nay rather in a certain manner it would be necessary, that there be certain assemblages of the Christian powers, where controversies might be settled by disinterested parties: and that steps even be taken for compelling the disputants to accept peace in accordance with just laws [DOA].

grounds of nullity   Bases on which the validity of an arbitration award may be challenged and vacation of the award sought [DOA]. Under most MODERN ARBITRATION STATUTES, the grounds of nullity for commercial arbitration awards are strictly limited. See VACATING AN AWARD.

group decision support systems (GDSS)   Systems that combine communication, computer, and decision technologies to support the decision making and related activities of work groups. GDSSs provide technical features aimed at removing common communication barriers, such as anonymous input of ideas and preferences, electronic message exchange between members, voting solicitation and compilation, and common viewing screens for idea display [Poole, Shannon, and DeSanctis, 1992, p. 48–49]. See COMPUTER-AIDED MEDIATION.

grouping   Technique used by mediators and facilitators in which common issues or ideas are combined into logical units. In addition to helping the disputants communicate more easily about the substantive issues, there are numerous possible benefits. For example, the grouping of common issues reduces the number of issues to resolve, while the grouping of common ideas may help package solutions and make decision making more efficient [Moore, 1986, p. 169].

groupthink   Phenomenon by which highly cohesive groups tend to make unwise decisions precisely because their high degree of cohesiveness leads individual members, who may be harboring private reservations about the wisdom of some recommended course of action, to keep those reservations to themselves. The result is often a group decision in favor of some risky course of action that is counter to the private views of dissenting group members [Rubin, 1991, p. 219]. Coined by George Orwell in *1984*.

haggling Often used synonymously with BARGAINING; connotes arguing, especially over terms or amounts of money. Sometimes referred to as *bazaar bargaining*. See BARGAINING.

Compromise technique in positional bargaining initiated by admittedly flexible starting positions followed by many alternating, incremental concessions until the point of compromise or settlement is reached [Iklé, 1964, p. 208].

Hague Convention for the Pacific Settlement of International Disputes, Hague Convention of 1899 and 1907 Common, less formal names for the CONVENTION ON THE PACIFIC SETTLEMENT OF INTERNATIONAL DISPUTES.

Hague Tribunal *International Relations:* Permanent Court of Arbitration established by the Hague Peace Conferences of 1899 and 1907. See PERMANENT COURT OF ARBITRATION.

haku **(Hawaiian)** Third party who guides the traditional Hawaiian dispute settlement technique, HO'OPONOPONO. Although the *haku* is usually a respectable family elder intimately known to the disputants, she may also be an outsider, such as a traditional healer, minister, or social worker [Pe, Sosmena, and Tadiar, 1988, pp. 4–5].

halo effect Favorable, sympathetic approach a person takes to evaluate those things that she identifies as being related to herself or as being related to people or events that she views favorably. EMPATHY in this latter sense can be achieved by demonstrating that she shares such things as attitudes, values, associations, conduct, and even vocabulary. Psychologists sometimes refer to this as *congruence*. The tactical method of congruence is to discover and call attention to the shared acquaintances, experiences, backgrounds, values, and the like so as to induce the other to assume that one will regard all matters from the same perspective [Goldman, 1991, pp. 176–177].

Hanseatic League Confederation of German cities (Hanse Town) formed to promote collective commercial interests and provide mutual protection. The league lasted from the second half of the twelfth century to the latter part of the seventeenth century. It promulgated a code of maritime law and provided for compulsory arbitration among its members.

hard-line *Negotiation:* Firm, uncompromising position.

hard-liner One who adopts a firm, uncompromising position.
   The term is mostly associated with foreign policy, such as "a person who supports militant internationalism but opposes cooperative internationalism" [Wittkopf, 1987, pp. 131–159].

Harmony Among Neighbors Dispute Service (HANDS) Community-based dispute resolution program in Minneapolis, Minnesota.
   Volunteer residents are trained to serve on panels that help their neighbors express and resolve disputes. They undergo a twenty-six-hour training in communication, teamwork, collaborative problem solving, prejudice reduction, and a structured panel process method of conciliation. The underlying vision of HANDS is not the mere settling of disputes. Instead, participants seek to strengthen neighborhoods and build the capacity of the community to solve its own problems [Gerber, 1991, p. 91–93].
   See NEIGHBORHOOD JUSTICE CENTER, COMMUNITY BOARDS, COMMUNITY DISPUTE RESOLUTION.

Harvard Program on Negotiation (PON) See PROGRAM ON NEGOTIATION (PON).

hearing Any proceeding in which witnesses or interested parties are heard for purposes of either adjudication or decision making.
   A hearing might be distinguished from a trial in that the former is relatively less formal than the latter. Sometimes a hearing may be used in reference to interim proceedings before a judge prior to a final trial before a jury, such as a hearing on a motion. Legislatures and administrative agencies hold hearings.

Hearings have some common characteristics: they are usually public or at least open to interested parties, adjudicators or decision makers are present, and persons affected are given notice and an opportunity to be heard.

Adversarial hearings are when all parties in a dispute are present and make arguments in support of their respective positions.

EX PARTE HEARINGS are when one or more of the disputing parties is absent from the presentation of arguments by others.

Arbitration: Oral presentation of a case, held privately in COMMERCIAL ARBITRATION.

hegemonic war   Mechanism for realigning through a newly emerged distribution of power the way in which the international system is governed. The war is a direct contest between the dominant power and the rising challenger in which all major powers and most of the minor powers become participants as well [Thompson and Rasler, 1989, p. 337].

hegemony   Dominance of one party over another, especially among states that are allied or interdependent. From the Greek *hegemonia,* meaning "high command," "kingship," and "leading position."

Hegemony is often associated with concepts such as *satellite states* and *sphere of influence* but can exist between equal and sovereign states. It is sometimes limited to measurements of relative military power [See Wolfson, Puri, and Martelli, 1992, p. 125]. It is a useful concept in conflict resolution to the extent that it denotes an inherently conflictual condition in coalitions and alliances, whether personal or international in context. Subordinate entities will usually perceive predominant influence or control, regardless of intentions, as a potential threat and seek to realign the power relationships [Pauling, Laszlo, and Jong, 1986, vol. 1, p. 409].

heightening   *Mediation:* Technique whereby a mediator highlights a neglected background issue by bringing it into focus [McIsaac, 1986–1987, p. 66].

See INTENSIFYING.

Hewlett Conflict Resolution Theory Building Centers   Interdisciplinary, university-based conflict centers for evaluating conflict resolution processes and developing new theoretical approaches. This lexicon was started under a research grant from one of these centers. A list of these centers funded by the William and Flora Hewlett Foundation is on the World Wide Web at www.colorado.edu/conflict/hewlett/index.html.

high-conflict couple   See LITIGIOUS FAMILY.

high-context communication   See LOW-CONTEXT AND HIGH-CONTEXT COMMU-
NICATION.

high-low arbitration   Form of arbitration, usually binding, in which the parties set a range for the award before the proceeding, thereby limiting the risks
in the outcome. The arbitrator may or may not be aware of the range. If the arbitrator is unaware of the range, an award over the high is reduced to the high
and an award under the low is increased to the low. Any award within the range
is not adjusted. High-low arbitration has become increasingly popular in third-
party insurance claim disputes where liability is admitted but damages are in
issue.

high-power language   Forceful, direct style of communication lacking hedges
("sort of"), hesitations ("er," "um"), tag questions ("It's a good price, isn't it?"),
polite forms ("Yes, ma'am"), and intensifiers ("It's an extremely good deal"),
used by speakers with high social status, particularly in legal settings. This style
sends a signal that the negotiator is more powerful, has greater resources than
her opponent, and is credible when stating her intention to adhere to a position
[Gibbons, Bradac, and Busch, 1992, p. 165, citations omitted].

ho'oponopono **(Hawaiian)**   Meaning "setting to right," a traditional dispute
settlement technique.
   Originally used by Hawaiian families to restore harmonious family relationships, the process has been expanded beyond the immediate familial sphere. A
third party, the HAKU, guides the disputants through a process involving prayer,
discussion, apology, and forgiveness. Though she is usually a respectable family elder intimately known to the disputants, she may also be an outsider, such
as a traditional healer, minister, or social worker [Pe, Sosmena, and Tadiar, 1988,
pp. 4–5; Shook and Kwan, 1988, p. 426].

horizontal bargaining   Primary *across-the-table* negotiation, bilateral or multilateral, between the parties in contention or their representatives, as opposed
to negotiations that may take place between members of the same negotiation
team or with their constituents [Colosi and Berkeley, 1986].
   Contrast VERTICAL BARGAINING, INTERNAL BARGAINING.

horizontal constituent approval   Decision making or settlement approval by
a nonbureaucratically organized constituency represented by a negotiator or negotiating team without ultimate settlement authority. The negotiator usually
must gain approval of the negotiated settlement through a form of ratification.
Voting and consensus are common procedures for obtaining approval [Moore,
1986, p. 290].

hot line   Method of direct access to primary decision makers for the purpose of resolving a problem.

The term is most familiar in the context of international relations wherein heads of state, particularly U.S. and Soviet, established a direct phone line in order to build confidence and engage in direct discussions to reduce conflict that may lead to nuclear confrontation. The term is also used in consumer dispute resolution interchangeably with ACTION LINE and in intraorganizational dispute resolution to denote direct access, usually by telephone, to an ORGANIZATIONAL OMBUDSPERSON or other complaint handler inside the organization. Some hot lines are established for *whistle blowing*, reporting malfeasance, by other people in the organization.

hozho **(Native North American/Navajo)**   Concept of harmony, everything being in its place and working well with everything else, incorporated into Navajo justice, which emphasizes restoration and reconciliation through consensus in order to reestablish *hozho*. See NAAT'AANII.

hozhooji naat'aanii **(Native North American/Navajo)**   Modern term for a Navajo peacemaker. Means "peace and harmony way leader," the key person in the NAVAJO PEACEMAKER COURT and its operation. Also a justice ceremony to restore disputants to harmony. The peacemaker's role in this ceremony is to guide the parties to HOZHO, or harmony. See NAAT'AANII.

hukihuki **(Hawaiian)**   Meaning "pull, pull," a totally damaging situation that exists when opposing individuals or groups tug, pull, and pressure to gain emotional ascendancy over another individual or group [Shook and Kwan, 1988, p. 430].

humanistic mediation   Specific practice of TRANSFORMATIVE MEDIATION emphasizing DIALOGUE over SETTLEMENT.

In this nondirective style of mediation, the mediator focuses on creating a safe place to foster direct dialogue among the parties. In preparation, the mediator meets with the parties individually and in person; however, during the mediation itself the mediator engages in minimal intervention and maintains an attitude of unconditional positive regard and connectedness to all the parties while remaining impartial. Written settlement agreements are possible but not central to the process [Umbreit, 1995].

human needs   See NEEDS THEORY.

hybrid.   Thing composed of dissimilar elements; having mixed origins.

In conflict resolution typologies, the term is used to denote a class of processes that derive their characteristics from both adjudicative and conciliatory processes. In most typologies, this class would include private, voluntary processes such as MED-ARB, variations of med-arb, and MINI-TRIALS, as well as court-related, evaluative processes such as MANDATORY NONBINDING ARBITRATION and SUMMARY JURY TRIALS.

Classification of a process as hybrid is sometimes difficult because the line between conciliatory and adjudicative process may be difficult to draw. For example, if a mediator makes nonbinding recommendations for settlement, Singer [1990] would classify the process as a hybrid—no longer "pure" mediation. Singer [1990, pp. 25–27] also classifies as hybrids dispute resolution systems and programs that provide choices of different, otherwise nonhybrid processes, such as ombudsmen, complaint programs, and grievance procedures. This use is probably too inclusive, however, because these terms describe sometimes sequential but always distinct processes that may or may not be hybrids themselves.

See ADJUDICATIVE PROCESSES and CONCILIATORY PROCESSES.

hyperlexis   Societal condition in which there is too much litigation. Coined in 1986 by Senator Mitch McConnell in a speech touting tort reform.

ICAR   See Institute for Conflict Analysis and Resolution.

ICC   See International Chamber of Commerce.

ICJ   See International Court of Justice.

ICSID   See International Centre for the Settlement of Investment Disputes.

ICSID Additional Facility   See International Centre for the Settlement of Investment Disputes.

***Ifugao* mediation (Philippine)**   Method of dispute resolution practiced by a peacemaking functionary known as a *MONKALUN* in a preliterate Philippine tribe studied by the eminent anthropologist R. F. Barton around the time of World War I. "To the end of a peaceful settlement," wrote Barton [(1919) 1969, p. 100], the monkalun represents the society at large's interest in restoring peace and

> exhausts every art of Ifugao diplomacy. He wheedles, coaxes, flatters, threatens, drives, scolds, insinuates. He beats down the demands of the plaintiffs or prosecution, and bolsters up the proposals of the defendants until a point be reached at which the two parties may compromise. If the culprit or accused be not disposed to listen to reason or "shows fight" when approached, the monkalun waits till the former ascends into his house, follows him, and war-knife in hand, sits in front of him and compels him to listen.

See Merry, 1989, pp. 72–74.

impartial, impartiality   "Freedom from favoritism or bias, either by word or by action, and a commitment to serve all parties as opposed to a single party" (from *Ethical Standards of Professional Responsibility* adopted by the Society of Professionals in Dispute Resolution in June 1986, which identifies impartiality as the first responsibility that neutrals have to disputing parties). The ability to interact in the absence of feelings, values, or agendas in oneself. The ability of the mediator (interventionist) to maintain an unbiased relationship with the disputants. Impartiality and EQUIDISTANCE are generally thought to be the primary components of mediator neutrality [Rifkin, Millen, and Cobb, 1991, p. 152]. In ADJUDICATION, the impartiality of the adjudicator is a fundamental tenet of natural law ("a person cannot judge his own cause" [*Bonham's Case*]). In some forms of arbitration, however, the PARTISAN ARBITRATOR is not expected to be completely impartial.

Compare EQUIDISTANCE, FAIRNESS, NEUTRALITY. Contrast BALANCED PARTIALITY, BIAS.

impartial arbitral institution   Organization that provides arbitration services impartially and independently from the disputing parties. See ADMINISTERING AGENCY.

impartial chairman   *Labor:* Permanent arbitrator who is the only impartial member of an arbitration board established jointly by a union and a company to resolve labor disputes.

An impartial chairman may not necessarily be the chair of an official board or committee. The decision of the impartial chairman is the final and binding step in the grievance procedure, subject always to the authority granted her by the COLLECTIVE BARGAINING AGREEMENT. Under some agreements, she may arbitrate some or all of the terms of a new contract. She may also take into account the long-term interests of the parties in deciding disciplinary cases [DOA].

See IMPARTIAL CHAIRMAN SYSTEM. Compare NEUTRAL ARBITRATOR.

impartial chairman, ad hoc   Arbitration: Sometimes used to designate the neutral member of a tripartite arbitration panel chosen by the mutual consent of the parties to serve in a single case only.

The other members of such an ad hoc arbitral tribunal are known as PARTY-APPOINTED or PARTISAN ARBITRATORS, each having been chosen by one of the parties. The award is usually rendered by the neutral arbitrator, with the concurrence or dissent of the party-appointed arbitrators merely noted. The party-appointed arbitrators may write a separate opinion, though this is seldom done in practice. Use of the title *impartial chairman* in this context is not to be confused with use of the title in the permanent arbitration procedure established in labor arbitration through the IMPARTIAL CHAIRMAN SYSTEMS in the early part of the twentieth century [DOA]. The term is mostly associated with labor arbitration, while the term NEUTRAL ARBITRATOR is more common in COMMERCIAL ARBITRATION.

impartial chairman arbitration   Arbitration conducted under an IMPARTIAL CHAIRMAN SYSTEM.

impartial chairman system   *Labor:* Historical method for settling labor disputes in which an impartial chairman selected by a union and an employer would be free to mediate as well as to arbitrate all disputes that occur during the life of a particular contract.

The impartial chairman system was one of two successful permanent labor arbitration procedures to be used in the United States. The impartial chairman system came into existence with the appointment of an impartial chairman in Chicago in 1911 by the clothing company Hart, Schaffner, and Marx and the Amalgamated Clothing Workers. Their COLLECTIVE BARGAINING AGREEMENT was brief and was stated in general terms. The scope of arbitration had much latitude, allowing any problem that might arise between management and labor to be submitted to the impartial chairman. Originally the settlements were most often mediated. The first impartial chairmen also participated actively in the contract negotiations of the parties. An earlier permanent arbitration procedure was the UMPIRE SYSTEM, which began with the award in 1903 made by the Anthracite Coal Strike Commission [DOA].

impartial expert   *Arbitration:* Expert appointed by the tribunal to give an unbiased opinion on a disputed matter. The applicable procedural law or arbitration procedures may provide express authority for the appointment. Parties usually have the right to examine or cross-examine such experts as witnesses before the tribunal. More common in international practice.

impasse   Standstill in negotiations.
Labor Relations: "The point at which further bargaining would be futile" [*Larsdale, Inc. and Int'l Union of Elecs., et al.,* 1993 WL 153703 (N.L.R.B.)]. An impasse is reached when collective bargaining has been brought to a standstill and unresolved issues are still on the bargaining table. An impasse may be resolved by pressure from strikes, lockouts, or arbitration, depending on the terms of the contract. Mediation or fact-finding panels are often used, particularly in public employee disputes, to try to resolve such an impasse [DOA]. An impasse must be reached before parties can proceed with INTEREST ARBITRATION. Compare DEADLOCKED.

implementation   Actions taken to make an agreement operational and thereby to terminate the dispute.

implicit bargaining   Dispute resolution method in which each adversary, without explicit negotiation and agreement, modifies her conduct toward the other until a stable condition is reached [Azar and Burton, 1986, p. 82].

implicit contract   Any action by an agent to enforce agreements that condition current actions on some past behavior that is not directly relevant to current and future payoffs. An example is a threat to end cooperation if an agreement is ever violated [Crawford, 1985, p. 212].

implicit mediation   Idea that there is always, in effect, mediation—if not by some individual directly then by an implicit mediator. Implicit mediation may be shared values without a physically present mediator, or system-preserving values that constitute an implied third party [Hamnett, 1977, p. 41].

incremental convergence   Pattern of gradual, alternating concessions within the BARGAINING RANGE during the final bargaining stage that terminates at a mutually satisfactory compromise [Gulliver, 1979; Walton and McKersie, 1965].

Indian Gaming Regulatory Act   Requires the states to negotiate in GOOD FAITH to resolve disputes over gambling on Native American reservations. In addition to the Labor Relations Act, it is one of the few U.S. statutes to mention the notion of *good faith* [25 U.S.C.A. §§ 2701–2721 (West 1997)].

Indifferent Gentlemen (archaic)   *Arbitration:* Phrase occasionally used to describe arbitrators as well as jurors, as early as Tudor England. *Indifferent* meaning strictly impartial, such a person is understood to be living in the county where the dispute occurred and would therefore be acquainted with the parties, would be able to judge the credibility of witnesses, and thus would ensure the settlement of the dispute without strife or disruption of the peace.

Many of the submissions to arbitration or ARBITRAMENT in Tudor England use such phrases as to achieve a "frendly and quyet end." Occasionally the arbitrators were described as "indyferent citizen[s] of London" or "gentlemen in the country" [DOA]. A similar concept in European civil law countries was that of the *bono viri*.

indigenization   *Ethnic/Civil Strife:* Set of strategies used to resolve ethnic conflict in which the state uses affirmative, unsolicited policies of cultivation of ethnic minorities in general. Crudely translated from the Russian term *korenizatsiya.* Examples include the standardization of many uncodified languages and the granting of autonomy to special regions that are marked by some form of cultural distinctiveness.

individualistic approach   Tactics and strategy used by negotiators who are self-centered about their interests and indifferent to the other side's needs. Such negotiators seek to maximize their position while being neutral about the opponent's position [Haydock and Mitchell, 1984, p. 6]. See COMPETITIVE, COOPERATIVE STRATEGY.

industrial mediation   Mediation of employment-related issues, usually in the context of COLLECTIVE BARGAINING AGREEMENTS and unionized labor. More commonly referred to as LABOR MEDIATION.

informal court-operated processing   Used by McGillis and Mullen [1977, p. 22] to describe the activities of court personnel in arranging informal settlements to disputes. For example, court clerks in some jurisdictions attempt to conciliate or mediate minor matters that appear before them. In criminal cases, a modified version of this type of processing occurs in prosecutorial plea negotiations.

informalism   Use of informal procedures by public tribunals with the power to make binding determinations; a more accurate term may be *judicial informalism*. A neo-Marxist critique of informalism defines it as a "movement to create avenues and means for the economically disinclined to have access to and efficacy within the legal system. Examples include the creation of legal aid clinics, small claims courts, and public defenders. Additionally, this movement has come to include the use of nonlegalistic channels of dispute resolution, such as mediation, conciliation, and negotiation" [Abel, 1985–1986, pp. 379–382].

Abel's expansive definition of an informalism movement includes players (legal aid and public defenders) and private, voluntary ADR processes, as well as court-related processes. This makes the term less useful for distinguishing between processes. Although legal-aid lawyers and public defenders engage in informal dispute resolution activities outside the courtroom, so do most disputants, even when engaged in formal litigation. This in fact begs the question of what formalism is, because the lines between formalism and informalism are increasingly blurred. For example, the line between informal forms of litigation and arbitration has been and often remains obscure. On the one hand, courts have incorporated consensual arbitration in their procedures and have adopted arbitration-like informality in their civil procedure. On the other hand, arbitration proceedings can take place before court judges, be more coercive than consensual, and reflect all the formality of classical litigation. See ARBITRATION.

Informalism might be distinguishable by the degree of coercion and lack of party control over process. For example, in judicial informalism, the parties may be forced to participate without mutual consent, may have little or no choice of tribunal, cannot create their own procedures, and cannot control the amount and effect of the determination. In contrast, the essence of private arbitration is nonjudicial, third-party judgment in which the parties choose the tribunal, mode of procedure, and extent to which they are bound by the solution. In arbitration, the parties determine the jurisdiction of the tribunal, while in judicial informalism, tribunal jurisdiction is frequently predetermined by statute. One notable feature of arbitration is that the tribunal cannot directly enforce its award, unlike much of judicial informalism, in which the tribunal can directly enforce its award. In many cases, however, the state has allowed private organizations to use arbitration as a form of self-government and self-regulation by sanctioning compulsory arbitration among the organization's membership and by approving the use of internal discipline by these tribunals as a mode of enforcing their own awards.

In contrast to Abel's definition, it may be more useful to exclude ADR processes, even court-related ADR processes, and to limit the definition to situations in which officials of the court or government make binding determinations while imposing their own informal procedure.

information exchange   *Negotiation:* Process of exchanging information among parties to understand the problem better or the other side's perspective on the problem [Gulliver, 1979].

Public Policy: Phase of consensus building in public policy mediation or facilitation. The goal of the phase is to get as much information as possible on the table so that people have a common understanding of the problem or an appreciation for the perspectives of the different stakeholders.

Arbitration: Process by which the disputants obtain information from each other in order to prepare for an arbitration hearing, especially under the administration of the American Arbitration Association, which uses the term instead of DISCOVERY. Formal discovery is not traditional in arbitration unless the parties agree to its use. However, as more arbitrations incorporate many of the formalities of litigation, the term becomes a somewhat euphemistic reference to discovery.

information procedures   Method of providing disputants, through the use of a database, with the characteristics and results of other, similar disputes in order to reduce the uncertainty about the likely outcome of the current dispute [Ury, Brett, and Goldberg, 1988, pp. 52–53].

See OBJECTIVE CRITERIA.

informed award   See AGREED AWARD.

injunctive relief   Remedy, usually issued by a court, prohibiting a person from continuing or initiating a course of conduct that damages or may damage another. The remedy issued is referred to as an *injunction* and may be either *temporary* (in effect until a final hearing and decision is made on the matter) or *permanent.*

Arbitration: Award an arbitrator may grant, if so empowered [DOA], more often as an interim measure to preserve evidence or the subject matter of the dispute until hearing and final award. Sometimes referred to as INTERIM MEASURES OF PROTECTION or PROVISIONAL MEASURES.

inquiry, enquiry   Process used when a court or other body endeavors to resolve a disputed issue of fact, especially in international law. In this sense, it is most similar to FACT-FINDING. Because most disputes contain contentions of fact, inquiry is a major component of most third-party settlement processes such as arbitration. The term is almost never used in domestic U.S. law or alternative dispute resolution practice.

International Relations: Particular process employed by COMMISSIONS OF INQUIRY established under the HAGUE CONVENTIONS OF 1899 AND 1907 to resolve international disputes. The UN Charter also mentions *enquiry* into facts as one of several procedures to solve disputes [art. 33]. States that are unwilling to be bound by a third-party determination or to consider third-party recommendations may select inquiry because they believe an independent, impartial investigation and determination of the facts may facilitate settlement.

Disputing states initiate inquiry by mutual consent, either ad hoc or through preexisting treaty commitments. As envisaged by the Hague Conventions, inquiry is initiated when either the parties or an international body appoints a commission. The commission makes an investigation that includes receipt of statements and information from the parties, possible examination of a locality, and examination of witnesses and experts. After conducting its investigation, the commission of inquiry issues a report of its findings to the disputants or to the international agency. Technically the report is restricted to factual conclusions. However, an expanded inquiry includes legal conclusions as well.

Unlike arbitration, the outcome is a nonbinding report rather than an award, and the parties are free to determine how to use it in subsequent negotiations or other processes. In rare cases, parties agree that the report is binding. *Inquiry* is used interchangeably with *fact-finding,* and to the extent that the inquiry is limited to a mere finding of facts, the processes are indistinguishable. If, however, the process is an *enlarged inquiry* including conclusions of law or recommendations, as in CONCILIATION, then it would not be equivalent to fact-finding.

Although the Hague Conventions refer to commissions, an individual can serve as the third party. Some treaties contemplate inquiry conducted jointly by officials of the disputing states rather than by an independent third party [*Handbook on the Peaceful Settlement of Disputes Between States*, 1992, p. 29].

Compare FACT-FINDING. Contrast, in the context of international disputes, CONCILIATION, MEDIATION, ARBITRATION.

inquisitorial   See INQUISITORIAL SYSTEM.

inquisitorial system, inquisitory system   *Law:* Legal system in which judges have power to investigate facts and question parties, in contrast to ADVERSARY SYSTEM.

Found in most European legal systems, the inquisitorial approach has been characterized as a *truth-seeking* system of justice in which specially trained judges (usually separate from advocates) actively investigate and ferret out the truth. Much of this activity involves a series of court-ordered submissions of material and evidence and possibly several brief hearings and examinations of witnesses. Questions are controlled and initiated by the judge. Often there is no large, single, all-conclusive hearing, typical of adversary systems. Parties play a rather passive role, while judges are far more active than is typical of the passive referee role in adversary systems. In practice, few European courts appear purely inquisitorial. Parties often make adversarial presentations and, with the judge's permission, direct the questioning of witnesses and the presentation of evidence.

Some commentators posit that judges in an inquisitorial system are more likely to make compromise verdicts and to emphasize societal needs and harmony among disputants than to vindicate individual rights [see Leeson and Johnston, 1988, p. 3]. This tendency, however, is more likely rooted in fundamental political and social principles typical of European countries using inquisitorial systems rather than in the innate characteristics of inquisitorial systems.

ARBITRATION is often characterized as an inquisitorial process to the extent that arbitrators have broad powers to question witnesses and seek information necessary to determine the truth.

Contrast ADVERSARY SYSTEM.

inside bargaining   Process of negotiation with one's superiors or subordinates within one's chain of command to meet the goals of the organization [Lax and Sebenius, 1986].

Institute for Conflict Analysis and Resolution (ICAR)   Based at George Mason University, ICAR is the longest-operating graduate academic program in the field.

Institute for Dispute Resolution   See CENTER FOR PUBLIC RESOURCES.

Institute of Arbitrators, Chartered Institute of Arbitrators (United Kingdom)
Organization established in 1915 and incorporated in 1925 to supply the business community with commercial arbitrators who are acquainted with the legal aspects of arbitration and skilled in various technical branches of commerce and industry [DOA].

institutional arbitration   Arbitration conducted under the rules of a permanent and impartial agency, either national or international, such as the AMERICAN ARBITRATION ASSOCIATION or the INTERNATIONAL CHAMBER OF COMMERCE.

Institutional arbitration is administered by many business organizations, chambers of commerce, commodity exchanges, trade associations, and intergovernmental agencies throughout the world. Access to the arbitration tribunal may or may not be restricted to the members of the institution, depending on its rules. Such agencies provide facilities for arbitration, including arbitrators or lists from which the parties may select arbitrators, as well as administrative personnel and rules of procedure. These services help to ensure that the arbitration will be conducted under strict procedural rules. Reference in an arbitration clause to the rules of a specific administering agency is one method of incorporating those rules as part of the agreement [DOA].

institutionalization   Term used loosely in DISPUTE SYSTEMS DESIGN to refer to the process of establishing or integrating dispute resolution mechanisms or procedures within an organization, culture, or social structure. See also MAINSTREAMING.

instructed committee   *Negotiation:* Tactic used by negotiation teams representing a group in a negotiation where final settlement is dependent on constituent approval, especially in labor negotiations. Immediately prior to a scheduled negotiation meeting, the negotiation team will give notice to either the other side or the mediator that the constituents met before the meeting and instructed the team to accept no less than a particular settlement. Therefore, the team is bound by this mandate, and unless the other side is prepared to meet this demand, there is no point in convening the meeting [Maggiolo, 1985, p. 184].

Compare BOULWAREISM, BRINKSMANSHIP, GOOD GUY/BAD GUY, CONDITIONAL MEETINGS. See HORIZONTAL CONSTITUENT APPROVAL.

instrumental interests   Where favorable terms on the issues are valued because of their effect on subsequent dealings among the parties [Lax and Sebenius, 1986, p. 71]. Contrast INTRINSIC INTERESTS.

Insurance Ombudsman Bureau (IOB)   Complaint-handling organization established by member insurance companies in the United Kingdom. The IOB receives complaints arising from insurance policies issued by member companies and attempts settlement or withdrawal of the matter. The individual ombudsman has a full range of dispute resolution powers, acting as counselor, conciliator, adjudicator, or arbitrator. Her determinations are subject to the supervision of a board and a council, which is a smaller unit of the board. The determination of the ombudsman is binding upon the entity against which restitution is sought, but the complainant is not bound to accept the award and may decide to take legal proceedings against the insurer.

insurance principle   Establishment of rules to deal with conflicts before the power relation and the winners and losers are known [Fogg, 1985, pp. 343–344].

intake session   *Mediation:* Prenegotiation session (especially in divorce mediation) in which the disputing parties determine the appropriateness of their specific mediator and the mediation arena in general. In the session, the mediator must explain the mediation process, establish control of that process while assuring the parties that they will control the content of the outcome, and assign the first tasks required to implement their resolution. The intake session generally lasts one to two hours and is sometimes called the *orientation session* [Haynes, 1984, p. 4].

in-team bargaining   See INTERNAL BARGAINING.

integrated conflict management system   Form of conflict management system within an organization that takes into account all types of complaints and conflicts among its members. An integrated system provides complainants with parallel options for dispute settlement. The system is open to both managers and employees, and possibly to those outside the organization who have a complaint. It offers both rights-based, formal grievance procedures and interest-based, often informal means of dispute resolution. For example, a certain type of complainant may trust the system only if it provides due process in an independent fact-finding procedure with an impartial decision maker and levels of appeal. Other complainants may fear reprisal or disapproval from peers or supervisors if such an action is instituted and may instead wish to pursue resolution of an issue without formal action. This latter path may help the complainant retain confidentiality and privacy.

   An integrated system also allows for grievances to be dealt with in either a representative or facilitative manner by a *gatekeeper* functioning within the system. The gatekeeper informs the complainant of the array of options for dispute settlement within the integrated system and stands ready to perform whatever role is chosen by the complainant or to refer the matter to another who can.

An integrated system may also provide multiple access points for complainants. The initial contact person, or gatekeeper, may be designated as a neutral who refers the complainant to the appropriate contact for different segments of the organizational population, such as for women, or for different segments of the organization itself; or there may be multiple gatekeepers of varying gender, race, and position [Rowe, 1995].

Compare ALTERNATIVE DISPUTE RESOLUTION SYSTEM, DISPUTE MANAGEMENT SYSTEM.

integrating, integrative   A situation or condition in which disputants can achieve joint gain or satisfy their respective interests without significant loss. Roughly analogous to NON-ZERO-SUM.

Also denotes a style of handling INTERPERSONAL CONFLICT in which there is a high concern for oneself and for the others. This involves openness, exchange of information, and examination of differences to reach an effective solution acceptable to both parties. It is associated with problem solving that may lead to creative solutions [Rahim, 1986, p. 83].

Contrast DISTRIBUTIVE. See INTEGRATIVE BARGAINING.

integrative agreement   Solution reached through INTEGRATIVE BARGAINING and sometimes referred to as a WIN-WIN SOLUTION.

integrative bargaining, problem-solving negotiation   Bargaining whereby parties seek a resolution that fully or substantially meets the needs of all the parties. The process of developing joint benefits [Whiting, 1992] and the opposite of DISTRIBUTIVE BARGAINING [see, generally, Walton and McKersie, 1965].

Integrative bargaining is associated with NON-ZERO-SUM situations involving multiple issues, the possibility of an ongoing relationship, and a high degree of commonality or compatibility among the parties' interests. Because individual gain does not have to be achieved at the direct expense of the other, parties do not have to view each other as strict competitors and can search beyond the compromise alternatives and make mutually beneficial trade-offs or joint gains. As a result, integrative bargaining is also called problem-solving negotiation and is characterized by more cooperative and collaborative behaviors and less hostile or adversarial behaviors.

The concept of integrative bargaining raises two interrelated issues. The first issue is whether integrative bargaining is an all-or-nothing process. Some commentators define the process as requiring that all needs be met, for example, "a technique of identifying the needs of conflicting parties and creating a solution which meets all the needs concerned" [Fogg, 1985, p. 332].

Similarly, other commentators see the process as requiring joint gain that exceeds the possible individual gains (the whole being greater than the sum of the parts) and individual maximum benefit being dependent on all participants' needs being met. See Raiffa [1982, p. 131]: "In integrative bargaining, it is no longer true that if one party gets more, the other necessarily has to get less: they both can get more"; and Goldman [1991, p. 10]: "Both sides stand to gain their maximum benefit if a resolution . . . meets the needs of all participants." Still other commentators point to the problem of *degree:*

> Bargaining always involves joint consideration of two or more "options" or potential agreements. Some options are more "integrative" than others in the sense of providing greater joint utility to the bargainers taken collectively. The term "integrative bargaining" refers to the processes by which bargainers locate and adopt such options. One process is considered to be more "integrative" than another to the extent that it is more capable of locating the best among the options available to the bargainers" [Pruitt and Lewis, 1977, p. 161].

The second issue is whether integrative bargaining behavior results from the nature of the situation or creates the situation. In other words, can a concerted effort at integrative bargaining make a seemingly distributive situation into an integrative one? This problem goes to the heart of the White [1984] and Fisher [1981] debate in which White argued that inherently distributive situations preclude integrative bargaining and Fisher argued the utility of integrative bargaining behaviors in such situations. Again, this may be a matter of degree. A purely distributive situation, such as ZERO-SUM, will require the parties to divide a limited resource so that gains come at the expense of others. Some situations that appear distributive, however, might be converted to integrative, perhaps through reframing. See FRAMING.

See WIN-WIN SOLUTION. Compare INTEREST-BASED NEGOTIATION, MUTUAL GAINS BARGAINING, PRINCIPLED NEGOTIATION. Contrast DISTRIBUTIVE BARGAINING.

integrative issues   Issues requiring continued contact and cooperation among the disputing parties; each decision is a prelude to new questions and answers. In the case of child custody disputes, these decisions are also profoundly influenced by the central concern of the best interest of the child, which establishes important limits to confidentiality [McIsaac, 1985, p. 60].

Contrast DISTRIBUTIVE ISSUES.

intensifying   *Mediation:* Technique whereby a mediator highlights a neglected background issue by bringing it into focus [McIsaac, 1985, p. 66].

See HEIGHTENING.

interactional monitoring   *Mediation:* Explicit comments made by the mediator concerning the character of ongoing interaction, especially behavior inimical to effective negotiation. A method whereby mediators may empower both parties by helping them to interact more effectively [Benjamin and Irving, 1992, p. 142]. See also Smart [1987] and Ricci [1985, pp. 49–61].

interactive problem solving   Occurs whenever parties in conflict, or their representatives, engage in direct communication to achieve resolution.

More specifically used to describe a form of third-party intervention as manifested particularly in problem-solving workshops. Problem-solving workshops try to create an environment conducive to conflict resolution and try to transform the relationship between the conflicting parties. As used in international disputes, the process is characterized by a panel of experts, often scientists, that facilitates a process whereby solutions emerge out of the direct communication and interaction between the parties. The task of the third party is to provide the setting, create the atmosphere, establish the norms, and offer occasional interventions that make it possible for such a process to evolve [Kelman, 1992, p. 65].

Inter-American Convention on International Commercial Arbitration (Panama Convention)   Multilateral international agreement providing for the recognition and enforcement of foreign arbitral agreements and awards from member states [O.A.S.T.S. No. 42, 14 I.L.M. 336 (1975)]. Also known as the Panama Convention, it has been ratified by the United States and many other countries in the Americas. Implementing U.S. legislation is codified at 9 U.S.C.A. §§ 301 et seq. (West 1998).

See CONVENTION ON THE RECOGNITION AND ENFORCEMENT OF FOREIGN ARBITRAL AWARDS.

Inter-Association Commercial Arbitration Agreements   Reciprocity agreements between international arbitral agencies making available the use of their arbitration facilities in the countries covered by the agreement. A typical arrangement would allow parties to arbitrate in Paris at the INTERNATIONAL CHAMBER OF COMMERCE COURT OF ARBITRATION under AMERICAN ARBITRATION ASSOCIATION (AAA) procedural rules, or in New York at the AAA under the ICC rules.

intercede, intercession   Interposing or pleading on another's behalf; mediation.

The term's two definitions may seem somewhat incongruous, particularly for mediators who conceive of their role as prohibiting pleading on either party's behalf. It often implies advocacy for a weaker party in relationship to a stronger one. The term is rarely used in conflict resolution literature. Contrast INTERMEDIATION, INTERPOSITION, INTERVENTION.

intercultural conflict resolution   See CULTURE.

interdisciplinary co-mediation   See CO-MEDIATION.

interest   Something for which one feels concern or in which one has a stake. The plural form, *interests,* is commonly used in conflict resolution interchangeably or jointly with *needs.* For conflict resolution theorists, interests are those real or perceived personal or corporate requirements from which goals and objectives as well as negotiation offers and demands are derived.

Arbitration/Law: The sum of money accrued and due with the passage of time on the amount that is awarded by the arbitrators or by a court. In many jurisdictions, arbitrators have the power to award interest [DOA].

interest arbitration   *Labor Relations:* Arbitration of the terms of a new labor contract.

When contract negotiations between a union and employer reach an impasse and cannot be resolved by normal collective bargaining, the issues in dispute are sometimes submitted to an arbitrator [DOA]. Many states provide a form of statutorily imposed interest arbitration on certain essential-service public employees, commonly called COMPULSORY or MANDATORY ARBITRATION. The type of interest arbitration procedure adopted in this context varies from state to state, ranging from conventional arbitration on each issue to FINAL-OFFER ARBITRATION. Some interest arbitrators are empowered to attempt settlement through mediation before resorting to adjudication (see MED-ARB).

Interest arbitration is distinguished from GRIEVANCE ARBITRATION in that the former covers arbitration over new contract terms while the latter covers disputes regarding compliance with an existing contract [*International Bhd. of Elec. Workers* v. *Graham County Elec. Coop.* (1986)].

interest-based negotiation   Act of back-and-forth communication focused on reconciling interests with the goal of reaching an agreement. Also known as *problem-solving negotiation* [Ury, Brett, and Goldberg, 1988, p. 6]. Same as or similar to PRINCIPLED NEGOTIATION and INTEGRATIVE BARGAINING but may differ with respect to focus. Interest-based negotiation focuses on interests and their reconciliation, while integrative bargaining can be seen as focused on outcomes that maximize JOINT GAINS. The result and behavior, however, may be indistinguishable.

See INTEGRATIVE BARGAINING.

intergroup conflict   See CONFLICT.

interim award   *Arbitration:* Partial or temporary award rendered on only part of the dispute.

Most arbitration statutes in the United States require that arbitration awards must be final and that they must determine all of the issues submitted. Partial or interim awards in this sense would therefore have no legal sanction, especially under the rule that once an arbitrator renders an award he is FUNCTUS OFFICIO [DOA]. There is substantial precedent, however, for enforcing partial final awards.

interim communications   *Negotiation:* Information exchange among the parties or their representatives that occurs between meetings or official working sessions. Can refer to communications between parties and neutrals outside official conferences or hearings.

interim measures of protection   See PROVISIONAL MEASURES.

interim relief   *Law:* Same as INJUNCTIVE RELIEF.
Arbitration: Same as PROVISIONAL MEASURES.

intermediary, intermediation   Someone who is in-between; go-between; broker.
Most dictionaries and many authorities use the term to encompass an entire class of third parties who are in-between others. Under these expansive definitions, an intermediary includes MEDIATORS and ARBITRATORS [see, for example, *Black's Law Dictionary*]. The following definition of *intermediary intervention* includes parties in interest as potential mediators, but distinguishes intermediaries as follows:

> Can be thought of as one of three forms of negotiation. Some negotiations are direct and bilateral. Others are multilateral where one member "mediates" in the sense of bringing others together to form a coalition. In such coalitional bargaining, all parties in multilateral negotiations are potential mediators. But they are not "in between"; they are not intermediaries. Negotiations with a third party who is not a direct party to the negotiations is what I term intermediary intervention [Princen, 1992, p. 6].

Law: A significantly different definition can be found in the American Bar Association's *Model Rules of Professional Conduct* [1995], in which "a lawyer acts as an intermediary . . . when the lawyer represents two or more parties with potentially conflicting interests" or "in seeking to establish or adjust a relationship between clients on an amicable and mutually advantageous basis" [Rule 2.2, Comments 1 and 3]. Under this definition, representation of both parties in common, arbitration, and mediation can be forms of intermediation [Id. at Comment 4]. The factor that distinguishes this from most definitions of arbitration and mediation is the attorney-client relationship. In this sense, intermediaries have a responsibility of joint representation and a form of fiduciary relationship that exceeds that found in most definitions of mediators. Most mediators would say that they represent neither party. If mediation was considered joint representation, then lawyer-mediators could rarely serve because of the ethical limitations based on conflicts of interest.

Compare INTERVENTION, INTERPOSITION, INTERCESSION.

intermediate   See INTERMEDIARY.

intermediate preference   Mutually acceptable point reached when two parties with different preferences come to an agreement through some form of resolution.

internal bargaining, in-team bargaining   Negotiations or bargaining among members of the same negotiating team [Colosi and Berkeley, 1986].

internal criteria   Criteria for evaluating mediation fairness that are often seen as subjective. Internal criteria include individual and joint feelings about fairness, personality factors, relationship patterns between the parties, intuition, spiritual and religious factors, family norms, short-term and long-term needs of family members, and best-interest issues [Dworkin and London, 1989, pp. 3–4]. See also Girdner [1986].

international arbitral tribunal   One or more arbitrators empowered by the parties to hear and determine a transnational dispute. The term includes tribunals established ad hoc or through an institution and tribunals hearing private commercial disputes, as well as those hearing disputes between states. Tribunals are constituted to hear a single case or several related cases submitted by the parties and under procedural and substantive rules adopted by the parties. Sometimes the term is rather loosely used to refer to the lists of arbitrators maintained by arbitral institutions for international cases, even though the arbitrators are not assigned to a specific case.

See JUDICIAL SETTLEMENT for distinction between international arbitral tribunals and international courts.

international arbitration   Term that embodies both arbitration of disputes between states and international commercial arbitration, usually between private entities residing in different countries. The distinction between the two terms is generally grounded in the parties, type of dispute, and institution used to settle the dispute.

See INTERNATIONAL COMMERCIAL ARBITRATION, INTERNATIONAL PUBLIC ARBITRATION, INTERSTATE ARBITRATION.

International Centre for Settlement of Investment Disputes (ICSID)   Public international organization jointly administered by representatives of participating states to provide a neutral forum for resolving disputes between states and foreign investors. Created in 1966 by the CONVENTION ON THE SETTLEMENT OF

INVESTMENT DISPUTES BETWEEN STATES AND NATIONALS OF OTHER STATES and functioning under the auspices of the World Bank, ICSID maintains panels of conciliators and arbitrators. Most of the conciliators and arbitrators are nominated by the contracting states. They administer conciliation and arbitration proceedings when a dispute between a contracting state and a national of another contracting state arising from an investment is submitted for resolution.

ICSID was formed in response to the increasing *nationalization* of private, often foreign-owned industries by states. In theory, it enhances private foreign capital flow to developing states by providing some assurance that foreigners investing in member states will have a forum for direct recourse. Unlike interstate arbitration processes, in which claims must be espoused by states themselves, foreign investors may make claims directly.

ICSID Additional Facility: Short for the ICSID Additional Facility for the Administration of Conciliation, Arbitration, and Fact-Finding Proceedings. Procedure for international arbitration of investment disputes in which one of the disputing parties is a member of the ICSID convention but the other is not.

See, generally, Morrison [1991, pp. 833–35] and Amerasinghe [1976].

International Chamber of Commerce (ICC)   Chamber founded in 1919 and headquartered in Paris, following a decision taken at the International Trade Conference of 1919 in Atlantic City, New Jersey, to establish a permanent organization of world business that provides dispute resolution.

International Chamber of Commerce Court of Arbitration   Organization in Paris that administers conciliation and arbitration to resolve international commercial disputes worldwide for the International Chamber of Commerce.

international claim   Claim that a government of one country makes on behalf of one of its citizens against another country for loss or injury the citizen sustained.

international commercial arbitration   Arbitration of disputes in international trade or business transactions between two private entities arising out of a transnational contract. The process may be ad hoc or administered under the auspices of a trade association or an independent, private arbitral institution such as the INTERNATIONAL CHAMBER OF COMMERCE, the AMERICAN ARBITRATION ASSOCIATION, or another body.

Whether a commercial arbitration is international depends on the applicable law or rules the parties adopt.

International Commission of Inquiry   See COMMISSION OF INQUIRY, INQUIRY.

International Court of Justice (ICJ)   Court whose function is to decide disputes between states in accordance with international law.

In permanent session at The Hague, the ICJ was established as the principal judicial organ of the United Nations under its 1945 charter and is governed by the statute of the ICJ, a component of the charter. Article 36 of the statute gives the court jurisdiction over all cases that the disputing member states jointly submit to it, and over all other legal matters specifically provided for in the charter or in treaties and conventions in force. The article also gives the court compulsory jurisdiction where the disputing parties have previously submitted declarations accepting the ICJ's jurisdiction.

Under Article 96 of the U.N. Charter and Article 65 of the statute, the court can issue an advisory opinion on any legal question submitted by the Security Council or the General Assembly. Although the United Nations cannot be a party or institute proceedings on a matter in dispute, it may obtain an opinion from the ICJ without necessarily obtaining the agreement of the interested states through majority vote in either body. By clarifying the legal issues, the nonbinding opinion may encourage the disputing states to conform to the norms expressed, and a state may choose to be bound by it.

The court is composed of fifteen judges nominated by the national groups of the PERMANENT COURT OF ARBITRATION and elected by the UN General Assembly and Security Council for a period of nine years with the possibility of re-election. The ICJ president is frequently authorized in arbitration agreements or treaties to appoint an arbitrator when the parties fail to do so [DOA].

international customary law   Body of law that acquired its authority through custom and practice rather than through treaties or conventions.

The three traditional sources of international law are treaties, custom, and general principles of law recognized by civilized nations. The distinctive characteristic of custom is that it does not require the express consent of states to render it into law [DOA].

international dispute   Most properly, a dispute between or among nations, but commonly used to denote any disagreement involving governments, institutions, juristic persons (corporations), or private individuals in different countries. The international character of the dispute derives either from the disputants representing or residing in different countries or from the subject matter of the dispute being located in a country different from that of the disputants. Private, nongovernmental disputes that transcend borders are sometimes referred to as *transnational.*

In addition to the United Nations and the International Court of Justice, many international organizations provide dispute settlement mechanisms. Examples include international and regional trade organizations such as the WORLD TRADE ORGANIZATION and the NORTH AMERICAN FREE TRADE AGREEMENT (NAFTA), specialized regimes such as the INTERNATIONAL TRIBUNAL FOR THE LAW OF THE SEA and the International Telecommunications Union, regional arrangements such as the arbitral and judicial mechanisms for European regional integration, and mechanisms allowing access by private, nongovernmental entities ranging from the INTERNATIONAL CENTRE FOR SETTLEMENT OF INVESTMENT DISPUTES and NAFTA to various human rights conventions.

international estoppel   *International Law:* Principle under which a nation may be banned from acting inconsistently with a previous unambiguous, voluntary, and unconditional statement on which others rely in good faith [Wagner, 1986, pp. 1977–1980].

internationalism   Willingness to tolerate international involvement in domestic matters [Wittkopf, 1987, pp. 131–159].

internationalist   In foreign policy, one who supports internationalism [Wittkopf, 1987, pp. 131–159]. Contrast ISOLATIONIST.

international judicial settlement   See JUDICIAL SETTLEMENT.

international law   Body of rules governing the relations between states and derived from custom, treaty, or general principles of law recognized by civilized nations, including arbitral and judicial opinions [DOA]. Sometimes referred to as *the Law of Nations.*

International Negotiation Network (INN)   Developed at the Carter Center of Emory University in Atlanta, Georgia, the INN seeks to establish ongoing connections between former heads of state, officials of international and regional organizations, and experienced mediators throughout the world. If someone in the INN is asked to mediate or agrees to function in such a role, he is encouraged to tap the other members of the INN for information or advice or simply to brainstorm strategy. The INN staff at the Carter Center is establishing a database on existing conflicts, on the assumption that all mediation efforts will need to draw quickly on available background information. The status of former U.S. President Jimmy Carter makes it possible to attract high-ranking officials, at Carter's invitation, to participate in off-the-record problem-solving sessions [Susskind and Babbitt, 1992, p. 47].

international public arbitration   Settlement of disputes between states by judges of their own choice. One of two forms of INTERNATIONAL ARBITRATION.

The modern history of international arbitration is traditionally said to have begun with JAY'S TREATY of 1794, under which Great Britain and the United States submitted certain important boundary disputes to arbitration by mixed commissions [DOA].

Compare INTERSTATE ARBITRATION. Contrast INTERNATIONAL COMMERCIAL ARBITRATION.

International Tribunal for the Law of the Sea (ITLS)   Body created by the Law of the Sea Convention of 1982 to resolve disputes arising under that treaty or when any agreement so provides. The convention has not been adequately ratified to bring it into force.

interpersonal conflict   See CONFLICT.

interpose   Insert something between others so as to intervene or interfere. Connotes use of authority, force, or a forcible interruption.

interposition   Act of coming between disputants to encourage them to resolve their differences.
   International Relations: Friendly and nonforceful involvement by a state in disputes among other states to encourage peace. Though the term refers to no specific process, it has more neutral and less coercive connotations than INTERVENTION.
   Compare INTERCESSION, INTERMEDIATION, INTERVENTION.

interpretation   *Law:* Process of determining the sense or meaning of legal instruments or expressions within such instruments through the application of legal standards or rationality. Often used interchangeably with, but distinguishable from, CONSTRUCTION, which is also concerned with the legal effect of the instrument.
   Communication: Meaning that the receiver of a message assigns to what was received. Miscommunication can result from the failure of the receiver to interpret the message as the sender intended.

interstate arbitration   Arbitration between two sovereign states using either an ad hoc or institutional panel [Caron, 1990, pp. 110–111].
   Sometimes the term is used to refer to domestic arbitration in the United States of a transaction involving commerce between the various U.S. states and therefore subject to federal law pursuant to § 2 of the UNITED STATES ARBITRATION ACT.
   Compare INTERNATIONAL ARBITRATION, INTERNATIONAL COMMERCIAL ARBITRATION.

intervenor   Person engaged in INTERVENTION. Used loosely in conflict resolution literature to refer to third parties engaged in dispute resolution, especially mediators. A specific legal meaning is third parties seeking to be accepted as a party in a pending suit or arbitration.

intervention   Coming between others for the purpose of self-interested manipulation or to modify the course of events.

Mediation: Any technique used by mediators to defuse destructive interactions between the parties and to promote cooperative behaviors.

Law, Arbitration: Procedure by which a third party requests to be acknowledged as a party in order to protect an alleged interest in a suit or an arbitration pending between two other parties.

International Relations: Used broadly to denote coercive interference by states, individually or in concert, in the affairs of another state. The extent of intervention can vary substantially and is often used merely to reduce the threat of violence or stabilize a crisis. In addition to the UN Charter, which justifies collective action when the target state commits an act of aggression or threatens to break the peace, justifications under international law include intervention rights granted by treaty, the target state's violation of international law, protection of the intervening state's citizens, and the right of self-defense. Intervention can be directed toward the target state's internal policies. Thus the United States is said to be intervening when it tries to influence human rights policies in the People's Republic of China.

A more specific use embodied in the broader definition just presented is the use of various coercive pressures, other than the direct use of military force, by third-party states to persuade states in conflict to DE-ESCALATE the conflict and move toward settlement. In this sense, actions are intended to help both sides toward peaceful solutions rather than to tip the balance toward one or the other side. Intervention does not require the consent of the protagonists or target state. See, generally, Young [1967].

Compare INTERCESSION, INTERMEDIATION, INTERPOSITION.

in the shadow of the law, shadow verdict   Effect of the legal environment on extrajudicial dispute resolution.

Lon Fuller [1978, p. 369] recognized the phenomenon by noting that the possibility of litigation can "cast a very long shadow" over other "modes of social ordering." Mnookin and Kornhauser [1979] coined the term to describe the "bargaining in the shadow of the law" that takes place when settling divorce actions. In legal disputes, legal standards create certain bargaining endowments. Parties shape their agreements in the context of probable outcomes in litigation (a form of BATNA). In addition, the procedural rules of litigation, such as discovery, motion practice, and cost shifting, change the strategic choices for the negotiators (see LITIGOTIATION).

intractable conflict   Usually long-lasting conflict resistant to attempts at resolution and typically involving a struggle to satisfy fundamental human needs (see NEEDS THEORY), a conflict of values, or issues that defy WIN-WIN SOLUTIONS.

Despite the use of *intractable,* such conflicts are not necessarily unresolvable. An alternative term that implies the possibility of resolution is *deep-rooted conflict.* Contrast PROTRACTED CONFLICT.

intragroup conflict   See CONFLICT.

intraorganizational conflict   Conflict characterized by opposition between and among persons from different groups or constituencies within the same organization. See CONFLICT.

intrinsic interests   Where favorable terms on the issues are valued independent of any subsequent dealings between or among the parties [Lax and Sebenius, 1986, p. 71]. Contrast INSTRUMENTAL INTERESTS.

inverse reciprocity   *Negotiation:* Broad strategy whereby a party starts out with a tough stand. If the other party stands firm, this indicates that he has been pushed too far and a concession would be the appropriate response. If, however, the other party makes concessions, this indicates that continuing firmness is likely to result in continuing concessions from him [Stoll and McAndrew, 1986, p. 317].

investigation   Exploration of the facts and nature of a dispute or situation [Lall, 1966, pp. 9, 11]. May involve systematic observation, examination, and questioning. Although used interchangeably with INQUIRY, an investigation is distinguishable technically from inquiry and from FACT-FINDING, in which factual conclusions are made in the final reports. Investigation may be an essential step in those two processes. However, investigation is merely the gathering of information that, if reported at all, does not contain conclusions.

investment referee (United Kingdom)   Person who resolves securities and investment disputes between customers and members of the two primary self-regulatory stock brokerage organizations (SBOs). There is a conciliation stage followed by an informal adjudication, if necessary, usually conducted by separate referees.

Unlike SECURITIES ARBITRATION before SBO arbitration panels in the United States, customers are not bound by the decision unless they expressly accept the decision, while member companies of the SBO in question are obligated to act in conformity with the decision. Points of law, however, may be referred or appealed to a court.

Iran–United States Claims Tribunal   Ad hoc international arbitral tribunal formed to resolve claims between the United States and Iran. Established in 1981 pursuant to a series of declarations referred to as the Algiers Accords, which brought an end to the Iran hostage crisis.

Governed by rules of the UNITED NATIONS COMMISSION ON INTERNATIONAL TRADE LAW, the nine-member tribunal (or any greater multiple of three by agreement of both the United States and Iran) performs binding arbitration, the result being enforceable in the courts of any nation in accordance with its laws [Caron, 1990, p. 104].

See JOINT CLAIMS COMMISSION.

Irenology   Science of peace, named for the ancient Greek word for peace and for Irene, the personification of peace.

That body of theories, concepts, hypotheses, principles, generalizations, general laws, deductions, and propositions concerning the subject of peace. Irenology serves to clarify the forces or conditions that (1) from a positive standpoint, are favorable to or necessary for the maintenance or establishment of a peaceful regime; and (2) from a negative standpoint, are unfavorable to, or may threaten or disturb such peaceful regime. Irenology includes analysis of the formal machinery or formal methods for securing peace. Irenology is then to some extent a correlative to *Polemology*, which means the study of war, after the ancient Greek word for war and after Polemo, the personification of war [Starke, 1968, p. 15]. Compare CONFLIGOLOGY.

irrationality   *Negotiation:* Tactic involving unreasonable, arbitrary, and often emotional acts, including a commitment to a position that cannot be logically justified.

This can be a powerful tactic for reducing the other side's willingness to tolerate uncertainty and punishment. However, reliance on irrational or illogical means over the long term may generate unpredictable and illogical sets of solutions [Murray, Rau, and Sherman, 1989, pp. 215–216].

iso-curve   Mathematical model in negotiation depicting all the points an individual holds in equal value of combinations between different amounts of two options in trade-offs, such as the cost to build a building and the time it takes to complete [Raiffa, 1982, pp. 156–158].

isolation effect   How individuals evaluate a set of potential options in decision making. Making choices among options typically follows a *sequential process of elimination* in which individuals choose the most important attribute of an option and eliminate alternatives that do not include this attribute [Putnam and Holmer, 1992, p. 133, citation omitted].

isolationist   *International Relations:* One who opposes internationalism [Wittkopf, 1987, pp. 131–159].

Contrast INTERNATIONALIST.

issue   Matter of concern; problem; situation requiring thought.

In conflict resolution the term is sometimes used as a less adversarial and less threatening term than *conflict* or *dispute*.

issue development   Way in which issues change during the negotiation process. Operating from the assumption that disputes are transformed through shifting frames or by altering the way problems are conceptualized, a focus on issue development helps to clarify the task and agenda continually [Putnam and Holmer, 1992, p. 137].

issue escalation   Negotiation strategy in which a dispute over a relatively concrete issue is transferred into a matter of principle. Also designed to illustrate to the opposing party one's commitment to that particular issue [Holsti, 1983, p. 182].

issue field   Subject of contention between disputing parties, including the ends they hope to achieve [Holsti, 1983, p. 400].

issue substitution   *Negotiation:* Tactic of focusing on an issue that is important to the other side and trading a concession on it for a concession on an issue that is important to oneself. This assumes, of course, that not all issues are of equal importance to all parties—but the truth is, they rarely are [Jandt and Gillette, 1985, p. 259]. Compare LOGROLLING.

iterative dynamics   Reaction of a system when outputs are a function of inputs, and outputs are repeatedly fed back into the system as inputs. Used by chaos theorists to make conclusions about the long-term, dynamic aspects of a system.

A similar approach can be used to study BARGAINING. Whenever a bargainer makes an offer, that offer becomes a stimulus that requires a response by the other bargainer, which in turn requires the first bargainer to counter with yet another offer. This process continues until the bargainers either agree or reach an impasse. The key theoretical problem is to determine the relationship between offer and response [Tutzauer, 1992, p. 76–78].

I-will-if-you-will (IFU) proposition   When one party offers to take a certain action if and only if the other side does so also [Mitchell, 1991, p. 414].

jaha **(Arabic, Palestinian)**   Delegation of respected elders, usually men, who are known for their diplomacy, tact, and negotiation skills, and who help resolve disputes among others in the community. See SULHA.

jali **(Arabic, Bedouin)**   Tradition of exiling an accused murderer and close kinsmen from their local community. The banishment prevents an escalating blood feud by putting the accused and kin out of reach of the victim's family.

Bedouin society considers it an honorable duty to avenge wrongdoings committed unto one's family. The custom of *jali* curtails what could become an ongoing blood feud by placing the offender and close kin outside the practical reach of the offended family. With the offender's family no longer a presence in the local community, the kin of the victim need not commit a parallel offense to salvage their sense of social honor and tribal chivalry [Khalaf, 1990, p. 228].

Related terms: DAKHALA.

jang **(China)**   COMPROMISE. Under Confucianism there is a high value on compromise in order to achieve social harmony. See CHINESE MEDIATION.

Janus quality of negotiation   Describes the juxtaposition of two aspects of negotiation: forward-looking, interest-based deal-making negotiations, and backward-looking, rights-based dispute settlement [Goldberg, Sander, and Rogers, 1992, p. 66]. Janus was a god with two faces, one looking forward and the other looking backward.

239

Jay's Treaty 1794 treaty between England and the United States that provided that various questions and disputes arising out of the American Revolutionary War of 1776 be referred to arbitration.

This treaty of friendship, commerce, and navigation gave great impetus to the institution of arbitration. Jay's Treaty marks the beginning of the modern period of international arbitration [DOA].

Jewish rabbinical tribunal (Jewish Conciliation Board, Jewish Conciliation Center, Jewish court) Adjudicative and conciliatory forums that resolve disputes within the Jewish community.

Like many close-knit, ethnic, and religious communities trying to preserve traditions and maintain cohesiveness and harmony within a larger, often hostile culture and society, the Jewish community has a long-standing proscription against submitting intragroup disputes to secular courts [Auerbach, 1983]. In the tradition of the BET DIN, forms of rabbinical arbitration have been widely used. See *Congregation B'nai Sholom* v. *Martin* (1986). Its modern form typically involves a board consisting of volunteer members of the Jewish religious and professional community hearing disputes that range from familial to commercial to religious. The typical panel hearing a submission consists of a lawyer, a rabbi, and a businessman. It proceeds in an informal, private, nonlegalistic manner and decides on the basis of religious custom, principles of equity, and common sense. The panel "may seek to compromise the parties' claims, and is not bound to decide strictly in accordance with the governing rules of Jewish law, but may more carefully weigh the equities of the situation" [*Kingsbridge Center of Israel* v. *Turk* (1983)]. Many of the cases heard in the United States concern divorce matters. See, for example, *Avitzur* v. *Avitzur* (1983).

Because members of the community are not required to participate and submission of the dispute is voluntary, these boards are most effective when disputants are active members of the Jewish community and subject to community coercion, and they are less effective if the disputants are relatively independent of the community [McGillis and Mullen, 1977, pp. 13–14]. Another commentator notes that often the effectiveness of lay board judges stems from the disputants' own need for an impartial outside force to COMPEL them to yield without sacrificing their pride [Silberman, 1979, pp. 226–227]. Where there has been a high degree of assimilation into the wider society, the role of these autonomous tribunals has declined. However, there are indications of a resurgence.

Jirga **(Pakistan)** Ad hoc adjudicative body of up to fifty well-respected male elders used in tribal areas of northwestern Pakistan.

The *Jirga* is not bound by codified laws. It makes its determinations by consensus; upon failing to reach consensus, the panel is reconstituted. Those who do not comply with the *Jirga*'s verdict may be subject to fines, ostracism, property damage, or property confiscation. Areas governed by the *Jirga* system have a lower crime rate compared to areas regulated by formalized legal codes [Afzal, 1988, p. 224].

See BARANGAY, PANCHAYAT.

joinder *Law:* Legal procedure in which a party not named in the original complaint enters or is brought into the lawsuit by subsequent pleadings.

Labor/Arbitration: Procedure whereby multiple grievances affecting many employees of the same company can be combined and arbitrated as a single case. When joinder is used, the arbitrator's award will then bind all involved and will therefore foreclose needless multiplicity and expense of proceedings. This term may also refer to the joining of two separate unions in a trilateral arbitration over a work assignment dispute, though only one of the unions has an arbitration agreement with the employer [DOA].

Compare CONSOLIDATION.

joint benefit That part of an agreement that is mutually beneficial.

joint board *Labor:* Grievance procedure using BIPARTITE BOARD.

joint claims commission *International:* TRIBUNAL for settling international claims.

International claims are those that a citizen of one country makes against the government of another for some infringement of the citizen's rights. Members of a joint claims commission are appointed by the disputing states. The states usually appoint their own nationals, thus maintaining a controlling influence. Joint claims commissions often fail to reach an agreement and tend to produce compromise settlements. When disputes cannot be resolved under such commissions, the parties may choose to use a MIXED ARBITRAL TRIBUNAL. A joint claims commission may sometimes be a quasi-permanent body, such as the CANADA–U.S. INTERNATIONAL JOINT COMMISSION, established by treaty in 1909 and relating to the boundary between the United States and Canada [DOA]. The most famous contemporary joint claims commission is the IRAN–UNITED STATES CLAIMS TRIBUNAL.

joint defense agreement *International Relations:* Agreement between states to join military resources for mutual defense.

Law: Agreement between multiple defendants to coordinate their defense strategies and perhaps pool resources. Such pretrial agreements may also include loss allocation, such as percentages that individual defendants will pay to satisfy a plaintiff's verdict. Alternatively, the defendants may agree to defer the exercise of their rights against each other to a subsequent negotiation or other ADR process [Dauer and Nyhart, 1984].

joint fact-finding   See FACT-FINDING.

joint gains   *Negotiation:* Additional value created through negotiation that would not have been achieved had the parties proceeded independently.

joint problem solving   See PROBLEM SOLVING.

joint session   Phase of decision making, negotiation, or mediation in which the parties are meeting together. Sometimes referred to as PLENARY SESSION in contrast to CAUCUS or PRIVATE POSITION.

Journal of Conflict Resolution   Scholarly periodical published by Sage Publications with an emphasis on international conflict and theory.

Journal of Dispute Resolution   Periodical of legal scholarship on dispute resolution sponsored by the law school at University of Missouri at Columbia.

judge   Adjudicator. Although commonly used to refer to any adjudicator, the term more properly refers to an adjudicator serving in the public courts as opposed to an ARBITRATOR, who is also an adjudicator but serves privately.

judge-mediator   Sitting judge who also works as a private, paid contractor for mediation services. The practice may not be allowed in some jurisdictions.

judge pro tem   Adjudicator serving ad hoc under the auspices of a court, usually as a REFEREE under a REFEREE SYSTEM or in a TRIAL ON ORDER OF REFERENCE.

judgment   Exercise of critical thinking and discernment yielding an opinion; also the opinion itself.
   Law: Decision of a court on a proceeding brought before it [DOA]. Commonly refers to a final, officially recorded decision on the parties' respective rights in criminal or civil matters brought before the court (compare RULING), although there are specific terms such as *final judgment* and *interlocutory judgment*. DECREE and judgment are often used interchangeably. However, there is a historical difference. A sentence or order of a court according to equity is a decree, while a decision based on law is a judgment. The difference is clearer when courts of law and equity are separate (as historically was the case in COMMON LAW systems). As distinctions between the two types of courts have eroded, however, *decree* has fallen out of use, in favor of judgment.
   Arbitration: Decision of an arbitrator, properly referred to as an AWARD rather than a judgment. Arbitrators do exercise judgment, however.

judgment-roll (archaic)   Record of court proceedings and judgments, at one time written on a roll of parchment. The term is still used in some jurisdictions, but has been largely replaced by *docket*.

Arbitration: Documents that must be filed in a court in order to make the arbitrator's award into a judgment that can be enforced. A judgment-roll may consist of the original or a copy of the contract containing the arbitration agreement, each written extension of time within which the award is to be made, and each paper submitted to the court in connection with the arbitration, as well as each order of the court concerned with confirming the award [DOA]. The applicable arbitration statute usually specifies the contents of the judgment roll.

judicial adjunct   Expert appointed by the court to facilitate a negotiation or trial by fact-finding, by directing the discovery procedure, by mediating, or by presiding over a settlement conference [BNA ADR Report, 1988, p. 130]. The term is broad, covering a range of third-party dispute resolution activities under the auspices of a court acting under the authority of either court rule or statute. See DISCOVERY REFEREE, JUDICIAL HOST, REFEREE.

judicial arbitration   Same as COURT-ANNEXED ARBITRATION or MANDATORY NON-BINDING ARBITRATION and "is obviously an inapt term for the system that it describes is neither judicial nor arbitration. A hearing that is not conducted by a judge, and the right to a trial de novo removes the finality of true arbitration" [*Dodd* v. *Ford* (1984)].

judicial host   Federal magistrate or judge who presides over a settlement conference.

Coined by Magistrate Wayne Brazil, the term connotes a third party who seeks to make the parties feel comfortable, to help the parties overcome barriers to settlement, and often to encourage consideration of ADR [Riskin, 1991, pp. 1081–1085].

judicial mediation   Mediation conducted by a judge or magistrate, typically court-connected mediation as required under local court rules.

judicial reference   Alternative term for TRIAL ON ORDER OF REFERENCE.

judicial review of ADR proceedings   Court monitoring and oversight of outcomes from ADR processes.

In general, courts have no review or *appellate* jurisdiction over private, voluntary ADR processes unless asked to enforce settlement agreements or arbitration awards. A court applies basic principles of contract law when a party contests the court's enforcement of an agreement and rarely examines the ADR process out of which the agreement arose. Judicial review of settlement agreements may extend to those affecting third parties (such as class action or child custody settlements) or involving divorce. Courts review arbitration awards at the request of one of the parties to determine whether or not the award can be enforced. However, the review cannot concern itself with the sufficiency of evidence or the merits of the award, nor can the court vacate the award because of alleged errors of law or fact. Most arbitration statutes are explicit on these points [DOA].

With respect to court-connected ADR programs established by statute or local rule, the court may exercise more oversight on the processes, but because such programs allow a trial de novo on request after the ADR process, there is little reason to review the outcome. Indeed, ADR proceedings are usually protected by a privilege of confidentiality and treated as settlement negotiations, making records made in conjunction with the ADR process inadmissible in court.

judicial review of arbitral awards   See AWARD.

judicial settlement   *International Law:* Submission of a dispute to an international judicial body for a final and binding decision.

Explicitly recognized in Article 33 of the UN Charter, judicial settlement implies the use of a standing, independent judicial body, such as the INTERNATIONAL COURT OF JUSTICE. However, it may include arbitral bodies if sufficiently independent arbitrators make their decision on the basis of applicable legal standards and employ accepted, equitable judicial procedure.

judicial settlement conference, judicially supervised settlement conference
Settlement discussion held with the presence and active participation of the trial judge or magistrate.

Conferences vary from informal and spontaneous to formal and scheduled. Although the degree of judicial intervention may vary, it could include the judge's active role as mediator [Harter, 1987, p. 11]. Because the pressures of case management and disappointment with a litigant's position in negotiation can affect how a judge conducts the settlement conference or rules in a subsequent adjudication, many courts designate a separate judge as a settlement judge [Schoenfield and Schoenfield, 1988, p. 201].

See SETTLEMENT CONFERENCE.

juge conciliateur (France)   Literally, "conciliator-judge," a volunteer who hears each disputant and proposes a nonbinding solution to promote a written settlement agreement.

In the tradition of the *COUR DE CONCILIATION*, a pilot program of *juges concil-iateurs* was established in 1977 to resolve small claims through AMICABLE AGREE-MENT and faster, cheaper, and less formally than litigation. Nationwide implementation followed the next year. *Juges conciliateurs* are most often called upon to resolve consumer, landlord-tenant, and neighborhood disputes, al-though their jurisdiction is not limited to such cases and even includes minor criminal offenses [Marshall, 1985, p. 83].

juridogenic problem   Result when the legal system exacerbates rather than helps solve an original problem [Menkel-Meadow, 1991, p. 45].

jurisdiction   Legal power or right to exercise authority; power of a court to de-cide a case.
   Contrast VENUE.

jury-determined settlement   Form of private, voluntary arbitration similar to the SUMMARY JURY TRIAL in its use of a jury except that the verdict is binding and the parties split the costs of the procedure [Vidmar and Rice, 1991, pp. 98–102]. If the parties are in litigation, they might voluntarily agree in advance to be bound by the court-connected summary jury trial procedure using the court's own jury pool. Essentially this would be just an informal, abbreviated trial. How-ever, this would be rare and constitutionally questionable in most states. The typical procedure is private and the parties must create their own private jury, often with the assistance of an ADMINISTERING AGENCY, or ad hoc using a tem-porary employment agency.

jury verdict reports, jury verdict research   Information service providing de-tails of the backgrounds and outcomes of cases that are adjudicated in public courts. Though often compared to claims in negotiation to provide some crite-ria for a settlement (a form of OBJECTIVE CRITERIA and an indicator of one's BATNA), they rarely provide enough detail to instill confidence in the compari-son and often show considerable variation among and even within jurisdictions.

just, justice   That which is due, proper, fair, or proportional; using authority to achieve what is right.
   Concepts of justice serve as moral criteria, helping to gauge specific actions of institutions and individuals. They are best established prior to and independently of the specific situation to be judged. The concept is problematic because it can vary significantly among different cultures. It can be highly subjective and indi-vidualistic, or objective to the degree that it consists of broadly shared norms that have been applied universally or with some consistency in comparable contexts.

For proponents of conciliatory forms of dispute resolution that rely on consensus and party autonomy, justice as a subjective concept might translate to "justice is what the parties agree to"; or as an objective concept, it could represent a principle deeply held by one or both parties that might impede resolution. If the concept is broadly held in the society at large and accepted by the disputants, it may facilitate resolution.

Concepts of *procedural justice* are often distinguished from *substantive justice*. Procedural justice is the process by which an outcome is reached and implemented. A primary tenet is that both parties must operate within the same procedures. If the procedures are to be different, the reasons for the difference should be mutually acceptable. Another tenet is that a person serving as adjudicator should be impartial and includes the corollary principle that the adjudicator cannot have a conflict of interest or an interest in the outcome. Again highlighting the tension between objective and subjective notions of justice, Peachey [1989, p. 301] notes that while within the legal system the common understanding of procedural justice is the right application of the right rules, it may also refer to the individual's perception of the fairness of the rules or procedures that regulate a process or give rise to a decision.

Substantive justice refers to the fairness of an outcome. *Distributive justice* examines ways of evaluating substantive outcomes by focusing on the allocation of resources or access to entitlements. Different approaches to distributive justice may use different criteria to determine the fairness of distribution. Thus, *equitable justice* would require apportionment on the basis of each party's particular characteristics [Zartman and Berman, 1982, p. 104]. *Compensatory justice* would remedy an unequal distribution of resources to the extent that one of the parties through past actions has deprived the other of a benefit previously enjoyed. For example, a husband may agree to pay spousal support and fund his ex-wife's school expenses so that she can earn an income and attain a standard of living equal to what she was accustomed to in the marriage. A developer may monetarily compensate the immediate neighbors of a new building project for potential damage to their lifestyle [O'Hare, Bacow, and Sanderson, 1983]. Under concepts of *subtractive justice* all parties are equally denied access to a resource. This might apply when denial of access to the other is more important than having access oneself. For example, if a divorcing couple cannot decide which of them should have the piano, both may agree to sell it and deny possession to each other rather than agree that one of them should have it. In contrast to distributive justice, which focuses on resource allocation, *restorative justice* focuses on redress for injury and suffering and restoring a situation or relationship as best as possible following a transgression [Peachey, 1989].

In some cases, procedural and substantive justice are overlapping concepts to the extent that one is difficult to determine without the other. The fairness of the procedure influences the parties' perceptions of the fairness of the outcome and vice versa.

Contrast with FAIRNESS; see also RESTORATIVE JUSTICE.

Justice of the Peace Subordinate magistrate elected or appointed as judge in a court of limited jurisdiction. Although the office is found in many COMMON LAW jurisdictions, these officials in the United States were historically LAY JUDGES who resolved disputes informally and by mediation as well as by formal process. Many states have abolished the office or require legal training to serve.

justiciable Liable to trial in a court.

Many disputes may not raise justiciable issues and therefore cannot be brought before a court for resolution. Such disputes are good candidates for private, voluntary ADR.

juvenile arbitration Program to resolve disputes involving youths without resorting to court. The programs may be sponsored by either public or private sources. Most referrals come from the police and the schools and involve offenses that would be minor crimes if committed by adults. Although mediation is more commonly used for such disputes, arbitration similarly diverts the youths from court and attempts to formulate a resolution that is expressly tailored to juvenile problems. Compare FAMILY GROUP CONFERENCE, JUVENILE CONFERENCE COMMITTEES, SENTENCING CIRCLES, VICTIM-OFFENDER RECONCILIATION PROGRAMS. See also RESTORATIVE JUSTICE.

juvenile conference committees (JCCs) Court-connected alternative dispute resolution process in which volunteer groups of community members dispose of usually minor, first-offense complaints against juveniles.

Though these committees serve as a diversion mechanism, releasing judges to concentrate their efforts on serious offenders and conserving valuable court resources, JCCs also express community sentiments and standards through sentencing. Under most models, JCCs meet with juveniles, their family members, and interested parties to determine the circumstances surrounding the complaint and to receive input and recommendations for appropriate punishment. The JCCs determination is referred to a judge for approval.

Compare FAMILY GROUP CONFERENCE, JUVENILE ARBITRATION, SENTENCING CIRCLES, VICTIM-OFFENDER RECONCILIATION PROGRAMS. See also RESTORATIVE JUSTICE.

juvenile mediation, juvenile restitution Mediation involving minor crimes committed by juvenile offenders. The aim is to provide the victims and the juvenile offenders with opportunity to work out restitution. See RESTORATIVE JUSTICE, VICTIM-OFFENDER MEDIATION.

keeping the peace Use of physical or moral suasion to restrain others from using violent forms of self-help to resolve conflict. Used mostly in the context of police action preventing and suppressing criminal activity.

Konfliktkomission See GERMAN SOCIAL COURTS.

Kpelle **Moot (Liberia)** Conciliatory process for the resolution of interpersonal and family disputes and the restoration of highly valued social harmony among the Kpelle tribe.

The procedure, in which a complainant aired a grievance at home among fellow disputants and other kinsmen, focused not on assigning blame but on rewarding peaceful behavior in accordance with tribal norms [Auerbach, 1983, pp. 118–119], and served as an alternative to the state court system. The state of this institution after the Liberian civil wars of the 1990s is unknown.

labor arbitration   Process for resolving labor-management disputes by an impartial third party.

The term is associated primarily with VOLUNTARY ARBITRATION between management and organized labor under contractual agreements to arbitrate future disputes reached through collective bargaining. Most COLLECTIVE BARGAINING AGREEMENTS provide for the arbitration of contract-related disputes and individual employee grievances. With its roots in the dispute resolution systems of medieval guilds, modern labor arbitration evolved with the emergence of workers' rights and organized labor in the early twentieth century as a method of preserving workplace harmony and avoiding the sometimes catastrophic effect of strikes.

The term is also used to refer to COMPULSORY ARBITRATION between labor and management mandated by statute, although the preferred term in this context is *compulsory labor arbitration.*

See ARBITRATION, INTEREST ARBITRATION, GRIEVANCE ARBITRATION, PUBLIC EMPLOYEE ARBITRATION.

labor court   Labor arbitration court of government origin and control for the purpose of resolving labor-management disputes.

Labor courts are common in many countries of the world. They may be bipartite (see BIPARTITE BOARD)or tripartite (see TRIPARTITE PANEL)[DOA].

labor dispute   Dispute between parties to a COLLECTIVE BARGAINING AGREE-MENT over the terms or the interpretation of the terms of their contract, work-place conditions, and disciplinary issues [DOA]. The Norris-LaGuardia Act of 1932, at § 13(c), 29 U.S.C.A. § 113, defines a labor dispute as follows: "Any controversy concerning terms or conditions of employment, or concerning the association or representation of persons in negotiating, fixing, maintaining, changing, or seeking to arrange terms or conditions of employment, regardless of whether or not the disputants stand in the proximate relation of employer and employee." The collective bargaining context distinguishes a labor dispute from other disputes between employees and employers.

labor-management committee   Decision-making body composed of super-visors and workers and formed to promote collaboration in solving workplace problems.

Generally these committees are formed outside the formal framework of collective bargaining agreements, thereby avoiding union representation and governmental regulation. Dunlop [1984, pp. 227–228] observes that these committees often limit their focus to the narrow issues of health and safety, quality of work life, waste, absenteeism, production efficiency, and training. Decisions over conflict in these areas may be reached in the committee only if both labor and management agree. Failure to agree at this stage may result in the conflict being moved to a collective bargaining stage or other, more formal procedure.

labor mediation   Mediation of employment-related issues, usually in the context of COLLECTIVE BARGAINING AGREEMENTS and unionized labor. Occasionally referred to as INDUSTRIAL MEDIATION.

laches   Undue or unreasonable delay in asserting a right that may prevent enforcement of that right or result in its loss [DOA]. An equitable concept in COMMON LAW, as opposed to a LIMITATIONS PERIOD imposed by contract or statute.

land for peace   *International Relations:* Compromise strategy whereby sovereignty over geographical territory is exchanged for a vow to refrain from violence.

Implementation of this concept has been suggested by various parties involved in the Israeli-Palestinian conflict.

land-use negotiation   *Public Policy:* Complex multiparty negotiation, typically facilitated, over the application of municipal regulation to the use of land. Land-use negotiation can be over the formation of land-use policy generally or it may be site specific.

language intensity *Communication:* Strength of affect, which often reflects the intensity of a speaker's position.

High-intensity language, characterized by strong affect, indicates a strong feeling and intense commitment to a position, whereas low-intensity language reflects weaker commitment and enthusiasm. "Your project sounds excellent," for example, is a more intense statement than "Your project sounds good" [Gibbons, Bradac, and Busch, 1992, p. 164].

largest number In GAME THEORY, social-trap game in which individuals submit a number as large as they wish; the participant who has picked the highest number gets a prize of a previously determined amount divided by the number she chose [Rapoport, 1988, p. 460]. Though participants feel competitive pressure to pick a high number to outbid the others, the reward is reduced proportionally.

last-best-offer arbitration Form of SPECIAL-FEATURE ARBITRATION in which the arbitrator may award only one or the other party's last or best offer. Same as FINAL-OFFER ARBITRATION, LAST-OFFER ARBITRATION, and BASEBALL ARBITRATION, unless the arbitrator is authorized to choose from best offers rather than only last offers.

Negotiation: Positional bargaining tactic in which the negotiator declares a final position, "This is my last and best offer." A form of "take it or leave it."

last-minute demand *Negotiation:* Pressure tactic whereby a party makes a demand toward the end of a negotiation, when all other major issues have been settled and an agreement has been reached.

If the other parties are satisfied with the agreement and anxious to conclude negotiations, they may simply concede to a last-minute demand in the interest of closing the deal [Iklé, 1964, pp. 221–222]. In Craver's [1988] list of dirty tricks, such a negotiator is referred to as the NIBBLER.

last-offer arbitration Type of SPECIAL-FEATURE ARBITRATION in which each party submits her final demand and final offer to the arbitrator, who must then select between the last offers in rendering the disputants' awards. Also called FINAL-OFFER ARBITRATION, LAST-BEST-OFFER ARBITRATION, and BASEBALL ARBITRATION. See also MEDALOA.

latent conflict Conflict that has not ripened into a dispute, as opposed to a MANIFEST CONFLICT. See CONFLICT and DISPUTE for important distinctions.

laundry list technique *Negotiation:* Positional bargaining technique of itemizing demands instead of presenting one's opponent with a lump sum.

An itemized list of demands can be more easily explained and appear more palatable than a lump sum. Also, it allows for trade-offs that may avoid impasse [Edwards, 1981, p. 55].

law   Rule or body of rules that prescribes actions.

The legal anthropologist Malinowski [1972] distinguished law from mere social order or norms by the existence of some social machinery of binding force reinforced through formal ceremony and public control and criticism. The rules of law are recognized as obligations and rights among persons based on mutual dependence rather than mere psychological motive [Gruter, 1991, p. 5].

The law is distinct from *a law* or *laws.* While *a law* refers to a particular rule, standard, or concrete legal precept, *the law* is a more abstract reference to a larger body of laws prescribed by government or some controlling authority. *The law* might also refer to the agents or social organizations that enforce and administer the law—judges and police, for example.

The term *law* is sometimes used to distinguish law from EQUITY, which are two different approaches to remedies and historically applied by different courts. In most jurisdictions, the distinction between *law courts* and *equity courts* has been abolished, obscuring the theoretical distinction between the two concepts. The term is also used opposite *fact,* particularly in adjudication, where a distinction is made between fact-finding and law-finding. For example, a judge decides questions of law, while a jury decides questions of fact.

lawday, law day (archaic, English)   Day for holding court.

Lawday was the day that a particular court—mainly a lower court, such as the Court Leet, Hundred Courts, and Sheriff's Tourns—would meet. It was often a partial holiday for local residents, who were required to attend. Many of these courts met only sporadically and were not courts of record; they served the important function of adjudicating minor misdemeanors and local interpersonal and community disputes. The social institution of the LOVEDAY emerged as an alternative to adjudication by governmental authority.

In the United States, May 1 is designated Law Day in recognition of the role of law in society.

law merchant, *lex mercatoria*   *International Commercial Arbitration:* Body of rules derived from custom and usage that governed the transactions of merchants who traveled throughout the civilized world during the Middle Ages. In current international commercial arbitration practice, parties may direct arbitrators to decide cases by applying these rules.

The *lex mercatoria* was applied as part of the COMMON LAW by the merchants in their special tribunals. This body of trade rules developed by the business community in PIEPOUDRE COURTS and other mercantile tribunals was almost as universal in medieval times as the law of the church. Later, this cosmopolitan and universal merchant law was incorporated into the national laws of various countries [DOA]. Whether or not a body of applicable trade law exists outside of national laws is a matter of continuing debate. However, specific industries could adopt a set of norms to govern behavior and promote predictability in relationships before the state recognizes such norms.

lawsuit   Same as CIVIL ACTION. There existed a distinction between *suits in equity* and *actions at law,* which were heard in separate courts of equity and of law, respectively. However, the distinction between such courts, and thus the terms, has largely been abolished.

lawyer   Person who practices law and typically is licensed to do so.

In the United States, *lawyer* and *attorney* are used synonymously. However, *attorney* is a broader term referring to anyone designated by someone else to transact business in their stead. Thus, an *attorney-at-law* is a lawyer with a client who is empowered to represent that client in his legal affairs. In England, lawyers can be *solicitors* (attorneys) or *barristers* (counsellors), the latter being a trial lawyer or *litigator,* while in the United States a lawyer is licensed to practice as both an attorney and a *counselor,* the latter referring more to someone who gives legal advice because there is no separate designation for litigator.

Lawyers Engaged in Alternative Dispute Resolution (LEADR)   Australian ADR membership organization.

lay judge   Person without formal training who fulfills a judicial role.

In the United States, lay judges are individuals who perform traditional judicial duties but lack formal qualifications for the bar. Many JUSTICES OF THE PEACE were lay judges as were some judges of higher courts prior to the latter half of the twentieth century. Also called *nonlawyer judge.*

In other countries, the term may also refer to laypersons who usually, after some training, serve on a mixed attorney-lay bench or act primarily as jurors [Silberman, 1979, pp. 2, 24–26].

league   Alliance or association between persons, organizations, or states.

League Council   *International Relations:* Now-defunct conciliatory body established by the League of Nations and charged with investigating and trying to resolve international disputes. Similar to COMMISSION OF INQUIRY, which it could appoint, the council employed a system of rapporteurs to clarify and report on the facts in support of CONCILIATION.

In the United Nations, by contrast, the Security Council's primary role is peacekeeping and its powers of investigation under Article 34 of the Charter are oriented to PEACEKEEPING rather than conciliation.

League of Nations   Association of states created in accordance with the Covenant of the Peace Conference at Paris, adopted on April 28, 1919, with the high purpose of reducing the likelihood of war, establishing a system of collective security and cooperation, and encouraging the adoption of the principle of arbitration.

The Covenant of the Peace Conference provided for judicial and arbitral settlement of international disputes as one way of securing the principal objective of the organization—the prevention of war and the maintenance of world peace. The League of Nations was officially dissolved on April 18, 1946 [DOA].

leap to agreement   *Negotiation:* Bargaining strategy consisting of a high opening demand, followed by minimal concessions, finalized by sudden presentation or support of a package that meets the needs of the other party.

Negotiators often use the leap-to-agreement approach when (1) no one proposal seems better than the rest; (2) they are anxious to conclude negotiations—to meet a deadline, for example; or (3) they want to reach a compromise, but only after educating the opponent on a principle consistent with their initial *hard line* [Zartman and Berman, 1982].

The final "leap" often comes in the form of a mutually acceptable YESABLE PROPOSITION or PACKAGE DEAL, which the opponent can merely sign her name to and thereby conclude the process [Fisher, 1969].

leave on the table   *Negotiation:* Psychological tension in positional negotiation over whether the negotiator has correctly estimated her opponent's RESERVATION PRICE, thereby getting the most concessions possible from the opponent, that is, "By accepting this offer, I hope we don't leave anything on the table."

Also can mean concluding a negotiation session with a verbal agreement, usually to be reviewed for approval by a negotiator's constituency, but leaving all issues technically unresolved until the signing of a formal agreement. Simkin [1971, p. 168] notes that this practice can be problematic if attitudes change or different interpretations evolve before formal signing.

legal   Pertaining to or in accordance with the applicable law; not prohibited by law.

legal audit   Process of weighing the costs and benefits of litigation as a method of dispute resolution against the relative efficiency and effectiveness of resolution through alternative means.

Applies to both individual cases and standardized dispute resolution mechanisms. In the latter case, a legal audit should include an assessment of the necessary steps for large-scale policy change, as well as an analysis of the current system's success [Riskin and Westbrook, 1987, p. 451]. Compare LITIGATION AUDIT.

legal dispute   Dispute grounded in a legal entitlement; dispute on which a claim would be recognized by law and be justiciable.

Courts can process a legal dispute. Many disputes, however, are not recognized by law and must be resolved through other processes. Whether a dispute is a legal dispute often depends on how it is framed.

legalism   Procedure or technique adopted from legal proceedings, such as formal litigation, and used in extrajudicial processes, such as arbitration or mediation [DOA].

Also, the ethical attitude that holds moral conduct to be a matter of rule-following, and moral relationships to consist of duties and rights determined by rules [Shklar, 1964, p. 1]. Contrasts with a focus on disputants' interests rather than on their rights.

legislative negotiation   Direct, usually facilitated negotiation among stakeholders in proposed legislation for the purpose of reaching a consensus recommendation on the content of legislation.

Related to REGULATORY NEGOTIATION, certainly the POLICY DIALOGUE version of it. The negotiation over amendments to the Federal Insecticide, Fungicide, and Rodenticide Act (FIFRA) is an important example of an attempt at legislative negotiation. Legislative negotiation raises many of the same issues as regulatory negotiation, such as adequate representation of interests and resolution of controversial issues [Nagel and Mills, 1991, p. 117].

legitimacy   To be in conformity with the law, recognized principles, or accepted norms as applicable to the context.

Negotiation: Recognition that the other side has genuine interests, concerns, and emotions and a right to be heard as a serious and equal bargaining partner. Sometimes referred to as *role legitimacy*. Fisher and Brown [1989] promote this acceptance as an element of being *unconditionally constructive*. See also Moore [1986, p. 137].

The term may also refer to the use of an independent standard rather than a subjective standard to judge options for settlement. Fisher and Ury [1981] refer to this concept as OBJECTIVE CRITERIA.

lemon law   Legislation designed to provide consumers with effective remedies when a motor vehicle or other product is defective and cannot be repaired.

In the typical statute on new motor vehicles, the manufacturer must refund the purchase price or provide the consumer with a new replacement vehicle if it cannot correct any defect after a "reasonable number of attempts." These remedies and direct recourse to the manufacturer are not easily available under other consumer protection laws. Many lemon laws also establish an independent arbitration procedure after the consumer has exhausted any informal dispute resolution process provided by the manufacturer (see, for example, AUTOLINE). Because participation is mandated by statute rather than agreed to by contract, the independent arbitration process is really a form of administrative procedure. The procedure is administered by the state's attorney general or consumer protection office or by private contractor such as the AMERICAN ARBITRATION ASSOCIATION. The binding nature of the process varies with jurisdiction.

level-of-aspiration theory   Theory that hard bargaining, characterized by a high opening bid and few concessions, leads the opponent to lower demands and aspire to a settlement less favorable than originally hoped for [Tutzauer, 1992, p. 71].

lex arbitri   *International Commercial Arbitration:* Law of the place of arbitration that may govern whether an arbitral award is valid. It is not necessarily the law governing the substance of the dispute or procedural rules applied by arbitrators, but the legal system of the situs that determines whether the award was arrived at properly. Compare LEX FORI.

lex fori   Law of the forum or jurisdiction within which a remedy is being pursued. Procedural rights are determined by the law of the place or forum. Compare LEX ARBITRI.

lexical diversity   *Communication:* Variety and quality of the language a speaker uses, measured by the percentage of "novel" words within the total of words used.

Speakers demonstrating high lexical diversity are often rated as confident, competent, effective, and credible. In negotiations, however, a party may choose to reiterate her position using the same words and phrases, a pattern that while classified as low in diversity may lead to being perceived as tough, firm, or committed [Gibbons, Bradac, and Busch, 1992, p. 164–165].

lexicon   Dictionary of specialized or unique vocabulary.

lex loci   Law of the location wherein the CAUSE OF ACTION arose and which determines substantive rights. Compare LEX ARBITRI, LEX FORI.

lex mercatoria   See LAW MERCHANT.

lex specialis   *International Arbitration:* Literally, "special law," refers to the substantive law agreed upon by the parties for arbitrators to apply in resolving disputes arising under a particular agreement.

The *lex specialis* is often a combination of legal systems, or it may be the law of a single nation or municipality. Parties can authorize the arbitrator to settle the case by supplementing a combination of international and municipal law with the parties' view of what seems reasonable and fair in the particular case [Merrills, 1991, pp. 91–92]. Compare LEX ARBITRI, LEX FORI, LEX LOCI. See also AMIABLE COMPOSITION, EX AEQUO ET BONO.

liability   *Law:* a legal obligation to perform or a condition in which one is responsible for some expense or loss.

li-lao **(China)**   Village leaders and elders who resolved minor local disputes through extrajudicial means.

Originally, referral of disputes to a *li-lao* was a voluntary alternative to the local magistrate. Overloaded magistrates and the Ming Dynasty (1368–1644) rulers actively encouraged this form of community mediation, and the *li-lao* began to seek out aggressively community disputes to mediate. Eventually, *li-lao* dispute resolution became the norm. According to one account, around 1500 A.D., ten years passed without the magistrate of a certain village handling a single case [Wall and Blum, 1991, pp. 4–5].

limitations periods   Period imposed either by statute (STATUTE OF LIMITATIONS) or by contract within which one may make a claim or assert a right. Failure to do so within the period may bar the assertion of the right or claim in a particular forum such as a court or arbitral tribunal. Compare to LACHES.

limited rationality   Decision-making model created as a more realistic alternative to pure or COMPREHENSIVE RATIONALITY.

Rather than attempting to discover and evaluate all possible alternatives in order to maximize their values, policymakers are usually content to choose the first alternative that appears to meet their needs. The model acknowledges that officials are fallible and that their assessment of available options and their consequences will be incomplete.

linkage   *Negotiation:* Making two agreements, or the resolution of two separate issues, contingent upon one another.

Typically, one agreement is exchanged for the other, so one party gives in on one issue under the condition that the other party gives in on another.

Compare LOGROLLING.

listen, listening   *Communication:* Hear or receive communications, usually oral, from another.

Listening implies giving one's attention to another and waiting or refraining from speech or action until the communication has been made. It is often referenced by degree, such as "half listening" or "listening intently." Good listening skills are considered essential in conciliatory forms of conflict resolution, particularly in negotiation. While it would certainly be naive to think that all conflicts can be resolved by better listening, poor listening can result in misperceptions and misinformation causing or aggravating the conflict. Much has been written on recognizing and overcoming the many impediments to good listening, such as excessive interruptions, inattention, hearing what you want to hear, mentally composing a response, overuse of jargon, and having a closed mind. Other terms refer to specific listening skills beyond the mere receipt and understanding of the common meaning of spoken words. See ACTIVE LISTENING, DIALOGIC LISTENING, EMPATHIC LISTENING.

litigate   Engage in LITIGATION; pursue or defend a legal action in a court in accordance with the applicable formal procedures.

litigation   Process of disputing, beginning with the filing of a lawsuit and ending with dismissal of the suit or enforcement of the judgment entered in the suit or of a final decision on appeal.

In litigation, the disputants take their claims to a court and engage in a contest involving pretrial, trial, and posttrial activities in the context of the rules of evidence and procedure in force in that court. As Galanter [1986, pp. 152] notes, disputants usually pursue the litigation process for two reasons. First, they are mobilizing the court's ADJUDICATION process. Although *adjudication* and *litigation* are often used interchangeably, the former implies an activity of the court, *judging,* while the latter connotes an activity of the disputants that eventually leads to judgment. Litigation and adjudication are perhaps merely two different aspects of the same overall process. Second, the disputants are using the court process in a strategic pursuit of settlement. In this sense, litigation presents opportunities to shift the power dynamics in negotiation in a way that promotes a negotiated settlement (see LITIGOTIATION). Thus litigation does not necessarily require adjudication.

Litigation embodies principles of the ADVERSARY SYSTEM. As a general rule, courts are passive—they do not initiate the activity and they judge largely on the basis of the parties' presentation of the facts and law. This is especially true in common law jurisdictions. In many civil law jurisdictions and in countries with other legal traditions, the court may be a more active or INQUISITORIAL participant in the process leading to adjudication.

Leeson and Johnston [1988, pp. 7–8] list five characteristics that distinguish litigation from other dispute resolution processes: (1) litigation can make law for society as a whole while resolving a particular dispute, (2) litigation has the authority to compel participation, (3) litigation is conducted according to rigidly enforced procedural and evidentiary rules enacted by legislatures or adopted by courts, (4) litigation is the only dispute resolution process with explicit enforcement powers, and (5) litigation is a public process.

litigation audit   Examination of a corporation's policies and procedures, usually conducted by outside legal counsel, for the purpose of identifying vulnerability to lawsuits [Lieberman and Lieberman, 1985, p. 104]. Compare LEGAL AUDIT.

litigation explosion   Much-publicized proliferation of lawsuit filings over the last several decades of the twentieth century.

The widespread perception of an increasingly litigious society overwhelming the courts with lawsuits has been a major factor in the *institutionalization* of ADR processes, particularly COURT-CONNECTED processes. The extent of this problem is debated. While civil case filings per capita have increased and litigation is more complex and expensive, the relative capacity of the courts has not expanded accordingly, and the percentage of cases actually reaching trial had decreased by the early 1980s. See Galanter, 1983. Also called *crisis in the courts*.

litigation risk analysis   Decision-making model using a decision tree to dissect elements of case proof at trial and assessing the probability of outcomes at each element.

Mediators and lawyers commonly use litigation risk analysis to REALITY TEST disputants and to assess BATNAS. Assigning probabilities is largely subjective, however, making this a weak method of predicting adjudicated outcomes. Litigation risk analysis is a useful way to visualize the steps in litigation and prepare accordingly. See DECISION-TREE ANALYSIS.

litigator   LAWYER representing someone before a court in the LITIGATION process.

litigious   Contentious and prone to engage in lawsuits.

litigious family   Divorced couple who have resigned themselves to a relationship characterized by perpetual conflict and feud and who cannot settle their dispute for years. Also called *high-conflict couple* [Duryee, 1985, p. 51]. Compare ENMESHED COUPLE.

litigotiation   Strategic pursuit of a settlement by combining litigation and negotiation [Galanter, 1984, p. 268].

The concept is similar to IN THE SHADOW OF THE LAW. However, litigotiation refers more to the procedural and tactical environment created by the court's rules of procedure, as opposed to merely the use of legal standards for reference in shaping an agreement. One may bargain "in the shadow of the law" without filing a lawsuit, but litigotiation requires mobilization of the judicial process.

lockout   *Labor:* Employer's refusal to allow regular employees access to the workplace until they concede on issues in dispute. The employer's version of a STRIKE.

loggerheads, at loggerheads (colloquial)   Disputing or in contention over an issue. Broader implication than IMPASSE, which is a deadlock in negotiations.

logrolling   *Negotiation:* Trade-offs among the issues; exchanges of concessions on issues of differing importance, allowing each bargainer to get her way on one issue in exchange for her concession on another of lesser importance to herself [Pruitt and Lewis, 1977]. Contrast LINKAGE.

Legislation: Bundling into one bill several pieces of distinct legislation that would not pass alone but that would be adopted as a group because a majority is reached by combining the minorities that support the separate propositions.

***Lok Adalats* (India)**   Form of people's court or community court that promotes settlements through conciliation and mediation between the disputing parties as an alternative to formal litigation.

Lok Adalats have evolved from voluntary efforts rather than through legislation or court rule, so there is no mandate for disputants to participate as a precondition to trial. The dispute does not have to be in litigation. Each *Lok Adalat* has a team of two or more *judges* (conciliators) assisted by a clerk provided locally by the presiding officer of the court. They meet at an appointed place and, in the presence of the public, call each case and discuss each matter with the disputants. Agreements are written up by the clerk and signed by the parties. If the matter is pending in court, the presiding officer reviews the agreement before dismissing the case. Shourie [1988, pp. 122–124] notes that the conciliators promote amicable resolution and, after listening to the parties, often suggest a solution.

Compare LOVEDAY, CHINESE MEDIATION.

London Court of International Arbitration (LCIA), London Court of Arbitration
ADMINISTERING AGENCY established in 1892 under the auspices of the London Chamber of Commerce to provide facilities for domestic and international commercial arbitration [DOA].

look-sniff arbitration   Binding third-party determination for resolving disputes over the quality or quantity of goods. Commonly employed in disputes arising between participants in transactions within commodities-trading associations.

The parties must agree, usually as part of the contract entered into prior to the dispute, that quality and quantity issues will be resolved by this process. However, the process is summarily conducted without the procedural requirements of ordinary arbitrations. Contrast APPRAISAL.

loop-back   *Systems Design:* Opportunity within a comprehensive dispute resolution system for disputants to leave rights-based processes, such as adjudication, or power contests and return to interest-based negotiation or mediation.

In addition to simply not impeding a return to negotiation, designers encourage loop-back by building procedural incentives into a dispute resolution process. Ury, Brett, and Goldberg [1988, pp. 52–55] cite the following examples: information procedures providing disputants with information about other, similar disputes, thereby reducing uncertainty about probable outcomes; ADVISORY ARBITRATION and MINI-TRIALS providing some REALITY TESTING about probable outcomes if the dispute is taken to arbitration or court; COOLING-OFF PERIODS specifying a time during which the disputants refrain from a power contest; and intervention by third parties.

loss aversion   In the context of decision making, the common tendency to view prospective gains as less significant than prospective losses of equal value [Ross and Stillinger, 1991, p. 392].

loveday (England)   Day when courts suspended cases to allow disputants to resolve their conflicts amicably.

The loveday was a recognized social institution, especially during the Anglo-Norman period but extending into the late Middle Ages. It gave influential members of the community an opportunity to mediate and arbitrate resolutions between local litigants and avoid the divisive effects of an imposed judgment, often by an outside judge, at a LAWDAY. If the dispute had been a case pending in court, a successful loveday was simply notated as having resolved the case. The term was more common in the records of the lowest civil courts, such as those of the manor, borough, and fair, while the term *day of concord* was used in the higher courts.

In one of the earliest legal treatises on arbitration, loveday was associated directly with the process of ARBITRAMENT. Kyd [1791, Preface] remarks that "arbitrament was once known as a 'love day' because of the peace and tranquility which followed." Also called *jour d'amour, dies amoris, dies ad concordandum, dies concordandi,* Day of Concord. Compare SETTLEMENT WEEK.

low-context and high-context communication   Hall [1976, p. 79] differentiates cultures on the basis of the communication that predominates in the culture. A high-context communication or message is one in which "most of the information is either in the physical context or internalized in the person, while very little is in the coded, explicit, transmitted part of the message." A low-context communication or message, in contrast, is one in which "the mass of information is vested in the explicit code" [p. 70]. Though no culture exists at either end of the continuum, the culture of the United States is placed toward the lower end, slightly above the German, Scandinavian, and Swiss cultures. Most Asian cultures, such as the Japanese, Chinese, and Korean, in contrast, fall toward the high-context end of the continuum [Gudykunst, 1991, p. 50].

LULU   Locally unwanted land use. Used in reference to land-use disputes, usually site-specific or NIMBY disputes.

lumping it   Dispute resolution strategy whereby an aggrieved party decides not to press her claim but to ignore the issue, accept the status quo, and maintain contact with the offending party. Most common response to conflict [Felstiner, 1974].

A party might "lump it" when she feels she has more to lose by making an issue of her complaint and hampering her relationship with the offender than she stands to gain through dispute resolution procedures [Nader and Todd, 1978, p. 9; Mackie, 1991a, p. 11].

lump-sum settlement   Payment of a single, undifferentiated amount of money in settlement of multiple claims made by one or more claimants. Ethically, lawyers cannot accept a lump-sum settlement for multiple claimants unless all claimants agree.

International Relations: Method of settling international claims through negotiation between governments of a single or lump sum to be paid without consideration for individual claims or recourse to international adjudication [DOA].

lying, lie   Utterance or impression that a speaker attempts to convey to a listener (speaker believes X) when the speaker really believes the opposite (speaker actually believes not X) [Gibbons, Bradac, and Busch, 1992, p. 161, citation omitted].

MACAP See Major Appliance Consumer Action Panel.

machiavellianism Political doctrine in which standards for individual ethical conduct do not apply to the conduct of public affairs. Instead, conduct is judged on the basis of whether the goals are achieved. Commonly understood, the term implies a high degree of deception.

mainstreaming Process of integrating ADR processes into the corporate culture; involves strategies to gain acceptance and make dispute-handling procedures operational. As used by Center for Public Resources.

Major Appliance Consumer Action Panel (MACAP) Consumer complaint mechanism for resolving disputes between individual consumers and manufacturers of major home appliances.

Funded by the leading manufacturers and private label marketers of appliances and located in the office of the Association of Home Appliance Manufacturers in Chicago, MACAP pursues only those complaints that are unresolved after consumers have first dealt with the dealer and manufacturer. Consumers may write or call to complain about their appliance problems. After the manufacturer is notified, qualifying complaints proceed through a structured process. Most disputes are satisfactorily resolved in the first step, called the *communications phase*. Only about 25 percent of complaints require further handling in the second step, called the *study phase* [Holding, 1983, p. 63].

265

malpractice screening   See MEDICAL MALPRACTICE SCREENING.

management rights   *Labor:* Rights that management retains in its contracts with a union or that management is prohibited from surrendering in the public sector.

Management rights can be divided into two categories: all decisions relating to the operation of the business, and those concerned with the supervision of employees [DOA].

managerial judging   Use by a court of a set of techniques for inducing settlements as a way to manage the caseload on the docket.

These techniques include COURT-CONNECTED ADR processes such as court-ordered mediation, mandatory nonbinding arbitration, summary jury trials, and the use of special masters [Elliot, 1986, p. 308].

Mandatory Alternative Dispute and Discovery Track (MADD Track)   Mandatory set of experimental pretrial civil procedures designed to promote settlement and reduce discovery costs and tactical delay.

Maricopa County, Arizona, began an experimental MADD Track program on January 2, 1991, for cases filed with four of its judges. The program combines presumptive discovery limits (uniform interrogatories, depositions limited to the parties, and one expert for each side), mandatory disclosure of evidence on a strict schedule, and nonbinding ADR. The parties must agree to some form of nonbinding ADR process within four months of the filing of the answer [Sander, 1991, p. 138].

mandatory arbitration   Alternative term for COMPULSORY ARBITRATION. Also used commonly in reference to one of its COURT-CONNECTED forms, MANDATORY NONBINDING ARBITRATION.

Both *compulsory* and *mandatory* are often used to describe *contractual* arbitration (see ARBITRATION) when the commitment to arbitrate is enforceable by statute and, derisively, when the agreement to arbitrate is imposed on consumers or employees either without their being aware or in an adhesive manner. It may be more accurate to distinguish *compulsory* as arbitration imposed by government without an arbitration agreement and *mandatory* as arbitration imposed by a court when enforcing an arbitration agreement.

mandatory mediation   COURT-CONNECTED mediation when required as a prerequisite to trial or mediation required as a prerequisite to litigation under the terms of an agreement.

mandatory nonbinding arbitration   COURT-CONNECTED form of COMPULSORY ARBITRATION used primarily as a reality-testing device to encourage settlement of cases before trial, but often binding and dispositive of a case if a party does not demand a trial within a specific period after the award is issued. Also referred to as COURT-ANNEXED or COURT-REFERRED arbitration, or sometimes less accurately but simply as MANDATORY ARBITRATION.

A typical statutory definition is as follows: "Process where certain specified types of court cases are automatically assigned to arbitration by the court where a third party hears evidence from each disputant and makes a final decision which is binding unless either party demands a trial de novo within a certain period of time" [Colo. Rev. Stat. Ann. §§ 13-22-403, 13-22-404 (West 1996)].

Although models vary by jurisdiction, most mandatory nonbinding arbitration programs share the following characteristics: after the suit is filed, cases involving monetary claims under a certain ceiling are automatically assigned to the program (timing and amounts vary); one or three volunteer arbitrators, usually local attorneys, conduct a summary hearing of the case (strict time limits and various evidentiary rules may apply); the arbitrators issue an award that becomes binding, usually within thirty days, unless an objecting party makes a timely request for trial; the trial judge is insulated from the process and the arbitrators' award has no evidentiary value; and if the party requesting trial does not substantially improve his position (usually measured by some percentage), that party will have to pay certain court costs.

If one limits the term *arbitration* limited to voluntary, contractual arbitration, this court-connected ADR process is not arbitration but rather an ADR HYBRID or judicial INFORMALISM, merely an aspect of civil procedure. Voluntary arbitration is governed by a particular statutory scheme distinct from the court rules and occasional statutes that govern mandatory nonbinding arbitration. This distinction is increasingly blurred, however, and is the cause of considerable confusion.

manifest conflict   Conflict that has ripened into an ongoing dispute [Moore, 1986, pp. 16–17], as opposed to a LATENT CONFLICT. See CONFLICT and DISPUTE for further distinction.

marchandage **(French)**   Same as HAGGLING.

Mary Carter agreement   *Negotiation:* Pretrial settlement agreement with certain multiple defendants limiting their liability while guaranteeing the plaintiff some monies and allowing him to continue litigation against any remaining defendants.

Named after *Booth* v. *Mary Carter Paint Co.* (1967), these agreements are analogous to loans and usually involve a formula whereby any subsequent recovery above a certain amount against the nonsettling defendants is credited to the settling defendants. The legality and effect of these settlement agreements varies by jurisdiction.

Mashkim Ancient Sumerian neutral whose duty it was to attempt to settle a case between parties; if a settlement was not reached, the case went before a judicial panel [Patterson, 1988, citations omitted].

master in chancery In some U.S. jurisdictions, person appointed by the court whose fees are paid by the parties and whose powers are enumerated by the courts on a case-by-case basis. Similar to *official* REFEREES. These court-appointed third parties can be empowered to encourage settlement or may promote settlement through their efforts to streamline the case for trial.
  England: Archaic title for assistants to the Lord Chancellor.

maximalist position *Negotiation:* Positional bargaining tactic of demanding more (sometimes much more) than one expects to obtain [Williams, 1983, pp. 70–72].

Mayordomo (Mexico) Person chosen within the community to oversee the cleaning and maintenance of the *acequias* (the ditches that make up the irrigation system of Northern New Mexico) who also settles disputes arising from the division of the water supply and the like.

MEDALOA From the family of MED-ARB variations, combination of mediation and LAST-OFFER ARBITRATION.
  The term was coined by the American Arbitration Association, which promotes the process. Parties agree in advance to mediation followed by an arbitration in which each party submits its final demand and final offer to the arbitrator, who must select between these last offers in rendering the reward. Depending on the agreement, the mediator or a separate neutral can serve as the arbitrator.

med-arb, med/arb Hybrid ADR process in which the parties agree first to mediate and then to arbitrate any unresolved issues using the same neutral both as mediator and as subsequent binding arbitrator. Also known as *expedited claims resolution* in some construction practices in which DISPUTE REVIEW BOARDS may be empowered to apply the process. A sample legal definition is as follows: "A process in which parties begin by mediation, and failing settlement, the same neutral third party acts as arbitrator over the remaining issues" [Colo. Rev. Stat. Ann. § 13-22-302(2.3)(West 1996)].
  The term *med-arb* or *med/arb* is a contraction of *mediation/arbitration* and is often used to designate an entire family of private, voluntary hybrids in which the conciliatory, nonbinding process of mediation is combined in some fashion with the adjudicative, often binding process of arbitration. This broad definition would include ARB-MED, CONCILIO-ARBITRATION, MED-ARB2, MED-REC, MED-

THEN-ARB, and MEDALOA. Feuille [1992, p. 133] suggests that the term also covers ad hoc mediation at the arbitration hearing. For purposes of clarity, the term is best used to designate a specific hybrid process rather than this entire family of hybrids, many of which are variations of med-arb.

The MED-ARB process is contractual, starting with a dispute resolution agreement between parties, usually contained in a contract, that empowers a neutral first to mediate and then to arbitrate any unresolved issues, usually in clearly delineated stages. The agreement commits the parties to a continuum of dispute resolution processes that will ensure a resolution. If disputants cannot negotiate a settlement, they are then bound to attempt mediation. If mediation does not achieve a mutually acceptable solution, they are then bound to arbitrate. The unique feature of the *pure* form of med-arb is that the same person who mediates the dispute is also authorized to arbitrate any issues remaining unresolved by the mediation. In addition to committing to both processes at the onset, the most obvious advantage is the cost savings in using only one neutral for both processes. As a mediator, the neutral will learn almost everything necessary to subsequently arbitrate, if needed. The neutral conducts the mediation process and is authorized by the agreement to determine when further mediation is fruitless and arbitration is required.

In one sense, med-arb is a natural extension of mediation—most mediators have been asked at one time or another to arbitrate remaining issues after exhausting the mediation process. A good mediator will have impressed the parties with his grasp of the dispute and his impartiality and may be a natural candidate to act as arbitrator if both parties agree. What distinguishes med-arb from a mere mediation followed by an agreement to arbitrate, however, is the preauthorization of the neutral to assume each role as needed. The disputants know that through mediation the neutral will acquire a more intimate view of the dispute than a conventional arbitrator, and thus any subsequent arbitration would likely be unconventional. Additionally, the mediator may reveal in caucus some of his own impressions as to the weaknesses and strengths of a party's case. Parties can easily draw conclusions as to how they think the mediator would award on the dispute. The realization that the mediator is authorized to adjudicate at any time may make med-arb even more effective at producing negotiated agreements than mediation alone.

In another sense, med-arb is a combination of two disparate ADR processes, and this very thing that purports to make med-arb so effective has generated the most criticism. Critics claim that it is inappropriate for one individual to serve as a neutral in a conciliatory process and then serve as a binding authority in an adversary procedure, thus raising legitimate fears of abuse. For example, the MED-ARBITRATOR has the potential power to coerce a settlement that the parties may not desire. The unique position of the med-arbitrator raises other legitimate concerns over the effectiveness of the process. On the one hand, it could undermine the neutral's ability to mediate. The neutral, as mediator, needs the complete confidence of the parties to obtain full confidential disclosures of their interests, positions, and willingness to compromise. This allows the neutral to help direct the parties toward a mutually acceptable solution. However, knowing that the neutral may ultimately act as arbitrator, the parties may not be as forthcoming. In addition, a lazy neutral may be inclined to jump prematurely to the arbitration phase when at an impasse in the mediation phase. On the other hand, the position of the med-arbitrator could undermine the arbitration process. After exposure to the intimate perspectives of mediation, the neutral's heuristic tendencies may encourage an award tainted by the mediation. Imagine how difficult it might be to hear the parties' confidential compromise positions for settlement during the mediation and yet have to turn around and make a noncompromising award. The tendency to "split the baby" may be very strong [Yarn, 1992].

Historically, collective bargaining labor disputes, particularly public sector interest disputes (new-contract negotiation disputes involving essential service public employees), have been the traditional proving ground for this process. For all practical purposes, there have been comparatively few detailed reports of med-arb applications in other disputes. For a labor relations viewpoint, see Henry, 1988; see also Bartel, 1991. Though there is no empirical evidence that the process is innately dysfunctional when used in its traditional context, criticisms of the pure form of med-arb (using the same neutral for both roles) have led to the development of alternative hybrids. For example, in MED-THEN-ARB the parties are still committed to successive processes, but the functions of mediator and arbitrator are performed by different individuals. In MED-ARB2, the participants, including the mediator, must unanimously agree at the transition to arbitration that the mediator will change roles; otherwise, a separate arbitrator is introduced. In MED-REC the arbitration award is advisory and nonbinding only, while in ARB-MED the arbitration precedes the mediation.

See also CO-MED-ARB, SHADOW MEDIATION.

med-arb2 Variation of MED-ARB and essentially the same as MED-THEN-ARB, with one exception: If during the course of the mediation phase one party requests the mediator to decide the remaining issues and all the other parties concur, then instead of shifting the proceeding to a different neutral acting as arbitrator, the mediator is empowered to decide the remaining issues unilaterally. If any party objects, then everyone goes to arbitration with a separate neutral.

In med-arb2, the use of a separate neutral is avoidable upon mutual consent and the parties will have the opportunity to decide, after mediation, whether the mediator should shift roles and arbitrate. This allows the parties to determine whether the criticisms of med-arb are valid in their situation. In one sense, this encourages the natural tendency for some parties in mediation to ask the mediator to resolve the intractable issues. For all practical purposes, however, disputants will make certain conclusions about a mediator's opinion on their positions despite the mediator's best efforts to conceal it. It is unlikely that all the disputants will feel comfortable authorizing the mediator to arbitrate after a thorough mediation.

media complaint center   Form of CONSUMER COMPLAINT MECHANISM administered by a newspaper, radio, or television station.

Called by such names as HOT LINE, *consumer advocate,* or media ACTION LINE, the center features a producer or reporter who solicits individual grievances, primarily consumer problems, and pursues resolution. Programs vary in assistance and volume. Some merely refer the consumer to another agency or social service; others contact the provider of goods or services that is the subject of the complaint while still others more actively intervene, including investigation and FACT-FINDING. While some respond to only that small percentage of grievances that are recurring or that may appeal to the media audience, others attempt to respond to all complaints. Flagrant abuses by governmental agencies and merchants are publicized, and the threat of adverse media exposure pressures the provider of goods or services to remedy the situation [Johnson, Kantor, and Schwartz, 1977, p. 71; McGillis and Mullen, 1977, p. 19].

mediate   Conduct a MEDIATION. Although the term is often used in reference to the parties, as in "the disputants have agreed to mediate," it seems more accurate to say that the "mediator mediates" and the parties "have agreed to participate in a mediation."

Mediate.com   On-line mediation information resource. Though there are innumerable World Wide Web and Internet sites that focus on various aspects of conflict resolution, this one has drawn considerable attention from the professional community.

mediated negotiations   Common alternative phrase for MEDIATION, especially in planning rather than dispute resolution settings.

Because mediation is negotiation assisted by an impartial third party, this term seems redundant. It does, however, put more (and perhaps appropriate) emphasis on the fact that the purposes of the mediator's actions are to facilitate and better manage the disputants' negotiations.

mediated settlement   Settlement voluntarily reached and accepted by the parties with the assistance of a mediator.

mediated settlement conference   COURT-CONNECTED MEDIATION in some jurisdictions.

The term is useful to the extent that it distinguishes mediation in the court-annexed or court-referred context from voluntary, contractual mediation. Because the former always involves concurrent litigation, often makes participation mandatory, and may limit the parties' control over the process and choice of mediator, its ethos is fundamentally different from the latter. Because the concept of court-ordered settlement conferences predates court-connected mediation, the term connotes a natural, process of evolution, out of court procedure rather than an extrajudicial, alternative import into court procedure.

In Virginia, the term has been proposed to denote a court-connected dispute resolution process that falls between mediation and EARLY NEUTRAL EVALUATION. In addition to using conflict resolution techniques that are characteristic of mediation, the third party may also give an opinion as to the merits of the parties' case, suggest solutions or settlement terms, or merely provide settlement ranges.

mediation   Generic term encompassing certain conciliatory or nonadjudicative dispute resolution processes that involve intervention by a party not involved in the dispute.

The Latin root, *medi* or *medio,* means "middle." *Mediatus,* a form of the verb *mediare* ("to halve" or "to be in the middle") and its medieval French and Anglo-French derivatives, *mediacioun* and *medyacyoun,* evolved into the present term and were used with similar meaning. For example, in 1386, Chaucer wrote, "By the popes mediacion . . . they been acorded." An archaic use of the term in mathematics denoted dividing a number by two or bisecting in geometry [Singer, 1992, p. 15].

Until the turn of the twentieth century, the term carried no particular meaning other than the generalized notion of intervening between conflicting parties in order to promote reconciliation. Unlike ARBITRAMENT—which even in its conciliatory, nonadjudicative form constituted a formal, societal mechanism recognized by law—there was no particular formal, institutionalized process that would give more particularized meaning to mediation. This does not imply that mediation has been unimportant. Forms of nonadjudicative, third-party intervention probably have existed in most human societies and have been observed in some non-human primate species [see de Waal, 1989]. Certainly nonadjudicative, third-party intervention predates formal legal adjudication, which may have evolved from it, while the participation of others in the resolution of a dyadic dispute may be a fundamental adaptation for human success as a social species. Such interventions are referenced on ancient Sumerian tablets, in the Bible, and in *The Iliad* and have been observed in most societies and cultures. Nonadjudicative, third-party intervention may be the preferred norm in many cultures and societies, but despite the many cultural variations, most Western observers use the label *mediation*—for example, IFUGAO MEDIATION, *Nuer mediation,* and CHINESE MEDIATION, without regard to their differences. In this most general and comprehensive sense, mediation includes the entire range of pacific, nonadjudicative, third-party interventions, and the mediator is the person or organization who employs all relevant methods to resolve a conflict peacefully [Pauling, Laszlo, and Jong, 1986, Vol. 1, p. 589].

In the United States and in most Western societies affected by the modern mediation movement, mediation is used to denote a range of nonadjudicative, third-party interventions that have evolved in a variety of disputing contexts and subcultures within which the term has acquired different and particularized meanings. These contexts include international relations, labor, community, family, commercial relations, and courts. Academics and practitioners with varying philosophies, heuristic tendencies, and biases use the term to denote their brand of nonadjudicative, third-party intervention. Indeed, most modern mediators have chosen mediation as a second or ancillary profession and began mediating in contexts that complimented or were somehow related to their primary professions. Thus diplomats and foreign service officers understand mediation as defined initially by the HAGUE CONVENTION FOR THE PACIFIC SETTLEMENT OF INTERNATIONAL DISPUTES and refined through a century of experience. Many mediators began as labor arbitrators or acquired their mediation experience in the specialized realm of COLLECTIVE BARGAINING and workplace disputes, a tradition that dates back to medieval guilds and that was revived during the nineteenth century for railway labor disputes. Many mediators started as volunteer mediators in COMMUNITY and NEIGHBORHOOD JUSTICE CENTER programs that evolved from the civil rights movements of the 1960s. Most psychologists, family therapists, and social workers who mediate acquired their experience mediating family and divorce disputes, sometimes diverted by the courts but also submitted voluntarily. By the early 1980s, many businesspeople and lawyers began adapting mediation to business disputes. Most lawyers who mediate acquired their experience by mediating commercial and tort claims diverted by the courts in programs that mostly started in the late 1980s and expanded significantly in the 1990s.

There are other contexts—schools and public policy/environmental decision making, for example. Mediation models, experience, and traditions from all these contexts have probably influenced the others. The important point is that the efficacy of different intervention strategies and mediation models varies by context. Indeed, the very notion of mediation efficacy may vary by context because the goals of the process may vary by context—negotiated monetary settlement might be the goal of a legal dispute between strangers, or reconciliation in a family or community dispute, or problem solving in a business dispute, or improving communications and adjusting behaviors in a sexual harassment complaint. Objectives and strategy may also be a function of the mediator's personal style and philosophy.

While studying mediation in particular contexts, observers have developed categories of mediation to describe particular styles or types of mediator strategy and behavior. Most of these categories are dichotomous and describe ends of a continuum of dispute resolution processes with increasing degrees of intervention. The most common dichotomies are *evaluative* (most interventionist) versus *facilitative* (least interventionist) mediation and *directive* versus *nondirective* mediation. Other dichotomies tend to match these roughly—for example, *bargaining* and *therapeutic* styles among community mediators [Silbey and Merry, 1986], *dealmakers* and *orchestrators* among labor mediators [Kolb, 1983], *settlement-orientation* and *problem-solving* styles among custody mediators [Kressel and others, 1994], and *task-oriented* and *socioeconomic* among mediators in some contexts [Kressel and Pruitt, 1989, pp. 423–424]. In their study of mediators who work in a variety of contexts, Kolb and Kressel [1994, p. 466] describe a dichotomy of *pragmatic problem-solving* and *transformative*. In the context of disputes in litigation, Galton [1994, pp. 2–4] distinguishes between *evaluative* and *pure form* mediation, which he finds synonymous with the terms *empowerment mediation* and *community model mediation*. Finding dichotomies to be insufficiently descriptive, other authorities have constructed more complex categories. For example, Carnevale [1986, pp. 44–45] distinguishes between four basic strategies: *integration, pressing, compensation,* and *inaction*. Riskin [1996, p. 7], imposes an additional continuum based on problem-definition approaches of mediators and derives four mediator orientations: *evaluative-broad, evaluative-narrow, facilitative-broad,* and *facilitative-narrow*. While a single mediator may be able to use any of these styles or exhibit a range of behaviors even in the same mediation, the common wisdom holds that an individual mediator will favor one particular category or style of mediation.

Because the current ADR movement and the emerging profession of dispute resolution consist of diverse people whose initial training, experience, and modalities of intervention vary by context and personal preference, it is not surprising that these people disagree as to what is *pure* or *real* mediation. The current debate is whether these differences constitute mere differences in style, different models, or fundamentally different processes. As Kovach [1996] notes, the ultimate question is, How are people in authority defining mediation now? This entry does not attempt to resolve that debate but rather to review the content of some authoritative definitions and highlight the various styles, models, or processes that are being labeled *mediation*.

Treatises, training materials, and other secondary authorities predate most legal definitions and have a strong influence on conceptions of mediation. Many definitions from these materials focus on mediation's relationship with negotiation. For example:

- "Mediation is negotiation carried out with the assistance of a third party" [Goldberg, Sander, and Rogers, 1992, p. 103].

- "Assistance of a 'neutral' third party to a negotiation" [Bingham, 1986, p. 5].

- "Mediation is an extension of negotiations" [BNA ADR Report, vol. 2, April 14, 1988, p. 191].

- "Third party dispute settlement technique integrally related to the negotiation process whereby a skilled, disinterested neutral assists parties in changing their minds over conflicting needs mainly through the noncompulsory applicants of various forms of persuasion in order to reach a viable agreement on terms at issue" [Davis and Dugan, 1982, p. 85].

- "Mediation is an extension and elaboration of the negotiation process. Mediation involves the intervention of an acceptable, impartial, and neutral third party who has no authoritative decision-making power to assist contending parties in voluntarily reaching their own mutually acceptable settlement of issues in dispute. As with negotiation, mediation leaves the decision-making power in the hands of the people in conflict" [Moore, 1986, p. 6].

- "Mediation is essentially negotiation that includes a third party who is knowledgeable in effective negotiation procedures, and can help people in conflict to coordinate their activities and to be more effective in their bargaining. Mediation is an extension of the negotiation process in that it involves extending the bargaining into a new format and using a mediator who contributes new variables and dynamics to the interaction of the disputants. Without negotiation, however, there can be no mediation" [Moore, 1986, p. 14].

- "Mediation is defined most simply as facilitated negotiation. An impartial third party (the mediator) facilitates negotiations between disputants or the disputants' representatives in their search for a resolution of their dispute. The disputants remain responsible for negotiating a settlement; the mediator's role is to assist the process in ways acceptable to the disputants. Sometimes this means merely providing a forum for negotiations or convening the negotiations. More often it means helping the disputants find areas of common ground for resolution, offering alternatives, supervising the bargaining, then drafting the final settlement" [Leeson and Johnston, 1988, pp. 133–134].

Many of the authorities that emphasize mediation as an extension of negotiation are proponents of the collaborative PROBLEM SOLVING model and discuss mediation as essentially an interest-based or PRINCIPLED NEGOTIATION process directed by the third party. Consistent with this approach, many definitions emphasize linear *stages* or *phases* of the mediation process that roughly correspond to these negotiation models. The *classic* mediation-phase model starts with the parties agreeing to mediate, choosing a mediator, and reaching agreement on the mediator's role, the ground rules, and the structure of the process. The latter is usually accomplished by the mediator making an introductory statement that includes a suggested procedure. After the parties agree on the procedure, each has an opportunity to share positions, information, and perspectives and identify issues and interests. Typically this interaction is facilitated by the mediator in joint session and often followed by separate confidential caucuses between the mediator and the separate parties. Settlement options are generated and evaluated in joint sessions or caucuses. With the help and encouragement of the mediator, parties select or bargain over the options and reach agreement. Consistent with this approach, Folberg and Taylor [1984] define mediation as "the process by which participants, together with the assistance of a neutral person or persons, systematically isolate disputed issues in order to develop options, consider alternatives, and reach a consensual settlement that will accommodate their needs" [1984, pp. 7–8]. Different authorities have identified more phases and describe them differently, and some practitioners skip or reject certain phases—the use of caucuses, for example—or they may reject the linear, problem-solving paradigm entirely.

Many authorities visualize mediation occupying the space between negotiation and arbitration along a continuum of dispute resolution processes with increasing degrees of intervention. Mediation differs from negotiation to the extent that an impartial third party assists in the negotiations. The introduction of the third party, however, can make the look, feel, and effectiveness of a mediation fundamentally different than a negotiation on the same dispute. For a discussion of how mediation compares to negotiation and what advantages mediation has over negotiation, see Bush, 1996. Mediation may cover a range of the continuum depending on the degree of intervention by the mediator. Mediators may engage in the same behaviors and use the same intervention strategies as conciliators and facilitators, but they are also empowered to intervene in the substantive dialogue and use their powers of persuasion to help the parties reach a mutually acceptable outcome. Mediation differs from adjudication not only in the different role for the third party (a judge orders, a mediator persuades), but also in that adjudication is oriented toward achieving conformity to norms while in mediation the disputants create the relevant norms for themselves [Fuller, 1971, p. 308]. Thus mediation is distinguishable from arbitration because the third-party mediator is without the power to decide for the disputants. The following definitions emphasize the latter distinction:

- "The mediator, in contrast to the arbitrator or judge, has no power to impose an outcome on disputing parties" [Goldberg, Sander, and Rogers, 1992, p. 103].

- Mediation is the intervention into a dispute or negotiation by an acceptable, impartial, and neutral third party who has no authoritative decision-making power to assist disputing parties in voluntarily reaching their own mutually acceptable settlement of issues in dispute" [Moore, 1986, p. 14].

- "A process in which the disputing parties select a neutral third party to assist them in reaching a settlement of the dispute. The process is private, voluntary, informal and nonbinding. The mediator has no power to impose a settlement" [*Corporate Counsel's Guide to Alternative Dispute Resolution Techniques*, 1989, Sec. 1.040].

- "The mediator is not empowered to render a decision. The mediator has no authority to impose a settlement on the parties" [Davis, 1984, pp. 3, 4]

- "Mediators do not make decisions FOR people. Their job is to help people make their OWN decisions" [Marshall, 1985, p. viii].

These definitions indicate that a fundamental characteristic of mediation is the third party's lack of authority to impose a binding solution. Some authorities attempt to define mediation by identifying this and other characteristics. Generally, most definitions include the NEUTRALITY of the third party. However, in international (see later discussion) and intraorganizational disputes, the mediator may be neutral in the sense of being free from favoritism toward one or the other parties, but may also have an interest in seeing the dispute resolved (SEE EMERGENT MEDIATION). Other commonly identified characteristics include voluntary, nonbinding, and confidential [Cooper and Meyerson, 1991, p. 34]; voluntary use of a facilitator to assist the structuring and conduct of the negotiations, private consultations (caucuses) with each disputant, flexible process in control of the parties, who can stop at any time; private, confidential, created and controlled by the parties, and oriented toward future action and relations rather than toward the past as in litigation [Leeson and Johnston, 1988, pp. 133–134]; voluntary, participatory, and informal [Sigurdson, 1986]. Though some of these additional characteristics may hold true in most mediations, they do not in others. As previously noted, not every mediator uses caucuses, while some mediations may appear extremely formal. One particular characteristic, party creation and control of the process, may be completely absent in many court-connected mediation models in which parties are ordered to participate and may have little influence over the procedures or even the choice of mediator. Some of the following legal definitions recognize this but emphasize the voluntary nature of settlement:

- "The process of resolving a dispute with the assistance of a mediator outside of a formal court proceeding" [Okla. Stat. Ann. tit. 12 § 1802 (West 1993)].

- "A forum in which one or more impartial persons, acting as mediators, facilitate communication between parties to a controversy to promote a mutually acceptable resolution or settlement among them" [Utah Code Ann. § 78-31B-1 (1953)].

- "A non-binding, voluntary process initiated by the parties or by a commission where the mediator serves to encourage voluntary settlement by the parties" [Wis. Stat. Ann. § 111.70(4)(c)(3) (West 1996)].

- "An intervention in dispute negotiations by a trained neutral third party with the purpose of assisting the parties to reach their own solution" [Colo. Rev. Stat. Ann. § 13-22-302(2.4) (West 1996)].

- "A voluntary process in which an impartial mediator actively assists disputants in identifying and clarifying issues of concern and in designing and agreeing to solutions for those issues" [710 Ill. Comp. Stat. Ann. 20/2 (West 1992)].

- "An informal process conducted by a mediator with the objective of helping parties voluntarily settle their dispute" [N.C. Gen. Stat. § 7A-38.1 (1996)].

- "Mediation involves a neutral third party to assist the parties in negotiating an agreement. The mediator has no independent authority and does not render a decision; any decision must be reached by the parties themselves" [1 C.F.R. § 305.86-3 App. (1993)].

- "A process whereby a neutral third person called a mediator acts to encourage and facilitate the resolution of a dispute between two or more parties. It is an informal and non-adversarial process with the objective of helping the disputing parties reach a mutually acceptable and voluntary agreement. In mediation, decision-making authority rests with the parties. The role of the mediator includes, but is not limited to, assisting the parties in identifying issues, fostering joint problem-solving, and exploring settlement alternatives" [Fla. Stat. Ann. § 44.1011 (West Supp. 1992)].

- "A process in which a neutral facilitates settlement discussions between parties. The neutral has no authority to make a decision or impose a settlement upon the parties. The neutral attempts to focus the attention of the parties upon their needs and interests rather than upon rights and positions. Although in court-annexed or court-referred mediation programs the parties may be ordered to attend a mediation session, any settlement is entirely voluntary. In the absence of settlement the parties lose none of their rights to a jury trial" [Georgia Supreme Court Alternative Dispute Resolution Rules, 1993].

Much of the current debate on the definition of mediation focuses on the tension at the edges of the dispute resolution process continuum. At what point do certain intervention strategies and behaviors exceed the bounds? Because a mediator cannot make a binding decision, can she question the parties' evaluation of their alternatives to a negotiated agreement, challenge the assumptions behind their positions, make recommendations for settlement, evaluate the legal case, give advice, share her own experience in resolving such cases, or otherwise attempt to influence the parties to accept certain settlement terms? Recognizing that some of these *evaluative* or *directive* tactics flirt on the adjudicative edge of the continuum, courts and professional associations have developed codes of conduct or standards of behavior that define mediation and prescribe appropriate mediator behavior or proscribe inappropriate behavior. Presumably, inappropriate behaviors would be outside the realm of mediation, thereby helping to define it. For example, the Preamble of the Standards of Conduct for Mediators developed by SPIDR, the AMERICAN ARBITRATION ASSOCIATION, and the AMERICAN BAR ASSOCIATION defines mediation as "a process in which an impartial third party—a mediator—facilitates the resolution of a dispute by promoting voluntary agreement (or 'self-determination') by the parties to the dispute." The Preamble concludes that "these standards give meaning to this definition of mediation." Of the standards that follow, *Standard I: Self-Determination* provides additional insight: "Self-determination is the fundamental principle of mediation. It requires that the mediation process rely upon the ability of the parties to reach a voluntary, uncoerced agreement. . . ." This purposely imprecise notion of *self-determination* is emerging as a critical element in defining the boundaries of mediation. Some critics argue that mediators who are using intervention strategies and behaviors that somehow impinge on party self-determination are coercing agreement and no longer mediating. Several states have refined this concept in their standards for court-connected mediators. For example:

> Mediation is a private and consensual process in which an impartial person, a mediator, works with disputing parties to help them explore settlement, reconciliation, and understanding among them. . . . The primary responsibility for the resolution of a dispute rests with the parties. . . . A mediator shall respect and encourage self-determination by the parties in their decision whether, and on what terms, to resolve their dispute, and shall refrain from being directive and judgmental regarding the issues in dispute and options for settlement. . . . He may assist them in making informed and thoughtful decisions, but shall not impose his judgment for that of the parties concerning any aspect of the mediation [*N.C. Standards of Professional Conduct*, 1996].

Under this definition, mediators are no longer mediating when they express their opinions on the issues and settlement options, and while it is permissible to be directive about process, it is not permissible to be directive about the outcome.

This limitation on what constitutes mediation is not yet broadly accepted, nor is it the norm in international (see later discussion) and some labor mediation. In the context of intraorganizational dispute resolution, for example, Blake and Mouton [1985, p. 15] define mediation as "the intervention of a third party who first investigates and defines the problem and then usually approaches each group separately with recommendations designed to provide a mutually acceptable solution." Many authorities accept a certain degree of such *evaluative mediation,* which is popularly ascribed to lawyer-mediators and retired judges who mediate, particularly in the context of court-connected programs and commercial disputes [see Menkel-Meadow, 1996, pp. 1, 4, opining that such mediation may simply be ancillary to the practice of law]. Other authorities reject it outright. Benjamin [1996, pp. 6–7], for example, argues that a mediator is no longer mediating when she evaluates, gives advice, or recommends.

While the debate over what mediation is focuses primarily on the adjudicative end of the continuum, few commentators question facilitative behaviors that border on therapeutic. This approach is attributed mainly to mental health professionals who mediate. Gold [1993, pp. 58–60], for example, characterizes mediation as part of a general healing paradigm. Attitudinal change, spirituality, and the nurturing of relationships have all been espoused as mediation goals. Bush and Folger's [1994] describe the process of TRANSFORMATIVE MEDIATION as an opportunity for personal growth. Mediation focused on individual healing and growth may contribute to dispute resolution; however, mediation without the primary goal of resolving the dispute between the parties is arguably no longer a dispute resolution process but rather a form of therapy. In distinguishing family mediation from psychotherapy, Kelly [1983, p. 43] warns that a successful mediation can be highly therapeutic, but the primary goal is negotiated settlement rather than psychological change. Shook and Kwan [1988, pp. 448–449] note that, unlike therapy and counseling, mediation does not attempt to understand or resolve underlying psychological issues. Indeed, the commentary to the *Model Standards of Conduct for Mediators* warns mediators of any professional background, psychologists as well as lawyers, from lapsing into their other professional modalities.

In psychology, however, mediation has been defined as "the intervention by independent or impartial third party or parties to promote the reconciliation, settlement, or compromise between conflicting parties" [Walker, 1991, p. 127]. This definition makes reconciliation a goal and draws the debate over the definition of mediation into the question of what constitutes *resolution. Settlement* may be a compromise on a narrow issue while *resolution* deals with the underlying causes of conflict [Keating and Shaw, 1990]. If the disputants' relationship is an important aspect of the dispute, reconciliation may be crucial to resolution. Lon Fuller [1971, p. 325] described the "central quality of media-tion" as "its capacity to reorient the parties toward each other, not by imposing rules on them, but by helping them to achieve a new and shared perception of their relationship, a perception that will redirect their attitudes and dispositions toward one another." Generally, interpersonal disputes among individuals who have some type of ongoing relationship and where the dispute may be part of recurring conflict symptomatic of deeper relationship problems seem best suited for facilitative mediation. In contrast, disputes where the parties randomly en-counter one another and are then forced to resolve some question of liability seem better suited to evaluative mediation, if not adjudication.

Here again, context may determine the goal and thereby influence the look and feel of the particular mediation. The mediation of a dispute between two employees with the goal of improving their relationship in the workplace may be different than one between a former employee and employer over a mone-tary claim. A mediation involving custody may entail an ongoing relationship between former spouses. The following statement of goals for such mediations hints at a particular type of intervention:

> The goals of custody and visitation disputes mediation are centered in the reduc-tion of the stress and anxiety experienced by children in separation and divorce, by furnishing an alternative way for the parties to settle custody and visitation disputes. A trained mediator helps the parties reorganize the family, to continue parenting their children despite separation, and begins an educational process which will allow parties to recognize and meet the needs of their children . . . reduce the acrimony between the parties, reducing attendant stress on both the parties and the child . . . will teach them to solve future problems without re-course to the courts, and thus reduce the stress of relitigation of custody and vis-itation disputes [N.C. Uniform Rules Regulating Mediation of Child Custody and Visitation Disputes Under the North Carolina Custody and Visitation Mediation Program, 1989].

Evaluation of the dispute makes little sense with such goals.

Finally, it could be argued that intervenor flexibility is the ethos of media-tion. Therefore, *mediation* alludes to a range of possible styles and strategies of third-party, nonadjudicative intervention that varies both by context and by party and mediator preferences. If one of the fundamental principles of media-tion is party self-determination, it would be consistent with that principle for *mediation* to be whatever the parties agree it is, either explicitly or implicitly—"There is no textbook definition of mediation. . . . Instead, the mediator allows himself to be created by the parties" [*BNA ADR Report*, 1988, p. 191]. Parties may agree to empower the mediator to evaluate, advise, and recommend, or to assist in healing, personal growth, and the reconciliation of relationships. If an-other fundamental principle is informed decision making, it would be consistent with that principle for the agreement on what mediation is to follow a discussion of what interventions are available, the pros and cons of such interventions, and the preferences of both the parties and the mediator.

International Relations: Conciliatory, nonadjudicative intervention by a third party in an INTERNATIONAL DISPUTE for the purposes of reconciling the claims of the disputants through a range of informal techniques, including advancement of proposals or recommendations aimed at encouraging a mutually acceptable compromise solution.

Like the definition of mediation in the domestic context, international mediation is used broadly to denote the entire range of nonadjudicative, pacific, third-party intervention strategies and styles. The following definitions of mediation are illustrative:

- "All services rendered, efforts made and steps taken by the government of a foreign State in connection with the conflict in question; or even by one of its nationals, not invested with an official capacity; or also through the organ of an international organization; with the object of reducing tensions, encouraging negotiation or recourse to all other means of peaceful settlement or to put an end to hostilities or, further, to help to eliminate the causes or the consequences of the conflict" [Probost, 1989, pp. 3–5].

- "The participation of a third state or a disinterested individual in negotiations between states in dispute" [*Report of a Study Group. . .,* 1966, p. 72].

- "Any action taken by an actor that is not a direct party to the crisis, that is designed to reduce or remove one or more of the problems of the bargaining relationship, and therefore to facilitate the termination of the crisis itself" [Young, 1967, p. 34].

- "Any intermediary activity . . . undertaken by a third party with the primary intention of achieving some compromise settlement of the issues at stake between the parties, or at least ending disruptive conflict behavior" [Mitchell, 1981, p. 287].

Under international law, mediation is a familiar method of pacific settlement included in treaties and conventions. Many international agreements, including the United Nations Charter [art. 33], contain references to mediation, usually as one of several pacific methods of dispute resolution to which the signatories agree to submit future disputes. Very few contain specific mediation procedures. Part Two of the Hague Conventions of 1899 and 1907 sets out simple guidelines for initiating and terminating mediation. Mediation is usually ad hoc and set in motion by either one of the disputing parties or by a third party that either suggests mediation or offers to mediate. The third party can be one or more states or individuals mutually agreed upon by the disputants [art. 4]. The parties or the mediator can terminate the mediation at any time, although in some cases the treaty or mediation agreement may set a limit on the duration of the mediation.

With respect to what the mediator actually does, the Hague Conventions provide only that "the part of the mediator consists in reconciling the opposing claims and appeasing the feelings of resentment which may have arisen between the States at variance" [art. 4]. Article 20 of the 1964 Protocol of the ORGANIZATION OF AFRICAN UNITY COMMISSION OF MEDIATION, CONCILIATION AND ARBITRATION confirms that reconciling the views of the parties is the primary function of international mediation. With respect to how the mediator goes about accomplishing this task, there is little guidance. The PACT OF BOGOTA, article 11, defines mediation as "the submission of the controversy to one or more American Governments not parties to the controversy, or to one or more eminent citizens of any American State not a party to the controversy . . . [and] chosen by mutual agreement between the parties." Article 12 outlines the functions of the mediator as "assist[ing] the parties in the settlement of controversies in the simplest and most direct manner, avoiding formalities and seeking an acceptable solution." This allows the mediator broad latitude in choosing techniques for reconciliation.

After discussing the substance of the dispute with the parties, international mediators will often propose or suggest terms of settlement that they think the parties will find acceptable. This technique has become controversial in domestic mediation (see earlier discussion). It is traditional, however, and even expected in international mediation [Merrills, 1991, pp. 27–28]. Articles 5 (termination) and 6 (nonbinding effect) of the Hague Convention allude to the mediator proposing or advising terms of settlement. Such proposals are made in confidence and not in the form of reports [art. 12, Pact of Bogota]. Unlike most international arbitration, the effect is nonbinding and the procedure is nonjudicial.

Most authorities describe international mediation as an extension of or ancillary to direct negotiations. Of course the participation of a third party distinguishes mediation from negotiation. Along with making substantive proposals for settlement, the mediator's ability to participate in the negotiations and bargain directly with the parties distinguishes the process from GOOD OFFICES. The Hague Conventions treat mediation and good offices as interchangeable procedures. However, other international instruments, such as the Pact of Bogota, make this distinction. In good offices, the third party merely brings the parties together for the purposes of negotiation, and although that third party can be present at the negotiations by invitation, he does not participate (Pact of Bogota, arts. 9, 10). In practice, however, the distinction is largely theoretical, because the mediator often performs the function of good offices, and good offices often evolves into mediation. CONCILIATION, as practiced in the international context, contains elements of both mediation and INQUIRY. In mediation, the mediator makes informal suggestions or proposals based on an understanding of the dispute derived from confidential discussions with the parties. In conciliation, the third party, usually a commission, engages in an objective investigation and evaluation of all aspects of the dispute and then attempts to clarify the issues in dispute in order to improve the parties' understanding of the situation and of each other. Proposals for terms of settlement are derived from the fact-finding function and may be issued formally and publicly. Again, such distinctions may be blurred in practice [Merrills, 1991, pp. 27, 28].

For a discussion of the neutrality of international mediators, see MEDIATOR.

Mediation Subterms: There are many terms for variations of mediation and of mediation as used in different contexts that are defined in this lexicon. See, for example, CO-MEDIATION, COMMUNITY MEDIATION, COMPREHENSIVE MEDIATION, CONTRACTUAL MEDIATION, CRIMINAL MEDIATION, CUSTODY MEDIATION, DIVORCE MEDIATION, DUAL MEDIATION, EMERGENT MEDIATION, FAMILY MEDIATION, FARMER-LENDER MEDIATION, GOVERNMENT MEDIATION, GRIEVANCE MEDIATION, IMPLICIT MEDIATION, INDUSTRIAL MEDIATION, LABOR MEDIATION, STRUCTURED MEDIATION, VICTIM-OFFENDER MEDIATION.

Mediation and Conciliation Service   See FEDERAL MEDIATION AND CONCILIATION SERVICE.

mediation clause, mediation article   Contract clause in which the parties agree to submit to mediation future disputes arising out of the contractual relationship. Mediation is a condition precedent to arbitration or litigation and begins after attempts at unassisted negotiation fail.

mediation communication   Communication, verbal or nonverbal, made by, between, or among any parties, mediators, mediation programs, or other persons present in order to further the mediation process; such communication occurs during a mediation session or outside such a session when made to or by the mediator or mediation program [Mastrofski, 1991, pp. 27–28]. The term has particular significance when used in the context of confidentiality. Statutes, court rules, evidentiary rules, and contractual agreements controlling the confidentiality of mediation communications vary by jurisdiction.

mediation panel   Stable of available mediators offered by an ADMINISTERING AGENCY from which disputants can choose.

Labor: Three mediators assigned to a labor dispute. Compare MEDIATION TEAM.

mediation privilege, mediator privilege   Evidentiary exclusion rule that protects the mediator from having to testify about what happened or was said in a mediation.

Though U.S. federal district courts rely on Federal Rule of Evidence 408, which has numerous exceptions, the rule varies in other jurisdictions and is established by the court or by statute. Unless a special rule applies, each of the parties, rather than the mediator, has the power to invoke the privilege.

mediation proceedings   Legalistic term for COURT-CONNECTED mediation in which the court orders the parties to participate.

Through common use the term is evolving to denote any aspect of the mediation process, whether voluntary or court-ordered.

Mediation Quarterly   Periodical focusing primarily on divorce and family mediation and sponsored by the ACADEMY OF FAMILY MEDIATORS.

mediation strategy   Overall plan or approach, including techniques and methods, with which the mediator intends to manage the case, parties, and issues toward resolution [Kolb, 1983, p. 38].

Mediation strategies have traditionally been viewed as either content or process strategies [Kolb, 1983, p. 39]. *Content strategies* are designed to change the substantive content of the dispute (through the use of such tactics as offering suggestions, encouraging concession-making, imposing deadlines, and so on), and *process strategies* are designed to affect the perceptual dimension of the dispute (by educating the parties, offering facilities for better communication, and so forth) [Bercovitch, 1992a, p. 16].

mediation team   Two or more mediators working together on a particular dispute. Term is more common in labor relations, while CO-MEDIATORS seems to be the preferred term in other mediation contexts. Alternatively, it could refer to a group of mediators and possibly nonmediators working collaboratively in a complex dispute.

Mediation UK (United Kingdom)   Membership organization promoting conflict resolution education, standards of practice, and services.

mediator   One who mediates. See MEDIATION.

An illustrative sample of legal definitions includes the following:

- "A person who assists parties involved in a minor dispute to reach a mutually acceptable resolution of their dispute" [Iowa Code § 679.1 (1996)].

- An impartial, neutral person responsible for reaching a resolution in each case" [Mich. Comp. Laws Ann. § 691.1552 et seq. (West Supp. 1993)].

- "An impartial person who assists in the resolution of a dispute" [N.Y. Judiciary Law § 849-a (McKinney 1994)].

- "A neutral facilitator whose function is to encourage communication and negotiation between all parties of a dispute" [40 C.F.R. § 131.7(f)(1)(ii) (1992)].

A mediator has no authority to impose a decision, grant a concession, or compel an agreement. A mediator is an impartial third party whose primary objective is to structure and conduct a settlement negotiation in a manner that maximizes the potential for resolution. To accomplish this, the mediator may serve in a number of important procedural and substantive roles that may vary considerably depending on the extent to which the parties empower the mediator or on the mediator's particular style or preference.

The mediator acts foremost as a facilitator, convening, refereeing, and moderating the meeting in a neutral and evenhanded manner. By assisting the disputants in developing an agenda and maintaining structure, order (sometimes decorum), and direction in the discussions, the mediator keeps the parties focused on joint resolution of the substantive issues in conflict. Unassisted negotiations are rarely as focused and therefore rarely as efficient as a mediation.

The mediator helps the disputants communicate. One of the first aspects of a relationship that deteriorates as conflict escalates is communication. Disputants tend to express themselves poorly or in hostile language while failing to listen to or negatively interpreting what is being said by the other. In negotiations, disputants have a tendency not to listen carefully to the other side because they are thinking ahead to their responses or strategy. Through probing, questioning, restating, and summarizing, mediators clarify poor communications and make sure that each disputant understands what the other is saying. In many cases the mediator acts as the messenger, restating adversarial messages in neutral tones or nonpolarizing terms so that they will be more credible and have a greater likelihood of being heard and understood.

The mediator can serve as an educator in both process and substance. He teaches process by instructing the parties in how to negotiate more constructively. The mediator can spot destructive and obstructive negotiation tactics and help the actors move away from inefficient positioning while saving face. The mediator teaches substance by helping the parties become more educated about their dispute, their respective interests, and the other side's perceptions of the problem. If the mediator is an expert in the disputed subject matter, he can provide insight that may assist the disputants in overcoming an impasse.

The mediator can be a creative force by inventing options for settlement that might not occur to disputants who have been more focused on simply defeating the other side. Such options might satisfy the interests of both parties better than a simple distributive or zero-sum solution. By objectively reviewing the details of an imminent agreement, the mediator may spot missing or flawed details important to the implementation and durability of the resolution. The mediator may be able to help disputants gain access to factual or legal information that has a bearing on the dispute or that is important to the settlement. In some cases, the mediator may help the parties understand and enter into another process, perhaps adjudicative, that will ensure efficient and just resolution of any remaining issues in dispute.

A mediator may serve as reality tester and devil's advocate. As an objective, neutral sounding board, the mediator can prevent disputants and their advocates from dangerously overcrediting their own points of view. The mediator may make each side think through and justify its factual assertions, demands, views, and positions while considering and dealing with the other side's arguments. The mediator assists the disputants in assessing the costs and benefits of continuing the dispute, of resolving the dispute, and of accepting various settlement alternatives. A mediator may serve as guardian of the details. In the heat of imminent resolution, disputants often overlook details necessary for the implementation and durability of the settlement. A mediator will monitor the details and bring to the disputants' attention issues that may impede implementation of an emerging agreement.

Because many of these functions reduce hostility, increase perception and empathy among the disputants, and reopen channels of communication, the mediator is a reconciler. Hostility, anger, and other emotions often impede productive discussion on substantive issues in dispute. A mediator may use a variety of techniques to manage destructive emotions and reconcile the disputants.

In private, voluntary, contractual mediation, anyone mutually selected by the parties can be a mediator. Presumably the parties will choose someone they trust and feel would be helpful in assisting them toward resolution. One or more individuals, states, or organizations can serve as mediator. *Impartiality, neutrality,* and *disinterest* are often-cited characteristics of mediators. These characteristics are useful and customary, but they are not required in private, voluntary mediation. Arguably, because the mediator cannot impose an outcome, impartiality is not as important as the disputants' mutual belief that the mediator will improve the prospects of an acceptable outcome, presuming that the parties are aware of the mediator's particular bias. Past partiality may not be related to current or future usefulness. Good relations with one of the parties may stimulate cooperative behavior on the part of that party or improve communications. In all cases, mediators bring with them, consciously or otherwise, ideas, knowledge, resources, and interests of their own or of the group or organization they represent. In many cases, the mediator may be an influential representative of the community to which both parties belong, and though he may not necessarily feel favoritism toward one of the parties, he may have his own assumptions and agenda or prefer an outcome that favors some broad community interest or notion of fairness or justice [Bercovitch, 1992a, pp. 4–5]. To the extent that a mediator can exert pressure on one or both parties, the mediator's sense of broader community interests may be reflected in the outcome. This is recognized in international mediation, particularly to the extent that a mediator can express preference for certain outcomes. As a practical matter, mediators who express favoritism toward one party or who are not sufficiently impartial will be less likely to achieve a mutually acceptable outcome. Because participation is voluntary and a mediator is empowered only to the extent that both parties are willing to tolerate the intervention, a party will withdraw if a mediator fully sides with the other party. International mediators may use the threat of siding with the other party or withdrawing and making a public expression of support for the other side to pressure a party. Mediators in private, voluntary mediation are not required to have any particular training or credentials.

In contrast, court-connected mediation and the emerging mediator codes of conduct (such as the *Model Standards of Conduct for Mediators*, discussed under MEDIATION) require a mediator to be both impartial and competent. With respect to competence, mediators in court-connected mediation programs must meet certain requirements, which usually include mediator training, as reflected in the following definitions:

- "A trained individual who assists disputants to reach a mutually acceptable resolution of their disputes by identifying and evaluating alternatives" [Colo. Rev. Stat. Ann. § 13-22-302(4) (West 1996)].

- "Any person certified pursuant to the provisions of the Dispute Resolution Act to assist in the resolution of a dispute" [Okla. Stat. Ann. tit. 12 § 1802 (West 1993)].

- "A person who has received at least 30 hours of training in the areas of negotiation, non-verbal communication, agreement writing, neutrality and ethics" [710 Ill. Comp. Stat. Ann. 20/2 (West 1992)].

More controversial requirements for competence include college and graduate degrees or particular professional backgrounds, such as law or psychology.

mediator-arbitrator, med-arbiter   Neutral third party selected to conduct a MED-ARB.

mediator liability   Legal responsibility of a mediator for willful or wanton misconduct that injures another.

Most state statutes or court rules that authorize mediation programs also grant mediators immunity from civil liability. However, like the privilege statutes, mediator immunity may be limited. Although lack of common standards for practice skills makes liability for malpractice unlikely, an action for negligence could be framed if the mediator violated a commonly accepted ethical standard. In some instances, a breach of confidentiality may be a breach of contract.

mediator privilege   See MEDIATION PRIVILEGE.

mediatress, mediatrice, mediatrix (archaic)   Female mediator.

medical malpractice arbitration   Use of voluntary, binding arbitration to resolve medical malpractice claims. As a matter of public policy, many jurisdictions will not enforce agreements to arbitrate medical malpractice claims arising in the future. Most jurisdictions will enforce SUBMISSION agreements. However, even these may be subject to special regulation [O.C.G.A. §§ 9-9-60 through 9-9-84 (1996)]. Managed-care plans involving health maintenance organizations (HMOs) and preferred provider organizations (PPOs) may include provisions for resolving any future medical malpractice claims made by beneficiaries through binding arbitration. The enforceability of such provisions may rest on special laws governing HMOs and PPOs.

Michigan Medical Malpractice Arbitration (MMAA) Act [Mich. Comp. Laws Ann. §§ 600.5040 to 600.5065, repealed by P. A. 1993, No. 78, § 2, eff. Apr. 1, 1994]. This important variation from most legislation governing voluntary medical malpractice arbitration required hospitals to offer arbitration agreements to patients before treatment, although the agreements were voluntary on the patient's part. The MMAA detailed the specific procedures governing the arbitration and, originally, delegated administration to the AAA. A three-person panel was selected by the parties from a list of five candidates in each of three categories: attorneys, health care licensees, and laypersons who are neither attorneys nor health care licensees.

The term is sometimes used to denote a variant of court-connected MANDATORY NONBINDING ARBITRATION adopted by some states specifically to expedite medical malpractice cases and not to be confused with voluntary, binding arbitration. More commonly referred to as a MEDICAL MALPRACTICE SCREENING PANEL.

medical malpractice screening, medical malpractice screening panel   Variant of MANDATORY NONBINDING ARBITRATION adopted by some states specifically to expedite medical malpractice cases. In some jurisdictions, referred to as MEDICAL MALPRACTICE ARBITRATION, but should not be confused with the voluntary, binding arbitration of medical malpractice claims.

Following the malpractice "crisis" in the mid-1970s, a number of states established special procedures for malpractice actions. The most common approach is the mandatory screening panel designed to screen out frivolous claims and facilitate settlements. These three-person panels are composed of some combination of attorneys, health care providers, and laypersons. In states using this approach, review by a screening panel either is required before the case can be filed in court or is a precondition to obtaining a trial date. The proceedings are private and result in an evaluation of liability or a determination of whether a prima facie case was established. Although the panel's findings are not binding on the parties, who may reject the decision and proceed to court, the panel's conclusions are admissible as a form of expert evidence in most states. In addition, although less common, some jurisdictions have required a plaintiff who wishes to proceed to trial after receiving an adverse decision from the screening panel to post bond to cover the defendant's costs. These aspects of screening panels distinguish them from most other variants of court-connected, mandatory nonbinding arbitration and have resulted in constitutional challenges and the abandonment of many screening programs. Other programs, however, claim success in weeding out spurious claims and expediting settlement [Saunders, 1986, pp. 267–272; Wilkinson, 1990, pp. 360–361; Kestner, Devonshire, and Kim, 1988, p. 9–10].

Medicine Wheel mediation model   Mediation model developed for use in urban aboriginal communities, particularly in Vancouver, British Columbia; based on the sacred Four Directions of the Medicine Wheel, an ancient Plains Nations symbol used by many aboriginal communities to explain certain complex concepts.

In the Four Directions of the Medicine Wheel, the East, home of the spiritual, is associated with the mediator's opening and orientation, grounded in spiritual rituals. The South, the home of emotions and sensitivity (the heart), is associated with the telling by the participants of their stories. The West, home of the physical, where people recognize their relationship to the Creator and to others, is associated with a phase of the mediation in which the mediator encourages the parties to focus inward and extend understanding to one another through reflection, introspection, honesty, humility, and sacrifice. The North, home of the intellect, is where parties think, imagine, and synthesize, searching for appropriate resolutions to the conflict at hand. After this stage, the parties move to the center of the wheel, the place of volition from which they put their solutions into action. A closing circle and prayer complete the process [Huber, 1993, pp. 355–360].

med-rec   From the family of MED-ARB variations, combination of mediation and nonbinding or ADVISORY ARBITRATION conducted by the same third-party neutral. Also known as *advisory med-arb*.

Nonbinding recommendations on unresolved issues following a mediation can be an effective form of reality testing and can induce settlement, particularly when the mediator has established a high degree of credibility and when parties are under political pressure to save face in a compromise. They can always say "the mediator recommended it" [Kagel and Kelly, 1989, p. 188]. In some court-connected contexts, the mediator may be charged with making a recommendation to the ultimate decision maker as to how the dispute should be resolved [Murray, Rau, and Sherman, 1989, p. 600].

As a practical matter and without commenting on the propriety of the practice, many mediators, particularly those using evaluative techniques, resort to informal judgments as a last resort in an impasse. In this context, med-rec's difference is an express grant of that power in advance of and as an integral part of the overall process.

med-then-arb   Variation of MED-ARB in which the parties agree to arbitrate any issues unresolved by mediation. The different functions of mediation and arbitration are performed by different individuals. If mediation fails, the dispute is then entrusted to a separate arbitrator who has the power to make a binding award. See Iowa Code §§ 20.20-20.22 (1996); Goldberg [1982].

Designed to avoid the criticism surrounding the use of a single neutral in two dissimilar processes, the dispute resolution agreement is similar to that method in that it requires a commitment to both processes, usually in advance of any disputes, and an authorization for the mediator to determine when arbitration is needed. The functional difference is that any arbitration is conducted under the aegis of a different neutral than the mediator. The theory is that the arbitrator, who was not privy to the mediation, will be unaffected by the discussions and material relating to that process. In addition to eliminating the danger of *role confusion* associated with med-arb, this variation allows the parties to select a mediator who is an expert in the mediation process and an arbitrator who is an expert in the substantive or technical issues in dispute. Because good, experienced mediators with technical expertise in many substantive areas are difficult to find, and because few technically expert arbitrators are currently trained as mediators, this variation can improve both phases of this hybrid process. If the mediation results in settlement, which is likely in most cases, then the parties bear only the cost of the first phase of the process.

Another advantage may be that the mediation can occur earlier in the dispute. In simple med-arb, the parties will probably be unwilling to start talking with the single neutral until they are prepared for both phases of the process. Compared to mediation, preparation for arbitration is more extensive and expensive. Parties can mediate whenever they have sufficient information to evaluate their positions. In med-then-arb, parties can mediate and if that fails they can then spend the time and effort preparing for the arbitration phase with the second neutral.

Even though this modification may address criticisms of med-arb, whether valid or invalid, it adds time and cost to the dispute resolution process. Additional time is wasted if the new neutral, the arbitrator, is called upon. Unless the arbitrator is waiting outside the doors of the mediation conference room, he must be contacted, scheduled, and introduced to the dispute, substantially duplicating the effort expended on the mediator. Additional cost results from incurring the additional neutral's fee. Transitions back and forth between neutrals caused by the issuance of interim awards would be ungainly. One way to reduce the added cost of this hybrid would be to have the parties give a joint presentation to both neutrals at the same time. The presentation should be designed to educate both neutrals about the case to the extent necessary to allow mediated negotiations to proceed. After this initial presentation, the arbitrator would retire until such time as he is needed. The obvious drawback of this last suggestion is that parties will have to pay the arbitrator for the time spent in the presentation even if the mediation results in a total settlement. So this technique would be useful only when the parties are fairly certain that not all issues will be resolved in the mediation. Another possible problem is that the parties will be inclined to start their mediation on a more adversarial note if the ultimate adjudicator is hearing the initial presentations. Conversely, the presence of the arbitrator at the start may be a good reminder that the mediation is the parties' last chance to fashion their own solution [Yarn, 1992].

meet-and-confer systems   *Labor:* Form of legislated general grievance-and-complaint processing used in labor-management relations with state and local government employees in some states.

Such legislation simply requires the unit of government to give its employees the opportunity to voice their concerns or to present their positions regarding employment-related issues. According to Deitsch and Dilts [1990], only three states—Alabama, Georgia, and Missouri—relied exclusively on meet-and-confer labor-management relations systems. Four other states—Indiana, Kansas, Nebraska, and Texas—had meet-and-confer statutes for specific groups of employees, the first two for state employees and the last two for teachers. Critics explain the rarity of this system by noting that failure to mandate bargaining or to establish exclusive bargaining representation gives employees no more input than the general public has.

memorandum of agreement   Written instrument memorializing the future actions to which the parties have committed themselves in order to resolve issues in dispute.

If the matter in dispute involves rights or responsibilities enforceable under law, a memorandum of agreement may constitute a settlement agreement enforceable under applicable principles of contract law, which may or may not require signatures. Mediators employ memoranda of agreement in both legal and nonlegal disputes to clarify the parties' understanding of the solutions reached and to encourage compliance by providing the parties with a document that they usually sign and retain as a reminder of their commitment. The drafting of the document itself is often done by the mediator with the direct participation of the parties. The mediator strives to use neutral language and provide balanced mutuality of commitment. The execution of the document, sometimes called a *memorandum of understanding* in nonlegal disputes, provides a degree of customary formality designed to impress upon the participants the seriousness of their commitments. In some jurisdictions, a memorandum of understanding is not enforceable as a settlement agreement and may be used as a precursor to a final memorandum of agreement. In divorce mediation, mediators customarily provide a draft memorandum to the parties for their use in consultation with legal counsel prior to committing to an enforceable agreement.

Mennonites   Christian sect whose members are active in peace and conflict resolution activities. Compare SOCIETY OF FRIENDS.

Founded in 1525 as part of the Anabaptist movement and named after an early Dutch leader, Menno Simons, the Mennonite congregation is devoted to the principles of loving the enemy, refusing to use violence or participate in military service, living peaceably with others at all levels, and taking risks to work actively for justice and mercy. They work actively to ameliorate the divisive and destructive aspects of nationalism, racism, tribalism, and class, and they practice reconciliation in human conflicts and warfare through passive and nonresistant methods.

The relief and development arm of the North American Mennonite and Brethren in Christ churches, the *Mennonite Central Committee,* assists in peace-related activities and in the area of crime, including services to offenders and mediation of offenses. CHRISTIAN PEACEMAKER TEAMS (CPT) is a collaborative program of Mennonite and Church of the Brethren congregations and Quaker meetings and focuses on international and civil war. Mennonites pioneered VICTIM-OFFENDER RECONCILIATION PROGRAMS.

metachange   Change in a person's ability to change. Among some mediators' goals for their clients [Fong, 1992, p. 212].

metacommunication   Communication about communication, or the way that language provides cues for interpreting both the content and substance of talk as well as the relationship between communicators [Putnam and Holmer, 1992, p. 144].

Implicit metacommunication is a part of all the messages we send to others. The implicit metacommunicative message is transmitted through our tone of voice and nonverbal behaviors. When we are communicating with strangers, implicit metacommunicative messages may lead to misunderstanding because people from other cultures or ethnic backgrounds may interpret our tone of voice or nonverbal behavior differently than we intended [Gudykunst, 1991, p. 40].

Michigan mediation   Process whereby a panel of lawyers evaluates cases upon referral from a judge and provides an advisory opinion as to value. Parties may continue their action in court but face assessment of costs if they do not improve their position.

Michigan mediation is a misnomer, for this type of dispute settlement technique is actually a hybrid of elements of mediation, case evaluation, and court-annexed arbitration. The system was established in 1978 in the Michigan state court in Detroit and was then adopted by the federal Eastern and Western Districts of Michigan. The goal of the system is to reduce case backlog in the courts by encouraging early settlement. Cases are diverted to Michigan mediation processes by trial judges upon the close of discovery. Referral in the Western District is available either if the judge requires it or if a party requests it (Local Rule 42). The Michigan state courts apply a set of criteria to determine whether referral is required (General Rule 316). Following referral, a three-member panel is established to evaluate the case and to suggest a settlement value. In the federal Eastern District (Local Rule 53.1) and the state court program, an independent, private group names a plaintiff lawyer, a defense lawyer, and a neutral lawyer to the panel. In the federal Western District, the parties each select one neutral, and the third is chosen either by the parties, the panel members, or the court clerk. Hearings before the panel are preceded by a submission of briefs and other evidence to the panel. The panel hearing itself is informal and limited to one hour. Neither clients nor witnesses may be present. Following the hearing, the panelists meet with each attorney separately to discuss the case and to serve in a mediator-like role. The panelists then meet among themselves and decide on a settlement recommendation. The parties may either accept the settlement or make an express rejection and request a trial de novo [Sander, 1991]. If the evaluation is challenged in court, the challenging party must gain a judgment that is at least 10 percent better than the mediation panel's evaluation. If they do not, challenging parties must pay actual costs, including court time and attorney fees. However, reports from the Western District of Michigan indicate that this latter provision has rarely been used.

Michigan mediation could be classified as a form of court-connected arbitration process (also arguably a misnomer; see MANDATORY NONBINDING ARBITRATION). However, the presentation of evidence is much briefer and there are no dollar amounts that trigger automatic case referral as in most court-connected arbitration models. Instead, cases are referred upon motion of either the parties or the judge [Harter, 1987, p. 87]. As in most court-connected processes, the nonbinding opinion of the neutrals serves to reality test the disputants, to focus their attention on negotiating, and to provide a range for bargaining. The more respected the neutrals are, the greater influence their evaluation will have.

Compare CASE EVALUATION, EARLY NEUTRAL EVALUATION, MANDATORY NON-BINDING ARBITRATION, TRIAL ON ORDER OF REFERENCE.

Michigan Medical Malpractice Arbitration Act   See MEDICAL MALPRACTICE ARBITRATION.

mid-mid solution   Means of dividing up a limited number of goods whereby each party receives the number of goods that would give him a utility equal to half of the utility he would have if he received all of the goods, plus half of the utility he could receive if he had all of the remaining goods after the initial equal distribution is determined [Raiffa, 1982, pp. 242–243].

mini-max, minimax   *Negotiation:* Approach to achieving acceptable trade-offs by minimizing losses and maximizing gains. Sometimes referred to as *minimax strategy* [Habeeb, 1988, p. 11].

As described by Jandt and Gillette [1985, p. 201], negotiators who employ mini-max do not begin negotiating until they have resolved four questions: (1) What is the minimum I can accept? (2) What is the maximum I can ask for without getting laughed out of the room? (3) What is the maximum I can give away? (4) What is the least I can offer without getting laughed out of the room? Maybe none of the adversaries will get all they want, but all of the adversaries should get enough of what they want to let them walk away from the negotiations feeling satisfied.

minimax strategy   Strategy to minimize one's losses and maximize one's gains [Habeeb, 1988, p. 11]. See MINI-MAX.

mini-trial, minitrial   Hybrid dispute resolution process combining elements of conciliatory and adjudicative processes. Typically involves an abbreviated adversarial presentation of the case before the parties who subsequently engage in negotiations. A neutral may be engaged to UMPIRE the presentation or to facilitate or mediate the negotiations, or to provide a case evaluation. Legal definitions include the following:

- "A structured settlement process in which each side presents a highly abbreviated summary of its case before senior officials of each party authorized to settle the case. A neutral advisor sometimes presides over the proceeding and will render an advisory opinion if asked to do so. Following the presentations, the officials seek to negotiate a settlement" [1 C.F.R. § 305.86-3 App. (1993)].

- "A structured settlement process in which the principals involved meet at a hearing before a neutral advisor to present the merits of each side of the dispute in an attempt to formulate a voluntary settlement" [Colo. Rev. Stat. Ann. § 13-22-302(4.3) (West 1996)].

- "A meeting of parties to a legal action where the parties present their positions to define the issues and develop a basis for realistic settlement negotiations" [Utah Code Ann. §§ 78-31B-1 et seq. (1953)].

The term is used indiscriminately to refer to any process with an abbreviated case presentation, particularly court-connected processes such as SUMMARY JURY TRIAL, MANDATORY NONBINDING ARBITRATION, or EARLY NEUTRAL EVALUATION. However, the classic mini-trial is a private, contractual dispute resolution process primarily employed in the resolution of commercial disputes among large organizations. In this sense, *mini-trial* is a misnomer because it is not a "small judicial proceeding" but rather a voluntary, nonbinding, and nonjudicial process like negotiation or mediation, yet one of its primary features is an adversarial presentation of each party's case, as in arbitration or litigation. The classic mini-trial's most distinguishing and essential characteristic, however, is the use of a hearing panel composed of top management representatives of the disputing organizations. Each party presents an abbreviated version of their case to the panel. A neutral third party, often a retired judge, can be appointed to serve on the panel as a procedural umpire. After hearing the case, these executives retire to negotiate a resolution. The neutral panel member may be asked to give an assessment of the strengths and weaknesses of the respective sides, to opine as to how a jury would respond, or to facilitate negotiations as a mediator. There is no set or accepted formula for a mini-trial. Typically, however, it is initiated after the dispute arises by an agreement that outlines a highly structured process involving a stay of court proceedings, if applicable; a period of limited discovery; a one- or two-day abbreviated "best case" presentation by the disputants' attorneys; a period for negotiation; and the use of a neutral advisor.

The rationale behind the mini-trial is that after obtaining an understanding of the significant legal issues and relevant facts, key decision makers with authority to settle the dispute are best able to assess the costs and benefits of pursuing litigation and to negotiate an out-of-court settlement in the context of broader organizational goals and interests. For more general commentary on the mini-trial process, see Edelman and Carr, 1987; see also "Comment: Whose Dispute Is It Anyway?" [1987]. For good practical advice on mini-trials, see Wilkinson, 1990, p. 171.

The first recognized mini-trial was used to resolve a dispute concerning infringement of a computer terminal patent. Telecredit had brought a $6 million suit against TRW, and after three years and $500 thousand in legal and expert fees, the frustrated disputants employed a mini-trial procedure. After a two-day mini-trial, they settled the case in thirty minutes [see Green, 1983]. Since then, the mini-trial has been used successfully in settings involving corporations, public institutions, and government agencies. The exact number of mini-trials and mini-trial agreements is unknown. However, many of the large corporate mini-trials are well documented and usually provide good anecdotal material on the relative effectiveness of ADR processes [see, for example, *The Effectiveness of the Mini-Trial. . .*, 1986].

Mini-trials have proven to be particularly popular in construction disputes involving federal government contracts, wherein there has been a tradition of reluctance by the government to enter into arbitration agreements. The U.S. Army Corps of Engineers' first mini-trial concerned an acceleration claim pending before the Armed Services Board of Contract Appeals (ASBCA). The claim of $630,000 was settled in three days for $380,000. The Corps' second mini-trial was over a $55.6 million claim involving changed site conditions in the construction of the Tennessee Tombigbee Waterway [Tennessee Tombigbee Constructors, Inc., 44 Fed. Cont. Rep. (BNA) 502 (1985)]. The mini-trial lasted three days, was followed by another one-day mini-trial, and resulted in a settlement of $17.2 million. The Department of Defense's inspector general affirmed the appropriateness of both the settlement and the procedure [Department of Defense, Inspector General, 1986]. This affirmation encouraged further use of mini-trials by the Corps [American Arbitration Association, 1990; Center for Public Resources, 1989]. Also note that the U.S. Army Corps of Engineers uses a model mini-trial agreement reprinted in U.S. Army Corps of Engineers, 1985.

The primary advantages of the mini-trial over litigation match those provided by negotiation or mediation, that is, they are nonbinding and private, they preserve business relationships, they allow party participation in and control over process, they provide the opportunity to create a win-win solution, and they afford savings in time, costs, and personnel. The primary disadvantage is that the mini-trial requires more expense and commitment than some forms of ADR. The concentrated effort of both counsel and top executives in a mini-trial is very expensive, and if the mini-trial does not settle the dispute, the disputants will also probably face an expensive piece of litigation. It is very important, therefore, to determine whether the process is suitable for a particular case. The best cases for a mini-trial are those that take advantage of the mini-trial's most distinctive characteristic: the use of top executives on the hearing panel and as subsequent negotiators. Many disputes persist because of a clash of personalities between and among middle management or opposing counsel. Where settlement is hampered by poor perspective or personality conflicts, mini-trials are useful. The best cases are concerned with disputes in which executives of higher authority have not been involved directly and that took place somewhere below them in the organization's structure but not directly in their chain of command. The likelihood of finding panel executives that are distanced from the dispute depends on the size of the disputing organizations, and the indications are that mini-trials are probably more effective in disputes between large organizations. If these organizations have or desire interdependence or long-term contractual relationships, so much the better.

One advantage of using *panel executives* is that they are usually knowledgeable in trade custom and practice and in technical matters of concern to their organization. For this reason, disputes involving complex technical issues or practices in the industry are amenable to mini-trials. Similarly, if the disputants are motivated to retranslate a business problem that has become a legal problem due to the litigation process back into a business problem and management issue, then a mini-trial is appropriate, particularly when the long-term goals of one or both of the organizations rely on nonadversarial business relationships. Such motivation usually comes from the in-house counsels' and panel executives' realization that it is important to curb or stop escalating legal costs.

If settlement negotiations will be enhanced by following an adversarial, trial-like case presentation, mini-trials are appropriate. They would be useful if settlement is impeded by the parties' differing assumptions about the merit or value of their claims if resolved by litigation. The case presentation could promote negotiations either by convincing a party of the weakness of its case or by creating significant uncertainty, and therefore risk, as to the outcome in litigation. Similarly, disputes that require the parties to unravel complex questions of mixed law and fact would be aided by the prenegotiation case presentation. The presentations may be useful in narrowing the issues by eliminating overly technical or collateral considerations that obscure the underlying problem. In such a case, even an unsuccessful mini-trial may be useful to reduce subsequent litigation costs.

Generally a mini-trial is inappropriate if a case hinges solely on legal issues. In such a case, a ruling by an outside party, usually a judge rendering summary judgment, is probably a more efficient means of resolving the matter. Similarly, if one of the parties' primary goals is to test a point of law or to create legal precedent, a mini-trial may not be productive. Arguably, mini-trials are not appropriate in disputes over factual issues that hinge solely on credibility. Typically the executives on the hearing panel are neither trained nor impartial enough to weigh credibility. Most mini-trial presentations—characterized by limited witness testimony, little if any cross examination, and use of affidavits—are not designed to verify the accuracy or veracity of testimony. It is possible, however, for the agreement to provide sufficient opportunity for cross-examination, while the neutral could communicate his observations on credibility. Finally, cases with small amounts at stake should be carefully analyzed to determine whether the amount in controversy justifies the costs of the mini-trial.

If the dispute is in litigation, then some discovery may be necessary before a mini-trial can take place. Experience indicates that the mini-trial should be used early in the discovery stage so that sufficient information is available but the higher costs of litigation have not been incurred. If scheduled toward the end of discovery, however, there may be more connection between the presentation and what a judge would hear, thereby facilitating settlement. Most reported mini-trials involve disputes in which the parties have turned to the process in the midst of costly and frustrating litigation. Arguably, some of the reputed success of mini-trials may be due to the fact that the parties are dissatisfied with the process of concurrent litigation. If the dispute is not in litigation, then some period of pre-mini-trial discovery and evaluation is necessary. In such cases, agreement on ground rules for discovery is important, and the neutral can be authorized to rule on contested discovery issues [Yarn, 1992].

One variation on the use of neutrals in this process is the creation of a jury to render an advisory opinion (see JURY-DETERMINED SETTLEMENT). This would entail more expense and probably would not be useful unless negotiations are at an impasse based on differing opinion as to how a real jury would respond to the case, if the credibility of a key witness is the major issue, or if the parties feel more comfortable with the opinion of more than one neutral. In the latter case, the mini-trial jury should be composed of experts in the disputed subject matter.

Mini-trials should not be confused with ARBITRATION, which in its contractual form usually involves a binding decision by the neutral third party without the participation of the principals in shaping the award. Some jurisdictions provide for a court-connected version of the mini-trial requiring key executives to hear the summary presentations and engage in subsequent negotiations. In British Columbia, for example, court-connected mini-trials are conducted before a judge [Bristow, 1992, p. 202].

mirror action *International Relations:* Unilateral rescission of an obligation under a treaty in response to another nation's failure to abide by the same provisions. Some treaties expressly permit this form of reciprocal action when a party to the treaty believes that another party has violated some portion [Rubin and Jones, 1989, p. 150].

mirror image *Negotiation:* Partisan perception of each party regarding the other's position as exactly opposite and wholly inimical to his own. This perception makes it difficult for parties to recognize opportunities for accommodation or compromise [Jandt and Gillette, 1985, p. 83].

misrepresentation False suggestion made by either words or action, or by the omission of words or a failure to act, or by affirmation or incorporation of the false statements of others. Although there is such a thing as an *innocent misrepresentation,* the term is associated with deliberate and knowing conduct.

Negotiation: Tactic, or DIRTY TRICK, more common to competitive positional bargaining. May connote a milder form of lying. Nevertheless, agreements reached through reliance on a misrepresentation may be unenforceable. Under prevailing codes of conduct, lawyers are required to be truthful in their representation. However, exceptions are drawn for representation in negotiations. The comment to the American Bar Association's *Model Rules of Professional Conduct,* Model Rule 4.1, provides the following:

> This Rule refers to statements of fact. Whether a particular statement should be regarded as one of fact can depend on the circumstances. Under generally accepted conventions in negotiation, certain types of statements ordinarily are not taken as statements of material fact. Estimates of price or value placed on the subject of a transaction and a party's intentions as to an acceptable settlement of a claim are in this category, and so is the existence of an undisclosed principal except where nondisclosure of the principal would constitute fraud.

This exception is consistent with generally accepted conventions of competitive positional bargaining in which some degree of deception over one's RESERVATION PRICE is crucial to the process [White, 1980].

mixed arbitral tribunal, mixed arbitration tribunal *International:* Special tribunal established by agreement to arbitrate mutual or unilateral claims in which states party to the agreement and their nationals can plead directly.

States may resort to mixed arbitral tribunals after wars or insurrections, or in peace time when established procedures for handling claims break down. The term is used interchangeably with MIXED CLAIMS COMMISSION, an identical concept. However, a technical distinction would be that tribunals are composed of three members, one from each of the disputing states and a president appointed jointly by the disputants or by some designated public figure or institution. The agreement establishing the tribunal may make it clear that arbitration is to take place without having to exhaust all other remedies [DOA]. Claims can be brought by one state against another state, by citizens of one state against another state, or by citizens of one state against the citizens of the other state.

The concept originated in the nineteenth-century claims commissions established between the United States and several Central American states to resolve damage to U.S. citizens resulting from war and revolution. The most important example of modern mixed arbitral tribunals was established after World War I pursuant to Article 304 of the Treaty of Versailles. The tribunal was empowered to settle disputes in connection with the rights and claims of private individuals who were affected by the war. Unlike the nineteenth-century claims commissions and most modern public international adjudicative processes, in which only states have standing, individuals are permitted to present their cases before the mixed arbitral tribunals themselves rather than relying on representation by their country.

mixed claims commissions   Bodies founded ad hoc on the basis of international agreements and established with the purpose to settle, in formal and final arbitration proceedings, claims that have arisen between citizens of different states, between citizens of one state and the other state, or between the states themselves.

The states involved in a dispute select equal numbers of members. An odd member is selected jointly by these members or by an authority appointed by them or designated by the constituting agreement. The power of decision may be by majority vote, or if no such agreement is reached, the final decision rests with the odd member acting as UMPIRE. The commission members decide claims based on the legal rules designated in the constituting agreement or on equitable principles. Nations usually do not require that local remedies be exhausted first before the parties resort to arbitration. Although this more common term is used interchangeably with MIXED ARBITRAL TRIBUNAL, the technical distinction is that commissions usually number more than three members. In addition, these commissions are created by treaty and are therefore distinguishable from commissions established by international organizations.

mixed commission   Institution set up by nations with common, ongoing interests for negotiating settlements to disputes that arise from those interests [Merrills, 1991, p. 8].

Mixed commissions usually consist of an equal number of representatives of both parties and may be given either a broad or indefinite duration or the task of dealing with a specific problem. Additionally, there may be a third party, a member of neutral nationality. A mixed commission may be established by agreement between states or with the direct participation of an international organization. One or more international organizations may establish mixed commissions as subsidiary organs to coordinate functions. The constituting agreement, either treaty or directive, defines the tasks and functions of the commission.

Unlike a MIXED CLAIMS COMMISSION, mixed commissions are not established to hear and decide claims by individual citizens but rather to resolve problems between states.

mixed processes   Processes that combine elements of negotiation, mediation, fact-finding, or adjudication—the primary dispute resolution processes [Riskin and Westbrook, 1987, p. 324]. Same as HYBRIDS.

MLATNA   Most Likely Alternative(s) to a Negotiated Agreement [Potapchuk and Carlson, 1987, p. 37]. See BATNA.

moderated settlement, moderated settlement conference   Term used in different jurisdictions to describe at least two distinct COURT-CONNECTED ADR processes that are similar to MANDATORY NONBINDING ARBITRATION.

One form, adopted in the U.S. District Court for the Northern District of California, is now better known as EARLY NEUTRAL EVALUATION. In another form, a panel of three attorneys who specialize in the area of law of the case being moderated facilitates the conference and issues a nonbinding award. This latter form is defined under Texas law as a "forum for case evaluation and realistic settlement negotiations. Each party presents their position before a panel of impartial third parties, and the panel issues a non-binding, advisory opinion regarding the liability of the parties" [Tex. Civ. Prac. & Rem. Code Ann. § 154.025 (West 1993)]. Similarly, Utah law defines it as follows: "A meeting of parties to a legal action where the parties present their positions to one or more ADR providers" [Utah Code Ann. § 78-31B-1 (1953)]. If requested, the panel may also facilitate the subsequent negotiations [Kestner, Devonshire, and Kim, 1988, p. 364].

modern arbitration statute, modern arbitration act   Legislative act providing for the enforcement of agreements to arbitrate future disputes.

Most modern arbitration statutes grant courts the authority to compel arbitration by reluctant parties, to stay any litigation on an arbitrable matter, to appoint arbitrators when parties fail to provide for appointment or when the method of appointment fails, to fill vacancies when the parties fail to make such appointments or when the arbitrators withdraw or are unable to serve, and to confirm the award so as to enforce it as if it were a final judgment of the court. A court is not free to review the facts and findings in the award and can modify or vacate an award on only very limited grounds. The UNITED STATES ARBITRATION ACT and various state adaptions of the UNIFORM ARBITRATION ACT are examples of modern arbitration acts.

modified final-offer arbitration   Variation of FINAL-OFFER ARBITRATION in which if both offers are unacceptable the arbitrator has the option of writing his own proposed settlement. If both parties agree to the arbitrator's settlement, it becomes the award. If either party refuses to accept it, then the arbitrator must choose from between the two parties' final offers [Baizley and Suche, 1986]. See SPECIAL-FEATURE ARBITRATION.

modifying the award   *Arbitration:* Correction of errors in an arbitration award by a court or an arbitrator.

Under most MODERN ARBITRATION STATUTES, an award may be corrected if there is a miscalculation of figures or a mistake in the description of any person, thing, or property referred to in the award. There is a limited period of time within which a disputant can petition for modification.

money judgment   Court's final determination that a defendant must pay a certain sum of money. Contrast with *equity judgment*, in which the court orders equitable relief such as an injunction.

monkalun **(Philippine)**   Peacemaking go-between in Ifugao society.

Although the *Monkalun* has no legal authority to bind the parties, he uses his considerable moral authority to act as judge, prosecuting and defending counsel, and the court record. Ultimately his duty is to promote consensual, peaceful settlement through the art of persuasion [Barton, 1969, p. 87]. See IFUGAO MEDIATION.

monolithic   Internal quality of an organizational unit whose members all hold similar beliefs, goals, and attitudes [Raiffa, 1982, p. 12]. This quality reduces opportunities for conflict among conforming members of the organization, but increases possibilities for conflict with nonconforming members. Monolithic organizations have difficulty resolving both internal and external conflict because they are not accustomed to internal conflict and because they fail to recognize that in external conflict other organizations may hold different, legitimate beliefs, goals, and attitudes.

moot   Unofficial public assembly at which grievances are publicly aired and often resolved through the conciliatory efforts of community members.

Procedure in which parties discuss an issue until consensus is achieved or pay the penalty of having no decision [Fogg, 1985, p. 349]. Historically it denotes a meeting of freemen in early England for the purposes of administering justice. Anthropologists have used the term to describe a range of public discussions employed mostly by preliterate societies as alternatives to the official courts of colonial powers (see, for example, KPELLE MOOT, TRIBAL MOOT. In contrast to formal courts, moots are informal (though not devoid of custom) and lack official judges (though influential members of the community may play key intervening roles). Like formal courts, moots provide an opportunity to express and disseminate publicly the societal norms and tenets of proper behavior, but in a much broader and unrestricted manner. In his study of moots among the Simbu of the New Guinea highlands, Podolefsky [1992, pp. 70, 71] notes that the primary difference between moots and courts is that moots focus on the settlement of the grievance and the restoration of at least a degree of harmony between the disputants.

moot councilor (New Guinea)   Third party in a Simbu moot who behaves much like a mediator in modern domestic mediation in the United States. Usually an influential member of the community who is respected for his knowledge of the formal state law as well as the customs and norms of the tribal groups. In contrast to a western mediator, a moot councilor may discuss or make public declarations about community problems that are similar to the case [Podolefsky, 1992, pp. 73, 74].

motion   *Law:* a formal request to a court asking it to do something.

motion to compel arbitration   Legal notice used by an aggrieved party to petition a court to compel the other party to arbitrate [DOA].

mukhtaar **(Lebanon)**   Mayor of a Sunni village whose official duties are administrative but who may take upon himself certain unofficial duties of a judicial nature, such as dispute settlement. The informal procedure usually involves hearing all information from disputing parties and then offering a suggestion on how to settle [Rothenberger, 1978, pp. 152–180, 160–161].

multicultural conflict resolution   See CULTURE.

multiculturalism   Adherence to a system or theory that values having many cultures within a society. It also means valuing the existence, maintenance, and extension of individual cultures, and ultimately suggests a society in which equal participation is unfettered by race, ethnicity, gender, or class [Duryea, 1992, p. 6, citations omitted].

multidoor courthouse (MDCH), multidoor center (MDC) (courthouse of many doors, multidoor program)   Primarily court-connected program through which litigants are provided with a choice of dispute resolution processes.

As initially proposed in 1976 by Frank E. A. Sander [1979, 1985] of Harvard Law School, disputants would go to a center offering an array of dispute resolution services under one roof. Each "door" would be a dispute resolution device, such as mediation, arbitration, or litigation. In the context of courthouses, potential litigants who go to court to settle their dispute would have the option to enter into ADR instead of pursuing a traditional adversarial trial process [Kessler and Finkelstein, 1988, p. 577].

The concept is premised on the notion that there are advantages and disadvantages in any specific case to using one or another dispute resolution process. The key feature of the multidoor courthouse is the initial intake, screening, and referral process in which an intake counselor helps the parties make choices by analyzing disputes to determine what process or combination of processes would be most appropriate for the problem [Goldberg, Sander, and Rogers, 1992, p. 432].

The concept has been implemented in a number of cities, including Houston, Tulsa, and Washington, D.C., as both court-annexed programs and free-standing centers handling both court-referred and voluntarily referred cases. Legal definitions include the following:

- "The multi-door courthouse is a concept rather than a process. It is based on the premise that the justice system should make a wide range of dispute resolution processes available to disputants. In practice, skilled intake workers direct disputants to the most appropriate process or series of processes, considering such factors as the relationship of the parties, the amount in controversy, anticipated length of trial, number of parties, and type of relief sought. Mediation, arbitration, case evaluation or early neutral evaluation, summary jury trial, mini-trial, and various combinations of these ADR processes would all be available in the multi-door courthouse" [Georgia Supreme Court Alternative Dispute Resolution Rules, 1993, Appendix 1].

- "That form of alternative dispute resolution in which the parties select any combination of problem-solving methods designed to achieve effective resolution, including but not limited to arbitration, early neutral evaluation, med-arb, mini-trials, settlement conference, special masters, and summary jury trials" [Colo. Rev. Stat. Ann. § 13-22-302(4.5) (West 1996)].

multilateral agreement   Compact involving three or more parties. Term most often used in public international law, as in treaties between nations. However, such an agreement need not rise to the level of a treaty.

multilateralism   Approach to dispute resolution in which a number of parties seek a settlement that is acceptable to all involved. The key characteristics are that discussions are open and subject to universal participation.

International: Normally contrasted with unilateralism, it involves trying to change or constrain the policies of two or more states through international negotiations and treaties, rather than by independent, unilateral actions [Pauling, Laszlo, and Jong, 1986, vol. 1, p. 627].

multilateral trade negotiations   Bargaining sessions among the participating contracting parties in search of mutually beneficial agreements. Most often found in international law, as when parties to a treaty or agreement (such as GATT) attempt to reduce barriers to world trade.

multilateral treaty   *International:* Treaty made between three or more nations as opposed to a *bilateral treaty* between two nations. Most special provisions in multilateral treaties organize settlement of disputes in the form of interstate procedures on the initiative of the member states. With the odd exception, conciliation is entrusted to the competent authorities mentioned in the treaties—administrative conciliation—or to a body set up in the treaty in which all member states are represented [de Waart, 1973, p. 65].

multiple grievances   *Labor/Arbitration:* Accumulation of many grievances by union and management that may be consolidated and heard in a single hearing by the same arbitrator.

multiple-issue dispute   Dispute in which more than one primary issue is involved. According to Raiffa [1982, pp. 251–255], parties to multiple-issue disputes tend to use integrative tactics and strategies rather than those of distributive bargaining (see BARGAINING). In such disputes, disputants no longer need to view themselves as strict competitors and can engage in cooperative negotiation. In such instances, the circumstances of the dispute have changed from a ZERO-SUM game, typically characterized as a fixed pie, to one in which the overall size of the pie varies and participants can arrange their circumstances in such a manner as to satisfy the bottom-line demands of both parties [Whiting, 1992, p. 59].

multiple-offer selection   Variation of FINAL-OFFER ARBITRATION in which each side presents the arbitrator with more than one final offer. Although the number could vary under the agreement, the arbitrator chooses the best from among the offers submitted and announces which side has made the best offer. The other party then selects one of the three offers the other side has made, which becomes the award. This technique may allow one side's position to be improved, with no detriment to the other side's position [Baizley and Suche, 1986].

multiplex relationship   Intimate or ongoing relationship. Much literature on courts discusses the relative utility and wisdom of judicial involvement in disputes arising in the context of what have been called multiplex relationships [Cavanagh and Sarat, 1980].

multistep ADR   Agreement by the parties to engage in a series of successive dispute resolution techniques until a resolution is reached. Typically, multistep ADR starts with negotiation and ends with binding arbitration. STEP NEGOTIATION and mediation might be included.

multitrack diplomacy   *International Relations:* Conceptual framework describing the various activities that contribute to international peacemaking.

Unlike the traditional view of DIPLOMACY as only activities of government representatives, this framework recognizes the contributions of many nongovernmental actors. Expanding on the concept of *Track One* (government representatives) and *Track Two* (nongovernmental actors) articulated in 1982 by Joseph Montville of the Foreign Service Institute, Diamond and McDonald [1993] described nine tracks that constitute a living system of interrelated parts (activities, individuals, institutions, and communities) consciously and unconsciously working together toward peace: governmental, professional conflict resolution, business, private citizen, research (including training and education), activism, religious, funding, and public opinion.

mutual agreement   Situation in which all parties to a negotiation are supportive of decisions reached, as contrasted with procedures whereby a decision is achieved through a voting process (resulting in "winners" and "losers") or through some individual or body making a unilateral decision (such as a designated decision maker or through administrative or judicial proceedings). Often characterized as CONSENSUS [Cormick, 1991, p. 363].

mutual criticism   Process of dispute resolution used during the nineteenth century at Oneida, a utopian community, that was an adaptation of Benedictine procedures that substituted communal scrutiny for formal rules. Discord was expressed openly; members were criticized by the community leader or, in extreme cases, before an assembly of the entire community. Criticism asserted the primacy of group norms over individual contentiousness [Auerbach, 1983, pp. 52–53].

mutual gains bargaining (MGB)   Term used in the labor context to describe interest-based negotiation in which the parties strive to realize joint gain in their final settlement. See BARGAINING, INTEGRATIVE BARGAINING.

mutually acceptable restatement of arguments   Technique whereby each side in a conflict states the arguments of the other side so clearly and persuasively that the other side will accept the wording. This technique increases each side's understanding of the other's perception of the dispute [Fogg, 1985, p. 350].

mutually assured destruction (MAD)   See DETERRENCE THEORY.

muxtaar   See *MUKHTAAR.*

NAA See NATIONAL ACADEMY OF ARBITRATORS.

naashaadei nukx'ee **(Native North American/Tlingit)** Ceremonial assembly of Alaskan native Tlingit clan leaders for conflict resolution. Literally, "heads of clans meeting together."

Such gatherings have long been a part of traditional Tlingit law and practice. Recently clan leaders have begun advising the tribal court of the southeastern *Sitka* region, base of the Tlingit clan [Connors, 1993, p. 379].

naat'aanii **(Native North American/Navajo)** Person who speaks strongly, wisely, and well. Describes Navajo *peace chiefs,* who are civil leaders known for their ability to guide others and plan for community solidarity and survival, and for their personal knowledge of Navajo values and morals and demonstrated practice of them.

Traditionally, *naat'aanii* are selected on a nonhereditary basis by local communities and exercise authority through their ability to persuade by speaking rather than through coercion. When a dispute occurs, the extended families involved try to resolve it themselves. If they are unsuccessful, the families bring the dispute to one or more respected members of the community, often the naat'aanii, for mediation. The disputants represent themselves, all of the people present may speak, and sessions frequently last for days. The mediators provide advice, moral exhortation, and instruction about Navajo traditions. The result, generally, is that the parties reach an agreement by consensus, often involving a payment in kind [Lieder, 1993, pp. 16–22].

The naat'aanii is not quite neutral; as a clan and kinship relative of the parties or as an elder, he has a point of view. He teaches values through prayer and a "lecture" to tell disputants what is right and wrong [Bluehouse and Zion, 1993]. In modern Navajo society, this person serves as a model for judges and guides the NAVAJO PEACEMAKER COURT. If a solution agreeable to the parties has been reached during the course of the peacemaking session, then the results may be written out and taken to the district judge for signature as a final judgment. If the parties cannot agree, Anglo-style litigation through the district court is still available to them.

The term has been inaccurately translated as *headman* or *principal leader*. See also HOZHO, HOZHOOJI NAAT'AANII.

NAFCM   See NATIONAL ASSOCIATION FOR COMMUNITY MEDIATION.

NAFTA   See NORTH AMERICAN FREE TRADE AGREEMENT.

naive procedure   Approach to allocating a limited amount of goods among several parties whereby each individual gets an equal portion of the goods, regardless of external factors [Raiffa, 1982, p. 289].

NAME   See NATIONAL ASSOCIATION FOR MEDIATION IN EDUCATION, now known as the CONFLICT RESOLUTION IN EDUCATION NETWORK.

naming   Process of acknowledging to oneself that a particular situation has caused injury; coming to perceive a situation as injurious [Felstiner, Abel, and Sarat, 1980–1981, pp. 631, 635].

Naming is recognizing a GRIEVANCE and is the initial step in the evolution of a CONFLICT into a DISPUTE, followed by BLAMING, CLAIMING, and claim rejection.

narrow arbitration clause   Agreement by which the parties agree to arbitrate only limited issues, as in "we will arbitrate X and Y," in contrast to a BROAD ARBITRATION CLAUSE, as in "we will arbitrate any and all disputes or claims that may arise." Compare RESTRICTED ARBITRATION CLAUSE, which designates certain issues to be nonarbitrable, as in "X and Y cannot be arbitrated."

NASD   See NATIONAL ASSOCIATION OF SECURITIES DEALERS.

Nash Point, Nash solution   Point in the range of possible bargaining outcomes at which the product of the two players' utilities is maximized; economic model of the bargaining problem.

Economist John Nash [1975a, 1975b] suggested this point as marking the ideal outcome of the bargaining process as he conceived it. Other theorists have examined the formulation and how the Nash point might be used as a guideline in the arbitration of bargaining conflicts [see Raiffa, 1982, pp. 244–246, 321–322].

National Academy of Arbitrators (NAA)   Nonprofit professional and honorary organization of arbitrators of labor-management disputes, formed to foster competence, establish ethical standards, and promote the understanding of labor-management arbitration.

national arbitrator   See PARTISAN ARBITRATOR.

National Association for Community Mediation (NAFCM)   Nonprofit membership organization composed of community mediation centers, their staff and volunteer mediators, and other individuals and organizations interested in the community mediation movement. Its purpose is to support the maintenance and growth of community-based mediation programs and processes; to present a compelling voice in appropriate policymaking, legislative, professional, and other arenas; and to encourage the development and sharing of resources for these efforts.

National Association for Mediation in Education (NAME)   Former name of the CONFLICT RESOLUTION IN EDUCATION NETWORK (CRENET).

National Association of Securities Dealers (NASD)   A self-regulatory organization, the NASD provides a forum for and has rules governing mediation and arbitration of disputes between its members or between its members and its customers. See also NEW YORK STOCK EXCHANGE.

National Conference on Peacemaking and Conflict Resolution (NCPCR)   International biennial gathering started in 1982 as a forum where individuals working and researching conflict resolution can gather to exchange ideas in order to promote the use and acceptance of nonviolent approaches to the resolution of conflict and the improvement of conflict resolution theory and practice. With a strong emphasis on collaboration, inclusiveness, and diversity, NCPCR is not member-based, so anyone interested in issues of peacemaking and conflict resolution may attend.

National Institute for Dispute Resolution (NIDR)   Public-interest organization created in 1982 for the purpose of furthering the development and use of conflict resolution programs and processes.

Based in Washington, D.C., NIDR served as a central administering agency for several foundations that made grants in conflict resolution. NIDR was instrumental in the establishment of many of the state offices of dispute resolution in the United States.

natural peace   State of peace, or lack of conflict, based on mutual dependency.

In a state of natural peace, parties' interdependence has boosted both the cost of conflict and incentives for cooperation [Polachek, 1980, p. 56]. This is in contrast to a peace resulting from a stalemate of opposing forces.

Navajo Peacemaker Court   Created in 1982 by the Navajo Nation Judicial Conference. Unique method of mediation and arbitration that uses Navajo values and institutions in local communities [Bluehouse and Zion, 1993, p. 328]. See HOZHO, NAAT'AANII.

NCPCR   See NATIONAL CONFERENCE ON PEACEMAKING AND CONFLICT RESOLUTION.

needs theory   Posits that fundamental human needs underlie certain conflicts.

Building from Maslow's famous hierarchy of human needs (1954, pp. 35–47), which identifies both physiological and psychological requirements, needs theory suggests that some intractable and deep-rooted conflicts are about needs that are nonnegotiable rather than about interests that are negotiable. Resolution of such conflicts is dependent on restructuring society to meet the needs of its constituent groups [Burton, 1990b].

need theory of negotiation   Theory that parties' needs are the driving force behind the negotiation process.

According to this theory, negotiation presupposes that each party needs something from the other; if they did not, they would disregard one another's demands from the start and refuse to participate in the process. A party's needs may consist solely of maintaining the status quo, which necessitates cooperation of the other [Nierenberg, 1968, p. 79].

negative reciprocity   See RECIPROCITY.

negative settlement   Settlement achieved without trial only because of parties' suspicions that they would have done worse in court [Menkel-Meadow, 1991]. Contrast POSITIVE SETTLEMENT.

negotiate   To engage in NEGOTIATION.

negotiated investment strategy (NIS)   *Public Policy:* Facilitated negotiation process that enables representatives from the public and private sectors jointly to address complex intergovernmental issues primarily about the effects and direction of future growth and public and private investment [Moore and Carlson, 1984].

In the mid-1970s, staff members at the Kettering Foundation developed the NIS to help urban communities handle serious conflicts over policy and community issues involving growth patterns and land use, maintenance and revitalization of neighborhoods, community investment, and social equality. NIS experiments in three Midwestern metropolitan areas yielded perceptible results, including written agreements for specific, coordinated public-private investment; expedited implementation of projects; improved working relationships both within the local community and among public officials at all levels; and the development of a new process for resolving public planning and policy differences [See Kettering Foundation, 1981].

Though often described as a form of mediation, the NIS might best be described as a form of strategic planning among governmental entities with overlapping responsibilities that emphasizes civic participation and uses some of the structure and techniques of formal mediation. While mediation is more commonly used after a formal dispute arises and the disputants reach an impasse in negotiations, the NIS is used by the parties from the beginning for identification of issues for discussion, collaborative problem solving, and joint action [Kunde and Rudd, 1988, p. 34]. A third party facilitates the process and may actively mediate as disputes and impasses arise. Participants are representatives, often teams, of governmental and nongovernmental stakeholders who are responsible for or affected by the issues to be discussed. Also, the private sector needs to be represented so that private and public resources can be coordinated and committed to the agreed-upon solutions. Bringing citizens directly into the decision-making process through an NIS can be very important in building broad consensus around strategies to address the public issues. Presumably consensus on strategies improves implementation and compliance. Typically the process involves identification of the stakeholders and invitations to participate, informal fact-finding and information exchange, face-to-face brainstorming and narrowing of options, formal agreement containing mutual commitments reduced to writing, public presentation and review of the recommended strategy followed by formal adoption, and some process for monitoring implementation.

NIS refers as much to the final product as to the process. The final product is an agreement that embodies a joint strategy for solving the selected problems and that defines the respective roles and commitments of the participants for carrying out that strategy. The list of problems accompanied by a detailed set of goals, objectives, and delegated action steps is in essence a strategic plan. Although an NIS can result in regulation, as can a REGULATORY NEGOTIATION, the agreement is primarily about commitments to action rather than restrictions on action. An NIS is useful in resolving public policy issues that involve dispersed authority and resources and that affect diverse interest groups whose opinions may differ but who are motivated to resolve conflicts because of the limited time or the severity of the problem. The NIS is more difficult, inefficient, and prone to failure when substantial stakeholders are not represented, participants lack authority to commit necessary resources, or one or more of the participants either benefits more by not having an agreement or believes that the stakes are too small to make the necessary commitment to the process [Carlson, 1990, pp. 141–142].

negotiated rulemaking   Rulemaking by U.S. federal agencies through the use of a negotiated rulemaking committee under the NEGOTIATED RULEMAKING ACT [5 U.S.C. § 562 (6) (1993)].

Negotiated Rulemaking Act (of 1990)   U.S. law providing procedures for federal agencies to use negotiated rulemaking (see also REGULATORY NEGOTIATION).

Under the Act, an agency may use negotiated rulemaking to develop a proposed rule whenever the agency determines that it would be "in the public interest" to do so. The agency must determine the stakeholders and determine whether they can be represented in a negotiated rulemaking committee. If so, the agency may establish such a committee composed of persons representing the various affected interests and at least one member of the agency. The committee tries to reach a consensus on a draft of the rule. The agency may use a convenor to determine whether a committee would be functional and to form the committee. The agency may use a facilitator to impartially chair the committee meetings and assist the negotiations.

Proponents believe such a process can reduce the time required to make a rule, decrease litigation over the final rule, and even yield a better rule than the traditional process or rulemaking. In practice, it is not at all clear that negotiated rulemaking achieves these objectives. The Environmental Protection Agency has the most experience under the Act. See, generally, Pritzker and Dalton (1995).

negotiation   Bilateral or multilateral process in which parties who differ over a particular issue attempt to reach agreement or compromise over that issue through communication.

Negotiation generally refers to the process of conferring with another party with the purpose of securing agreement on some matter of common interest [Morley and Stephenson, 1977, p. 19]. Negotiation is a CONCILIATORY PROCESS in which participants engage in back-and-forth communications in an effort to adjust differences. It is typically consensual and private, with minimal third-party involvement. It is one of the most common approaches to making decisions and managing disputes. Informal negotiation occurs daily among friends, family, and coworkers for the purpose of adjusting or redefining relationships.

There are as many definitions for negotiation as people who write about it. In no particular order, the following is a sample of definitions in use in the conflict resolution literature:

- "An explicit or tacit process of potentially opportunistic interaction by which two or more parties, with some apparent conflict, seek to do better through joint decided action than they could do otherwise" [Lax and Sebenius, 1986, p. 11].

- "The process of engaging in good-faith efforts to reach an agreement or resolve a dispute, through the confidential exchange of factual statements and representations" [Haydock and Mitchell, 1984].

- "A process of adjustment in existing differences, with a view to the establishment of a mutually more desirable legal relation by means of barter and compromise of legal rights and duties and of economic, psychological, social and other interests. It is accomplished consensually as contrasted with the force of law" [Bellow and Moulton, 1981, p. 11].

- "A field of knowledge and endeavor that focuses on gaining the favor of people from whom we want things" [Cohen, 1991, p. 15].

- "Negotiating is a basic means of getting what you want from others. It is back-and-forth communication designed to reach an agreement when you and the other side have some interests that are shared and others that are opposed" [Fisher and Ury, 1981, p. xi].

- "One kind of problem-solving process—one in which people attempt to reach a joint decision on matters of common concern in situations where they are in disagreement and conflict" [Gulliver, 1979, p. xiii].

- "Concerned with situations in which two or more parties recognize that differences of interest and values exist . . . and in which they want (or in which one or more are compelled) to seek a compromise agreement" [Raiffa, 1982, p. 7].

- "A process in which divergent values are combined into an agreed decision" [Zartman and Berman, 1982, p. 1].

- "A process whereby parties with conflicting aims establish the terms on which they will co-operate" [Hawkins, Hudson, and Cornall, 1991, pp. 6–7].

- "A process in which explicit proposals are put forward ostensibly for the purpose of reaching agreement on an exchange or on the realization of a common interest where conflicting interests are present" [Iklé, 1964, pp. 3–4].

- "The voluntary process of distributing the proceeds from cooperation" [Cross, 1969, p. 3].

- "A process by which a joint decision is made by two or more parties. The parties first verbalize contradictory demands and then move toward agreement by a process of concession making or search for new alternatives" [Pruitt, 1981, p. 1].

- "Negotiation is a bargaining relationship between parties who have a perceived or actual conflict of interest. The participants voluntarily join in a temporary relationship designed to educate each other about their needs and interests, to exchange specific resources, or to resolve one or more intangible issues such as the form their relationship will take in the future or the procedure by which problems are to be solved" [Moore, 1986, p. 6].

- "A process in which explicit proposals are put forward ostensibly for the purpose of reaching agreement on an exchange or on the realization of a common interest where conflicting interests are present" [Iklé, 1964, pp. 3, 4].

- "Negotiation is a process through which parties determine whether an acceptable agreement can be reached" [Schoenfield and Schoenfield, 1988, p. 3].

The common elements of most definitions are that negotiators are involved in a process of joint decision making, that they differ as to the actions to take, that compromise is required to reach agreement, and that negotiators engage in communications in an effort to seek or influence the joint decision. Some definitions focus on the strategic interaction, typically referring to the exchange of proposals. Some include the implicit assumption that each party may try to misrepresent its own position in one way or another [for example, Bartos, 1967]. Though many authorities focus on offers and counteroffers, arguments and counterarguments as the familiar central feature of negotiation, the process also includes the formation and adjustment of the negotiating relationship, the clarification of issues, other methods of sharing information, persuasion and accommodation, the analysis and evaluation of information, settlement options, and the consequences of not settling [Schoenfield and Schoenfield, 1988, p. 3]. Participation in negotiation implies that the parties would like to resolve the matter without third-party involvement and cannot resolve the matter unilaterally or would prefer to resolve the matter bilaterally. The objective of reaching agreement is motivated by the underlying goal to satisfy needs or interests.

Parties can use negotiation in either transactional or disputational contexts. The Latin roots are *neg* (not) and *otium* (leisure), which also form *negotiatus*, the past participle of *negotiari* (to engage in business). Under this origin, the term, like BARGAINING, is strongly linked to business transactions or sales that have less overt disputational characteristics but do imply a disagreement over terms and conditions and the existence of an underlying conflict of interests. With respect to transactions or legislation (or deciding on a dispute processing mechanism), parties use negotiation to reach agreement on what will happen. With respect to disputes, negotiation is usually focused on what already happened, but with the objective of reaching agreement on the parameters of a future settlement. Because a settlement is a transaction and a transaction is rarely reached without some disagreement, the conceptual difference between negotiating a transaction and negotiating a settlement is indistinct. The practical difference is marked. Disputational negotiation typically is more adversarial and hostile than transactional negotiation and is usually conducted in the shadow of adjudicatory processes or under the threat of violence and the assertion of unilateral power that can be resorted to should negotiations fail [Leeson and Johnston, 1988, p. 103].

Negotiation is easy to distinguish from adjudicative processes. Negotiation is conciliatory; the parties determine the outcome rather than a third party. Third parties can be involved in negotiation. Other forms of conciliatory, third-party intervention, such as good offices or nondirective forms of conciliation, can induce the communications necessary for negotiation, and a third party can facilitate the negotiation process. Many authorities refer to mediation as a special case of negotiation, and say that negotiation between parties takes place within the context of a mediation.

It is more difficult to distinguish other dispute resolution processes not involving third parties from negotiation. In common usage, BARGAINING and negotiation are treated as synonymous. Morley and Stephenson [1977, p. 23] note unhelpfully that "negotiation may denote a special case of bargaining, or vice versa." In dispute resolution, bargaining is best regarded as a more narrow concept than negotiation, referring only to the process of exchanging offers with the intent of finding an agreeable point of settlement. In contrast, negotiation is broader in scope and includes, in addition to bargaining, identification of issues, exchanges of information, and other activities that generally precede actual bargaining [Iklé, 1964, pp. 3–4]; or according to Cross [1969, p. 7], *bargaining* is the process of demand formation and revision that provides the basic mechanism whereby the parties converge toward an agreement, while *negotiation* is the whole situation within which the bargaining occurs. Conversely, Stevens [1963, p. 1] argues that bargains may be stuck without any negotiation, so negotiation is more restricted than bargaining.

Some authorities attempt to distinguish negotiation from problem solving, other decision-making processes requiring communication, and informal discussions. Moore [1986, p. 6] believes that negotiation is more intentional and structured than informal discussions and problem solving. Focusing on negotiation as a special form of communication, Putnam and Roloff [1992, p. 2] note that it is similar to decision making or joint problem solving but distinguished by different goals, relationships, and normative practices. Winham [1989] and Tedeschi and Bonoma [1977] stress that other forms of decision making involve choices against the environment rather than choices against another person. Lax and Sebenius [1986] distinguish negotiation as requiring conflict while decision processes without conflict are merely problem solving. Though other decision-making processes may involve persuasion, that is, attempting to convince someone to do something he would not ordinarily do, Druckman [1977] sees negotiation as a combination of persuasion and HAGGLING. Along these same lines, Putnam and Roloff [1992] contend that while negotiation employs problem solving and persuasion, negotiation centers on perceived incompatibilities and employs strategies and tactics.

Many authorities discuss negotiation as occurring in phases or of having component parts. These may vary considerably depending on the type of negotiation. For example, a discussion of negotiation in the context of distributive or positional bargaining (see BARGAINING) might emphasize a series of offers and counteroffers leading to agreement. In contrast, a discussion of integrative bargaining and principled negotiation might focus on problem definition, interest identification, and option creation leading to agreement.

International Negotiation: It is important to note that commentators may differ on the range of processes included in international negotiation. Though the term refers to negotiation between countries, it may also extend to negotiation between any entities recognized under international law, including international organizations and, in limited contexts, individuals negotiating with a country of which they are not citizens. Most references, however, focus on *diplomatic negotiation,* involving formal discussions, public or secret, between states through official representatives seeking to arrive at a mutually acceptable outcome on some issue or issues of shared concern. Such discussions may take place in the absence of a dispute simply because the parties recognize the need for a decision or concerted action on a matter of common interest [Morley and Stephenson, 1977, p. 19]. On the spectrum of diplomatic activity, Cohen [1991, p. 7] defines international negotiation as more than the simple exchange of views and as distinct from any unilateral coercive action. Lall [1966] defines it broadly to include any consideration of an international situation by peaceful means, other than adjudicative, with the goal of reaching an understanding, adjustment, or settlement among concerned parties. Thus all forms of discussion, meeting, conference, mediation, conciliation, good offices, and other direct or indirect liaison among the parties would be classified as negotiation. Every conscious effort for the peaceful settlement, adjustment, amelioration, or better understanding of international situations or disputes is in essence a negotiation.

Negotiation Subterms: Much of the literature on negotiation is specific to a particular context, such as negotiating collective bargaining agreements, environmental disputes, international commercial contracts, or peace treaties. Specialized negotiation terms have been created in particular contexts but are too limited for inclusion in this lexicon. Many commentators on negotiation also provide lists of strategic moves, TACTICS, or DIRTY TRICKS. Though most of these lists cover the same range of tactics, the names assigned to them vary by commentator and are not reproduced in this lexicon [see, for example, Craver, 1988, 1993; and Fisher and Ury, 1981].

negotiation analysis   Refers generally to several theoretical models used to examine, explain, and predict patterns and behaviors in negotiation.

There are five "families" of negotiation analysis models: structural, strategic, process, behavioral, and integrative. *Structural analysis* focuses on the distribution of power or the relative strength of the parties. *Strategic analysis* employs game-theory approaches to examine preset utilities and options. GAME THEORY typically models utilities while reducing the number of options that players can consider at once. *Process analysis* focuses on links between concession behavior and negotiated outcomes. *Behavioral analysis* focuses on the goals, personality traits, and predispositions of negotiators. *Integrative analysis* centers on negotiation as a process that develops either through stages or through changes in bargaining over time [Putnam and Roloff, 1992, pp. 5–6, citations omitted]. Other analytical models are discipline specific, such as anthropological, economic, and sociological analysis. The *phase model* used in communications research combines aspects of the five models just presented and classifies communication interaction as falling into either an initiation, problem-solving, or resolution phase [Holmes, 1992, p. 83].

negotiation cycle   Conceptualization of the negotiation process as progression through certain basic events, or stages.

One cycle, for example, poses negotiation as a sequence from ideas to positions to concessions to resolutions to concrete action. Another negotiation cycle, formulated with regard to COLLECTIVE BARGAINING contract negotiation, patterns the negotiation process as a transition from competitive tactics to cooperative ones [Stevens, 1963, pp. 10–11]. Compare summary of *phase model* under NEGOTIATION ANALYSIS.

Negotiation Journal   Conflict resolution periodical sponsored by the HARVARD PROGRAM ON NEGOTIATION.

negotiation jujitsu   Term coined by Fisher and Ury [1981] to describe useful tactics for PRINCIPLED NEGOTIATION with difficult or *hard* positional bargainers. The recommended tactics include looking behind positions to uncover interests, inviting criticism and advice rather than being defensive over one's own proposals, refocusing personal attacks onto attacking the problem, and using silence until questions are answered. Contrast COERCION.

negotiator's dilemma   Whether to reveal information so as to explore the possibility for joint gains or to conceal information to maintain a strong positional bargaining stance.

In a negotiation, each side confronts a tension between two strategies. a party can attempt to create value by clearly and honestly communicating her interests and exploring possible joint gains, or she can try to claim value by obscuring her interests and taking a position. By revealing interests, the party can open herself up to claiming tactics, thereby weakening her bargaining position. The negotiator's dilemma, then, is that there seems to be an incentive to take a position and to seek to deceive the opponent as to one's interests, thus avoiding exposure of weaknesses. However, this tactic will result in possibilities of joint gains being forever ignored [Lax and Sebenius, 1986, pp. 29–45].

neighborhood justice center (NJC)   COMMUNITY DISPUTE RESOLUTION CENTER that handles conflicts arising within a certain geographic area.

NJCs emerged in the 1960s as part of a movement toward community-based justice. Some were funded by federal government grants under antipoverty efforts and other Great Society programs and either served as adjuncts of prosecutors' offices or local legal services offices. Private foundations funded a multicity NJC experiment managed by the AMERICAN ARBITRATION ASSOCIATION. By the mid-1970s, local attempts to establish NJCs as alternatives to court came to the attention of the American Bar Association, which defined NJCs as "facilities . . . designed to make available a variety of methods of processing disputes, including arbitration, mediation, referral to small claims courts as well as referral to courts of general jurisdiction" [*Report of the Pound Conference. . .,* 1976, p. 1].

Neighborhood justice center was the title given to each of the three community dispute resolution centers (Atlanta, Kansas City, and Los Angeles) funded by the Department of Justice in a pilot program in the late 1970s. These pilots and most of the several hundred NJCs and other community dispute resolution centers were based predominately on Sander's [1976] *dispute resolution centre* model (see COMMUNITY DISPUTE RESOLUTION CENTER for a discussion of the various models). NJCs deal primarily with disputes between individuals with ongoing relationships (such as landlord-tenant, domestic, and backyard conflicts) but usually draw their caseloads from referrals from police, local courts, and prosecutors' offices with which they are affiliated. They are also known as *community mediation centers, citizen dispute centers,* and similar titles. The Atlanta NJC now goes by *the Justice Center of Atlanta.*

neutral   Condition of IMPARTIALITY; lack of bias, favoritism, or opinion; from the Latin *neuter,* meaning "neither of them." See NEUTRALITY.

Also denotes a third party engaged to help resolve a dispute who is NEUTRAL, that is, can act in an impartial and unbiased manner because she has no conflict of interest in the matter. The following legal definition reflects the common meaning that excludes judges acting in their judicial capacity: "a qualified individual or organization who facilitates the resolution of a dispute by serving as, for example, arbitrator, mediator, conciliator, trainer, special master, or factfinder" [1 C.F.R. § 316.101(d) (1993)]. A third party can be designated as a neutral by informed consent of the parties, despite apparent conflicts of interest, as reflected in this definition: "a neutral must not have any official, personal, or financial conflict of interest in the contested matter, unless such interest is fully disclosed in writing to all primary parties and they agree that the neutral may serve. A neutral serves only at the mutual will of the parties" [48 C.F.R. § 33.201 (1992)]. This indicates that the parties' perception of the third party's neutrality is more important than its actuality.

Compare BALANCED PARTIALITY. Contrast BIAS.

neutral advisor   *Mini-trials:* Third party selected by the parties to a MINI-TRIAL to help conduct the process.

Not all mini-trials include neutral advisors. Parties engage neutral advisors to participate in the hearing phase and, at the parties' option, to help in later settlement discussions. Depending on the mini-trial agreement, a neutral advisor may preside at the presentation, question witnesses, mediate settlement negotiations, and render an advisory opinion to the parties. If a neutral advisor is given the power to make a binding decision, the process is no longer a mini-trial but an arbitration, and the third party is an arbitrator.

neutral arbitrator   Usually the third or impartial arbitrator selected by both parties to serve on an arbitration board after each party has already appointed a member of her own.

The neutral arbitrator is the chair of the arbitral tribunal. She may also be appointed jointly by the partisan arbitrators or by an impartial official, in accordance with the agreement of the parties. This latter manner of appointment is frequent in international public arbitration [DOA], although the term is commonly associated with commercial arbitration (see IMPARTIAL CHAIRMAN, which is associated more closely with labor arbitration). In some arbitral traditions, the neutral arbitrator evolved from the concept of the UMPIRE, who in ARBITRAMENT would be selected by party-appointed arbitrators to render an award when those arbitrators deadlocked and failed to render an award.

neutral case evaluation   See CASE EVALUATION and EARLY NEUTRAL EVALUATION.

neutral expert   Person or organization that is NEUTRAL with respect to the parties, called on to apply its particular knowledge or expertise to a legal or factual issue in dispute and to opine as to what the facts or law might be.

A neutral expert should be distinguished from other NEUTRALS and from an expert engaged directly by one of the disputants. Unlike a neutral who is typically engaged to conduct a dispute resolution process, neutral experts merely provide, upon request, their disinterested and objective opinion or advice on a matter in dispute. Although neutral experts can be used ad hoc, they are usually engaged in conjunction with another process, such as mediation or arbitration. In mediation, the parties can agree to use a neutral expert to opine on a discrete issue that may be causing an impasse. The use of neutral experts is associated primarily with arbitration. Parties can engage or empower the arbitrators to engage a neutral expert whose opinions on discrete factual or legal issues will help the arbitrators in their determination of an award. Unlike arbitrators and neutral evaluators, neutral experts do not determine how a dispute should be resolved. An expert hired by a party is not considered neutral, because the parties pay such experts to opine in favor of their positions.

Compare FACT-FINDING, NEUTRAL EXPERT FACT-FINDING, NEUTRAL FACT EVALUATION.

neutral expert fact-finding   Process whereby disputing parties appoint a neutral expert to collect factual information relevant to the conflict.

In the broadest sense, a fact-finder (see FACT-FINDING) is a neutral expert. However, the role of fact-finder can be distinguished from the role of neutral expert if the fact-finding process requires proactive investigation or is designed to establish the "true facts" or yield recommendations for resolution.

neutral fact evaluation   Objective, fact-based evaluation of a dispute as made by a neutral expert. May not include investigation and data collection as in NEUTRAL EXPERT FACT-FINDING.

neutrality   From the Latin *neuter,* meaning "neither of them," condition in which attitude and action reflect a refusal to take sides in a dispute, or a lack of bias or favoritism. Compare BALANCED PARTIALITY.

Neutrality is traditionally understood as incorporating two qualities that a mediator ought to be able to employ: IMPARTIALITY and EQUIDISTANCE [Rifkin, Millen, and Cobb, 1991, p. 152].

International Relations: Condition or status claimed by a state that refuses to support or take sides in a dispute, typically armed conflict, among other states.

neutral mediator   Third party who facilitates negotiations between disputants (see MEDIATOR) but has no interest, direct or indirect, in the disputed issues or outcome. See NEUTRAL.

In common conceptualizations of mediation, the mediator is believed to be neutral by definition. A distinction can be made, however, between neutral mediators and PRINCIPAL MEDIATORS. While the latter have an interest, usually indirect, in the dispute and have the capacity to influence the outcome by making side deals and changing the payoffs for the disputants (President Jimmy Carter in the Camp David Accords, for example), neutral mediators have neither the interest nor the capacity to bargain directly with the disputants. As a consequence, neutral mediators try to adjust the disputants' interaction by focusing on their relationship, communication, and patterns of negotiation [Princen, 1992, pp. 25, 26].

See PRINCIPAL MEDIATOR for a discussion of the relative advantages and disadvantages of the two types of·mediators.

neutral process consultant   Term coined by Lax and Sebenius [1986] to denote a particular type of third-party intervenor who facilitates the negotiation process.

Unlike mediators in classic mediation models in which the third party brings the disputants together, the neutral process consultant allows each party to tell her story, then shifts into a series of caucuses and plenary meetings designed to move the parties toward resolution. Lax and Sebenius [1986] describe a process in which the neutral process consultant initially meets with the parties separately to discuss their stories, then brings them together to improve mutual understanding of viewpoints, followed by an attempt to create a norm for peaceful problem solving.

news blackout   Technique to prevent conflict escalation in which the parties to a negotiation agree not to make statements to the news media or agree that any public statements regarding the negotiation will be issued by the mediator alone.

The technique is common in negotiations of labor disputes and disputes involving issues of great public interest (note that barring the public from meetings involving public officials is increasingly difficult under *open-meetings laws* and *government-in-the-sunshine acts*). The purpose of the technique is to prevent parties to a negotiation from using the media to attack opponents, or in an attempt to gain bargaining leverage, from using practices that can undermine the negotiation by escalating tensions and distrust. News blackouts are established by party agreement, often at the onset of negotiations and sometimes at the suggestion of a mediator. Ground rules for a news blackout often require parties to give notice before they abrogate the agreement [Maggiolo, 1985, p. 240].

New York Convention   See CONVENTION ON THE RECOGNITION AND ENFORCEMENT OF FOREIGN ARBITRAL AWARDS.

New York Stock Exchange (NYSE)   Self-regulatory organization. The NYSE administers and provides rules governing arbitration of disputes between its members or between its members and its members' customers. See SELF-REGULATORY ORGANIZATION, NASD.

Neve Shalom/Wahat al-Salam   Village in Israel established jointly by Jews and Palestinian Arabs of Israeli citizenship whose members are engaged in educational work for peace, equality, and understanding between the two peoples.

The *School for Peace* was established in 1979 as Neve Shalom/Wahat al-Salam's foremost institution for outreach educational work. Through a variety of courses and seminars for many strata of Jewish and Palestinian society, the School for Peace works to heighten awareness toward the complexity of the conflict and to improve understanding between Palestinians and Jews through education. It also conducts conflict resolution courses in English for other groups and individuals. By 1996, some sixteen thousand young people had attended School for Peace encounters. More than two hundred adults had received training in conflict management skills, many of whom are now active in other organizations involved in conflict work. The school has won local and international recognition.

nibbler   *Negotiation:* Tactic of reaching an agreement on the whole but continuing to ask for additional concessions [Craver, 1993]. Also called SALAMI TACTICS.

NIDR   See NATIONAL INSTITUTE FOR DISPUTE RESOLUTION.

night baseball arbitration   Variation of FINAL-OFFER or LAST-BEST-OFFER ARBITRATION in which the arbitrator devises a settlement proposal before seeing what the parties proposed, then renders an award on the terms of the offer closest to the proposal. See BASEBALL ARBITRATION.

NIMBY   *Environmental/Public Policy:* "Not in my backyard." Reference to an existing or proposed land use by someone in the surrounding community who considers it undesirable to live close or adjacent to it.

Common NIMBYs include chemical plants and solid waste management facilities. Stamato and Jaffe [1991, p. 166] observe that the term connotes an attitude that a particular facility or land use is important in principle but undesirable as a presence in one's own community. Members of a community may not want to live beside a NIMBY, but some may desire some of its attendant benefits, such as employment or a place to dump garbage. Compare LULU.

no!   Blunt negative response to an offer, demand, or proposal; exclamation signaling rejection.

Cross-Cultural: Cohen [1991, pp. xi, 113] notes that *no* is a term that, because of its many nuances, can cause considerable misunderstanding in cross-cultural negotiation. Negotiators in some cultures—such as Arab, Asian, and Latin American—are reluctant to say no and may be shocked by the use of such an overtly negative term by negotiators who have few qualms in using it to reject a proposal, such as Americans. In their reluctance to say no, negotiators from some cultures may use phrases that can be misunderstood as affirmative, while at the opposite end of the spectrum, some negotiators, such as Israelis, may issue an emphatic rejection while seriously considering the offer.

no-agreement alternative   Likely outcome if parties in negotiation fail to reach agreement.

Parties can use the no-agreement alternative as a standard for evaluating proposed agreements instead of trying to estimate the other side's RESERVATION PRICE or BOTTOM LINE. In this sense, the concept is very similar to that of BATNA (although it may be closer to PATNA). Brett [1991, p. 294] notes that a party with a good no-agreement alternative is less dependent on reaching a negotiated agreement and therefore more powerful, while a party with a poor no-agreement alternative is motivated to try harder and to be more creative in constructing agreements that are superior to the no-agreement alternative. See also SECOND AGREEMENT.

nominal group process   Two-stage process for group problem solving, premised on the theory that individuals invent and groups evaluate.

During the first stage, individuals independently brainstorm possible solutions to the problem at hand. During the second stage, participants gather into small subgroups and share their ideas, which the subgroup discusses, elaborates on, and evaluates according to such criteria as feasibility and effectiveness [Delbecq, Vandeven, and Gustafson, 1975].

nonbinding arbitration   Process in which the parties submit their dispute to a neutral person who renders a decision that the parties may either accept or reject.

The term includes the COURT-CONNECTED process of MANDATORY NONBINDING ARBITRATION, and voluntary, contractual arbitration in which the parties have agreed not to make the award enforceable in a court. Agreements to submit disputes for a nonbinding opinion are enforceable. See *AMF Inc. v. Brunswick Corp.* (1985). Unlike BINDING ARBITRATION, which results in a final, imposed, third-party solution, the process is somewhat abridged and merely a method of nudging the parties toward agreement. The decision provides the parties with information about the likely results if the dispute is resolved by binding adjudication. This REALITY TESTING gives the parties a neutral perspective on their case and a clearer notion of their risk exposure in a binding forum. In theory this promotes settlement and overcomes previous negotiation impasses based on disparate predictions of outcomes in binding adjudication. In addition, it gives negotiators an excuse to withdraw from hardened positions while saving face, or offers justification for compromise to reluctant clients or constituents.

It is the same as ADVISORY ARBITRATION except to the extent that the latter implies advice. Traditional advisory arbitration, used historically to resolve public employee disputes, can result in one or more recommended solutions. Nonbinding arbitration entails only a single award.

noncontingent moves   *Mediation:* General interventions used by mediators in all disputes. These moves correspond to the stages of mediation, are linked to the overall pattern of conflict development and resolution, and respond only to the broadest categories of critical situations [Moore, 1986, p. 25]. Compare CONTINGENT MOVES.

non liquet   *Arbitration:* Literally, "it is not clear." Refers to the refusal by an arbitrator to render an award on the grounds that the law that has been invoked to apply to the case does not exist.

The doctrine of *non liquet* derives from a theory of law that has been largely abandoned. a large number of municipal codes, as well as the majority of writers on international law, now hold that in case of a "gap" in the law, it is the arbitrator's duty to supplement the law and render a decision [DOA].

non-zero-sum   In GAME THEORY, situation in which a gain for one side does not entail a corresponding loss for the other side.

North American Free Trade Agreement (NAFTA)   Trade liberalization treaty among Canada, Mexico, and the United States containing a variety of international dispute resolution mechanisms.

Chapter Twenty of the agreement provides a multistep method of resolving disputes over the interpretation of provisions and the application of the treaty. Chapter Nineteen contains a separate mechanism for the resolution of disputes over antidumping and countervailing duties decisions made by signatory governments. Article 2022 directs each signatory country to facilitate and encourage private mechanisms, such as arbitration and mediation, to resolve international commercial disputes between private parties. Provisions of the side agreements on the environment and labor contain mechanisms to resolve disputes over the enforcement of environmental and labor regulations.

no-strike clause   *Labor Relations:* Contractual clause stating a union's agreement not to strike during the life of the contract.

The U.S. Supreme Court held in *Textile Workers Union of America* v. *Lincoln Mills of Alabama* (1957) that an agreement to arbitrate grievances in a COLLECTIVE BARGAINING AGREEMENT is the quid pro quo for a union's promise not to strike. The presence of an arbitration provision has been held to imply a promise not to strike when the contract itself is silent on that point [DOA]. See GRIEVANCE ARBITRATION and INTEREST ARBITRATION for important distinctions.

notice   *International Relations*: Prior to taking an action, the act of informing interested or potentially affected parties of the impending action. Compare CONSULTATION.

notice of hearing   *Arbitration:* Formal notification of the time and place of a hearing, sent to both parties to a dispute by an arbitrator or administering agency.

A notice of hearing is issued after the notice of intention to arbitrate has been sent by one disputing party to the other. Arbitration laws may specify the time allowed between such notice of hearing and the hearing itself [DOA].

notice of intention to arbitrate   Document submitted by one disputing party to the other to initiate an arbitration procedure. Usually filed with the administering agency when an arbitration is to be held under the rules of that agency [DOA].

Also called DEMAND FOR ARBITRATION or request for arbitration.

NYSE   See NEW YORK STOCK EXCHANGE.

objective   n. Something sought or pursued, or accomplishment necessary to achieve a GOAL.

adj. Independent of personal emotions and individual perceptions or idiosyncracies; external to self, in contrast with SUBJECTIVE, as used in OBJECTIVE CRITERIA or OBJECTIVE REVIEW.

objective criteria   *Negotiation:* Criteria used in negotiation to assess positions and proposals impartially.

Fisher and Ury [1981] promote the use of objective criteria in PRINCIPLED NEGOTIATION to legitimize positions, proposals, and outcomes. In theory, the negotiator who relies on objective as opposed to subjective indices of value and fairness will be more persuasive in gaining acceptance of his proposal. In his critique of principled negotiation, White [1984] argues that positional negotiation cannot be avoided; negotiation merely shifts to positioning over the applicable criteria.

objective review   *Public Policy:* Defined by federal regulation as a "thorough examination and assessment of a proposal by an expert, neutral individual or group" [48 C.F.R. § 935.016-3 (1992)].

This procedure is increasingly used to inform participants in public policy facilitation processes of the consequences, legal and otherwise, of a proposed solution before its adoption.

obligatory *compromis* *International Public Arbitration:* Document to take the place of the *compromis* or submission agreement when the parties cannot agree on one or more issues or clauses of the original agreement to arbitrate.

An obligatory *compromis* may permit the parties to request a third power to appoint an individual or group to draw up the *compromis*. If this procedure fails, the arbitral tribunal, if one with jurisdiction is available, draws it up. In Articles 53 and 54 of the HAGUE CONVENTIONS ON THE PACIFIC SETTLEMENT OF INTERNATIONAL DISPUTES OF 1899 AND 1907, provision is made for the *compromis* to be settled by a commission consisting of five members [DOA].

See COMPROMIS.

obliging Conflict management strategy whereby a party places more emphasis on the satisfaction and concerns of the other party than on his own needs [Rahim, 1986, p. 84].

This strategy is closely associated with an ACCOMMODATING personality, cooperative but nonassertive. It can, however, be useful independent of personal style preferences when one seeks to move away from a previous position or to concede on an issue of more importance to the other side.

observations *International Relations:* Statement or report on treaty violations made by an international organization or enforcement body.

Observations are made for the purpose of bringing international pressure on the noncomplying party. Treaties and conventions may contain provisions that specifically empower an enforcing body to make periodic observations. An example of such a treaty provision is found in the conventions of the International Labor Organization, whose constitution provides for a Committee of Experts to make such publication in their annual report prior to the annual conference.

offer Proposal that one person makes to another for either acceptance or rejection and which, if accepted, will form a CONTRACT between them.

officiate Perform a ceremony or administer the rules of the game or sport.

Ohio Commission on Dispute Resolution and Conflict Management Government agency that assists Ohioans with ways to deal with disputes and conflict. Its mission is to disseminate information about constructive ways to manage conflict and to help Ohio residents to build the foundations for making conflict resolution a part of social institutions as well as individual lives. Working in partnership with communities, schools, and state and local government, the staff of the commission acts as a resource center, consultant, catalyst, trainer, and evaluator. One of several STATE OFFICES OF DISPUTE RESOLUTION, the

Ohio commission has pioneered the concept and been very influential in the development of both practice and theory.

Ohio State Journal of Dispute Resolution   Periodical of legal scholarship on dispute resolution and related legal issues cosponsored by the Ohio State College of Law and the American Bar Association's Dispute Resolution Section.

ombudsman (ombuds, ombudsperson)   Person appointed by an institution to investigate complaints within or against the institution and to help resolve and prevent disputes. The English plural is *ombudsmen*; the gender neutral terms are *ombuds* or *ombudsperson*.

Ombudsman may refer to either a person or an office containing one or more people who perform ombudsman functions. The person is either an employee or a temporary appointee of the institution—a government body, private corporation, or other organization. The person or office serves as a point of contact for the receipt of complaints and grievances about the institution that are raised by individuals who either work within or are served by the institution. Ombuds are often described as representing the individual's interests against the larger, often impersonal organization. However, most ombudsmen have direct responsibilities to the larger organization within which they operate, and they probably perceive themselves as impartial problem solvers rather than as advocates. Ombudsmen who handle complaints by clients, customers, or citizens are sometimes referred to as *external ombudsmen*, while those who primarily handle disputes and complaints among and by employees or members of an institution are known as *internal ombudsmen*. This latter term is being gradually replaced in practice with *organizational ombudsmen* (see later discussion); however, the internal/external distinction may still be applicable to an ombudsman serving an organization. Ombudsmen can have any or all of the functions of complaint handlers, ranging from merely serving as a sounding board, information source, and self-help advisor to more active intervention as conciliator, mediator, fact-finder, and arbiter. Ombudsman may be called upon to interpret policy, make recommendations to management on how to resolve a case, or suggest systematic changes to reduce conflict recurrence. To maintain the integrity of the role, the ombudsman may function independently of the normal hierarchy and may have certain privileges to facilitate inquiry and to uphold confidentiality when approached in confidence.

Although the institution originated in Sweden, different traditions in ombudsmanship, varying by country and by type of institution, favor different ranges of functions. While the Scandinavian ombudsman has traditionally focused on designing ways to avoid future conflicts, the American ombudsman has assumed greater responsibility for resolving disputes within the organization and actively mediates and negotiates settlements. Kahana [1994, p. 222] opines that the divergence in the roles played by different ombudsmen can be explained by reference to the level of conflict between the disputants, so when the degree of conflict between parties increases or as the political culture diverges from a consensus orientation, there is a greater need to develop alternatives to the classical ombudsman.

Government ombudsman: An external ombudsman employed or appointed by government to investigate and help resolve complaints by citizens about maladministration by government agencies; sometimes called a *citizen ombudsman.* The historical roots of the term and the functions of the office originated in Sweden, where the king would appoint an ombudsman to help citizens process complaints against the government. Now formalized in the constitutions of most Scandinavian countries and appointed by the legislature, the office is also referred to as *parliamentsman* (Sweden) and *parliamentary commissioner of justice* (Finland). Traditionally the government ombudsman received complaints, conducted an investigation, and submitted findings, often accompanied by nonbinding recommendations to the complainant and the relevant government agency. Johnson, Kantor, and Schwartz [1977, p. 58] characterize a governmental ombudsman as an "independent, impartial, high-level public official stationed between the citizen and government. He is concerned equally with protecting the rights of the public and government officials by receiving and investigating allegations of bureaucratic abuse and reporting and publicizing the findings." If an agency fails to respond to the findings and recommendations, the ombudsman may be empowered to issue the findings to the public or report directly to a higher governmental authority. As a general rule, the government ombudsman cannot mandate policy changes or other outcomes. However, the powers can be more expansive. Under Finnish law, for example, the primary government ombudsman, the parliamentary commissioner of justice, has the duty of supervising the functioning of all courts and other authorities in the country. In addition to collecting information, making inspections, and receiving complaints, the ombudsman's responses to maladministration may vary from simple reminders to prosecution in court.

In addition to these national ombudsman offices, the Maastricht Treaty establishes an independent ombudsman for the European Union. Appointed by the European Parliament, he is empowered to receive complaints from any citizen of the union or any person residing in a member state concerning instances of maladministration in the activities of the community institutions or bodies. He conducts inquiries either on his own initiative or on the basis of complaints. In an instance of maladministration, he refers the matter to the institution concerned, which has three months to respond, after which he forwards a report to the European Parliament and the institution concerned. The person lodging the complaint is informed of the outcome [Article 107d, Treaty of European Unity].

Government ombudsmen have not been broadly institutionalized at the federal or state level in the United States. However, they are not uncommon in local or municipal governments. The U.S. version seems to put less emphasis on the fact-finding, inquiry, and reporting role, as illustrated in the following legal definition:

> An individual used in settling disputes with a local government. The ombudsperson is available to receive issues or grievances from individuals, public agencies, or organizations and in turn brings such issues to the attention of the public agency with whom the public has a dispute. The ombudsperson also provides advice regarding available resources and options, proposes a resolution, or proposes a systematic change related to the issues [Cal. Educ. Code § 56101(b)(1) (West 1993)].

As the source of this definition indicates, the ombudsman concept has found some acceptance in institutions of higher education, particularly public ones. However, the role of ombudsmen in higher education more closely resembles the corporate ombudsman discussed shortly than the traditional Scandinavian or European model of a government ombudsman.

Some governments have established subspecialties of government ombudsman concerned with complaints made by certain categories of persons who are vulnerable with regard to their civil rights: prisoners, children, patients in mental institutions, conscripts in the military, and so on. An interesting hybrid is the *long-term care ombudsman,* empowered by many U.S. state governments to investigate alleged abuses of nursing-home residents by staff. Although the office is created by legislation and funded by the government, this type of ombudsman is empowered through the policing powers of the state to investigate maladministration and abuse in private institutions that are either funded or licensed by the state.

Corporate or Organizational Ombudsman: Usually an *internal* ombudsman employed by a corporation to give employees a way to raise concerns or to complain about how they have been treated by other employees or by the system generally. A corporate ombudsman can, however, be assigned the task of receiving complaints from the institution's external constituencies. In the United States, corporate ombudsmen are increasingly used as part of the conflict management systems of private, commercial corporations, press organizations, and institutions of higher education. Early forms of the corporate ombudsman resembled government ombudsmen with their emphasis on investigating and reporting. Such ombudsmen often functioned in corporations with a public service orientation or strong contractual ties to the government, such as defense contractors, for whom public accountability was an issue. Instead of focusing on internal disputes, these ombudsman offices provided opportunities for employees to engage in confidential whistle-blowing. Although it still functions to uncover mismanagement, the corporate ombudsman model has evolved with greater emphasis on dispute resolution among employees and managers. Rowe [1987] defines a corporate ombudsman as "a neutral and impartial manager within a corporation who may provide confidential and informal assistance to managers and employees in resolving work-related concerns." In addition to investigating and reporting on complaints by employees and providing feedback to senior management, the functions of such an ombudsman can include merely listening, confidential counseling, answering routine inquiries about company policies and practices, informal conciliating, facilitating, mediating, and general organizational consulting and problem solving. There is some tension in the ombudsman role when the office functions both as a confidential source for employee dispute resolution counseling and as a fact-finder or inspector general. The ombudsman has responsibilities both to the employee who approaches the office in confidence and to the corporation that needs feedback and recommendations. To alleviate this tension, many corporate ombudsmen limit their intervention activities to informal mediation at the most and do not engage in formal inquiries. Feedback to management is put in generic form that does not identify the complainant. In addition, ombudsmen operate outside the traditional corporate structure and independent of line management and of the human resources and corporate legal departments. The prefix *corporate* is gradually giving way to *organizational*.

Consumer ombudsman: Form of CONSUMER COMPLAINT MECHANISM established by television or radio stations, by newspapers, and occasionally by a local or state government. Sometimes called ACTION LINES.

one-text method, one-text document   *Negotiation:* Technique in which a party, often a neutral third party, passes a single *text* containing the framework of an agreement back and forth between the parties for adjustment until a mutually acceptable and sufficiently detailed agreement is formed. Also known as SINGLE NEGOTIATING TEXT.

open bargaining style   Alternative term for COOPERATIVE bargaining style in POSITIONAL BARGAINING. Described as generally pragmatic and based on the assumption that compromise is the only possible reason for and outcome of bargaining [Holsti, 1983, p. 187]. Contrast CLOSED BARGAINING STYLE.

open-door policy   *Organizational:* Conflict management strategy in which employees are allowed to circumvent normal rank-and-file or command hierarchies to voice complaints and grievances.

The theory behind open-door policies is that conflicts involving employees who have grievances against their immediate supervisor or ones to which their immediate supervisor is unresponsive will escalate, sharply raising the costs of resolution. By providing unrestricted access to other supervisors and managers, often trained in conflict management techniques, the policy is designed to identify and resolve these problems early and at the lowest possible level. Open-door policies are being implemented as components of comprehensive conflict management systems in some organizations and serve to disperse duties and skills usually associated with an internal OMBUDSMAN.

open-end grievance procedure *Labor Relations:* Grievance procedure that has as its final step the right to strike rather than to arbitrate [DOA].

opening offer *Negotiation:* In bargaining, point among the range of possible outcomes that a party claims as his desired outcome at the onset of a bargaining session. See OFFER. Also called *opening demand.*

opening statement Brief statement traditionally made by the parties at the opening of a trial or an arbitration hearing to acquaint the adjudicator with the nature of the dispute and with the evidence they intend to present [DOA].

open space meeting, open space technology (OST) Minimalist meeting-facilitation concept in which an *agendaless meeting* is held and the participants develop and work through a set of issues.

The concept is credited to a management consultant, Harrison Owen (1997), and was designed for large corporate personnel and association meetings. It has, however, attracted the attention of facilitators and mediators who work with public policy and other large public participation dispute resolution processes. It has the advantage of inclusiveness, giving the participants *ownership* of the process, and allows for problem identification and solving by large groups.

opinion Judgment or belief formed without conclusive evidence. In contrast, the term also denotes a written document in which adjudicators set forth their decision and their reasoning supporting it regarding a matter submitted to them.

Arbitration: Written judgment that almost invariably precedes an arbitrator's award in labor arbitration. As the award itself states, the opinion is not considered to be part of the award. The practice of giving an opinion is not common in commercial arbitration in the United States or in countries of the British Commonwealth. In France and The Netherlands, reasons usually accompany the award. In international arbitration cases, any use of the word *opinion* refers to the advisory opinions that judges of the PERMANENT COURT OF INTERNATIONAL JUSTICE, and subsequently the INTERNATIONAL COURT OF JUSTICE, may deliver under certain circumstances. Reasons for the award are usually required in international public arbitration, or are necessary for enforcement in foreign jurisdiction in international commercial arbitration [DOA]. An award accompanied by an opinion is called a *reasoned award,* while an award without opinion is known as an *unreasoned award.*

opportunistic interaction   Bargaining behavior in which parties pursue their own interests through manipulative maneuvering instead of through straight-forward problem-solving methods to reach a mutually agreeable resolution. Par-ties interacting as such often attempt to influence outcomes to their benefit by, for example, refusing to cooperate or resisting completely [Lax and Sebenius, 1986, pp. 10–11].

Optional Clause   *International Relations:* Provision outlined in Article 36 of the Statute of the INTERNATIONAL COURT OF JUSTICE through which states submit in advance of disputes to the compulsory jurisdiction of the court.

Without compulsory jurisdiction, the court is powerless to exercise jurisdic-tion over sovereign states that would refuse to submit a matter after it arises. Acceptance without reservation gives the court power to hear all legal disputes involving international obligations, the interpretation of treaties, and repara-tions in the event of a breach.

Although many states have accepted compulsory jurisdiction, most have done so with reservations or on the condition of reciprocity. See CONNALLY RESERVATION.

options rehearsal   *Negotiation:* Method of preparation in which a party con-siders several different options for handling the negotiation while rehearsing how he will present his case and answer to the other party.

According to its advocates, options rehearsals boost negotiators' skills and confidence, leaving them more prepared for unexpected twists that may occur in the actual session [Hawkins, Hudson, and Cornall, 1991, pp. 95–96].

oral agreement   Agreement by word of mouth as opposed to one that is writ-ten. Also known as a *parol agreement.* Many jurisdictions have *statutes of fraud* that render oral agreements on certain matters unenforceable.

oral arbitration agreement   Agreement by word of mouth, as opposed to one that is written, to submit a matter to arbitration.

Under most MODERN ARBITRATION STATUTES, courts will only enforce a writ-ten arbitration agreement. In COMMON LAW, an oral agreement to arbitrate is suf-ficient to permit an enforceable award [DOA].

ordeal (trial by fire, trial by water, trial by combat, medieval ordeal)   Ar-chaic method of determining the truth or the moral superiority of a disputant's claim.

The predominant form of unilateral ordeal to determine truthfulness was the ordeal of the cauldron, or the ordeal of hot water, in which an object, usually a stone or a ring, had to be plucked from a bubbling cauldron. To blister or fail to retrieve the item raised doubt. There is a strong likelihood that the custom has Frankish origins [Bartlett, 1986, p. 1]. The best-known form of bilateral ordeal was trial by battle, found in the early law codes of many Germanic peoples [Bartlett, 1986, p. 104].

Organization of African Unity Commission of Mediation, Conciliation, and Arbitration Commission of twenty-one members elected by heads of the thirty-four member states, designed to help peacefully resolve conflicts among its member states.

The commission has a bureau consisting of the president and two vice presidents who are similarly elected and full-time members of the commission; the other eighteen members are part-time. A dispute may be referred to the commission (1) jointly by the parties, (2) by one party alone, or (3) by the Council of Ministers or the Assemblies of the Heads of States and Governments. Should one of the parties decline to submit to the commission's jurisdiction, the bureau must refer the matter to the Council of Ministers, presumably with a view to diplomatic action to persuade the recalcitrant state to accept some form of peaceful procedure to solve the dispute. In other words, the African states have adopted a system of institutionalized persuasion to accept the commission's jurisdiction, rather than a system of compulsory jurisdiction.

If no party objects to the exercise of the commission's jurisdiction, the bureau will consult with the parties regarding the mode of settlement to be used. In the case of mediation, the president appoints, with the agreement of the parties, one or more members of the commission to act as mediators. In the case of conciliation, the president establishes a board of five conciliators, three appointed by him and one by each party. In the case of arbitration, each party selects one arbitrator from among the legally qualified members of the commission, and these two choose a third as chairman of the tribunal; if they fail to agree, the bureau appoints the chairman.

organizational ombudsperson Confidential and informal information resource, communications channel, complaint-handler, and dispute resolver within an organization.

Employed by public and private institutions, agencies, and corporations, his purpose is to foster values and decent behavior—fairness, equity, justice, equality of opportunity, and respect. The ombudsperson will often be especially concerned with respect for those who are or who see themselves as less powerful than others in a given situation. The organizational ombudsperson is a designated neutral within an organization and usually reports at or near the top of that organization, outside ordinary management channels. An *outside* organizational ombudsperson works on contract as an ombuds service provider and may report to the chief executive officer or to the head of the division with whom he is contracting. Outside ombudspeople work under the same precepts as internal ombudspeople [Rowe, 1995b, p. 103]. See OMBUDSMAN.

orientation session   See INTAKE SESSION.

ouster doctrine   In common law, policy of U.S. courts to refuse to enforce agreements to arbitrate future disputes prior to the passage of MODERN ARBITRATION STATUTES, on the grounds that such agreements were counter to public policy. The doctrine is associated with the COMMON LAW HOSTILITY toward arbitration, and the term derives from the well-worn phrase, "nothing would be easier than for the more astute party to oust the courts of their jurisdiction. By first making the contract and then declaring who should construe it, the strong could oppress the weak, and in effect so nullify the law as to secure enforcement of contracts usurious, illegal, immoral, and contrary to public policy" [*Parsons* v. *Ambos* (1904)].

Common law hostility is traceable to a misreading of an old English case, VYNIOR'S CASE (1610).

outcome   Results of a dispute-processing mechanism, sometimes used more narrowly to refer to the terms of a settlement agreement.

In its broader sense, an outcome might not involve SETTLEMENT or RESOLUTION. Some common classifications and descriptions for outcomes in negotiation are as follows:

- *Win-Lose:* One person's interests are satisfied at the expense of another's.
- *Impasse:* No party succeeds in accomplishing his objectives.
- *Compromise:* All parties give up some of their objectives to obtain others.
- *Win-Win:* All parties feel that their interests have been satisfied.

Compare AGREEMENT. See also BATNA.

out-of-court settlement   Resolution of a matter pending in court achieved without judicial determination.

An out-of-court settlement implies that the dispute reached the stage of pending litigation—that is, a suit was filed—and the resolution reached privately does not require approval by the court. Technically the parties are said to have compromised and settled their respective claims, and the suit is withdrawn, usually by motion.

overconfidence bias   *Negotiation:* Tendency of parties involved in an uncertain or otherwise difficult negotiation to rely too heavily on their instincts and initial estimates [Neale and Bazerman, 1991].

A negotiator with an overconfidence bias may feel so secure with his instinctual judgment that he neglects to second-guess his decision and even overlooks disconfirming evidence.

overdirection   *Mediation:* When a mediator becomes so active in the process and outcome that it effectively deprives the parties of control over and responsibility for their dispute [Haynes, 1986b, pp. 5–6].

While noting that what a mediator's job entails and what a mediator may and may not do are highly debated, Haynes [1986b] considers the generally accepted rule to be that the parties should remain in control of their own conflict. Thus a mediator can be said to overstep his bounds and overdirect when he attempts to inform the parties of what is in their best interests, to define what he thinks those interests are, to offer too many suggestions, or to disrupt a mutually agreeable settlement because he does not think it does justice to one side.

overman   See UMPIRE.

pacific Tranquil, peaceful; as in "pacific methods of dispute resolution." Used as an adjective primarily in the context of international relations.

pacific settlement See PEACEFUL SETTLEMENT.

package deal, packaging *Negotiation:* Proposal that attempts to settle multiple issues simultaneously rather than single issues in sequence [Iklé, 1964, p. 222].

While some authorities simply define packaging as a technique of bundling issues and solutions, others examine it as a method of facilitating mutual gain through systematic trade-offs [Brett, 1991, p. 305]. Though the idea is that everybody gets something, it does not imply that everyone gains equally. In some contexts, the package may include procedural or insignificant substantive matters that help mitigate the effects of one party gaining at the other's expense. For example, giving a party with little negotiation leverage control over the time and location of negotiations may function to save face and provide a symbolically and psychologically significant *consolation award* for such parties. Packaging becomes a more conspicuous feature of negotiations as the number of issues and parties increases.

pact Promise, contract, agreement. More commonly used in the context of international relations to denote an agreement between states that is similar to but less formal than a treaty.

Pact of Bogota   Agreement codifying all previous inter-American agreements concerned with the pacific settlement of international disputes. Known formally as the American Treaty of Pacific Settlement, entered into April 30, 1948 [30 U.N.T.S. 55 (1949)].

pacta sunt servanda   *International Relations:* Literally, "agreements must be observed." A principle of international law that treaties are binding and that each state is responsible for its own adherence. Because there is no international agency that enforces treaty compliance, the principle is fundamental to the functioning of international law. See REBUS SIC STANTIBUS.

Panama Convention   Same as INTER-AMERICAN CONVENTION ON INTERNATIONAL COMMERCIAL ARBITRATION.

panchayat **(South Asia, Indian subcontinent)**   Assembly of respected village elders that engages in dispute resolution.

The *panchayat* is found in rural Nepal and India and is of ancient origin. It has served as the primary institution for administrating village affairs, among them resolving grievances and disputes among villagers. The institution is rooted in Hindu and Buddhist traditions of CONCILIATION. Originally the *panchayat* consisted of five persons of recognized social and moral authority. However, variations included as many as eleven members. Reportedly, the group's favored method of dispute resolution was conciliatory rather than adjudicative, and some commentators describe the old *panchayat* system as exemplifying institutionalized mediation. A *panchayat,* however, could easily compel conformity by threatening social ostracism [Shourie, 1988, p. 115]. Also note that the DOA describes *panchayats* as "territorial arbitration boards . . . who act as the sole and final judges of the matter referred to them by the parties," and the odd number of members (five or eleven) denotes a method of avoiding vote deadlock in adjudication.

The modern *panchayat* is enshrined in the Indian Constitution (Art. 40 of the Directive Principles) as a method of promoting decentralized self-governance. Though the *panchayat* still functions as an instrument of conciliation, authorities note that the formalized, elective nature of the office has undermined its effectiveness as a mediating body, and disputants in rural areas increasingly avail themselves of the courts. Consequently, legal aid and advice boards are credited with preserving some of the conciliatory traditions of the *panchayat* [Pe, Sosmena, and Tadiar, 1988, pp. 23–31; Shourie, 1988, p. 116].

panel   Collection of adjudicators.
Law: May be used to refer to the list of jurors available or to three-member divisions of a larger court, for example, a nine-member court of appeals that hears some cases in panels of three appellate judges.

Arbitration: Used to refer either to the larger list of arbitrators available to the parties through an ADMINISTERING AGENCY or to the smaller three- or four-person group that is chosen to arbitrate.

Because of the adjudicative connotations of this term, some providers of dispute resolution services with a list of neutrals other than just arbitrators have changed to using the term *roster.*

panel evaluation   *Court-Connected ADR:* As described by Leeson and Johnston [1988, p. 26], a hybrid of CASE EVALUATION and MANDATORY NONBINDING ARBITRATION because it includes abbreviated presentations of arguments and evidence at a hearing before a three-person panel that comments on the perceived strengths and weaknesses of both sides' cases and announces a nonbinding verdict to facilitate further negotiations. A unique aspect of this process is the composition of the panel, which in addition to including a member of the plaintiff bar and a member of the defense bar, includes a judge.

parachuting   *Labor Relations:* Practice of assigning an additional mediator without notifying the originally assigned mediator in advance. Maggiolo [1985, p. 90] describes this as a detrimental, political ploy once used by the United States Conciliation Service. A national office representative would appear at the scene of the negotiations amid attendant publicity and announce that she was joining in the mediation efforts.

paraphrasing   Communication technique often used by mediators in which the listener repeats to the speaker the substantive portion of the message in language virtually identical to that used by the speaker.

Paraphrasing can serve several purposes in promoting clear communication: (1) it allows the initial speaker an opportunity to determine whether what he said properly communicated what he intended, to judge the effect of that communication, and to modify it to better communicate the intention; (2) it allows the mediator to check whether she clearly understood what was said and to show the speaker that she heard; and (3) it allows any other parties hearing the initial communication to hear it again from a neutral third party [Bartunek, Benton, and Keys, 1975, pp. 532–557]. See FORMULATION.

parent-child mediation   Form of FAMILY MEDIATION that focuses on resolving disputes between parents and their children (usually adolescents).

Parent-child mediation differs from most other applications of family mediation (as in such areas of family conflict as separation, divorce, and child custody) in that parent-child mediation involves an adult and a minor as disputants rather than two adults, and involves families that wish to remain intact rather than to separate. Parent-child conflicts that come to mediation are typically identified as arising from the adolescents' problematic behavior, which often involves the juvenile justice system. In these instances, mediation is used as an alternative to such standard interventions as adjudication, probation, and counseling for resolving these parent-child disputes. The fundamental goal of parent-child mediation is to assist family members in defining the underlying issues in their conflict and to facilitate their movement toward a common agreement focusing on future behavior [Van Slyck, Newland, and Stern, 1992, p. 193, citations omitted].

parenting agreement, parenting plan, co-parenting agreement   *Family Mediation:* Agreements made as a result of custody mediation, visitation mediation, or both.

The term *parenting agreement* is preferred by some family mediators over *visitation agreement* because important parenting issues can arise in the course of a visitation mediation that do not fall under the strictly defined domain of visitation. For example, an agreement may include a clause that specifies the right of the noncustodial parent to be invited to parent conferences at the child's school [Prather, 1990, p. 27].

The term *parenting plan* is increasingly favored as connoting a more positive, proactive statement of future parental objectives. Parenting plans are required by law in many states without regard to whether mediation is involved. In addition to the best interests of the child, the typical statutory objectives of the plan include providing for the child's physical care and financial needs, maintaining the child's emotional stability, encouraging and protecting the child's intellectual and moral development, providing for the child's changing needs as it matures, establishing the authority and responsibilities of each parent, minimizing exposure to harmful parental conflict, and encouraging agreement without judicial intervention. Plans often must include provisions for the resolution of future disputes between the parents [Tenn. Code Ann. § 36-6-410 (West 1999)].

parenting plan mediation   Refers to CHILD CUSTODY MEDIATION in some jurisdictions, most notably Florida.

pareto-optimal (pareto frontier, utility frontier)   Most efficient solution (or set of solutions) attainable through joint action that maximize the parties' utilities. Alternative solutions are not possible unless one party gains at the expense of another.

An agreement is pareto-optimal for the bargainers if it places them at some point on the locus where, for any given attainable utility for one person, the other's utility is a maximum [Raiffa, 1982].

parliamentary diplomacy   *International Relations:* Form of CONFERENCE DIPLOMACY imitative of some national legislative processes in which majorities are formed to promote agreements. Found in ongoing international conferences, such as the UN General Assembly, the formation of majorities by states with regional or shared interests may create sufficient leverage to force negotiation. It is just as likely, however, to harden opposition and create an adversarial atmosphere.

parol agreement   See ORAL AGREEMENT.

parol award   *Arbitration:* Award issued verbally rather than written.

Arbitration laws in the United States declare that an award is not enforceable unless it is in writing. In COMMON LAW in the United States, if the submission requires that the award be in writing, that requirement must be met. In Great Britain, a parol award is usually valid unless the submission agreement or governing rules have provided that the award be in writing [DOA].

partial award   See INTERIM AWARD.

partisan arbitrator   Arbitrator chosen by one of the parties.

More commonly known in U.S. domestic commercial arbitration as the PARTY-APPOINTED ARBITRATOR. In international arbitration, the partisan arbitrator is called the *national* arbitrator or the national member of the tribunal in order to emphasize the mixed character of her role. Though a degree of partiality toward the appointing nation is tolerated, the international arbitrator is otherwise subject to the same requirements that apply to the third or neutral arbitrator [DOA].

Traditionally it was common for the partisan arbitrator to act in the interest of the appointing party, although she was also free to make determinations against that party. The practice derives from old forms of ARBITRAMENT and from Roman law arbitration. Partisan arbitrators were expected to enlighten the panel as to the norms, laws, and perceptions that may have motivated the appointing party in the contested matters. In some forms of maritime arbitration, such arbitrators are known as ARBITRATOR-ADVOCATES and, while free to award against the appointing party, are expected actually to advocate her case.

partnering   Dispute prevention process involving team-building activities to help define common goals, improve communication, and foster a problem-solving attitude among a group that must work together throughout contract performance. The primary goal is to encourage contracting parties who are about to work together on a project to be less adversarial and more cooperative. Partnering was developed and is used primarily in the construction industry.

party   Principal participant in a transaction or dispute resolution process.

In law, the term denotes either a person who files suit or the person against whom a suit is filed. Although any number of people may participate in a dispute resolution process and therefore be considered *participants,* not all of them are principals in the process. Thus the disputants, who had the primary authority to agree to engage in a dispute resolution process, are parties while their representatives are merely participants. Others who may be affected by the process are at best *interested parties.* Compare DISPUTANT.

party-affiliated arbitrator   Alternative term for PARTISAN ARBITRATOR. Also used to refer to representatives of the parties that serve on BIPARTITE BOARDS and JOINT BOARDS. See also ARBITRATOR-ADVOCATES.

party-appointed arbitrator   Increasingly preferred term for the PARTISAN ARBITRATOR in U.S. domestic commercial arbitration, wherein such arbitrators are bound to ethical rules that allow ex parte communications but are expected to decide substantive matters in a neutral fashion.

party autonomy   Principle that parties to an agreement to use voluntary forms of ADR, such as mediation or arbitration, will retain their mutual rights to control the rules and procedures that will govern the process to which they have agreed.

In arbitration, party autonomy is rarely absolute. It is often limited by various statutes, governing conventions, or the general principles of law recognized by civilized nations [DOA]. Parties empower the arbitrator to control the outcome, although parties can limit the effect of the award and the remedies available to the arbitrator. In many forms of court-connected ADR, party autonomy over procedures and choice of neutral may be severely limited. In both voluntary and court-connected mediation, however, most mediators subscribe to ethical rules that emphasize party autonomy. In this context, the principle of autonomy restrains the mediator from imposing undue influence on the outcome and extends to notions of party capacity to contract and, in some cases, to problems of unequal negotiating power.

party capability   Individual's ability and willingness to participate in a particular dispute resolution process.

The concept was coined by Galanter [1984] to explain how differences in the use of legal process, particularly litigation, are a function of the differing abilities of litigants to make use of the process. It refers to the individual's disposition regarding the process as well as the resources she can apply [Sarat, 1986, p. 537].

passive settlement   Resolution without formal agreement wherein the conflict may persist until the disputants merely accept a new status quo.

pass-the-buck phenomenon   Tendency of disputants to want to shift responsibility for the outcome onto third-party neutrals.

In labor relations, some issues go to arbitration instead of being resolved through less formal, less expensive means, particularly where an agent must answer to her principal, as between a union negotiator and the rank and file. The agent may choose to enter arbitration in order to lay the blame of an unfavorable position on the arbitrator and not on the agent. Similarly, in mediation it is not uncommon for a disputant to want the mediator to approve of a particular solution in order to justify the outcome to some critic or constituency not at the table. Sometimes known as the *cathartic* or *therapeutic* effect of arbitration.

pathological clause   *Arbitration:* Refers to an arbitration clause that, while enforceable, is so poorly drafted that the process is subject to unilateral abuses and uncharacteristic delays and costs.

The term was coined by Frederic Eisemann, the late secretary-general of the ICC Court of Arbitration (now the INTERNATIONAL COURT OF ARBITRATION).

PATNA   Probable alternative to a negotiated agreement. Contrast BATNA, WATNA.

pattern bargaining   Tendency of negotiators to agree on terms identical to or substantially the same as those negotiated earlier by other bargainers.

Simkin [1971, p. 180], in the context of COLLECTIVE BARGAINING, noted that pattern bargaining involves a conscious intent to match some other *key* bargain rather than an analysis of positions in other bargains. An example might be the attempt by an auto workers union to pattern all of its contracts with auto manufacturers on a contract it recently reached with a single manufacturer. Because no particular employer, union, or facility is identical, pattern bargaining carried to its extreme would have inefficient if not irrational results. Therefore the pattern must be modified as differences between the model and the situation in negotiation are revealed.

peace   State or condition of quiet, security, justice, and tranquility.

The term is problematic. Although commonly associated with the nonviolent resolution of international conflict [Holsti, 1983], peace is not defined in the UN Charter or other primary international law documents. States or nonstate groups, as in a civil war, are often said to achieve peace through the official cessation of hostilities; thus peace is sometimes defined as the absence of war [Treverton, 1991, p. 24]. This is also referred to as a *negative peace* because conditions of animosity or latent conflict can exist despite the absence of open, direct violence, and war may cease without resolving the underlying conflicts, thereby creating a continuing threat of violence. In addition, people who are too weak or otherwise reluctant to wage war may be pressed into a status quo that is fundamentally unfair. Note also that war is not the absence of peace, and nations can be engaged in armed strife while technically not being in a state of war.

In contrast, a *positive peace* is said to exist when states or nonstate groups continually engage in the nonviolent, constructive management of their differences with the goal of mutually satisfying relations [Holsti, 1983, p. 301]. Peace is directly linked to several other concepts (see PEACEFUL SETTLEMENT), primary of which are security and justice. *Security* implies lack of threats of violence or civil disorder and stable relations among stable societies. *Justice* implies that the stability is fair, equitable, and cognizant of fundamental human rights rather than merely a product of coercion and domination. St. Augustine's idea of peace as *tranquilitas ordinis,* the "tranquility in order," led to defining peace as "the condition of a community in which order and justice prevail, internally among its members and externally in its relations with other communities" [Starke, 1968, pp. 21–23, citation omitted].

Finally, peace may be defined as a nonviolent process rather than as a condition or state of affairs [Dahlen, Westas, and Wood, 1988, p. 15]. This is consistent with the concept of positive peace, which is oriented toward achieving desirable conditions, and it parallels the notion of war as both a process and a condition.

See also PEACEBUILDING, PEACEKEEPING, and PEACEMAKING.

peace brigade   Team of people trained in nonviolent peacemaking who intervene as third parties to resolve disputes. Associated with both international and intranational conflict resolution.

Peace Committee of the Organization of American States   Dispute resolution panel composed of representatives of five member states and authorized to suggest ways of resolving disputes among member states. Its recommendations are nonbinding.

peacebuilding   Proactive approach to developing and maintaining peace in which the focus is on developing structural and institutional mechanisms that favor nonviolent, constructive means of resolving differences [Dahlen, Westas, and Wood, 1988, pp. 29–30] and achieve a more extensive reconciliation. Compare PEACEKEEPING, PEACEMAKING.

peace-by-pieces   Technique of focusing peacemaking negotiations on attainable agreements around limited issues, such as military disengagement, rather than by convening a general peace conference. The technique is associated with former U.S. Secretary of State Kissinger's strategy in the Middle East negotiations after the 1973 war [Pendergast, 1990, pp. 137–138].

peaceful settlement, pacific settlement   Resolution of disputes without resort to force.

International Relations: Principle of peaceful settlement embodied in the UN Charter under which member states are obligated to settle disputes by peaceful means [Art. 2, ¶ 3]. Peaceful means of settlement are elaborated on in Chapter 6 of the charter and listed in Art. 33, ¶ 1. These include arbitration, judicial adjudication, negotiation, good offices, mediation, inquiry, conciliation, resort to regional agencies or arrangements, and other peaceful means.

The concept of peaceful settlement includes acting in a manner so as not to endanger international peace and security or to violate principles of justice. This links the concept to a number of other principles, such as refraining from the threat or use of force against another state, nonintervention in another state's external or internal affairs, a duty to cooperate, good faith in fulfilling international obligations, recognition of equal rights and the right of self-determination by peoples, and respect for fundamental human rights and freedoms.

peacekeeping   Method of reducing conflict by keeping conflicting parties away from each other, thereby achieving some level of security. Often involves restoring the previous status quo even if that preserves the underlying conflict and structural violence [Dahlen, Westas, and Wood, 1988, pp. 29–30]. Compare PEACEBUILDING, PEACEMAKING.

peacemaking   Process of modifying the behavior of actors and institutions in order to achieve more peaceful relations. Because it involves an attempt actually to resolve the issues in dispute, it goes beyond PEACEKEEPING, which is a more narrow and technically specified set of procedures for maintaining specific conflict resolution measures [Holsti, 1983, p. 301]; it falls short of PEACEBUILDING, however, which attempts a broader normalization of relationships.

Also an ad hoc approach to resolving an existing conflict, with its focus on cessation of hostilities [Dahlen, Westas, and Wood, 1988, pp. 29–30]. Compare PEACEBUILDING, PEACEKEEPING.

peer mediation   Process in which a peer of the disputants serves as a mediator to help them resolve their dispute. Though the term could have broader application, it is used almost exclusively in reference to mediation programs in schools where a trained student-mediator helps students resolve their own conflicts [Davis, 1986a]. Proponents promote peer mediation as empowering students to resolve their own problems and as providing an alternative to punishment imposed by supervising adults [Burrell and Vogl, 1990, p. 237].

peer review   Process used in the workplace or within professional associations that closely resembles ADVISORY ARBITRATION. It allows a disgruntled employee or member of an association or profession to present a dispute to a panel of peers. In the employment setting, the employee usually gets to chose one or more peers and the employer gets to chose one. The disputants present the matter to the panel, which issues a nonbinding recommendation.

permanent arbitration   Standing form of arbitration that is established to resolve dispute during the life of a continuing relationship rather than forming ad hoc as disputes arise.

permanent arbitrator   Arbitrator who is selected in advance to resolve disputes that may arise during the course of a continuing relationship.

A permanent arbitrator serves under the terms of a contract, often a COLLECTIVE BARGAINING AGREEMENT, for the life of that contract or for a specified period. The specific functions and responsibilities of the permanent arbitrator are determined by the contract [DOA].

permanent chairman   Neutral arbitrator on a TRIPARTITE PANEL in PERMANENT ARBITRATION. See BOARD OF ARBITRATION.

Permanent Court of Arbitration, The Hague   International agency established on July 29, 1899, by the CONVENTION ON THE PACIFIC SETTLEMENT OF INTERNATIONAL DISPUTES to provide facilities for arbitrating international disputes that have not been settled by diplomacy or negotiation.

The Permanent Court of Arbitration also makes available commissions of inquiry and conciliation. The court provides administrative facilities and a list of qualified arbitrators. Each member nation may designate four qualified persons for terms of six years on the court. Procedures are established by the Convention on the Pacific Settlement of International Disputes of July 28, 1899, as revised October 18, 1907. The administrative facilities are supported by contributions from member governments. Although the machinery of the Permanent Court of Arbitration was originally devised for settling disputes between governments, rules were drafted in 1962 for arbitrating disputes between a state and a private individual or corporation [DOA].

Permanent Court of International Justice, The Hague   Court established under the auspices of the Council of the League of Nations according to Article 14 of the constituting document, and under the Statute of the Court, which was annexed to a Protocol of Signature of December 16, 1920.

The Permanent Court was one of the first international courts. It functioned continuously from January 1922, when it held its first session at The Hague, until it was succeeded in 1945 by the INTERNATIONAL COURT OF JUSTICE. Sixty-five international disputes were brought before the court, most of them European in origin and related to European questions. The Permanent Court was not a court of arbitration. The president of the court might be designated in an arbitration agreement to appoint an arbitrator in cases where parties failed to agree. Judges of the Permanent Court did not officiate as arbitrators [DOA].

permanent umpire   Alternative term used to denote a PERMANENT ARBITRATOR. Technically, an umpire exists only where there are two party-appointed arbitrators, and she does not act until the other arbitrators fail to reach agreement. See UMPIRE.

persuade, persuasion   Convince or influence someone to act or think in a certain way, usually through appeals to rationality or emotions.

In negotiation, a party tries to influence another to act in a manner that will benefit herself. In this sense, her effort to persuade could be viewed as an attempt to control the other by operating on the other's expectations and preferences [Stevens, 1963, p. 67]. In another sense, persuasion can be viewed as a method of communication in negotiation; by trying to persuade each other, the parties become more aware of common interests and ways to use this knowledge to seek an optimum outcome [Young, 1967, p. 51]. In a less positive sense, persuasion can involve coercion.

In PRINCIPLED NEGOTIATION, the concept of *objective criteria* or the legitimacy of a proposed solution is closely linked to the concept of persuasion. To influence the other side to accept a particular outcome, a principled negotiator seeks to legitimize that outcome with criteria that would be most persuasive to the other party [Fisher and Ury, 1981].

PIES   Perceived injurious experiences. Concept developed to explain why some experiences lead to GRIEVANCES and develop into new types of disputes. Certain experiences through human interaction are *unPIES* until they are perceived as injurious. An analogy is that a person may have cancer but will not seek treatment until she is aware of being sick. For disputes to emerge and remedial action to be taken, an unPIE must be transformed into a PIE [Felstiner, Abel, and Sarat, 1980–1981, p. 633]. Sex discrimination is a good example of transformation from unPIE to PIE.

Piepoudre (Dusty-Footed) Court   Court of laymen set up at fairs and markets to decide on the spot all disputes between buyers and sellers. The origins of the Piepoudre Court reach back to Saxon times and did not die out until well into the nineteenth century [DOA]. See COURT OF PIEDPOUDRE.

PINS mediation   Mediation conducted in cooperation with the New York Family Courts for matters involving PINS (person in need of supervision) juveniles under sixteen who, because of repeated and patterned noncriminal acts (such as running away, incorrigible behavior, insubordination, or truancy), are considered by family, school, police, courts, or all of these parties as in need of additional supervision.

pipelines   Procedures designed to divert categories of disputes regularly to dispute resolution programs. Such procedures would direct disputes away from the adversarial paths they normally follow toward new paths leading to dispute resolution screening, and then on to mediation, arbitration, or another dispute resolution process [O'Connor, 1992, p. 85].

plaintiff   Person who complains and files a civil lawsuit.

plea bargaining   Method of processing criminal cases in which the accused and the state negotiate the exchange of official concessions, such as reduced charges or a lesser sentence, in exchange for a plea of guilty, often to a lesser offense than originally charged.

Plea bargaining includes a range of processing patterns that may involve protracted explicit bargaining or tacit reference to established understandings or custom among prosecution, judiciary, and defense [Galanter, 1986, pp. 199–200]. The impetus for the accused is to avoid the risk of conviction on a more serious charge or of receiving a harsher sentence than attainable through the plea bargain. The prosecution is motivated to avoid the expense and perhaps the unconstitutional delay of taking every contested criminal case through formal trial. In addition to the offer of a guilty plea in exchange for official concessions, the accused may have other bargaining endowments, such as offering victim restitution, public service, resignation from public office, or providing testimony or valuable information regarding other alleged offenders.

plenary session   Phase of dispute resolution process in which all the participants meet together, as opposed to a CAUCUS. Also known in mediation as a JOINT SESSION at which the parties express their PUBLIC POSITION as opposed to their PRIVATE POSITION.

polarization   Movement by parties toward extreme, opposing POSITIONS, usually occurring during CONFLICT ESCALATION.

polarized single-issue positions   *Negotiation:* Condition in which parties focus on one issue and perceive each other as representing the opposite extremes on that issue. Thus they see the conflict as having only one source, and they regard their task as forcing their adversaries to surrender unconditionally [Jandt and Gillette, 1985, p. 84].

policy dialogue   See PUBLIC POLICY DIALOGUE.

political discipline   Method by which conflicts are often resolved by the hierarchy of an alliance shared by the parties to the conflict. The alliance might be a political party or it might be a fraternal order, a group of business or professional associates, members of the same family, and the like. Form of communal coercion in hierarchical organizations and societies that tend to suppress rather than resolve conflict.

polycentric   Literally "many centered," describes a type of problem that is ill-suited for adjudication because it has many possible "right" solutions and therefore is not amenable to a win-lose, all-or-nothing outcome.

The term was coined by Fuller [1963, pp. 32–33], who cites as an example the testator who leaves a collection of paintings in equal but nonspecific parts to several museums. Obviously a judicially imposed division of the paintings is inferior to a negotiated solution that accommodates the museums' interests.

It should be noted that polycentricity exists in most disputes involving resource division (division of property in a divorce would have high polycentricity), as well as those involving multiple parties, causation, interests, and issues. Fuller recognized, however, that courts are obligated to resolve these polycentric conflicts daily. The concept simply identifies disputes that pose special difficulty for courts and for which a court-imposed remedy may exacerbate the initial dispute because of the dispute's complexity [Cavanagh and Sarat, 1980, p. 384].

position   Proposal or point of view that is adopted and held onto; in negotiation, the demands made of opponents. In PRINCIPLED NEGOTIATION, positions mask parties' interests [Fisher and Ury, 1981].

positional bargaining   Style of BARGAINING named after the pattern of positional demands, offers, and sequential concession making toward a mutually acceptable position. Also called DISTRIBUTIVE BARGAINING. Contrast INTEGRATIVE BARGAINING.

positive reciprocity   See RECIPROCITY.

positive settlement   Settlement created because the parties believe they have reached a consensual and wise solution, as opposed to a NEGATIVE SETTLEMENT [Menkel-Meadow, 1991, p. 11].

possibilistic decision making   Making of decisions by considering only possibilities rather than estimated probabilities.

The concept was articulated by Osgood [1971], who analogized to paranoid schizophrenics to explain certain irrational behaviors in international conflict. By analogy, if the paranoid knows it is possible that his doctor belongs to the secret society that is persecuting him, he leaps to the conclusion that he does belong and acts accordingly. Similarly, in the international arena, if the *we's* know that the *they's* could be cheating, lying, or planning a surprise attack, it is easy for the *we's* to conclude that the *they's* are doing these immoral things. Then the *we's* are liable to do the same immoral things first in order to protect themselves, firmly proclaiming their motives benign [p. 518].

post-settlement settlement   Process of deciding on an outcome first, then determining the particulars later.

Parties reach a simple settlement, then engage a third party who suggests outcomes that are better for both parties than the initial settlement. Either party is usually able to veto the post-settlement settlement in favor of the initial draft. This is a way of reaching the PARETO-OPTIMAL.

pourparler **(archaic)**   *Diplomacy:* Informal discussions, generally preliminary to substantive negotiations and having the objective of promoting peaceful settlement discussions.

Pourparler is used to prepare the groundwork and a conciliatory atmosphere for more substantive discussions. It is conducted directly rather than through a third party, although it can be initiated by a third party [Lall, 1966, pp. 18, 19].

power   Capacity to act or exert force; in negotiation, capacity to influence the behavior of others.

Power may be defined generally in terms of potential to influence the condition of others: "the possibility of imposing one's will upon the behavior of other persons" [Galbraith, 1983, pp. 4–5]; the ability to change the outcome, benefits, or costs of others in a relationship [Thibaut and Kelly, 1959]; the ability to withhold the benefits of a relationship [Ury, Brett, and Goldberg, 1988, p. 8]; or the ability to control "access to emotional, economic, and physical resources desired by the other person" [Neumann, 1990, p. 287]. In conflict resolution, therefore, power can be harnessed to achieve agreement and conciliation, or it can be used for self-enhancement—to get what one wants—or to prevent the other from getting what she wants.

Authorities have attempted to distinguish among different types of power. Galbraith [1983] describes three types: *condign power* (the ability to influence through the use or threat of harm); *compensatory power* (the ability to influence through reward); and *conditioned power* (the ability to harness another's willingness to submit or belief in submitting to authority). Mayer [1987, p. 78] identified several types of power, including formal authority, expert/information power, associational power, resource power, procedural power, sanction power, nuisance power, habitual power, moral power, and personal power. Drawing on earlier conceptualizations of social influence, Bercovitch [1992b, p. 107] identifies six types of resources, or *bases of power:* reward, coercion, referent, legitimacy, expertise, and information.

Power derives from different sources. In the context of PRINCIPLED NEGOTIATION, for example, Fisher [1983a] defines six sources of a negotiator's power: (1) knowledge of the dispute and skill in the negotiation, (2) a good relationship with the other side based on trust and communication, (3) an attractive alternative to a negotiated agreement (see BATNA), (4) ability to generate options that satisfy the interests of all parties, (5) independent standards that legitimate those options, and (6) commitment to accept a satisfactory offer and reject an unsatisfactory offer. A disputant's power may be a function of her material possessions, such as money or property, as well as her normative or symbolic resources, such as authority and social status [Hart, 1990, pp. 318–319]. Therefore disputants usually enter a dispute with differing amounts and types of power. Severe differences in power among disputants in a mediation may force the mediator to intervene to maintain the integrity of the process, or failing that, to end the mediation as inappropriate for achieving a fair result. See POWER-BALANCING TECHNIQUES.

power-balancing techniques *Mediation:* Various methods by which mediators intentionally affect the disputants' use of power in the process.

Commonly accepted techniques include controlling seating and other aspects of location and physical space (such as neutral location, similar chair height, round table) and establishing and monitoring behavioral ground rules to discourage the use of certain negotiation tactics (such as no name-calling, interrupting, lying, or physical violence; see DIRTY TRICKS).

Although these common techniques are considered an accepted if not essential part of the mediation process, others require more subjective judgment by the mediator and may raise ethical questions about the degree to which a mediator can empower weaker parties and disempower stronger parties. Although the introduction of a mediator into the disputants' relationship inherently changes their relative power, any active attempt at changing the balance of power puts two ethical principles in tension. On the one hand, mediators should treat the parties in an impartial manner, while on the other hand, mediators should be concerned about how abuses of power might undermine the integrity of the process. Arguably, mediation provides no protection from social, economic, or political power imbalances inherent in the disputants' relationship. In some cases of severe power imbalance, a mediator might determine that another process might provide more protection for the weaker party or yield a fairer resolution. Some mediators may be motivated to address imbalances, either because of ideology or because they identify the imbalance as the impediment to resolution. The propriety of mediator attempts to change the balance of power might depend on the type of power involved, on the way the disputants are using it, on the method of intervention, and on the degree to which the disputants empower the mediator to intervene.

power preponderance theory   *International Relations:* Theory that when power is highly concentrated, the likelihood of war is lower than when power is disbursed.

Two varieties of this theory revolve around whether one looks only to the power distribution between the two major powers (dyadic approach) or to the distribution among all the major actors in the system. The latter variety holds that a low concentration of power among the nations deters war because of the possibility of coalitions among groups [Mansfield, 1992, pp. 4–5].

practitioner   Someone who practices a particular technique, art, occupation, or profession, as opposed to someone who teaches it. In conflict resolution, practitioners include diplomats, judges, lawyers, arbitrators, mediators, conciliators, fact-finders, facilitators, and professional negotiators.

predictive settlement procedure   Refers to REALITY TESTING or *evaluative* ADR devices used to affect the parties' beliefs about what may happen at trial and thereby encourage settlement (for example, MANDATORY NONBINDING ARBITRATION, EARLY NEUTRAL EVALUATION, SUMMARY JURY TRIAL, MINI-TRIAL, AND SETTLEMENT CONFERENCE) [McEwen, 1991, p. 77].

predisputes clause   See FUTURE DISPUTES CLAUSE.

preemptive disposition of conflict   Methods of resolving specific problems by establishing in advance a mandatory outcome or procedure that will solve the problem without further dispute resolution efforts. Examples include BLOCK SOLUTIONS established by law, such as LEMON LAWS, or mechanisms for anticipated problems in contractual relations, such as procedures for buying out a disgruntled shareholder or partner. These should be distinguished from laws or contract provisions that merely direct parties to various dispute resolution processes, such as mediation or arbitration. These preemptive dispositions require no decision making or third-party intervention [Practising Law Institute, 1987, pp. 21–22].

prehearing conference   *Arbitration:* Meeting of the arbitrator or administrator with the parties before the formal hearing in order to sift through the issues in the case, particularly matters of procedure and information exchange to be determined and completed in advance of the hearing, and to give the arbitrator an opportunity to gather some of the information necessary to conduct the hearing [DOA].

prejudice   Bias; having preconceived opinions.
   Law: To harm.

premature negotiating   When the parties begin negotiating without having acquired sufficient information to negotiate effectively.
   This problem is usually indicated by the blocking behavior of one party [Haynes, 1986b, p. 6]. The term raises the general question of when a matter is "ripe" for negotiation (see RIPENESS). Factors in addition to information come into play, such as the parties' emotional readiness.

prenegotiation   Period or activities used by the parties to prepare for negotiation.
   Prenegotiation activities can be bilateral or unilateral. According to Druckman [1973, p. 21], social psychologists identify two general processes: bilateral agenda formation, including mutual assurances in maintaining the viability of the relationship; and unilateral and bilateral caucusing for position formation and for learning the other side's position. The difficulty with the term resides in determining where the negotiation process actually begins, and this may depend on the definition of negotiation. See NEGOTIATION.

prenegotiation conference   Formal meeting between parties to prepare for negotiations.
   Labor Relations: Some collective bargaining relationships feature a prenegotiation conference arrangement. The advantage of this procedure is that the parties start their actual negotiations with agreed-upon facts. The prenegotiation conference is designed primarily to get agreement as to the facts before negotiation begins [Stevens, 1963, p. 42].

presiding arbitrator   Arbitrator voted by an impartial arbitration board or tribunal to act as chairman of that board when there is more than one arbitrator.
   When there is a neutral or public arbitrator who is a member of a tripartite board, that neutral arbitrator presides. The presiding arbitrator in international arbitration is often designated in the agreement, either by name or to be chosen by the authority so specified [DOA].

pretrial conference   Meeting of opposing attorneys before trial, either required by rule or called at the discretion of the court and usually presided over by the judge.
   As opposed to a SETTLEMENT CONFERENCE, the express purpose of which is to promote settlement before trial, a pretrial conference is used to make the trial

more efficient by narrowing the issues and stipulating on factual and evidentiary matters. However, an additional goal can be to promote settlement.

pretrial settlement conference   See SETTLEMENT CONFERENCE.

pretrial review   Judge-assisted, hybrid dispute resolution process combining adjudicative and conciliatory elements.

Litigants make summary presentations of their cases before a judge and then retire to begin negotiations. They may return to the judge for help identifying or clarifying the issues. On request, the judge may make settlement suggestions and, in the last resort, express a view. The expression of views is not binding, and the judge who serves in pretrial review will not be the judge who conducts the trial.

preventive mediation   Mediation designed to discuss potential problems and conflicts before they undermine the parties' relationship and develop into disputes (see CONFLICT and DISPUTE for distinctions).

Such preventive mediation may be found in long-term contractual relations, as in a large construction project, a joint venture, or a long-term supplier agreement. They have been most common in collective bargaining arrangements, under which neutrals continuously consult or advise joint labor-management committees throughout the contract term. This is somewhat similar to the role the IMPARTIAL CHAIRMAN played in the early part of the century. Mediation may be employed in contract discussions before any direct negotiation takes place [DOA].

prevote meeting   *Labor Relations:* Meeting held before formal balloting to allow people to vent their views on the proposal and to reduce the psychological pressures inherent in voting during the course of an open meeting.

According to Maggiolo [1971, pp. 94–95], organized dissident groups have disrupted meetings to ratify tentative collective bargaining agreements by shouting down the negotiating committee's report and effectively blocking any opportunity to vote. In response, unions began holding the reporting meeting on one day and the vote by secret ballot a few days later. While providing the dissident group an opportunity to vent its opposition, it reduced the amount of immediate peer pressure on those who would otherwise vote to approve the settlement.

primacy   Heuristic tendency of people to commit themselves to first impressions and resist subsequent conflicting information.

Primacy impedes conflict resolution by creating resistance to new ideas or to the reduction of stereotypes. In negotiation, primacy makes it difficult for parties to change positions. In adjudicative processes, it explains why advocates want to be first to address the adjudicator, knowing that if they are initially persuasive, belief preservation will work in their favor during the rest of the process [Coulson, 1968, p. 38].

principal mediator Third-party intervenor who, unlike an impartial mediator, has an indirect interest in the dispute and brings her own bargaining endowments into the negotiations.

While a principal mediator may facilitate negotiations in a manner similar to that of an impartial mediator, she cannot claim to be interested solely in helping the disputants resolve their own dispute. The principal mediator has a substantive though less direct interest in the matter and, when necessary, will promote her interest over those of the parties. Because she has no independent bargaining leverage, such as the ability to grant or withhold benefits or to threaten harm, the impartial mediator can only facilitate the disputants' interaction. In contrast, the principal mediator is a fellow bargainer but not a disputant. She can use her resources to strike her own bargains with the parties individually, thus influencing the outcome of negotiations between them. Such a bargain would be trilateral instead of bilateral. An example of a principal mediator would be the United States in the Middle East, illustrated by the mediating role of President Jimmy Carter in the Camp David Accord negotiations [Princen, 1992, pp. 20–26].

principled Motivated by or based on collective standards, especially praiseworthy conduct or behavior. Sometimes associated with behavior that has an objective, rational basis.

principled negotiation Method of negotiation that focuses on satisfying the mutual interests of all the parties to a dispute, rather than on haggling and trying to prevail over each other's negotiating stances; articulated by Roger Fisher and William Ury [1981] at the Harvard Negotiation Project as an alternative to traditional POSITIONAL BARGAINING.

Principled negotiation, as conceived by Fisher and Ury [1981, p. xii],

> deals with the drawbacks inherent in the familiar forms of "hard" and "soft" negotiation. A hard negotiator approaches each negotiation as a war to be fought by establishing a firm position and defending it through any necessary means. While she may often "win," the hard bargainer pays the price by exhausting her resources and damaging her relationship with the other party. A soft negotiator, on the other hand, prefers to make concessions in order to avoid confrontations. While a soft bargainer may preserve her relationship with the other party, she often "loses," particularly when negotiating with a hard bargainer, and ends up feeling exploited and taken advantage of.

In contrast, principled negotiators strive to achieve a mutually "wise" and efficient agreement by (1) concentrating on solving the problem, rather than on the people with the problem; (2) focusing on satisfying the parties' interests instead of haggling over their positions; (3) inventing a variety of options together that satisfy the parties' mutual interests; and (4) agreeing on and using objective criteria, such as fair market value, to legitimize the agreement [Fisher and Ury, 1981, pp. 17–98].

In this sense, principled negotiation is simply a well-articulated form of interest-based bargaining. It should be distinguished, however, by its emphasis on *principled* conduct. While Fisher and Ury do not explicitly define their concept of principled negotiation, commentators have offered their own definitions along these lines. For example, Lax and Sebenius [1986, p. 256] observe that negotiation is principled when "one's claims are grounded in what is right, legitimate, or moral," and disputes are settled "by a process of normative conformity." White's [1984, pp. 115] criticism of principled negotiation as unrealistic because all negotiation ultimately is or becomes positional, prompted a response from Fisher that is perhaps the best clue as to what *principled* means in principled negotiation. Fisher emphasizes the behavioral aspect of principled negotiation and stresses that principled negotiation is not incompatible with a distributive situation that entails positional bargaining patterns. However, the principled negotiator adheres to a praiseworthy code of conduct rather than reverting to traditional deception and psychological tactics favored by stereotypical hard bargainers [White, 1984, pp. 119–122].

principle of least interest   Concept that the party with the least interest in reaching a settlement has the most negotiating power and is able to attain the greatest reward for the least cost [Parker, 1991, p. 124].

private adjudication   Process by which disputing parties empower a private individual to hear and decide their case.

More commonly and precisely used in reference to TRIAL ON ORDER OF REFERENCE or RENT-A-JUDGE proceedings that follow the formal rules of litigation and provide for appeal on the same grounds as a decision by a regular trial court.

The term is occasionally, perhaps facetiously but less accurately, used in reference to a private, voluntary arbitration in which the parties have agreed to proceed in imitation of formal litigation, that is, by using the Federal Rules of Civil Procedure. However, the award is subject not to appeal but rather to vacation on the limited grounds provided in the applicable arbitration law. See ARBITRATION.

private arbitration   Sometimes referred to as *voluntary* or *contractual* arbitration. See ARBITRATION.

private judging   Process in which the court, at the request of the litigants and under a statutory general order of reference or similar rule of court, refers the case to a private judge (usually a retired former judge) chosen and compensated by the litigants themselves. The judgment rendered is enforceable and appealable in the public courts for errors of law or on the ground that the judgment is against the weight of the evidence. Same as TRIAL ON ORDER OF REFERENCE and RENT-A-JUDGE. See REFEREE SYSTEM.

private position   *Mediation:* Portion of a mediation session in which a disputant discusses specific problems only in the presence of her representative and the mediator, that is, without the other party present.

Used in contrast to PUBLIC POSITION, the term implies that a disputant will present a different *position* when in the presence of the other side than when alone with the mediator. Similarly, it implies POSITIONAL BARGAINING. The term could be limited to denote the different way in which a disputant might characterize the situation when alone with the mediator rather than used as a label for a portion of the mediation process. A preferable term might be CAUCUS.

privilege   Special immunity granted to a particular person or class of people.

By law, certain third-party intervenors, such as arbitrators and mediators, especially in court-connected processes, are granted immunity from having to testify at a subsequent trial on a matter they handled. Most jurisdictions have exceptions to the privilege.

Privilege may be absolute or conditional. An absolute privilege prevents a court from requiring covered people to testify. A conditional privilege allows a court to force covered people to testify only if the public benefits of requiring the testimony outweigh the potential harms.

probability of performance   *Negotiation:* Perception of the likelihood that others will in fact do what they promise to do [Goldman, 1991, p. 22.]

An offer is discounted by the extent to which the offeree believes the offerer may fail to comply. Goldman [1991, pp. 187–188] identifies several ways to improve the perception of probability of performance, including *indemnification* (a guarantee of performance or its monetary equivalent), *self-annihilation* (assurance that nonperformance will injure the promisor), and efficient enforcement (degree to which an agreement can be quickly, cheaply, and easily enforced).

problem   Difficult or doubtful matter requiring a solution.

problem solving   Approach to dispute resolution in which the dispute is reframed as a mutual problem to be solved by the parties jointly through consensus.

Often referred to as *collaborative problem solving* and *collaborative negotiation,* it connotes a negotiation theory as well as strategy. As a negotiation theory, its efficacy rests on a variety of related assumptions. It assumes that parties will be able to agree on a definition of the problem and are willing to cooperate in seeking solutions [Potapchuk and Carlson, 1987, p. 32]. The potential for cooperation assumes a NON-ZERO-SUM situation in which there are multiple issues and varying interests that are not mutually exclusive. Presumably this allows the parties to search for integrative solutions and the maximization of joint gain. The more underlying needs and objectives they uncover, the more and better quality solutions they will discover [Kritzer, 1991, p. 175]. It also assumes that people make rational decisions based on an enlightened self-interest that recognizes interdependence, values relationships, acknowledges legitimacy in the other side, and shares goals of fairness and efficiency [Murray, Rau, and Sherman, 1989, pp. 82–84].

As a strategy, it is similar if not the same as *integrative bargaining* (see BARGAINING) or *interest-based negotiation,* popularly illustrated by Fisher and Ury [1981] as PRINCIPLED NEGOTIATION. It requires parties to reframe the dispute as a joint problem, to explore this problem from all possible points of view, to focus on the parties' interests and needs, to generate the full range of possible solutions, and to choose the solution that best satisfies all the interests and maximizes gains for all as judged by an objective standard that seems mutually fair and just.

Contrast COMPETITIVE, *distributive bargaining* under BARGAINING.

procedural arbitrability   See ARBITRABILITY.

procedural fairness   Extent to which the process of reaching an agreement is fair.

At a minimum, procedural fairness includes the opportunity to participate as fully as the other side does. In adjudication, this is reflected in the right to receive notice of the hearing, to present one's case, and to be treated in an evenhanded, impartial manner by the adjudicators. Dworkin and London [1989, pp. 4–5] posit more extensive criteria for procedural fairness in mediation, including impartiality of the mediator, voluntary decisions by the parties, sufficient factual data on which to base decisions, participant understanding of both information and decisions, noncoercive negotiations, power balance, full financial disclosure, and access to independent legal counsel. See FAIRNESS; compare JUSTICE.

procedural justice   See JUSTICE.

procedural timeline approach   Negotiating a time-sensitive formula to determine the substantive outcomes of a dispute.

This approach allows the parties to avoid a specific substantive decision on issues in dispute by creating a procedural formula for decision making. For example, parties may be at an impasse over the amount and timing of payment. This might be overcome by reaching an agreement linking amount due to time paid. Thus, before a specific date a certain amount is due from the payer; after this date, she must pay a penalty charge as well. Under this approach, negotiators shift their emphasis from creating a specific substantive solution to developing a process and timeline for reaching various outcomes and defining consequences for reaching or breaching those deadlines [Moore, 1986, p. 236]. Compare PREEMPTIVE DISPOSITION OF CONFLICT.

procedure   Established or agreed upon manner of conducting a process.

Program on Negotiation (PON)   Dispute resolution theory-building program originally funded by the William and Flora Hewlett Foundation. Based in the Harvard Law School, participants include faculty members from numerous schools in the Boston area.

In addition to activities such as research and theory building, postgraduate education and training, the development of teaching materials, and numerous publications, the program offers dispute resolution teaching materials, including role-play exercises, books, discussion problems, curricula, videotapes, and working papers addressing a wide range of negotiation and dispute resolution theories and practice issues through its clearinghouse.

project neutral   See STANDING NEUTRAL.

proposal and counterproposal   Alternative term for POSITIONAL BARGAINING, in which an initial proposal is followed by a counterproposal, which is then itself countered; the process continues to an agreement or impasse [Simkin, 1971, pp. 167–168].

pro se   On behalf of one's self. Litigants are said to appear pro se when they are not represented by an attorney.

protective contracts   Formal agreements to negotiate in "good faith" that parties make to maintain negotiations in the face of internal or external pressures to withdraw [Druckman, 1973, p. 22].

protracted conflict   *International Relations:* Hostile interactions that extend over long periods with sporadic outbreaks of open warfare fluctuating in frequency and intensity. Contrast INTRACTABLE CONFLICT.

provention   Removal of causes of conflict and promotion of environments conducive to collaborative relationships. A combination of *prevention* and *promotion.*

Coined by Burton [1990a, pp. 3, 18], *provention* avoids the connotation of containment found in *prevention* while shifting emphasis to the positive acts of removing sources of conflict and promoting conditions for collaboration. In this context, *conflict provention* includes an understanding not only of what causes conflict but also of what fosters cooperation.

provider, ADR provider   Person or organization that provides dispute resolution services commercially. Includes ADMINISTRATIVE AGENCIES. The term seems to have been coined during the early 1980s by the insurance industry.

provisional measures   Temporary or interim relief granted by a court so as to prevent imminent and irreparable injury or to preserve the status quo until the matter is resolved amicably or by adjudication. Also referred to as *interim measures of protection* and *interim relief.* The term is favored in international law, while *interim relief* or *interim remedy* is more common in domestic U.S. law.

Provisional measures prevent a party to a dispute from acting so as to prejudice the final outcome of an adjudication. The relief must be limited to preserving only those rights that are to be adjudicated while not itself prejudicing the final outcome. The threat of irreparable damage must be imminent, and the petitioner must have some prospects for ultimately prevailing on the merits.

proxy advocate   Government organization or representative empowered to represent the interests of particular groups of people before another government organization.

In contrast to an OMBUDSMAN, a proxy advocate represents a class of people, not an individual with a complaint. While an ombudsman's concerns are particular, the proxy advocate's concerns are general [Gormley, 1981].

psychodrama   Therapeutic, improvised role-playing by groups or individuals that is used by psychologists to explore underlying emotions, frustrations, and attitudes and to solve individual problems.

Recommended by Nierenberg [1968, p. 56] as a negotiation-preparation technique in which a negotiator not only acts out her role but also acts out the role of the other party.

psychological distance   Degree of directness and intensity of interaction between communicators.

Donohue, Weider-Hatfield, Hamilton, and Diez [1985, pp. 390–391] identify and describe four types of verbal markers that create psychological distance: spatial, temporal, denotative-specificity, and agent-action-object relationships.

Spatial markers either confirm or disavow direct communication to define a spatial distance, such as in reference to the same person ("I don't agree with you," or conversely, "I don't agree with that person sitting across the table"). *Temporal markers* use verb tense to define the distance between the speaker and the object or activity (such as "I want to do that," or conversely, "I wanted to do that"). *Denotative-specificity markers* define distance through variations in overinclusiveness or underinclusiveness, thereby making the speaker's participation more or less direct (such as "I agreed" rather than "we agreed" or "the group agreed"). Finally, verbal markers using *agent-action-object relationships* define distance through modifiers or qualifiers that indicate the speaker's willingness to own or disown a particular statement.

public employee arbitration, public employment arbitration Arbitration between government entities and their employees over terms and conditions of employment. Such arbitration is required by statute rather than by a collective bargaining agreement or voluntary arbitration agreement. In addition to conventional arbitration in which the arbitrator may craft her own solution, different types of arbitration may be used, including FINAL-OFFER ARBITRATION (in which the arbitrator chooses one of two proposed solutions). See COMPULSORY ARBITRATION.

public law board, special adjustment board Adjudicative panel established and empowered by legislation to resolve certain labor disputes. The best known is the National Railway Adjustment Board formed pursuant to 45 U.S.C. 153 (1994) for the resolution of certain railroad labor disputes.

public law dispute Controversy over issues that broadly affect the public, the resolution of which may require government action.

Public law disputes involve a broad range of issues, including civil rights, consumer protection, land use, environment, public services, and resource allocation. Typically a governmental entity is involved in its legislative or regulatory capacity (compare PUBLIC POLICY DISPUTE). In public law litigation, judicial relief for the plaintiffs assumes the guise of "complex forms of ongoing relief, which have widespread effects on persons not before the court and require the judge's continuing involvement in administration and implementation" [Cavanagh and Sarat, 1980, p. 396]. These disputes often involve unsettled law, costly litigation, and potentially negative political ramifications, and with a multiplicity of stakeholders and issues they are considered by some to be ideal candidates for mediation.

public member *Arbitration/Labor Relations:* Neutral member of an arbitration board in cases where the public interest is affected.

The public member is the nonpartisan arbitrator, as distinguished from the arbitrators chosen by labor and management respectively. Such arbitration courts are normally composed of three members but may sometimes have as many as five or more [DOA].

public policy dialogue   *Public Policy:* Complex process in which multiple parties seek consensus on broad public issues. Facilitated process in which stakeholders and others who have interests that are or may become the subject of regulation identify issues of concern and points of agreement and disagreement. The process yields recommendations for either regulation or self-regulatory behavior and should be distinguished from a public hearing, which receives only citizen comment, and from a REG-NEG, which is concerned with the shaping of actual regulations through negotiation.

The theory behind public policy dialogues is that any agreement is more easily implemented if parties that have a stake in the agreement (see STAKEHOLDERS) help write the agreement. Participants may be chosen for their influence over their constituencies, for their immediate involvement with the problem, and for their ability to affect the implementation of the agreement. Most early experiments with this process involved environmental policy and were sponsored by nongovernmental nonprofit organizations. Although problems with a particular site may have been the impetus for the dialogue, the dialogue itself is usually not site-specific. Today, policy dialogues include a range of other social issues and are sponsored mostly by government agencies that contract with a nonpartisan team of facilitators and mediators to convene and manage the process. The sponsoring government agency gets a broader perspective and range of ideas than attainable through traditional lobbying [Ehrmann and Lesnick, 1988, pp. 94–95].

public policy dispute   Form of PUBLIC LAW DISPUTE; controversy over issues that broadly affect the public, the resolution of which may require nonjudicial government action in the form of legislation or regulation.

public policy mediation   Form of mediation for PUBLIC POLICY DISPUTES that aims at bringing together affected representatives of business, public interest groups and government to negotiate agreements on policy development, implementation, or enforcement. Facilitators or mediators are usually used to organize and guide the process [Dillon, 1994].

public position   *Mediation:* Those parts of the mediation in which disputants meet together in the presence of the mediator.

Used in contrast to PRIVATE POSITION, the term implies that a disputant will present a different *position* when in the presence of the other side than when alone with the mediator. Similarly, it implies POSITIONAL BARGAINING. The term could be limited to refer only to those portions, usually initial, of the mediation in which parties confront each other about their differences, and not to subsequent portions wherein disputants are together but engaged in interest-based, integrative negotiation or collaborative problem solving. Alternatively, the term could be limited to denote the different way in which a disputant might characterize the situation when facing the other side, rather than as a label for a portion of the mediation process. Preferable terms might be PLENARY SESSION or JOINT SESSION.

puffing *Negotiation:* Statement regarding value that the negotiator making the statement knows is an exaggeration or at least inaccurate. Under conventional bargaining norms, such statements are not considered misrepresentations of material fact. The line between puffing and lying, however, is a thin one, particularly because the puffer is attempting to deceive the puffee.

punitive damages In adjudication, damages awarded as punishment for the defendant's acts rather than as compensation to make a plaintiff whole.

Policy on punitive damages varies. In some jurisdictions, punitive damages are "capped," or limited by laws created under tort reform. Similarly, in other jurisdictions a portion of punitive damages goes to the state rather than to the plaintiff. In arbitration, some courts have concluded that public policy precludes an arbitral award of punitive damages because the sanction is reserved to the state. Many jurisdictions, however, allow arbitrators to award punitive damages unless the arbitral agreement provides otherwise. Federal arbitration law may preempt state limitations on the award of punitive damages in arbitration. See *Mastrobuono* v. *Shearson Lehman Hutton, Inc.* (1995).

Quakers See SOCIETY OF FRIENDS.

quarrel Angry dispute. To disagree in a combative and rancorous manner.

quasi-judicial "As if" or seemingly judicial. Having powers, functions, or characteristics similar to courts or judges.

quasi-judicial bodies Adjudicative institutions that make binding findings through procedures that apply rules of law to facts established by due process. Such bodies should be distinguished from those that engage in fact-finding or that apply rules of law but only to make recommendations.

quasi-judicial immunity Legal principle that limits the liability of quasi-judicial officers and third-party intervenors, such as arbitrators and mediators, for their actions that were within the scope of their authority; also limits the extent to which they are required to respond to subpoenas or discovery requests in subsequent litigation of disputes in which they intervene. The principle is derived from the judicial immunity afforded to judges.

quasi-judicial officers Persons who perform certain judicial functions, such as REFEREES, often appointed ad hoc. In private, voluntary ADR, arbitrators and mediators may perform certain judgelike functions and enjoy certain QUASI-JUDICIAL IMMUNITY, but they are not quasi-judicial officers. Arbitrators and mediators empowered by the court to conduct COURT-CONNECTED ADR mechanisms might be referred to as quasi-judicial officers. However, though they may be granted limited judicial powers by the court, neither are granted the power to make a binding determination through procedures applying rules of law to facts established by due process. Thus neither are technically quasi-judicial officers.

quasi-mediator   Member of a negotiating team who is committed to the process and to creating a mutually acceptable, rational settlement. During INTERNAL BARGAINING, quasi-mediators mediate between STABILIZERS and DESTABILIZERS within the team in order to keep the team effective in its negotiations with other parties [Colosi and Berkeley, 1986].

Rabattderegulierungsgesetz **(German)**   Reform law to legalize HAGGLING in retail business.

rapprochement   Reconciliation or resumption of compatible relations after a period of estrangement or tensions. More common in the context of international relations in reference to a policy of trying to establish normal relations.

rationality   Use of reason to guide action and decision making.

Much of conflict resolution theory and recommended practice, particularly PROBLEM SOLVING, depends on notions of rationality. Most models of rationality focus on outcomes that are objectively most advantageous to the individual and assume that the individual with full information will seek that outcome. In contrast, *instrumental rationality* focuses on means instead of ends; thus if a desired outcome is best attained through the cooperation of the other side, the parties will choose to negotiate. When decision makers conflate concepts of doing what is "right" with doing what is in their best interests, they are operating under the *normative rationality of ends* [Daly, 1991, p. 37].

rationalization   Act of justifying a possibly irrational choice by interpreting a situation in a manner that will place one in the most favorable light [Nierenberg, 1968, p. 37], especially after the fact.

Rawls' difference principle Concept that a bargained end is fair if the party who does worst nevertheless does better than she would in any other available bargain [Luban, 1989, pp. 391–392]. This measurement of fairness is thus similar to a party's BATNA.

reactive devaluation Psychological process whereby a proposed settlement to a conflict appears less desirable simply because an adversary has offered it [Ross and Stillinger, 1991, p. 394].

Reactive devaluation serves as a barrier to conflict resolution, particularly in direct negotiations. Mediators can reduce the intensity of this response by obscuring the source of proposals.

reality testing Techniques used to adjust perceptions that do not conform to the realities of the situation.

Disputants may deceive themselves about the relative merits of each other's positions by being blind to their own weaknesses and to the other side's strengths. Parties misperceive their BATNAS or overestimate the possible negotiated outcome. In divisive legal disputes, it is common for both parties to believe that the adjudicated outcome will be in their favor. Clearly both estimates cannot be correct; one party will win and one will lose. Nevertheless, the parties will emphasize, if not exaggerate, different positions based on their estimated outcome, positions that gradually harden in the adversarial climate. As a result, many court-connected ADR mechanisms emphasize reality testing, especially MANDATORY NONBINDING ARBITRATION, EARLY NEUTRAL EVALUATION, and SUMMARY JURY TRIALS. These mechanisms are "trial runs" in front of third parties whose unbiased judgment will serve as persuasive evidence of a more realistic view of the situation. The more authoritative and credible the third parties are, the more effective the technique will be. Several private, voluntary ADR mechanisms also emphasize reality testing, for example, MINI-TRIALS, FACT-FINDING, and ADVISORY ARBITRATION. All of these court-connected and private processes have a nonbinding adjudicative element involving judgment or evaluation by third parties.

In contrast, MEDIATION is a conciliatory process in which overt revelation of the mediator's perspective on the relative merits of the case puts impartiality at risk. Certain styles of mediation, however, commonly associated with court-connected mediation, are *evaluative* [Riskin, 1996] and serve a reality-testing function. In nonevaluative models of mediation, mediators use other reality-testing techniques that do not rely on evaluation. These include ROLE REVERSAL (asking each side to place itself in the other's position to consider the opposing perspective), restatement of the other side's perspective and position, and referral to other independent, objective criteria of legitimacy. The simple technique of asking questions about the underlying reasoning or logic of a position or proposal can serve as a powerful reality-testing tool.

reasoned award   *Arbitration:* AWARD accompanied by a written statement of the reasoning behind the arbitrator's decision. See OPINION.

reassurance   *International Relations:* Conflict de-escalation strategy of dispelling apprehensions by communicating benign intentions, showing an interest in nonthreatening ways to resolve issues, and trying generally to reduce the insecurities, fears, and misunderstandings that escalate conflict.

This strategy assumes that hostility is often rooted in perceptions of vulnerability, and while DETERRENCE seeks to discourage hostility by raising the costs of hostile action, reassurance seeks to convince adversaries that there is little to be gained by hostile action.

rebus sic stantibus   *International Law:* Literally, "under the circumstances," a principle that allows states to renounce treaty obligations unilaterally in response to substantive changes in the conditions present when entering into the obligations.

Although there is a general principle that treaty obligations should be observed (*PACTA SUNT SERVANDA*), *rebus sic stantibus* serves as an exception to that principle when performing the obligation would be too onerous to bear because of the changed conditions. Although renegotiating obligations is an acceptable response to essential changes, the principle is open to abuse by states wishing to relieve themselves of inconvenient treaty obligations.

reciprocal altruism theory   Concept from social psychology and evolutionary biology used to explain altruistic behavior among nonkin. A helps B so that B will help A in return at some point in the future.

Moreover, the theory provides an explanation for why such behavior would be favored by selection: to the degree that the benefits of helping nonkin equal or exceed the costs of helping, and to the degree that such benefits contribute to increased reproductive success, helping behavior should be selected [Gruter, 1991, p. 35]. This theory is compatible with theories of positive reciprocity derived from GAME THEORY.

reciprocity   Mutuality of action.

One of the most fundamental concepts in conflict resolution theory, reciprocity is used to explain a variety of behaviors in negotiation and decision making. Using iterated prisoners' dilemma games (see GAME THEORY,) Axelrod [1984] determined that reciprocity explains cooperative behavior. As the possibility for repeated encounters increases, so does the chance for reciprocal action by the players. This action can take the form of positive or negative reciprocity:

• *Positive Reciprocity:* Provision of reward to a person who has previously provided reward to oneself. The level of reward provided to the other person is a positive function of the level of reward previously received from her. Research indicates that this principle is a common element in human behavior (see REC-IPROCAL ALTRUISM THEORY). It is often associated with the GOLDEN RULE: "Do unto others as you would have them do unto you."

- *Negative Reciprocity:* Negative norm of reciprocity; may be defined in terms of two minimal demands: harm those who harm you, and do not help those who harm you. This normative demand to extract "an eye for an eye" requires a person to retaliate. This is a defensive norm that restricts the actor to making his response in proportion [Tedeschi and Bonoma, 1977, p. 228, citation omitted].

The promise of positive reciprocity and the threat of negative reciprocity work together to create incentives for cooperative behavior over time. However, if one or more of the players perceives little chance of repeat encounters, there is little incentive to cooperate.

A negotiation strategy associated with reciprocity is TIT-FOR-TAT, wherein a player attempts to encourage cooperative behavior by leading with a unilateral positive concession in expectation of a cooperative response (positive reciprocity). If the recipient defects, then the player responds with a defection (negative reciprocity). Haydock and Mitchell [1984, p. 95] observed that in the positional bargaining that typifies lawyer-to-lawyer negotiations, reciprocity usually produces a counteroffer because of a high expectation of sequential reciprocal concessions. Verbalizing this expectation of reciprocity may force a counteroffer: "We have made this concession; now it's your turn." Strategies based on reciprocity have several weaknesses. They are wholly reactive, being based on the other side's actual or anticipated responses. Additionally, the other side may not follow a unilateral positive concession, or the players can easily get stuck in a cycle of negative punishing moves.

International Relations: Principle wherein one country mirrors its law or policy to that of another country regarding matters of mutual concern. The concept is most often associated with mutual concessions in trade or other commercial interests granted by one country in exchange for special advantages granted to it by another nation, and with treaty reservations and the rights of foreign nationals.

recognition   *Mediation:* Evocation in individuals of acknowledgment and empathy for the situation and problems of others [Bush and Folger, 1994, p. 2]. In TRANSFORMATIVE MEDIATION, recognition and EMPOWERMENT are two crucial elements.

recognition clause   *Labor Relations:* Clause in a collective bargaining contract that states that the employer will bargain only with a particular union as the exclusive bargaining agent of the employees who have selected this union to represent them, subject to and in accordance with the provisions of law [DOA].

recommendation   Advice or suggestion for a course of action that the recipient is free to accept or reject.

Recommendation refers to techniques used by third parties to induce settlement. Although in certain processes the neutrals may be specifically empowered to make substantive recommendations—as in fact-finding, mini-trial, and early neutral evaluation—other neutrals, such as mediators and facilitators, are empowered to recommend procedures that may induce settlement. The nonbinding award in an advisory arbitration is sometimes referred to loosely as a *recommendation*. OMBUDS make recommendations for policy changes or other generic responses in order to reduce recurring problems. Attorneys recommend to their clients appropriate procedural means to achieve resolution or substantive terms for settlement.

International Relations: Nonbinding suggestions made by an international organization to promote PACIFIC SETTLEMENT of international disputes. Under the UN Charter, specified organs of the United Nations are empowered to make recommendations to induce settlement of disputes among states. Under Article 14, the General Assembly may use substantive or procedural measures for the pacific adjustment of any situation that seems likely to threaten friendly relations between states. The Security Council has similar powers to make specific recommendations under Articles 36(1) (procedures) and 37(2) (substantive terms) or in response to referral by the disputants [Articles 37(1) and 38]. Under Article 33(2), the Security Council may simply make general recommendations to use the existing means of pacific settlement listed in Article 33. Although the disputants are free to reject a recommendation, additional recommendations to other member states to intervene or create sanctions and other pressures may invoke compliance [David Davies Memorial Institute of International Studies, 1972, pp. 183, 184].

reconciliation   Renewal of applicable relations between persons who have been at variance. In animal behavior, refers to friendly reunions between the former opponents and implies a behavior that serves the function of restoring social relationships and reducing social tension due to aggressive incidences [de Waal, 1989]. Reconciliation implies the restoration of a relationship and therefore should be distinguished from SETTLEMENT or RESOLUTION. Contrast FORGIVENESS.

reconciliation room (Korea)   Room used for conciliation by the Korea Legal Aid Center for Family Relations and furnished as though it were an inner room of a typical Korean house.

The center is very conscious about the role of ambiance in conciliation, believing that this homelike room neutralizes power disparity and decreases the participants' anxieties [Pe, Sosmena, and Tadiar, 1988, p. 15].

recovery   Vindication of a right, amount awarded, or thing obtained through civil suit.

In the negotiation of legal disputes, the parties often focus on the expectation of recovery at trial. See BATNA, SHADOW OF THE LAW.

referee   Third party to whom a dispute is or may be referred for a decision; person appointed to exercise certain judicial powers to whom all or part of a legal dispute is referred by a court under the authority of a REFEREE SYSTEM; sometimes known as a JUDGE PRO TEM. See TRIAL ON ORDER OF REFERENCE, DISCOVERY REFEREE.

referee system   Authority and procedures established by constitutional or statutory provisions allowing a court to refer all or part of a matter before it to a special judge known as a REFEREE or JUDGE PRO TEM.

Generally not regular judicial officers, referees are appointed on an ad hoc basis to serve as an arm of the court. Some form of referee system exists in most states. Variations include the power to refer, the scope of matters that can be referred, and the legal effect of the referee's decision. In some states, courts are empowered to refer certain matters on their own motion, while in others referral takes place only on motion and agreement by the parties (see REFERRAL BY AGREEMENT). In several jurisdictions, the court can refer either the entire case or specific issues of law or fact (popularly known as RENT-A-JUDGE), while in other jurisdictions the scope of matters subject to referral is limited to procedural disputes, discovery matters, or complex evidentiary determinations, for example. Finally, the referee's determinations or orders may be binding subject to appeal to the referring court or to the appellate court (see TRIAL ON ORDER OF REFERENCE) or nonbinding either as a mere recommendation to the judge or as expert testimony admissible at subsequent trial.

referral, reference   Presentation of a matter to a referee or other authoritative third party for consideration. Technically, cases are referred by court order.

Court-connected: Diverting a case in litigation to mediation or some other court-connected ADR process, as in "the judge referred this case to mediation."

Mediation: When a mediator makes use of psychological, educational, medical, financial, or legal resources to facilitate the mediation process or the postresolution stage [Baker-Jackson and others, 1985, p. 69].

referral by agreement   Process available under a REFEREE SYSTEM whereby litigants, on a motion by a party and with the full agreement of the other party, submit specific issues of law, fact, or both to a special judge. The referral must include the parties' waiver of a jury trial on these issues. Additionally, the person named to hear the issues must agree to be the special judge. The hearing before the special judge is conducted just like a regular trial expect for the lack of a jury. A court reporter is present. The parties split all general trial costs and individually pay their own special costs, such as witness expenses. The resulting verdict stands as if decided by a trial court, with the right to appeal to an appellate court preserved. See, for example, Tex. Civ. Prac. Code § 151.001 et seq. (West 1993). Referral by agreement is distinguished from a referral made by the court under its own authority and without the mutual consent of the parties.

reframing   Technique of relabeling or redefining a particular concept or reality so as to give it a slightly different and more constructive perspective [Saposnek, 1983, p. 42]. A mediation technique that the mediator uses to recast conflictual issues in neutral terms [Van Slyck, Newland, and Stern, 1992, p. 196]. Other terms for the technique include *framing, characterizing, reconceptualizing,* or *redefining the issues in dispute* [Moore, 1986, p. 175, citations omitted]. See FRAMING.

regional organizations   International political and economic organizations composed of states sharing common resources or geographic interests. They provide important forums for preventing and settling disputes between member states through parliamentary and bilateral diplomacy.

reg-neg   See REGULATORY NEGOTIATION.

regulatory negotiation   Process of negotiating in any decision-making process by an administrative agency. In its more restricted and better-known sense, it is also known as NEGOTIATED RULEMAKING: "The process of creating a governmental regulation whereby all interested parties are represented at meetings at which all parties attempt to reach consensus on what form that particular rule should take. The supervisory agency has the final responsibility of issuing the rule" [5 U.S.C. § 562 (1993); 1 C.F.R. § 305.82-4(3) (1993)].

Regulatory negotiation is an alternative to the traditional rulemaking process in which government agencies draft a regulation, give notice and an opportunity for public comment, and then issue the regulation through publication. In the traditional process, affected parties often challenged the regulation in court, increasing the costs and delay in regulatory effect. Regulatory negotiation tries to avoid these problems and enhance fairness, speed, and legitimacy by involving potentially affected parties in drafting the regulations. Representatives of affected parties, with help from a neutral facilitator or mediator, negotiate over the rules.

Despite its intuitive attraction, regulatory negotiation is not a panacea. It can be time-consuming and expensive, particularly for nonprofit, public-interest, consumer, or environmental organizations with limited resources. Ultimately, the various constituencies have little power to restrain an individual constituent who objects to the negotiated rule and sues to enjoin its enforcement.

rehearing   To hold another hearing to reconsider a matter already heard. An adjudicative body may order a rehearing if important new evidence comes to light. In arbitration, a court order for a rehearing may result in a new arbitration before the same or different arbitrators and may occur when an award is wholly or partly vacated.

relational distance   Physical and psychological orientations that parties exhibit toward one another with respect to power, solidarity, formality, and attraction [Donohue and Ramesh, 1992, p. 219, citations omitted].
   Relational distance is determined through three parameters:

- *Role distance*: the power and solidarity of the disputants as they seek to establish their roles in the negotiation
- *Social distance*: the formality or informality of the relationship
- *Psychological distance*: the degree to which individuals like each other

The concept can be used to examine the interpersonal and communication dynamics of a negotiation relationship. The concept has also been used to explain why disputes that arise in relationships characterized by a high degree of mutual interdependence or ongoing interaction are ill-suited to litigation [Cavanagh and Sarat, 1980, p. 394].

release   Relinquishment of a claim or right to the party against whom the claim exists or against whom the right is to be enforced. A voluntary act, as opposed to one imposed by law. Releases are commonly negotiated as part of the settlement of legal disputes. Though a release can be unilateral, parties can also surrender all claims and defenses through a mutual release.

render   Officially announcing an adjudicative decision, as in "the arbitrators have rendered their award" or "the court has rendered judgment."

renegotiation   Negotiating again. Many types of contracts provide for renegotiation of their terms at the end of the contract period.

rent-a-judge   See TRIAL ON ORDER OF REFERENCE.

repeated-offer selection   Variation of FINAL-OFFER ARBITRATION where, after determining that selecting either party's offer would be grossly unfair, the arbitrator advises the parties that the offers are unacceptable and each should submit a new final offer [Baizley and Suche, 1986].

res judicata   *Law:* Legal principle under which a matter that has been settled by legal judgment on its merits cannot be subject to litigation again between the same parties. The principle also applies to matters decided by binding arbitration. Compare COLLATERAL ESTOPPEL.

reservation price   Party's minimum or maximum acceptable settlement price within a negotiation, depending on whether the negotiator is a seller or buyer, respectively.

The term was coined by Raiffa [1982] to replace the Walton and McKersie [1965] concept of RESISTANCE POINT when applying the CONTRACT ZONE model to noncollective bargaining negotiations. A negotiator's reservation price is influenced by his or her BATNA, while the ZONE OF AGREEMENT is the area between the parties' reservation prices. Thus the probability of settlement depends on the degree to which the parties' reservation prices overlap. Raiffa [1982, p. 46] states, "In the abstraction . . . each bargainer knows his or her reservation price, but has only probabilistic information about the other party's reservation price. Very often in practice the parties have but an imprecise feel for their own reservation price and make no formal attempt to assess a probability distribution of the other party's reservation price."

residual disagreement   Issue that remains unsettled despite an explicit agreement on most if not seemingly all of the matter. The residual disagreement can be *explicit* in that certain issues are marked "for future negotiation," *implicit* in the agreement's equivocal language, or *latent* if differences originally ignored or viewed as unimportant later turn into serious disputes [Iklé, 1964, p. 16].

residual principle   *Labor Arbitration:* Principle that anything regarding the operation of an agency or business that is not limited or forfeited by the contract or statute remains a right of management.

Arbitrators may limit the application of the residual principle if they find that past practice establishes unwritten contract rights for the union [Deitsch and Dilts, 1990, pp. 75–76].

residual rights   *Labor Relations:* Those powers that an employer has held in the past and that have not been reduced or eliminated by court decisions, statute, or the collective bargaining agreement [DOA]. See RESIDUAL PRINCIPLE.

resistance force   Force that deters concession making and must be overcome before a bargainer lowers her offer [Tutzauer, 1992, p. 74, citation omitted].

resistance point   *Negotiation:* Least favorable outcome that is needed to satisfy a negotiating party's constituency [White and Neale, 1991, p. 380].

Walton and McKersie [1965] are generally credited with articulating the concept and coining the term in their work on the application of the contract zone model to collective bargaining negotiations. See CONTRACT ZONE. Compare RESERVATION PRICE, BATNA.

resolution   Solution or the act of solving; determination or the act of determining; in music, causing discord to move to concord.

Commonly used, as in *conflict resolution* and *dispute resolution,* this is a problematic term. *Resolution* implies finality or conclusion, when in fact that may be neither desirable nor possible. Though determination of the matter by a third party is clearly an act of resolution within the meaning of the term, such determination may fall short of actually ending the dispute or the underlying conflict. A third-party determination may not be binding or may merely address the legal issues without solving the cause of the dispute (see later discussion distinguishing *resolution* from *settlement*). In cases of intractable or deep-seated conflict, the only degree of resolution possible may be temporary periods in which the disputants' interests are adjusted to be less directly opposed. For these reasons, the term CONFLICT MANAGEMENT may be preferable. Similarly, Felstiner [1974] favors *dispute processing* over *dispute resolution,* and Deng and Zartman [1991] favor *conflict reduction* over *conflict resolution.* Nevertheless, the term is common currency in the field, so rather than quibbling over its correct use, it may be preferable to adopt a meaning that implies transition rather than conclusion. Thus, *resolution* coupled with *conflict* or *dispute* indicates a range of transitional action that, as in its musical meaning, moves away from discord but may or may not reach pure harmony.

According to Holsti [1983], a conflict may be said to be resolved when all the parties freely accept a solution that satisfies the interests and needs underlying the conflict, when it does not sacrifice any party's important values, when it will not provoke repudiation of the solution even if the parties are in a position to do so later, when it meets the standards of justice and fairness, and when it is sufficiently advantageous to all the parties that it becomes self-supporting or self-enforcing.

Although resolution is commonly used interchangeably with SETTLEMENT, it is useful to distinguish the terms. Though a settlement may put an end to a DISPUTE, it may not resolve or even alter the underlying CONFLICT giving rise to the dispute. See CONFLICT MANAGEMENT, CONFLICT REDUCTION, CONFLICT RESOLUTION, CONFLICT SETTLEMENT, DISPUTE PROCESSING, DISPUTE RESOLUTION, for examples of the distinction. Compare RECONCILIATION.

Legislation: Formal declaration of a legislature or other public body as voted on and adopted by that body. In this sense, a resolution is not enforceable law but rather an expression of will or a statement of opinion of the adopting body.

respondent   *Arbitration:* Adverse party who receives from the claimant a notice of intention to arbitrate.

responsive listening   Listening technique using head nods, eye contact, PARA-PHRASING, and other verbal and nonverbal signals to indicate to the speaker that she is being heard and to induce continued communication. See LISTEN. Compare ACTIVE LISTENING, DIALOGIC LISTENING, EMPATHIC LISTENING.

restorative justice   Criminal justice concept that views crime as a violation of people, not as a violation of the state, and creates an obligation to the victim and to the community to make things right. It focuses on the crime's harm rather than on the broken rule and emphasizes redress for the victim and the community for the effects of the wrongdoing over punishment imposed by the state. Restorative justice models may provide for appropriate dialogue, direct or indirect, between the victim and offender in the form of VICTIM-OFFENDER ME-DIATION. See BALANCED AND RESTORATIVE JUSTICE, JUST.

restricted arbitration clause   Agreement to arbitrate that limits the arbitrabil-ity of certain issues, as in "X and Y are not arbitrable," as compared to a NAR-ROW ARBITRATION CLAUSE, which makes only certain issues arbitrable, as in "Only X and Y are to be arbitrated." Contrast BROAD ARBITRATION CLAUSE, as in "Any and all disputes or claims arising shall be arbitrated."

rigged award   See AGREED AWARD.

rights arbitration   See GRIEVANCE ARBITRATION. Contrast INTEREST ARBITRATION.

ripeness   The extent to which circumstances are conducive for change.
   A metaphorical way to refer to timing when undertaking an effort to negoti-ate. If the situation is not ripe, there is insufficient motivation to bring about a settlement and the negotiation process is likely to fail. If the situation is too ripe, the parties may be too deeply entrenched to reach agreement. Prerequisites of ripeness include realization by the parties that in the absence of an agreement, time does not work in their favor; sufficient authority for a negotiator to com-promise; and a mutually acceptable process [Haass, 1988, pp. 232–251].

risk aversion   Degree to which a person dislikes or is unwilling to accept the possibility of suffering a loss.
   Described in the context of a game of chance, the risk-averse player will ac-cept less than the *expected value* of the gamble in lieu of playing the game; that is, given a fifty-fifty chance at $10, a risk-averse player will accept something

less than $5 in lieu of playing the game. The degree of risk aversion is reflected in the level of discount the player is willing to accept [Kritzer, 1991, p. 166]. In negotiation, a risk-averse person would accept less than might be gained outside of negotiation, such as in litigation, rather than risk an unfavorable jury verdict. A person with little or no risk aversion would be willing to reject any offer that does not approach or equal the expected value obtainable in a non-negotiated solution. Compare RISK PREFERENCE.

risk preference   Degree to which a person is willing to accept the possibility of suffering a loss.

A party could be risk neutral, risk averse, or risk prone depending on how they rank their options. A *risk-neutral* party ranks options in order of their expected values, without adjustment for subjective preferences favoring one more than another. A *risk-averse* party prefers an option with a lower expected value because of the higher risk (stakes or uncertainty) involved with the other choices. A *risk-prone* party prefers those options that include more risk [Murray, Rau, and Sherman, 1989, p. 143].

Applying the concept in negotiation, a risk preferrer would demand a premium to settle in lieu of the expected value to be possibly gained outside of a negotiated agreement. Compare RISK AVERSION.

rival   One of two or more parties who are seeking to possess something that only one can have.

role reversal   Negotiation technique in which one party tries to conceive of the dispute from another party's perspective. Sometimes called *flip side.*

The technique is associated with PROBLEM SOLVING and other cooperative or collaborative negotiation styles. It may be used in preparation as an exercise to gain insight into the other side's interests and their perceived barriers to agreement. During interactive phases of negotiation, a party or a third party, such as a mediator, may initiate the exercise to encourage cooperation. It involves stating the opponent's case as clearly as possible to the opponent's satisfaction, exploring the areas of agreement in the opponent's position, identifying acceptable principles and criteria of validity, and inducing assumptions of similarity in background and values (empathy) [Hopmann, 1991, p. 282, citing Rapoport's (1988) formulation].

Roster of Neutrals   Name for the former AMERICAN ARBITRATION ASSOCIATION's Panel of Neutrals, effective July 1, 1996; a list of people who have qualified to serve as arbitrators, mediators, fact-finders, and so forth through the AAA.

rotating panels   List of arbitrators in a COLLECTIVE BARGAINING AGREEMENT that is drawn up to function on a rotating basis for the life of the contract. See PERMANENT ARBITRATIONS.

The number of names in a rotating panel varies from three to five, with alternates to be used if necessary. These are variously called *contract arbitrators* or *rotating panels*. By such means, parties to a contract are able to expedite their arbitration caseload and take advantage at the same time of the benefits of a permanent arbitrator [DOA].

rule   Prescribed guide or general standard for conduct; a determination by a court or by a provision of law, legal doctrine, or precept.

Rule 16: judicial promotion of settlement   Rule of procedure in federal civil litigation that authorizes a judge to meet formally with the litigants' attorneys before trial so she can help manage, conduct, and dispose of the case efficiently and appropriately. Many states have adopted similar rules.

Pretrial conferences may be used by the judge and the parties to, among other purposes, explore "the possibility of settlement or the use of extrajudicial procedures to resolve the dispute" [(c)(7)]. In settlement negotiations, a federal judge or other judicially authorized officer may attempt to facilitate a settlement in much the same way as a mediator.

After any Rule 16 pretrial conference, the judge issues a pretrial order reciting any action to be taken [(f)]. If a party or her attorney disobeys a pretrial order, does not appear at a pretrial conference, is unprepared for the conference, or does not participate in good faith, the judge may issue remedial orders as she feels necessary and just. Also, the party, her attorney, or both will be liable for "the reasonable expenses incurred because of any noncompliance . . . including attorney's fees, unless the judge finds that the noncompliance was substantially justified or that other circumstances make an award of expenses unjust" [(f)].

Rule 68: offer of settlement   Rule of procedure in federal civil litigation that encourages and provides a procedure for parties in a lawsuit to initiate and negotiate settlement of their case. Many states and the District of Columbia have similar rules.

Under Rule 68, any defendant may offer to settle with a plaintiff at any time more than ten days before the trial date. The offer must specify monetary and nonmonetary relief for the plaintiff's claims and costs that the defendant is willing to pay. The plaintiff may accept or reject the defendant's offer. If the plaintiff accepts, the case will be deemed resolved as between that plaintiff and that defendant. If the plaintiff rejects the offer and wins a judgment that is not more favorable than the defendant's settlement offer, the plaintiff must pay the costs the defendant incurred after she made the offer. If the plaintiff wins a judgment that is more favorable than the defendant's offer, or wins nothing, or if the defendant's offer was in bad faith, the parties are bound by the judgment alone.

Rule 408: confidentiality of information Rule of evidence in federal civil litigation that prohibits certain information disclosed during settlement negotiations from being used against the disclosing party if negotiations break down and the dispute goes to trial. The rule encourages settlement by offering parties some protection for their frank communications and is presumed to extend over mediation.

The rule excludes from evidence offers to compromise and conduct, or statements made in compromise negotiations when they are used "to prove liability for or invalidity of the claim or its amount." The information revealed, however, may be offered as evidence for some other purpose, such as to prove bias or prejudice of a witness.

The rule may be invoked only in the trial phase of litigation to bar inclusion as evidence, and only by the participants in the negotiation or mediation who are parties to the litigation. It does not apply in administrative or legislative hearings or in the discovery phase of litigation, and it imposes no duty to keep information revealed in negotiation or mediation confidential. Most states have adopted similar rules.

ruling *Law:* Interpretation of law made by adjudicator to decide a substantive or procedural issue. A court can rule, for example, that a law does not apply to the particular case or that a piece of evidence is admissible. Unlike a legal JUDGMENT, which disposes of the case before the court, a ruling does not necessarily dispose of the case although a "final" ruling would. Also contrast a judicial OPINION, which sets out the reasons for the ruling.

saints (Pakistan)   In the Swat valley of Pakistan, religious leaders who serve as mediators, occasionally calling upon armed followers to reinforce their authority through military means in the event of noncooperation [Barth, 1959].

salami tactics   *Negotiation:* Offensive strategy of asking for what amounts to major concessions in small parts, "slice by slice."

A defensive party can accuse the opposition of salami tactics as an excuse to deny small concessions, claiming that a minor request, if met, will be followed by a slew of others—that giving in to one slice is in effect surrendering to the slicing process [Iklé, 1964, pp. 83–84]. Compare NIBBLER.

Samoan circle   Meeting facilitation technique to manage discussion of controversial or complex issues by a large number of people.

The technique involves a single table with a limited number of chairs, four to six, for example. All participants are seated in concentric circles around the table. If someone wishes to speak or make any comment or verbal expression, they must sit in one of the chairs at the table. If the chairs are full, participants must stand near the table until a chair is vacated.

This is a method of exchanging facts, perspectives, and other information about a problem rather than a method of dispute resolution. It may also serve to allow people to vent their emotions about an issue in public, allowing for some catharsis. It may or may not be facilitated. It seems particularly useful, however, when a facilitator or mediator is not available or cannot be agreed upon by the parties.

sanction Penalty for disobeying (*negative sanction*) or reward for obeying (*positive sanction*) a law, regulation, or custom. Prior to an offense, the threat of sanctions serves both to deter noncompliance and to encourage compliance. After an offense, however, negative sanctions serve to punish, to persuade the actor to return to compliance, and to discourage further noncompliance.

International Relations: Unilateral action by a single state or a collective effort of states to force an offending state to comply with international law or to punish a state for treaty violations. Usually states revert to sanctions only when other diplomatic techniques fail, because without an international enforcement mechanism such as a police force, participating states must accept a military or economic burden. Effective nonmilitary sanctions often involve areas of mutual interdependence. Sanctions will fail if there is inadequate collective will or if the penalty imposes greater hardships on the participating states than on the offending state [Doxey, 1987].

Law: Most commonly, penalties meted out by a court as a consequence of failure to follow court orders or to engage in proper conduct in the context of litigation. The power to impose sanctions is usually explicit in applicable law.

saving face See FACE.

***Schiedsstellen* (German)** *Consumer:* Literally, conciliation boards. In Germany, special boards created by trade, business, or professional associations to cope with customer claims and balance consumer-provider interests.

Schiedsstellen generally include an expert in the relevant field, as well as other employees of the association. So far, they have been most prominent within small to medium-sized enterprises, the building trade, and such white-collar professions as architecture, law, and medicine [Eidmann and Plett, 1991].

Also called SCHLICHTUNGSSTELLEN.

***Schlichtungsstellen* (German)** See SCHIEDSSTELLEN.

***Schoeffen* (German)** People chosen from the German community of the thirteenth and fourteenth centuries who were considered worthy of trust and qualified to make decisions concerning the law, thus functioning very much like modern arbitrators.

The *Schoeffen* were permanent officers of good repute and influence who were required to be selected from the landowning class. These early arbitrators sat in groups of perhaps seven to fifteen. Later the *Schoeffen* evolved into a secret and almost inquisitorial society, delivering decisions and penalties that marked these private judges as full of pride, believing as they did that they represented the highest court in the world. They created such a delusive law unto themselves that they soon withered and exhausted their usefulness [DOA].

school-based mediation   Mediation program within a school, usually PEER MEDIATION, in which a student serves as a neutral third party in helping fellow students resolve their own conflicts [Davis, 1986a; 1986b]. Although the term could cover any variety of mediation processes based in the schools, it is used mainly in reference to peer mediation in the elementary and secondary schools.

scientific reviewer   In disputes over awards of federal research grants, professional with expertise in the relevant scientific or technical field who objectively reviews the contested proposal [48 C.F.R. § 935.016-3 (1992)].

scope of the arbitration agreement   Number and extent of issues, as specifically outlined in the arbitration agreement, that can be referred to arbitration in case of a dispute.

A BROAD ARBITRATION CLAUSE is drafted so as to include "any controversy or claim arising out of or relating to this contract, or the breach thereof." A RESTRICTED ARBITRATION CLAUSE limits the arbitrability of some issues. A NARROW ARBITRATION CLAUSE severely restricts the arbitrability to only certain issues and may include only that which would relate to the validity, interpretation, or performance of the agreement itself.

Seabed Disputes Chamber   *International Relations:* Special body subordinate to the INTERNATIONAL TRIBUNAL OF THE LAW OF THE SEA to resolve disputes between nations and other entities that involve activities in the international seabed, such as mineral exploitation [U.N. Convention on the Law of the Sea (1982), arts. 186–191, 285; Annex VI, arts. 35–40].

search model   Set of criteria that a decision maker can use to screen settlement options. In COLLABORATIVE PROBLEM SOLVING, negotiators who agree on the criteria that their joint decision must meet, that is, on their search model, may more easily engage in a joint search for a solution [Brett, 1991, p. 305, citation omitted]. Compare OBJECTIVE CRITERIA.

second agreement   *Negotiation:* Agreement that is superior to the parties' first agreement.

After parties reach agreement, they may be able to improve on the agreement by continuing to deliberate. Improvement might be gauged by the degree to which the second agreement meets the parties' interests better than the first does, or fulfills a more broadly accepted norm. First agreements may be driven by the majority or by the more powerful parties and reached hastily before all views are shared, assumptions tested, and consequences considered. Better alternatives and a more durable consensus may be possible in a second agreement [Brett, 1991, p. 294].

second-tier negotiation   *Negotiation:* Most common form of STEP NEGOTIA-TION, involving only one level of referral up the organizational hierarchy for negotiation.

The first tier consists of negotiations among those closest to the dispute; if they cannot agree, the matter is then referred to the second-tier negotiators, who are at least one level higher in the disputing organizations.

International Relations: Form of negotiation established in the Canada-U.S. FREE TRADE AGREEMENT. Article 1804 requires notification for any proposed measure that a party believes will materially affect the operation of the treaty. Then a consultation is held in which the parties are to make every attempt to arrive at a mutually satisfactory resolution. The treaty does not state, however, who is to conduct the consultation or whether it is to be referred to an authority that is necessarily higher if the dispute proceeds to the next stage. If the parties fail to resolve the dispute within thirty days of a request for a consultation, either party may call for a meeting of the Commission, a body established by the treaty and composed of representatives of both countries (principally the cabinet-level ministers or officers responsible for international trade or their designees). The Commission's purpose is to supervise the implementation of the agreement, to resolve disputes that arise over its interpretation and application, and to consider any other matter that may affect its operation. If a dispute referred to the Commission has not been resolved within thirty days, the Commission may refer the matter to binding arbitration on the terms the Commission chooses to adopt [Bernier and Lapointe, 1990–1993, pp. 432–435].

securities arbitration   Arbitration of disputes involving securities.

Although any parties involved in a dispute over stocks, bonds, and other securities may voluntarily agree to resolve the dispute through arbitration, the term has become associated with arbitration between brokerage companies and their customers. After the U.S. Supreme Court's landmark decision in *Shearson/ American Express, Inc.* v. *McMahon* (1987), which enforced arbitration agreements involving federal securities fraud claims, such clauses have become standard BOILERPLATE in most engagement agreements with brokerage companies. Many SELF-REGULATORY ORGANIZATIONS in the securities industry, such as the New York Stock Exchange, and trade associations, such as the NATIONAL ASSO-CIATION OF SECURITIES DEALERS, are named as the exclusive ADMINISTERING AGENCY for the resolution of customer claims.

Security Council *International Relations:* UN organ with specific powers to investigate disputes, to appoint subsidiary organs, and under certain conditions, to act as a conciliatory body itself. The council has the power to recommend terms of settlement for disputes referred to it under Article 37 of the UN Charter.

seed arbitration Arbitration, usually required by statute, for disputes between vendors and purchasers of seeds. Statutory definitions include the following: "A non-binding process, which is mandatory for any purchaser of seed before being allowed to proceed to court action, whereby a third party hears evidence of both disputants and makes a finding as to its belief of the proper resolution" [710 Ill. Comp. Stat. Ann. 25/1-25-80 (West 1992)].
This form of arbitration has a long historical precedent in commodities trade associations.

self-executing agreement Agreement the execution of which requires no affirmative action by a party.
Arbitration: Clause that allows the arbitration to take place despite the refusal of a party to cooperate or participate. An arbitration clause incorporating the American Arbitration Association's arbitration rules is self-executing because it empowers the administering agency to appoint an arbitrator when a party refuses to make an appointment.
International Relations: Agreement, such as a treaty, that needs no enabling domestic legislation to function.

self-executing commitment procedures Term used by Moore [1986, p. 254] to describe mostly informal activities initiated by the mediator or the negotiators that enhance subsequent compliance with the settlement. Examples include private oral exchanges of promises in front of the mediator or authority figures, public declaration of promises, symbolic gestures of friendship, and both formal and informal written agreements.

self-help Strategy of taking unilateral and direct action to achieve one's goals and objectives.
Self-help includes various forms of direct action, such as taking or retaining possession of property as well as physical retaliation, overt or covert [Galanter, 1984, p. 168]. Some forms of self-help rely on public institutions. For example, in response to the neighbor's dog escaping its pen and digging up your garden you could call the dog catcher or initiate a civil action in court. Resort to courts is a limited, legalistic form of self-help. It serves, however, as an alternative to the many forms of self-help constrained by law, such as physical violence, threats, and so on. Many forms of self-help, however, do not rely on social institutions

and are legal, for example, chasing the dog off your property or putting a fence around your garden. Available and acceptable forms of self-help may differ significantly in different cultures.

Marshall [1985, p. 28] defines self-help as "the simplest level of settlement, the purely private, [which] consists of the case where a person takes action on his/her own to put things to rights." While noting that other authorities differ, his definition excludes AVOIDANCE, which involves not SETTLEMENT but rather withdrawal from the relationship or a decision not to address the conflict.

Self-help is most effective when achieving an objective does not rely on the actions of others, either because there is no interdependence involved or because the actor has sufficient power to achieve the desired result without or in spite of the actions of others. Self-help is more efficient when the costs of achieving the objective through alternatives such as avoidance or negotiation exceed the costs of self-help.

self-presentation   *Negotiation:* Presentation, explanation, and justification of one's own position.

Parties to a negotiation who focus unduly on self-presentation may be perceived as more interested in reaping as many personal benefits as possible from the process than in trying to identify a mutually acceptable solution [Walcott, Hopmann, and King, 1977, p. 194].

self-regulatory organization (SRO)   Organization allowed by the state to police or discipline its members through application of its own private regulations, especially stock and commodities exchanges. The legal definition is as follows: "any national securities exchange, registered securities association, or registered clearing agency, or . . . the Municipal Securities Rulemaking Board. . . ." [§ 2(3) of the 1934 Securities Exchange Act of 1934; 15 U.S.C. § 78b].

Federal law regarding securities regulation provides for the institution of SROs to regulate the business of securities underwriting and sales by broker-dealers as well as to provide oversight of the securities markets. While the Securities and Exchange Commission has ultimate veto power over any rules or rulings of the SROs, as a practical matter the SROs perform the bulk of day-to-day regulation. By virtue of Section 15A of the 1934 Act, the NATIONAL ASSOCIATION OF SECURITIES DEALERS (NASD) has primary authority over broker-dealers and their employees [15 U.S.C. § 78o]. In addition, the national and regional securities markets, such as the New York Stock Exchange, the American Stock Exchange, and the Chicago Board Options Exchange, among others, are registered as SROs under Section 6 of the 1934 Act [15 U.S.C. § 78f]. Each self-regulatory organization has the obligation to police its members to ensure compliance with its rules and regulations. Each body has its own set of arbitration rules. See, for example, the NASD Manual (CCH) ¶¶ 3712–3720; the New York Stock Exchange

Guide (CCH) ¶¶ 4311–4317; and the American Stock Exchange Guide (CCH) ¶¶ 9540–9575.

Section 28(b) of the 1934 Act specifically states that, as between members of the SROs, nothing in the act shall be construed so as to limit arbitrability of securities-related claims [15 U.S.C. § 78bb(b)]. The courts have confirmed that claims between members of the SROs, such as between a broker and his employer or between broker-dealers, are arbitrable. The 1934 act makes claims between members of the Municipal Securities Rulemaking Board specifically arbitrable [15 U.S.C. § 78o-4(b)(2)].

Brokers, also known as *registered representatives,* sign contracts as part of their registration with the SRO, subjecting all disputes arising either between themselves and their employer or between themselves and a customer to binding arbitration under the rules of the appropriate SRO. Disputes between registered representatives and their employers that are subject to arbitration under the general arbitration clause include issues of compensation, responsibility for customer losses, right to work-product, enforceability of contracts not to compete, unjust termination, sexual harassment, and discrimination.

In *Shearson/American Express, Inc.* v. *McMahon* (1987), the U.S. Supreme Court held that claims under the Securities Exchange Act were arbitrable. Since this decision, arbitration clauses have been included in most brokerage contracts with customers. Thus customer claims for churning, misappropriation, or other fraud, are subject to mandatory arbitration. As stated earlier, the SROs require their registered representatives to arbitrate all claims regarding customers. Although many brokerage contracts allow the customer to select a forum from among the various SROs in which to have his claim arbitrated, few provide the nonindustry-related American Arbitration Association as an option. See SECURITIES ARBITRATION, NYSE, NASD.

sentencing circles   Process in which victims, offenders, their families, and representatives of the community use peacemaking, mediation, and consensus-building techniques to deal with serious crimes. Pioneered and used primarily by aboriginal (or First Nations) peoples in Canada. Contains elements of RESTORATIVE JUSTICE. Compare FAMILY GROUP CONFERENCE.

separability doctrine   *Arbitration:* Principle that an arbitration clause is an agreement separate and apart from the contract in which it appears [DOA]. Also known as SEVERABILITY.

separation   Reframing technique whereby a negotiator or mediator divides an idea or issue into smaller component parts in order to make a seemingly intractable or unwieldy dispute more manageable [Moore, 1986, p. 169]. See FRACTIONING, REFRAMING.

settlement   Agreement or arrangement ending a dispute.

Although settlement is commonly used interchangeably with RESOLUTION, it is useful to distinguish the terms. Though a settlement may put an end to a DISPUTE, it may not resolve or even alter the underlying CONFLICT. See CONFLICT MANAGEMENT, CONFLICT REDUCTION, CONFLICT RESOLUTION, CONFLICT SETTLEMENT, DISPUTE PROCESSING, DISPUTE RESOLUTION for examples of the distinction.

Settlement may by imposed by an external party or intervening force, such as a court or police. A binding decision by a court is sometimes referred to as a *settlement,* or more accurately, as a JUDICIAL SETTLEMENT. At a minimum, settlement requires that the disputants accept, however reluctantly, some solution and refrain from further disputing on the matter settled. A court decision is effective in settling a dispute only to the extent that the parties accept the competence and legitimacy of the court in determining the matter [Azar and Burton, 1986, pp. 153, 154].

settlement brochure   Document, often with pictures, outlining proposed terms of settlement and their justifications. Commonly used in lawyer-to-lawyer negotiations in personal injury claims.

As a negotiating tactic, settlement brochures create auras of legitimacy. A brochure enables a party to establish a highly principled initial position to bolster his confidence and to force his opponent to argue from the document [Craver, 1993, p. 176–177].

settlement conference   Broad term covering a variety of court-connected procedures designed to encourage the settlement of civil suits before adjudication.

Definitions vary considerably. One authority defines *settlement conference* as "a judicially supervised procedure in the litigation which combines elements of mediation, evaluation and negotiation to achieve the end of a lawsuit by agreeing to a compromise and settlement" [Conn, 1988, p. 1]. One legal definition more closely resembles that of CASE EVALUATION: "An informal assessment and negotiation session conducted by a legal professional who hears both sides of the case and may advise the parties on the law and precedent relating to the dispute and suggest a settlement" [Colo. Rev. Stat. Ann. § 13-22-302(4.3) (West 1996)].

Settlement conferences can be provided by court rule, ordered by the court, or merely coerced by a judge. In many jurisdictions, unassisted pretrial settlement conferences are required by court rule as a condition precedent to trial. A judge or other court official may or may not supervise or facilitate the discussions. If a judge or federal magistrate is directly involved in the negotiation, it is technically more accurate to refer to the process as a JUDICIAL SETTLEMENT CONFERENCE. However, settlement conferences may not involve assistance by a third party.

settlement judge   In the broadest sense, judicial officer assigned to promote settlement of a lawsuit. Some jurisdictions have experimented with assigning a special settlement judge to facilitate settlement discussions and insulate the actual trial judge from settlement activities and from any possible bias resulting from his participation in them.

Administrative Law: Administrative law judge appointed by the chief administrative law judge to conduct settlement negotiations. The settlement judge convenes and presides over the conferences and settlement negotiations and assesses the practicalities of a potential settlement. He may also recommend to the chief administrative law judge whether to terminate or continue the settlement negotiations [18 C.F.R. § 385.603 (1993)].

In slang, the term refers to a judge who has a reputation for coercing or cajoling parties into settlement.

settlement range   Field of options, any one of which the disputants would prefer over the consequences of ceasing negotiations. Often referred to as the BARGAINING RANGE when applied to options generated by positional bargaining [Moore, 1986, p. 219]. Related terms: BARGAINING SET, CONTRACT ZONE, ZONE OF AGREEMENT.

settlement week   Period when judges suspend their trial calendars and, in cooperation with volunteers from the local bars, concentrate on settling cases.

Settlement week began as a mechanism to reduce court congestion in Orange County, California, in the late 1970s. In 1986, the bar and courts in Columbus, Ohio, borrowed the idea and added their own concepts to create a program that has been modeled around the country. Ohio's Settlement Week includes the following interdependent concepts: (1) full or partial trial moratorium, (2) mediation, (3) mediation training, (4) bench-bar cooperation, and (5) effective timing [Paddock, 1990]. Although Ohio focuses on the use of mediation, other courts that have experimented with settlement weeks have engaged a combination of court-connected ADR processes. The success of settlement weeks depends on numerous factors, including the commitment of the judges and court administrators, an effective method of determining which cases should be routed to which processes, and the quality of the volunteer bar members serving as neutrals [see Woodward, 1990]. Note that some settlement weeks have been held for less than a week and without the suspension of trial calendars. Sometimes referred to as DISPUTE RESOLUTION WEEK.

severability   See SEPARABILITY DOCTRINE.

shadow bargain   Bargain achieved through SHADOW BARGAINING. "Side" deal, secret agreement between one side and a representative of the other that may be but not always is unbeknownst to that representative's team members and is sometimes detrimental to their common cause.

The term also denotes an unmediated, unsupervised, yet fair negotiation that some hold as the measure of success for ADR. It is often measured as the expected value of a litigated outcome (probability of winning multiplied by the likely award) [Luban, 1989, pp. 389–390].

shadow bargaining   Occurs when one or more members of a negotiating team informally, and possibly privately, explore alternatives for settlement with members of another team.

Shadow bargaining can occur with the full knowledge of the team to promote more fruitful full-team bargaining. Usually this is done by moderates or quasi-mediators who identify and approach an individual from the other team who is similarly moderate or has commonality. Shadow bargaining can also occur covertly, without the knowledge of other team members and for the sole benefit of one or more team members at the expense of the whole team, a wider constituency, or the organization at large. Shadow bargainers can come from outside the team—for example, high-level executives from the disputing companies [Colosi and Berkeley, 1986]. Compare *unilateral vested interest bargaining* under BARGAINING.

shadow mediation   When a mediator participates in the arbitration process as an observer until such time as the parties agree to suspend the arbitration and attempt mediation.

The AMERICAN ARBITRATION ASSOCIATION's Orlando office experimented with the concept and coined the term. Although parties may not be prepared initially to submit to mediation, they may be willing to allow a mediator to "shadow" the arbitral proceedings. During the course of these proceedings, the parties may reconsider the possibility of negotiated settlement or the mediator may convince them that there is such a possibility. If they engage the mediator at that point, the mediator is already familiar with the dispute. Obviously this may be more important in complex, technical disputes where the stakes are sufficient to merit the additional cost of a shadow mediator who may not be used.

Compare *standby conciliator* under CONCILIATOR.

shadow of the law   See IN THE SHADOW OF THE LAW.

shadow verdict   Anticipated result of a trial; baseline against which some parties measure an ADR outcome to determine its acceptability. The use of shadow verdicts presupposes the moral significance of legal norms [Luban, 1989, pp. 387–388]. Compare IN THE SHADOW OF THE LAW, SHADOW BARGAIN.

shake up the game board   Technique for overcoming impasse wherein a mediator tries to get the disputants to look at and attack the problem from a different perspective.

Described as throwing the game pieces in the air and starting over again. It requires the mediator to keep track of the avenues the parties have been traveling in their attempt to settle the case and to suggest that another route might provide settlement [Erikson and McKnight Erikson, 1988, p. 202; Prather, 1990, p. 58].

shalish **(Southeast Asia)**   Group of village elders who served as traditional dispute resolvers in the area of present-day Bangladesh. Somewhat similar to the village PANCHAYATS of rural Nepal and India, the *shalish* engaged in conciliatory activities but had the power to make decisions that were enforced by social coercion and usually obeyed.

Colonial rule neither integrated nor reinforced the *shalish*. The institution deteriorated because outcomes were influenced by local elites and village politics. The *shalish* became a divisive factor in rural society in Bangladesh and raised issues of individual justice. Successful institutionalization of local courts further undermined the institution.

Recent discontent with the court system because of growing delay, expense, and frustration, coupled with a nostalgia for self-government, has made some quarters in Bangladesh call for village autonomy and its concomitant dispute-resolving processes as alternatives to the judicial machinery [Pe, Sosmena, and Tadiar, 1988, pp. 24–25, 32].

share bargaining   Process by which opponents share or ration the SETTLEMENT RANGE between themselves. If one party gets more, the other gets less [Karrass, 1970, p. 66]. Compare *distributive bargaining* under BARGAINING.

Shariah Council   Arbitration panel created in 1994 by Montreal Muslim leaders to provide a forum in which disputes among the Muslim community could by resolved according to Islamic law [WAMR, 5(3)], or *Shariah*.

shuo ho ti **(China)**   "One who talks harmony." Mediator responsible for promoting societal harmony. Such a mediator fine-tunes harmony instead of imposing it and is expected to speak for society, to serve as moral force, and to advise people on their legal obligations as well as the consequences of their behavior [Wall and Blum, 1991, p. 19, citation omitted]. See CHINESE MEDIATION.

shuttle diplomacy   *Negotiation:* Technique in which an intermediary shuttles back and forth between the disputants to lower hostilities or reach agreement. Avoiding direct contact between the disputants overcomes impediments to direct negotiation, such as the need to save face. Although best known in international dispute resolution, the term is also used by mediators and ombudsmen to describe analogous third-party techniques.

side bar   *Negotiation:* Unassisted negotiation among negotiation team members either out of the presence of the other side or in their presence but without their participation. See INTERNAL BARGAINING.

Mediation: Private meeting with the mediator and out of hearing of other participants [Feuille, 1992, p. 138]. Same as CAUCUS.

Also denotes private meeting between one or more principals with or without the mediator. Distinguished from caucus by the absence of the parties' negotiating representatives, lawyers, or committees. Introduced by mediators as an impasse-breaking strategy when direct negotiation and caucuses fail to produce movement on basic issues. Maggiolo [1985, p. 155] notes that once the principals are freed from the need to maintain a bargaining-table facade, they frequently take on more constructive roles and enter into more candid discussion toward mutual accommodation and problem solving.

Law/Litigation: Position beside the judge's bench where the trial counsel and the judge discuss matters out of the jury's hearing.

Silver Rule   In GAME THEORY, equivalent to TIT-FOR-TAT.

Players start out constructively (Golden Rule: do unto others) but make subsequent moves by mirroring the other player, such as by being nice to begin with and responding to niceness with niceness, but answering meanness with meanness.

See TIT-FOR-TAT, GOLDEN RULE, BRASS RULE.

simulation   Imitated or artificial conditions created for learning, experimentation, evaluation, or prediction.

Device containing the central features of reality in order to arrive at the best or most feasible solution to a problem [Nagel and Mills, 1991, p. 145]. According to Morley and Stephenson [1977, pp. 42–43], there are at least two types of simulation. The first requires an explicit and precise imitation of the system or reality to be imitated and would be developed to test assumptions about the simulated system. The second incorporates only the essential aspects of the task situation and thus provides a simple experimental analogue of a more complex real-life task. It is hoped that the behavior observed in the simulated system will replicate behavior that is harder to observe in the referent system, so that the study of the former can to some extent be substituted for the study of the latter. The gaming simulation of negotiation behavior involves simulation in this second sense.

single negotiating text (SNT) *Negotiation:* Facilitation technique in which a draft of an agreement written by a third party is subsequently criticized by the parties but not evaluated or accepted. The third party then revises the draft in light of the criticisms and repeats the process until he believes the document has been improved as much as possible, at which point the negotiating parties decide for or against the document as a whole.

Also called *one-text document.* See ONE TEXT METHOD.

small claims court Special court of limited jurisdiction that handles civil disputes involving small monetary amounts. Known for their cheap, fast, and informal adjudication, small claims courts have also been called *conciliation courts* (not to be confused with CONCILIATION COURTS that handle family matters), and in civil law, *courts of reconciliation.*

The small claims court model initially adopted in the United States included six major components: low court costs, simplified pleadings, informality (no rules of evidence), discretionary trial procedure, preparation and presentation help for litigants to eliminate their need for attorneys, and the power to direct installment payment of judgments [Weller, Ruhnka, and Martin, 1990; Whelan, 1990].

social conflict Term used by sociologists and social psychologists to denote a broad range of conflict situations—dyadic, multiparty, and intergroup. Examples include the following:

- "When two or more persons or groups manifest the belief that they have incompatible objectives" [Kreisberg, 1998b, p. 2].
- "The intentional mutual exchange of negative sanctions, or punitive behaviors, by two or more parties" [Blalock, 1989, p. 7].
- "A struggle over values and claims to scarce status, power and resources in which the aims of the opponents are to neutralize, injure or eliminate their rivals" [Coser, 1956, p. 8].

Although Coser and Blalock's definitions include means by which the parties might respond to conflict, particularly violent means, Kreisberg and others [Pruitt and Zubin, 1986, for example] focus on the awareness or perception of incompatible goals or divergent interests, thereby leaving open the possibility that the parties may or may not be in actual competition, that the conflict could resolve though adjustments in perceptions, and that they could employ noncoercive as well as coercive means of resolution. Generally these authorities do not distinguish CONFLICT from DISPUTE as an expression of conflict. Kreisberg's definition limits conflict to those situations in which the parties are aware of incompatible objectives [1998b, p. 7, citation omitted].

In many respects, the term differs little from the way in which many authorities use *conflict,* leaving the addition of *social* as an indication of the user's academic discipline and predominant analytical thrust.

social dilemma   From GAME THEORY, situation that presents a conflict between the pursuit of one's individual gain and the pursuit of the welfare of one's group.

The individual must decide whether to cooperate to maintain a public good, or to defect to achieve individual gain at the expense of the group. Other terms are *collective action dilemma* and *n-person prisoner's dilemma.* An example of a social dilemma is found in the familiar problem called TRAGEDY OF THE COMMONS.

social distance   *Communication:* Relative degree of formality in an interaction. Might be communicated through eye contact and body position, through verbal markers, or by such aspects of communication as length of utterance, structural complexity, syntactical complexity, and readability [Donohue, Weider-Hatfield, Hamilton, and Diez, 1985, pp. 390–391].

See RELATIONAL DISTANCE.

social trap   From GAME THEORY, situation in which an individual must make a decision, the outcome of which is dependent on choices made by someone else. The trap exists because an individually rational decision by every member of the set results in an outcome that is not collectively rational [Rapoport, 1988, pp. 457–458].

Society of Friends (Quakers)   Christian sect whose adherents are active in peacemaking and consensus-based approaches to dispute resolution.

Founded in seventeenth-century England by George Fox as a radically egalitarian alternative to the traditional churches, Society doctrine holds that all persons are children of God and have God's "light within." The Peace Testimony, which is a very important Quaker principle of opposition to war, arose out of this belief. To take up arms against another would be to take up arms against God's light within one's enemies. Similarly, Society practice does not permit domination of one person over another. Therefore, Friends value consensus building and promote discussion and acceptance of other points of view as leading to organic unity of the "light." When they meet for business, Friends strive to obtain the "sense of the meeting" from those present before taking action— a concept that is very familiar to most facilitators. Also, Friends believe in making manifest expressions of the light within through outward actions. This has led Friends into pioneering social reforms of prisons, schools, and mental institutions, and into supporting refugees and others in need.

See CHRISTIAN PEACEMAKER TEAMS; compare MENNONITE.

Society of Professionals in Dispute Resolution (SPIDR)　Membership organization organized in 1972 as a professional association of NEUTRALS (mediators, arbitrators, dispute resolution professionals) for the purpose of promoting alternative dispute resolution and enhancing the profession. SPIDR's broad and diverse membership is representative of all types of neutrals and all sectors of practice. See www.igc.apc.org/spidr.

sociolegal informalism　Ideological underpinning of the ALTERNATIVE DISPUTE RESOLUTION MOVEMENT. Poses that the responsibility of the state is to facilitate private accords rather than actually to adjudicate or manage disputes [Araki, 1990, p. 52]. See Adler, 1987, p. 65.

sole arbitrator　Arbitrator appointed to be solely responsible for making a final and binding award [DOA], as opposed to a three-arbitrator board.

solicitor　See LAWYER.

sovereign arbitration　Currently rare practice of referring a dispute to a foreign head of state or government for decision.

Soviet Comrades' Courts　See WORKER'S COURTS OF THE SOVIET UNION.

special case (Great Britain)　*Arbitration:* Referral by an arbitrator to a court for a legal opinion on a point of law that has arisen during the course of an arbitration.

A special case may be stated in the form of a consultative case, as an interim award, or as an alternative final award. An arbitrator cannot refuse to state a special case in an arbitration in which a point of law arises, because to do so would constitute misconduct and be cause for vacating the award. The parties may request an arbitrator to state a special case. If the arbitrator refuses, either party may apply for a court order directing the arbitrator to do so, as provided in English law [DOA]. The special-case stated procedure is subject to abuse and has received considerable criticism for delaying arbitration. In response, the Arbitration Act of 1979 provided exceptions to and a method of opting out of the procedure.

special-feature arbitration　Binding arbitration modified by procedures that encourage parties to reach voluntary settlements or to accomplish some other policy goal. The best known form is BASEBALL ARBITRATION, designed to resolve player salary disputes, which operates to drive disputants' final positions closer to a reasonable range in which they can voluntarily agree [Practising Law Institute, 1987, pp. 20–21]. For examples of special-feature arbitration, see FINAL-OFFER ARBITRATION, MED-ARB, MODIFIED FINAL-OFFER ARBITRATION, MULTIPLE-OFFER SELECTION, REPEATED-OFFER SELECTION.

specialized dispute resolution ADR initiatives developed in response to the needs of specialized areas.

For the most part, modern uses of ADR have been specialized, such as mediation in divorce, mediation and arbitration in labor, and arbitration in construction. Recent initiatives in court-annexed ADR, however, have generalized use across a range of substantive matters.

special judge Individual who meets statutory or judicial requirements to hear a case that litigants have agreed to have heard outside of court. Person who hears a trial by reference; an official referee.

The special judge is generally a retired or former district judge, statutory county court judge, or appellate judge who has met certain other requirements, such as experience in a certain field or completion of continuing legal education courses. See Tex. Civ. Prac. & Rem. Code Ann. § 151.003 (West 1993). The verdict of the special judge stands as a verdict by the district court [Tex. Civ. Prac. & Rem. Code Ann. § 151.011 (West 1993)].

See TRIAL ON ORDER OF REFERENCE, RENT-A-JUDGE.

special master Quasi-judicial, ad hoc appointee of the court who assists in the judicial management of the case. An example of a legal definition is the following: "A court-appointed magistrate, auditor or examiner who, subject to specifications and limitations stated in the court order, shall exercise the power to regulate all proceedings in every hearing before such special master, and to do all acts and take all measures necessary or proper for compliance with the court's order" [Colo. Rev. Stat. Ann. § 13-22-302(7)(West 1996)].

Judges use special masters to help manage discovery, settlement, creation of remedial plans, and other aspects of litigation. In federal court, the typical special master is an experienced private attorney, retired judge, or law professor to whom the court delegates frontline judicial responsibility on a *pro hoc vice* basis. Usually paid by one or more of the parties [Levine, 1985].

In the Northern District of California, the third-party attorney who works with and assesses positions of parties by EARLY NEUTRAL EVALUATION is designated as a special master [Brazil, Kahn, Newman, and Gold, 1986].

SPIDR   See SOCIETY OF PROFESSIONALS IN DISPUTE RESOLUTION.

split the difference   *Negotiation:* Common tactic whereby the parties resolve an issue by splitting a certain quantity in half. The quantity split is the difference between the parties' respective demands or positions on that issue and may be money, time, or anything else capable of being split in half [Schoenfield and Schoenfield, 1988, p. 147].

Splitting the difference may be a legitimate way of overcoming impasse when the parties are within the contract zone and there is no objective standard for dividing the difference. When an objective standard exists, however, splitting the difference is a potentially abusive tactic promoted as "fair" because of its seemingly arbitrary impact, but used to gain at the expense of the other.

SRO   Self-regulatory organization. See SELF-REGULATORY ORGANIZATION, NYSE, NASD.

stabilizer   Negotiating team member committed to the process and often eager to reach a settlement. One of three generic roles identified by Colosi and Berkeley [1986] that are assumed by members of a negotiating team, also including DE-STABILIZERS and QUASI-MEDIATORS. Various team members may have different degrees of knowledge, authority, skill, or resources. They will always have different personality traits and negotiation styles. Because different team members have different interests, their roles could change as the issues under negotiation change; however, they could maintain the same roles throughout.

stakeholder   One who is directly affected by the outcome of a decision-making process.

The term is commonly used in public policy facilitation, wherein participation by representatives of all affected groups is sought. A stakeholder should be distinguished from a PARTY, because the former may not be a participant in the process.

standby conciliator   See CONCILIATOR. Compare SHADOW MEDIATION.

standing neutral   Third party contracted to resolve disputes as they arise during the course of a relationship. Best known in construction as performing the same functions as a DISPUTE REVIEW BOARD during the course of a construction project (also called a *project neutral*).

stare decisis   Literally, "to stand by that which has been decided"; the doctrine of following rules or principles laid down in previous judicial decisions, accepting them as obligatory and binding precedents [DOA].

state board of mediation   *Labor Relations:* Board vested by state law with authority to mediate labor disputes and, if mediation fails, to urge fact-finding and voluntary arbitration as means of settlement.

Such state boards are variously known as state boards of arbitration and conciliation, boards of mediation, or industrial commissions. Some states that have no special boards authorize the director of the Department of Labor to promote voluntary mediation and conciliation in resolving labor disputes. The Taft-Hartley Act requires that state mediation agencies be notified of certain types of labor disputes, and in § 203(b), in describing the duties of the FEDERAL MEDIATION AND CONCILIATION SERVICE, states, "The Director and the Service are directed to avoid attempting to mediate disputes which would have only a minor effect on interstate commerce if State or other conciliation services are available to the parties. . . ." Some state mediation boards volunteer their services whenever they learn of a labor dispute. Other boards wait until one or both parties specifically request help [DOA].

state office of dispute resolution   In the United States, government agency in many states that promotes and in some cases administers alternative dispute resolution in the public sector.

The mandates of these offices vary by state. Some focus only on the development and administration of court-connected ADR processes, others concentrate only on public disputes (land use and the environment, for example), and still others have broad responsibility for the institutionalization of ADR across a broad range of public institutions, including schools. One of the most influential of these offices is the OHIO COMMISSION ON DISPUTE RESOLUTION AND CONFLICT MANAGEMENT.

statute of limitations   Statute that delineates the fixed period after which an action cannot be taken to enforce a legal claim or right [DOA]. Under the arbitration law in some jurisdictions, a party can raise limitations periods as a defense before either the court or the arbitrator. Compare LACHES, LIMITATIONS PERIODS.

statutory arbitration   Arbitration for which state or federal law provides the rules and procedures for conduct and for enforcement of arbitration agreements and awards [DOA]. This is in contrast to COMMON LAW ARBITRATION, wherein the rules and procedures are provided by a body of court decisions. This is also in contrast to COMPULSORY ARBITRATION, wherein a statute requires parties to arbitrate without express submission to the jurisdiction of the arbitrators. Most commercial arbitration is statutory arbitration because the enforcement of the arbitral agreement and award is dictated by MODERN ARBITRATION STATUTES.

Steelworkers' Trilogy   *Arbitration:* Three 1960 decisions of the U.S. Supreme Court that articulated the circumstances under which an arbitrator's award could be enforced and limited the intervention of courts in the arbitration process to determining whether the parties must go to arbitration. These decisions greatly enhanced the status of arbitration and the power of arbitrators in the United States.

step negotiation   Process wherein hierarchical entities, corporations, governments, and so on, agree to move responsibility for a negotiation step by step up their respective hierarchies until the matter is resolved.

The first step of negotiation is the level at which the dispute arose or was noticed. This step usually involves those closest to the dispute. If they fail to reach agreement, the negotiation is referred a level up—to superiors—for negotiation, and so on. Step negotiation is often mechanistic, activated by notice and automatically referred to the immediate, respective superiors of the negotiators if they fail to resolve the dispute within a set period. Typically the steps are timed to conclude during a COOLING-OFF PERIOD. The theory is that lower-level people will probably reach agreement because they will not want to concede to their superiors that they have been unable to do so. Moreover, if the first attempt fails, the second-tier negotiators, who are further removed from the actual dispute, may be in a more favorable position to effect settlement. Step negotiation agreements are usually found in long-term contracts, such as joint ventures and construction.

See SECOND-TIER NEGOTIATION.

Stockholm Chamber of Commerce Arbitration Institute (Sweden)   Independent entity within the Stockholm Chamber of Commerce that administers arbitrations and provides education and training. It has been the preferred site for international commercial arbitration between communist countries (including the former Soviet Union) and noncommunist, private entities.

storytelling   *Mediation:* Phase of the mediation process in which each disputant tells his version of the conflict [Fuller, Kimsey, and McKinney, 1992, p. 188].

strategic interaction   Set of behavior patterns manifested by individuals whose choices are interdependent, that is, when two or more individuals find that the outcomes associated with their choices are partially controlled by each other [Princen, 1992, p. 32].

strategy   Plan of action, usually associated with war.

In dispute resolution, parties may adopt strategies, such as a negotiation strategy or litigation strategy. Strategies are based on underlying assumptions and on an understanding of the situation, coupled with relevant goals, rules, and guiding principles. A strategy lays out the plan of action, conduct, and interim objectives for achieving the goals. Strategies are executed through TACTICS.

strike   *Labor Relations:* Concerted work stoppage to protest or to force employer accession to an unmet demand. Strikes or the threat of strikes is a common way to seek leverage in a labor-management negotiation. See STRIKE DEADLINE. Contrast LOCKOUT.

strike deadline, lockout deadline   *Labor Relations:* In collective bargaining negotiation, a fixed deadline after which negotiations proceed under strike (employee action) or lockout (employer action) conditions. More than just a threat to strike if some agreement is not reached by a certain time, the deadline serves as an (implied) promise not to strike prior to that time. This gives the parties a set time to negotiate without the threat of sudden withdrawal of the benefits of the basic relationship [Stevens, 1963, pp. 45–46.]

structured mediation   Form of divorce mediation that attempts to use a complex set of rules and procedures to guide a rational process of problem solving.

Developed in 1974 by O. J. Coogler, an Atlanta lawyer generally credited with starting the divorce mediation movement in the United States, the first major nonlabor mediation program in modern times. The system he conceived, which was propagated through training programs conducted by the FAMILY MEDIATION ASSOCIATION, involved a single mediator who would methodically guide the divorcing couple through the issues of property division, alimony, and child support and custody. The parties would not be represented by separate attorneys; instead, an advisory attorney, drawn from a panel, would answer legal questions and prepare documents. Coogler believed that attorneys lacked sufficient training in behavioral sciences, were constrained by their ethical restrictions, and would create too much hostility and make the process too adversary. While rejecting notions of fault and promoting party autonomy in the decision-making process, structured mediation relied on normative guidance, Coogler's "Rules and Guidelines." Should mediation result in impasse, the couple were required to submit their entire divorce to binding arbitration. Compare THERAPEUTIC FAMILY MEDIATION. Contrast COMPREHENSIVE MEDIATION.

structured settlements   Method of paying a monetary settlement in periodic payments.

The typical structured settlement provides for payment of expenses, legal fees, and certain periodic payments, in addition to an initial up-front cash payment to the client. Structured settlements are integrative solutions of a sort. For the recipient, the payment plan may be designed to meet certain of the recipient's anticipated needs—for example, future medical or rehabilitative expenses, college tuition for children, and so on—or to avoid the squandering of settlement proceeds. For the payer, annuities form the basis of the typical structured settlement, allowing the payer to deposit an initial sum that is less than the amount eventually paid out over time. Negotiators and mediators use structured settlements to bridge the difference between demands and offers.

structuring Technique whereby a mediator helps a speaker organize and arrange his thoughts and speech into a coherent message [Moore, 1986, p. 169].

subjective Dependent on personal emotion or opinion and individual perceptions or idiosyncracies, in contrast with OBJECTIVE.

subjectively expected utility (SEU) *Negotiation:* Particular part of the spectrum of outcomes between the target or aspiration point and the resistance point or reservation price that has particular influence on the negotiator's decision making [Walton and McKersie, 1965, p. 25]. It implies that the negotiator's minimum goals can be a vague set of points rather than a single, clearly defined resistance point or minimum goal below which the negotiator will cease negotiating and refuse to settle [Iklé and Leites, 1962]. As the SEU is approached, concessions become increasingly meaningful and difficult [Walton and McKersie, 1965, p. 88]. The concept is more applicable in positional bargaining [Morley and Stephenson, 1977, pp. 37–38]. Compare BATNA, BOTTOM LINE, RESERVATION PRICE, RESISTANCE POINT.

submission-deterrence *International Relations:* When one side withdraws from a previously held value, position, or interest because the opponent makes effective threats to push him out by force [Holsti, 1983, p. 410].

submission, submission agreement *Arbitration:* Document used to initiate an arbitration of an existing dispute, stating the nature of the dispute and affirming the parties' intention to arbitrate and abide by the award.

Parties not originally bound by an arbitration clause may use a submission agreement to refer their dispute to arbitration. The submission agreement establishes the extent and limit of the arbitrator's authority [DOA]. Less common today, submission agreements were once the primary method of agreeing to arbitrate, the term itself being synonymous with the arbitration process. Early legal commentators tended to define and distinguish the process by focusing either on the *submission* (the agreement to submit to and abide by the judgment of another) or on the award itself. One of the oldest treatises, West's *Symboleography* [1601–1603], provides quite simply that a "Compromise or Submission, Arbitrium, Compromissum, Submissio, is the faciltie or power of pronouncing

Sentence betweene persons at controversie, given to Arbitrators by the parties mutuall private consent, without publike authoritie" [p. 163, citing Y.B. 8 Eliz. 4, pl. 2].

The first modern treatise on the subject also defines the process by its elements:

> That act, by which parties refer any matter in dispute between them to the decision of a third person, is called a submission; the person to whom the reference is made, an arbitrator; when the reference is made to more than one, and provision made, that in case they shall disagree, another shall decide, that one is called an umpire; the judgment pronounced by an arbitrator, or arbitrators, an award; that by an umpire, an umpirage, or, less properly, an award [Kyd, 1791, pp. 4–5].

Recently the term has been extended to refer to any agreement to submit to various forums, such as submission to mediation. This is a less accurate usage, however.

subpoena   Legal document ordering the person designated in it to appear in court or at an arbitration hearing under a penalty for failure to do so.

A subpoena may also request that the person designated bring with him certain specified documents. Modern arbitration statutes of most states give the arbitrator the power to issue subpoenas [DOA].

subpoena duces tecum   Subpoena compelling a witness to appear in court or at an arbitration hearing along with any books or documents he may have that may illustrate or explain the subject matter of the trial or arbitration [DOA].

substantive arbitrability   Judicial determination of whether an agreement to arbitrate exists, and if it does, whether the parties agreed to arbitrate.

Arbitrability questions can be raised in the courts and arbitration hearings. *Arbitrability* refers to two aspects of the same issue: first, whether the parties in their contract intended to arbitrate the matter under dispute, and second, whether all the procedural requirements in the labor agreement were complied with before arbitration [DOA].

substantive fairness   Whether the content of an agreement or outcome is fair, as opposed to the fairness of the process of an agreement (procedural fairness)[Dworkin and London, 1989, pp. 5–7]. See FAIRNESS. Compare JUSTICE.

sulha (**Arabic**)   Traditional tribal process of resolving disputes and returning peace to the broader community.

In Arab society an interpersonal offense is quickly transformed into an interfamilial offense, thereby threatening the broader communal fabric. The family of the offender visits the family of the offended in the company of a JAHA, a group of men known for their diplomacy, tact, and negotiating skills. The offender asks forgiveness from various family members of the offended party. Ritual sharing of coffee is offered to seal a truce. The two parties tie a knot in a white flag carried by the *jaha* to signify that an agreement has been reached. Sometimes this is followed by a ritual shared meal. See related terms: DAKHALA, JALI.

summary jury trial (SJT)   COURT-CONNECTED hybrid ADR procedure in which the parties' lawyers present a summary version of their evidence and arguments to a jury drawn from the court's regular jury pool and receive a nonbinding advisory verdict to facilitate settlement negotiations.

District Court Judge Thomas D. Lambros [1986] of the Northern District of Ohio is credited with inventing the SJT. A case that could take many days or weeks of ordinary trial is truncated to one day of summation or less. A judge or magistrate presides, and rules of evidence are revised to restrict use of objections and, often, use of live witnesses. The jury is empaneled under ordinary procedures and not explicitly informed that its verdict is merely advisory. Principles or representatives with sufficient settlement authority are usually required to attend. In many cases, the parties settle soon after the advisory verdict. However for those who do not, some judges will hold *post summary trial conferences* to maintain momentum toward settlement.

Because the SJT functions primarily as a reality-testing device, it is most useful in cases where settlement is impeded by differences of opinion about the value a jury would assign to the case. SJTs provide little pretrial cost savings because they are most effective after pretrial discovery and motions and because they require almost as much pretrial preparation as a regular trial. Presumably they are most suitable in complex civil cases that require a lengthy time for trial. Some appellate courts have questioned the constitutionality of using regular jurors for SJTs and the judge's authority to order unwilling parties to participate in SJTs.

SJTs are used in a number of state and federal courts and are recognized by the Civil Justice Reform Acts of 1990 and 1996 and by numerous state statutes. Variation has accompanied this expansion. For example, the following statutory provision provides for binding results as well: "Summary presentations in complex cases before a jury empaneled to make findings which may or may not be binding" [Colo. Rev. Stat. Ann. § 13-22-302(8) (West 1996)].

A binding verdict from an SJT would either be submitted to voluntarily in advance to avoid the expense of a long trial or be imposed in the same manner as awards from another court-connected process, such as MANDATORY NONBINDING

ARBITRATION. Other variations from the original SJT model include the use of more than one advisory jury. In any case, the SJT verdict should not bias a subsequent trial on the matter, a principle embodied in this sample statute: "Neither the fact that parties used the SJT process nor the verdict that resulted, if any, shall be admissible as evidence in any subsequent trial of the action unless otherwise admissible under the rules of evidence" [Neb. Rev. Stat. § 25-1157 (1992)].

The court may not impose sanctions for failure to follow the SJT verdict [*McCay* v. *Ashland Oil Co.* (1988) at 46].

The term MINI-TRIAL is sometimes used interchangeably with or in lieu of SJT. Both are hybrids using a summary presentation of evidence and arguments coupled with subsequent settlement negotiations. It is useful, however, to distinguish a MINI-TRIAL as a distinct, nonjury process requiring the active participation of high-ranking corporate or government officials. In this context, a mini-trial is a voluntary, private ADR process. In contrast, an SJT is a court-connected and usually court-ordered process requiring a regular jury pool. The distinction may be less clear if a court orders high-ranking corporate or government officials to participate in a mini-trial or if parties create a *private* SJT by hiring a "mock jury" off the street or through a temporary employment agency.

summary proceeding   Swift and simplified procedure for hearing and resolving a dispute [DOA]. Usually associated with formal adjudicative processes.

summit diplomacy, summit discussions   *International Relations:* Diplomacy conducted personally by heads of state or government, as opposed to diplomacy conducted by ambassadors, cabinet members, or ministers.

Summit diplomacy is usually reserved for major issues in which the purpose is to establish agreement on broad principles that will require later detailed negotiations by lower-level diplomats, or to bring closure to or formalize agreements that have been negotiated in advance by lower-level diplomats. It is sometimes used to merely improve the relationship, without other substantive purpose. Sometimes it is resorted to after the established machinery fails to reach a settlement. Usually it is the culmination of a great deal of conventional negotiation.

sunshine law   Statutory provision that mandates openness and public access in governmental decision making.

Also called *government-in-the-sunshine acts,* sunshine laws include *open-meetings laws,* which require public access to all meetings of government or municipal officials at which official action will be taken, and *open-records acts,* which require public access to government records.

When mediation involves a governmental unit, it may have to be public under the applicable sunshine laws. However, if the government unit's participation includes no substantial delegation of decision-making authority, sunshine laws may not apply. It is undecided whether full mediation with public bodies as parties falls within sunshine laws.

supergame   From GAME THEORY, where the same game with the same players is played time and again.

In each round of the supergame, each player is informed about the opponent's behavior in the previous round and thus knows the complete history of the game. The players then presumably choose a course of action based not only on the situation at hand but also on the opponent's pattern of behavior [Siebe, 1991, p. 197]. Same as *repeated (or iterated) prisoner's dilemma.*

superordinate goal   Goal sought by all the disputants that requires their joint effort to attain. Because it is impossible for each of the parties to achieve this goal separately, it creates a level of interdependence between disputants that can promote cooperation [Nye, 1973, p. 168].

supplemental award   Award in which the arbitrator corrects or supplements his original decision.

A supplemental award may be made only if the parties have agreed to give the arbitrators the authority to do so. If the supplemental award is a correction, modification, or amendment of the earlier award, the final award should read, "In all other respects the Award dated . . . shall remain in full force and effect" [DOA]. The power to issue a supplemental award differs from the power provided by MODERN ARBITRATION STATUTES to make very limited modifications to an award to correct obvious mistakes that do not go to the substance of the decision.

***suq* (Arab/Middle Eastern)**   *Negotiation:* Archetypal market or bazaar bargaining model preceded by elaborate ritual and social courtesies establishing a personal relationship and followed by positional bargaining.

Although the bargaining may start with extreme positions for which the negotiators have no expectation, patient HAGGLING brings about progressive convergence. Cohen [1991, pp. 86–87] notes that the purpose is to make customers satisfied by making them feel they have gained something. Americans, however, tend to be uncomfortable with the exaggerated posturing of the *suq.*

surprise tactic   *Negotiation:* Tactic of introducing startling new terms during a negotiation.

The terms are structured to be, at least superficially, much more attractive to the other side. They are presented to catch the other party off guard. The negotiator introducing the surprise offer then presses for an immediate agreement. He points out—through a seemingly spontaneous and innocent but well-planned presentation—the ways in which the new proposal meets the other side's prior objections or problems and how it fulfills the other party's needs, interests, and goals [Schoenfield and Schoenfield, 1988, p. 178].

symmetrical power relations Condition of roughly equal power among disputants.

Practical experience and social psychological experimentation indicate that when negotiators have an equal or symmetrical power relationship, they behave more cooperatively, function more effectively, and behave in a less exploitive or manipulative manner than when there is an asymmetrical power relationship [Rubin and Brown, 1975]. Disputes in which parties have roughly equal power are amenable to mediation techniques to achieve settlement [Moore, 1986, p. 278].

systemic war Military conflict fought over such serious and fundamental issues that the stakes involved draw in all of the major actors as combatants. The duration of the war is long, the casualty count is high, and the intensity of the conflict is such that a substantial portion of the civilian population becomes involved in the combat. See WORLD WAR.

tactic Procedure, method, or move adopted to carry out a strategy to accomplish a particular goal; has military or adversarial connotations.

Negotiation or Bargaining Tactic: Position to be taken or maneuver to be made at a specific point in the bargaining process. As distinguished from STRATEGY, a bargaining strategy consists of a series of bargaining tactics to be used throughout the bargaining process. It implies a commitment to a long-range position to be taken with the bargaining opponent from initial contact [Hamner and Yukl, 1977, p. 138].

Litigation Tactic: Maneuver made at a specific point in the litigation process. As distinguished from *negotiation tactic*, although either type of tactic can be used to gain an advantage over an opponent, litigation tactics are derived largely from the formal rules and procedures of the forum.

See STRATEGY.

***tamazai* (Tuareg/Central Sahara, North Africa)** Condition of depression specifically resulting from a failure to express one's sentiments and conflicts openly [Rasmussen, 1991, p. 35].

target point Position in the bargaining range that the negotiator has predetermined to be the optimum realistic settlement point [Harbaugh and Britzke, 1988]. Aspirational, as opposed to the BOTTOM LINE or RESERVATION PRICE. Carries the same meaning as LEVEL OF ASPIRATION.

team negotiation   Negotiation through use of a group consisting of two or more persons with similar interest in the disputed matter who negotiate as a single entity to gain the best advantage for the collective group [Moore, 1986, p. 283]. Also called *team bargaining*.

telephone mediation   Mediation conducted by telephone.

Telephone mediation makes participating in the dispute resolution process more convenient for mediators as well as for parties, often with less cost. However, it lacks the visual element. If a face-to-face meeting is likely to deteriorate the atmosphere, telephone mediation may be mutually advantageous. If direct confrontation and nonverbal cues are of strategic or emotional importance, the process has disadvantages. Nonvisual communication skills are crucial. Advocates and mediators should be sure that the parties clearly understand the dynamics of this process. Early uses of telephone mediation were at the Merit System Protection Board, the U.S. Department of Health and Human Services' Early Complaint Resolution Process, and the Council of Better Business Bureau's AUTOLINE program [Schweber, 1989, pp. 192–194].

tentative award   Provisional award presented by the arbitrator to the parties for their consideration.

A tentative award is an effective means of testing principles and arguments not fully covered by the parties in the hearing. It might also impel the parties to explore certain implications of an award, to which they might be more sensitive [DOA]. This increasingly rare practice is a remnant of arbitration as a conciliatory process in which the parties had some control or input as to the nature of the final award. See ARBITRAMENT. Variations of this practice have recently been suggested as an effective means to induce negotiations, thereby resolving the matter without the imposition of a final, binding award. See CONCILIO-ARBITRATION.

terminal resistance value   Same or similar to RESERVATION PRICE [Tutzauer, 1992, p. 74].

terms of reference   *International Commercial Arbitration:* Preliminary framing of issues for arbitral determination.

Terms of reference are best known in INTERNATIONAL CHAMBER OF COMMERCE (ICC) arbitration, which requires that the parties and the arbitrators enter into written *Terms of Reference* before proceeding with the presentation of evidence on the merits (ICC Rules of Arbitration, Art. 18) (1998).

territorial dispute   *International Relations:* Controversy between states over the sovereignty of territory that each claims as its own [DOA].

tertius gaudens   Literally, "the third who rejoices." Situation in which inter-action among negotiators and between negotiators and the media suits the media's own purposes [Douglas, 1992, p. 251].

therapeutic family mediation (TFM)   Mediation model designed to accom-modate the full range of client couple interactions. Applying distinct theory, val-ues, and practice, TFM differs from other models of mediation in its greater emphasis on in-take assessment, selective use of premediation, integration of therapeutic approaches in the phases of the process, and use of LOOP-BACK and loop-forward between phases.

TFM involves four phases—assessment, premediation, negotiation, and follow-up—linked by a series of feedback loops:

- *Assessment:* Screening process to determine the readiness of client cou-ples to enter mediation.

- *Premediation:* Postassessment treatment process to prepare client cou-ples to engage in fruitful negotiations. Used on client couples who are amenable to but incapable of negotiating because of their relational dys-function. The mediator may loopback to premediation during negotia-tion when clients' relational problems cause impasse.

- *Negotiation:* Process whereby client couples seek to reach agreement on disputed issues. If successful, they prepare a draft agreement for review by their respective lawyers. If unsuccessful, they are referred out for treatment, litigation, or both.

- *Follow-up:* Routine checkup within a specific period after termination. The mediator uses this phase to monitor the couple's progress, to evalu-ate the utility of the present agreement, and to determine whether it should be modified or abrogated. If indicated, the mediator may suggest a return to premediation, negotiation, or both.

Initially developed by Irving in the late 1970s, the same period in which Coogler developed the contrasting method of STRUCTURED MEDIATION, TFM has undergone significant refinement [Irving and Benjamin, 1987].

third arbitrator   Neutral member of the arbitration board.

As the neutral member, the third arbitrator is most frequently used in tripar-tite boards to which one of the arbitrators is elected by each of the parties and the third is chosen according to the agreement or the rules of the administering agency. The parties may appoint the third arbitrator, or the two arbitrators se-lected by each of the parties may appoint her, or the administering agency may designate her [DOA]. Same as NEUTRAL ARBITRATOR. Compare UMPIRE.

third party   Someone other than the principals to an agreement, a transaction, a legal action, or a dispute. A third party may or may not have an interest or rights in the matter between the principals.

As an adjective, *third-party* is hyphenated. Thus mediators and arbitrators might be referred to as *third-party neutrals*. In insurance, *third-party* refers to coverage of an injury or damage incurred by someone other than the insured.

third-party consultation   Generally, use of a third party by one or more principals for consultation.

In a common and more specific usage, the term refers to methods of conflict resolution, such as mediation, that involve the use of an outside third party by consent and invitation of all principals.

third-party decision maker   Third party to whom the parties refer a disputed matter for determination. Some forms of third-party decision maker are adjudicators—such as judge, jury, and arbitrator—while other forms are evaluative—such as appraiser. Most common use is in reference to adjudicators.

third-party intervention   Intervention into a dispute by a person or agency whose purpose is to act as an instrument for bringing about a peaceful settlement of the dispute, or by an actor who is not a direct party to the crisis. The purpose of the intervening action is to facilitate resolution [Treverton, 1991, p. 193].

Third Wave Environmentalism   Philosophy of environmental advocacy that emphasizes the need to engage government and industry in a collaborative, problem-solving approach to environmental problems and sustainable development rather than relying solely on adversarial, confrontational tactics and litigation.

Thomas/Kilmann Conflict Mode Instrument   Psychological instrument that measures degrees of assertiveness and cooperativeness in individuals' personal conflict resolution styles. See ACCOMMODATING, ASSERTIVE, AVOIDING, COLLABORATING, COMPETING, COMPROMISING, COOPERATIVE.

threat   Declaration of intent to punish or injure; person or thing perceived as likely to punish or injure.

Threats are efforts to change another's position or behavior by making conditional commitments to do something undesirable [Lax and Sebenius, 1986, p. 128]. They can be examined from two perspectives: the target and the threatener. From the perspective of the target, a threat works when it induces the target to vary from preferred behavior. The cost of the sanction to the target must exceed the value of the preferred behavior. The target must perceive the threat as one that cannot be avoided other than by doing something he does not want to do. From the perspective of the threatener, Schelling [1960, pp. 35–36] observes that "the distinctive feature of a threat is that the threatener has no incentive to carry it out either before the event or after. . . . The threat is ineffectual unless the threatener can rearrange or display his own incentives so as to demonstrate that he would, *ex post,* have an incentive to carry it out." Thus the key to an effective threat is commitment [Mnookin and Birke, 1992, p. 43].

International Relations: Explicit communication by one state declaring an intent to use force against another state for other than strictly defensive purposes, or overt mobilization of armed forces by a state during periods of dispute or high tension, clearly directed at another state for other than strictly defensive purposes.

threat point   Same as BATNA. From Sebenius, 1992, p. 50.

thromise   *Negotiation:* Hybrid form of communication that is simultaneously a promise and a threat. For example, the promise "stay with me and succeed" carries the implied threat "leave me and fail" [Gibbons, Bradac, and Busch, 1992, p. 160, cite omitted].

tie-in   *Negotiation:* Strategy whereby a party introduces an issue considered extraneous by the opponent and offers to accept a certain settlement provided that the issue will also be settled to the party's satisfaction [Iklé, 1964, p. 222]. The introduction of the issue might occur before or after the proffered settlement.

tit-for-tat   *Negotiation:* Strategy of initial cooperation followed by mirroring of the other party's subsequent actions.

Tit-for-tat is identified with GAME THEORY, particularly Axelrod's [1984] repeated Prisoner's Dilemma scenarios. It seeks to induce cooperation by the other player by signaling a willingness to cooperate and to reward cooperation with cooperation (positive reciprocity) and to punish defection with defection (negative reciprocity). The first move in tit-for-tat is the GOLDEN RULE (positive reciprocity), "do unto others as you would have them do unto you," while the remaining moves are rooted in the concept of negative reciprocity, "an eye for an eye." This reveals two problems with such game theory strategies: first, you cannot depend on the other side to follow your positive lead; and second, it is easy to fall into a spiraling pattern of defections that will destroy the negotiating relationship. Kritzer [1991, pp. 80–82] notes that the lessons of the Repeated Prisoner's Dilemma (see GAME THEORY) have limited applicability to bargaining in civil litigation because of the fixed payoff, lack of explicit negotiation, repeat plays, exclusion of third-party decision makers, and choice between only two strategies.

touching   *Mediation:* Minor physical contact, such as a handshake or a pat on the back, initiated by a mediator toward a party [Neumann, 1990, p. 285]. The purpose of touching may be to encourage or reward positive behavior or to develop the relationship between the mediator and the party. It may have negative consequences if perceived as an indicator of bias.

Toyota Reversal Arbitration Board   Mechanism developed for resolving disputes between Toyota Motor Sales, USA, and its automobile dealerships regarding sales credits to dealerships.

The program operates under rules and guidelines developed by Toyota that are specific to the nuances of dealer sales-credit disputes. The board is composed of outside neutral arbitrators trained to decide sales-credit disputes. No counsel is allowed to the disputants during hearings, which may take place via conference call. The board's procedure is characterized by ASYMMETRICALLY BINDING ARBITRATION awards. Toyota is bound by the decision of the arbitrator, whereas the dealer may pursue the case in court. This feature is designed to counter any perceived or real imbalance of power between Toyota and its dealers [Ellis, Ravindra, Vidmar, and Davis, 1994]. See ASYMMETRICALLY BINDING ARBITRATION.

track-two diplomacy   Informal interaction among members of adversarial groups or nations without reliance on official efforts, to search for and promote peace. Supplements official diplomacy and may include a number of nontraditional processes [Azar, 1990, p. 19].

tractability   Extent to which parties' aspirations, expectations, and opportunities permit the formulation of mutually advantageous deals. Tractable conflicts are ones in which changes in the joint status of the adversaries can be proposed that both adversaries recognize as preferable to the status quo and that they can obtain merely by agreeing to do so. Such conflicts can be conceived of as *non-zero-sum* games [Ross and Stillinger, 1991, pp. 389–390]. Derived from *intractable*.

trade association   Private, nonprofit organization of businesspeople or manufacturers in a particular trade or industry for the protection and advancement of their common interests.

Trade associations differ from chambers of commerce in that membership is by industry rather than by locality. Many trade associations maintain their own arbitration facilities for use by their members, or in some cases for use by the general public [DOA].

tragedy of the commons SOCIAL TRAP game whereby a renewable resource becomes depleted by excessive harvesting by a number of exploiters (for example, commercial fisheries and jointly owned pastureland) [Rapoport, 1988].

The Theory of the Commons was first stated in 1833 by William Lloyd in response to the dominant laissez faire economic and social theories of Adam Smith. A half-century earlier in *The Wealth of Nations* (1976, originally published 1776), Adam Smith stated that "insatiable desires" would not escalate prices indefinitely because the "invisible hand" of interpersonal competition would keep prices under control. Smith ultimately concluded that pursuit of individual self-interest would produce the best results for society as a whole. Lloyd developed his theory in terms of a model of a meadow open to anybody in the village. Each villager could pasture as many cattle as he wanted on the property held in common. Given this rule, Lloyd said, the invisible hand would lead to disaster because there is nothing to prevent greedy herdsmen from overusing the commons to the point of destruction. Although it is in the interest of all herdsmen that the caring capacity of the commons not be exceeded, if every herdsman makes his decisions individually, the aggregation of decision makers will end up doing the wrong thing. Whenever the limit of caring capacity has been reached, each participating herdsman can, by adding one more animal to his herd, gain proportionately, because the added animal is his private property. But the loss caused by degradation of the pasture is shared by many herdsmen because the pasture is common property. Seeing that his gain is greater than his loss, each individual would be tempted to add more and more animals to the herd and to the common pasture land. The utility of the commons would be destroyed, and the herdsman who exercised restraint would lose out in competition with the selfish ones. Therein lies the "tragedy of the commons." Losses are commonized while profits are privatized. In the long run, all players would lose.

The tragedy-of-the-commons concept was revived in 1968 by ecologist Garrett Hardin [1968] and applied to negotiation subsequently. See Lloyd, 1833.

transactional analysis (TA) School of psychotherapy derived from psychoanalysis.

TA provides a means for analyzing the stimulus-response patterns of human interactions so as to enable people to understand better what they are doing when they interact with others and how they can change what they are doing if change is desired. Applying TA concepts to negotiation, Goldman [1991, pp. 90–112] concludes that the external realities of the negotiation may be secondary to, if not undermined by, the ulterior emotional needs of the participants.

transformative mediation   Mediation in which disputants have the opportunity to increase their own capacity to work through their own problems and to understand the perspectives of others.

Articulation of this concept and the term are credited to Bush and Folger [1994], who promote the use of mediation to help individuals experience personal growth, find their personal strengths, think through their points of view, understand the need for and consequences of decisions, and make and take responsibility for decisions. Such a mediation would generate EMPOWERMENT (increase in personal capacity) and RECOGNITION (acknowledgment of and empathy toward the other) and become a transformative experience through which individuals increase their personal sense of power, capacity, and effectiveness while also reaching beyond their own perspective and interests to understand the other person's perspective.

Kolb and Kressel [1994, pp. 459, 466–79] refer to a *transformative* frame that mediators use that emphasizes a communicative orientation over the problem-solving orientation.

transmission of final offer   Communication of an offer in which the offerer states that there will be no improvement in favor of the offeree.

In mediation, commentators recommend that mediators transmit final offers only in the presence of both parties. This procedure eliminates any possibility of misunderstanding. If there is any doubt as to the meaning or import of the offer, it can be clarified then and there [Maggiolo, 1971, p. 67].

transparency   Clearly expressing what one intends to do in the future depending on a variety of contingencies. An essential characteristic of TIT-FOR-TAT strategy, which relies on the other side's awareness of the negative consequences of uncooperative behavior and the benefits of cooperative behavior. See RECIPROCITY.

International Relations: Degree to which a party's compliance with a treaty can be determined; usually measured by the availability of information, disclosure of activities, or submission to observation and inspection. Transparency induces compliance by reassuring a party that others are in compliance and deters defections by providing the basis for embarrassing and shaming a party who fails to comply. Transparency facilitates negotiations by building trust or providing verification without dependence on trust [Chayes and Chayes, 1991, p. 321].

treaty   *International Relations:* Pact or written agreement between sovereign states, between states and international organizations, or between international organizations that establishes, defines, or modifies their mutual rights and obligations or their legal relationship.

Treaties usually refer to agreements between two nations and are bilateral. CONVENTIONS are usually international agreements between more than two signatory nations. Customary usage allows the term *multilateral treaty* to be used instead of *convention*. Treaties may involve peace, territorial cession, alliance, friendship, commerce, or other matters of international concern. Treaties may be of a specific or indefinite duration or may terminate upon conditions, mutual consent, or unilateral denunciation, as in the case of war or changed circumstances.

International organizations such as the United Nations or the International Bank for Reconstruction and Development may themselves have the authority to conclude international agreements with states or other international organizations. Though a treaty or convention may be defined as a written instrument, states may incur legal obligations other than through such written agreements [DOA]. For example, other types of international agreements include act, *aide memoire,* charter, covenant, convention, *entente, modus vivendi,* and protocol.

Many treaties are called *declarations, communiques,* or *regulations;* the juridical effect, or binding nature (see PACTA SUNT SERVANDA), however, does not dependent on the name of the instrument. The substance alone decides whether the instrument is a treaty. International organizations may be empowered to create regulations regarding a matter of international concern. However, such unilateral actions are not treaties.

treaty making *International Relations:* Process involving negotiation, signature, ratification, exchange of ratifications, publication and proclamation, and execution of a TREATY.

trend reciprocity *Negotiation:* Increasing or decreasing one's concessions in response to the other party's increase or decrease in concessions from the past several rounds of bargaining [Druckman and Harris, 1989, p. 236]. Similar to TIT-FOR-TAT.

trial Adjudicative hearing before a court in which the parties present their issues of law and fact for examination and determination. Should be distinguished from the larger LITIGATION process of which it is a part.

trial on order of reference, trial by reference Voluntary, court-connected process, provided by statutory or constitutional law in some states, that allows parties to opt out of court and select a private judge (REFEREE) to hear their proofs and arguments and make a binding decision that has the force and effect of a regular court judgment. Typically the parties choose and pay for a retired judge or influential lawyer to serve as the neutral. The parties have a fair amount of control over the process, including location and scheduling. This process is considered court-connected because the parties have to initiate suit to access the process and because the decision is binding and appealable for full review through the normal appellate system.

Trial by reference, also known as *private judging,* was well known in common law. One of the earliest recorded cases using this process was *Honesti* v. *Chartres* [1291 A.D.; reprinted in Arnold, 1987], a complex accounting action in which the Exchequer Court entered judgment on the findings of three merchants and two auditors [*Select Cases Concerning the Law Merchant,* 1930, pp. 53–62, 148–50]. The practice was common particularly in the equity courts and became routinized by the late seventeenth century and under later statutory provisions. In the nineteenth-century United States, the scarcity of judges led some states to create REFEREE SYSTEMS that permitted parties to engage private judges. Today, at least forty-eight states permit reference of at least some issues of fact or law or both to a referee. Provisions can vary widely between jurisdictions, circumscribing the subject matter triable by reference, providing methods of neutral compensation, and specifying the qualifications of the referees. Generally these statutes are liberal in allowing reference by mutual consent of the parties. Unlike arbitration statutes, these statutes usually require trial procedure as in a court (California allows the parties to agree to less formal procedures in advance) and a decision that includes findings of fact and conclusions of law. Perhaps ten or more states permit reference of all issues of law and fact in all cases and give the referee's decision the weight of a jury verdict or trial judgment. The most notable uses of trials by reference have occurred in California [Cal. Civ. Proc. Code §§ 638, 639 (West 1976 and West Supp. 1987)] where the process has become popularly known as *rent-a-judge* and allows a judge to be hired under either statutory or constitutional provisions. See also DISCOVERY REFEREE.

triangulation   *Mediation:* Occurs when the mediator adopts an adversarial stance toward one party, is seduced by one party into paying too much attention to him or her, or accepts only one party's definition of the problem. See Hocker and Wilmot, 1995, pp. 146–149. See BIAS, BALANCED PARTIALITY, IMPARTIALITY.

Also, when divorcing parents draw their child into the marital dispute.

tribal moot   Alternative method of dispute resolution used by societies after imposition of colonial law, particularly in Africa.

In contrast to colonial courts, tribal moots were informal and involved participation by the broader community. Instead of focusing on blame, moots tended toward open discussion and the airing of issues and tensions with a focus on the restoration of relationships or communal harmony. As such, they performed a conciliatory function in these societies. See MOOT.

tribunal   One or more adjudicators who together exercise jurisdiction over a matter. In arbitration, a tribunal is composed of one or more arbitrators with the authority to hear and decide disputes.

Tribunal may also be used to refer to the site of a court or arbitration, also often referred to as an arbitration court, or the seat of a judge [DOA]. The term referred to the elevated seat of the *praetor* in Roman law.

tripartite arbitration   Arbitration conducted by a TRIPARTITE PANEL.

tripartite panel, tripartite board   Arbitration board usually composed of one or more members selected by each party and a neutral member selected by both parties or by the party-appointed arbitrators to act as chair [DOA]. If there is a distinction between *panel* and *board,* it is not clear. *Board* is more common in labor arbitration and almost unknown in commercial arbitration. *Panel* is common in commercial arbitration. In American Arbitration Association parlance, *panel* also has been a reference to a larger body of arbitrators (known today as the AAA ROSTER OF NEUTRALS) from which the parties may choose their three arbitrators for a tripartite board.

truce   Cessation of hostilities for a period, usually temporary; agreement for the temporary cessation of hostilities. Compare TREATY.

trust vacuum   When disputants lack the degree of trust necessary to negotiate or to reach a negotiated agreement.

In mediation, the mediator bridges the trust vacuum sometimes by merely serving as a third party whom both sides can trust even if they cannot trust each other. Colosi [1983] refers to this phenomenon in the labor and collective bargaining sphere. In family mediation, a trust vacuum occurs when parents feel they cannot trust their children because the children have not been trustworthy, and children in turn lament the lack of trust their parents place in them. In these situations, the mediator can bridge the gap created by the lack of trust between parent and child by acting as a third party whom both sides can trust [Zetzel, 1985, p. 57].

two-track approach   Use of an ADR process or traditional settlement negotiations in conjunction with litigation.

The ADR efforts may proceed concurrently with the litigation or during an agreed-upon suspension of litigation. A disputant may initiate a two-track approach to induce the other disputant to participate in ADR, to toll a statute of limitations, or to gain certain bargaining endowments available through civil procedure. This approach can be more costly and cast a more adversarial atmosphere over negotiations.

umbrella groups   *Public Policy:* Formal organizations or ad hoc gatherings of various individuals, groups, or other organizations formed for discussion or action on issues of mutual interest. Members may share concerns or interests only on the issues around which the umbrella group is formed. The purpose of many umbrella groups is to try to reach a consensus about and take action on crucial issues on which the members may have different perspectives.

These groups can be organized and sanctioned by government or organized independently by the interested parties. In forming governmental or regulatory policy, such groups provide a forum outside the formal regulatory process for interested parties to discuss policy. Examples include the National Coal Policy Project, created to bring together parties with specific interests concerning the mining of coal and its use by industry, and the National Institute of Building Sciences, formed to develop proposals concerning the regulation of the construction industry through a consensus of industry, labor, architectural groups, and consumer organizations [Rose, 1983, pp. 382–383].

umpire   *Arbitration:* Arbitrator who makes the final decision alone when the arbitrators appointed by the parties disagree on the merits of the dispute.

Historically the umpire evolved from premodern uses of party-appointed arbitrators in ARBITRAMENT and similar processes. Typically the parties would each choose an arbitrator, usually a friend, and the umpire was selected by those arbitrators only when the two arbitrators reached an impasse in their determinations.

Technically, even today an umpire is empowered to act only when the party-appointed arbitrators fail to agree on an award. Unlike most modern commercial arbitration practice, in which the NEUTRAL ARBITRATOR participates with the party-appointed arbitrators to issue a unanimous or majority award, an umpire issues a sole determination. Some arbitration statutes in the United States still refer to umpires [such as La. Rev. Stat. Ann. § 9:4204 (West 1997)]. The technical distinction, however, between an umpire and a NEUTRAL ARBITRATOR is rarely recognized in U.S. practice. The use of an umpire in commercial cases is more common to European trade association arbitration. In Scots law, an umpire is sometimes referred to as an OVERMAN, or as an arbitrator to settle disputes between arbitrators.

Labor Relations: Permanent arbitrator appointed jointly by labor and management who is given limited jurisdiction under the terms of the contract and is solely responsible for his decision. The umpire is appointed by the parties to serve for a specified time and fee [DOA].

umpire system   *Arbitration:* Any institutionalized use of umpires to resolve disputes. See UMPIRE.

Labor: Method of dispute settlement by means of a neutral arbitrator, chosen by the parties, whose authority is restricted to interpreting and applying the existing collective bargaining agreement between the parties and who arrives at his decision based on evidence presented at a formal hearing. The umpire serves for a specified time according to the will of the parties. His jurisdiction is limited by a detailed and specific collective bargaining agreement [DOA].

Also used more specifically in the labor context to denote a system whereby a third party settles a dispute if the board of commission established to settle the dispute could not reach a solution.

Modern use in this context originated in the anthracite coal industry, with the award made in 1903 by the Anthracite Coal Strike Commission. This award provided for a board of conciliation with equal representation of management and labor, to which unresolved grievances were to be referred. Unsettled grievances were to be referred to a neutral outsider known as the umpire. Unlike present practice, the umpire did not then meet with the board. Transcripts of hearings and other relevant documents were mailed to him. The umpire arrived at his decision and then mailed it to the parties. His jurisdiction was limited to interpreting and applying an existing agreement [DOA].

UN   See UNITED NATIONS.

unbalancing   *Mediation:* Technique whereby a mediator changes the balance of power between mediating parties by tactically shifting his support between them, in an effort to prevent the negotiations from stalemating [McIsaac, 1986–1987, p. 67].

unconfirmed award *Arbitration:* Award that has not yet been confirmed as a judgment in a court action so that it can be judicially enforced. Modern arbitration acts provide a mechanism for parties to ask the court, usually with time limitations, to convert an arbitration award into a court judgment. The award can then be enforced through the mechanisms available to enforce court judgments. See, for example, 9 U.S.C. § 9 (1994).

Uniform Arbitration Act (UAA) (United States) Uniform modern arbitration act covering voluntary agreements to arbitrate future and existing disputes, drafted by a committee appointed by the National Conference of Commissioners on Uniform State Laws, approved at Philadelphia, Pennsylvania, August 15–20, 1955, amended at Dallas, Texas, August 24, 1956, and recommended for enactment in all states [DOA].

Most states have adopted a version of the UAA as their modern arbitration statute. In addition to having authority to enforce valid arbitration agreements, the UAA provides guidelines for confirming or vacating an arbitration award, as well as jurisdiction, venue, and division of the costs of arbitration. These provisions are generally gap fillers for those points that the private arbitration agreement does not explicitly cover. See MODERN ARBITRATION STATUTE.

unilateral decision-making system *Labor Relations:* System in which management has the exclusive right to set and enforce whatever terms and conditions of employment it deems appropriate, limited only by specific regulatory statute and constitutional provision [Deitsch and Dilts, 1990, p. 7].

uninsured motorist arbitration Arbitration between an insured and his insurance carrier to resolve disputed claim arising out of the insured's accident with an uninsured motorist.

Arbitration is encouraged in this situation to reduce the time and cost of resolving such claims through the court system. It is also believed that a less adversarial process will be less detrimental to the insured-insurer relationship and result in speedier payment of claims, greater loss distribution, and the possibility of lower insurance premiums. Because of their perceived adhesive nature, however, such arbitration agreements are subject to stringent requirements in some states. Some states will allow arbitration only of issues concerning the liability of the uninsured motorist; other states broaden the jurisdiction to allow arbitration of all issues related to the dispute [Johnson, Kantor, and Schwartz, 1977, p. 50]. Generally, enforcement of such arbitration provisions contained in the uninsured motorist endorsement of the policy requires modification of the common law or enactment of a special statute [DOA].

United Nations (UN) *International Relations:* International organization composed of member states and established "to maintain international peace and security, and to that end: to take effective collective measures for the prevention and removal of threats to the peace, and for the suppression of acts of aggression or other breaches of the peace, and to bring about by peaceful means, and in conformity with principles of justice and international law, adjustments or settlement of international disputes or situations which might lead to a breach of the peace" [Art. 1, ¶ 1, Charter of the United Nations].

Member states are to "settle their international disputes by peaceful means" [Art. 2, ¶ 3, Charter of the United Nations], some of which are listed in Chapter 4, Article 33, which provides that the parties to a dispute should "first of all, seek a solution by negotiation, inquiry, mediation, conciliation, arbitration, judicial settlement, resort to regional agencies or arrangements, or other peaceful means of their own choice." If these traditional pacific settlement approaches fail or are inappropriate, the dispute may be brought before the principal organs, the UN Security Council or UN General Assembly, by a member state, or by a nonmember if it agrees to accept charter obligations relating to dispute settlement. The UN Secretary-General, under the Charter (Art. 99), may also bring any situation that threatens peace and security to the attention of the Security Council. See also INTERNATIONAL COURT OF JUSTICE.

United Nations Commission on International Trade Law (UNCITRAL) Commission established by Resolution 2205 (XXI) of the General Assembly on December 17, 1966, to harmonize all laws concerned with international trade [DOA].

UNCITRAL chose international commercial arbitration as a priority at its opening session in 1968. In 1976 it produced the UNCITRAL Arbitration Rules, which are widely used in ad hoc arbitrations or in arbitrations administered by institutions such as the American Arbitration Association (Resolution 31/98 adopted by the General Assembly on Dec. 15, 1976). In 1983, it finalized the UNCITRAL Conciliation Rules. An UNCITRAL Model Law on International Commercial Arbitration (as adopted by the UNCITRAL on June 21, 1985) has been adopted by many countries and by U.S. states as an international commercial arbitration statute.

United Nations Commission on International Trade Law (UNCITRAL) Arbitration Rules Arbitration rules adopted and promoted by UNCITRAL (Resolution 31/98 adopted by the General Assembly on Dec. 15, 1976) and widely used in ad hoc arbitrations or in arbitrations administered by institutions conducted by the AMERICAN ARBITRATION ASSOCIATION, the LONDON COURT OF ARBITRATION, and the INTERNATIONAL CHAMBER OF COMMERCE.

United Nations Convention on the Recognition and Enforcement of Foreign Arbitral Awards See CONVENTION ON THE RECOGNITION AND ENFORCEMENT OF FOREIGN ARBITRAL AWARDS.

United States Arbitration Act (USAA)   First federal modern arbitration statute in the United States; also known as the Federal Arbitration Act (FAA) [9 U.S.C. §§ 1 et seq.].

Approved by President Calvin Coolidge on February 12, 1925, the USAA made written agreements to arbitrate valid and specifically enforceable for the arbitration of disputes arising out of maritime transactions, out of contracts relating to commerce among states or territories, or with foreign nations. The act was similar to the state arbitration laws of New York, New Jersey, Oregon, and Massachusetts. It provided for the enforcement of arbitration agreements and awards in federal courts. To invoke the act in federal court, some independent ground of federal court jurisdiction must exist. Unless the agreement provides otherwise, or if state arbitration law is in conflict with federal arbitration law and policy, state courts must also follow the USAA when the kind of contract invoked is enforceable under the act [DOA].

United States Institute of Peace (USIP)   Independent, nonpartisan federal institution created and funded by Congress to strengthen the nation's capacity to promote the peaceful resolution of international conflict.

Established in 1984, the institute is governed by a bipartisan, fifteen-member board of directors, including four members *ex officio* from the executive branch of the federal government and eleven individuals appointed from outside federal service by the president of the United States and confirmed by the Senate. Its congressional mandate is to expand available knowledge about ways to achieve a more peaceful world. Its programs include grantmaking, a three-tiered fellowship program, research and studies projects, development of library resources, and a variety of citizen education activities [Cohen, 1991].

unpacking   Technique of identifying all the sources of dissatisfaction and dealing with them as separate issues [Jandt and Gillette, 1985, p. 231].

unreasoned award   See OPINION.

USIP   See UNITED STATES INSTITUTE OF PEACE.

utility   Generally, value or usefulness; more specifically used in negotiation theory as an indicator of relative value to the bargainers.

utility function   Number assigned to a specific proposal that defines and quantifies its utility and worth to a particular bargainer relative to other proposals. It has the property that if a bargainer prefers proposal A to proposal B, then the utility of A will be larger than the utility of B [Tutzauer, 1992, p. 70, citation omitted].

vacating an award   Court ruling to set aside an arbitration award.

Under U.S. law, an award can be vacated in whole or in part on proof of partiality of an arbitrator appointed as a neutral, when the arbitrator exceeds her powers that the parties established in their agreement, or when she imperfectly executes the award. Other grounds for vacating an award are corruption, fraud, or other misconduct on the part of the arbitrator, or when the arbitration failed to follow the procedure established by the applicable statute. The right to object to such irregular procedure may be lost if the party shall have proceeded with the arbitration without making his objection known. See 9 U.S.C. § 10 [DOA].

Some federal courts have recognized several nonstatutory bases for vacating an arbitration award:

- An arbitration award can be vacated if it is *arbitrary* and *capricious* [*Ainsworth* v. *Skurnick* (1993); *Raiford* v. *Merrill Lynch Pierce Fenner and Smith, Inc.* (1990)].

- An arbitration award may be vacated if enforcement is contrary to public policy [*Delta Air Lines, Inc.* v. *Airline Pilots Ass'n* (1989)].

- An award might be vacated if the arbitrators show a "manifest disregard of law" [see *Jenkins* v. *Prudential-Bache Sec., Inc.* (1988)]. The Eleventh Circuit, however, has expressly declined to adopt the manifest-disregard-of-law standard as a basis for vacating an arbitration award. [See *Robbins* v. *Paine-Webber* (1992); *Brown* v. *Rauscher Pierce Refsnes, Inc.* (1993); Yarn, 1992.]

venting   Giving free flow to emotion and expression.

Mediators encourage disputants to vent because the release of emotional tension and the need for recognition of their feelings is often considered a necessary prelude to more rational problem solving.

venue   *Law:* Possible or proper geographic area in which a court with jurisdiction may hear a case. Venue refers to the locale in which the suit can be brought in contrast with jurisdiction, which refers to the authority of a court to hear the case.

verbal aggression   Attack or attempt to dominate or overpower another verbally.

In disputing, verbal aggression might be characterized as an attack on opponent's self-concept instead of, or in addition to, his or her position [Keough, 1992, p. 120, citation omitted]. In the language of principled negotiation, an attack on the person rather than on the problem.

verbal immediacy   *Communication:* Degree to which a participant's language reflects commitment to the proposition stated or matter referred to. High immediacy language embraces its referents, while low immediacy language is indirect, avoiding, or noncommittal [Gibbons, Bradac, and Busch, 1992, p. 163].

Also, verbal immediacy characterizes the use of language when a negotiator seeks to move close to a person he likes or away from one he dislikes [Donohue and Ramesh, 1992].

verbal response mode (VRM)   General framework for coding different types of negotiation. This taxonomy features such categories as edifications, disclosures, confirmations, questions, and interpretations [Gibbons, Bradac, and Busch, 1992, p. 170, citation omitted].

verdict   Answer given to the court by the jury in any cause, civil or criminal, committed to its determination.

vertical bargaining   Level of internal bargaining that occurs when the negotiator or team is responsible to a bureaucratic, corporate, or agency hierarchy, a broad-based constituency, or both. The team may have to negotiate with higher authority to obtain settlement approval. In some cases, the team may be responsible to several constituencies, each of which may have differing interests [Colosi and Berkeley, 1986]. Also called *constituencies bargaining.* Compare BACK CHANNEL COMMUNICATIONS. Contrast HORIZONTAL BARGAINING, SHADOW BARGAINING.

Victim Offender Mediation Association (VOMA)   Membership organization that promotes the understanding and use of VICTIM-OFFENDER MEDIATION.

victim-offender mediation, victim-perpetrator mediation   Facilitated interaction between the victim of a crime and the perpetrator to help bring some closure to the emotional, psychological, and social wounds resulting from the offense [Umbreit, 1994].

victim-offender reconciliation programs (VORPs)   Programs that provide appropriate interaction between victims and offenders in criminal matters.

Such programs provide the victim with an opportunity to confront the offender, thereby allowing some psychological or emotional catharsis. Conversely, the encounter may contribute to the offender's rehabilitation and give opportunities for penitent offenders to compensate the victim in an appropriate manner. The underlying philosophy of such programs is closely associated with RESTORATIVE JUSTICE. VORPs can be traced back to a MENNONITE project in Kitchener, Ontario in 1974. Although it is difficult to accurately track the number of VORPs because the name and approach may vary, there are at least 120 programs in the United States, 20 to 30 in Canada, and a large number in Europe [Umbreit, 1994].

voluntariness   Characterizes an act brought about by the actor's free will, without compulsion.

In a dispute resolution process such as mediation, voluntariness depends on the participants' understanding of and consent to the process on which they are embarking [Roberts, 1992, p. 8]. Arguably, voluntariness is an essential characteristic of conciliatory processes seeking CONSENSUS and underlies the rationale for enforcing agreements to use arbitration and other forms of private adjudication. There may, however, be varying degrees of consent and free choice.

Voluntariness, in negative terms, simply means that the parties are free to withdraw from a dispute resolution process. Moreover, the parties, rather than neutrals, must set the agenda. Each side must be granted the autonomy to pursue any alternatives that are in their interest. In effect, the voluntariness of the parties ensures that the parties will engage in a dispute resolution process openly rather than in a defensive posture. If voluntariness is absent, it is unlikely that consensus can be reached, and the conflict will likely continue [Jones, 1994]. In mediator ethics, the concept of voluntariness is sometimes expressed as *party self-determination*.

voluntary arbitration   See ARBITRATION.

voluntary impasse resolution   Under Wisconsin law, an agreement between a municipal employer and a collective bargaining unit to use ADR. The process entered into may either be binding or nonbinding [Wis. Stat. Ann. § 111.70(4)(c) (West 1996)].

VOMA   See VICTIM OFFENDER MEDIATION ASSOCIATION.

VORPs   See VICTIM-OFFENDER RECONCILIATION PROGRAMS.

voting   Method for collective self-determination used to select among specified alternatives. Once those alternatives have been selected, however, voting usually provides no flexibility. Moreover, while the result reflects a defined level of consensus (such as majority, plurality, two-thirds), it does not necessarily represent the wisest solution, offer an accommodation of a competing party's interests, or reflect standards of fairness or justice beyond those of the participating voters.

Vynior's Case   Landmark case [(1610) 8 Co. Rep. 81b, 77 E.R. 597 (K.B.)] that allegedly reflected in its decision an early judicial hostility to the enforcement of arbitration agreements. See also COMMON LAW HOSTILITY and OUSTER DOCTRINE.

In dictum, Lord C. J. Coke declared for the English court that an arbitral agreement was revocable until it resulted in an award. This became a crucial principle of common law arbitration and undermined agreements to arbitrate until modern arbitration statutes were enacted. Despite this apparently damaging opinion, the court actually enforced the performance bond given by the defaulting party. Though the decision covers only recovery on the bond, the dictum seems to represent the common law of that time. Vynior's Case was rarely cited as authority for a court to refuse to enforce agreements to arbitrate until *Scott* v. *Avery* (1856).

waiting period *Labor Relations:* Period provided by law for parties to negotiate, between the notice of an intention to strike and when the strike may lawfully start. Compare COOLING-OFF PERIOD.

war, warfare Hostility among persons, usually accompanied by violence.

International Relations: Generally refers to a period of publicly declared hostilities among nations involving military force directed by the respective governments, and the suspension of ordinary diplomatic relations. War is *civil war* if the combatants are organized factions internal to a nation and one of the factions purports to be the recognized national government or is the internationally recognized government.

WATNA Worst Alternative to a Negotiated Agreement.

Negotiation: "Worst case" scenario if one fails to reach a negotiated agreement; supplement or alternative to BATNA. Compare PATNA.

In mediation, some mediators encourage disputants to identify their WATNA and mutually agree to eliminate it from the list of options in order to "free up creative energy for solutions" [Haynes, 1988, p. 29]. Other mediators use WATNA in addition to or in place of BATNA for reality testing or to identify the acceptable range of offers.

what if? *Negotiation:* Common phrase used to test proposals without necessarily committing to the proposal stated, or used merely to gauge reaction; preface to a *trial balloon.*

whittle down   *Negotiation:* Gradual resolution of multiple issues in dispute, by either AGREEMENT or WITHDRAWAL.

Observed as a systematic method of procedure in the context of labor management negotiations, it may be initialed by the principal negotiators. The issues in dispute are gradually reduced, until only a few remain. According to one commentator, it is the practical equivalent of "proposal and counterproposal" [Simkin, 1971, p. 168].

wigless litigation (Great Britain)   *Arbitration:* Arbitration in which the complex, formal, and adversarial civil procedure of the High Court is used to conduct the proceedings.

Much arbitration in England is highly formalized. According to one commentary, no formal provisions of English law currently require such procedures to be used in arbitral hearings, despite the common assumption to the contrary [WAMR, 5(3)]. The practice has persisted, however, for at least a century. In addition, English courts will not enforce an arbitration award issued by a tribunal in England unless the proceeding was conducted using the rules of evidence and the arbitrators made their decision by proper application of English law. Some exceptions to this general rule exist under the Arbitration Act of 1979. Because of their similar levels of formality, arbitration and formal litigation in England appear to have few differences or advantages over each other. In 1935, Lord Hailsham, formerly Q.M. Hogg, devoted nine pages to defining arbitration, which he summarized "with some hesitation" as follows: "arbitration is the reference for binding judicial determination of any matter in controversy capable of being compromised by way of accord and satisfaction or rendered arbitrable by statute between two or more parties to some person or persons other than a Court of competent jurisdiction."

Hogg's definition was barely distinguishable from court judgment. In fact, he was forced to distinguish arbitration by noting that the decision maker is "other than a Court" [p. 16]. The imposition of law and the ingrained societal habits of disputing practice, however, imposed upon arbitration most of the characteristics found in English litigation, leading one court to observe, "the whole difference [between judicial determination and arbitration] is that [arbitration] is a tribunal chosen by the parties themselves" [*Doe d. Lloyd* v. *Evans* (1827), per Chief Justice Vaughan, who said also that "a matter comes as adversely before arbitrators as before any another tribunal"].

Wilko doctrine   Legal principle that certain federal statutory claims, especially those involving securities fraud and antitrust, were not arbitrable.

The doctrine was derived from a decision by the U.S. Supreme Court, *Wilko* v. *Swan* (1953), in which the court held that a customer of a brokerage house was entitled to litigate his claim for fraud under the Securities Act of 1933, despite an agreement in the margin contract to arbitrate future disputes. At the time, the court perceived the private dispute resolution function of arbitration as inconsistent with the public policy functions of security fraud and antitrust law. Subsequent cases have significantly eroded the applicability of the Wilko doctrine. See *Shearson/American Express, Inc. v. McMahon* (1987)(securities claim); *Mitsubishi Motors Corp. v. Soler Chrysler-Plymouth, Inc.* (1985)(anti-trust claim); *Gilmer v. Interstate/Johnson Lane Corp.* (1991)(age discrimination claim).

willingly   Performed of free choice, engaged in voluntarily. Used in the context of determining whether a person is acting under compulsion; similar to VOLUNTARINESS. Has positive connotations, while *willfully* often describes entering into a negative action voluntarily and with conscious appreciation of the consequences.

winner's curse   *Negotiation:* Psychological tendency to feel taken advantage of when the other side accepts one's offer. When, for example, a buyer begins to think he has overpaid as soon as the seller agrees to accept the offer [Stuart and Jacobson, 1986–1987, p. 82; Bazerman, 1983, pp. 211–228]. Winner's curse is particularly prevalent when agreement is reached with few or no concessional moves in positional patterned bargaining.

win-set   *International Relations:* Set of potential agreements that would be accepted by a party's relevant domestic constituencies. For the international negotiation to succeed at both domestic and international levels, there must be an overlap between the win-sets of the parties [Chayes and Chayes, 1991, p. 325]. Similar to BARGAINING RANGE and CONTRACT ZONE.

win-win solution   Solution from which both parties to a negotiation benefit, emerging as "winners." One commentator opines that a true win-win solution is not possible without additional resource contribution from some source, often a third party. Another term for a win-win solution is INTEGRATIVE AGREEMENT.

   Contrast DISTRIBUTIVE AGREEMENT, FIXED PIE, ZERO-SUM.

withdrawal   Dispute resolution mechanism in which a party retires or disengages from active disputing. Form of AVOIDANCE occurring after the dispute has arisen. Unless the withdrawing party is also the claiming party, this process is not likely to result in resolution.

   Term can also refer to a retraction or revocation of a disputed claim by the claiming party. This action ends the dispute but may not resolve the underlying conflict or source of the dispute.

   Negotiation: Revocation by parties of offers, demands, or proposals. Withdrawal can be in response to an action taken by another party or can be used as a threat to gain leverage.

"wolf under the bed" reaction   *Mediation:* When the mediator, influenced by his own experiences, perceives something as a problem regardless of whether it is objectively an issue [Zetzel, 1985, p. 64]. In addition to experience, most mediation training emphasizes uncovering hidden agendas or sources of conflict deeper than those initially expressed.

Workers' Courts of the Soviet Union (community courts of the Soviet Union, Soviet Comrades' Courts)   System of localized, informal courts that emphasized voluntary resolution of disputes, or in the case of minor criminal offenses, voluntary atonement, over adjudication.

Prototype for the various *workers' courts, comrades' courts,* and *community courts* found in many socialist countries during the twentieth century, the original Soviet Comrades' Court was established in the military in 1917 and quickly reproduced in other social institutions and communities. Workers' Courts were established to handle disputes and petty offenses in the workplace, while community courts focused on residential neighborhoods. Variations in other countries may reflect their own distinct cultural backgrounds, for example, CHINESE MEDIATION COMMITTEE. Although they had adjudicative, decision-making powers backed by the power of state sanction, these courts were not formally part of the judicial system and relied on persuasion and education, backed by community pressure, coupled with informal sanctions to encourage reconciliation or behavior change. Hearings were recorded, public, and scheduled within two or three weeks of filing; most cases were voluntarily settled before the hearing. The courts also served as alternative mechanisms for communist indoctrinalization and social control [Marshall, 1985, pp. 57–59] and probably disbanded as the Soviet system was abandoned.

World Court   *International Relations:* Term that refers to both the PERMANENT COURT OF INTERNATIONAL JUSTICE (1922–1946), set up as part of the 1919 peace settlement, and its successor, the INTERNATIONAL COURT OF JUSTICE (ICJ) (1946–present), founded in 1945 as the principal judicial organ of the UNITED NATIONS.

World Trade Organization (WTO)   International body for negotiation of a liberalized international trade regime that provides a formal trade dispute settlement mechanism.

Settlement of international trade disputes among nation-states that are signatories to the GENERAL AGREEMENT ON TARIFFS AND TRADE (GATT) is provided for by Article 22 and 23 of GATT and is governed by the Dispute Settlement Understanding that emerged from the Uruguay Round of GATT talks. Prior to the Dispute Settlement Understanding, there was no formal mechanism to resolve disputes among GATT members regarding international trade. The United States, during the Reagan and Bush administrations, had pursued a policy of *unilateralism* in addressing its trade disputes, while at the same time seeking the establishment of the WTO as a formal, legalistic means of trade dispute settlement. The actions of the United States ultimately led to an international consensus on the need for formalized dispute settlement, which led to the formation of the WTO and the Dispute Settlement Understanding [Bello and Holmer, 1994, pp. 1099–1102].

The system for international trade-dispute settlement under the WTO consists of four phases: consultation; a panel phase, review by the Appellate Body; and as an alternative procedure, arbitration. A party to a dispute may elect to have *consultations*, or settlement negotiations, under the auspices of the Dispute Settlement Body (DSB), which is made up of the representatives of all members of the WTO.

A request for consultations must be answered by the respondent, or else the complaining party may seek the institution of a panel. The DSB must form a panel following such a request, unless it agrees by consensus not to do so. Panel members are qualified individuals who are not citizens of any of the parties to the dispute, unless the parties agree to appoint their own citizens. The panel phase of dispute settlement resembles adjudication in that the panel accepts pleadings, sets deadlines, hears oral arguments, and takes part in confidential deliberations. In addition, the panel must render an award with reasons, which is then submitted to the DSB for review. The DSB will accept the award unless it decides by consensus not to do so.

Following this, a party may request Appellate Body review. The proceedings of the Appellate Body also resemble judicial review of the panel's award. The parties do not have the ability to appoint Appellate Body members, as they do with the panels. Appellate Body decisions are adopted without revision by the DSB, unless it decides by consensus not to do so.

The Dispute Settlement Understanding also recognizes the right of the parties to turn to conciliation, good offices, or mediation at any time during this process. Additionally, the parties may at any time submit their dispute to binding arbitration. In this fashion, the parties may avoid the scrutiny of the DSB, but may still face review by a panel or by the Appellate Body [Dillon, 1995]. See GENERAL AGREEMENT ON TARIFFS AND TRADE.

world war *International Relations:* International warfare that involves most of the major military powers at some point in the fighting and produces a new period of hegemony in a restructured interstate system.

worth analysis *Negotiation:* Approach to analyzing a situation or potential outcome focusing on those elements considered useful or desirable to the affected parties. Created in contrast to cost analysis, which characterizes a situation strictly according to costs, regardless of whether the data is significant to the parties. Cost is only one of many elements that may be considered in assigning worth, which includes any number of economic and psychological factors. In Karrass's [1970, pp. 154–155] example, if a $100 part is required on an assembly line and a one-day delay costs $2,000, a buyer is justified in paying $2,000 for the part if he can save a single day. It would make no difference if the supplier's cost were 1¢ or $10,000.

WTO   See WORLD TRADE ORGANIZATION.

xadsitl **(Native North America/Salish)** "Crowding against you." Formalized fight arranged by a host of an important ceremony to alleviate tensions between families or communities. Other gambling or challenge contests and games were also introduced for the same purpose [Mansfield, 1993, pp. 347–348, citation omitted].

xotla **(South Africa)** Community meeting held among Bushmen of the Kalahari desert for the purpose of settling disputes. Adult men and women of the community participate in the *xotla,* which is held in the center of the encampment and is marked by a circle of poles. Because everyone is given the chance to have their say, it is sometimes days before a resolution to the dispute is finally reached [Ury, 1990, p. 229].

yes Usually denotes affirmation or agreement. However, some cultures discourage the use of *no* and negative signals so much that the use of *yes* and many nonverbal affirmative signals may not mean agreement or even understanding in those cultures. Contrast NO.

yesable proposition *Negotiation:* Proposal or offer that will invoke an acceptance or that leaves little room for refusal because it is stated in such a way as to appeal to the offeree's interests, concerns, and values. Attributable to Fisher (1969), the concept is a natural extension of the Currently Perceived Choice and Target Balance Sheet tools introduced in *Getting to Yes* by Fisher and Ury [1981, p. 45]

yielding See ACCOMMODATION.

yoloxalgwic **(Native North America/Lushootseed)** "Justice by council where there are two sides to a situation that need to be addressed" [Mansfield, 1993, p. 344, citation omitted].

yo-yo principle *Negotiation:* Tendency for specific bargaining relationships, particularly long-term, to have variation (ups and downs) in the success of their contract bargaining. Although these variations may be influenced by general economic trends and other external factors, the yo-yo effect may be substantially independent of external forces [Simkin, 1971, p. 163].

Zeuthen/Harsanyi model *Negotiation:* Mathematical model that calculates a party's comparative bargaining strength by determining the ratio between the utility difference to the party between his own demand and that of his opponent, and the utility difference to the party between his own demand and no agreement. The party for whom this fraction is smaller has to yield or make a concession. This criterion leads to the NASH POINT, that is, the outcome that maximizes the product of each party's own gain over no agreement [Harsanyi, 1975].

zero-sum *Negotiation:* In game theory, descriptive of a situation in which one's gains come only at the expense of another's equal loss. Game or system in which any gains made by one party are accompanied by a corresponding loss of equal value endured by another, making the sum of gains and losses equal to zero after each transaction.

Although zero-sum situations can be modeled, there are arguably few if any pure zero-sum situations in real life. Even if the parties are dividing a fixed resource, they often have different utilities regarding the resource. It is the varying perceptions of interests that determine whether the negotiations on a particular issue will be approached as a zero-sum game. The factors determining perceptions of interests are varied and variable.

See also FIXED PIE; contrast NON-ZERO SUM.

zone of agreement, zone of overlap *Negotiation:* Range of possible agreements created when the minimum one party will accept is less than the maximum the other party will pay. Similar if not identical concept as CONTRACT ZONE. As expressed on a graph, the concept is one-dimensional and thus limited to conceptualizing ZERO-SUM situations or classic positional bargaining over a fixed, limited resource of identical utility to the negotiators.

Conflict Resolution
Organizations and Programs

This appendix lists organizations and programs in conflict resolution. The organizations include not-for-profit associations and government agencies. A few larger for-profit providers of conflict resolution services are included in the listing. Not-for-profit associations include international, national, and local organizations devoted to conflict resolution, including providers of conflict resolution services such as the American Arbitration Association. Foundations with an interest in conflict resolution are listed. Government agencies include federal, national, provincial, tribal, and state agencies involved in conflict resolution. The programs listed are research or advanced degree-granting programs based in institutions of higher education. Some of these programs also provide conflict resolution services.

This does not purport to be a complete listing of all organizations and programs in conflict resolution. For example, there are an estimated 350 community or neighborhood mediation centers in the United States alone and no attempt is made here to list such local organizations. Though we have attempted to include only the most current information, the field is so dynamic and rapidly changing that certain information may no longer be accurate. Please help us by providing details on organizations and programs we have missed or that have recently formed, and any corrections and updates to the information provided herein.

A. A. White Dispute Resolution Institute
University of Houston, College of Business Administration
325 Melcher Hall
Houston, TX 77204-6283
Phone: (713) 743-4933
Fax: (713) 743-4934
E-mail: aawewt@rics1.cba.uh.edu
www.cba.uh.edu/center/aawdri.html

The Abraham Fund
477 Madison Avenue, 4th Floor
New York, NY 10022
Phone: (212) 303-9421
Toll Free: (800) 301-3863
Fax: (212) 935-1834
E-mail: abrahamfun@aol.com
www.coexistence.org

Academy of Family Mediators
5 Militia Drive
Lexington, MA 02421
Phone: (781) 674-2663
Fax: (781) 674-2690
E-mail: afmoffice@mediators.org
www.igc.org/afm

African Centre for the Constructive Resolution of Disputes (ACCORD)
c/o University of Durban–Westville
Private Bag X018
2 Golf Course Drive, Mount Edgecombe
Umhlanga, 4320, South Africa
Phone: +27 (31) 262-9340
Fax: +27 (31) 204-4815
www.accord.org.za

Alternative Dispute Resolution Centre–Vancouver
Broadway Plaza
905—601 West Broadway
Vancouver, British Columbia
Canada V5Z 4C2
Phone: (604) 708-9990
Toll Free: (800) 606-2378

Fax: (604) 708-3388
E-mail: postmaster@adrc.com
www.adrc.com/vanmap.htm

American Arbitration Association
1655 Broadway, 10th Floor
New York, NY 10019-6709
Phone: (212) 484-3266
Fax: (212) 307-4387
www.adr.org

American Bar Association
Section of Dispute Resolution
740 Fifteenth Street NW
Washington, DC 20005-1009
Phone: (202) 662-1720
Fax: (202) 662-1755
E-mail: dispute@abanet.org
www.abanet.org/dispute/dispute.html

Arkansas Alternative Dispute Resolution Commission
625 Marshall Street, Justice Building
Little Rock, AR 72201-1020
Phone: (501) 682-9400
Fax: (501) 682-9410
courts.state.ar.us/adr/index.html

Association of Family and Conciliation Courts
329 West Wilson Street
Madison, WI 53703
Phone: (608) 251-4001

Auckland University
See CENTRE FOR PEACE STUDIES

California Dispute Resolution Council
P.O. Box 55020
Los Angeles, CA 90055
Phone: (213) 896-6540
Fax: (213) 627-1426
www.conflict-resolution.net/cdrc

The Carter Center
453 Freedom Parkway
Atlanta, GA 30307
Phone: (404) 331-3900
www.CarterCenter.org

CDR Associates
100 Arapahoe Avenue, Suite 12
Boulder, CO 80302
Phone: (303) 442-7367
Toll Free: (800) MEDIATE
Fax: (303) 442-7442
E-mail: mmgolten@mediate.org
www.mediate.org

The Center for Alternative Dispute Resolution
130 Ontario Street
Albany, NY 12206
Phone: (518) 463-3686
Fax (518) 463-3680

Center for Analysis of Alternative Dispute Resolution Systems
11 East Adams Street, Suite 500
Chicago, IL 60603
Phone: (312) 922-6475, ext. 924
Fax: (312) 922-6463
www.caadrs.org

Center for Dispute Settlement
1666 Connecticut Avenue NW, Suite 500
Washington, DC 20009
Phone: (202) 265-9572
Fax: (202) 328-9162

Center for Environmental Dispute Resolution
1255 Twenty-Third Street NW, Suite 275
Washington, DC 20037
Phone: (202) 944-2300
Fax: (202) 338-1264

Center for Health Dispute Resolution
1 Fisher Road, 2nd Floor
Pittsford, NY 14534

Phone: (716) 586-1770
E-mail: info@healthappeal.com
www.healthappeal.com

Center for Negotiation and Conflict Resolution
Rutgers–State University of New Jersey
Bloustein School of Planning and Public Policy
33 Livingston Avenue, #104
New Brunswick, NJ 08901-1985,
Phone: (732) 932-2487
Fax: (732) 932-2493
E-mail: cncr@rci.rutgers.edu or lstamato@rci.rutgers.edu

Center for Peacemaking and Conflict Studies
Fresno Pacific University
1717 South Chestnut Avenue
Fresno, CA 93702
Phone: (559) 455-5840
Toll Free: (800) 909-8677
Fax: (559) 252-4800
E-mail: pacs@fresno.edu
www.fresno.edu/pacs

Center for Research in Conflict and Negotiation
Pennsylvania State University
313 Beam Business Administration Building
University Park, PA 16802
Phone: (814) 865-0197
Fax: (814) 856-0123
E-mail: b9g@psuvm.psu.edu

Center for Restorative Justice & Mediation
University of Minnesota
School of Social Work
386 McNeal Hall
1985 Buford Avenue
St. Paul, MN 55108-6134
Phone: (612) 624-4923
Fax: (612) 625-8224
E-mail: ctr4rjm@che2.che.umn.edu
ssw.che.umn.edu/ctr4rjm

Center for the Study of Dispute Resolution
University of Missouri School of Law
206 Hulston Hall
Columbia, MO 65211
Phone: (573) 882-2052
Fax: (573) 882-3343
E-mail: umclawedr@missouri.edu
www.law.missouri.edu/esdr

Center on Conflict and Negotiation
Stanford University Law School
Crown Quadrangle
Stanford, CA 94305-8610
Phone: (415) 723-1931
Fax: (415) 723-9421
E-mail: bland@leland.stanford.edu

Centre for Conflict Resolution
Macquarie University
Sydney, NSW 2109
Australia
Phone: (02) 850-8873
Fax: (02) 850-8230
E-mail: atidwell@laurel.ocs.mq.edu.au

Centre for Conflict Resolution International Ltd.
428 Portage Avenue, Suite 210
Winnipeg, Manitoba
Canada R3C 0E2
Phone: (204) 943-7588
Fax: (204) 943-7592
www.escape.ca/ ~ resolve/main.html

Centre for Peace and Conflict Studies
The University of Sydney
Mackie Building, K01
Sydney, NSW 2006
Australia
Phone: (02) 660-0862
Fax: (02) 351-3783
E-mail: wendyl@bullwinkle.econ.su.oz.au

Centre for Peace Studies
Auckland University
Private Bag 92019
Auckland, New Zealand
Phone: (64) 9373-7599
Fax: (64) 9373-7445
E-mail: r.white@auckland.ac.nz or p.wills@auckland.ac.nz

Centre for Peace Studies
The University of New England
Armidale, NSW 2351
Australia
Phone: (067) 73-2414
Fax: (067) 73-3280
E-mail: gharris@metz.une.edu.au

The Chartered Institute of Arbitrators
24 Angel Gate
City Road
London EC1V 2RS
Phone: (0171) 837-4483
Fax: (0171) 837-4185
E-mail: 71411.2735@Compuserve.com
www.arbitrators.org

City University of New York
Dispute Resolution Consortium
445 West Fifty-Ninth Street
New York, NY 10019
Phone: (212) 237-8693
Fax: (212) 237-8742
E-mail: mvolpe@faculty.jjay.cuny.edu

Coalition for Conflict Resolution in Education
Nova Southeastern University
School of Social and Systemic Studies
3301 College Avenue
Fort Lauderdale, FL 33314-7796
Phone: (800) 986-3223 ext. 8713
E-mail: ccre@nsu.nova.edu
www.nova.edu/ssss

Columbia University
School for International Affairs
See INTERNATIONAL CONFLICT RESOLUTION PROGRAM

Commission for Conciliation, Mediation, and Arbitration
20 Anderson Street
Johannesburg
Private Bag X94
Marshalltown 2107 South Africa
Phone: (011) 377-6650
Fax: (011) 834-7351
E-mail: infoservices@CCMA.org.za
www.ccma.org.za

Community Boards of San Francisco
1540 Market Street, Room 490
San Francisco, CA 94102
Phone: (415) 552-1250
Fax: (415) 626-0595
E-mail: cheetham@igc.apc.org

Community Dispute Resolution Centers Program
New York State Unified Court System
P.O. Box 7039
Alfred E. Smith Office Building
Albany, NY 12225
Phone: (518) 473-4160
Fax: (518) 473-6861

Community Dispute Resolution Program
State Court Administrative Offices
Michigan Supreme Court
309 North Washington Square
Lansing, MI 48909
Phone: (517) 373-0130
Fax: (517) 373-8922

Community Dispute Services
140 West Fifty-First Street
New York, NY 10020
Phone: (212) 484-4000

Conflict and Change Center
University of Minnesota
252 Hubert H. Humphrey Center
301 Nineteenth Avenue South
Minneapolis, MN 55455
Phone: (612) 625-0362 or 625-3046
Fax: (612) 625-3513
E-mail: ccc@gold.tc.umn.edu or fiuta001@maroon.tc.umn.edu

Conflict Management Group
20 University Road
Cambridge, MA 02138
Phone: (617) 354-5444
Fax: (617) 354-8467
E-mail: info@cmgonline.org
www.cmgonline.org

ConflictNet
Institute for Global Communications
P.O. Box 29904
San Francisco, CA 94129-0904
Phone: (415) 561-6100
Fax: (415) 561-6101
E-mail: conflictnet@igc.org
www.igc.org/igc/conflictnet

Conflict Research Consortium
University of Colorado
1560 Thirtieth Street
Room 232 Litman Building
Boulder, CO 80309
Phone: (303) 492-1635
Fax: (303) 492-2154
E-mail: crc@colorado.edu or burgess@colorado.edu
www.colorado.edu/conflict

Conflict Resolution Center
University of North Dakota
P.O. Box 8009
Grand Forks, ND 58202-8009
Phone: (701) 777-3664
Fax: (701) 777-6184
E-mail: udcrc@badlands.nodak.edu
www.und.nodak.edu/dept/crc

Conflict Resolution Center International
2205 East Carson Street
Pittsburgh, PA 15203-2107
Phone: (412) 481-5559

Conflict Resolution Education Network
1527 New Hampshire Avenue NW
Washington, DC 20036
Phone: (202) 667-9700
Fax: (202) 667-8629
E-mail: nidr@crenet.org

Conflict Resolution Program
Washington State University
P.O. Box 641018
Pullman, WA 99164-1018
Phone: (509) 335-6648
Fax: (509) 335-7092
E-mail: crp@wsu.edu or paqui@wsu.edu
www.wsu.edu:8080/ ~ paqui/homepage.htm

Conflict Resolution, Research and Resource Institute
705 South Ninth Street, Suite 206
Tacoma, WA 98405
Phone: (253) 597-8100
Fax: (253) 597-8103
E-mail: critacwa@sprynet.com
www.cri.cc/index.html

Connecticut Community Mediation Network
c/o Community Mediation, Inc.
134 Grand Avenue
New Haven, CT 06513
Phone: (203) 782-3500
Fax: (203) 782-3503

Consortium on Dispute Resolution
Management and Human Resources
Ohio State University
304C Hagerty Hall
1775 College Road
Columbus, OH 43210

Phone: (614) 292-0258
Fax: (614) 488-0546
E-mail: lewickir@babble.cob.ohio-state.edu

Consortium on Negotiation and Conflict Resolution
Georgia State University
College of Law
P.O. Box 4037
Atlanta, GA 30302-4037
Phone: (404) 651-1588
Fax: (404) 651-2092
E-mail: cncr@gsu.edu
law.gsu.edu/CNCR

The Consortium on Peace Research, Education and Development
c/o Institute for Conflict Analysis and Resolution
George Mason University
Fairfax, VA 22030-4444
Phone: (703) 993-2405
Fax: (703) 993-3070
www.gmu.edu/departments/ICAR/copred

CONVENOR Dispute Resolution
590 Madison Avenue, 21st Floor
New York, NY 10022
Phone: (212) 521-4321
Fax: (212) 504-8399
E-mail: webmaster@convenor.com
www.convenor.com

Council of Better Business Bureaus
Dispute Resolution Division
4200 Wilson Boulevard, Suite 800
Arlington, VA 22203-1838
www.bbb.org/complaints/index.html

CPR Institute for Dispute Resolution
366 Madison Avenue
New York, NY 10017-3122
Phone: (212) 949-6490
Fax: (212) 949-8859
www.cpradr.org

The Danish Institute of Arbitration
Frederiksborggade 1,3
DK-1360 Copenhagen K
Denmark
Phone: (+45) 3313-37-00
Fax: (+45) 3313-0403
www.denarbitra.dk/facts.html

Dispute Avoidance and Resolution Task Force (DART)
1150 Connecticut Avenue NW, Suite 600
Washington, DC 20036
Phone: (202) 296-5775

Dispute Resolution Institute
Hamline University School of Law
1536 Hewitt Avenue
St. Paul, MN 55104
Phone: (612) 641-2897
Fax: (612) 641-2435
www.hamline.edu/law/adr

Dispute Resolution Research Center
J.L. Kellogg Graduate School of Management
Northwestern University
Leverone Hall 386
2001 Sheridan Road
Evanston, IL 60208-2011
Phone: (847) 491-8068
Fax: (847) 491-8896
E-mail: drrc@kellogg.nwu.edu
www.kellogg.nwu.edu/research/disp_res

Disputes Processing Research Program
University of Wisconsin–Madison Law School
975 Bascom Mall
Madison, WI 53706
Phone: (608) 262-2244
Fax: (608) 262-5486
E-mail: galanter@law.wisc.edu

Environmental Conflict Resolution Programs
Udall Center for Studies in Public Policy
University of Arizona
803 East First Street
Tucson, AZ 85719

Phone: (520) 621-7189
Fax: (520) 621-9234
E-mail: emersonk@u.arizona.edu
vpr2.admin.arizona.edu/udall-center/programs/ecr/ecrprogram.htm

Family Mediation Canada
123 Woolwich Street
Guelph, Ontario
Canada N1H 3V1
Phone: (519) 836-7750
Fax: (519) 836-7204
E-mail: faltom@aol.com
www.mediate.com/fmc

Federal Mediation and Conciliation Service
2100 K Street NW
Washington, DC 20427
Phone: (202) 606-8100
Fax: (202) 606-4216
E-mail: publicinformation@fmcs.gov
www.fmcs.gov

Federal Mediation and Conciliation Service
Canada/New Brunswick Business Service Centre
165 Hotel de Ville
Place du Portage, Phase II
Ottawa, Québec
Canada K1A 0J2
Phone: (819) 994-1519
Fax: (819) 953-4899
www.cbsc.org/nb/bis/1539.html

Florida Conflict Resolution Consortium
Florida State University
P.O. Box 2850
Tallahassee, FL 32306-2850
www.ispa.fsu.edu/growth_man.html

Florida Dispute Resolution Center
Supreme Court Building
Tallahassee, FL 32399-1905
Phone: (904) 921-2910
justice.courts.state.fl.us/courts/adr/brochure.html

Florida State University
See FLORIDA CONFLICT RESOLUTION CONSORTIUM

Fresno Pacific University
See CENTER FOR PEACEMAKING AND CONFLICT STUDIES

The Fund for Peace
1701 K Street NW, 11th Floor
Washington, DC 20006
Phone: (202) 223-7940
Fax: (202) 223-7947
E-mail: Comments@fundforpeace.org

George Mason University
See INSTITUTE FOR CONFLICT ANALYSIS AND RESOLUTION

Georgia Office of Dispute Resolution
800 The Hurt Building
50 Hurt Plaza
Atlanta, GA 30303
Phone: (404) 527-8789
Fax: (404) 527-8711
E-mail: gaodr@mindspring.com
www.doas.state.ga.us/courts/adr/odr.htm

Georgia State University College of Law
See CONSORTIUM ON NEGOTIATION AND CONFLICT RESOLUTION

Hamline University School of Law
See DISPUTE RESOLUTION INSTITUTE

Hong Kong International Arbitration Centre
38th Floor, Two Exchange Square
8 Connaught Place
Hong Kong, China
Phone: (852) 2525-2381
Fax: (852) 2524-2171
E-mail: adr@hkiac.org

ICC International Court of Arbitration
38 Cours Albert 1er
75008 Paris, France

Phone: +33 1 49 53 28 28
Fax: +33 1 49 53 29 33
E-mail: arb@iccwbo.org
www.iccwbo.org/arb/2.htm

Indian Ocean Centre for Peace Studies
The University of Western Australia
Nedlands, WA 6007
Australia
Phone: (09) 380-3993
Fax: (09) 380-1074
E-mail: iocps@uniwa.uwa.edu.au

Indiana Conflict Resolution Institute
University of Indiana
School of Public and Environmental Affairs
1315 East Tenth Street
Bloomington, IN 47405
Phone: (812) 855-3774
Toll Free: 800) 765-7755
E-mail: speainfo@indiana.edu
www.spea.indiana.edu/icri

Initiative on Conflict Resolution and Ethnicity
Aberfoyle House
University of Ulster
Magee College
Northland Road
Derry (Londonderry) BT48 7JA
Northern Ireland
Phone: +44 0 1504 375501
Fax: +44 0 1504 375510
E-mail: incore@incore.ulst.ac.uk
www.incore.ulst.ac.uk

Institute for Conflict Analysis and Resolution
George Mason University
4400 University Drive
Fairfax, VA 22030-4444
Phone: (703) 993-1300
Fax: (703) 993-1302
E-mail: kclement@gmu.edu
www.gmu.edu/depts/ICAR

Institute for Conflict Resolution Studies
Vietnam Veterans of America Foundation
2001 South Street NW, Suite 740
Washington, DC 20009
Phone: (202) 483-2063
Fax: (202) 483-9314

Institute for Dispute Resolution
University of Victoria
P.O. Box 2400, STN CSC
Victoria, British Columbia
Canada V8W 3H7
Phone: (250) 721-8777
Fax: (250) 721-6607
E-mail: uvicidr@uvic.ca
dispute.resolution.uvic.ca

Institute on Global Conflict and Cooperation
University of California
9500 Gilman Drive, Mail Code 0518
La Jolla, CA 92093-0518
Phone: (619) 534-3352
Fax: (619) 534-7655
E-mail: ph13@sdcc12.ucsd.edu
www-igcc.ucsd.edu

Institute for International Mediation and Conflict Resolution
2708 Cathedral Avenue NW
Washington, DC 20008
Phone: (202) 462-9544
Fax: (202) 462-6151
www.iimcr.org

Institute for Multi-Track Diplomacy
1819 H Street NW
Washington, DC 20006
Phone: (202) 466-4605
Fax: (202) 466-4607
E-mail: imtd@imtd.org

Institute for Peace Science
See PEACE STUDIES ASSOCIATION OF JAPAN

Institute of World Affairs
1321 Pennsylvania Avenue SE
Washington, DC 20003
Phone: (202) 544-4141
Fax: (202) 544-5115
E-mail: info@iwa.org
www.iwa.org

The International Conflict Resolution Centre
School of Behavioural Science
University of Melbourne
Parkville, VIC 3052
Australia
Phone: +61 3 9344 7035
Fax: +61 3 9347 6618
E-mail: icrc@psych.unimelb.edu.au
www.psych.unimelb.edu.au/icrc/index.html

International Conflict Resolution Program
Columbia University
School for International Affairs
Box 23, International Affairs Building
420 West 118th Street
Columbia University, Mail Code 3369
New York, NY 10027
Phone: (212) 854-5623
Fax: (212) 854-6171
E-mail: ICRP@Columbia.edu
www.columbia.edu/cu/sipa/RESOURCES/ICRP

International Peace Academy
777 UN Plaza
New York, NY 10017
Phone: (212) 687-4300
Fax: (212) 983-8246
E-mail: ipa@ipacademy.org

International Peace Research Association
c/o Copenhagen Peace Research Institute
Fredericiagade 18
1310 Copenhagen K
Denmark
Phone: (+45) 3345-5050
Fax: (+45) 3332-6554
www.copri.dk/ipra/ipra.html

ISN–International Relations and Security Network
Center for Security Studies and Conflict Research
ETH-Zentrum/SEI
CH-8092 Zurich, Switzerland
Phone: + +41 (0) 1 632 40 25
Fax: + +41 (0) 1 632 19 41
E-mail: postmaster@sipo.reok.ethz.ch

JAMS/Endispute
New York Dispute Resolution Panel
345 Park Avenue, 8th Floor
New York, NY 10154
Phone: (212) 751-2700
Toll Free: (800) 352-52677
Fax: (212) 751-4099
E-mail: info@jams-endispute.com
www.jams-endispute.com

Joan B. Kroc Institute for International Peace Studies
University of Notre Dame
P.O. Box 639
Notre Dame, IN 46556-0639
Phone: (219) 631-6970
Fax: (219) 631-6973
E-mail: kroc-admissions.1@nd.edu
www.nd.edu/~krocinst/index.html

The Key Bridge Foundation
1117 North Nineteenth Street, Suite 903
Arlington, VA 22209
E-mail: keybfound@aol.com

La Marsh Centre for Research on Violence and Conflict Resolution
217 York Lanes
York University
4700 Keele Street
Toronto, Ontario M3J 1P3 CANADA
Phone: (416) 736-5528
Fax: (416) 736-5647
E-mail: lamarsh@yorku.ca
www.yorku.ca/research/lamarsh

Lawyers Engaged in Dispute Resolution
National Dispute Centre
Level 4, 233 Macquarie Street
Sydney NSW 2000
Australia
Phone: 61 2 9233 2255
Toll Free: (800) 651-6500
Fax: 61 2 9232 3024
E-mail: leadr@fl.asn.au
www.leadr.com.au

Macquarie University
See CENTRE FOR CONFLICT RESOLUTION

Mediation Association of Tennessee
Knoxville Chapter
P.O. Box 414
Knoxville, TN 37901-0414
Phone: (423) 525-1099
Fax: (423) 525-7494
E-mail: matk@cide.com
www.cide.com/matk

Mediation Centers of Hawaii
c/o Neighborhood Justice Center of Honolulu, Inc.
200 North Vineyard Boulevard, Suite 320
Honolulu, HI 96817
Phone: (808) 521-6767
Fax: (808) 538-1454

The Mediation Information and Resource Center
440 East Broadway, Suite 340
P.O. Box 51090
Eugene, OR 97405
Phone: (541) 302-6254
Fax: (541) 345-4024
www.mediate.com

Mediation Network of North Carolina
P.O. Box 241
Chapel Hill, NC 27514-0241
Phone: (919) 929-6333
Fax: (919) 933-4465

Mediation Programs
Administrative Office
District Court Department of the Trial Court of Massachusetts
Holyoke Square
Salem, MA 01970
Phone: (508) 745-9010
Fax: (508) 745-9019

National Academy of Arbitrators
503 Lowder Building
College of Business
Auburn University, AL 36849
Phone: (334) 844-6523
www.cornell.edu/Campus/Infobase/National.Academy.of.Arbitrators.html

National Academy of Conciliators
1111 West Mockingbird Lane, Suite 300
Dallas, TX 75247
Phone: (214) 638-5633

National Association for Community Mediation
1726 M Street NW, Suite 500
Washington, DC 20036
Phone: (202) 467-6226
Fax: (202) 466-4769
E-mail: nafcm@nafcm.org
www.igc.org/nafcm

National Association for Mediation in Education
University of Massachusetts
205 Hampshire House, Box 33635
Amherst, MA 01003-3635
Phone: (413) 545-2462
Fax: (413) 545-4802
www.nonprofits.org/gallery/alpha/name

National Institute for Dispute Resolution
1527 New Hampshire Avenue NW
Washington, DC 20036
Phone: (202) 667-9700
Fax: (202) 667-8629
E-mail: nidr@crenet.org
www.nidr.org

National Resource Center for Youth Mediation
800 Park Avenue SW
Albuquerque, NM 87102
Toll Free: (800) 249-6884
Fax: (505) 247-0572

Neighbourhood Coalition for Conflict Resolution
1061 Merivale Road
Room 5, Second Floor
Ottawa, Ontario
Canada K1Z 6A9
Phone: (613) 724-6058
Fax: (613) 724-4950
www.web.net/ ~ nccr/frame.html

New Mexico Center for Dispute Resolution
800 Park Avenue SW
Albuquerque, NM 87102
Phone: (505) 247-0571
Fax: (505) 242-5966

New Mexico Mediation Association
P.O. Box 82384
Albuquerque, NM 87198
Phone: (505) 881-1141

New York State Dispute Resolution Association
244 Hudson Avenue
Albany, NY 12210
Phone: (518) 465-2500
Fax: (518) 465-0840

New York State Mediation Association
c/o Westchester Mediation Center
P.O. Box 1248
20 South Broadway
Yonkers, NY 10701
Phone: (914) 963-6440
Fax: (914) 963-4566

Northern California Mediation Association
Box 544
Corte Madera, CA 94976-0544
Phone: (415) 927-4308
www.mediate.com/organize/ncma

Northwestern University
J.L. Kellogg Graduate School of Management
See DISPUTE RESOLUTION RESEARCH CENTER

Nova Southeastern University
See COALITION FOR CONFLICT RESOLUTION IN EDUCATION

Ohio Commission on Dispute Resolution and Conflict Management
77 South High Street, 24th Floor
Columbus, OH 43266
Phone: (614) 752-9595
Fax: (614) 752-9682

Ohio State Consortium on Dispute Resolution
Ohio State University College of Law
55 West Twelfth Avenue
Columbus, OH 43212-1194
Phone: (614) 292-4223 or 292-2631
Fax: (614) 292-1383
E-mail: nrogers@magnus.acs.Ohio-State.edu

Ohio State University
See CONSORTIUM ON DISPUTE RESOLUTION

Oregon Dispute Resolution Commission
1174 Chemeketa Street NE
Salem, OR 97310
Phone: (503) 378-2877
www.open.org/odrc

Oregon Mediation Association
P.O. Box 2951
Portland, OR 97208
Phone: (503) 294-1017
www.mediate.com/organize/oma

Peace and Conflict Studies Programme
Department of Government
University of Queensland
St. Lucia, Queensland 4072
Australia
Phone: (07) 3365-2090
Fax: (07) 3365-1388
E-mail: r.sumny@mailbox.uq.oz.au

Peace Research Centre
Research School of Pacific and Asian Studies
The Australian National University
Canberra, ACT 0200
Australia
Phone: (06) 249-3098
Fax: (06) 249-0174
E-mail: peace@cooms.anu.edu.au

Peace Studies Association of Japan
c/o Institute for Peace Science
Hiroshima University
1-1-81 Higashisenda, Naka-ku
Hiroshima 730 Japan
Phone: +81-82-241-1221 ext. 3829
E-mail: psaj@ue.ipc.hiroshima-u.ac.jp
133.67.70.210/IPRA/IPRN_30.html

Peace Studies Program
Department of French
University of Canterbury
Christchurch 1, New Zealand
Phone: (64)(33) 66-7001
Fax: (64)(33) 64-2999

Peace Studies Program
School of English
University of New South Wales
Kensington, NSW 2053
Australia
Phone: (02) 697-2298
Fax: (02) 662-2148

Peace Studies Programme
La Trobe University
Bundoora, VIC 3083
Australia
Phone: (03) 9479-1111
Fax: (03) 9479-1607

Pearson Peacekeeping Centre
P.O. Box 100
Cornwallis Park
Clementsport, Nova Scotia
Canada B0S 1E0
Phone: (902) 638-8611
Fax: (902) 638-8888
E-mail: president@ppc.cdnpeacekeeping.ns.ca

Pennsylvania State University
See CENTER FOR RESEARCH IN CONFLICT AND NEGOTIATION

Pepperdine University School of Law
See INSTITUTE FOR DISPUTE RESOLUTION

Program on the Analysis and Resolution of Conflicts
Syracuse University
410 Maxwell Hall
Syracuse, NY 13244
Phone: (315) 423-2367
Fax: (315) 443-3818
E-mail: rar@mailbox.syr.edu
www.maxwell.syr.edu/parc/parcmain.htm

Program on Conflict Management Alternatives
Center for Research on Social Organization
University of Michigan
4016 LSA Building
Ann Arbor, MI 48109
Phone: (313) 763-0472

Program on Conflict Resolution
Spark M. Matsunaga Institute for Peace
University of Hawaii at Manoa
2424 Maile Way, Porteus 523
Honolulu, HI 96822
Phone: (808) 956-7792
Fax: (808) 956-9121
E-mail: program@uhunix.uhcc.hawaii.edu

Program on Mediating Theory and Democratic Systems
Wayne State University
2325 Faculty-Administration Building
Detroit, MI 48202

Phone: (313) 577-5313
Fax: (313) 577-8269
E-mail: FPEARSO@cms.cc.wayne.edu

Program on Negotiation at Harvard Law School
500 Pound Hall
Cambridge, MA 02138
Phone: (617) 495-1684
Fax: (617) 495-7818
E-mail: PON@law.harvard.edu
www.pon.harvard.edu

RAND Institute for Civil Justice
The Rand Corporation
1700 Main Street
P.O. Box 2138
Santa Monica, CA 90406-2138
Phone: (310) 451-6916
Fax: (310) 451-6979
E-mail: deborah_hensler@rand.org

RESOLVE, Inc.
1255 Twenty-Third Street NW, Suite 275
Washington, DC 20037
Phone: (202) 944-2300
www.resolv.org

Rutgers–State University of New Jersey
Bloustein School of Planning and Public Policy
See CENTER FOR NEGOTIATION AND CONFLICT RESOLUTION

Schleswig-Holstein Institute for Peace Research at the Christian-Albrechts-University Kiel
Phone: +49 431 77572-860
E-mail: Potthoff@schiff.uni-kiel.de

Singapore International Arbitration Centre
1 Coleman Street, no. 05-08
The Adelphi, Singapore 179803
Phone: (65) 334-1277
Fax: (65) 334-2942
E-mail: sinarb@singnet.com.sg
siac.tdb.gov.sg

Society of Professionals in Dispute Resolution
1527 New Hampshire Avenue NW, 3rd Floor
Washington, DC 20036
Phone: (202) 667-9700
Fax: (202) 265-1968
E-mail: spidr@spidr.org
www.igc.apc.org/spidr

Software and Information Association
(Software Publishers Association)
1730 M Street NW, Suite 700
Washington, DC 20036-4510
Phone: (202) 452-1600 ext. 311
Fax: (202) 223-8756
E-mail: mediation@spa.org
www.spa.org/mediation

South Dakota Mediation Association
625 Minnesota Avenue, Suite 101
Sioux Falls, SD 57104
Phone: (605) 339-3310
Fax: (605) 339-3243

Southern California Mediation Association
P.O. Box 15982
Long Beach, CA 90815-0982
Phone: (562) 425-1721
Fax: (562) 425-0199
E-mail: scma@scmediation.org
www.scmediation.org

Stanford University Law School
See CENTER ON CONFLICT AND NEGOTIATION

Straus Institute for Dispute Resolution
Pepperdine University School of Law
24255 Pacific Coast Highway
Malibu, CA 90263
Phone: (310) 317-7455
Fax: (310) 456-4000
www.pepperdine.edu/idrweb

Syracuse University
See PROGRAM ON THE ANALYSIS AND RESOLUTION OF CONFLICTS

United States Institute of Peace
1200 Seventeenth Street NW, Suite 200
Washington, DC 20036-3011
Phone: (202) 457-1700
Fax: (202) 429-6063
E-mail: usip_requests@usip.org

University of Arizona
Udall Center for Studies in Public Policy
See ENVIRONMENTAL CONFLICT RESOLUTION PROGRAMS

University of California
See INSTITUTE ON GLOBAL CONFLICT AND COOPERATION

University of Colorado
See CONFLICT RESEARCH CONSORTIUM

University of Durban–Westville
See ACCORD

University of Hawaii at Manoa
Spark M. Matsunaga Institute for Peace
See PROGRAM ON CONFLICT RESOLUTION

University of Indiana
See INDIANA CONFLICT RESOLUTION INSTITUTE

University of Michigan
Center for Research on Social Organization
See PROGRAM ON CONFLICT MANAGEMENT ALTERNATIVES

University of Minnesota
See CENTER FOR RESTORATIVE JUSTICE & MEDIATION;
CONFLICT AND CHANGE CENTER

University of Missouri School of Law
See CENTER FOR THE STUDY OF DISPUTE RESOLUTION

University of North Dakota
See CONFLICT RESOLUTION CENTER

University of Notre Dame
See JOAN B. KROC INSTITUTE FOR INTERNATIONAL PEACE STUDIES

University of Sydney
See CENTRE FOR PEACE AND CONFLICT STUDIES

University of Victoria
See INSTITUTE FOR DISPUTE RESOLUTION

University of Wisconsin–Madison Law School
See DISPUTES PROCESSING RESEARCH PROGRAM

Victim Offender Mediation Association
4624 Van Kleeck Drive
New Smyrna Beach, FL 32169
Phone: (904) 424-1591
Fax: (904) 423-8099
E-mail: voma@voma.org
www.igc.org/voma

Washington State University
See CONFLICT RESOLUTION PROGRAM

Wayne State University
See PROGRAM ON MEDIATING THEORY AND DEMOCRATIC SYSTEMS

Resources for Court-Connected Alternative Dispute Resolution Arranged by State

ALABAMA

Alabama Center for Dispute Resolution
415 Dexter Avenue
P.O. Box 671
Montgomery, AL 36101
Phone: (334) 269-0409
Fax: (334) 261-6310

ALASKA

Court Rules Attorney
820 West Fourth Avenue
Anchorage, AK 99501
Phone: (907) 264-8239
Fax: (907) 264-8291
E-mail: cjohnson@courts.state.ak.us

ARIZONA

Court Services Division
1501 West Washington Street, Suite 410
Phoenix, AZ 85007-3330
Phone: (602) 542-9453

ARKANSAS

State Court Administrator
Justice Building
625 Marshall Street
Little Rock, AR 72201-1020
Phone: (501) 682-9400
Fax: (501) 682-9010

Arkansas ADR Commission
Hon. Warren O. Kimbrough (Retired), Chair
2600 South Forty-Sixth Street
Fort Smith, AR 72903-3529
Phone: (501) 783-7733

Arkansas Bar Association ADR Committee
Hon. Sidney McCollum, Chair
ADR, Inc.
1104 South Walton Boulevard
Bentonville, AR 72712-6291
Phone: (501) 271-2237

CALIFORNIA

Judicial Council Task Force on Quality of Justice
Subcommittee on ADR
Judicial Council of California
Administrative Office of the Courts
303 Second Street, South Tower
San Francisco, CA 94107
Phone: (415) 396-9129
Fax: (415) 396-9358

COLORADO

Office of Dispute Resolution
Colorado Judicial Department
1301 Pennsylvania Street, Suite 110
Denver, CO 80203-2416
Phone: (303) 837-3667
Fax: (303) 837-2340

CONNECTICUT

Dispute Resolution Program
Judicial Branch
Court Operations Division
75 Elm Street
Hartford, CT 60106
Phone: (860) 722-1640
Fax: (860) 722-5817

DELAWARE

Administrative Office of the Court
Carvel State Office Building, 11th Floor
820 North French Street
Wilmington, DE 19801
Phone: (302) 577-2480

DISTRICT OF COLUMBIA

Multi-Door Dispute Resolution Division
Superior Court of the District of Columbia
500 Indiana Avenue NW, John Marshall Level
Washington, DC 20001
Phone: (202) 879-1479

FLORIDA

Florida Dispute Resolution Center
Supreme Court Building
500 South Duval Street
Tallahassee, FL 32399-1905
Phone: (850) 921-2910

GEORGIA

Georgia Office of Dispute Resolution
800 The Hurt Building
50 Hurt Plaza
Atlanta, GA 30303
Phone: (404) 527-8789

HAWAII

Center for Alternative Dispute Resolution
417 South King Street, Room 207
Ali'iolani Hale
Honolulu, HI 96813
Phone: (808) 539-4980

IDAHO

Administrative Director of the Courts
Supreme Court Building
451 West State Street
P.O. Box 83720
Boise, ID 83720-0101
Phone: (208) 334-2246
Fax: (208) 334-2146

ILLINOIS

Executive Office
Administrative Office of the Illinois Courts
840 South Spring Street
Springfield, IL 62704
Phone: (217) 785-2125
Fax: (217) 785-3793

INDIANA

Mediation Office Manager
115 West Washington Street
Indianapolis, IN 46204-3417
Phone: (317) 233-2581
Fax: (317) 233-1442

IOWA

ADR Grant Fund
Supreme Court of Iowa
State Capital Building
Des Moines, IA 50312
Phone: (515) 281-5174
Fax: (515) 281-3043

KANSAS

Jason Oldham
Kansas Judicial Center
301 West Tenth Street, Room 337
Topeka, KS 66612-1507
Phone: (785) 291-3748
Fax: (785) 296-1804

KENTUCKY

Administrative Office of the Courts
100 Millcreek Park
Frankfort, KY 40601
Phone: (502) 573-2350
Fax: (502) 695-1759

LOUISIANA

Supreme Court of Louisiana
301 Loyola Avenue
New Orleans, LA 70112
Phone: (504) 568-5747

MAINE

Center for Alternative Dispute Resolution
RR1, Box 310
West Bath, ME 04530-9704
Phone: (207) 442-0227
Fax: (207) 442-0228

MARYLAND

Maryland Alternative Dispute Resolution Commission
120 East Chesapeake Avenue
Second Floor Chambers 6
Towson, MD 21286
Phone: (410) 321-2398
Fax: (410) 321-2399
E-mail: rachel.wohl@courts.state.md.us

MASSACHUSETTS

Administrative Office of the Trial Courts
Two Center Plaza
Boston, MA 02108
Phone: (617) 742-8575
Fax: (617) 742-0968

Council for Policy Development
Massachusetts Supreme Judicial Court
1400 New Courthouse
Boston, MA 02108
Phone: (617) 557-1156
Fax: (617) 557-1052

MICHIGAN

State Court Administrative Office
309 North Washington Square
P.O. Box 30048
Lansing, MI 48909
Phone: (517) 373-4835

MINNESOTA

Supreme Court of Minnesota
140 Minnesota Judicial Center
25 Constitution Avenue
St. Paul, MN 55155
Phone: (612) 297 7591

MISSISSIPPI

Administrative Office of the Courts
P.O. Box 117
Jackson, MS 39205
Phone: (601) 354-7449
Fax: (601) 354 7459
E-mail: santhony@mssc.state.ms.us

MISSOURI

Family Preservation Project Specialist
Office of the State Courts Administrator
2112 Industrial Drive
P.O. Box 104480
Jefferson City, MO 65110
Phone: (573) 751-4377
Fax: (573) 751-5540

MONTANA

Clerk of the Supreme Court
Justice Building, Room 323
215 North Sanders
Helena, MT 59620
Phone: (406) 444-3858
Fax: (406) 444-5705

NEBRASKA

Office of Dispute Resolution
State Capitol Building, Room 1207
P.O. Box 98910
Lincoln, NE 68509-8910
Phone: (402) 471-3148
Fax: (402) 471-2197

NEVADA

Family Mediation and Assessment Center
Family Court and Services Center
601 North Pecos Road
Las Vegas, NV 89101
Phone: (702) 455-4186

Phil Bushard
Director of Court Mediation
Family Mediation Program
Courthouse
75 Court Street
Reno, NV 89501
Phone: (702) 328-3556

NEW HAMPSHIRE

Chair of Superior Court ADR Committee
22 Main Street
Newport, NH 03773
Phone: (603) 863-3450
Fax: (603) 863-3204

NEW JERSEY

CDR Program Operations
Administrative Office of the Courts
Hughes Justice Complex CN-988
Trenton, NJ 08625
Phone: (609) 984-2337
Fax: (609) 633-7142

Marylin C. Slivka
Acting Manager, Special Program Unit
Administrative Office of the Courts
Hughes Justice Complex CN-988
Trenton, NJ 08625
Phone: (609) 984-2172
Fax: (609) 633-7142

NEW MEXICO

Clerk, Second District Court
County Courthouse
P.O. Box 488
Albuquerque, NM 87103
Phone: (505) 841-7425
Fax: (505) 841-7446

NEW YORK

Alternative Resolution Dispute Coordinator
Office of Court Administration
25 Beaver Street, Room 1024
New York, NY 10004
Phone: (212) 428-2756
Fax: (212) 428-2513

Mark Collins
Deputy State Coordinator
Community Dispute Resolution Centers Program
Alfred E. Smith Office Building, 1st Floor
P.O. Box 7039
Albany, NY 12225-0039
Phone: (518) 473-4160
Fax: (518) 473-6861

NORTH CAROLINA

State of North Carolina Dispute Resolution Commission
P.O. Box 2448
Raleigh, NC 27602
Phone: (919) 715-1676
Fax: (919) 733-1845

Arbitration
Miriam Saxon
Administrative Office of the Courts
P.O. Box 2448
Raleigh, NC 27602
Phone: (919) 733-7107

Custody Mediation
Jan Hood
Custody Mediation Program Administrator
Administrative Office of the Courts
P.O. Box 2448
Raleigh, NC 27602
Phone: (919) 733-7107

NORTH DAKOTA

Deborah Knuth
Liaison to ADR Committee
State Bar Association of North Dakota
P.O. Box 2136
Bismarck, ND 58502
Phone: (701) 255-1404
Fax: (701) 224-1621

OHIO

Dispute Resolution Programs
Supreme Court of Ohio
30 E. Broad Street
Columbus, OH 43266-0419
Phone: (614) 752-4700
Fax: (614) 466-6652

Maria Mone
Ohio Commission on State Government Dispute
Resolution and Conflict Management
77 South High Street, 24th Floor
Columbus, OH 43266
Phone: (614) 752-9595

OKLAHOMA

Alternative Dispute Resolution Systems
Administrative Office of the Courts
1915 North Stiles, Suite 305
Oklahoma City, OK 73105
Phone: (405) 521-2450
Fax: (405) 521-6815
E-mail: tates@oscn.net

OREGON

ADR Advisor
Oregon Judicial Department
Oregon Supreme Court Building
1163 State Street
Salem, OR 97310
Phone: (503) 986-5935
Fax: (503) 986-5503

PENNSYLVANIA

Supreme Court of Pennsylvania
5035 Ritter Road, Suite 700
Mechanicsburg, PA 17055
Phone: (717) 795-2000
Fax: (717) 795-2116

RHODE ISLAND

State Court Administrator
Supreme Court of Rhode Island
250 Benefit Street
Providence, RI 02903
Phone: (401) 222-3263
Fax: (401) 222-3599

State has no official ADR program

SOUTH CAROLINA

Chair, Joint Commission on ADR
P.O. Box 1037
Charleston, SC 29402
Phone: (803) 577-5083
Fax: (803) 723-9037

Andy Surles
ADR Programs
1015 Sumter Street
Columbia, SC 29201
Phone: (803) 734-1800
Fax: (803) 734-1821

SOUTH DAKOTA

No contact

TENNESSEE

Tennessee ADR Commission
Nashville City Center, Suite 600
511 Union Street
Nashville, TN 37243-0607
Phone: (615) 741-2687
Fax: (615) 741-6285

TEXAS

Center for Public Policy on Dispute Resolution
University of Texas School of Law
727 East Dean Keeton Drive
Austin, TX 78705
Phone: (512) 471-3507
Fax: (512) 471-1191

UTAH

Director of ADR.
Administrative Office of the Courts
230 South 500 East, S-300
Salt Lake City, UT 84102
Phone: (801) 578-3800
Fax: (801) 578-3843

VERMONT

Office of State Court Administrator
109 State Street
Montpelier, VT 05609-0701
Phone: (802) 828-3276
Fax: (802) 828-3457

VIRGINIA

Department of Dispute Resolution Services
Supreme Court of Virginia
100 North Ninth Street
Richmond, VA 23219
Phone: (804) 786-6455
Fax: (804) 786-4542

WASHINGTON

No contact

WEST VIRGINIA

No contact

WISCONSIN

Randy Sproule
Medical Mediation Panels Coordinator
110 East Main Street, Room 320
Madison, WI 53703
Phone: (608) 266-7711
Fax: (608) 267-0911

WYOMING

Supreme Court Administrator
Supreme Court Building
2301 Capital Avenue
Cheyenne, WY 82002
Phone: (307) 777-7581
Fax: (307) 777-3447

Conflict Resolution Degree-Granting Programs in Higher Education

The education programs listed here include only degree-granting programs in institutions of higher education. Numerous certificate programs exist but are not listed. Most conflict resolution and peace studies programs are housed in a more traditional academic department, such as political science or sociology; there are a few programs, however, offered by peace or conflict studies departments. Each year some programs cease while new ones emerge, so this list is in constant flux. Please see the following Web sites for partial listings and links:

csf.Colorado.EDU/peace/academic.html

www.gradschools.com/listings/out/peace_out.html

www.gradschools.com/listings/all/peace.html

UNDERGRADUATE DEGREE PROGRAMS

Bethel College
Peace Studies Department
300 East Twenty-Seventh Street
North Newton, KS 67117
Degree: Major, minor, concentration
Phone: (316) 283-2500 ext. 353

Bridgewater College
Peace Studies Minor
Department of Philosophy and Religion
Bridgewater, VA 22812
Degree: Major, minor
Phone: (703) 828-2501

California State University at Sacramento
Peace and Conflict Resolution Studies
6000 J Street
Sacramento, CA 95819
Degree: Major
Phone: (916) 278-6574

Chapman University
Peace Studies Program
333 North Glassell Street
Orange, CA 92666
Degree: Major, minor
Phone: (714) 997-6620
E-mail: will@nexua.chapman.edu

City College of New York
International Studies Program
NAC 6/109, Covenant Avenue at 138th
New York, NY 10031
Degree: B.A.
Phone: (212) 650-6909

Colgate University
Peace Studies Program
Hamilton, NY 13346
Degree: Major, minor
Phone: (315) 824-7574, 824-7550, 824-7806

Depauw University
Peace and Conflict Management Studies
500 East Seminary Street
Greencastle, IN 46135
Degree: Major, minor
Phone: (317) 658-4358

Earlham College
Peace and Global Studies Program
Richmond, IN 47374
Degree: Major
Phone: (765) 983-1305

Edgewood College
Independent Studies in Peace Education
855 Woodrow Street
Madison, WI 53711
Degree: Major
Phone: (608) 257-4861

Georgetown University
Program of Justice and Peace
Philosophy Department
225 New North
Washington, DC 20057
Degree: Major
Phone: (202) 687-7647
Fax: (202) 687-4493
www.georgetown.edu/departments/pjp

Hiroshima University
Institute for Peace Science
1-1-81 Higashisenda, Naka-ku
Hiroshima 730 Japan
Degree: Major
Phone: +81-82-241-1221 ext. 3829
E-mail: psaj@ue.ipc.hiroshima-u.ac.jp
133.67.70.210/IPRA/IPRN_30.html

Juniata College
The Baker Institute
Peace and Conflict Studies
Huntington, PA 16652
Degree: Major
Phone: (814) 643-4310

Kent State University
Center for Applied Conflict Management
Political Science Department
P.O. Box 5190
302 Bowman Hall
Kent, OH 44242-0001
Degree: Major, minor
Phone: (330) 672-3143
Fax: (330) 672-3362
E-mail: cacm@kent.edu
www.kent.edu/cacm

La Trobe University
Peace Studies
Martin Bldg SS251
Bundoora, VIC 3083
Australia
Degree: Major
Phone: (03) 9479-1111

Manchester College
Peace Studies Institute and Program in Conflict Resolution
North Manchester, IN 46962
Degree: Major
Phone: (219) 982-5343

Molloy College
Program for International Peace and Justice Studies
1000 Hempstead Avenue
P.O. Box 5002
Rockville Centre, NY 11570-5002
Degree: Major, minor
Phone: (516) 678-500 ext. 307

Northland College
Studies in Conflict and Peacemaking
Ashland, WI 54806
Degree: Major
Phone: (715) 682-4531

The Ohio State University
Undergraduate International Studies Program
Peace Studies
Department of International Studies
2186 Derby Hall
154 North Oval Mall
Columbus, OH 43210
Degree: Major, minor, certificate
Phone: (614) 292-9657
E-mail: IntStds@osu.edu

Purdue University
International Relations/Political Science
West Lafayette, IN 47907
Degree: B.A.
Phone: (317) 494-8462, 494-4169

Russian Christian Institute
Department of Philosophy
Voznesenski prospekt 34 "b," 190068
St. Petersburg, Russia
Degrees: Major
Phone: (812) 315-70-86

Saint John's University
Peace Studies
Collegeville, MN 56321
Degree: Major
Phone: (612) 363-2698

Syracuse University
Program on Nonviolent Conflict and Change
712 Ostrom Avenue
Syracuse, NY 13244
Degree: Major, minor, concentration
Phone: (315) 443-2367

Temple University
Communication Sciences
Emphasis in Conflict Studies
Weiss Hall
Philadelphia, PA 19122
Degree: B.A.
Phone: (215) 204-1890
Fax: (215) 204-5954
E-mail: folger@vm.temple.edu

Universiti Sains Malaysia
Research and Education for Peace
School for Social Sciences
11800 Minden
Penang, Malaysia
Degree: Major in Social Science
Phone: (604) 657-7888
Fax: (604) 657-7888

University of Bradford
Department of Peace Studies
Richmond Road
West Yorkshire BD7 1DP
United Kingdom
Degree: Major
Phone: +44 1274 235235
Fax: +44 1274 235240
E-mail: H.C.Swaine1@bradford.ac.uk
www.brad.ac.uk/acad/peace/home.html

University of California at Berkeley
Peace and Conflict Studies Program
Room 110, Building T-5
Berkeley, CA 94720
Degree: Major
Phone: (510) 463-6465

University of Canterbury
Peace Studies
Department of Sociology
Christchurch 1, New Zealand
Degree: Major, minor, concentration
Phone: (643) 366-7001
E-mail: plowe@canterbury.ac.nz

University of Denver
School of International Studies
2201 South Gaylord
Denver, CO 80208
Degree: Major
Phone: (303) 871-2539

University of Hawaii
Spark M. Matsunaga Institute for Peace
2424 Maile Way, 717 Porteus
Honolulu, HI 96822
Degree: Major, minor
Phone: (808) 956-6433

University of North Dakota
Center for Peace Studies
Box 8131, University Station
Grand Forks, ND 58202
Degree: Major
Phone: (701) 777-3250

University of Portland
Peace Studies Program
Department of History, Political Science and Theology
5000 North Willamette Boulevard
Portland, OR 97203
Degree: Interdisciplinary major, minor, certificate
Phone: (503) 943-7541
Fax: (503) 943-7399

University of Saint Thomas
Justice and Peace Studies Program
Mail Code 4137
St. Paul, MN 55105-1096
Degree: Major, minor
Phone: (651) 962-5325

University of Toronto
Erindale College
Peace and Conflict Studies Programme
Room 1145
Mississauga, Ontario
Canada L5L 1C6
Degree: Major
Phone: (416) 828-3938

University of Toronto
University College
Peace and Conflict Studies
Toronto, Ontario
Canada M5S 1A1
Degree: Major
Phone: (416) 978-8148
E-mail: hdixon@gpu.utcs.utoronto.ca

University of Ulster
Magee College
Peace Studies Programme
Northland Road
Derry (Londonderry) BT48 7JL
Northern Ireland
Degree: Major
Phone: (011) 44-504-265-621

University of Washington
Peace and Strategic Studies Program
Psychology Department
Seattle, WA 98195
Degree: Major
Phone: (206) 543-8784

University of Waterloo
Conrad Grebel College
Institute for Peace and Conflict Studies
Waterloo, Ontario
Canada N2L 3G6
Degree: Major, minor, diploma
Phone: (519) 885-0220

Uppsala University
Department of Peace and Conflict Research
Box 514, 751 20
Uppsala, Sweden
Degree: Major
Phone: (+46) 018 18 23 49
Fax: (+46) 018 69 51 02
E-mail: info@pcr.uu.se
www.peace.uu.se/index.html

Wayne State University
Center for Peace and Conflict Studies
2320 Faculty-Administration Building
Detroit MI 48202
Degree: Co-major, minor
Phone: (313) 577-3453
E-mail: fpearson@cms.cc.wayne.edu

Whitworth College
Peace and Studies Program
300 West Hawthorne Rd.
Spokane, WA 99251
Degree: Major, certificate
Phone: (509) 777-1000

Wilmington College
Peace Studies and Certificate Program in Applied Peace Studies
Box 1262, Pyle Center
Wilmington, OH 45177
Degree: Major, minor
Phone: (513) 382-6661 ext. 388

World University of America
Institute of Avasthology
World Education Program
107 North Ventura Street
Ojai, CA 93023
Degree: Major
Phone: (805) 646-1444

GRADUATE DEGREE PROGRAMS

American University
Peace and Conflict Resolution Studies
School of International Service
4400 Massachusetts Avenue NW
Washington, DC 20016-8071
Degree: M.A., concentration for Ph.D. in International Affairs
Phone: (202) 885-1622
E-mail: peace@american.edu
www.american.edu/academic.depts/sis/peace/

Antioch University
The McGregor School
Master of Arts Program in Conflict Resolution
800 Livermore Street
Yellow Springs, OH 45387
Degree: M.A.
Phone: (513) 767-6321

Associated Mennonite Biblical Seminaries
Master of Arts and Peace Studies Program
3003 Benham Avenue
Elkhart, IN 46517-1999
Degree: M. Div., M. Theol.
Phone: (219) 295-3726

Australian National University
Peace Research Centre
Research School of Pacific Studies
Canberra, ACT 0200 Australia
Degrees: M.A. and Ph.D.
Phone: (616) 249-3089
E-mail: peace@coombs.anu.edu.au

Basque Peace Studies Center
Guernika Gogoratuz
Guernika-Lumoko Udala
Plaza de los Fueros, s/n 48300
Guernika, Spain
Degree: Ph.D.
Phone: (34-43) 28-08-00

Beaver College
Peace Studies
450 South Easton Road
Glenside, PA 19038
Degree: M.A. in International Peace and Conflict Management
Phone: (888) BEAVER-3 or (215) 572-2925
Fax: (215) 572-2126
www.beaver.edu/programs/mast_peace.htm

Bethany Theological Seminary
Peace Studies Program
615 National Road West
Richmond, IN 47374-4095
Degree: M.A. Div., M.A. Theol.
Phone: (317) 983-1800

Bhagalpur University
Department of Ghandhian Thought
Bhagalpur-7 India
Degree: M.A., Ph.D. in Ghandhian Thought
Phone: (0641) 20659

California State University at Dominguez Hills
Negotiation and Conflict Management
Behavioral Science Graduate Programs Department
1000 East Victoria
Carson, CA 90747
Degree: M.A., certificate in Negotiation and Conflict Management
E-mail: dchurchman@dhvx20.csudh.edu

Clark University
Global Peace Studies Program
Department of Psychology
950 Main Street
Worcester, MA 01610-1477
Degree: M.A., Ph.D.
Phone: (508) 793-7259

Duquesne University
McAnulty College and Graduate School of Liberal Arts
Conflict Resolution and Peace Studies
600 Forbes Avenue
Pittsburgh, PA 15282
Degree: M.A.
Phone: (800) 456-0590 or (412) 396-6220
Fax: (412) 396-5644

Eastern Mennonite University
Conflict Analysis and Transformation Program
1200 Park Road
Harrisonburg, VA 22801
Degree: M.A. in Conflict Transformation
Phone: (703) 432-4450
www.emu.edu/ctp/ctp.htm

European University
Center for Peace Studies
Rochusplatz 1, A-7461
Stadtschlaining, Austria
Degree: M.A. in Peace and Conflict Studies
Phone: + +43 (0) 3355-2498
Fax: + +43 (0) 3355-2381
E-mail: epu@epu.ac.at
www.aspr.ac.at/welcome.htm

George Mason University
Institute for Conflict Analysis and Resolution
4400 University Drive
Fairfax, VA 22030-4444
Degree: M.A., Ph.D. in Conflict Resolution
Phone: (703) 993-1300
E-mail: icarinfo@osf1.gmu.edu
web.gmu.edu/departments/ICAR

Göteborg University
Padrigu, Brogatan 4
S-413 01 Göteborg
Sweden
Degree: Ph.D. in Peace and Development Research
Phone: (031) 773 14 28
Fax: (031) 773 49 10
E-mail: Info@padrigu.gu.se
www.padrigu.gu.se

Hiroshima University
Institute for Peace Science
1-1-81, Higashisenda, Naka-ku
Hiroshima 730 Japan
Degree: M.A., Ph.D.
Phone: +81-82-241-1221 ext. 3829
E-mail: psaj@ue.ipc.hiroshima-u.ac.jp
133.67.70.210/IPRA/IPRN_30.html

Holy Names College
Institute in Cultural and Creation Spirituality
3500 Mountain Boulevard
Oakland, CA 94619
Degree: M.A., certificate
Phone: (510) 436-1046

Immaculate Heart College Center
Masters in Global Studies
425 Shatto Place, Suite 401
Los Angeles, CA 30020-1721
Degree: M.A.
Phone: (213) 386-3116
Fax: (213) 386-6334

Incarnate Word College
Peace and Justice Studies Program
4301 Broadway
San Antonio, TX 78209
Degree: M.A.
Phone: (210) 829-3889
Fax: (210) 829-3197

International Peace University Programme
c/o Copenhagen Peace Research Institute
M.A. in Peace and Culture Studies
Fredericiagade 18
1310 Copenhagen K
Denmark
Phone: (45) 3345-5050
Fax: (45) 3345-5060
E-mail: IPU@peaceuniversity.com
www.peaceuniversity.com/IPUhome.htm

Jain Vishva Bharati Institute
Deemed University
Faculty of Social Sciences
Ladnun 341306
Rajasthan, India
Degree: M.A. in Non-Violence and Peace Research

Kyung Hee University
Graduate Institute of Peace Studies
Jinjobup, Namyangjukun, Kyonggido
South Korea 473-860
Degree: M.A.
Phone: (02) 233-2992 or 234-0220

Lancaster University
The Richardson Institute
Department of Politics and International Relations
Lancaster LA1 4YF
United Kingdom
Degree: M.A. in Peace Studies and Conflict Resolution
Phone: +44 (0) 1524-594261
Fax: +44 (0) 1524-594238
E-mail: ri@lancaster.ac.uk
www.lancs.ac.uk/users/richinst/riweb1.htm

La Trobe University
The Institute for Peace Research
Martin Building SS251
Bundoora, VIC 3083
Australia

Degree: M.A., Ph.D.
Phone: (03) 9479-1111
Fax: (03) 9479-1607
www.latrobe.edu.au

Maryknoll School of Theology
Master of Arts in Theology Program
Maryknoll, NY 10545-0305
Degree: M.A., Ph.D.
Phone: (914) 941-7590 ext. 2229

New York University
Program on Negotiations and Conflict Resolution
Robert F. Wagner Graduate School of Public Service
4 Washington Square North
New York, NY 10003-6671
Degree: M.A.
Phone: (212) 998-7400

Nova Southeastern University
Department of Dispute Resolution
School of Social and Systemic Studies
3301 College Avenue
Fort Lauderdale, FL 33314-7796
Degree: M.S., Ph.D. in Dispute Resolution
Phone: (954) 262-3000
Toll Free: (800) 262-7978
Fax: (954) 262-3968
E-mail: cr@ssss.nova.edu
www.nova.edu/ssss

Pepperdine University
Straus Institute for Dispute Resolution
School of Law
24255 Pacific Coast Highway
Malibu, CA 90263
Degree: Ph.D.
Phone: (310) 317-7455
Fax: (310) 456-4000
www.pepperdine.edu/idrweb

Royal Roads University
2005 Sooke Road
Victoria, British Columbia
Canada V9B 5Y2
Degree: M.A. in Conflict Analysis and Management
Phone: (250) 391-2511
Fax: (250) 391-2500
E-mail: webmaster@royalroads.ca
www.royalroads.ca/macam/information/default.htm

Temple University
Communication Sciences, Department of Conflict Studies
Weiss Hall, 13th Cecil B. Moore Ave.
Philadelphia, PA 19122
Degree: M.A., Ph.D.
Phone: (215) 204-1890
Fax: (215) 204-5954
E-mail: folger@vm.temple.edu

Union Institute
Doctoral Program
440 East McMillan Street
Cincinnati, OH 45206-1947
Degree: Ph.D.
Phone: (513) 861-6400

The United Nations University
53-70, Jingumae
5-chome, Shibuya-ku
Tokyo 150-8925
Phone: (+81-3) 3499-2811
Fax: (+81-3) 3499-2828
E-mail: webmaster@hq.unu.edu
www.unu.edu

Universitat Jaume I
Bancajo International Centre for Peace and Development
Fundación Caja Castellón
C/ Enmedio 82
12001 Castellón, Spain
Degree: M.A. in Peace and Development Studies

Phone: (+34) 964 23 25 51
Fax: (+34) 964 23 02 12
E-mail: epd@guest.uji.es
www1.uji.es/epd/master/index.html

Universite du Benin
Irenology
B. P. 1515 Lome-Togo, West Africa
Degree: M.A.
Phone: (228) 22-14-33 or 25-07-48

University of Bradford
Department of Peace Studies
Richmond Road
West Yorkshire BD7 1DP
United Kingdom
Degree: M.A., Ph.D., Diploma
Phone: 027-384175

University of Denver
Conflict Resolution Program
Ben Cherrington Hall
2201 South Gaylord
Denver, CO 80208
Degree: M.A.
Phone: (303) 871-2305
Fax: (303) 871-4566
www.du.edu/con-res

The University of Dublin
Trinity College
The Irish School of Ecumenics
Milltown Park, Dublin 6
Ireland
Degree: M.Phil. in Peace Studies
Phone: +353 1 2601144
Fax: +353 1 2601158
E-mail: ise.peace@tcd.ie
www2.tcd.ie/Senior.Lecturer/Courses/sch_ecum/isempeac.html

University of Granada
Department of Peace and Conflict Resolution
Departamento de Filosophia del Derecho, Moral y Politica
Plaza de la Universidad 1, E-18100
Granada, Spain
Degree: Ph.D.
Phone: +34-958-243-431

University of Hawaii at Manoa
Spark M. Matsunaga Institute for Peace
2424 Maile Way, Porteus 523
Honolulu, HI 96822
Degree: M.A., Ph.D.
Phone: (808) 948-6433, 948-6459

The University of Kent at Canterbury
Graduate School of Politics and International Relations
The Graduate Office, The Registry
Canterbury CT2 7NZ
United Kingdom
Degree: M.A. in International Conflict Analysis
Phone: +44 (0) 1227 764000 ext. 7561/3692
Fax: +44 (0) 1227 452196
E-mail: graduate-office@ukc.ac.uk
snipe.ukc.ac.uk/international/

University of Limerick
Centre for Peace and Development Studies
Robert Schuman Building
Limerick, Republic of Ireland
Degree: M.A. in Peace and Development Studies
Phone: + 353 61 202015
Fax: +353 61 334859
E-mail: admissions@ul.ie
www.ul.ie/~ipirc

University of Massachusetts at Boston
Dispute Resolution Program
100 Morrissey Boulevard
Boston, MA 02125-3393
Degree: M.A. in Dispute Resolution

Phone: (617) 287-7421
Fax: (617) 287-7099
E-mail: krajewski@umbsky.ccumb.edu
www.umb.edu/EXPLORE_ACADEMIC_PROG/CPCS/DisputeResolution/index.html

University of Missouri School of Law
206 Hulston Hall
Columbia, Missouri 65211
Degree: LL.M. in Dispute Resolution
Phone: (573) 882-2052
Fax: (573) 882-3343
E-mail: umclawcdr@missouri.edu
www.law.missouri.edu/csdr

University of Notre Dame
Joan B. Kroc Institute for International Peace Studies
P.O. Box 639
Notre Dame, IN 46556-0639
Degree: M.A., Ph.D. in Peace Studies
Phone: (219) 631-6970
Fax: (219) 631-6973
E-mail: kroc-admissions.1@nd.edu
www.nd.edu/ ~ krocinst/index.html

University of Oregon
Joint Master of Arts Degree in Peace and Conflict Resolution/Dean's Office
College of Liberal Arts and Sciences
Portland State University
P.O. Box 751
Portland, OR 97207-0751
Degree: M.A.
Phone, Fax: (503) 233-4703

University for Peace (Universidad Para La Paz)
Masters Programs
Apartado 138, Escazu
San Jose, Costa Rica
Degree: M.A.
Phone: + 506 49-10-72 or + 506 49-15-11

University of Pennsylvania
Conflict Analysis and Peace Science
3718 Locust Walk
Philadelphia, PA 19104
Degree: Ph.D.
Phone: (215) 898-6750

University of Tubingen
Institut fur Politikwissenschaft
Center for International Relations
Peace and Conflict Studies
Melanchthonstrasse 36 D-72074
Tubingen, Germany
Degree: M.A., State Exam
Phone: 07071-294957

University of Ulster
Magee College
Peace Studies Programme
Northland Road
Derry (Londonderry) BT48 7JL
Northern Ireland
Degree: Diploma, M.A., Ph.D.
Phone: 011-44-504-265-621

University of Western Cape
Conflict Studies
Private Bag X17, Bellville 7535
South Africa
Degree: M.A.
Phone: (27) 21 959-3360 or 959-3361

Uppsala University
Department of Peace and Conflict Research
Box 514, 751 20
Uppsala, Sweden
Degree: M.A., Ph.D. in Peace and Conflict Research
Phone: (+46) 018 471 25 00
Fax: (+46) 018 69 51 02
E-mail: info@pcr.uu.se
www.peace.uu.se/index.html

Wayne State University
College of Urban, Labor & Metropolitan Affairs
Program on Mediating Theory and Democratic Systems
3198 Faculty-Administration Building
Detroit, MI 48202
Degree: M.A. in Dispute Resolution
Phone: (313) 577-3221
E-mail: L.Keashly@wayne.edu
www.pcs.wayne.edu/madr/index.htm

World University of America
Institute of Avasthology
Institute of World Peace
Department of Peace Studies
107 North Ventura Street
Ojai, CA 93023
Degree: M.A.
Phone: (805) 646-1444

BIBLIOGRAPHY

This bibliography lists materials used as authority for definitions contained in the dictionary. It does not purport to be a complete listing of authorities in the field of conflict resolution, and it excludes a large body of material that was reviewed during the compilation of the dictionary but that otherwise provided no help with terms or definitions. In addition to referencing all works cited in the text, the bibliography includes for general reference a number of key publications in the field that are not cited in the text, to make it more useful as a research and reference tool.

TREATIES AND STATUTORY
AND ADMINISTRATIVE MATERIALS

Archaic

Corpus Iuris Civilis, Dig. 4.8.1 and 4.8.13 § 2.

International and Non-U.S. Law

Acts 30 and 31 Vict., c.105.

Antarctic Treaty, Dec. 1, 1959, 12 U.S.T. 794, 402 U.N.T.S. 71.

Convention on the Execution of Foreign Arbitral Awards, Sept. 26, 1927, 92 L.N.T.S. 301, 1930 Gr. Brit. T.S. No. 28 (Cmd. 3655).

Convention on the Pacific Settlement of International Disputes, The Hague, July 28, 1899, 32 Stat. 1779, 187 Consol. T.S. 410, as amended, Oct. 18, 1907, 36 Stat. 2199, 205 Consol. T.S. 233.

Convention on the Recognition and Enforcement of Foreign Arbitral Awards, June 10, 1958, 21 U.S.T. 2517, 330 U.N.T.S. 3.

Convention on the Settlement of Investment Disputes Between States and Nationals of Other States, Mar. 18, 1965, 17 U.S.T. 1270, 575 U.N.T.S. 159.

Convention on the Succession of States in Respect of Treaties, Aug. 22, 1978, U.N. Doc. NCONF.80/31, 17 ILM 1488 (1978).

Inter-American Convention on International Commercial Arbitration, done at Panama City, Jan. 30, 1975 (O.A.S.T.S. No. 42, 14 I.L.M. 336 (1975)).

Pact of Bogota (American Treaty on Pacific Settlement), Apr. 30, 1948, 30 U.N.T.S. 55 (1949).

Regulations on the Procedure of International Conciliation, adopted 11 Sept 1961, Institut de Droit International.

Revised Geneva General Act for the Pacific Settlement of International Disputes, 1949.

Treaty of European Unity (Maastricht Treaty), Feb. 7, 1992, 1992 O.J. (C224)1.

U.N. Convention on the Law of the Sea, opened for signature Dec. 10, 1982, U.N. Doc A/CONF.62/122 (1982), 21 I.L.M. 1261.

U.S. Federal

1 C.F.R. § 305.82–4(1993).

1 C.F.R. § 305.86–3 App. (1993).

1 C.F.R. § 316.101 (1993).

18 C.F.R. § 385.603 (1993).

40 C.F.R. § 131.7(f) (1992).

48 C.F.R. § 33.201 (1992).

48 C.F.R. § 935.016–3 (1992).

Fed. R. Civ. P. Rule 13.

5 U.S.C. § 562 (1993).

5 U.S.C. §§ 581–593 (Administrative Dispute Resolution Act) (1993).

5 U.S.C.A. § 551(7) (West 1993).

5 U.S.C.A. § 571(3) (West 1993).

5 U.S.C.A. § 7103(9) (West 1993).

9 U.S.C. §§ 1 et seq. (United States Arbitration Act/Federal Arbitration Act) (1994).

9 U.S.C.A. §§ 301 et seq. (West 1998).

15 U.S.C. §§ 78a et seq. (Securities Exchange Act of 1934) (1994).

25 U.S.C.A. §§ 2701–2721 (West 1997).

28 U.S.C. §§ 471 et seq. (1994).

29 U.S.C.A. § 113 (Norris-La Guardia Act of 1932) (West 1998).

41 U.S.C.A. § 601 (West 1987).

41 U.S.C.A. §§ 605(a)–605(b) (West 1987).

45 U.S.C. § 153 (1994).

U.S. District Court Rules, D. Mass., Expense and Delay Reduction Rule 4.03.

U.S. State

Ala. Code § 27-9-1 (1993).

Cal. Civ. Proc. Code §§ 638, 639 (West 1976 and West Supp. 1987).

Cal. Educ. Code § 56101(b)(1) (West 1993).

Cal. Family Code § 2451 (West 1993).

Colo. Rev. Stat. Ann. § 13-22-302 (West 1996).

Colo. Rev. Stat. Ann. § 13-22-403 (West 1996).

Colo. Rev. Stat. Ann. § 13-22-404 (West 1996).

Fla. Stat. Ann. § 44.1011 (West Supp. 1992).

Georgia Supreme Court Order on Alternative Dispute Resolution Rules, Mar. 9, 1993, as amended Dec. 2, 1993.

Georgia Supreme Court Alternative Dispute Resolution Rules (effective Oct. 22, 1992, as amended by the Georgia Supreme Court, Jan. 8, 1993).

Haw. Rev. Stat. § 613–1 (1992 Supp.).

710 Ill. Comp. Stat. Ann. 25/1-25-80 (West 1992).

710 Ill. Comp. Stat. Ann. 20/2 (West 1992).

Iowa Code § 679.1 (1996).

Iowa Code §§ 20.20–20.22 (1996).

Kan. Stat. Ann. § 23–601 et. seq. (1991).

La. Rev. Stat. Ann. § 9:4204 (West 1997).

Maine Supreme Judicial Court Administrative Order to Establish Alternative Dispute Resolution Pilot Project (1995).

Mich. Comp. Laws Ann. §§ 600.5040–600.5065, repealed by P. A. 1993, No. 78, § 2, eff. Apr. 1, 1994.

Mich. Comp. Laws Ann. § 691.1552 et seq. (West Supp. 1993).

Minn. Stat. Ann. § 494.01 (West Supp. 1993).

N.C. Gen. Stat. § 7A-38.1 (1996).

N.C. Standards of Professional Conduct [for mediators]. Adopted by the North Carolina Dispute Resolution Commission, May 10, 1996.

N.C. Uniform Rules Regulating Mediation of Child Custody and Visitation Disputes Under the North Carolina Custody and Visitation Mediation Program (1989).

Neb. Rev. Stat. § 25-1157 (1992).

N.J. Stat. Ann. § 34:13A-16 (West 1992).

N.Y. Judiciary Law § 849-a (McKinney 1994).

O.C.G.A. § 9-9-6(e) (1996).

O.C.G.A. §§ 9-9-60–9-9-84 (1996).

Ohio Rev. Code Ann. § 4117.14 (c) (Banks-Baldwin, 1990).

Ohio Rev. Code Ann. § 179.01 (Banks-Baldwin, 1990).

Okla. Stat. Ann. tit. 12 § 1802 (West 1993).

Ore. Rev. Stat. § 243.722(3) (1993).

43 Pa. Cons. Stat. §§ 1101.801, 1101.802 (1993).

Tenn. Code Ann. § 36-6-410 (West 1999).

Tenn. Supreme Court Rule 31(f) (1996).

Tex. Civ. Prac. & Rem. Code Ann. §§ 151.001 et. seq. (West 1993).

Tex. Civ. Prac. & Rem. Code Ann. § 152-001 (West 1993).

Tex. Civ. Prac. & Rem. Code Ann. § 154.001 (West 1993).

Tex. Civ. Prac. & Rem. Code Ann. § 154.025 (West 1993).

Utah Code Ann. §§ 58-39A-1 et seq. (Supp. 1992).

Utah Code Ann. §§ 78-31B-1 et seq. (1953).

Wis. Stat. Ann. § 111.70(4)(West 1996).

CASE LAW

Ainsworth v. *Skurnick,* 960 F.2d 939, 941 (11th Cir. 1992), cert. denied, 507 U.S. 915 113 S. Ct. 1269, 122 L.Ed. 2d 665 (1993).

AMF Inc. v. *Brunswick Corp.,* 621 F. Supp. 456, 462 (E.D.N.Y. 1985).

Avitzur v. *Avitzur,* 446 N.E.2d 136 (N.Y. 1983).

Barcon Assocs., Inc. v. *Tri-County Asphalt Corp.,* 86 N.J. 179, 430 A.2d 214 (1981).

Bonham's Case, 8 Co. Rep. 107a, 77 Eng. Rep. 638 (K.B. 1610).

Booth v. *Mary Carter Paint Co.,* 202 So. 2d 8 (Fla. Dist. Ct. App. 1967).

Brown v. *Rauscher Pierce Refsnes, Inc.,* 994 F.2d 775, 775 n. 3 (11th Cir. 1993).

Congregation B'nai Sholom v. *Martin,* 382 Mich. 659, 173 N.W.2d 504 (1986).

Delta Air Lines, Inc. v. *Airline Pilots Ass'n,* 861 F.2d 665, 671 (11th Cir. 1988), cert. denied, 493 U.S. 871, 1100 S. Ct. 201, 107 L. Ed. 2d 154 (1989).

Dodd v. *Ford,* 153 Cal. App. 3d 425 (1984).

Doe d. Lloyd v. *Evans* (1827) 3 Car. and P. 219; 172 E.R. 394, 395 (N.P.).

Gilmer v. *Interstate/Johnson Lane Corp.,* 500 U.S. 20, 111 S. Ct. 1647, 114 L. Ed. 2d 26 (1991).

Honesti v. Chartres (1291 A.D.), reprinted in M. S. Arnold (ed.), *Select Cases Concerning the Law Merchant.* Vol. II. London: Selden Society, 1987.

International Bhd. of Elec. Workers v. *Graham County Elec. Coop.,* 783 F.2d 897 (9th Cir. 1986).

Jenkins v. *Prudential-Bache Sec., Inc.,* 847 F.2d 631 (10th Cir. 1988).

Kingsbridge Center of Israel v. *Turk,* 469 N.Y.S.2d 732, 734 (1983).

Larsdale, Inc. and Int'l Union of Elecs., et al., 1993 WL 153703 (N.L.R.B.).

Mastrobuono v. *Shearson Lehman Hutton, Inc.,* 514 U.S. 52, 115 S. Ct. 1212, 131 L. Ed. 2d 76 (1995).

McCay v. *Ashland Oil Co.,* 120 F.R.D. 43 (E.D. Ky. 1988).

Mitsubishi Motors Corp. v. *Soler Chrysler-Plymouth, Inc.,* 723 F.2d 155 (1st Cir. 1983), rev'd in part 473 U.S. 614, 105 S. Ct. 3346, 87 L. Ed. 2d 444 (1985).

N.L.R.B. v. *General Elec. Co.,* 418 F.2d 736 (2d Cir. 1969), cert. den. 397 U.S. 965 (1970).

Parsons v. *Ambos,* 121 Ga. 98, 101, 48 S.E. 696 (1904).

Raiford v. *Merrill Lynch Pierce Fenner and Smith, Inc.,* 903 F.2d 1410, 1413 (11th Cir. 1990).

Robbins v. *PaineWebber,* 954 F.2d 679, 684 (11th Cir.), cert. denied, 506 U.S. 870, 113 S. Ct. 201, 121 L. Ed. 2d 143 (1992).

The Schooner Exchange v. *M'Faddon,* 11 U.S. 116, 3 L. Ed. 287, 7 Cranch 116 (1812).

Scott v. *Avery* (1856) 5 H.L.C. 811, 10 E.R. 1121 (H.L.).

Shearson/American Express, Inc. v. *McMahon,* 482 U.S. 220, 107 S. Ct. 2332, 96 L. Ed. 2d 185 (1987).

Tennessee Tombigbee Constructors, Inc., 44 Fed. Cont. Rep. (BNA) 502 (1985).

Textile Workers Union of America v. *Lincoln Mills of Alabama,* 353 U.S. 448, 77 S. Ct. 912, 1 L. Ed. 2d 972 (1957).

Thomas Crimmins Contracting Co. v. *City of New York,* 542 N.E.2d 1097 (N.Y. 1989).

United States v. *Woodcrest Nursing Home,* 706 F.2d 70 (2d Cir. 1983), *cert. denied,* 464 U.S. 849 (1983).

United Steelworkers v. *Enterprise Wheel and Car Corp.,* 363 U.S. 593, 597, 80 S. Ct. 1358, 4 L. Ed. 2d 1424 (1960).

Volt Information Sciences, Inc. v. *Board of Trustees of Leland Stanford Junior University,* 489 U.S. 468, 109 S. Ct. 1248, 103 L. Ed. 2d 488 (1988).

Vynior's Case (1610), 8 Co. Rep. 81b, 77 E.R. 597 (K.B.).

Wilko v. *Swan,* 346 U.S. 427, 74 S. Ct. 182, 98 L. Ed. 168 (1953).

BOOKS, ARTICLES, AND REPORTS

Abel, R. (ed.). *The Politics of Informal Justice: The American Experience.* Orlando: Academic Press, 1982.

Abel, R. "Informalism: A Tactical Equivalent to Law?" *Clearinghouse Review,* 1985–1986, *19,* 375–383.

Adler, P. S. "Is ADR a Social Movement?" *Negotiation Journal,* 1987, *3*(1), 59–71.

Afzal, M. "Community-Based Conflict Resolution (Pakistan Experience)." In C. L. Pe, G. C. Sosmena Jr., and A. F. Tadiar (eds.), *Transcultural Mediation in the Asia-Pacific.* Manila, Philippines: Asia-Pacific Organization for Mediation, 1988.

Agid-Ben Yehuda, H., and Auerbach, Y. "Attitudes to an Existence Conflict: Allon and Peres on the Palestinian Issue, 1967–1987." *Journal of Conflict Resolution,* 1991, *35*(3), 519–546.

Albin, C. "The Role of Fairness in Negotiation." *Negotiation Journal,* 1993, *9*(3), 223–244.

Amerasinghe, C. F. "The International Centre for Settlement of Investment Disputes and Development Through the Multinational Corporation." *Vanderbilt Journal of Transnational Law,* 1976, *9*(4), 793–816.

American Arbitration Association. *Corporate By-Laws.* 1926.

American Arbitration Association. *Mini-Trial Procedures.* (rev. ed.) New York: American Arbitration Association, 1990.

American Bar Association. *Model Rules of Professional Conduct.* Chicago: American Bar Association Center for Professional Responsibility, 1995.

American Stock Exchange Guide. Chicago: Commercial Clearing House, 1994.

Applebey, G. "Alternative Dispute Resolution and the Civil Justice System." In K. J. Mackie (ed.), *A Handbook of Dispute Resolution: ADR in Action.* New York: Routledge, 1991.

Araki, C. T. "Dispute Management in the Schools." *Mediation Quarterly,* 1990, *8*(1), 1990, 51–62.

Arnold, M. S. (ed.). *Select Cases Concerning the Law Merchant.* Vol. 2. London: Selden Society, 1987.

Arnold, T. *Alternative Dispute Resolution: How to Use It to Your Advantage—A Vocabulary of ADR Procedures.* C976 ALI-ABA 19. Philadelphia: American Law Institute-American Bar Association, Dec. 15, 1994.

Atkin, W. R. "New Zealand: 1991 Controversy Surrounds Policies on Children." *Journal of Family Law,* 1993–94, *32*(2), 377–393.

Aubert, V. "Competition and Dissensus: Two Types of Conflict and Conflict Resolution." *Journal of Dispute Resolution,* 1963, *7*, 26.

Auerbach, J. S. *Justice Without Law?* New York: Oxford University Press, 1983.

Avruch, K., and Black, P. W. "Ideas of Human Nature in Contemporary Conflict Resolution Theory." *Negotiation Journal,* 1990, *6*(3), 221–228.

Avruch, K., Black, P. W., and Scimecca, J. A. *Conflict resolution: Cross-Cultural Perspectives.* Westport, Conn.: Greenwood Press, 1991.

Axelrod, R. M. *Conflict of Interest: A Theory of Divergent Goals with Applications to Politics.* Chicago: Markham, 1970.

Axelrod, R. M. *The Evolution of Cooperation.* New York: Basic Books, 1984.

Azar, E. E. *The Management of Protracted Social Conflict: Theory and Cases.* Aldershot, Hampshire, England: Dartmouth; Brookfield, Vt.: Gower, 1990.

Azar, E. E., and Burton, J. W. *International Conflict Resolution: Theory and Practice.* Sussex: Wheatsheaf Books; Boulder, Colo.: Rienner, 1986.

Bailey, S. D. *Peaceful Settlement of International Disputes.* (3rd ed.) New York: United Nations Institute for Training and Research, 1971.

Baizley, Q. C., and Suche, P. C. "Final Offer Arbitration." In R. J. Scott and S.G. Sigurdson (eds.), The 1986 Isaac Pitblado Lectures on Alternative Dispute Resolution: Emerging Mechanisms and Professional Responsibilities in Dispute Resolution. Manitoba, Canada: Law Society of Manitoba, 1986.

Baker-Jackson, M., and others. "Ethical Standards for Court-Connected Mediators." *Mediation Quarterly,* 1985, *8,* 67–72.

Balto, B. "Mediator Directiveness in Child Custody Mediation: An Exploration of Alternatives and Decision Making." *Mediation Quarterly,* 1990, *7*(3), 215–227.

Bartel, B. C. "Med-Arb as a Distinct Method of Dispute Resolution: History, Analysis, and Potential." *Willamette Law Review,* 1991, *27,* 661–692.

Barth, F. *Political Leadership Among Swat Pathans.* London: University of London, Athlone Press, 1959.

Bartlett, R. *Trial by Fire and Water: The Medieval Judicial Ordeal.* Oxford: Clarendon Press, 1986.

Barton, R. F. *Ifugao Law.* Berkeley: University of California Press, 1969. (Originally published 1919.)

Bartos, O. "How Predictable Are Negotiations?" *Journal of Conflict Resolution,* 1967, *2,* 481–496.

Bartunek, J. M., Benton, A. A., and Keys, C. B. "Third Party Intervention and the Bargaining Behavior of Group Representatives." *Journal of Conflict Resolution,* 1975, *19*(3), 532–557.

Bartunek, J. M., and Reid, R. D. "The Role of Conflict in a Second Order Change Attempt." In D. M. Kolb and J. M. Bartunek (eds.), *Hidden Conflict in Organizations: Uncovering the Behind-the-Scenes Disputes.* Thousand Oaks, Calif.: Sage, 1992.

Bazerman, M. H. "Negotiator Judgment: A Critical Look at the Rationality Assumption." *American Behavioral Scientist,* 1983, *27,* 211–228.

Becker-Haven, J. F. "Analyzing the Process of Child Custody Mediation: An Heuristic Model." Paper presented at the ninety-first annual convention of the American Psychological Association, Anaheim, Calif., Aug. 28, 1983.

Bello, J. H., and Holmer, A. F. "U.S. Trade Law and Policy Series No. 24: Dispute Resolution in the New World Trade Organization: Concerns and Net Benefits." *International Lawyer,* 1994, *28,* 1095–1104.

Bellow, G., and Moulton, B. *The Lawyering Process: Negotiation.* Westbury, N.Y.: Foundation Press, 1981.

Benjamin, M., and Irving, H. H. "Toward a Feminist-Informed Model of Therapeutic Family Mediation." *Mediation Quarterly,* 1992, *10*(2), 129–153.

Benjamin, R. D. "What Is Mediation Anyway?" *AFM Mediation News,* Summer 1996, pp. 6–7.

Bercovitch, J. "The Structure and Diversity of Mediation in International Relations." In J. Bercovitch and J. Z. Rubin (eds.), *Mediation in International Relations: Multiple Approaches to Conflict Management.* New York: St. Martin's Press, 1992a.

Bercovitch, J. "Mediators and Mediation Strategies in International Relations." *Negotiation Journal,* 1992b, *8*(2), 99–112.

Bernier, I., and Lapointe, B. *Free Trade Agreement Between Canada and the United States Annotated.* Cowansville, Quebec: Editions Y. Blais, 1990–1993.

Betz, B. "Response to Strategy and Communication in an Arms Race–Disarmament Dilemma." *Journal of Conflict Resolution,* 1991, *35*(4), 678–690.

Bienenfeld, F. *Child Custody Mediation: Techniques for Counselors, Attorneys, and Parents.* Palo Alto, Calif.: Science and Behavior Books, 1983.

Bilder, R. B. "International Third Party Dispute Settlement." *Denver Journal of International Law and Policy,* 1989, *17,* 471–503.

Bingham, G. *Resolving Environmental Disputes: A Decade of Experience.* Washington, D.C.: Conservation Foundation, 1986.

Black's Law Dictionary. (5th ed.) St. Paul, Minn.: West, 1979.

Blackstone, W. *Commentaries on the Laws of England.* [4 vols.] Oxford: Clarendon Press, 1765–1769.

Blake, R. R., and Moulon, J. S. *The Managerial Grid III.* Houston: Gulf, 1985.

Blalock, H. M. *Power and Conflict: Toward a General Theory.* Thousand Oaks, Calif.: Sage, 1989.

Bluehouse, P., and Zion, J. W. "Naat'aanii, Hozhooji: The Navajo Justice and Harmony Ceremony." *Mediation Quarterly,* 1993, *10*(4), 327–337.

BNA ADR Report, vol. 2. Washington, D.C.: Bureau of National Affairs, 1988.

Bohannan, P. (ed.). *Law and Warfare: Studies in the Anthropology of Conflict.* Austin: University of Texas Press, 1967.

Borisoff, D., and Victor, D. A. *Conflict Management: A Communication Skills Approach.* Englewood Cliffs, N.J.: Prentice-Hall, 1989.

Bossey, J. (ed.). *Disputes and Settlements: Law and Human Relations in the West.* Cambridge: Cambridge University Press, 1983.

Boulding, K. E. *Conflict and Defense: A General Theory.* New York: HarperCollins, 1962.

Bradley, R. H. "Managing Major Metropolitan Areas: Applying Collaborative Planning and Negotiation Techniques." *Mediation Quarterly,* 1988, *20,* 45–56.

Brazil, W. D., Kahn, M. A., Newman, J. P., and Gold, J. Z. "Early Neutral Evaluation: An Experimental Effort to Expedite Dispute Resolution." *Judicature,* 1986, *69*(5), 279–285.

Breggin, P. R. *Beyond Conflict: From Self-Help and Psychotherapy to Peacemaking.* New York: St. Martin's Press, 1992.

Brett, J. M. "Negotiating Group Decisions." *Negotiation Journal,* 1991, *7*(3), 291–310.

Bristow, D. I. "Alternative Methods of Dispute Resolution in Canada." *The Arbitration and Dispute Resolution Law Journal,* 1992, *4,* 194–210.

Britton, R. L. *The Arbitration Guide: A Case-Handling Manual of Procedures and Practices in Dispute Resolution.* Englewood Cliffs, N.J.: Prentice-Hall, 1982.

Broches, A. "Recourse Against an Award: Enforcement of the Award." In P. Sanders (ed.), *UNCITRAL's Project for a Model Law on International Commercial Arbitration.* Boston: Kluwer Law and Taxation, 1984.

Brougham, L. "Proposal on Courts of Conciliation." *Law Magazine,* 1831, *5,* 33.

Brown, B. R. "Face-Saving and Face-Restoration in Negotiation." In D. Druckman (ed.), *Negotiations: Social-Psychological Perspectives.* Thousand Oaks, Calif.: Sage, 1977.

Buhring-Uhle, C. "Co-Med-Arb Technique Holds Promise for Getting Best of Both Worlds." *World Arbitration and Mediation Report,* 1992, *3*(1), 21.

Burr, A., and Lofthouse, S. "The Interrelationship Between Section 4 and Orders 14 and 29." *The Arbitration and Dispute Resolution Law Journal,* 1992, *1,* 2–12.

Burrell, N. A., and Vogl, S. M. "Turf-Side Conflict Mediation for Students." *Mediation Quarterly,* 1990, *7*(3), 237–250.

Burton, J. W. *Conflict and Communication: The Use of Controlled Communication in International Relations.* New York: Free Press, 1969.

Burton, J. W. *Conflict: Resolution and Provention.* New York: St. Martin's Press, 1990a.

Burton, J. W. *Conflict: Human Needs Theory.* London: Macmillan, 1990b.

Burton, J. W., and Dukes, F. *Conflict: Practices in Management, Settlement and Resolution.* New York: St. Martin's Press, 1990.

Bush, R.A.B. "'What Do We Need a Mediator For?' Mediation's 'Value-Added' for Negotiators." *Ohio State Journal on Dispute Resolution,* 1996, *12,* 1–36.

Bush, R.A.B., and Folger, J. P. *The Promise of Mediation: Responding to Conflict Through Empowerment and Recognition.* San Francisco: Jossey-Bass, 1994.

Cappelletti, M., and Jolowicz, J. *Public Interest Parties and the Active Role of the Judge in Civil Litigation.* Dobbs Ferry, N.Y.: Oceana, 1975.

Carbonneau, T. E. *Alternative Dispute Resolution: Melting the Lances and Dismounting the Steeds.* Urbana: University of Illinois Press, 1989.

Carlson, C. "Mediating Public Policy Disputes: Negotiated Investment Strategy." In V. Prather (ed.), *Family Dispute Resolution: Options for All Ages.* Washington, D.C.: American Bar Association Standing Committee on Dispute Resolution, Division of Public Services, Governmental Affairs and Public Services Group, 1990.

Carnevale, P.J.D. "Strategic Choice in Mediation." *Negotiation Journal,* 1986, *2*(1), 41–56.

Carnevale, P.J.D., and Lawler, E. J. "Time Pressure and the Development of Integrative Agreements and Bilateral Negotiations." *Journal of Conflict Resolution*, 1986, *30*, 636–659.

Caron, D. D. "The Nature of the Iran–United States Claims Tribunal and the Evolving Structure of International Dispute Resolution." *American Journal of International Law*, 1990, *84*(1), 104–156.

Cavanagh, R., and Sarat, A. "Thinking About Courts: Toward and Beyond a Jurisprudence of Judicial Competence." *Law and Society Review*, 1980, *14*(2), 371–420.

Center for Public Resources. *Model ADR Procedures: Minitrial.* (Rev. ed.) New York: Center for Public Resources, 1989.

Chandler, D. B. "Violence, Fear, and Communication: The Variable Impact of Domestic Violence on Mediation." *Mediation Quarterly*, 1990, *7*(4), 331–346.

Chatterji, M. *Analytical Techniques in Conflict Management.* Brookfield, Vt.: Dartmouth, 1992.

Chayes, A., and Chayes, A. H. "Compliance Without Enforcement: State Behavior Under Regulatory Treaties." *Negotiation Journal*, 1991, *7*(3), 311–330.

Cobb, S. "Empowerment and Mediation: A Narrative Perspective." *Negotiation Journal*, 1993, *9*(3), 245–259.

Cohen, R. *Negotiating Across Cultures: Communication Obstacles in International Diplomacy.* Washington, D.C.: U.S. Institute of Peace Press, 1991.

Colosi, T. "Negotiation in the Public and Private Sectors: A Core Model." *American Behavioral Scientist*, 1983, *27*(2), 229–253.

Colosi, T., and Berkeley, A. E. *Collective Bargaining: How It Works and Why.* New York: American Arbitration Association, 1986.

"Comment: Whose Dispute Is It Anyway? The Propriety of the Mini-Trial in Promoting Corporate Dispute Resolution." *Journal of Dispute Resolution*, 1987, 133–148.

Conn, K. E. *Settlement Conference: A Handbook for Judges and Lawyers.* Visalia, Calif.: San Joaquin Eagle, 1988.

Connors, J. F. "Resolving Disputes Locally in Rural Alaska." *Mediation Quarterly*, 1993, *10*(4), 367–386.

Coombs, R. M. "Noncourt-Connected Mediation and Counseling in Child-Custody Disputes." *Family Law Quarterly*, 1984, *17*, 469–494.

Cooper, C., and Meyerson, B. (eds.). *A Drafter's Guide to Alternative Dispute Resolution.* Chicago: American Bar Association, Business Section, Committee on Dispute Resolution, 1991.

Corcoran, K. O., and Melamed, J. C. "From Coercion to Empowerment: Spousal Abuse and Mediation." *Mediation Quarterly*, 1990, *7*(4), 303–316.

Cormick, G. W. "Crafting the Language of Consensus." *Negotiation Journal*, 1991, *7*(4), 363–368.

Corporate Counsel's Guide to Alternative Dispute Resolution Techniques. Chesterland, Ohio: Business Laws, 1989.

Coser, L. *The Functions of Social Conflict.* New York: Free Press, 1956.

Costantino, C. A., and Merchant, C. S. *Designing Conflict Management Systems: A Guide to Creating Productive and Healthy Organizations.* San Francisco: Jossey-Bass, 1996.

Coulson, R. *How to Stay Out of Court.* New York: Crown, 1968.

Cramer, C., and Schoeneman, R. "A Court Mediation Model with an Eye Toward Standards." *Mediation Quarterly,* 1985, *8,* 33–46.

Craver, C. B. "The Judicial Enforcement of Public Sector Interest Arbitration." *Boston College Law Review,* 1980, *3*(21), 557–577.

Craver, C. B. "Effective Legal Negotiation and Settlement." In J. D. Harbaugh (ed.), *Negotiation: Winning Tactics and Techniques.* New York: Practising Law Institute, 1988.

Craver, C. B. *Effective Legal Negotiation and Settlement.* (2nd ed.) Charlottesville, Va.: Michie, 1993.

Crawford, V. P. "Dynamic Games and Dynamic Contract Theory." *Journal of Conflict Resolution,* 1985, *29,* 195–224.

Cross, J. G. *The Economics of Bargaining.* New York: Basic Books, 1969.

Curle, L. *Making Peace.* London: Tavistock, 1971.

Curtis, F. A., and Bailey, B. "A Mediation-Counseling Approach to Marriage Crisis Resolution." *Mediation Quarterly,* 1990, *8*(2), 137–149.

Dahlen, O., Westas, B., and Wood, D. *Peaceful Resolution of Conflicts: Non-Governmental Organizations in the International System.* Uppsala, Sweden: Life and Peace Institute, 1988.

Daly, J. P. "The Effects of Anger on Negotiations over Mergers and Acquisitions." *Negotiation Journal,* 1991, *7*(1), 31–40.

Danzig, R. "Toward the Creation of a Complementary, Decentralized System of Criminal Justice." *Stanford Law Review,* 1973, *26,* 1ff.

Dauer, E. A., and Nyhart, D. "An ADR Procedure for Loss Allocation in a Joint Defense Agreement." *Alternatives to the High Cost of Litigation,* 1984, *2,* 14.

David Davies Memorial Institute of International Studies. *International Disputes: The Legal Aspects.* London: Europa Publications, 1972.

David, R. *Arbitration in International Trade.* Boston: Kluwer Law and Taxation, 1985.

Davis, A. *Mediation: An Alternative That Works.* (2nd ed.) Salem, Mass.: Law-Related Education Program, 1984.

Davis, A. *Community Mediation in Massachusetts.* Report to the Massachusetts District Court. Salem, Mass.: n.p., 1986a.

Davis, A. M. "Dispute Resolution at an Early Age." *Negotiation Journal,* 1986b, *2*(3), 287–298.

Davis, H. E., and Dugan, M. A. "Training the Mediator." *Peace and Change,* 1982, *8*(2/3), 85–90.

Dawkins, R. *The Selfish Gene.* Oxford: Oxford University Press, 1989.

de Pierola, N. "The Andean Court of Justice." *Emory Journal of International Dispute Resolution,* 1987, *2,* 11–37.

de Waal, F.B.M. *Peacemaking Among Primates.* Cambridge: Harvard University Press, 1989.

de Waart, P.J.I.M. *The Element of Negotiation in the Pacific Settlement of Disputes Between States: An Analysis of Provisions Made and/or Applied Since 1918 in the Field of the Pacific Settlement of International Disputes.* The Hague, The Netherlands: Martinus Nijhoff, 1973.

Deitsch, C. R., and Dilts, D. A. *The Arbitration of Rights Disputes in the Public Sector.* Westport, Conn.: Greenwood Press, 1990.

Delbecq, A., Vandeven, A., and Gustafson, A. *Group Techniques for Program Planning.* Glenview, Ill.: Scott, Foresman, 1975.

Deng, F. M., and Zartman, W. *Conflict Resolution in Africa.* Washington, D.C.: Brookings Institution, 1991.

Department of Defense, Inspector General. *Report of Investigation, Tennessee Tombigbee Claim Settlement.* Washington, D.C.: Department of Defense, 1986.

Deutsch, M. *The Resolution of Conflict: Constructive and Destructive Processes.* New Haven, Conn.: Yale University Press, 1973.

Diamond, L., and McDonald, J. *Multi-Track Diplomacy: A Systems Guide and Analysis.* Washington, D.C.: U.S. Institute for Peace, 1993.

A Dictionary of Arbitration. [K. Seide, ed.] Dobbs Ferry, N.Y.: Oceana, 1970.

Diehl, P. F., and Goertz, G. "Territorial Changes in Militarized Conflict." *Journal of Conflict Resolution,* 1988, *32,* 103–122.

Dillon, K. L. *Statewide Offices of Dispute Resolution: Initiating Collaborative Approaches to Dispute Resolution in State Government.* Washington, D.C.: National Institute for Dispute Resolution, 1994.

Dillon, T. "The World Trade Organization: A New Legal Order for World Trade?" *Michigan Journal of International Law,* 1995, *16*(2), 349–402.

Dingwall, R. "Some Observations on Divorce Mediation in Britain and the United States." *Mediation Quarterly,* 1986, *11,* 5–24.

Donohue, W. A., and Kolt, R. *Managing Interpersonal Conflict.* Thousand Oaks, Calif.: Sage, 1992.

Donohue, W. A., and Ramesh, C. N. "Negotiator-Opponent Relationships." In L. L. Putnam and M. E. Roloff (eds.), *Communication and Negotiation.* Thousand Oaks, Calif.: Sage, 1992.

Donohue, W. A., Weider-Hatfield, D., Hamilton, M., and Diez, M. E. "Relational Distance in Managing Conflict." *Human Communication Research,* 1985, *11,* 387–406.

Douglas, A. *Industrial Peacemaking.* New York: Columbia University Press, 1962.

Douglas, S. U. "Negotiation Audiences: The Role of the Mass Media." In L. L. Putnam and M. E. Roloff (eds.), *Communication and Negotiation.* Thousand Oaks, Calif.: Sage, 1992.

Doxey, M. P. *International Sanctions in Contemporary Perspective.* New York: St. Martin's Press, 1987.

Doyle, M., and Straus, D. *How to Make Meetings Work.* Chicago: Playboy Press, 1984.

Druckman, D. *Human Factors in International Negotiations: Social-Psychological Aspects of International Conflict.* Thousand Oaks, Calif.: Sage, 1973.

Druckman, D. "Social-Psychological Approaches to the Study of Negotiation." In D. Druckman (ed.), *Negotiations: Social-Psychological Perspectives.* Thousand Oaks, Calif.: Sage, 1977.

Druckman, D., and Harris, R. "Alternative Models of Responsiveness in International Negotiation." *Journal of Conflict Resolution,* 1989, *34*(2), 234–251.

Dunlop, J. T. *Dispute Resolution: Negotiation and Consensus Building.* Westport, Conn.: Auburn House, 1984.

Durie-Hall, D., and Metge, J. "Kua Tutu Te Puehu, Kia Mau: Maori Aspirations and Family Law." In M. Henaghan and W. Atkin (eds.), *Family Law and Policy in New Zealand.* Oxford: Oxford University Press, 1992.

Duryea, M. L. *Conflict and Culture: A Literature Review and Bibliography.* Victoria, B.C.: University of Victoria Institute for Dispute Resolution, 1992.

Duryee, M. A. "Public-Sector Mediation: A Report from the Courts." *Mediation Quarterly,* 1985, *8*, 47–56.

Dworkin, J., and London, W. "What Is a Fair Agreement?" *Mediation Quarterly,* 1989, *7*(1), 3–13.

Eckhoff, T. "The Mediator, the Judge, and the Administrator in Conflict Resolution." In B. P. Blegvad (ed.), *Contributions to the Sociology of Law.* Copenhagen: Munksgaard, 1966.

Edelman, L., and Carr, F. "The Mini-Trial: An Alternative Dispute Resolution Procedure." *Arbitration Journal,* 1987, *42*(1), 7–16.

Edwards, H. T., and White, J. J. *The Lawyer as a Negotiator: Problems, Readings and Materials.* St. Paul, Minn.: West, 1977.

Edwards, M. F. (ed.) *Settlement and Plea Bargaining.* Washington, D.C.: Association of Trial Lawyers of America Education Fund, 1981.

The Effectiveness of the Mini-Trial in Resolving Complex Commercial Disputes: A Survey. Report of the Subcommittee on Alternate Means of Dispute Resolution, ABA Section of Litigation Subcommittee on Alternate Means of Dispute Resolution. Chicago: American Bar Association, Section of Litigation, 1986.

Ehrmann, J. R., and Lesnick, M. T. "The Policy Dialogue: Applying Mediation to the Policy-Making Process." *Mediation Quarterly,* 1988, *20*, 93–99.

Eidmann, D., and Plett, K. "Non-Judicial Dispute Processing in West Germany." In K. J. Mackie (ed.), *A Handbook of Dispute Resolution: ADR in Action.* New York: Routledge, 1991.

Elliot, E. D. "Managerial Judging and the Evolution of Procedure." *University of Chicago Law Review,* 1986, *53*(2), 306–336.

Ellis, R., Ravindra, G., Vidmar, N., and Davis, T. "The Reversal Arbitration Board: An ADR Model for Resolving Intra-Corporate Disputes." *Journal of Dispute Resolution,* 1994, *1*, 93–110.

Encyclopedia of Public International Law. Published under the auspices of the Max Planck Institute for Comparative Public Law and International Law. [Under direction of R. Bernhardt. 12 vols.] Amsterdam, New York: North-Holland, 1992.

Engram, P. S., and Markowitz, J. R. "Ethical Issues in Mediation: Divorce and Labor Compared." *Mediation Quarterly,* 1985, *8*, 1–32.

Enright, R. D., Freedman, S., and Rique, J. "The Psychology of Interpersonal Forgiveness." In R. D. Enright and J. North (eds.), *Exploring Forgiveness.* Madison: University of Wisconsin Press, 1998.

Erikson, S. K., and McKnight Erikson, M. S. *Family Mediation Casebook: Theory and Process.* New York: Brunner/Mazel, 1988.

Etzioni, A. "Compliance Structure." In A. Etzioni and E. W. Lehman (eds.), *A Sociological Reader on Complex Organizations.* Austin, Tex.: Holt, Rinehart and Winston, 1980.

Faurot, D. J., and McAllister, S. "Salary Arbitrations and Pre-Arbitration Negotiation in Major League Baseball." *Industrial and Labor Relations Review,* 1992, *45*(4), 697–710.

Felstiner, W.L.F. "Influences of Social Organization on Dispute Processing." *Law and Society Review,* 1974, *9*(1), 63–94.

Felstiner, W.L.F., Abel, R. L., and Sarat, A. "The Emergence and Transformation of Disputes: Naming, Blaming, Claiming." *Law and Society Review,* 1980–1981, *15*(3–4), 631–654.

Feuille, P. "Why Does Grievance Mediation Resolve Grievances?" *Negotiation Journal,* 1992, *8*(2), 131–145.

Fiorino, D. J. "Dimensions of Negotiated Rule-Making: Practical Constraints and Theoretical Implications." In M. K. Mills (ed.), *Conflict Resolution and Public Policy.* Westport, Conn.: Greenwood Press, 1990.

Fisher, R. *International Conflict for Beginners.* New York: HarperCollins, 1969.

Fisher, R. "Negotiating Power: Getting and Using Influence." *American Behavioral Scientist,* 1983a, *27*, 149–166.

Fisher, R. J. "Third Party Consultation as a Method of Inter-Group Conflict Resolution: A Review of Studies." *Journal of Conflict Resolution,* 1983b, *27*, 301–334.

Fisher, R., and Brown, S. *Getting Together: Building Relationships as We Negotiate.* New York: Penguin Books, 1989.

Fisher, R., and Ury, W. *Getting to Yes: Negotiating Agreement Without Giving In.* Boston: Houghton Mifflin, 1981.

Fishkin, F. "The *Bet Din* as an Arbitration Model." *Case and Comment,* 1979, *84*(6), 50–54.

Fizel, J. L. "Play Ball: Baseball Arbitration at Twenty." *Dispute Resolution Journal,* 1994, *49*(2), 42–47.

Fogg, R. W. "Dealing with Conflict: A Repertoire of Creative, Peaceful Approaches." *Journal of Conflict Resolution,* 1985, *29,* 330–358.

Folberg, H. J. "Divorce Mediation: A Workable Alternative." In H. Davidson, L. Ray, and R. Horowitz (eds.), *Alternative Means of Family Dispute Resolution.* Washington, D.C.: American Bar Association, 1982.

Folberg, J., and Taylor, A. *Mediation: A Comprehensive Guide to Resolving Conflicts Without Litigation.* San Francisco: Jossey-Bass, 1984.

Folger, J. P., Poole, M. S., and Stutman, R. K. *Working Through Conflict: Strategies for Relationships, Groups and Organizations.* New York: HarperCollins, 1993.

Fong, L. S. "New Paradigms in Mediation: Thinking About Our Thinking." *Mediation Quarterly,* 1992, *10*(2), 209–212.

Foster, M. L., and Rubenstein, R. A. (eds.). *Peace and War: Cross-Cultural Perspectives.* New Brunswick: Transaction, 1986.

Fowler, [n.i.]. "Forms of Arbitration." In S. Kuttner (ed.), *Proceedings of the Fourth International Congress of Medieval Canon Law, Toronto, 21–25 August 1972.* Citta del Vaticano: Biblioteca Apostolica Vaticana, 1976.

Frangi, A. T. "The Internationalized Noninternational Armed Conflict in Lebanon, 1975–1990: Introduction to Confligology." *Capital University Law Review,* 1993, *22,* 965–1040.

Friedman, R. A. "The Culture of Mediation: Private Understandings in the Context of Public Conflict." In D. M. Kolb and J. M. Bartunek (eds.), *Hidden Conflict in Organizations: Uncovering the Behind-the-Scenes Disputes.* Thousand Oaks, Calif.: Sage, 1992.

Frohlich, N., and Oppenheimer, J. "Beyond Economic Demand: Altruism, Egalitarianism, and Difference Maximizing." *Journal of Conflict Resolution,* 1984, *28,* 3–24.

Fuller, L. L. "Collective Bargaining and the Arbitrator." *Wisconsin Law Review,* 1963, *1963*(1), 3–46.

Fuller, L. L. "Mediation: Its Forms and Functions." *Southern California Law Review,* 1971, *44,* 305–339.

Fuller, L. L. "The Forms and Limits of Adjudication." *Harvard Law Review,* 1978, *92,* 353–409.

Fuller, R. M., Kimsey, W. D., and McKinney, B. C. "Mediator Neutrality and Storytelling Order." *Mediation Quarterly,* 1992, *10*(2), 187–192.

Galanter, M. "Reading the Landscape of Disputes: What We Know and Don't Know (and Think We Know) About Our Allegedly Contentious and Litigious Society." *UCLA Law Review,* 1983, *31*(1), 4–71.

Galanter, M. "Worlds of Deals: Using Negotiation to Teach About Legal Process." *Journal of Legal Education,* 1984, *34*(2), 268–276.

Galanter, M. "Adjudication, Litigation, and Related Phenomena." In L. Lipson and S. Wheeler (eds.), *Law and the Social Sciences.* New York: Russell Sage Foundation, 1986.

Galbraith, J. K. *The Anatomy of Power.* Boston: Houghton Mifflin, 1983.

Galton, E. *Representing Clients in Mediation.* Dallas: Texas Lawyer Press, 1994.

Gamson, W. "A Theory of Coalition Formation." In C. G. Smith (ed.), *Conflict Resolution: Contributions of the Social Sciences.* Notre Dame, Ind.: University of Notre Dame Press, 1971.

Garth, B. "The Movement Toward Procedural Informalism in North America and Western Europe." In R. L. Abel (ed.), *The Politics of Informal Justice.* Orlando: Academic Press, 1982.

Geller, D. S. "Nuclear Weapons, Deterrence, and Crisis Escalation." *Journal of Conflict Resolution,* 1990, *34,* 291–310.

Gerber, S. G. "The HANDS Program of Minneapolis: A Grassroots, Community-Based Conflict Resolution Program Contrasted with One Other Alternative Dispute Resolution Model." *Hamline Journal of Public Law and Policy,* 1991, *12,* 91–116.

Gibbons, P., Bradac, J. J., and Busch, J. D. "The Role of Language in Negotiations: Threats and Promises." In L. L. Putnam and M. E. Roloff (eds.), *Communication and Negotiation.* Thousand Oaks, Calif.: Sage, 1992.

Gilpin, R. *War and Change in World Politics.* Cambridge: Cambridge University Press, 1981.

Girdner, L. K. "Family Mediation: Toward a Synthesis." *Mediation Quarterly,* 1986, *13,* 21–29.

Goffman, E. "On Face Work." *Psychiatry,* 1955, *18,* 213–231.

Goffman, E. *Strategic Interaction.* Philadelphia: University of Pennsylvania Press, 1969.

Gold, L. *Between Love and Hate: A Guide to Civilized Divorce.* New York: Plenum, 1992.

Gold, L. "Influencing Unconscious Influences: The Healing Dimension of Mediation." *Mediation Quarterly,* 1993, *11*(1), 55–66.

Gold, N. "Considering Dispute Resolution: A Research Prospectus." In K. J. Mackie (ed.), *A Handbook of Dispute Resolution: ADR in Action.* New York: Routledge, 1991.

Goldberg, S. B. "The Mediation of Grievances Under a Collective Bargaining Contract: An Alternative to Arbitration." *Northwestern University Law Review,* 1982, *77,* 270–315.

Goldberg, S., Sander, F., and Rogers, N. *Dispute Resolution: Negotiation, Mediation, and Other Processes.* (2nd ed.) New York: Little Brown, 1992.

Goldman, A. L. *Settling for More: Mastering Negotiating Strategies and Techniques.* Washington, D.C.: Bureau of National Affairs, 1991.

Gormley, W. T. "Public Advocacy in Public Utility Commission Proceedings." *The Journal of Applied Behavioral Science,* 1981, *17*(4), 446–462.

Graham, J. L., and Sano, Y. *Smart Bargaining: Doing Business with the Japanese.* (Rev. ed.) New York: HarperCollins, 1989.

Green, E. D "Recent Developments in Alternative Forms of Dispute Resolution." [Federal Rules Decisions.] 100 F.R.D. 513 (1983).

Greenhalgh, L. "Relationships in Negotiations." *Negotiation Journal,* 1987, *3*(3), 235–243.

Greenstone, J. L., and Leviton, S. C. "Crisis Management for Mediators." *Mediation Quarterly,* 1987, *17,* 39–54.

Grotius, H. *De Jure Belliac Pacis (The Law of War and Peace).* [3 vols. F. W. Kelsey, trans.] Indianapolis: Bobbs-Merrill, 1925.

Gruter, M. *Law and the Mind: Biological Origins of Human Behavior.* Thousand Oaks, Calif.: Sage, 1991.

Gudykunst, W. B. *Bridging Differences: Effective Intergroup Communication.* Thousand Oaks, Calif.: Sage, 1991.

Gulliver, P. H. *Disputes and Negotiations: A Cross-Cultural Perspective.* Orlando: Academic Press, 1979.

Haas, M. *International Conflict.* New York: Bobbs-Merrill, 1974.

Haass, R. "Ripeness and the Settlement of International Disputes." *Survival,* 1988, *30,* 232–251.

Habeeb, W. M. *Power and Tactics in International Negotiation.* Baltimore, Md.: Johns Hopkins University Press, 1988.

Hall, E. T. *Beyond Culture.* New York: Doubleday, 1976.

Hamner, W. C., and Yukl, G. A. "The Effectiveness of Different Offer Strategies in Bargaining." In D. Druckman (ed.), *Negotiations: Social-Psychological Perspectives.* Thousand Oaks, Calif.: Sage, 1977.

Hamnett, I. (ed.). *Social Anthropology and the Law.* Orlando: Academic Press, 1977.

Hancock, W. (ed.). *Laws of International Trade.* Chesterland, Ohio: Business Laws, 1987.

Handbook on the Peaceful Settlement of Disputes Between States. New York: UN Office of Legal Affairs OLA/COD/2394, 1992.

Harbaugh, J. D., and Britzke, B. "The Negotiation Process." In J. D. Harbaugh (ed.), *Negotiation: Winning Tactics and Techniques.* New York: Practising Law Institute, 1988.

Hardin, G. "The Tragedy of the Commons." *Science,* 1968, *162*(3859), 1243–48.

Hare, A. P. "Informal Mediation by Private Individuals." In J. Bercovitch and J. Z. Rubin (eds.), *Mediation in International Relations: Multiple Approaches to Conflict Management.* New York: St. Martin's Press, 1992.

Harrington, C. *Shadow Justice: The Ideology and Institutionalization of Alternatives to Court.* Westport, Conn.: Greenwood Press, 1985.

Harsanyi, J. C. "Bargaining and Conflict Situations in Light of a New Approach to Game Theory." In O. R. Young (ed.), *Bargaining: Formal Theories of Negotiation.* Urbana: University of Illinois Press, 1975.

Hart, B. J. "Gentle Jeopardy: The Further Endangerment of Battered Women and Children in Custody Mediation." *Mediation Quarterly,* 1990, *7*(4), 317–330.

Harter, P. (ed.). *Alternative Dispute Resolution: A Handbook for Judges.* Chicago: American Bar Association, 1987.

Harvey, M. *An Evaluation of the Organization and Operation of Care and Protection Family Group Conferences: Interim Report of Findings from the FGC Statistical Information Questionnaires.* Wellington, New Zealand: Evaluation Unit, Department of Social Welfare, Feb. 1991.

Hawkins, L., Hudson, M., and Cornall, R. *The Legal Negotiator: A Handbook for Managing Legal Negotiations More Effectively.* [n.p.], Australia: Longman Professional, 1991.

Haydock, R. S., and Mitchell, W. *Negotiation Practice.* New York: Wiley, 1984.

Haynes, J. M. "Mediated Negotiations: The Function of the Intake." *Mediation Quarterly,* 1984, *6,* 3–15.

Haynes, J. M. "Consultation in Mediation." *Mediation Quarterly,* 1986a, *12,* 3–15.

Haynes, J. M. "Supervision Issues in Mediation." *Mediation Quarterly,* 1986b, *13,* 31–42.

Haynes, J. M. "John and Mary: Sharing Parenting After Divorce." *Mediation Quarterly,* 1988, *21,* 23–29.

Helper, B. "Resolution Facilities in the Queen's Bench, Family Division." In R. J. Scott and S. G. Sigurdson (eds.), *The 1986 Isaac Pitblado Lectures on Alternative Dispute Resolution: Emerging Mechanisms and Professional Responsibilities in Dispute Resolution.* Manitoba, Canada: Law Society of Manitoba, 1986.

Henry, J. F. "Remarks Prepared for the Consumer Dispute Resolution Conference." In L. Ray and D. Smolover (eds.), *Consumer Dispute Resolution: Exploring the Alternatives.* Chicago: American Bar Association, Special Committee on Alternative Dispute Resolution, Public Services Group; Washington, D.C.: U.S. Department of Consumer Affairs, National Association of Consumer Agency Administrators, 1983.

Henry, K. L. "Med-Arb: An Alternative to Interest Arbitration in the Resolution of Contract Negotiation Disputes." *Ohio State Journal on Dispute Resolution,* 1988, *3*(2), 385–398.

Hensler, D. R. "A Glass Half Full, a Glass Half Empty: The Use of Alternative Dispute Resolution in Mass Personal Injury Litigation." *Texas Law Review,* 1995, *73,* 1587–1626.

Hocker, J. L., and Wilmot, W. W. *Interpersonal Conflict.* (4th ed.) Madison, Wis.: Brown & Benchmark, 1995.

Hoffman, R. B. "The Bureaucratic Spectre: Newest Challenge to the Courts." *Judicature,* 1982, *66*(2), 60–72.

Hogg, Q. M. (Viscount Hailsham). *The Law of Arbitration.* [n.p.], 1935.

Holding, R. L. "MACAP: The Appliance Industry's Solution to Consumer Disputes." In L. Ray and D. Smolover (eds.), *Consumer Dispute Resolution: Exploring the Alternatives.* Chicago: American Bar Association, Special Committee on Alternative Dispute Resolution, Public Services Group; Washington, D.C.: U.S. Department of Consumer Affairs, National Association of Consumer Agency Administrators, 1983.

Holdsworth, W. S. *A History of English Law.* [17 vols.] London: Methuen, 1909–1972.

Holmes, M. E. "Phase Structures in Negotiation." In L. L. Putnam and M. E. Roloff (eds.), *Communication and Negotiation.* Thousand Oaks, Calif.: Sage, 1992.

Holsti, K. J. *International Politics: A Framework for Analysis.* (4th ed.) Englewood Cliffs, N.J.: Prentice Hall, 1983.

Holsti, O. R., and Rosenau, J. N. *American Leadership in World Affairs: Vietnam and the Breakdown of Consensus.* Boston: Unwin Hyman, 1984.

Hopmann, P. T. "Arms Control and Arms Reduction: View I." In V. A. Kremenyuk (ed.), *International Negotiations: Analysis, Approaches, Issues.* San Francisco: Jossey-Bass, 1991.

Houweling, H., and Siccana, J. G. "Power Transitions as a Cause of War." *Journal of Conflict Resolution,* 1988, *32,* 87–102.

Howard, A. "Dispute Management in Rotuma." *Journal of Anthropological Research,* 1990, *46*(3), 263–292.

Howell, W. S. *The Empathic Communicator.* Belmont, Calif.: Wadsworth, 1982.

Huber, M. "Mediation Around the Medicine Wheel." *Mediation Quarterly,* 1993, *10*(4), 355–365.

Huleatt-James, M. "The Avoidance of Delay in Dispute Resolution for International Projects." *The Arbitration and Dispute Resolution Law Journal,* 1992, *4,* 211–218.

ICC. *Rules of Arbitration.* [In effect on Jan. 1, 1998.] International Chamber of Commerce, 1998.

Ihromi, T. O. "Informal Methods of Dispute Settlement in Indonesia." In C. L. Pe, G. C. Sosmena Jr., and A. F. Tadiar (eds.), *Transcultural Mediation in the Asia-Pacific.* Manila, Philippines: Asia-Pacific Organization for Mediation, 1988.

Iklé, F. C. *How Nations Negotiate.* New York: HarperCollins, 1964.

Iklé, F. C., and Leites, N. "Political Negotiation as a Process of Modifying Utilities." *Journal of Conflict Resolution,* 1962, *6,* 19–28.

Irving, H. H., and Benjamin, M. *Family Mediation: Theory and Practice of Dispute Resolution.* Toronto: Carswell, 1987.

Irving, H. H., and Benjamin, M. "Therapeutic Family Mediation: Fitting the Service to the Interactional Diversity of Client Couples." *Mediation Quarterly,* 1989, *7*(2), 115–131.

Irving, H. H., and Benjamin, M. "An Evaluation of Process and Outcome in a Private Family Mediation Service." *Mediation Quarterly,* 1992, *10*(1), 35–55.

Isaacson, B., and Wigoder, D. *The International Jewish Encyclopedia.* Englewood Cliffs, N.J.: Prentice Hall, 1973.

Jacob's Law Dictionary. (10th ed.) London: [n.p.], 1797.

Jandt, F. E., and Gillette, P. *Win-Win Negotiating.* New York: Wiley, 1985.

Johnson, E. Jr., Kantor, V., and Schwartz, E. *Outside the Courts: A Survey of Diversion Alternatives in Civil Cases.* Denver: National Center for State Courts, 1977.

Jones, B. "A Comparison of Consensus and Voting in Public Decision Making." *Negotiation Journal,* 1994, *10*(2), 161–171.

Kagel, S., and Kelly, K. *The Anatomy of Mediation: What Makes It Work.* Washington, D.C.: Bureau of National Affairs, 1989.

Kahana, J. S. "Reevaluating the Nursing Home Ombudsman's Role with a View Toward Expanding the Concept of Dispute Resolution." *Journal of Dispute Resolution,* 1994, 2, 217–233.

Kahn, R. L., and others. *Organizational Stress: Studies in Role Conflict and Ambiguity.* New York: Wiley, 1964.

Kanowitz, L. *Cases and Materials on Alternative Dispute Resolution.* St. Paul, Minn.: West, 1986.

Kantor, D., and Lehr, W. *Inside the Family: Toward a Theory of Family Process.* New York: HarperCollins, 1976.

Karrass, C. L. *The Negotiating Game.* Cleveland: World, 1970.

Katz, D., and Kahn, R. L. *The Social Psychology of Organizations.* New York: Wiley, 1964.

Keating, J. M., and Shaw, M. L. "Compared to What? Defining Terms in Court-Related ADR Programs." *Negotiation Journal,* 1990, *6*(3), 217–220.

Kelly, K. "Mediation and Psychotherapy: Distinguishing the Differences." In J. Lemmon (ed.), *Dimensions and Practice of Divorce Mediation.* San Francisco: Jossey-Bass, 1983.

Kelman, H. C. "Informal Mediation by the Scholar/Practitioner." In J. Bercovitch and J. Z. Rubin (eds), *Mediation in International Relations: Multiple Approaches to Conflict Management.* New York: St. Martin's Press, 1992.

Keough, C. M. "Bargaining Arguments and Argumentative Bargainers." In L. L. Putnam and M. E. Roloff (eds.), *Communication and Negotiation.* Thousand Oaks, Calif.: Sage, 1992.

Kesner, I. F., and Shapiro, D. L. "Did a 'Failed' Negotiation Really Fail? Reflections on the Arthur Andersen–Price Waterhouse Merger Talks." *Negotiation Journal,* 1991, *7*(4), 369–377.

Kessler, G., and Finkelstein, L. J. "The Evolution of a Multi-Door Courthouse." *Catholic University Law Review,* 1988, *37,* 577–590.

Kestner, P. B., Devonshire, J., and Kim, U. (eds.). *Education and Mediation: Exploring the Alternatives.* Washington, D.C.: American Bar Association Standing Committee on Dispute Resolution, Public Services Division, Governmental Affairs Group, 1988.

Kettering Foundation. "Mediation and New Federalism: Proceedings of a Roundtable on the Negotiated Investment Strategy." Washington, D.C.: Kettering Foundation, July 8, 1981.

Khalaf, S. N. "Settlement of Violence in Bedouin Society." *Ethnology*, 1990, *29*(3), 1990, 225–242.

Kiely, L. S., and Crary, D. R. "Effective Mediation: A Communication Approach to Consubstantiality." *Mediation Quarterly*, 1986, *12*, 37–50.

Kittay, E. F., and Meyers, D. T. *Women and Moral Theory.* Lanham, Md.: Rowman and Littlefield, 1987.

Knight, H. W. "Role of the Private Judge or Neutral Advisor in Alternative Dispute Resolution." In L. Ray and D. Smolover (eds.), *Consumer Dispute Resolution: Exploring the Alternatives.* Chicago: American Bar Association, Special Committee on Alternative Dispute Resolution, Public Services Group; Washington, D.C.: U.S. Department of Consumer Affairs, National Association of Consumer Agency Administrators, 1983.

Kolb, D. M. *The Mediators.* Cambridge, Mass.: MIT Press, 1983.

Kolb, D. M. "Corporate Ombudsman and Organization Conflict." *Journal of Conflict Resolution*, 1987, *31*, 673–692.

Kolb, D. M. "Labor Mediators, Managers, and Ombudsmen: Roles Mediators Play in Different Contexts." In K. Kressel, D. G. Pruitt, and Associates, *Mediation Research: The Process and Effectiveness of Third-Party Intervention.* San Francisco: Jossey-Bass, 1989.

Kolb, D. M., and Bartunek, J. M. (eds.). *Hidden Conflict in Organizations: Uncovering the Behind-the-Scenes Disputes.* Thousand Oaks, Calif.: Sage, 1992.

Kolb, D. M., and Kressel, K. "Conclusion: The Realities of Making Talk Work." In D. M. Kolb, and Associates (eds.), *When Talk Works: Profiles of Mediators.* San Francisco: Jossey-Bass, 1994.

Kovach, K. K. "What Is Real Mediation, and Who Should Decide?" *Dispute Resolution Magazine*, 1996, *3*(2), pp. 5, 8.

Kressel, K., and Pruitt, D. G. "Conclusion: A Research Perspective on the Mediation of Social Conflict." In K. Kressel, D. G. Pruitt, and Associates, *Mediation Research: The Process and Effectiveness of Third-Party Intervention.* San Francisco: Jossey-Bass, 1989.

Kressel, K., and others. "The Settlement-Orientation Versus the Problem-Solving Style in Custody Mediation." *Journal of Social Issues*, 1994, *50*, 67–84.

Kriesberg, L. "Coexistence and the Reconciliation of Communal Conflicts." In E. Weiner (ed.), *The Handbook of Interethnic Coexistence.* New York: Continuum, 1998a.

Kriesberg, L. *Constructive Conflicts: From Escalation to Resolution.* Lanham, Md.: Rowman & Littlefield, 1998b.

Kritzer, H. M. *Let's Make a Deal: Understanding the Negotiation Process in Ordinary Litigation.* Madison: University of Wisconsin Press, 1991.

Kunde, J. E., and Rudd, J. E. "The Role of Citizens Groups in Policy Conflicts." *Mediation Quarterly,* 1988, *20,* 33–44.

Kyd, S. *A Treatise on the Law of Awards.* Dublin: G. Burnett, 1791.

Ladinsky, J., and Susmilch, C. "Major Findings of the Milwaukee Consumer Dispute Study." In L. Ray and D. Smolover (eds.), *Consumer Dispute Resolution: Exploring the Alternatives.* Chicago: American Bar Association, Special Committee on Alternative Dispute Resolution, Public Services Group; Washington, D.C.: U.S. Department of Consumer Affairs, National Association of Consumer Agency Administrators, 1983.

Lall, A. S. *Modern International Negotiation: Principles and Practice.* New York: Columbia University Press, 1966.

Lall, A. S. (ed.). *Multilateral Negotiation and Mediation: Instruments and Methods.* New York: International Peace Academy, Pergamon Press, 1985.

Lambros, T. D. "The Summary Jury Trial: An Alternative Method of Resolving Disputes." *Judicature,* 1986, *69,* 286–290.

Lauer, E. J. "Conciliation: A Cure for the Law's Delay." *Massachusetts Law Quarterly,* 1930, *15,* 3.

Lax, D. A., and Sebenius, J. K. *The Manager as Negotiator: Bargaining for Cooperation and Competitive Gain.* New York: Free Press, 1986.

Lederach, J. P. *Preparing for Peace: Conflict Transformation Across Cultures.* Syracuse, N.Y.: Syracuse University Press, 1995.

Leeson, S. M., and Johnston, B. M. *Ending It: Dispute Resolution in America— Descriptions, Examples, Cases, and Questions.* Cincinnati, Ohio: Anderson, 1988.

Lemmon, J. A. "The Mediation Method Throughout the Family Life Cycle." *Mediation Quarterly,* 1985, *7,* 5–21.

Levine, D. I. "Calculating Fees of Special Masters." *Hastings Law Journal,* 1985, *37,* 141–200.

Levinger, G., and Rubin, J. Z. "Bridges and Barriers to a More General Theory of Conflict." *Negotiation Journal,* 1994, *10*(3), 201–215.

Levy, J. S. "Theories of General War." *World Politics,* 1985, *37*(3), 344–374.

Lewin, D., and Peterson, R. B. *The Modern Grievance Procedure in the United States.* Westport, Conn.: Quorum/Greenwood, 1988.

Li Mei Qin, and He Wei. "Mediation (or Conciliation) in China." In C. L. Pe, G. C. Sosmena Jr., and A. F. Tadiar (eds.), *Transcultural Mediation in the Asia-Pacific.* Manila, Philippines: Asia-Pacific Organization for Mediation, 1988.

Lieberman, H., and Lieberman, J. *The Manager's Guide to Resolving Legal Disputes.* New York: HarperCollins, 1985.

Lieberman, J. K., and Henry, J. F. "Lessons from the Alternate Dispute Resolution Movement." *University of Chicago Law Review,* 1986, *53,* 424–439.

Lieder, M. D. "Navajo Dispute Resolution and Promissory Obligations: Continuity and Change in the Largest Native American Nation." *American Indian Law Review,* 1993, *18,* 1–71.

Lloyd, W. F. "Two Lectures on the Checks to Population. *In Lectures on Population, Value, Poor-Laws, and Rent.* [Delivered at the University of Oxford during the years 1832, 1833, 1834, 1835, and 1836.] New York: A. M. Kelley, 1968.

Lockhart, C. *Bargaining in International Conflicts.* New York: Columbia University Press, 1979.

Lowy, M. J. "A Good Name Is Worth More Than Money: Strategies of Court Use in Urban Ghana." In L. Nader and H. F. Todd Jr. (eds.), *The Disputing Process: Law in Ten Societies.* New York: Columbia University Press, 1978.

Luban, D. "The Quality of Justice." *Denver University Law Review,* 1989, *66,* 381–417.

Mack, R. W., and Snyder, R. C. "The Analysis of Social Conflict: Toward an Overview and Synthesis." In C. G. Smith (ed.), *Conflict Resolution: Contributions of the Behavioral Sciences.* Notre Dame, Ind.: University of Notre Dame Press, 1971.

Mackie, K. J. "Conclusion: Dispute Resolution Futures." In K. J. Mackie (ed.), *A Handbook of Dispute Resolution: ADR in Action.* New York: Routledge, 1991a.

Mackie, K. J. (ed.). *A Handbook of Dispute Resolution: ADR in Action.* New York: Routledge, 1991b.

Maggiolo, W. A. *Techniques of Mediation in Labor Disputes.* Dobbs Ferry, N.Y.: Oceana, 1971.

Maggiolo, W. A. *Techniques of Mediation.* Dobbs Ferry, N.Y.: Oceana, 1985.

Malinowski, B. *Crime and Custom in Savage Society.* Totowa, N.J.: Littlefield, Adams, 1972.

Mansfield, E. "Balance and Harmony: Peacemaking in Coast Salish Tribes of the Pacific Northwest." *Mediation Quarterly,* 1993, *10*(4), 339–353.

Mansfield, E. D. "The Concentration of Capabilities and the Onset of War." *Journal of Conflict Resolution,* 1992, *36*(1), 3–24.

Marcus, R. L., and Sherman, E. F. "The Asbestos Claims Agreement." In R. L. Marcus and E. F. Sherman (eds.), *Complex Litigation: Cases and Materials on Advanced Civil Procedure.* St. Paul, Minn.: West, 1985.

Marshall, T. F. *Alternatives to Criminal Courts: The Potential for Non-Judicial Dispute Settlement.* Hampshire, England: Gower, 1985.

Maslow, A. *Motivation and Personality.* New York: HarperCollins, 1954.

Mastrofski, J. A. "Reexamination of the Bar: Incentives to Support Custody Mediation." *Mediation Quarterly,* 1991, *9*(1), 21–31.

Mayer, B. "Conflict Resolution in Child Protection and Adoption." *Mediation Quarterly,* 1985, *7,* 69–81.

Mayer, B. "The Dynamics of Power in Mediation and Negotiation." *Mediation Quarterly,* 1987, *16,* 75–86.

Mayer, B. "Mediation in Child Protection Cases: The Impact of Third-Party Intervention on Parental Compliance Attitudes." *Mediation Quarterly,* 1989, *24,* 89–106.

McConnell, M. [Speech to U.S. Congress.] 132 Cong. Rec. S9, daily ed., Feb. 5, 1986.

McEwen, C. A. "Pursuing Problem-Solving or Predictive Settlement." *Florida State University Law Review,* 1991, *10*(9), 77–88.

McGillis, D., and Mullen, J. *Neighborhood Justice Centers: An Analysis of Potential Models.* Washington, D.C.: U.S. Government Printing Office, 1977.

McIsaac, H. "Confidentiality: An Exploration of Issues." *Mediation Quarterly,* 1985, *8,* 57–66.

McIsaac, H. "Toward a Classification of Child Custody Disputes: An Application of Family Systems Theory." *Mediation Quarterly,* 1986–1987, *14/15,* 39–50.

Menkel-Meadow, C. "Pursuing Settlement in an Adversary Culture: A Tale of Innovation Co-opted or 'The Law of ADR.'" *Florida State University Law Review,* 1991, *19*(1), 1–46.

Menkel-Meadow, C. "Is Altruism Possible in Lawyering?" *Georgia State University Law Review,* 1992, *8*(2), 385–419.

Menkel-Meadow, C. "Is Mediation the Practice of Law?" *NIDR News,* 1996, *3*(2), 1, 4.

Menzel, K. E. "Judging the Fairness of Mediation: A Critical Framework." *Mediation Quarterly,* 1991, *9*(1), 3–20.

Mernitz, S. *Mediation of Environmental Disputes: A Sourcebook.* New York: Praeger, 1980.

Merrills, J. G. *International Dispute Settlement.* (2nd ed.) Cambridge: Grotius, 1991.

Merry, S. E. "Mediation in Nonindustrial Societies." In K. Kressel, D. G. Pruitt, and Associates, *Mediation Research: The Process and Effectiveness of Third-Party Intervention.* San Francisco: Jossey-Bass, 1989.

Merry, S. E., and Milner, N. *The Possibility of Popular Justice: A Case Study of Community Mediation in the United States.* Ann Arbor: University of Michigan Press, 1993.

Midgaard, K., and Underdal, A. "Multiparty Conferences." In D. Druckman (ed.), *Negotiations: Social-Psychological Perspectives.* Thousand Oaks, Calif.: Sage, 1977.

Miller, R. E., and Sarat, A. "Grievances, Claims, and Disputes: Assessing the Adversary Culture." *Law and Society Review,* 1980–1981, *15*(3–4), 525–566.

Miller, W. I. "Avoiding Legal Judgment: The Submission of Disputes to Arbitration in Medieval Iceland." *American Journal of Legal History,* 1984, *28,* 95–134.

Mills, M. K. (ed.). *Conflict Resolution and Public Policy.* Westport, Conn: Greenwood Press, 1990.

Mitchell, C. R. *The Structure of International Conflict.* London: Macmillan, 1981.

Mitchell, C. R. "A Willingness to Talk: Conciliatory Gestures and De-Escalation." *Negotiation Journal,* 1991, *7*(4), 405–430.

Mnookin, R. H., and Birke, R. "Saddam's Folly: Playing Chicken with George Bush." *Negotiation Journal,* 1992, *8*(1), 41–47.

Mnookin, R. H., and Kornhauser, L. "Bargaining in the Shadow of the Law: The Case of Divorce." *Yale Law Journal,* 1979, *88,* 950–997.

Mnookin, R. H., Peppet, S. R., and Tulumello, A. S. "The Tension Between Empathy and Assertiveness." *Negotiation Journal,* 1996, *12*(3), 217–229.

Modelski, G. "Global Wars and World Leadership Selection." Speech delivered at the Second World Peace Society Congress, Rotterdam, June 4–10, 1984.

Montrose, S. P. "Comment: To Police the Police—Functional Equivalence to the EIS Requirement and EPA Remedial Actions Under Superfund." *Catholic University Law Review*, 1984, *33*, 863–897.

Moore, C. M., and Carlson, C. *Public Decision Making: Using the Negotiated Investment Strategy.* Washington, D.C.: Kettering Foundation, 1984.

Moore, C. W. *The Mediation Process: Practical Strategies for Resolving Conflict.* San Francisco: Jossey-Bass, 1986.

Morley, I. E., and Stephenson, G. M. *The Social Psychology of Bargaining.* Boston: Unwin Hyman, 1977.

Morrison, F. L. "The Future of International Adjudication." *Minnesota Law Review,* 1991, *75*(3), 827–847.

Murray, J. S., Rau, A. S., and Sherman, E. F. *Processes of Dispute Resolution: The Role of Lawyers.* Westbury, N.Y.: Foundation Press, 1989.

Mustill, M. J., and Boyd, S. C. *The Law and Practice of Commercial Arbitration in England.* London: Butterworths, 1987.

Nader, L., and Singer, L. "Dispute Resolution and Law in the Future: What Are the Choices?" *California State Bar Journal,* 1976, *51*, 281.

Nader, L., and Todd, H. F. Jr. (eds.). *The Disputing Process: Law in Ten Societies.* New York: Columbia University Press, 1978.

Nagel, S. S. "Multi-Criteria Dispute Resolution Through Computer-Aided Mediation." In M. K. Mills (ed.), *Conflict Resolution and Public Policy.* Westport, Conn.: Greenwood Press, 1990.

Nagel, S. S., and Mills, M. K. "Multicriteria Dispute Resolution Through Computer-Aided Mediation Software." *Mediation Quarterly,* 1989, *7*(2), 175–189.

Nagel, S. S., and Mills, M. K. *Systematic Analysis in Dispute Resolution.* Westport, Conn.: Quorum/Greenwood, 1991.

Nash, J. F. "The Bargaining Problem." In O. R. Young (ed.), *Bargaining: Formal Theories of Negotiation.* Urbana: University of Illinois Press, 1975a.

Nash, J. F. "Two-Person Cooperative Games." In O. R. Young (ed.), *Bargaining: Formal Theories of Negotiation.* Urbana: University of Illinois Press, 1975b.

National Association of Securities Dealers. *NASD Manual.* Chicago: Commerce Clearing House, 1954.

Neal, F. W. "Diplomacy." In J. Gould and W. L. Kolb (eds.), *A Dictionary of the Social Sciences.* Glencoe, N.Y.: Free Press of Glencoe, 1964.

Neale, M. A., and Bazerman, M. H. *Cognition and Rationality in Negotiation.* New York: Free Press, 1991.

Nergård, T. B. "Solving Conflicts Outside the Court System: Experiences with the Conflict Resolution Boards in Norway." *British Journal of Criminology,* 1993, *33*, 81–94.

Neumann, D. "The Advanced Technique of Touching: Notes from a Training Seminar." *Mediation Quarterly,* 1990, *7*(3), 285–289.

New York Stock Exchange Guide. Chicago: Commerce Clearing House, 1994.

Newton, D. A. "Alternative Dispute Resolution in Australia." In K. J. Mackie (ed.), *A Handbook of Dispute Resolution: ADR in Action.* New York: Routledge, 1991.

Nicholson, M. B. "The Resolution of Conflict." In O. R. Young (ed.), *Bargaining: Formal Theories of Negotiation.* Urbana: University of Illinois Press, 1975.

Nierenberg, G. I. *The Art of Negotiating.* New York: Hawthorne Books, 1968.

Nye, R. D. *Conflict Among Humans: Some Basic Psychological and Social-Psychological Considerations.* New York: Springer, 1973.

O'Connor, D. "The Design of Self-Supporting Dispute Resolution Programs." *Negotiation Journal,* 1992, *8*(2), 85–89.

O'Hare, M., Bacow, L., and Sanderson, D. *Facility Sitting and Public Opposition.* New York: Van Nostrand Reinhold, 1983.

Oliver, P. "Rewards and Punishments as Selective Incentives: An Apex Game." *Journal of Conflict Resolution,* 1984, *28,* 123–148.

Orme, J. D. "U.S. Mediation in Revolutionary Conflicts, 1944–1986." *Mediation Quarterly,* 1989, *7*(1), 59–72.

Orwell, G. *1984.* Orlando: Harcourt Brace, 1982.

Osgood, C. E. *An Alternative to War or Surrender.* Urbana: University of Illinois, 1962.

Osgood, C. E. "Graduated Unilateral Initiatives for Peace." In C. G. Smith (ed.), *Conflict Resolution: Contributions of the Social Sciences.* Notre Dame, Ind.: University of Notre Dame Press, 1971.

Owen, H. *Expanding Our Now: The Story of Open Space Technology.* San Francisco: Berrett-Koehler, 1997.

Paddock, H. *Settlement Week: A Practical Manual for Resolving Civil Cases Through Mediation.* Washington, D.C.: Bureau of National Affairs, 1990.

Parker, R. G. "Mediation: A Social Exchange Framework." *Mediation Quarterly,* 1991, *9*(2), 121–135.

Patterson, R. J. "Dispute Resolution in a World of Alternatives." *Catholic University Law Review,* 1988, *37*(3), 591–604.

Pauling, L., Laszlo, E., and Jong, Y. Y. (eds.). *World Encyclopedia of Peace.* [2 vols.] Oxford: Pergamon Press, 1986.

Pe, C. L., Sosmena, G. C. Jr., and Tadiar, A. F. (eds.). *Transcultural Mediation in the Asia-Pacific.* Manila, Philippines: Asia-Pacific Organization for Mediation, 1988.

Peachey, D. E. "What People Want from Mediation." In K. Kressel, D. G. Pruitt, and Associates, *Mediation Research: The Process and Effectiveness of Third-Party Intervention.* San Francisco: Jossey-Bass, 1989.

Pendergast, W. R. "Managing the Negotiation Agenda." *Negotiation Journal,* 1990, *6*(2), 135–145.

Pennell, J., and Burford, G. "Widening the Circle: Family Group Decision Making." *Journal of Child and Youth Care,* 1994, *9*(1), 1–11.

Perkovich, R. "A Comparative Analysis of Community Mediation in the United States and the People's Republic of China." *Temple International and Comparative Law Journal,* 1996, *10*(2), 313–328.

Podolefsky, A. *Simbu Law: Conflict Management in the New Guinea Highlands.* Orlando: Harcourt Brace, 1992.

Polachek, S. W. "Conflict and Trade." *Journal of Conflict Resolution,* 1980, *24*, 55–78.

Pollock, F., and Maitland, F. W. *History of English Law.* [2 vols.] Cambridge: Cambridge University Press, 1895.

Poole, M. S., Shannon, D. L., and DeSanctis, G. "Communication Media and Negotiation Processes." In L. L. Putnam and M. E. Roloff (eds.), *Communication and Negotiation.* Thousand Oaks, Calif.: Sage, 1992.

Potapchuk, W., and Carlson, C. "Using Conflict Analysis to Determine Intervention Techniques." *Mediation Quarterly,* 1987, *16*, 31–43.

Powell, D. E. "Legal Perspective." In V. A. Kremenyuk (ed.), *International Negotiation: Analysis, Approaches, Issues.* San Francisco: Jossey-Bass, 1991.

Practising Law Institute. *Alternative Dispute Resolution and Risk Management.* [J. Sands, ed.] New York: Practising Law Institute, 1987.

Prather, V. F. (ed.). *Family Dispute Resolution: Options for All Ages.* Washington, D.C.: American Bar Association, 1990.

Price, J., and Woods, K. *Legislation on Dispute Resolution.* Washington, D.C.: American Bar Association, 1990.

Princen, T. *Intermediaries in International Conflict.* Princeton, N.J.: Princeton University Press, 1992.

Pritzker, D. M., and Dalton, D. S. (eds.). *Negotiated Rulemaking Sourcebook.* (2nd ed.) Washington, D.C.: U.S. Government Printing Office, 1995.

Probost, R. R. *"Good Offices" in the Light of Swiss International Practice and Experience.* Dordrecht, The Netherlands: Martinus Nijhoff, 1989.

Pruitt, D. G. *Negotiation Behavior.* Orlando: Academic Press, 1981.

Pruitt, D. G. "Achieving Integrative Agreements." In M. Bazerman and R. J. Lewicki (eds.), *Negotiation in Organizations.* Thousand Oaks, Calif.: Sage, 1983.

Pruitt, D. G., and Lewis, S. A. "The Psychology of Integrative Bargaining." In D. Druckman (ed.), *Negotiations: Social-Psychological Perspectives.* Thousand Oaks, Calif.: Sage, 1977.

Pruitt, D. G., McGillicuddy, N. B., Welton, G. L., and Fry, W. R. "Process of Mediation in Dispute Settlement Centers." In K. Kressel, D. G. Pruitt, and Associates, *Mediation Research: The Process and Effectiveness of Third-Party Intervention.* San Francisco: Jossey-Bass, 1989.

Pruitt, D. G., and Zubin, J. Z. *Social Conflict: Escalation, Stalemate, and Settlement.* New York: Random House, 1986.

Putnam, L. L., and Holmer, M. "Framing, Reframing, and Issue Development." In L. L. Putnam and M. E. Roloff (eds.), *Communication and Negotiation.* Thousand Oaks, Calif.: Sage, 1992.

Putnam, L. L., and Jones, T. S. "The Role of Communication in Bargaining." *Human Communication Research,* 1982b, *8,* 262–280.

Putnam, L. L., and Roloff, M. E. "Communication Perspectives on Negotiation." In L. L. Putnam and M. E. Roloff (eds.), *Communication and Negotiation.* Thousand Oaks, Calif.: Sage, 1992.

Rabe, B. G. "The Hazardous Waste Dilemma and the Hazards of Institutionalizing Negotiation." In M. K. Mills (ed.), *Conflict Resolution and Public Policy.* Westport, Conn.: Greenwood Press, 1990.

Rahim, M. A. *Managing Conflict in Organizations.* New York: Praeger, 1986.

Raiffa, H. *The Art and Science of Negotiation: How to Resolve Conflicts and Get the Best Out of Bargaining.* Cambridge, Mass.: Harvard University Press, 1982.

Raman, K. V. (ed.). *Dispute Settlement Through the United Nations.* Dobbs Ferry, N.Y.: Oceana, 1977.

Rapoport, A. "Experiments with N-Person Social Traps I: Prisoner's Dilemma, Weak Prisoner's Dilemma, Volunteer's Dilemma, and Largest Number." *Journal of Conflict Resolution,* 1988, *32*(3), 457–472.

Rasmussen, S. J. "Modes of Persuasion: Gossip, Song, and Divination in Tuareg Conflict Resolution." *Anthropological Quarterly,* 1991, *64*(1), 35–46.

"Records of the Fair Court of St. Ives (1287 A.D.)." In C. Gross (ed.), *Select Cases Concerning the Law Merchant.* Vol. 1. London: Selden Society, 1908.

Report of a Study Group on the Peaceful Settlement of International Disputes. London: David Davies Memorial Institute of International Studies, 1966.

Report of the Committee on One-Parent Families. Cmnd. 5629. London: Her Majesty's Stationery Office, 1974.

"Report of the Pound Conference Follow-Up Task Force." In A. L. Levin and R. R. Wheeler (eds.), *Proceedings of the National Conference on the Causes of Popular Dissatisfaction with the Administration of Justice.* St. Paul, Minn.: West, 1976.

Resnik, J. "Managerial Judges." *Harvard Law Review,* 1982, *96*(2), 374–448.

Reuben, R. C. "Are We Creating a Monster? The Dark Side of Alternative Dispute Resolution." *California Lawyer,* Feb. 1994, pp. 53–58.

Ricci, I. "Mediator's Notebook: Reflections on Promoting Equal Empowerment and Entitlements for Women." *Journal of Divorce,* 1985, *8*(3–4), 49–61.

Rifkin, J., Millen, J., and Cobb, S. "Toward a New Discourse for Mediation: A Critique of Neutrality." *Mediation Quarterly,* 1991, *9*(2), 151–163.

Riskin, L. L. "The Represented Client in a Settlement Conference: The Lessons of *G. Heileman Brewing Co.* v. *Joseph Oat Corp.*" *Washington University Law Quarterly,* 1991, *69*(4), 1059–1116.

Riskin, L. L. "Understanding Mediators' Orientations, Strategies, and Techniques: A Grid for the Perplexed." *Harvard Negotiation Law Review,* Spring 1996, pp. 7–51.

Riskin, L. L., and Westbrook, J. E. *Dispute Resolution and Lawyers.* St. Paul, Minn.: West, 1987.

Roberts, M. "Systems or Selves? Some Issues in Family Mediation." *Mediation Quarterly,* 1992, *10*(1), 3–19.

Rose, J. C. "Conflict with the Government: The Need for New Approaches." In L. Ray and D. Smolover (eds.), *Consumer Dispute Resolution: Exploring the Alternatives.* Chicago: American Bar Association, Special Committee on Alternative Dispute Resolution, Public Services Group; Washington, D.C.: U.S. Department of Consumer Affairs, National Association of Consumer Agency Administrators, 1983.

Ross, L. "The Intuitive Psychologist and His Shortcomings: Distortions in the Attribution Process." In L. Berkowitz (ed.), *Advances in Experimental Social Psychology.* Vol 10. Orlando: Academic Press, 1977.

Ross, L., and Stillinger, C. "Barriers to Conflict Resolution." *Negotiation Journal,* 1991, *7*(4), 389–404.

Rothenberger, J. E. "The Social Dynamics of Dispute Settlement in a Sunni Muslim Village in Lebanon." In L. Nader and H. F. Todd Jr. (eds.), *The Disputing Process: Law in Ten Societies.* New York: Columbia University Press, 1978.

Rothman, J. "Reflexive Dialogue as Transformation." *Mediation Quarterly,* 1996, *13*(4), 345–52.

Rowe, M. P. "The Corporate Ombudsman: An Overview and Analysis." *Negotiation Journal,* 1987, *3*(2), 127–140.

Rowe, M. P. "Options, Functions and Skills: What an Organizational Ombudsman Might Want to Know." *Negotiation Journal,* 1995, *11*(2), 103–116.

Rowe, M. P. "Dispute Resolution in the Nonunion Environment: An Evolution Toward Integrated Systems for Conflict Management?" In S. Gleason (ed.), *Frontiers in Dispute Resolution in Labor Relations and Human Resources.* Ann Arbor: University of Michigan Press, 1997.

Rubin, J. Z. "Negotiation: An Introduction to Some Issues and Themes." *American Behavioral Scientist,* 1983, *27*, 135–147.

Rubin, J. Z. "The Actors in Negotiation." In V. A. Kremenyuk (ed.), *International Negotiation: Analysis, Approaches, Issues.* San Francisco: Jossey-Bass, 1991.

Rubin, J. Z., Brockner, J., Small-Weil, S., and Nathanson, S. "Factors Affecting Entry into Psychological Trends." *Journal of Conflict Resolution,* 1980, *24*, 405–426.

Rubin, J. Z., and Brown, B. R. *Social Psychology of Bargaining and Negotiation.* Orlando: Academic Press, 1975.

Rubin, J. Z., Pruitt, D. G., and Kim Sung Hee. *Social Conflict: Escalation, Stalemate, and Settlement.* (2nd ed.) New York: McGraw-Hill, 1994.

Rubin, J. Z., and Sander, F. A. "When Should We Use Agents? Direct Versus Representative Negotiation." *Negotiation Journal,* 1988, *4*(4), 395–401.

Rubin, S. J., and Jones, M. L. *Conflict and Resolution in US-EC Trade Relations at the Opening of the Uruguay Round.* Dobbs Ferry, N.Y.: Oceana, 1989.

Ruhnka, J. C., and Weller, S. *Small Claims Courts: A National Examination.* Williamsburg, Va.: National Center for State Courts, 1978.

Salem, R. A. "Mediating Political and Social Conflicts: The Skokie-Nazi Dispute." *Mediation Quarterly,* 1984, *5,* 65–76.

Sander, F.E.A. "Varieties of Dispute Processing." [Federal Rules Decisions.] 70 F.R.D. 111, 1976.

Sander, F.E.A. "Varieties of Dispute Processing." In A. L. Levin and R. R. Wheeler (eds.), Proceedings of the National Conference on the Causes of Popular Dissatisfaction with the Administration of Justice. St. Paul, Minn.: West, 1979.

Sander, F.E.A. "ADR in the U.S.: An Overview." *Mediation Quarterly,* 1985, *11,* 40.

Sander, F.E.A. (ed.). *Emerging ADR Issues in State and Federal Courts.* Chicago: American Bar Association, 1991.

Saposnek, D. T. "Strategies in Child Custody Mediation: A Family Systems Approach." *Mediation Quarterly,* 1983, *2,* 29–54.

Saposnek, D. T. "Aikido: A Systems Model for Maneuvering in Mediation." *Mediation Quarterly,* 1986–1987, *14/15,* 119–136.

Sarat, A. D. "Access to Justice: Citizen Participation and the American Legal Order." In L. Lipson and S. Wheeler (eds.), *Law and the Social Sciences.* New York: Russell Sage Foundation, 1986.

Satir, V. *Conjoint Family Therapy.* Palo Alto, Calif.: Science and Behavior Books, 1964.

Saunders, L. K. "The Quest for Balance: Public Policy and Due Process in Medical Malpractice Arbitration Agreements." *Harvard Journal on Legislation,* 1986, *23*(1), 267–285.

Schelling, T. C. *The Strategy of Conflict.* Cambridge, Mass.: Harvard University Press, 1960.

Schoenfield, M. K., and Schoenfield, R. M. *Legal Negotiations: Getting Maximum Results.* Colorado Springs: Shepard's/McGraw-Hill, 1988.

Schuessler, R. "Threshold Effects and the Decline of Cooperation." *Journal of Conflict Resolution,* 1990, *34,* 476–498.

Schweber, C. "Your Telephone May Be a Party Line: Mediation by Telephone." *Mediation Quarterly,* 1989, *7*(2), 191–196.

Sebenius, J. K. "On 'Offers That Can't Be Refused.'" *Negotiation Journal,* 1992, *8*(1), 49–57.

Select Cases Concerning the Law Merchant. Vol. II. [H. Hull, ed.] London: Selden Society, 1930.

Shapiro, M. M. *Courts: A Comparative and Political Analysis.* Chicago: University of Chicago Press, 1981.

Sheppard, B. H., Blumenfeld-Jones, K., and Roth, J. "Informal Thirdpartyship: Studies of Everyday Conflict Intervention." In K. Kressel, D. G. Pruitt, and Associates,

Mediation Research: The Process and Effectiveness of Third-Party Intervention. San Francisco: Jossey-Bass, 1989.

Shklar, J. N. *Legalism.* Cambridge, Mass.: Harvard University Press, 1964.

Shonholtz, R. "The Role of Minorities in Establishing Mediating Norms and Institutions in the New Democracies." *Mediation Quarterly,* 1993, *10*(3), 231–241.

Shook, V., and Kwan, L. K. "Straightening Relationships and Resolving Disputes in Hawaii: Ho'oponopono and Mediation." In C. L. Pe, G. C. Sosmena, Jr., and A. F. Tadiar (eds.), *Transcultural Mediation in the Asia-Pacific.* Manila, Philippines: Asia-Pacific Organization for Mediation, 1988.

Shourie, H. D. "Mediation Sans Legislation: An Experiment in India." In C. L. Pe, G. C. Sosmena, Jr., and A. F. Tadiar (eds.), *Transcultural Mediation in the Asia-Pacific.* Manila, Philippines: Asia-Pacific Organization for Mediation, 1988.

Siebe, W. "Game Theory." In V. A. Kremenyuk (ed.), *International Negotiation: Analysis, Approaches, Issues.* San Francisco: Jossey-Bass, 1991.

Sigurdson, S. G. "Lessons from Two Canadian Environmental Disputes." In R. J. Scott and S. G. Sigurdson (eds.), *The 1986 Isaac Pitblado Lectures on Alternative Dispute Resolution: Emerging Mechanisms and Professional Responsibilities in Dispute Resolution.* Manitoba, Canada: Law Society of Manitoba, 1986.

Silberman, L. J. *Non-Attorney Justice in the United States: An Empirical Study.* New York: Institute of Judicial Administration, 1979.

Silbey, S. S., and Merry, S. E. "Mediator Settlement Strategies." *Law and Policy,* 1986, *8,* 7–32.

Simkin, W. E. *Mediation and the Dynamics of Collective Bargaining.* Washington, D.C.: Bureau of National Affairs, 1971.

Singer, D. "Mediation: Nothying Els But Deuidyng By Two." *Arbitration Journal,* 1992, *47*(3), 15.

Singer, L. R. "Nonjudicial Dispute Resolution Mechanisms: The Effects on Justice for the Poor." In L. Ray and D. Smolover (eds.), *Consumer Dispute Resolution: Exploring the Alternatives.* Chicago: American Bar Association, Special Committee on Alternative Dispute Resolution, Public Services Group; Washington, D.C.: U.S. Department of Consumer Affairs, National Association of Consumer Agency Administrators, 1983.

Singer, L. R. "The Quiet Revolution in Dispute Resolution." *Mediation Quarterly,* 1989, *7*(2), 105–113.

Singer, L. R. *Settling Disputes: Conflict Resolution in Business, Families, and the Legal System.* Boulder, Colo.: Westview Press, 1990.

Smart, L. "Mediator Strategies for Dealing with Dirty Tricks." *Mediation Quarterly,* 1987, *16,* 53–63.

Smith, A. *An Inquiry into the Nature and Causes of the Wealth of Nations.* [R. H. Campbell and A. S. Skinner, gen. eds.; W. B. Todd, textual ed. 2 vols.] Oxford: Clarendon Press, 1976. [originally published 1776]

Smith, C. G. (ed.). *Conflict Resolution: Contributions of the Social Sciences.* Notre Dame, Ind.: University of Notre Dame Press, 1971.

Smith, K. K., Simmons, V. M., and Thames, T. B. "Fix the Women: An Intervention into Organizational Conflict Based on Parallel Process Thinking." *Journal of Applied Behavioral Science,* 1989, *25,* 11–30.

Society of Professionals in Dispute Resolution. *Ethical Standards of Professional Responsibility.* Washington, D.C.: Society of Professionals in Dispute Resolution, June 1986.

Stamato, L., and Jaffe, S. "Mediation and Public Policy: Variations on a Consensus Theme." *Mediation Quarterly,* 1991, *9*(2), 165–178.

Starke, J. G. *An Introduction to the Science of Peace (Irenology).* Leyden, The Netherlands: A. W. Sijthoff, 1968.

Stein, P. *Legal Institutions: The Development of Dispute Settlement.* London: Butterworths, 1984.

Stern, L. W., Bagozzi, R. P., and Dholakia, R. R. "Mediational Mechanisms in Interorganizational Conflict." In D. Druckman (ed.), *Negotiations: Social-Psychological Perspectives.* Thousand Oaks, Calif.: Sage, 1977.

Stevens, C. M. *Strategy and Collective Bargaining Negotiation.* New York: McGraw-Hill, 1963.

Stewart, J., and Thomas, M. "Dialogic Listening." In J. Stewart (ed.), *Bridges Not Walls.* (5th ed.) New York: McGraw-Hill, 1990.

Stoll, R. J., and McAndrew, W. "Negotiating Strategic Arms Control, 1969–1979: Modeling the Bargaining Process." *Journal of Conflict Resolution,* 1986, *30,* 315–326.

Stuart, R, B., and Jacobson, B. "Principles of Divorce Mediation: A Social Learning Theory Approach." *Mediation Quarterly,* 1986–1987, *14/15,* 71–85.

Sur, M. *Collective Bargaining: A Comparative Study of Developments in India and Other Countries.* New York: Asia, 1965.

Susskind, L., and Babbitt, E. "Overcoming the Obstacles to Effective Mediation of International Disputes." In J. Bercovitch and J. Z. Rubin (eds.), *Mediation in International Relations: Multiple Approaches to Conflict Management.* New York: St. Martin's Press, 1992.

Susskind, L., and Cruikshank, J. *Breaking the Impasse: Consensual Approaches to Resolving Public Disputes.* New York: Basic Books, 1987.

Swingle, Paul G. (ed.). *The Structure of Conflict.* Orlando: Academic Press, 1970.

Tedeschi, J. T., and Bonoma, T. V. "Measures of Last Resort: Coercion and Aggression in Bargaining." In D. Druckman (ed.), *Negotiations: Social-Psychological Perspectives.* Thousand Oaks, Calif.: Sage, 1977.

Les Termes de la Ley. (Abr. ed.) London: [n.p.], 1533. (Ascribed to William Rastell by Lord Coke in his preface to his Tenth Report according to page A3 of the 1671 ed.).

Thibaut, J. W., and Kelly, H. H. *The Social Psychology of Groups.* New York: Wiley, 1959.

Thomas, K. "Conflict and Conflict Management." In M. D. Dunnette (ed.), *Handbook of Industrial and Organizational Psychology.* Skokie, Ill.: Rand McNally, 1976.

Thomas/Kilmann Conflict Mode Instrument. Palo Alto, Calif.: Consulting Psychologists Press, 1974.

Thompson, W. R., and Rasler, K. A. *War and Statemaking: The Shaping of the Global Powers.* Boston: Unwin Hyman, 1989.

Tomasic, R., and Feeley, M. M. (eds.). *Neighborhood Justice: Assessment of an Emerging Idea.* White Plains, N.Y.: Longman, 1982.

Treverton, G. F. "Deterrence and Collective Security." In W. S. Thompson, K. M. Jensen, R. N. Smith, and K. M. Schraub (eds.), *Approaches to Peace: An Intellectual Map.* Washington, D.C.: United States Institute of Peace, 1991.

Tripp, C. J. "Intraorganizational Conflict Mediation: The Effects of Communication, Complaints, Compliance, and Confidence." *Mediation Quarterly,* 1985, *7,* 83–99.

Turner, D. B. "Negotiator-Constituent Relationships." In L. L. Putnam and M. E. Roloff (eds.), *Communication and Negotiation.* Thousand Oaks, Calif.: Sage, 1992.

Tutzauer, F. "The Communication of Offers in Dyadic Bargaining." In L. L. Putnam and M. E. Roloff (eds.), *Communication and Negotiation.* Thousand Oaks, Calif.: Sage, 1992.

Umbreit, M. S., with Coates, R. B., and Kalanj, B. *Victim Meets Offender: The Impact of Restorative Justice and Mediation.* Monsey, N.Y.: Criminal Justice Press, Willow Tree Press, 1994.

Umbreit, M. S. "Moving to a Higher Plane: A Humanistic Model of Mediation." In M. Umbreit, *Mediating Interpersonal Conflicts: A Pathway to Peace.* West Concord, Minn.: CPI, 1995.

Umbricht, V. H. *Multilateral Mediation Practical Experiences and Lessons.* Dordrecht, The Netherlands: Martinus Nijhoff, 1989.

Ury, W. L. "Dispute Resolution Notes from the Kalahari." *Negotiation Journal,* 1990, *6*(3), 229–238.

Ury, W. L. *Getting Past No: Negotiating Your Way from Confrontation to Cooperation.* (Rev. Ed.) New York: Bantam Books, 1993.

Ury, W. L., Brett, J. M., and Goldberg, S. B. *Getting Disputes Resolved: Designing Systems to Cut the Costs of Conflict.* San Francisco: Jossey-Bass, 1988.

U.S. Army Corps of Engineers. Alternative Dispute Resolution: Mini Trials, E. C. 27-1-3. Sept. 23, 1985.

Van Slyck, M. R., Newland, L. M., and Stern, M. "Parent-Child Mediation: Integrating Theory, Research, and Practice." *Mediation Quarterly,* 1992, *10*(2), 193–208.

Vidmar, N., and Rice, J. "Jury-Determined Settlements and Summary Jury Trials: Observations About Alternative Dispute Resolution in an Adversary Culture." *Florida State University Law Review,* 1991, *19*(1), 89–103.

Volkema, R. J. "The Mediator as Face Manager." *Mediation Quarterly,* 1988, *22,* 5–14.

Wagner, M. L. "Comment: Jurisdiction by Estoppel in the International Court of Justice." *California Law Review,* 1986, *74*(5), 1777–1804.

Walcott, C., Hopmann, P. T., and King, T. D. "The Role of Debate in Negotiation." In D. Druckman (ed.), *Negotiations: Social-Psychological Perspectives.* Thousand Oaks, Calif.: Sage, 1977.

Walker, A. Jr. *Thesaurus of Psychological Index Terms.* (6th ed.) Arlington, Va.: American Psychological Association, 1991.

Walker, J. A. "Assessment in Divorce Conciliation: Issues and Practice." *Mediation Quarterly,* 1986, *11,* 43–56.

Wall, J. A. Jr., and Blum, M. "Community Mediation in the People's Republic of China." *Journal of Conflict Resolution,* 1991, *35*(1), 3–20.

Wall, V. D. Jr., and Dewhurst, M. L. "Mediator Gender: Communication Differences in Resolved and Unresolved Mediations." *Mediation Quarterly,* 1991, *9*(1), 63–85.

Wallerstein, I. *Politics of the World Economy.* Cambridge: Cambridge University Press, 1984.

Walton, R. E. *Interpersonal Peacemaking: Confrontations and Third-Party Consultation.* Reading, Mass.: Addison-Wesley, 1969.

Walton, R., and McKersie, R. *A Behavioral Theory of Labor Negotiations: An Analysis of a Social Interaction System.* New York: McGraw-Hill, 1965.

Wehr, P. *Conflict Regulation.* Boulder, Colo.: Westview Press, 1979.

Weiner, E. "Coexistence Work: A New Profession." In E. Weiner (ed.), *The Handbook of Interethnic Coexistence.* New York: Continuum, 1998.

Weller, S., Ruhnka, J. C., and Martin, J. A. "American Small Claims Courts." In C. J. Whelan (ed.), *Small Claims Courts: A Comparative Study.* Oxford: Clarendon Press, 1990.

Welton, G. L., Pruitt, D. G., and McGillicuddy, N. B. "An Exploratory Examination of Caucusing: Its Role in Community Mediation." *Journal of Conflict Resolution,* 1988, *32,* 181–202.

West, W. *Symboleography.* London: Thomas Wright, 1601–1603.

Westin, A. F., and Feliu, A. G. *Resolving Employment Disputes Without Litigation.* Washington, D.C.: Bureau of National Affairs, 1988.

Whelan, C. J. "Small Claims Courts: Heritage and Adjustment." In C. J. Whelan (ed.), *Small Claims Courts: A Comparative Study.* Oxford: Clarendon Press, 1990.

White, J. J. "Machiavelli and the Bar: Ethical Limitations on Lying in Negotiation." *American Bar Foundation Research Journal,* 1980, *1980*(4), 926–930.

White, J. J. "The Pros and Cons of 'Getting to Yes.'" *Journal of Legal Education,* 1984, *34,* 115–124.

White, S. B., and Neale, M. A. "Reservation Prices, Resistance Points, and BATNAs: Determining the Parameters of Acceptable Negotiated Outcomes." *Negotiation Journal,* 1991, *7*(4), 380–388.

Whiting, R. A. "The Single-Issue, Multiple-Issue Debate and the Effect of Issue Number on Mediated Outcomes." *Mediation Quarterly,* 1992, *10*(1), 57–74.

Wilkenfeld, J. "Trigger-Response Transitions in Foreign Policy Crises, 1929–1985." *Journal of Conflict Resolution,* 1991, *35*(1), 143–169.

Wilkinson, J. H. (ed.). *Donovan Leisure Newton & Irvine ADR Practice Book.* New York: Wiley Law Publications, 1990.

Williams, G. R. *Legal Negotiation and Settlement.* St. Paul, Minn.: West, 1983.

Williams, R. *Concilio-Arbitration Handbook: Rules and Commentary.* London: Concilio-Arbitration, 1986.

Wilson, S. R. "Face and Facework in Negotiation." In L. L. Putnam and M. E. Roloff (eds.), *Communication and Negotiation.* Thousand Oaks, Calif.: Sage, 1992.

Winham, G. R. "The Prenegotiation Phase of the Uruguay Round." In J. G. Stein (ed.), *Getting to the Table: The Processes of International Prenegotiation.* Baltimore, Md.: Johns Hopkins University Press, 1989.

Wittkopf, E. G. "Elites and Masses: Another Look at Attitudes Towards America's World Role." *International Studies Quarterly,* 1987, *31,* 131–159.

Wolfson, M., Puri, A., and Martelli, M. "The Nonlinear Dynamics of International Conflict." *Journal of Conflict Resolution,* 1992, *36*(1), 119–149.

Woodward, J. G. "Settlement Week: Measuring the Promise." *Northern Illinois University Law Review,* 1990, *11,* 1–54.

World Arbitration and Mediation Report. Various issues.

Wright, Q. "The Escalation of International Conflicts." In C. G. Smith (ed.), *Conflict Resolution: Contributions of the Social Sciences.* Notre Dame, Ind.: University of Notre Dame Press, 1971.

Wu, S.S.G. "To Attack or Not to Attack: A Theory and Empirical Assessment of Extended Immediate Deterrence." *Journal of Conflict Resolution,* 1990, *34,* 531–552.

Yarn, D. H. *Alternative Dispute Resolution: Practice and Procedure in Georgia.* Norcross, Ga.: Harrison, 1992.

Yngvesson, B., and Hennessey, P. "Small Claims, Complex Disputes: A Review of the Small Claims Literature." *Law and Society Review,* 1975, *9*(2), 219–274.

Young, O. R. *The Intermediaries: Third Parties in International Crisis.* Princeton, N.J.: Princeton University Press, 1967.

Young, O. R. "The Bargainer's Calculus." In O. R. Young (ed.), *Bargaining: Formal Theories of Negotiation.* Urbana: University of Illinois Press, 1975.

Zartman, I. W., and Berman, M. *The Practical Negotiator.* New Haven, Conn.: Yale University Press, 1982.

Zeif, R. A. "Negotiation: The Key to Resolving Disputes and Conflicts." In L. Ray and D. Smolover (eds.), *Consumer Dispute Resolution: Exploring the Alternatives.* Chicago: American Bar Association, Special Committee on Alternative Dispute Resolution, Public Services Group; Washington, D.C.: U.S. Department of Consumer Affairs, National Association of Consumer Agency Administrators, 1983.

Zetzel, G.W.K. "In and Out of the Family Crucible: Reflections on Parent-Child Mediation." *Mediation Quarterly,* 1985, *7,* 47–67.

Zisk, K. M. "Soviet Academic Theories on International Conflict and Negotiation: A Research Note." *Journal of Conflict Resolution,* 1990, *34,* 678–693.

Williams, G. R. *Legal Negotiation and Settlement.* St. Paul, Minn.: West, 1983.

Williams, R. *Concilio-Arbitration Handbook: Rules and Commentary.* London: Concilio-Arbitration, 1986.

Wilson, S. R. "Face and Facework in Negotiation." In L. L. Putnam and M. E. Roloff (eds.), *Communication and Negotiation.* Thousand Oaks, Calif.: Sage, 1992.

Winham, G. R. "The Prenegotiation Phase of the Uruguay Round." In J. G. Stein (ed.), *Getting to the Table: The Processes of International Prenegotiation.* Baltimore, Md.: Johns Hopkins University Press, 1989.

Wittkopf, E. G. "Elites and Masses: Another Look at Attitudes Towards America's World Role." *International Studies Quarterly,* 1987, *31,* 131–159.

Wolfson, M., Puri, A., and Martelli, M. "The Nonlinear Dynamics of International Conflict." *Journal of Conflict Resolution,* 1992, *36*(1), 119–149.

Woodward, J. G. "Settlement Week: Measuring the Promise." *Northern Illinois University Law Review,* 1990, *11,* 1–54.

World Arbitration and Mediation Report. Various issues.

Wright, Q. "The Escalation of International Conflicts." In C. G. Smith (ed.), *Conflict Resolution: Contributions of the Social Sciences.* Notre Dame, Ind.: University of Notre Dame Press, 1971.

Wu, S.S.G. "To Attack or Not to Attack: A Theory and Empirical Assessment of Extended Immediate Deterrence." *Journal of Conflict Resolution,* 1990, *34,* 531–552.

Yarn, D. H. *Alternative Dispute Resolution: Practice and Procedure in Georgia.* Norcross, Ga.: Harrison, 1992.

Yngvesson, B., and Hennessey, P. "Small Claims, Complex Disputes: A Review of the Small Claims Literature." *Law and Society Review,* 1975, *9*(2), 219–274.

Young, O. R. *The Intermediaries: Third Parties in International Crisis.* Princeton, N.J.: Princeton University Press, 1967.

Young, O. R. "The Bargainer's Calculus." In O. R. Young (ed.), *Bargaining: Formal Theories of Negotiation.* Urbana: University of Illinois Press, 1975.

Zartman, I. W., and Berman, M. *The Practical Negotiator.* New Haven, Conn.: Yale University Press, 1982.

Zeif, R. A. "Negotiation: The Key to Resolving Disputes and Conflicts." In L. Ray and D. Smolover (eds.), *Consumer Dispute Resolution: Exploring the Alternatives.* Chicago: American Bar Association, Special Committee on Alternative Dispute Resolution, Public Services Group; Washington, D.C.: U.S. Department of Consumer Affairs, National Association of Consumer Agency Administrators, 1983.

Zetzel, G.W.K. "In and Out of the Family Crucible: Reflections on Parent-Child Mediation." *Mediation Quarterly,* 1985, *7,* 47–67.

Zisk, K. M. "Soviet Academic Theories on International Conflict and Negotiation: A Research Note." *Journal of Conflict Resolution,* 1990, *34,* 678–693.

DOUGLAS HURT YARN is an associate professor of law at Georgia State University, College of Law, where he teaches alternative dispute resolution and professional responsibility. He holds degrees from Duke University, the University of Georgia, and Cambridge University. An experienced litigator, mediator, facilitator, and arbitrator, Yarn served as in-house attorney, mediator, and panelist trainer for the American Arbitration Association from 1989 to 1994. He has trained mediators and arbitrators nationwide and has designed conflict management systems for private and public entities. As a member of the Georgia Supreme Court's Commission on Dispute Resolution, he hears ethics cases and chairs the committee on evaluation. He is the executive director of the Consortium on Negotiation and Conflict Resolution, a multidisciplinary theory-building center partially funded by the Hewlett Foundation. Yarn drafted the current Georgia Arbitration Code and is the author of *Alternative Dispute Resolution: Practice and Procedure in Georgia* (Harrison 1997), *Alternative Dispute Resolution: Practice and Procedure in North Carolina* (Harrison 1998), and numerous book chapters and articles.